THE
1989
ALMANAC

A Comprehensive Review
Of The 1988 Season,
Featuring Statistics
And Commentary

PUBLISHED BY
BASEBALL
AMERICA

Editor: Allan Simpson
Publisher: Miles Wolff

<u>**Associate Editors:**</u>
Danny Knobler, Mary Jo Monnin,
John Royster, Jon Scher

<u>**Contributing Editors:**</u>
Tracy Ringolsby, Jayson Stark, Tim Kurkjian,
George Rorrer, Patti Singer, Brian Hilderbrand,
Kevin Iole, Rubin Grant, Mike Knobler,
Jim Alexander, David Jones, Mike Koolbeck,
Gene Sapakoff, Gary Piccirillo, Vince Bruun,
Ken Leiker, Wayne Graczyk

<u>**Statistical Production Consultant:**</u>
Howe News Bureau

© 1989 American Sports Publishing, Inc.

No portion of this book may be reprinted or reproduced without the written consent of the publishers. For additional copies, send $7.95 to American Sports Publishing, P.O. Box 2089, Durham, NC, 27702.

Contents

The Year In Review

Major Leagues

Minor Leagues

Other Pro Baseball

College Baseball

Amateur Baseball

The Draft

Contributing photographers

J. Anthony Alderman, Mel Bailey, Tom DiPace, Wayne Graczyk, Keith Grayson, Fred J. Griffith, Bob Gwaltney, Kathy Hennesy, Mary Jo Monnin, Michael Ponzini, Bruce Schwartzman, John Spear, Wade Thrall, Bernard Troncale, Frank Varga, Ron Vesely, Larry Woolis.

Editor's note

All professional statistics are based on final, unofficial 1988 averages. The statistics include all players who participated in at least one game during the 1988 season. Pitchers' batting statistics are not included, nor are the pitching stats of minor league field players who pitched on rare occasions. For players who played with more than one team in the same league, the number of games he played with his first team is listed in parentheses after his name; his two-team totals follow.

Ueberroth leaves baseball healthy

By JON SCHER

When Peter Ueberroth became commissioner of baseball Oct. 1, 1984, he promised to work to improve the financial health of the game. Ueberroth kept his promise.

Major league attendance shattered records in each of the last four seasons. Many franchises now are appraised at more than $100 million. Revenues are way up, and the number of clubs thinking about relocation is down.

Still, Ueberroth, the man behind the successful 1984 Los Angeles Olympics, was perceived by baseball insiders as a cold, distant commissioner. Popular with fans, his reception among owners and players has been lukewarm at best. Realizing this, Ueberroth made it clear from the start he planned to be a one-term commissioner.

Again, he was true to his word. At an owners meeting Sept. 8 in Montreal, Ueberroth announced his intention to leave office April 1, 1989—six months before his five-

Peter Ueberroth
. . . outgoing

year contract officially expires. Then, Ueberroth orchestrated the owners' unanimous approval of National League president A. Bartlett Giamatti as his successor.

A pure baseball man

It was a rare display of unity by the Lords of Baseball, who awarded Giamatti a five-year contract as baseball's seventh commissioner.

Giamatti, a former Yale University president, has been NL president since December 1986. Unlike Ueberroth, whose primary attribute is his strong business background, Giamatti is known for a lifelong love affair with baseball.

"Bart is the perfect choice for the time," Ueberroth said. "His passion for the game will keep it on a steady course through the 1990s and into the next century."

Giamatti, 50, grew up a fan of the Boston Red Sox and is an unabashed foe of the designated-hitter rule. An advocate of civility on the field, Giamatti made news in 1988 when he handed Cincinnati Reds manager Pete Rose a 30-day suspension and a $10,000 fine after Rose shoved NL umpire Dave

A. Bartlett Giamatti
. . . incoming

Pallone (Pallone was later fired).

Tough times ahead

Despite the financial legacy Ueberroth leaves, there are dark clouds on the horizon. The Basic Agreement between players and owners expires at the end of 1989, and bitter negotiations are expected. Relations between Major League Baseball and the Players Association have reached a new low.

Arbitrators' rulings in 1987 and '88 upheld the Players Association's contention that Ueberroth and the owners conspired to curtail free agency after the 1985 and '86 seasons. Free agent status was restored to players like Detroit's Kirk Gibson (who wound up signing with the Dodgers) and Boston's Rich Gedman (among several players freed after the '88 season).

Although there was some movement in the regular free agent market after the 1987 season, with Jack Clark switching from the Cardinals to the Yankees and Bob Horner returning from Japan to sign with the Cards, the Players Association again charged the owners with collusion.

Commissioners
Kenesaw Mountain Landis 1920-44
A.B. "Happy" Chandler 1945-1951
Ford C. Frick 1951-1965
William D. "Spike" Eckert 1965-68
Bowie K. Kuhn 1969-84
Peter V. Ueberroth 1984-89
A. Bartlett Giamatti 1989-

A ruling on the '87 free agent class, which includes Detroit's Jack Morris, was expected during the winter of 1988-89, along with possible damage awards for all players whose free agency has been unfairly restricted. All these developments portend major labor strife in 1990.

Still, Giamatti was upbeat as he accepted the owners' mandate.

"The institution of baseball is getting stronger," he said, "and I intend to affirm its manifest strengths and to build new ones."

Year of the Pitcher

The Minnesota Twins, long one of the game's weak links, became one of its manifest strengths in 1988. The Twins were unable to defend their 1987 World Series championship, but they broke an American League record when they sold 3,030,672 tickets. A late-season buyout by area businesses helped the Twins become the first AL team to go over three million.

In the NL, the Mets (3,047,724) joined Minnesota as the only members of the three million club in 1988.

Overall, Major League Baseball attracted 52,957,752 fans, breaking the record set in 1987 by more than 900,000. In addition to the Twins, four other clubs set records: Boston (2,464,851), New York (2,633,703) and Oakland (2,287,335) in the AL and Pittsburgh (1,865,713) in the NL.

Fans who packed major league parks witnessed some of the best pitching in baseball history. A year after the game broke a record with 4,458 home runs, pitchers struck back.

The major league composite ERA fell from 4.28 to 3.72. Offensive production dropped dramatically—Tony Gwynn of the Padres hit just .313 to lead the NL. In 1987, rumors of a juiced-up "rabbit ball" were rampant. By the end of 1988, fans were wondering whether that wascally wabbit had wun off to Miami Beach.

Perhaps hot air from the silly 1988 presidential campaign was keeping balls from flying out of parks. Perhaps it was the new definition of the strike zone, which supposedly was expanded by changes in the wording of the rules during the offseason. Or maybe, just maybe, the pitchers simply figured out how to keep hitters off balance.

Whatever the reason, there were some memorable performances on the mound.

Tom Browning of the Reds pitched the 14th perfect game in baseball history Sept. 16 against the Dodgers, and near no-hitters abounded. Eight times, pitchers held the opposition hitless for eight or more innings, only to surrender a hit in the ninth. Pascual Perez of the Expos avoided that problem, pitching a five-inning no-hitter against the Phillies Sept. 24 in a game shortened by rain.

But the year's biggest achievement was by perhaps the game's nicest guy. Orel Hershiser broke one of baseball's unbreakable records, pitching 59 straight scoreless innings down the stretch as the Dodgers held on to win the NL West. Hershiser, of course, went on to lead Los Angeles to the World Series title, and he'll enter 1989 with the 59-inning streak still alive.

Only in the AL were hitters able to salvage some respect. Jose Canseco became the first player to hit 40 home runs and steal 40 bases in a season (42-40), and Wade Boggs hit .366 to win his fourth batting title.

Highlights and lowlights

■ Just like farmers in the Midwest, baseball experienced a drought in 1988. After impact players like Oakland's Canseco and Mark McGwire, San Francisco's Will Clark, Kansas City's Kevin Seitzer, Boston's Ellis Burks and Mike Greenwell, and San Diego's Benito Santiago emerged as rookies in 1986 and '87, that flow of talent slowed to a trickle.

In the NL, the top rookies included minor league journeyman Tim Belcher of the Dodgers and kamikaze third baseman Chris

---

Steinbach stars

Terry Steinbach, the Oakland catcher who was voted into the starting lineup in fan balloting despite a .217 batting average, upstaged baseball's biggest names during the 1988 major league all-star game.

Steinbach homered and hit a sacrifice fly, driving in both runs as the AL beat the NL 2-1 in the 59th all-star game, played July 12 in Cincinnati.

It was the third loss by the NL since 1971, and Cardinals manager Whitey Herzog was in charge of the National League team all three times (1983, 1986 and '88). The AL still trails in the series 37-21 (one tie).

★ ★ ★

American 2, National 1

AMERICAN	ab	r	h	bi	bb	so	NATIONAL	ab	r	h	bi	bb	so
Henderson cf	2	0	1	0	1	0	Coleman lf	2	1	1	0	0	0
Lansford 3b	1	0	0	0	0	0	Galarraga 1b	2	0	0	0	0	1
Molitor 2b	3	0	0	0	0	1	Sandberg 2b	4	0	1	0	0	2
Puckett cf	1	0	0	0	0	0	Worrell p	0	0	0	0	0	0
Boggs 3b	3	0	1	0	0	0	Dawson cf	2	0	1	0	0	0
Reynolds 2b	1	0	0	0	0	0	McGee pr-cf	2	0	0	0	0	0
Canseco lf-rf	4	0	0	0	0	1	Strawberry rf	4	0	1	0	0	1
Winfield rf	3	1	1	0	0	0	Bonilla 3b	4	0	0	0	0	0
Stieb p	0	0	0	0	0	0	Clark 1b	2	0	0	0	0	0
Russell p	0	0	0	0	0	0	Cone p	0	0	0	0	0	0
Jones p	0	0	0	0	0	0	Larkin ss	2	0	0	0	0	1
Plesac p	0	0	0	0	0	0	Carter c	3	0	1	0	0	1
Brett ph	1	0	0	0	0	0	Sabo pr	0	0	0	0	0	0
Stillwell ss	0	0	0	0	0	0	Parrish c	1	0	0	0	0	0
Ripken ss	3	0	0	0	1	0	Smith ss	2	0	0	0	0	1
Eckersley p	0	0	0	0	0	0	Gross p	0	0	0	0	0	0
McGwire 1b	2	0	1	0	0	0	Davis p	0	0	0	0	0	0
Mattingly 1b	2	0	0	0	0	0	Walk p	0	0	0	0	0	0
Steinbach c	1	1	1	2	0	0	Palmeiro ph-lf	0	0	0	0	1	0
Greenwell lf	1	0	0	0	0	0	Gooden p	0	0	0	0	0	0
Viola p	0	0	0	0	0	0	Perry ph	1	0	0	0	0	0
Gaetti ph	1	0	0	0	0	0	Knepper p	0	0	0	0	0	0
Clemens p	0	0	0	0	0	0	Van Slyke lf	2	0	0	0	0	0
Ray ph	1	0	0	0	0	0	Hershiser p	0	0	0	0	0	0
Gubicza p	0	0	0	0	0	0	Law 2b	0	0	0	0	0	0
Laudner c	1	0	1	0	0	0							
TOTALS	**31**	**2**	**6**	**2**	**2**	**3**	**TOTALS**	**33**	**1**	**5**	**0**	**1**	**7**

American	. . . .	001 100 000—2
National	. . . .	000 100 000—1

Game-winning RBI—Steinbach.

E—Steinbach, Mattingly. DP—National 1. LOB—American 5, National 6. 2B—Winfield, Laudner. HR—Steinbach. SB—Coleman, Sabo. SF—Steinbach.

American	IP	H	R	ER	BB	SO	National	IP	H	R	ER	BB	SO
Viola W	2	0	0	0	0	1	Gooden L	3	3	1	1	1	1
Clemens	1	0	0	0	0	1	Knepper	1	2	1	1	1	0
Gubicza	2	3	1	1	0	2	Cone	1	0	0	0	0	1
Stieb	1	1	0	0	0	0	Gross	1	0	0	0	0	1
Russell	1	1	0	0	1	0	Davis	⅔	1	0	0	0	0
Jones	⅔	0	0	0	0	0	Walk	⅓	0	0	0	0	0
Plesac	⅓	0	0	0	0	1	Hershiser	1	0	0	0	0	0
Eckersley S	1	0	0	0	0	1	Worrell	1	0	0	0	0	0

WP—Gubicza. Balk—Gooden. T—2:26. A—55,837.

Sabo of the Reds. In the AL, the pickings were even slimmer. The most significant newcomer may have been Oakland shortstop Walt Weiss, who hit .250 and played well in the field. Not exactly a glamorous group.

■ Willie Stargell, who hit 475 home runs and batted .282 in 21 years with the Pittsburgh Pirates, was inducted into the Baseball Hall of Fame in ceremonies July 31 in Cooperstown, N.Y. Stargell became the 200th Hall of Famer. He was the 17th to win admission in his first year of eligibility.

■ Pam Postema, professional baseball's second female full-time umpire, nearly became the first woman to call balls and strikes in the major leagues. Postema, 33, was one of seven umpires invited by the NL to audition for two openings during spring training.

Postema called a number of major league exhibition games and received intense publicity, but still wound up back in the minors for the 12th straight year.

■ Chicago was the center of attention for much of the summer—but not for the on-field antics of the constantly rebuilding Cubs and White Sox.

First, the Sox announced plans to move to a domed stadium

Willie Stargell became the 200th Hall Of Fame inductee, as the only player inducted in 1988.

in St. Petersburg, Fla., unless the Illinois legislature allocated money for a $150 million ballpark to replace aging Comiskey Park. The lawmakers waited until the last possible moment, then narrowly approved the stadium proposal. It seems the Sox will stay put.

Then the Cubs defied tradition, installing lights at venerable Wrigley Field. The Tribune Co., which owns the Cubs, finally overcame legal challenges by neighborhood residents who fought for years against night games. The Cubs plan to play as many as 18 night games a year at the North Side park.

The much-ballyhooed first game under the lights, Aug. 8 against the Phillies, was rained out after 3½ innings. An Aug. 9 game against the Mets became the first official night game at Wrigley Field.

■ Major league salaries continued their climb. According to a New York Times study based on Opening Day rosters, the average salary was $449,862. The Cardinals' Ozzie Smith was the highest-paid player, earning $2.34 million in 1988. Nine other players made $2 million or more. The major league minimum salary was $62,500.

Milestones

Thanks to stricter interpretation of the balk rule, fans thrilled to a record 924 balks, up from 356 in 1987. Both leagues broke records: 366 in the NL, 558 in the AL. The old records, 219 in the NL and 137 in the AL, were set in 1987 ... A year after the Al Campanis affair focused attention on the lack of minorities in positions of responsibility in baseball, only one black manager was named: Frank Robinson, baseball's first black manager when he was hired by the Indians in 1974, became manager of the Orioles in April. According to Ueberroth, more blacks were being hired for coaching, front-office and minor league jobs, but the evidence had yet to filter into the managers' ranks ... Baltimore's Cal Ripken Jr. kept his ironman streak alive, extending it to 1,088 consecutive games played—sixth on the all-time list. If Ripken plays 162 games in 1989, he will pass Joe Sewell (1,103), Billy Williams (1,117) and Steve Garvey (1,207), and move into third place behind Lou Gehrig (2,130) and Everett Scott (1,307) ... Randy Johnson, the Expos' 6-foot-10 lefthander, became the tallest player in major league history when he appeared in his first game Sept. 15 ... Dave Johnson of the Mets became the first NL manager to win 90 or more games in each of his first five seasons ... Boston's Wade Boggs became the first player since 1900 to record 200 or more hits in six straight seasons.

Deaths

■ **Edward Bennett Williams,** 68, a noted attorney and owner of the Baltimore Orioles since 1979, died of cancer Aug. 13. The club was left in the hands of Williams' estate, and is likely to be sold.

■ **Lee Weyer,** 51, a National League umpire since 1963, died of a heart attack July 4.

■ **Ralph Salvon,** 60, Orioles trainer for the past 23 years, died July 7 from complications after heart bypass surgery.

■ **Bob Fishel,** 74, special assistant to AL president Bobby Brown, died June 30 of complications after an asthma attack. Fishel had been public relations director for the St. Louis Browns, Baltimore Orioles, New York Yankees and the AL.

E.B. Williams
... Orioles owner

■ **Ted Kluszewski,** 63, who hit 279 home runs during a 15-year major league career with the Reds, Pirates, White Sox and Angels, died March 29 of a heart attack. He spent 18 years as a Reds' major league and minor league coach, before retiring in 1987.

■ **Harvey Kuenn,** 57, who compiled a .303 batting average in 15 major league seasons, died Feb. 28. Kuenn, who managed the Milwaukee Brewers to their only AL pennant in 1982, had myriad health problems while scouting for the Brewers in recent years.

■ **Nino Espinosa,** 34, a former Mets, Phillies and Blue Jays pitcher who had become a scout and minor league instructor for the Chicago Cubs, died Dec. 25, 1987, of an apparent heart attack.

■ **Dick Stello,** 53, an NL umpire since 1969, was killed Nov. 18, 1987, in an automobile crash.

■ **Jim Brewer,** 49, who spent 17 years as a major league pitcher, mostly for the Los Angeles Dodgers, died Nov. 16, 1987, after an automobile wreck. Brewer also had been a minor league pitching coach for the Dodgers.

THE
MAJOR
LEAGUES

The World Series

Hershiser's heroes shock
the baseball world

American League

Boston overtakes Detroit
to win the East, but West
champ Oakland rolls past
the Sox in the playoffs

National League

The Mets' return to greatness
was short-circuited by those
amazing Dodgers

The Dodgers' Orel Hershiser won both his World Series starts in convincing fashion.

Los Angeles' Bulldog has one heck of a bark

By TRACY RINGOLSBY

He was a skinny kid with a live arm. Orel Hershiser could light up radar guns in the 90-mph range. He could make his ball sink and rise. He could hit the corners, inside and out.

But as well as Hershiser pitched as a rookie with the Los Angeles Dodgers in 1984—a 2.66 ERA, only 160 hits in 190 innings and a 3-to-1 strikeout/walk ratio—he still had only an 11-8 record.

"You've got the ability," manager Tommy Lasorda recalls telling Hershiser. "You've got to be a bulldog out there."

Lasorda never let up. Orel Leonard Hershiser IV became Bulldog Hershiser. Whenever he would waver, Lasorda would be there to slap him on the back, shout from the dugout and issue not-so-subtle reminders.

The transformation of the puppy into a junkyard dog reached fruition in the summer of 1988.

What a performance!

The warning was issued first to the National League West, then to the New York Mets in the NL playoffs and finally to the Oakland Athletics in the World Series. When the Dodgers are around, beware of the Dog.

The Series began with the Dodgers heavy underdogs. But thanks to the Bulldog, it ended with Los Angeles as baseball's top dogs, champions for the first time since 1981, the only team to have won two titles in the last 11 years. Baseball had a record streak of 10 different champions in 10 years.

Hershiser, whose record streak of 59 scoreless innings came to an end only because the regular season did, brought the postseason to an end with a flurry. He pitched complete games in both his World Series starts, a three-hitter in Game Two and four-hitter in Game Five. He was the catalyst for a Dodger pitching staff which defused the Athletics in five games.

While the Dodgers became the ninth team in history to rebound from a losing record in one season to World Series champions the next, Hershiser became the first pitcher and the third player overall in 20 years of divisional play to earn MVP honors in both the playoffs and World Series.

To his regular-season resume of a 23-8 record, 2.26 ERA, 15 complete games and eight shutouts, Hershiser added a postseason record of 3-0 with a save and 1.05 ERA, three complete games in four starts and two shutouts.

The transformation was complete.

"The Orel Hershiser I knew about had good talent, but no one was sure if he had enough guts to come to the mound with it," said Oakland pitcher Dave Stewart, a minor-league teammate of Hershiser's in the Dodger organization. "But he's a bulldog now. He's a finisher."

Stopped Oakland cold

The Dodger pitchers certainly finished off an Oakland lineup which had scored 800 runs in 162 regular season games, and

		World Series Champs
1988—Los Angeles (NL)	1945—Detroit (AL)	
1987—Minnesota (AL)	1944—St. Louis (NL)	
1986—New York (NL)	1943—New York (AL)	
1985—Kansas City (AL)	1942—St. Louis (NL)	
1984—Detroit (AL)	1941—New York (AL)	
1983—Baltimore (AL)	1940—Cincinnati (NL)	
1982—St. Louis (NL)	1939—New York (AL)	
1981—Los Angeles (NL)	1938—New York (AL)	
1980—Philadelphia (NL)	1937—New York (AL)	
1979—Pittsburgh (NL)	1936—New York (AL)	
1978—New York (AL)	1935—Detroit (AL)	
1977—New York (AL)	1934—St. Louis (NL)	
1976—Cincinnati (NL)	1933—New York (NL)	
1975—Cincinnati (NL)	1932—New York (AL)	
1974—Oakland (AL)	1931—St. Louis (NL)	
1973—Oakland (AL)	1930—Philadelphia (AL)	
1972—Oakland (AL)	1929—Philadelphia (AL)	
1971—Pittsburgh (NL)	1928—New York (AL)	
1970—Baltimore (AL)	1927—New York (AL)	
1969—New York (NL)	1926—St. Louis (NL)	
1968—Detroit (AL)	1925—Pittsburgh (NL)	
1967—St. Louis (NL)	1924—Washington (AL)	
1966—Baltimore (AL)	1923—New York (AL)	
1965—Los Angeles (NL)	1922—New York (NL)	
1964—St. Louis (NL)	1921—New York (NL)	
1963—Los Angeles (NL)	1920—Cleveland (AL)	
1962—New York (AL)	1919—Cincinnati (NL)	
1961—New York (AL)	1918—Boston (AL)	
1960—Pittsburgh (NL)	1917—Chicago (AL)	
1959—Los Angeles (NL)	1916—Boston (AL)	
1958—New York (AL)	1915—Boston (AL)	
1957—Milwaukee (NL)	1914—Boston (NL)	
1956—New York (AL)	1913—Philadelphia (AL)	
1955—Brooklyn (NL)	1912—Boston (AL)	
1954—New York (NL)	1911—Philadelphia (AL)	
1953—New York (AL)	1910—Philadelphia (AL)	
1952—New York (AL)	1909—Pittsburgh (NL)	
1951—New York (AL)	1908—Chicago (NL)	
1950—New York (AL)	1907—Chicago (NL)	
1949—New York (AL)	1906—Chicago (AL)	
1948—Cleveland (AL)	1905—New York (NL)	
1947—New York (AL)	1903—Boston (AL)	
1946—St. Louis (NL)		

Kirk Gibson made his only World Series at-bat count, hitting a game-winning home run.

19 more in a four-game sweep of Boston in the AL playoffs. They scored only 11 runs in five World Series games, just two in the 18 innings Hershiser pitched.

The Dodgers found just enough hitting to complement that pitching, despite the fact that:

■ Kirk Gibson, troubled with a strained hamstring and sprained knee, was limited to one at-bat (albeit a very important one),

■ John Tudor was forced out in the second inning of Game Three, and later underwent Tommy John surgery (the transplant of a ligament from his right wrist to his left elbow),

■ Mike Marshall had to depart in the fourth inning of Game Three, and missed most of Game Four with a stiff back,

■ and catcher Mike Scioscia was knocked out of Game Four with a knee injury that had him scheduled for surgery.

"We didn't have all the talent in the world, but we believed in ourselves," Lasorda said. "This club has to be an influence to everybody in the world. If you don't quit, if you believe in yourself, you can get the job done.

"They said we couldn't win the division. They said we couldn't beat the Mets and they said we couldn't beat Oakland. It's David and Goliath. David was the first underdog ever, and we're the latest."

David had his slingshot and the Dodgers had their slingers. There was Hershiser, and there was a bullpen that was big on relief. The relievers, called on to work seven innings in each of two games, allowed just two runs in 16⅔ World Series innings.

Hatcher's heroics

And the Dodgers had the Stuntmen, as their reserves nicknamed themselves, ready to step into prime-time roles. Mickey Hatcher, who had only one regular season home run, replaced Gibson in left field and the No. 3 spot in the order, and had as many home runs (two) as Oakland's two big bashers, Jose Canseco and Mark McGwire, combined.

Canseco, who led the majors with 42 home runs, and McGwire, whose 32 was third in the AL, each had a dramatic blast. But neither had any other hits, going a collective 2-for-36 for an Oakland team which hit only .177 in the Series.

The A's had to feel they were going to get off to a big start against onetime Oakland farmhand Tim Belcher, who started the opener intent on proving the A's wrong for giving up on him.

Belcher lasted two innings, just long enough to serve up the first grand slam of Canseco's career. But it was nothing more than a prelude to the agony of the A's. Oakland took a 4-3 lead into the bottom of the ninth in that game, but then the Dodgers found their inspiration.

With two out and one on in the bottom of the ninth, Gibson limped to the plate, fell behind 0-2, worked Oakland reliever Dennis Eckersley to a 3-2 count and unloaded a game-winning home run. It will rank among the most dramatic in World Series history.

Game Two was Hershiser's from start to finish. He pitched the 32nd three-hitter in World Series history, and become the first pitcher to throw a shutout in both the playoffs and World Series.

He had as many hits as he allowed. Hershiser went 3-for-3, including two doubles, becoming the sixth pitcher to have three hits in a World Series game. The last one was Art Nehf of the 1924 New York Giants.

Oakland's only salvation

It was the A's turn for the dramatic in Game Three. Tudor was gone after throwing just 21 pitches and retiring the first four batters. Tim Leary and Alejandro Pena came on to allow just one run in 6⅔ innings.

But then Jay Howell, whose postseason had been one of attention but little action, came on in the ninth. After retiring Canseco on a pop fly, Howell served up a home run to Mark McGwire that gave Oakland a 2-1 win. It was second game-ending home run of this World Series, but only the eighth all-time.

Still, the A's had only five hits. Oakland manager Tony LaRussa said he wasn't concerned about the lack of offense, that his team was swinging the bat well, just not getting results.

By the end, LaRussa gave credit to the Dodgers for putting his hitters in a slump.

"Early on, I thought we were going to be fine, but when we started piling up the at-bats without success, it was obvious we started pressing," LaRussa said.

The problem was underscored in Game Four. The A's managed nine hits, and Dave Henderson became the 47th player in Series history to have a four-hit game. But eight of the A's hits were singles, and Oakland came up a run short, 4-3.

Merely mortal

It was up to Hershiser to finish things off in Game Five. He wasn't as dominating as he had been earlier in the postseason. He allowed two runs, but when the challenge was issued, he met it.

When the A's closed to 5-2 (which proved to be the final score) with one out and two on in the eighth, Hershiser got Canseco to pop up, then struck out Dave Parker on four pitches.

"I looked over at Tommy and gave him the high sign," said Hershiser, referring to the moment Canseco walked to the plate. "I wanted him to know I had enough left."

An uneasy Lasorda watched.

"I thought he was losing it," Lasorda said. "I told Ron (Perranoski, pitching coach), that if he didn't get Canseco out I was going to bring in (Jesse Orosco) to face Parker. I don't know where he got it, but Bulldog got it when we needed it."

Hershiser got Canseco to pop up on a 2-2 pitch. After bouncing his first pitch to Parker in the dirt, moving runners to second and third, Hershiser came back to strike out Parker on the next three.

And the warning was issued. Batters beware. This bulldog has more bite than bark.

World Series: Box Scores

Game One: Dodgers 5, Athletics 4

OAKLAND	ab	r	h	bi	bb	so	LOS ANGELES	ab	r	h	bi	bb	so
Lansford 3b	4	1	0	0	1	1	Sax 2b	3	1	1	0	0	0
Henderson cf	5	0	2	0	0	2	Stubbs 1b	4	0	0	0	0	0
Canseco rf	4	1	1	4	0	1	Hatcher lf	3	1	1	2	1	1
Parker lf	2	0	0	0	2	0	Marshall rf	4	1	1	0	0	1
Javier lf	1	0	1	0	0	0	Shelby cf	4	0	1	0	0	1
McGwire 1b	3	0	0	0	2	0	Scioscia c	4	0	1	1	0	0
Steinbach c	4	0	1	0	0	1	Hamilton 3b	4	0	0	0	0	2
Hassey c	0	0	0	0	0	0	Griffin ss	2	0	1	0	1	0
Hubbard 2b	4	1	2	0	0	0	MDavis ph	0	1	0	0	1	0
Weiss ss	4	0	0	0	0	1	Belcher p	0	0	0	0	0	0
Stewart p	3	1	0	0	1	3	Heep ph	1	0	0	0	0	0
Eckersley p	0	0	0	0	0	0	Leary p	0	0	0	0	0	0
							Woodson ph	1	0	0	0	0	0
							Holton p	0	0	0	0	0	0
							Gonzalez ph	1	0	0	0	0	1
							Pena p	0	0	0	0	0	0
							Gibson ph	1	1	1	2	0	0
TOTALS	34	4	7	4	6	9	TOTALS	32	5	7	5	3	6

```
Oakland . . . . . . . . . . . . . . . . . . . . . . . . . . . . . . . . . 040  000  000—4
Los Angeles . . . . . . . . . . . . . . . . . . . . . . . . . . . . . . 200  001  002—5
```

Two out when winning run scored
Game-winning RBI—Gibson.
DP—Oakland 1. LOB—Oakland 10, Los Angeles 5. 2B—Henderson. HR—Hatcher, Canseco, Gibson. SB—Canseco, Sax, MDavis.

Oakland	IP	H	R	ER	BB	SO	Los Angeles	IP	H	R	ER	BB	SO
Stewart	8	6	3	3	2	5	Belcher	2	3	4	4	4	3
Eckersley L	⅔	1	2	2	1	1	Leary	3	3	0	0	1	3
							Holton	2	0	0	0	0	0
							Pena W	2	1	0	0	0	3

HBP—Canseco by Belcher, Sax by Stewart. WP—Stewart. Balk—Stewart. T—3:04. A—55,983.

Game Two: Dodgers 6, Athletics 0

OAKLAND	ab	r	h	bi	bb	so	LOS ANGELES	ab	r	h	bi	bb	so
Lansford 3b	3	0	0	0	1	1	Sax 2b	4	1	1	0	0	0
Henderson cf	4	0	0	0	0	2	Stubbs 1b	2	1	1	1	1	0
Canseco rf	4	0	0	0	0	1	Woodson 1b	1	0	0	0	0	0
Parker lf	4	0	3	0	0	1	Hatcher lf	4	1	2	1	0	1
McGwire 1b	3	0	0	0	0	0	Marshall rf	4	1	2	3	0	2
Hassey c	3	0	0	0	0	0	Gonzalez rf	0	0	0	0	0	0
Hubbard 2b	2	0	0	0	1	0	Shelby cf	4	0	0	0	0	2
Weiss ss	3	0	0	0	0	1	Scioscia c	4	0	0	0	0	1
SDavis p	1	0	0	0	0	1	Hamilton 3b	4	0	0	0	0	1
Nelson p	0	0	0	0	0	0	Griffin ss	4	1	1	0	0	1
Polonia ph	1	0	0	0	0	0	Hershiser p	3	1	3	1	0	0
CYoung p	0	0	0	0	0	0							
Plunk p	0	0	0	0	0	0							
Baylor ph	1	0	0	0	0	1							
Honeycutt p	0	0	0	0	0	0							
TOTALS	29	0	3	0	2	8	TOTALS	34	6	10	6	1	8

```
Oakland . . . . . . . . . . . . . . . . . . . . . . . . . . . . . . . . . 000  000  000—0
Los Angeles . . . . . . . . . . . . . . . . . . . . . . . . . . . . . . 005  100  00x—6
```

Game-winning RBI—Stubbs.
E—Hamilton. DP—Los Angeles 2. LOB—Oakland 4, Los Angeles 5. 2B—Hershiser 2. 3B—Marshall. HR—Marshall. SB—Weiss.

Oakland	IP	H	R	ER	BB	SO	Los Angeles	IP	H	R	ER	BB	SO
SDavis L	3⅓	8	6	6	0	2	Hershiser W	9	3	0	0	2	8
Nelson	1⅔	1	0	0	1	1							
CYoung	1	1	0	0	0	0							
Plunk	1	0	0	0	0	3							
Honeycutt	1	0	0	0	0	2							

T—2:30. A—56,051.

Game Three: Athletics 2, Dodgers 1

LOS ANGELES	ab	r	h	bi	bb	so	OAKLAND	ab	r	h	bi	bb	so
Sax 2b	5	0	1	0	0	0	Phillips lf	1	0	0	0	0	0
Stubbs 1b	4	0	1	1	0	3	Polonia ph-lf	3	0	0	0	0	1
Woodson 1b	1	0	0	0	0	0	Henderson cf	4	0	0	0	0	2
Hatcher lf-rf	4	0	1	0	0	1	Canseco rf	4	0	0	0	0	1
Marshall rf	1	0	0	0	0	1	McGwire 1b	4	1	1	1	0	2
Heep lf	3	0	1	0	0	1	Steinbach dh	3	0	2	0	0	0
Shelby cf	3	0	2	0	1	1	Lansford 3b	3	0	0	0	0	0
MDavis dh	2	0	0	0	1	0	Hubbard 2b	3	1	1	0	0	0
Anderson dh	1	0	0	0	0	1	Hassey c	1	0	1	1	2	0
Scioscia c	4	0	1	0	0	1	Weiss ss	3	0	0	0	0	0
Hamilton 3b	3	1	1	0	1	1							
Griffin ss	3	0	0	0	0	2							
TOTALS	34	1	8	1	3	12	TOTALS	29	2	5	2	2	6

| Los Angeles | | | | | | | | 000 | 010 | 000—1 |
| Oakland | | | | | | | | 001 | 000 | 001—2 |

One out when winning run scored
Game-winning RBI—McGwire.
E—Scioscia. DP—Los Angeles 1. LOB—Los Angeles 10, Oakland 4. 2B—Steinbach, Stubbs, Heep, Hatcher. HR—McGwire. SB—Hubbard, Shelby. S—Griffin.

Los Angeles	IP	H	R	ER	BB	SO		Oakland	IP	H	R	ER	BB	SO
Tudor	1⅓	0	0	0	0	1		Welch	5	6	1	1	3	8
Leary	3⅔	3	1	1	1	1		Cadaret	⅓	0	0	0	0	0
Pena	3	1	0	0	1	4		Nelson	1⅔	2	0	0	0	1
Howell L	⅓	1	1	1	0	0		Honeycutt W	2	0	0	0	0	3

Welch pitched to 3 batters in 6th; Nelson pitched to 1 batter in 8th.
Balk—Leary. T—3:21. A—49,316.

Game Four: Dodgers 4, Athletics 3

LOS ANGELES	ab	r	h	bi	bb	so		OAKLAND	ab	r	h	bi	bb	so
Sax 2b	4	1	1	0	1	1		Polonia lf	5	1	1	0	0	1
Stubbs 1b	3	1	1	0	0	0		Henderson cf	5	1	4	1	0	0
Woodson ph-1b	1	0	0	1	0	0		Javier pr	0	0	0	0	0	0
Hatcher lf	4	1	1	0	0	0		Canseco rf	3	0	0	1	2	1
Marshall rf	0	0	0	0	0	0		Parker dh	5	0	0	0	0	2
MDavis rf	3	0	0	0	0	0		McGwire 1b	3	0	0	1	1	1
Gonzalez ph-rf- lf	1	0	0	0	0	1		Lansford 3b	4	0	1	1	0	0
Shelby cf	4	0	1	0	0	0		Steinbach c	4	0	1	0	0	1
Scioscia c	2	0	1	0	0	0		Hubbard 2b	3	0	0	0	0	2
Dempsey c	1	0	0	0	1	1		Hassey ph	1	0	1	0	0	0
Heep dh	4	0	1	0	0	1		Gallego pr-2b	0	0	0	0	0	0
Hamilton 3b	4	0	1	0	0	0		Weiss ss	4	1	1	0	0	1
Griffin ss	3	1	1	0	1	0								
TOTALS	34	4	8	2	3	4		TOTALS	37	3	9	3	3	9

| Los Angeles | | | | | | | | 201 | 000 | 100—4 |
| Oakland | | | | | | | | 100 | 001 | 100—3 |

Game-winning RBI—None.
E—Hubbard, Weiss, Griffin. LOB—Los Angeles 6, Oakland 10. 2B—Stubbs, Henderson, Shelby. SB—MDavis.

Los Angeles	IP	H	R	ER	BB	SO		Oakland	IP	H	R	ER	BB	SO
Belcher W	6⅔	7	3	2	2	7		Stewart L	6⅓	6	4	2	3	0
Howell S	2⅓	2	0	0	1	2		Cadaret	1⅔	1	0	0	3	3
								Eckersley	1	1	0	0	0	1

PB—Steinbach, Scioscia. T—3:05. A—49,317.

Game Five: Dodgers 5, Athletics 2

LOS ANGELES	ab	r	h	bi	bb	so		OAKLAND	ab	r	h	bi	bb	so
Sax 2b	4	0	2	0	0	0		Javier lf	3	0	1	2	0	1
Stubbs 1b	4	1	0	0	0	0		Henderson cf	2	0	0	0	2	1
Hatcher lf	4	2	2	2	0	0		Canseco rf	4	0	0	0	0	1
Gonzalez lf	0	0	0	0	0	0		Parker dh	4	0	0	0	0	1
Marshall rf	4	0	0	0	0	1		McGwire 1b	4	0	0	0	0	1
Shelby cf	3	0	0	0	1	3		Hassey c	3	0	0	0	1	2
MDavis dh	2	2	1	2	2	0		Lansford 3b	4	1	2	0	0	0
Dempsey c	4	0	1	1	0	1		Phillips 2b	3	1	1	0	1	2
Hamilton 3b	4	0	0	0	0	0		Weiss ss	2	0	0	0	0	0
Griffin ss	4	0	0	0	0	1								
TOTALS	33	5	8	5	3	6		TOTALS	29	2	4	2	4	9

| Los Angeles | | | | | | | | 200 | 201 | 000—5 |
| Oakland | | | | | | | | 001 | 000 | 010—2 |

Game-winning RBI—Hatcher.
DP—Oakland 1. LOB—Los Angeles 4, Oakland 6. 2B—Dempsey. HR—Hatcher, MDavis. S—Weiss. SF—Javier.

Los Angeles	IP	H	R	ER	BB	SO		Oakland	IP	H	R	ER	BB	SO
Hershiser W	9	4	2	2	4	9		SDavis L	4⅔	6	4	4	1	5
								Cadaret	0	1	0	0	0	0
								Nelson	3	1	1	1	2	1
								Honeycutt	⅓	0	0	0	0	0
								Plunk	⅔	0	0	0	0	0
								Burns	⅓	0	0	0	0	0

WP—Hershiser. T—2:51. A—49,317.

World Series: Composite Box

LOS ANGELES

Player, Pos.	AVG	G	AB	R	H	2B	3B	HR	RBI	BB	SO	SB
Orel Hershiser, p	1.000	2	3	1	3	2	0	0	1	0	0	0
Kirk Gibson, ph	1.000	1	1	1	1	0	0	1	2	0	0	0
Mickey Hatcher, lf-rf	.368	5	19	5	7	1	0	2	5	1	3	0
Steve Sax, 2b	.300	5	20	3	6	0	0	0	0	1	1	1
Franklin Stubbs, 1b	.294	5	17	3	5	2	0	0	2	1	3	0
Danny Heep, ph-lf-dh	.250	3	8	0	2	1	0	0	0	0	2	0
Mike Marshall, rf	.231	5	13	2	3	0	1	1	3	0	5	0
John Shelby, cf	.222	5	18	0	4	1	0	0	1	2	7	1
Mike Scioscia, c	.214	4	14	0	3	0	0	0	1	0	2	0
Rick Dempsey, c	.200	2	5	0	1	1	0	0	1	1	2	0
Alfredo Griffin, ss	.188	5	16	2	3	0	0	0	0	2	4	0
Mike Davis, ph-dh-rf	.143	4	7	3	1	0	0	1	2	4	0	2
Jeff Hamilton, 3b	.105	5	19	1	2	0	0	0	0	1	4	0
Tracy Woodson, ph-1b	.000	4	4	0	0	0	0	0	1	0	0	0
Jose Gonzalez, ph-rf-lf	.000	4	2	0	0	0	0	0	0	0	2	0
Dave Anderson, dh	.000	1	1	0	0	0	0	0	0	0	1	0
TOTALS	.246	5	167	21	41	8	1	5	19	13	36	4

Pitcher	W	L	ERA	G	GS	CG	SV	IP	H	R	ER	BB	SO
Alejandro Pena	1	0	0.00	2	0	0	0	5	2	0	0	1	7
Brian Holton	0	0	0.00	1	0	0	0	2	0	0	0	1	0
John Tudor	0	0	0.00	1	1	0	0	1⅓	0	0	0	0	1
Orel Hershiser	2	0	1.00	2	2	2	0	18	7	2	2	6	17
Tim Leary	0	0	1.35	2	0	0	0	6⅔	6	1	1	2	4
Jay Howell	0	1	3.38	2	0	0	1	2⅔	3	1	1	1	2
Tim Belcher	1	0	6.23	2	2	0	0	8⅔	10	7	6	6	10
TOTALS	4	1	2.03	5	5	2	1	44⅓	28	11	10	17	41

OAKLAND

Player, Pos.	AVG	G	AB	R	H	2B	3B	HR	RBI	BB	SO	SB
Stan Javier, lf-pr	.500	3	4	0	2	0	0	0	2	0	1	0
Terry Steinbach, c-dh	.364	3	11	0	4	1	0	0	0	0	2	0
Dave Henderson, cf	.300	5	20	1	6	2	0	0	1	2	7	0
Ron Hassey, c-ph	.250	5	8	0	2	0	0	0	1	3	3	0
Glenn Hubbard, 2b	.250	4	12	2	3	0	0	0	0	0	2	1
Tony Phillips, lf-2b	.250	2	4	1	1	0	0	0	0	1	2	0
Dave Parker, lf-dh	.200	5	15	0	3	0	0	0	0	2	3	0
Carney Lansford, 3b	.167	5	18	2	3	0	0	0	1	2	2	0
Luis Polonia, ph-lf	.111	3	9	1	1	0	0	0	0	0	2	0
Walt Weiss, ss	.063	5	16	1	1	0	0	0	0	0	3	1
Mark McGwire, 1b	.059	5	17	1	1	0	0	1	1	3	4	0
Jose Canseco, rf	.053	5	19	1	1	0	0	1	5	2	5	1
Dave Stewart, p	.000	2	3	0	0	0	0	0	0	1	3	0
Storm Davis, p	.000	2	1	0	0	0	0	0	0	0	1	0
Don Baylor, ph	.000	1	1	0	0	0	0	0	0	0	1	0
Mike Gallego, pr-2b	—	1	0	0	0	0	0	0	0	0	0	0
TOTALS	.177	5	158	11	28	3	0	2	11	17	41	3

Pitcher	W	L	ERA	G	GS	CG	SV	IP	H	R	ER	BB	SO
Rick Honeycutt	1	0	0.00	3	0	0	0	3⅓	0	0	0	0	5
Greg Cadaret	0	0	0.00	3	0	0	0	2	2	0	0	0	3
Eric Plunk	0	0	0.00	2	0	0	0	1⅔	0	0	0	0	3
Curt Young	0	0	0.00	1	0	0	0	1	1	0	0	0	0
Todd Burns	0	0	0.00	1	0	0	0	⅓	0	0	0	0	0
Gene Nelson	0	0	1.42	3	0	0	0	6⅓	4	1	1	3	3
Bob Welch	0	0	1.80	1	1	0	0	5	6	1	1	3	3
Dave Stewart	0	1	3.14	2	2	0	0	14⅓	12	7	5	5	5
Dennis Eckersley	0	1	10.80	2	0	0	0	1⅔	2	2	2	1	2
Storm Davis	0	2	11.25	2	2	0	0	8	14	10	10	1	7
TOTALS	1	4	3.92	5	5	0	0	43⅔	41	21	19	13	36

Los Angeles	6	0	6		3	1	2		1	0	2	—	21
Oakland	1	4	2		0	0	1		1	1	1	—	11

Game-winning RBIs—Gibson, Stubbs, McGwire, Hatcher.
E—Hamilton, Scioscia, Hubbard, Weiss, Griffin. DP—Los Angeles 3, Oakland 2. LOB—Los Angeles 30, Oakland 34. S—Griffin, Weiss. SF—Javier. PB—Steinbach, Scioscia. HBP—Canseco by Belcher, Sax by Stewart. WP—Stewart, Hershiser. Balk—Stewart, Leary. Umpires—Harvey (NL), Merrill (AL), Froemming (NL), Cousins (AL), Crawford (NL), McCoy (AL). Official Scorers—Jack Lang, New York Daily News; Dave Nightingale, The Sporting News; Vern Plagenhoef, Booth Newspapers.

Good Oakland team enjoys a great year

By TIM KURKJIAN

Forget, for a minute, the 1988 World Series. Forget Dennis Eckersley's hanging slider, the 1-for-19 by Jose Canseco, the 11 Oakland runs in five games.

The A's deserve better than that. After all, they blasted through their division, winning by 13 games and winning more games (104) than any American League West team ever. The last team to win more than Oakland was the '70 Orioles (108).

Remember the A's for beating Boston in four straight to win the pennant. Remember them for Canseco's three home runs in the championship series, including the monstrous blast off Roger Clemens in Game Two, tying the score and turning the tide. Remember how hard they hit Mike Boddicker in Game Three, how they beat Lee Smith in Game Two, how they managed to strike out Wade Boggs two times in Game One.

Remember them for Eckersley's four saves in the ALCS, giving him 49 this season. Remember their ace, Dave Stewart, winning Game Four. Remember rookie shortstop Walter Weiss' game-winning single off Smith in Game Two. Remember Mike Gallego turning the double play.

Don't label them as anything else but a good team that had a great year. As Red Sox general manager Lou Gorman put

League Champions
(Playoff Champions, Where Applicable)

1988—Oakland	1958—New York	1928—New York
1987—Minnesota	1957—New York	1927—New York
1986—Boston	1956—New York	1926—New York
1985—Kansas City	1955—New York	1925—Washington
1984—Detroit	1954—Cleveland	1924—Washington
1983—Baltimore	1953—New York	1923—New York
1982—Milwaukee	1952—New York	1922—New York
1981—New York	1951—New York	1921—New York
1980—Kansas City	1950—New York	1920—Cleveland
1979—Baltimore	1949—New York	1919—Chicago
1978—New York	1948—Cleveland	1918—Boston
1977—New York	1947—New York	1917—Chicago
1976—New York	1946—Boston	1916—Boston
1975—Boston	1945—Detroit	1915—Boston
1974—Oakland	1944—St. Louis	1914—Philadelphia
1973—Oakland	1943—New York	1913—Philadelphia
1972—Oakland	1942—New York	1912—Boston
1971—Baltimore	1941—New York	1911—Philadelphia
1970—Baltimore	1940—Detroit	1910—Philadelphia
1969—Baltimore	1939—New York	1909—Detroit
1968—Detroit	1938—New York	1908—Detroit
1967—Boston	1937—New York	1907—Detroit
1966—Baltimore	1936—New York	1906—Chicago
1965—Minnesota	1935—Detroit	1905—Philadelphia
1964—New York	1934—Detroit	1904—Boston
1963—New York	1933—Washington	1903—Boston
1962—New York	1932—New York	1902—Philadelphia
1961—New York	1931—Philadelphia	1901—Chicago
1960—New York	1930—Philadelphia	
1959—Chicago	1929—Philadelphia	

Jose Canseco of the Oakland A's became the first player to hit 40 homers and steal 40 bases in the same year.

it, "We played lousy. We had no momentum. We had a lot of guys in slumps. We didn't hit. If we had played up to our capabilities, we could have won."

Instead, they got stomped.

"I think Oakland has the best team in baseball," said Gorman after the Straight A's rout. "But I don't think that what they did they'll do forever."

AL East race

The Knife The Mac chants began in May, when the Red Sox were floundering. They were fighting on the team bus, they were back-biting, they were out of control.

A team with great talent stumbled into the all-star break nine games out of first. Manager John McNamara had to be replaced.

Gorman announced the firing July 14. McNamara was in uniform, filling out the lineup card, when he was told.

His replacement was Joe Morgan, a coach of many years, a man fired as the organization's Triple-A manager years earlier. A man who was misidentified in Boston's 1988 media guide. His picture and that of coach Rac Slider were transposed.

Who was this guy? At 57, he had waited patiently for this chance. He drove a snow plow on the Mass Pike in the offseason. From little Walpole, Mass., he was Boston's first manager from New England in 57 years.

He spun funny tales of the old days in Class A ball. He talked to his players. He had fun, they had fun. He placed shortstop Jody Reed and first baseman Todd Benzinger in the lineup. In most every way, he was exactly the opposite of McNamara.

And that's what the Red Sox needed.

They won their first 12 games, and 19 of their first 20 under Morgan—going from nine games out to a first-place tie with

AL Champs

Members of the American League pennant winning Oakland Athletics included top row, l to r, Walt Weiss, Don Baylor, Ron Hassey, Dave Henderson, Steve Ontiveros, Matt Young, Terry Steinbach, Greg Cadaret, Rick Honeycutt, Gene Nelson, Dave Stewart, Todd Burns, Curt Young. Second row, director of team travel Mickey Morabito, equipment manager Frank Cienscizyk, visiting clubhouse manager Steve Vucinich, Jose Canseco, Bob Welch, Carney Lansford, Storm Davis, Dennis Eckersley, Eric Plunk, Mark McGwire, Dave Parker, trainer Barry Weinberg, assistant trainer Larry Davis. Third row, Doug Jennings, Mike Gallego, bullpen coach Mike Paul, fitness instructor Dave McKay, first base coach Rene Lachemann, manager Tony LaRussa, third base coach Jim Lefebvre, bench coach Bob Watson, Glenn Hubbard, Matt Sinatro, Luis Polonia, Stan Javier.

Tony LaRussa (left) and rookie manager Joe Morgan guided their teams to division titles.

Detroit.

The only fight came between outfielder-DH Jim Rice and Morgan. Morgan, an ex-hockey player, won. Rice pushed Morgan after being lifted for a pinch hitter. Morgan pushed back—Mac wouldn't have—and won the total respect of his entire team.

"I'm the manager of this nine," he said.

From Aug 4. on, the Red Sox went 27-30, lost six of their last seven games and won by one game over Detroit. The Tigers, ravaged by injuries, collapsed. The Yankees' usual turmoil and lack of pitching did them in. Milwaukee fell apart in early September, then didn't have enough time to regroup. Toronto fell apart in early April and didn't have time to come back either.

The Indians were bad.

The Orioles were the worst.

AL West race

What race?

The A's moved into first place April 20, and stayed there for the final 165 days of the season. They won 14 straight and 18 of 19. By May 9, they led by eight. With each home run, they mashed forearms. With each save, Eckersley fired his fist in the air.

The Twins did make a run. They cut the lead to 5½ at the all-star break, then to three on July 17. But Oakland won six of its next seven to fend them off. By the end of August, the lead was nine again.

Leading the way was Canseco, the first player ever to hit 40 home runs and steal 40 bases in one season. He drove in 100 runs for the third straight season. No Oakland player had done that two straight years.

Stewart won 21 games, making him only the second Oakland pitcher to post back-to-back 20-win seasons. Eckersley saved 45 games. The deep, rich A's bullpen saved 64 games, tops in major league history.

The A's blended speed and power and starting pitching and bullpen. Dave Henderson, a free-agent outfielder, had his career year. So did a few others. There was no doubt it was the A's year.

The Twins won 91, the second most in the league. They became the first team in history to win more games the year after a championship season, and not win the division.

The Royals baffled many by not being better. The Rangers baffled more by being so bad. The White Sox and Mariners were bad, boring and never a factor.

Then again, no one was.

Hitting

Well, what a surprise.

Wade Boggs led the league in hitting (.366) for the fourth straight year. He became the first player in the modern era to record five straight 200-hit seasons. (Ironically, No. 200 came off Toronto's Jeff Musselman, who gave up No. 200 in 1986).

He reached base more than 300 times for the fifth time. In major league history, only Lou Gehrig, Babe Ruth, Ted Williams and Stan Musial have done that more times. And Boggs did it with a $6 million palimony suit hanging over his head (He said of that, "Well, it's not like I killed the president or anything, right?")

Boggs didn't lead the league in hits. Minnesota's Kirby Puckett

Wade Boggs of the Boston Red Sox had 200 or more hits for a record fifth straight season.

did, in another huge season. Canseco led in home runs, RBIs and slugging. He was expected to win the most valuable player award, perhaps unanimously.

Despite some great years, runs and home runs were down about 20 percent from 1987. In '87, nine teams scored 770 or more runs. In '88, three teams did. In '87, 20 players hit 30 or more home runs. In '88, three players did.

Pitching

What a comeback. The league ERA went from 4.46 to 3.96. Either the ball was dead or the pitchers got mad and got even.

Minnesota's Frank Viola was expected to run away with the Cy Young Award after a 24-7 season. But he didn't win the ERA title. That went to his teammate, Allan Anderson, who was taught Viola's change-up and suddenly emerged.

Anderson protected his 2.45 ERA by not making his last scheduled start, thereby depriving Milwaukee's Ted Higuera a shot at the title. Anderson was announced on CNN as the ERA champ—only he was announced as Andy Allanson, who catches for the Indians.

Eckersley saved 45 games, one short of Dave Righetti's major league record. Minnesota's Jeff Reardon saved 42, making him the only man to save 40 in both leagues. Cleveland's Doug Jones saved 37.

Special accomplishment

In many ways, the Orioles really were the story of 1988. They lost 21 straight to start the season, demolishing the record for the worst start in major league history.

They were 1-22 in April (worst month of any team in history), and 6-34 after 40 games. Their manager, Cal Ripken Sr., was fired after six games—believed to the earliest firing in history.

Ripken wasn't the only manager to go. Boston's McNamara, Seattle's Dick Williams, California's Cookie Rojas, and the New York Yankees' Billy Martin were fired during the season. After the season, the Yankees' Lou Piniella and Jim Fregosi of the Chicago White Sox were axed.

Milestones and miscellany

Chicago's Jerry Reuss, 38, won his 200th career game, and became the second pitcher ever to win 200 in a career, yet never 20 in a season (Milt Pappas was the other). After No. 200, teammate Dave LaPoint told Reuss "You can tell your grandchildren about it—tomorrow." . . . Blue Jays pitcher Mike Flanagan won his 150th career game, or so he thought. An error in the media guide was detected, so Flanagan actually had won his 149th. When he won the real No. 150 a few days later, Flanagan said "Well, I guess I'm down to 137 now." . . . Detroit's Darrell Evans hit his 400th career home run . . . Milwaukee's Rob Deer had three at-bats left, and needed three strikeouts to tie Texas' Pete Incaviglia for the AL strikeout title with 153. He struck out three times in a row. Incaviglia set a major league record for fewest games played by a strikeout (or co-strikeout) champ . . . The Angels' Devon White set some sort of record by not being at his position—center field, of all places—when the game began. He was in the clubhouse making a phone call when the first pitch was delivered. It had to be replayed. When asked how no one noticed, right fielder Chili Davis said "I yelled to the umpires, but they didn't hear. Not only are they blind, they're deaf, too." . . . Boggs swung at 1,032 pitches, and missed 33 . . . Blue Jays shortstop Tony Fernandez, in his last swing one game and his first swing the next game, hit two balls that resulted in five errors—four by outfielders . . . The Yankees' Tommy John became the first pitcher since Jay Bentley Seymour in 1898 to make three errors in one inning. Said the 44-year-old John: "Jay Bentley Seymour? I think I played against him in the Eastern League." . . . Cleveland outfielder Cory Snyder finally hit the ball off Roger Clemens. He was 0-for-9 with nine strikeouts against Clemens before flying out to right in his first at-bat against him this season. Snyder was greeted by high-fives when he returned to the Cleveland bench . . . Milwaukee's Jim Adduci batted 94 times without a walk, Milwaukee's Juan Castillo batted 90 times without an extra base hit and the Twins' Tom Nieto had 60 at-bats without an RBI . . . The Mariners' Steve Trout, in one start, threw 29 pitches, 22 balls. His line:⅔ IP, 0 H, 4 ER, 5 BB, 0 SO, 2 WP. The wild pitches came on successive pitches, one of which hit the screen on the fly.

What a great year.

East	W	L	Pct.	GB	
Boston..............	89	73	.549	—	
Detroit.............	88	74	.543	1	
Milwaukee..........	87	75	.537	2	
Toronto............	87	75	.537	2	
New York	85	76	.528	3½	
Cleveland	78	84	.481	11	
Baltimore	54	107	.335	34½	1988
West					Final
Oakland.............	104	58	.642	—	Standings
Minnesota..........	91	71	.562	13	
Kansas City	84	77	.522	19½	
California	75	87	.463	29	
Chicago............	71	90	.441	32½	
Texas	70	91	.435	33½	
Seattle.............	68	93	.422	35½	

1988: General Information

League Championship Series: Oakland defeated Boston 4-0 in a best-of-7 series for the league pennant.

Regular Season Attendance: Minnesota, 3,030,672; New York, 2,633,703; Toronto, 2,595,175; Boston, 2,464,851; Kansas City 2,350,181; California, 2,340,865; Oakland, 2,287,335; Detroit, 2,081,162; Milwaukee, 1,923,238; Baltimore, 1,660,738; Texas, 1,581,901; Cleveland, 1,411,610; Chicago, 1,115,525; Seattle, 1,020,354.

Managers: Baltimore—Cal Ripken Sr., Frank Robinson; **Boston**—John McNamara, Joe Morgan; **California**—Cookie Rojas, Moose Stubing; **Chicago**—Jim Fregosi; **Cleveland**—Doc Edwards; **Detroit**—Sparky Anderson; **Kansas City**—John Wathan; **Milwaukee**—Tom Trebelhorn; **Minnesota**—Tom Kelly; **New York**—Billy Martin, Lou Piniella; **Oakland**—Tony LaRussa; **Seattle**—Dick Williams, Jim Snyder; **Texas**—Bobby Valentine; **Toronto**—Jimy Williams.

1988 All-Star Team (by Baseball America): C—Bob Boone, California. **1B**—George Brett, Kansas City; **2B**—Marty Barrett, Boston. **3B**—Wade Boggs, Boston. **SS**—Alan Trammell, Detroit. **OF**—Jose Canseco, Oakland; Kirby Puckett, Minnesota; Mike Greenwell, Boston. **DH**—Jack Clark, New York. **P**—Frank Viola, Minnesota; Dave Stewart, Oakland; Mark Gubicza, Kansas City; Roger Clemens, Boston; Dennis Eckersley, Oakland. **Player of the Year**—Jose Canseco, Oakland. **Pitcher of the Year**—Frank Viola, Minnesota. **Rookie of the Year**—Walt Weiss, Oakland. **Manager of the Year**—Tony LaRussa, Oakland. **Executive of the Year**—Sandy Alderson, Oakland.

1988: Batting, Pitching Statistics

CLUB BATTING

	AVG	G	AB	R	H	2B	3B	HR	BB	SO	SB
Boston	.283	162	5545	813	1569	310	39	124	623	728	65
Minnesota	.274	162	5510	759	1508	294	31	151	528	832	107
Toronto	.268	162	5557	763	1491	271	47	158	521	935	107
New York	.263	161	5592	772	1469	272	12	148	588	935	146
Oakland	.263	162	5602	800	1474	251	22	156	580	926	129
California	.261	162	5582	714	1458	258	31	124	469	819	86
Cleveland	.261	162	5505	666	1435	235	28	134	416	866	97
Kansas City	.259	161	5469	704	1419	275	40	121	486	944	137
Seattle	.257	161	5436	664	1397	271	27	148	461	787	95
Milwaukee	.257	162	5488	682	1409	258	26	113	439	911	159
Texas	.252	161	5479	637	1378	228	39	112	542	1023	130
Detroit	.250	162	5433	703	1358	213	28	143	588	841	87
Chicago	.244	161	5449	631	1327	224	35	132	446	908	98
Baltimore	.238	161	5358	550	1275	199	20	137	504	869	69

CLUB PITCHING

	ERA	G	CG	SHO	SV	IP	H	R	ER	BB	SO
Oakland	3.44	162	22	9	64	1489	1376	620	569	553	984
Milwaukee	3.45	162	30	8	51	1449	1355	616	555	437	832
Kansas City	3.65	161	29	12	32	1428	1415	648	580	465	886
Detroit	3.71	162	34	8	36	1446	1361	658	596	497	890
Toronto	3.80	162	16	17	47	1449	1404	680	611	528	904
Minnesota	3.93	162	18	9	52	1432	1457	672	625	493	1085
Boston	3.97	162	26	14	37	1446	1415	689	629	629	912
Texas	4.05	161	41	11	31	1439	1467	757	659	654	912
Chicago	4.12	161	11	9	43	1439	1467	757	659	533	754
Seattle	4.15	161	28	11	28	1428	1384	744	659	558	981
Cleveland	4.16	162	35	10	46	1434	1501	731	663	442	812
New York	4.24	161	16	5	43	1456	1512	748	686	487	861
California	4.32	162	26	9	33	1456	1503	771	698	568	817
Baltimore	4.54	161	20	7	26	1416	1506	789	714	523	709

INDIVIDUAL BATTING LEADERS
(Minimum 502 Plate Appearances)

	AVG	G	AB	R	H	2B	3B	HR	RBI	BB	SO	SB
*Boggs, Wade, Bos	.366	155	584	128	214	45	6	5	58	125	34	2
Puckett, Kirby, Minn	.356	158	657	109	234	42	5	24	121	23	83	6
*Greenwell, Mike, Bos	.325	158	590	86	192	39	8	22	119	87	38	16
Winfield, Dave, NY	.322	149	559	96	180	37	2	25	107	69	88	9
Molitor, Paul, Mil	.312	154	609	115	190	34	6	13	60	71	54	41
*Hrbek, Kent, Minn	.312	143	510	75	159	31	0	25	76	67	54	0
Trammell, Alan, Det	.311	128	466	73	145	24	1	15	69	46	46	7
*Mattingly, Don, NY	.311	144	599	94	186	37	0	18	88	41	29	1
Canseco, Jose, Oak	.307	158	610	120	187	34	0	42	124	78	128	40
Yount, Robin, Mil	.306	162	621	92	190	38	11	13	91	63	63	22

* indicates lefthanded batter   # indicates switch hitter

INDIVIDUAL PITCHING LEADERS
(Minimum 162 Innings)

	W	L	ERA	G	GS	CG	SV	IP	H	R	ER	BB	SO
*Anderson, Allan, Minn	16	9	2.45	30	30	3	0	202	199	70	55	37	83
*Higuera, Ted, Mil	16	9	2.45	31	31	8	0	227	168	66	62	59	192

Minnesota's Frank Viola had his best year, going 24-7 with a 2.64 ERA.

	W	L	ERA	G	GS	CG	SV	IP	H	R	ER	BB	SO
*Viola, Frank, Minn	24	7	2.64	35	35	7	0	255	236	80	75	54	193
Gubicza, Mark, KC	20	8	2.70	35	35	8	0	270	237	94	81	83	183
Clemens, Roger, Bos	18	12	2.93	35	35	14	0	264	217	93	86	62	291
Robinson, Jeff, Det	13	6	2.98	24	23	6	0	172	121	61	57	72	114
Stieb, Dave, Tor	16	8	3.04	32	31	8	0	207	157	76	70	79	147
*Leibrandt, Charlie, KC	13	12	3.19	35	35	7	0	243	244	98	86	62	125
*Swindell, Greg, Cle	18	14	3.20	33	33	12	0	242	234	97	86	45	180
Stewart, Dave, Oak	21	12	3.23	37	37	14	0	276	240	111	99	110	192

* indicates lefthanded pitcher

BALTIMORE

BATTING	AVG	G	AB	R	H	2B	3B	HR	RBI	BB	SO	SB
*Anderson, Brady, of (41 Bos)	.212	94	325	31	69	13	4	1	21	23	75	10
Davis, Butch, of	.240	13	25	2	6	1	0	0	0	0	8	1
Gerhart, Ken, of	.195	103	262	27	51	10	1	9	23	21	57	7
Gonzales, Rene, 3b-2b	.215	92	237	13	51	6	0	2	15	13	32	2
*Hughes, Keith, of	.194	41	108	10	21	4	2	2	14	16	27	1
Kennedy, Terry, c	.226	85	265	20	60	10	0	3	16	15	53	0
Landrum, Tito, of	.125	13	24	2	3	0	1	0	2	4	6	0
#Murray, Eddie, 1b-dh	.284	161	603	75	171	27	2	28	84	75	78	5
Nichols, Carl, c	.191	18	47	2	9	1	0	0	1	3	10	0
*Orsulak, Joe, of	.288	125	379	48	109	21	3	8	27	23	30	9
Ripken, Billy, 2b	.207	150	512	52	106	18	1	2	34	33	63	8
Ripken, Cal, ss	.264	161	575	87	152	25	1	23	81	102	69	2
Rowdon, Wade, 3b-of	.100	20	30	1	3	0	0	0	0	0	6	1
Schu, Rick, 3b	.256	89	270	22	69	9	4	4	20	21	49	6
*Sheets, Larry, of-dh	.230	136	452	38	104	19	1	10	47	42	72	1
#Stanicek, Pete, of-2b	.230	83	261	29	60	7	1	4	17	28	45	12
*Stone, Jeff, of	.164	26	61	4	10	1	0	0	1	4	11	4
*Tettleton, Mickey, c	.261	86	283	31	74	11	1	11	37	28	70	0
*Traber, Jim, 1b-dh	.222	103	352	25	78	6	0	10	45	19	42	1
Worthington, Craig, 3b	.185	26	81	5	15	2	0	2	4	9	24	1

PITCHING	W	L	ERA	G	GS	CG	SV	IP	H	R	ER	BB	SO
Aase, Don	0	0	4.05	35	0	0	0	47	40	22	21	37	28
*Ballard, Jeff	8	12	4.40	25	25	6	0	153	167	83	75	42	41
Bautista, Jose	6	15	4.30	33	25	3	0	172	171	86	82	45	76
*Dillard, Gordon	0	0	6.00	2	1	0	0	3	3	2	2	4	2
Habyan, John	1	0	4.30	7	0	0	0	15	22	10	7	4	4
Harnisch, Pete	0	2	5.54	2	2	0	0	13	13	8	8	9	10
*McGregor, Scott	0	3	8.83	4	4	0	0	17	27	18	17	7	10

	W	L	ERA	G	GS	CG	SV	IP	H	R	ER	BB	SO
Milacki, Bob	2	0	0.72	3	3	1	0	25	9	2	2	9	18
Morgan, Mike	1	6	5.43	22	10	2	1	71	70	45	43	23	29
Niedenfuer, Tom	3	4	3.51	52	0	0	18	59	59	23	23	19	40
Noles, Dickie	0	2	24.30	2	2	0	0	3	11	10	9	0	1
Olson, Gregg	1	1	3.27	10	0	0	0	11	10	4	4	10	9
Peraza, Oswald	5	7	5.55	19	15	1	0	86	98	62	53	37	61
*Scherrer, Bill	0	1	13.50	4	0	0	0	4	8	6	6	3	3
Schilling, Curt	0	3	9.82	4	4	0	0	15	22	19	16	10	4
Schmidt, Dave	8	5	3.40	41	9	0	2	130	129	58	49	38	67
Sisk, Doug	3	3	3.72	52	0	0	0	94	109	43	39	45	26
*Thurmond, Mark	1	8	4.58	43	6	0	3	75	80	43	38	27	29
Tibbs, Jay	4	15	5.39	30	24	1	0	159	184	103	95	63	82
Williamson, Mark	5	8	4.90	37	10	2	2	118	125	70	64	40	69

BOSTON

BATTING	AVG	G	AB	R	H	2B	3B	HR	RBI	BB	SO	SB
Barrett, Marty, 2b	.283	150	612	83	173	28	1	1	65	40	35	7
#Benzinger, Todd, 1b-of	.254	120	405	47	103	28	1	13	70	22	80	2
*Boggs, Wade, 3b	.366	155	584	128	214	45	6	5	58	125	34	2
Burks, Ellis, of	.294	144	540	93	159	37	5	18	92	62	89	25
Cerone, Rick, c	.269	84	264	31	71	13	1	3	27	20	32	0
*Dodson, Pat, 1b	.178	17	45	5	8	3	1	1	6	17	0	
Evans, Dwight, of-1b	.293	149	559	96	164	31	7	21	111	76	99	5
*Gedman, Rich, c	.231	95	299	33	69	14	0	9	39	18	49	0
*Greenwell, Mike, of	.325	158	590	86	192	39	8	22	119	87	38	16
*Horn, Sam, dh	.148	24	61	4	9	0	0	2	8	11	20	0
Kutcher, Randy, of-3b	.167	19	12	2	2	1	0	0	0	0	2	0
Marzano, John, c	.138	10	29	3	4	1	0	0	1	1	3	0
#Owen, Spike, ss	.249	89	257	40	64	14	1	5	18	27	27	0
Parrish, Larry, dh-1b (68 Tex)	.217	120	406	32	88	14	1	14	52	28	111	0
Quintana, Carlos, of	.333	5	6	1	2	0	0	2	2	3	0	
Reed, Jody, ss	.293	109	338	60	99	23	1	1	28	45	21	1
Rice, Jim, dh-of	.264	135	485	57	128	18	3	15	72	48	89	1
Romero, Ed, inf	.240	31	75	3	18	3	0	0	5	3	8	0
Romine, Kevin, of	.192	57	78	17	15	2	1	1	6	7	15	2

PITCHING	W	L	ERA	G	GS	CG	SV	IP	H	R	ER	BB	SO
Boddicker, Mike (21 Balt)	13	15	3.39	36	35	5	0	236	234	102	89	77	156
*Bolton, Tom	1	3	4.75	28	0	0	1	30	35	17	16	14	21
Boyd, Oil Can	9	7	5.34	23	23	1	0	130	147	82	77	41	71
Clemens, Roger	18	12	2.93	35	35	14	0	264	217	93	86	62	291
*Crouch, Zach	0	0	6.75	3	0	0	0	4	1	1	2	0	
Curry, Steve	0	1	8.18	3	3	0	0	11	15	10	10	14	4
Ellsworth, Steve	1	6	6.75	8	7	0	0	36	47	29	27	16	16
Gardner, Wes	8	6	3.50	36	18	1	2	149	119	61	58	64	106
*Hurst, Bruce	18	6	3.66	33	32	7	0	217	222	98	88	65	166
Lamp, Dennis	7	6	3.48	46	0	0	0	83	92	39	32	19	49
*Rochford, Mike	0	0	0.00	2	0	0	0	2	4	0	0	1	1
Sellers, Jeff	1	7	4.83	18	12	1	0	86	89	49	46	56	70
Smith, Lee	4	5	2.80	64	0	0	29	84	72	34	26	37	96
Smithson, Mike	9	6	5.97	31	18	1	0	127	149	87	84	37	73
Stanley, Bob	6	4	3.19	57	0	0	5	102	90	41	36	29	57
Trautwein, John	0	1	9.00	9	0	0	0	16	26	17	16	9	8
Woodward, Rob	0	0	13.50	1	0	0	0	1	2	1	1	1	0

CALIFORNIA

BATTING	AVG	G	AB	R	H	2B	3B	HR	RBI	BB	SO	SB
Armas, Tony, of	.272	120	368	42	100	20	2	13	49	22	87	1
Bichette, Dante, of	.261	21	46	1	12	2	0	0	8	0	7	0
Boone, Bob, c	.295	122	352	38	104	17	0	5	39	29	26	2
*Bosley, Thad, of (15 KC)	.260	50	96	10	25	5	0	0	9	8	18	1
Brown, Mike, of	.220	18	50	4	11	2	0	0	3	1	12	0
#Davis, Chili, of	.268	158	600	81	161	29	3	21	93	56	118	9
Davis, Doug, 3b-c	.000	6	12	1	0	0	0	0	0	0	3	0
Dorsett, Brian, c	.091	7	11	0	1	0	0	0	2	1	5	0
Downing, Brian, dh	.242	135	484	80	117	18	2	25	64	81	63	3
*Eppard, Jim, of-1b	.283	56	113	7	32	3	1	0	14	11	15	0
Hendrick, George, of-1b	.244	69	127	12	31	1	0	3	19	7	20	0
*Howell, Jack, 3b	.254	154	500	59	127	32	2	16	63	46	130	2
*Joyner, Wally, 1b	.295	158	597	81	176	31	2	13	85	55	51	8
#McLemore, Mark, 2b	.240	77	233	38	56	11	2	2	16	25	28	13
Miller, Darrell, c-of	.221	70	140	21	31	4	1	2	7	9	22	2
Noboa, Junior, 2b	.063	21	16	4	1	0	0	0	0	0	1	0
Polidor, Gus, ss-3b	.148	54	81	4	12	3	0	0	4	3	11	0
Ramos, Domingo, inf (22 Cle)	.230	32	61	10	14	1	0	0	5	3	7	0
#Ray, Johnny, 2b-of	.306	153	602	75	184	42	7	6	83	36	38	4
Redfield, Joe, 3b	.000	1	2	0	0	0	0	0	0	0	0	0
Schofield, Dick, ss	.239	155	527	61	126	11	6	6	34	40	57	20
*Walker, Chico, of-2b	.154	33	78	8	12	1	0	0	2	6	15	2
#White, Devon, of	.259	122	455	76	118	22	2	11	51	23	84	17
#Wynegar, Butch, c	.255	26	55	8	14	4	1	1	8	8	7	0

PITCHING	W	L	ERA	G	GS	CG	SV	IP	H	R	ER	BB	SO
Buice, Dewayne	2	4	5.88	32	0	0	3	41	45	29	27	19	38
Clark, Terry	6	6	5.07	15	15	2	0	94	120	54	53	31	39
Cliburn, Stu	4	2	4.07	40	1	0	0	84	83	45	38	32	42
Cook, Mike	0	1	5.40	3	0	0	0	4	2	2	1	2	

	W	L	ERA	G	GS	CG	SV	IP	H	R	ER	BB	SO
*Corbett, Sherm	2	1	4.14	34	0	0	1	46	47	23	21	23	28
*DiMichele, Frank	0	0	9.64	4	0	0	0	5	5	5	5	2	1
*Finley, Chuck	9	15	4.17	31	31	2	0	194	191	95	90	82	111
Fraser, Willie	12	13	5.41	34	32	2	0	195	203	129	117	80	86
Harvey, Bryan	7	5	2.13	50	0	0	17	76	59	22	18	20	67
Krawczyk, Ray	0	1	4.81	14	1	0	1	24	29	13	13	8	17
Lazorko, Jack	0	1	3.35	10	3	0	0	38	37	15	14	16	19
*Lovelace, Vance	0	0	13.50	3	0	0	0	1	2	2	2	3	0
Lugo, Urbano	0	0	9.00	1	0	0	0	2	2	2	2	1	1
McCaskill, Kirk	8	6	4.31	23	23	4	0	146	155	78	70	61	98
Minton, Greg	4	5	2.85	44	0	0	7	79	67	37	25	34	46
Monteleone, Rich	0	0	0.00	3	0	0	0	4	4	0	0	1	3
Moore, Donnie	5	2	4.91	27	0	0	4	33	48	20	18	8	22
Petry, Dan	3	9	4.38	22	22	4	0	140	139	70	68	59	64
Witt, Mike	13	16	4.15	34	34	12	0	250	263	130	115	87	133

CHICAGO

BATTING	AVG	G	AB	R	H	2B	3B	HR	RBI	BB	SO	SB
*Baines, Harold, dh	.277	158	599	55	166	39	1	13	81	67	109	0
*Boston, Daryl, of	.217	105	281	37	61	12	2	15	31	21	44	9
Calderon, Ivan, of	.212	73	264	40	56	14	0	14	35	34	66	4
Diaz, Mike, 1b	.237	40	152	12	36	6	0	3	12	5	30	0
Fisk, Carlton, c	.277	76	253	17	70	8	1	19	50	37	40	0
Gallagher, Dave, of	.303	101	347	59	105	15	3	5	31	29	40	5
Guillen, Ozzie, ss	.261	156	566	58	148	16	7	0	39	25	40	25
#Hairston, Jerry, ph	.000	2	2	0	0	0	0	0	0	0	0	0
#Hill, Donnie, 2b-3b	.217	83	221	17	48	6	1	2	20	26	32	3
*Johnson, Lance, of	.185	33	124	11	23	4	1	0	6	6	11	6
Karkovice, Ron, c	.174	46	115	10	20	4	0	3	9	7	30	4
*Lyons, Steve, 3b-of	.269	145	472	59	127	28	3	5	45	32	59	1
Manrique, Fred, 2b	.235	140	345	43	81	10	6	5	37	21	54	6
Martinez, Carlos, 3b	.164	17	55	5	9	1	0	0	0	0	12	1
Morman, Russ, 1b-of	.240	40	75	8	18	2	0	0	3	3	17	0
Paris, Kelly, 1b-3b	.250	14	44	6	11	0	0	3	6	0	6	0
*Pasqua, Dan, of	.227	129	422	48	96	16	2	20	50	46	100	1
#Randall, Sap, 1b-of	.000	4	12	1	0	0	0	0	1	2	3	0
Redus, Gary, of	.263	77	262	42	69	10	4	6	34	33	52	26
*Salas, Mark, c	.250	75	196	17	49	7	0	3	9	12	17	0
*Walker, Greg, 1b	.247	99	377	45	93	22	1	8	42	29	77	0
Williams, Ken, of-3b	.159	73	220	18	35	4	2	8	28	10	64	6
*Woodard, Mike, 2b	.133	18	45	3	6	0	1	0	4	1	5	1

PITCHING	W	L	ERA	G	GS	CG	SV	IP	H	R	ER	BB	SO
Bittiger, Jeff	2	4	4.23	25	7	0	0	62	59	31	29	29	33
Davis, Joel	0	1	6.75	5	2	0	0	16	21	12	12	5	10
Davis, John	2	5	6.64	34	1	0	1	64	77	58	47	50	37
Hillegas, Shawn	3	2	3.15	6	6	0	0	40	30	16	14	18	26
*Horton, Ricky	6	10	4.86	52	9	1	2	109	120	64	59	36	28
Jones, Barry	2	2	2.42	17	0	0	1	26	15	7	7	17	17
*LaPoint, Dave	10	11	3.40	25	25	1	0	161	151	69	61	47	79
Long, Bill	8	11	4.03	47	18	3	2	174	187	89	78	43	77
*Manzanillo, Ravelo	0	1	5.79	2	2	0	0	9	7	6	6	12	10
McCarthy, Tom	2	0	1.38	6	0	0	1	13	9	2	2	2	5
McDowell, Jack	5	10	3.97	26	26	1	0	159	147	85	70	68	84
Pall, Donn	0	2	3.45	17	0	0	0	29	39	11	11	8	16
*Patterson, Ken	0	2	4.79	9	2	0	1	21	25	11	11	7	8
Pawlowski, John	1	0	8.36	6	0	0	0	14	20	14	13	3	10
Perez, Melido	12	10	3.79	32	32	3	0	197	186	105	83	72	138
Peterson, Adam	0	1	13.50	2	2	0	0	6	6	9	9	6	5
*Reuss, Jerry	13	9	3.44	32	29	2	0	183	183	79	70	43	73
Rosenberg, Steve	0	1	4.30	33	0	0	1	46	53	22	22	19	28
*Segura, Jose	0	0	13.50	4	0	0	0	9	19	17	13	8	2
Thigpen, Bobby	5	8	3.30	68	0	0	34	90	96	38	33	33	62
Willis, Carl	0	0	8.25	6	0	0	0	12	17	12	11	7	6

CLEVELAND

BATTING	AVG	G	AB	R	H	2B	3B	HR	RBI	BB	SO	SB
Allanson, Andy, c	.263	133	434	44	114	11	0	5	50	25	63	5
Allen, Rod, dh	.091	5	11	1	1	1	0	0	0	0	2	0
Bell, Jay, ss	.218	73	211	23	46	5	1	2	21	21	53	4
Carter, Joe, of	.271	157	621	84	168	36	6	27	98	35	82	27
Castillo, Carmen, of	.273	66	176	12	48	8	0	4	14	5	31	6
*Clark, Dave, of	.263	63	156	11	41	4	1	3	18	17	28	0
Franco, Julio, 2b	.305	152	613	88	186	23	6	10	54	56	72	25
*Francona, Terry, dh	.311	62	212	24	66	8	0	1	12	5	18	0
*Hall, Mel, of	.280	150	515	69	144	32	4	6	71	28	50	7
Jacoby, Brook, 3b	.241	152	552	59	133	25	0	9	49	48	101	2
Jimenez, Houston, 2b-ss	.048	9	21	1	1	0	0	0	1	0	2	0
Jordan, Scott, of	.111	7	9	0	1	0	0	0	0	1	3	0
Kittle, Ron, dh	.258	75	225	31	58	8	0	18	43	16	65	0
*Lampkin, Tom, c	.000	4	4	0	0	0	0	0	0	1	0	0
Medina, Luis, 1b	.255	16	51	10	13	0	0	6	8	2	18	0
Snyder, Cory, of	.272	142	511	71	139	24	3	26	75	42	101	5
Tingley, Ron, c	.167	9	24	1	4	0	0	1	2	2	8	0
*Upshaw, Willie, 1b	.245	149	493	58	121	22	3	11	50	62	66	12
Washington, Ron, ss	.256	69	223	30	57	14	2	2	21	9	35	3

	AVG	G	AB	R	H	2B	3B	HR	RBI	BB	SO	SB
Williams, Eddie, 3b	.190	10	21	3	4	0	0	0	1	0	3	0
Williams, Reggie, of	.226	11	31	7	7	2	0	1	3	0	6	0
Zuvella, Paul, ss	.231	51	130	9	30	5	1	0	7	8	13	0

PITCHING	W	L	ERA	G	GS	CG	SV	IP	H	R	ER	BB	SO
*Bailes, Scott	9	14	4.90	37	21	5	0	145	149	89	79	46	53
*Black, Bud (17 KC)	4	4	5.00	33	7	0	1	81	82	47	45	34	63
Candiotti, Tom	14	8	3.28	31	31	11	0	217	225	86	79	53	137
Codiroli, Chris	0	4	9.31	14	2	0	1	19	32	22	20	10	12
Dedmon, Jeff	1	0	4.54	21	0	0	1	34	35	20	17	21	17
Farrell, John	14	10	4.24	31	30	4	0	210	216	106	99	67	92
Gordon, Don	3	4	4.40	38	0	0	1	59	65	33	29	19	20
*Havens, Brad	2	3	3.14	28	0	0	1	57	62	22	20	17	30
Jones, Doug	3	4	2.27	51	0	0	37	83	69	26	21	16	72
*Kaiser, Jeff	0	0	0.00	3	0	0	0	3	2	0	0	1	0
Laskey, Bill	1	0	5.18	17	0	0	1	24	32	16	14	6	17
Nichols, Rod	1	7	5.06	11	10	3	0	69	73	41	39	23	31
Perlman, Jon	0	2	5.49	10	0	0	0	20	25	12	12	11	10
Rodriguez, Rick	1	2	7.09	10	5	0	0	33	43	28	26	17	9
Swindell, Greg	18	14	3.20	33	33	12	0	242	234	97	86	45	180
Walker, Mike	0	1	7.27	3	1	0	0	9	8	7	7	10	7
Yett, Rich	9	6	4.62	23	22	0	0	134	146	72	69	55	71

DETROIT

BATTING	AVG	G	AB	R	H	2B	3B	HR	RBI	BB	SO	SB
#Bando, Chris, c (32 Cle)	.125	33	72	6	9	1	0	1	8	8	12	0
*Bean, Billy, of	.182	10	11	2	2	0	1	0	0	0	2	0
Beane, Billy, of	.167	6	6	1	1	0	0	0	1	0	2	0
*Bergman, Dave, 1b-of	.294	116	289	37	85	14	0	5	35	38	34	0
Brookens, Tom, 3b	.243	136	441	62	107	23	5	5	38	44	74	4
DeJesus, Ivan, ss	.176	7	17	1	3	0	0	0	0	1	4	0
*Evans, Darrell, 1b-dh	.208	144	437	48	91	9	0	22	64	84	89	1
Heath, Mike, c	.247	86	219	24	54	7	2	5	18	18	32	1
Herndon, Larry, dh-of	.224	76	174	16	39	5	0	4	20	23	37	0
Knight, Ray, 1b-3b	.217	105	299	34	65	12	2	3	33	20	30	1
Lemon, Chet, of	.264	144	512	67	135	29	4	17	64	59	65	1
#Lovullo, Torey, 2b	.381	12	21	2	8	1	1	1	2	1	2	0
*Lusader, Scott, of	.063	16	16	3	1	0	0	1	3	1	4	0
*Lynn, Fred, of (87 Balt)	.246	114	391	46	96	14	1	25	56	33	82	2
Morrison, Jim, dh	.216	24	74	7	16	5	0	0	6	0	14	0
*Murphy, Dwayne, of	.250	49	144	16	36	5	0	4	19	24	26	1
*Nokes, Matt, c	.251	122	382	53	96	18	0	16	53	34	58	0
*Pettis, Gary, of	.210	129	458	65	96	14	4	3	36	47	85	44
Salazar, Luis, of-inf	.270	130	452	61	122	14	1	12	62	21	70	6
*Sheridan, Pat, of	.254	126	347	47	88	9	5	11	47	44	64	8
Trammell, Alan, ss	.311	128	466	73	145	24	1	15	69	46	46	7
#Walewander, Jim, 2b	.211	88	175	23	37	5	0	0	6	12	26	11
*Whitaker, Lou, 2b	.275	115	403	54	111	18	2	12	55	66	60	2

PITCHING	W	L	ERA	G	GS	CG	SV	IP	H	R	ER	BB	SO
Alexander, Doyle	14	11	4.32	34	34	5	0	229	260	122	110	46	126
*Gibson, Paul	4	2	2.93	40	1	0	0	92	83	33	30	34	50
Heinkel, Don	0	0	3.96	21	0	0	1	36	30	17	16	12	30
Henneman, Mike	9	6	1.87	65	0	0	22	91	72	23	19	24	58
*Hernandez, Guillermo	6	5	3.06	63	0	0	10	68	50	24	23	31	59
Huismann, Mark	1	0	5.06	5	0	0	0	5	6	3	2	4	6
King, Eric	4	1	3.41	23	5	0	3	69	60	28	26	34	45
Morris, Jack	15	13	3.94	34	34	10	0	235	225	115	103	83	168
Power, Ted (22 KC)	6	7	5.95	26	14	2	0	98	121	67	65	38	57
Robinson, Jeff	13	6	2.98	24	23	6	0	172	121	61	57	72	114
*Searcy, Steve	0	2	5.63	2	2	0	0	8	8	6	5	4	5
*Tanana, Frank	14	11	4.21	32	32	2	0	203	213	105	95	64	127
Terrell, Walt	7	16	3.97	29	29	11	0	206	199	101	91	78	84
Trujillo, Mike	0	0	5.11	6	0	0	0	12	11	7	7	5	5

KANSAS CITY

BATTING	AVG	G	AB	R	H	2B	3B	HR	RBI	BB	SO	SB
*Brett, George, 1b-dh	.306	157	589	89	180	42	3	24	103	82	51	14
*Buckner, Bill, dh-1b (19 Cal)	.249	108	285	19	71	14	0	3	43	17	19	5
Capra, Nick, of	.138	14	29	3	4	1	0	0	0	2	3	1
Delos Santos, Luis, 1b	.091	11	22	1	2	2	0	0	1	5	4	0
*Eisenreich, Jim, of-dh	.218	83	202	26	44	8	1	1	19	6	31	9
Hearn, Ed, c	.222	7	18	1	4	2	0	0	1	0	1	0
Jackson, Bo, of	.246	124	439	63	108	16	4	25	68	25	146	27
Macfarlane, Mike, c	.265	70	211	25	56	15	0	4	26	21	37	0
#Madison, Scotti, c-1b	.171	16	35	4	6	2	0	0	2	4	5	1
#Owen, Dave, ss	.000	8	5	0	0	0	0	0	0	0	3	0
Owen, Larry, c	.210	40	81	5	17	1	0	1	3	9	23	0
Palacios, Rey, c	.091	5	11	2	1	0	0	0	0	0	4	0
Pecota, Bill, ss-3b	.208	90	118	25	37	3	3	1	15	18	34	7
*Quirk, Jamie, c	.240	84	196	22	47	7	1	8	25	28	41	1
Seitzer, Kevin, 3b	.304	149	559	90	170	32	5	5	60	72	64	10
#Stillwell, Kurt, ss	.251	128	459	63	115	28	5	10	53	47	76	6
Tabler, Pat, dh-1b (41 Cle)	.282	130	444	53	125	22	3	2	66	46	68	3
Tartabull, Danny, of	.274	146	507	80	139	38	3	26	102	76	119	8
Thurman, Gary, of	.167	35	66	6	11	1	0	0	2	4	20	5
Wellman, Brad, 2b-ss	.271	71	107	11	29	3	0	1	6	6	23	1

Departmental Leaders

BATTING

RUNS
Wade Boggs, Boston 128
Jose Canseco, Oakland 120
Rickey Henderson, New York .. 118
Paul Molitor, Milwaukee 115
Kirby Puckett, Minnesota 109

HITS
Kirby Puckett, Minnesota 234
Wade Boggs, Boston 214
Mike Greenwell, Boston 192
Paul Molitor, Milwaukee 190
Robin Yount, Milwaukee 190

TOTAL BASES
Kirby Puckett, Minnesota 358
Jose Canseco, Oakland 347
Mike Greenwell, Boston 313
George Brett, Kansas City 300
Joe Carter, Cleveland 297

DOUBLES
Wade Boggs, Boston 45
Johnny Ray, California 42
Kirby Puckett, Minnesota 42
George Brett, Kansas City 42
Tony Fernandez, Toronto 41

TRIPLES
Harold Reynolds, Seattle 11
Willie Wilson, Kansas City 11
Robin Yount, Milwaukee 11
Mike Greenwell, Boston 8
Four tied at 7

HOME RUNS
Jose Canseco, Oakland 42
Fred McGriff, Toronto 34
Mark McGwire, Oakland 32
Gary Gaetti, Minnesota 28
Eddie Murray, Baltimore 28

RUNS BATTED IN
Jose Canseco, Oakland 124
Kirby Puckett, Minnesota 121
Mike Greenwell, Boston 119
Dwight Evans, Boston 111
Dave Winfield, New York 107

GAME-WINNING RBIs
Mike Greenwell, Boston 23
Mark McGwire, Oakland 20
George Bell, Toronto 17
Jose Canseco, Oakland 16
Jack Clark, New York 16

SACRIFICE BUNTS
Marty Barrett, Boston 20
Jim Gantner, Milwaukee 18
Fred Manrique, Chicago 16
Steve Lyons, Chicago 15
Scott Fletcher, Texas 15

SACRIFICE FLIES
Chili Davis, California 10
Cal Ripken, Baltimore 10
Kirby Puckett, Minnesota 9
Seven tied at 8

WALKS
Wade Boggs, Boston 125

Jack Clark, New York.......... 113
Cal Ripken, Baltimore.......... 102
Alvin Davis, Seattle 95
Mike Greenwell, Boston 87

INTENTIONAL WALKS
Wade Boggs, Boston 18
Mike Greenwell, Boston 18
Greg Brock, Milwaukee 16
George Brett, Kansas City 15
Five tied at...................... 14

HIT BY PITCH
Gene Larkin, Minnesota 15
Brian Downing, California 14
Don Baylor, Oakland 12
Scott Fletcher, Texas 12
Jose Canseco, Oakland......... 10

STRIKEOUTS
Rob Deer, Milwaukee 153
Pete Incaviglia, Texas 153
Fred McGriff, Toronto 149
Bo Jackson, Kansas City 146
Jack Clark, New York.......... 141

STOLEN BASES
Rickey Henderson, New York ... 93
Gary Pettis, Detroit............. 44
Paul Molitor, Milwaukee 41
Jose Canseco, Oakland........ 40
Harold Reynolds, Seattle 35
Willie Wilson, Kansas City 35

CAUGHT STEALING
Harold Reynolds, Seattle 29
Jose Canseco, Oakland 16
Ozzie Guillen, Chicago 13
Rickey Henderson, New York ... 13
Julio Franco, Cleveland 11

GIDP
Wade Boggs, Boston 23
Harold Baines, Chicago 21
George Bell, Toronto 21
Robin Yount, Milwaukee 21
Kelly Gruber, Toronto 20
Eddie Murray, Baltimore........ 20

ERRORS
Steve Lyons, Chicago.......... 29
Dale Sveum, Milwaukee 27
Kevin Seitzer, Kansas City 26
Rey Quinones, Seattle 23
Jim Presley, Seattle........... 22
Rafael Santana, New York 22

SLUGGING PERCENTAGE
Jose Canseco, Oakland....... .569
Fred McGriff, Toronto .... .552
Gary Gaetti, Minnesota .... .551
Kirby Puckett, Minnesota ..... .545
Mike Greenwell, Boston ...... .531

ON-BASE PERCENTAGE
Wade Boggs, Boston.......... .476
Mike Greenwell, Boston ...... .416
Alvin Davis, Seattle .... .412
Dave Winfield, New York ...... .398
Rickey Henderson, New York . .394

	AVG	G	AB	R	H	2B	3B	HR	RBI	BB	SO	SB
White, Frank, 2b	.235	150	537	48	126	25	1	8	58	21	67	7
#Wilson, Willie, of	.262	147	591	81	155	17	11	1	37	22	106	35

PITCHING	W	L	ERA	G	GS	CG	SV	IP	H	R	ER	BB	SO
Anderson, Rick	2	1	4.24	7	3	0	0	34	41	17	16	9	9
Aquino, Luis	1	0	2.79	7	5	1	0	29	33	15	9	17	11
*Bannister, Floyd	12	13	4.33	31	31	2	0	189	182	102	91	68	113
DeJesus, Jose	0	1	27.00	2	1	0	0	3	6	10	8	5	2
Farr, Steve	5	4	2.50	62	1	0	20	83	74	25	23	30	72
Garber, Gene	0	4	3.58	26	0	0	6	33	29	15	13	13	20
*Gleaton, Jerry Don	0	4	3.55	42	0	0	3	38	33	17	15	17	29
Gordon, Tom	0	2	5.17	5	2	0	0	16	16	9	9	7	18
Gubicza, Mark	20	8	2.70	35	35	8	0	270	237	94	81	83	183
*Lee, Mark	0	0	3.60	4	0	0	0	5	6	2	2	1	0
*Leibrandt, Charlie	13	12	3.19	35	35	7	0	243	244	98	86	62	125
Montgomery, Jeff	7	2	3.45	45	0	0	1	63	54	25	24	30	47
Quisenberry, Dan	0	1	3.55	20	0	0	1	25	32	11	10	5	9
Saberhagen, Bret	14	16	3.80	35	35	9	0	261	271	122	110	59	171
*Sanchez, Israel	3	2	4.54	19	1	0	1	36	36	20	18	18	14

MILWAUKEE

BATTING	AVG	G	AB	R	H	2B	3B	HR	RBI	BB	SO	SB
*Adduci, Jim, of	.266	44	94	8	25	6	1	1	15	0	15	0
Braggs, Glenn, of	.261	72	272	30	71	14	0	10	42	14	60	6
*Brock, Greg, 1b	.212	115	364	53	77	16	1	6	50	63	48	6
#Castillo, Juan, inf	.222	54	90	10	20	0	0	0	2	3	14	2
Deer, Rob, of	.252	135	492	71	124	24	0	23	85	51	153	9
*Felder, Mike, of	.173	50	81	14	14	1	0	0	5	0	11	8
*Gantner, Jim, 2b	.276	155	539	67	149	28	2	0	47	34	50	20
*Hamilton, Darryl, of	.184	44	103	14	19	4	0	1	11	12	10	7
Kiefer, Steve, 2b-3b	.300	7	10	2	3	1	0	1	1	2	3	0
Leonard, Jeffrey, of	.235	94	374	45	88	19	0	8	44	16	68	10
Meyer, Joey, dh-1b	.263	103	327	22	86	18	0	11	45	23	88	0
Molitor, Paul, 3b-dh	.312	154	609	115	190	34	6	13	60	71	54	41
O'Brien, Charlie, c	.220	40	118	12	26	6	0	2	9	5	16	0
*Riles, Ernest, 3b-ss	.252	41	127	7	32	6	1	1	9	7	26	2
*Robidoux, Billy Joe, 1b	.253	33	91	9	23	5	0	0	5	8	14	1
Schroeder, Bill, c	.156	41	122	9	19	2	0	5	10	6	36	0
Sheffield, Gary, ss	.238	24	80	12	19	1	0	4	12	7	7	3
*Surhoff, B.J., c	.245	139	493	47	121	21	0	5	38	31	49	21
#Sveum, Dale, ss	.242	129	467	41	113	14	4	9	51	21	122	1
#Young, Mike, dh	.000	8	14	2	0	0	0	0	0	2	5	0
Yount, Robin, of	.306	162	621	92	190	38	11	13	91	63	63	21

PITCHING	W	L	ERA	G	GS	CG	SV	IP	H	R	ER	BB	SO
August, Don	13	7	3.09	24	22	6	0	148	137	55	51	48	66
Birkbeck, Mike	10	8	4.72	23	23	0	0	124	141	69	65	37	64
Bosio, Chris	7	15	3.36	38	22	9	6	182	190	84	68	38	84
Clear, Mark	1	0	2.79	25	0	0	0	29	23	12	9	21	26
Crim, Chuck	7	6	2.91	70	0	0	9	105	95	38	34	28	58
Filer, Tom	5	8	4.43	19	16	2	0	102	108	54	50	33	39
*Higuera, Ted	16	9	2.45	31	31	8	0	227	168	66	62	59	192
Jones, Odell	5	0	4.35	28	2	0	1	81	75	47	39	29	48
Knudson, Mark	0	0	1.13	5	0	0	0	16	17	3	2	2	7
*Mirabella, Paul	2	2	1.65	38	0	0	4	60	44	12	11	21	33
*Nieves, Juan	7	5	4.08	25	15	1	1	110	84	53	50	50	73
Plesac, Dan	1	2	2.41	50	0	0	30	52	46	14	14	12	52
*Stapleton, Dave	0	0	5.93	6	0	0	0	14	20	9	9	9	6
Wegman, Bill	13	13	4.12	32	31	4	0	199	207	104	91	50	84

MINNESOTA

BATTING	AVG	G	AB	R	H	2B	3B	HR	RBI	BB	SO	SB
#Baker, Doug, ss	.000	11	7	1	0	0	0	0	0	0	5	0
Brunansky, Tom, of	.184	14	49	5	9	1	0	1	6	7	11	1
*Bullock, Eric, of	.294	16	17	3	5	0	0	0	3	3	1	1
*Bush, Randy, of-dh	.261	136	394	51	103	20	3	14	51	58	49	8
Christensen, John, of	.263	23	38	5	10	4	0	0	5	3	5	0
Davidson, Mark, of	.217	100	106	22	23	7	0	1	10	10	20	3
*Dwyer, Jim, dh (35 Balt)	.255	55	94	9	24	1	0	2	18	25	19	0
Gaetti, Gary, 3b	.301	133	468	66	141	29	2	28	88	36	85	7
Gagne, Greg, ss	.236	149	461	69	109	20	6	14	48	27	110	15
Gladden, Dan, of	.269	141	576	91	155	32	6	11	62	46	74	28
Harper, Brian, c	.295	60	166	15	49	11	1	3	20	10	12	0
#Herr, Tom, 2b	.263	86	304	42	80	16	0	1	21	40	47	10
*Hrbek, Kent, 1b-dh	.312	143	510	75	159	31	0	25	76	67	54	0
#Larkin, Gene, dh-1b	.267	149	505	65	135	30	2	8	70	68	55	3
Laudner, Tim, c	.251	117	375	38	94	18	1	13	54	36	89	0
Lombardozzi, Steve, 2b	.209	103	287	34	60	15	2	3	27	35	48	2
*Lowry, Dwight, c	.000	6	7	0	0	0	0	0	0	0	2	0
#Moses, John, of	.316	105	206	33	65	10	3	2	12	15	21	11
#Newman, Al, inf	.223	105	242	21	54	7	0	0	19	29	34	12
Nieto, Tom, c	.067	24	60	1	4	0	0	0	0	1	17	0
Puckett, Kirby, of	.356	158	657	109	234	42	5	24	121	23	83	6
*Torve, Kelvin, 1b	.188	12	16	1	3	0	0	0	1	2	1	0

PITCHING	W	L	ERA	G	GS	CG	SV	IP	H	R	ER	BB	SO
*Anderson, Allan	16	9	2.45	30	30	3	0	202	199	70	55	37	83
Atherton, Keith	7	5	3.41	49	0	0	3	74	65	29	28	22	43
Berenguer, Juan	8	4	3.96	57	1	0	2	100	74	44	44	61	99
Best, Karl	0	0	6.00	11	0	0	0	12	15	9	8	7	9
Blyleven, Bert	10	17	5.43	33	33	7	0	207	240	128	125	51	145
*Carlton, Steve	0	1	16.76	4	1	0	0	10	20	19	18	5	5
Gladden, Dan	0	0	0.00	1	0	0	0	1	0	0	0	0	0
Gonzalez, German	0	0	3.38	16	0	0	1	21	20	8	8	8	19
Lea, Charlie	7	7	4.85	24	23	0	0	130	156	79	70	50	72
*Martinez, Tippy	0	0	18.00	3	0	0	0	4	8	9	8	4	3
*Mason, Mike	0	1	10.80	5	0	0	0	7	8	8	9	9	7
Niekro, Joe	1	1	10.03	5	2	0	0	12	16	13	13	9	7
Portugal, Mark	3	3	4.53	26	0	0	3	58	60	30	29	17	31
Reardon, Jeff	2	4	2.47	63	0	0	42	73	68	21	20	15	56
*Schatzeder, Dan (15 Cle)	0	3	6.49	25	0	0	3	26	34	21	19	7	17
Smith, Roy	3	0	2.68	9	4	0	0	37	29	12	11	12	17
Straker, Les	2	5	3.92	16	14	1	1	83	86	39	36	25	23
Toliver, Fred	7	6	4.24	19	16	0	0	115	116	57	54	52	69
*Viola, Frank	24	7	2.64	35	35	7	0	255	236	80	75	54	193
Winn, Jim	1	0	6.00	9	0	0	0	21	33	15	14	10	9

Departmental Leaders

Dennis Eckersley
...45 saves

Roger Clemens
...291 K's

Allan Anderson
...ERA leader

PITCHING

GAMES
Chuck Crim, Milwaukee 70
Bobby Thigpen, Chicago 68
Mitch Williams, Texas 67
Mike Henneman, Detroit 65
Duane Ward, Toronto 64
Lee Smith, Boston 64

GAMES STARTED
Dave Stewart, Oakland.......... 37
Bob Welch, Oakland 36
Seven tied at 35

COMPLETE GAMES
Roger Clemens, Boston 14
Dave Stewart, Oakland.......... 14
Bobby Witt, Texas 13
Greg Swindell, Cleveland 12
Mike Witt, California............. 12

SHUTOUTS
Roger Clemens, Boston 8
Greg Swindell, Cleveland........ 4
Dave Stieb, Toronto 4
Mark Gubicza, Kansas City 4
Three tied at 3

SAVES
Dennis Eckersley, Oakland...... 45
Jeff Reardon, Minnesota 42
Doug Jones, Cleveland 37
Bobby Thigpen, Chicago 34
Dan Plesac, Milwaukee 30

WINS
Frank Viola, Minnesota 24
Dave Stewart, Oakland.......... 21
Mark Gubicza, Kansas City 20
Roger Clemens, Boston 18
Greg Swindell, Cleveland 18
Bruce Hurst, Boston 18

LOSSES
Bert Blyleven, Minnesota 17
Charlie Hough, Texas 16
Bret Saberhagen, Kansas City . 16
Walt Terrell, Detroit 16
Mike Witt, California............. 16

INNINGS PITCHED
Dave Stewart, Oakland 276
Mark Gubicza, Kansas City 270
Roger Clemens, Boston........ 264
Mark Langston, Seattle 261
Bret Saberhagen, Kansas City . 261

HITS ALLOWED
Mike Witt, California 263

Doyle Alexander, Detroit 260
Charlie Leibrandt, Kansas City . 244
Bert Blyleven, Minnesota 240
Dave Stewart, Oakland 240

RUNS ALLOWED
Mike Witt, California 130
Willie Fraser, California 129
Bert Blyleven, Minnesota 128
Doyle Alexander, Detroit 122
Bret Saberhagen, Kansas City . 122

HOME RUNS ALLOWED
Willie Fraser, California 33
Mark Langston, Seattle 32
Doyle Alexander, Detroit 30
Richard Dotson, New York 27
Jim Clancy, Toronto 26
Melido Perez, Chicago 26

WALKS
Charlie Hough, Texas 126
Mark Langston, Seattle 110
Dave Stewart, Oakland 110
Bobby Witt, Texas 101
Storm Davis, Oakland.......... 91

HIT BATSMEN
Bert Blyleven, Minnesota 16
Mike Boddicker, Balt.-Boston... 14
Dave Stieb, Toronto 13
Charlie Hough, Texas 12
Paul Kilgus, Texas 10
Bob Welch, Oakland 10

STRIKEOUTS
Roger Clemens, Boston........ 291
Mark Langston, Seattle 235
Frank Viola, Minnesota 193
Ted Higuera, Milwaukee 192
Dave Stewart, Oakland 192

WILD PITCHES
Storm Davis, Oakland.......... 16
Bobby Witt, Texas 16
Dave Stewart, Oakland 14
Willie Fraser, California 13
Kirk McCaskill, California 13
Melido Perez, Chicago 13

BALKS
Dave Stewart, Oakland 16
Bob Welch, Oakland 13
Jose Guzman, Texas 12
John Candelaria, New York 12
Three tied at.................... 11

NEW YORK

BATTING	AVG	G	AB	R	H	2B	3B	HR	RBI	BB	SO	SB
Aguayo, Luis, 3b	.250	50	140	12	35	4	0	3	8	7	33	0
*Chambliss, Chris, ph	.000	1	1	0	0	0	0	0	0	0	1	0
Clark, Jack, dh	.242	150	496	81	120	14	0	27	93	113	141	3
*Cruz, Jose, dh-of	.200	38	80	9	16	2	0	1	7	8	8	0
Espinoza, Alvaro, 2b-ss ..	.000	3	3	0	0	0	0	0	0	0	0	0
Geren, Bob, c	.100	10	10	0	1	0	0	0	0	0	2	0
Henderson, Rickey, of ..	.305	140	554	118	169	30	2	6	50	82	54	93
Kelly, Roberto, of	.247	38	77	9	19	4	1	1	7	3	15	5
*Mattingly, Don, 1b	.311	144	599	94	186	37	0	18	88	41	29	1
Meacham, Bobby, ss-2b .	.217	47	115	18	25	9	0	0	7	14	22	7
*Morris, Hal, of	.100	15	20	1	2	0	0	0	0	0	9	0

	AVG	G	AB	R	H	2B	3B	HR	RBI	BB	SO	SB
*Pagliarulo, Mike, 3b	.216	125	444	46	96	20	1	15	67	37	104	1
*Phelps, Ken, dh (72 Sea) .	.263	117	297	54	78	13	0	24	54	70	61	1
Randolph, Willie, 2b	.230	110	404	43	93	20	1	2	34	55	39	8
Santana, Rafael, ss	.240	148	480	50	115	12	1	4	38	33	61	1
Skinner, Joel, c	.227	88	251	23	57	15	0	4	23	14	72	0
Slaught, Don, c	.283	97	322	33	91	25	1	9	43	24	54	1
#Tolleson, Wayne, 2b-3b .	.254	21	59	8	15	2	0	0	5	8	12	1
Velarde, Randy, 2b	.174	48	115	18	20	6	0	5	12	8	22	1
Ward, Gary, of-dh	.225	91	231	26	52	8	0	4	24	24	41	0
*Washington, Claudell, of .	.308	126	455	62	140	22	3	11	64	24	74	15
Winfield, Dave, of	.322	149	559	96	180	37	2	25	107	69	88	9

PITCHING	W	L	ERA	G	GS	CG	SV	IP	H	R	ER	BB	SO
Allen, Neil	5	3	3.84	41	2	0	0	117	121	51	50	37	61
*Candelaria, John	13	7	3.38	25	24	6	1	157	150	69	59	23	121
*Clements, Pat	0	0	6.48	6	1	0	0	8	12	8	6	4	3
Dotson, Richard	12	9	5.00	32	29	4	0	171	178	103	95	72	77
Eiland, Dave	0	0	6.39	3	3	0	0	13	15	9	9	4	7
*Guetterman, Lee	1	2	4.65	20	2	0	0	41	49	21	21	14	15
*Guidry, Ron	2	3	4.18	12	10	0	0	56	57	28	26	15	32
Hudson, Charles	6	6	4.49	28	12	1	2	106	93	53	53	36	58
*John, Tommy	9	8	4.49	35	32	0	0	176	221	96	88	46	81
*Leiter, Al	4	4	3.92	14	14	0	0	57	49	27	25	33	60
Mohorcic, Dale (43 Tex) .	4	8	4.22	56	0	0	6	75	83	42	35	29	44
Nielsen, Scott	1	2	6.86	7	2	0	0	20	27	16	15	13	4
*Pena, Hipolito	1	1	2.51	16	0	0	0	14	10	8	4	9	10
Rhoden, Rick	12	12	4.20	30	30	5	0	197	206	107	92	56	94
*Righetti, Dave	5	4	3.52	60	0	0	25	87	86	35	34	37	70
Shields, Steve	5	5	4.37	39	0	0	0	82	96	44	40	30	55
Stoddard, Tim	2	2	6.38	28	0	0	3	55	62	41	39	27	33

OAKLAND

BATTING	AVG	G	AB	R	H	2B	3B	HR	RBI	BB	SO	SB
Baylor, Don, dh	.220	92	264	28	58	7	0	7	34	34	44	0
Blankenship, Lance, 2b .	.000	10	3	1	0	0	0	0	0	0	1	0
Canseco, Jose, of	.307	158	610	120	187	34	0	42	124	78	128	40
Gallego, Mike, 2b-ss	.209	129	277	38	58	8	0	2	20	34	53	2
*Hassey, Ron, c	.257	107	323	32	83	15	0	7	45	30	42	2
Henderson, Dave, of	.304	146	507	100	154	38	1	24	94	47	92	2
Hubbard, Glenn, 2b	.255	105	294	35	75	12	2	3	33	33	50	1
#Javier, Stan, of	.257	125	397	48	102	13	3	2	35	32	63	20
*Jennings, Doug, of-1b	.208	71	101	9	21	6	0	1	15	21	28	0
*Jose, Felix, of	.333	8	6	2	2	1	0	0	1	0	1	1
Jurak, Ed, 3b	.000	3	1	1	0	0	0	0	0	0	0	0
Lansford, Carney, 3b	.279	150	556	80	155	20	2	7	57	35	35	29
McGwire, Mark, 1b	.260	155	550	87	143	22	1	32	99	76	117	0
Mercado, Orlando, c	.125	16	24	3	3	0	0	1	1	3	8	0
*Parker, Dave, dh-of	.257	101	377	43	97	18	1	12	55	32	70	0
*Phillips, Tony, of-2b	.203	79	212	32	43	8	4	2	17	36	50	0
#Polonia, Luis, of	.292	84	288	51	84	11	4	2	27	21	40	24
Sinatro, Matt, c	.333	10	9	1	3	2	0	0	5	0	1	0
Steinbach, Terry, c	.265	104	351	42	93	19	1	9	51	33	47	3
#Weiss, Walt, ss	.250	147	452	44	113	17	3	3	39	35	56	4

PITCHING	W	L	ERA	G	GS	CG	SV	IP	H	R	ER	BB	SO
Bordi, Rich	0	1	4.70	2	2	0	0	8	6	6	4	5	6
Burns, Todd	8	2	3.16	17	14	2	1	103	93	38	36	34	57
*Cadaret, Greg	5	2	2.89	58	0	0	3	72	60	26	23	36	65
Corsi, Jim	0	1	3.80	11	1	0	0	21	20	10	9	6	10
Davis, Storm	16	7	3.70	33	33	1	0	202	211	86	83	91	127
Eckersley, Dennis	4	2	2.35	60	0	0	45	73	52	20	19	11	70
*Honeycutt, Rick	3	2	3.50	55	0	0	7	80	74	36	31	25	47
Nelson, Gene	9	6	3.06	54	1	0	3	112	93	42	38	38	67
Ontiveros, Steve	3	4	4.61	10	10	0	0	55	57	32	28	21	30
*Otto, Dave	0	0	1.80	3	2	0	0	10	9	2	2	6	7
Plunk, Eric	7	2	3.00	49	0	0	5	78	62	27	26	39	79
Shaver, Jeff	0	0	0.00	1	0	0	0	1	0	0	0	0	0
Stewart, Dave	21	12	3.23	37	37	14	0	276	240	111	99	110	192
Welch, Bob	17	9	3.64	36	36	4	0	245	237	107	99	81	158
*Young, Curt	11	8	4.15	26	26	0	1	156	162	77	72	50	69

SEATTLE

BATTING	AVG	G	AB	R	H	2B	3B	HR	RBI	BB	SO	SB
Balboni, Steve, 1b-dh (21 KC)	.235	118	413	46	97	17	1	23	66	24	87	0
*Bradley, Scott, c	.257	103	335	45	86	17	1	4	33	17	16	1
Brantley, Mickey, of	.263	149	577	76	152	25	4	15	56	26	64	18
*Briley, Greg, of	.250	13	36	6	9	2	0	1	4	5	6	0
Buhner, Jay, of (25 NY)	.215	85	261	36	56	13	1	13	38	28	93	1
Coles, Darnell, of	.292	55	195	32	57	10	1	10	34	17	26	3
Cotto, Henry, of	.259	133	386	50	100	18	1	8	33	23	53	27
*Davis, Alvin, 1b	.295	140	478	67	141	24	1	18	69	95	53	1
Diaz, Mario, ss	.306	28	72	6	22	5	0	0	9	3	5	0
*Fields, Bruce, of	.269	38	67	8	18	5	0	1	5	4	11	0
Hengel, Dave, of	.167	26	60	3	10	1	0	2	7	1	15	0
*Kingery, Mike, of	.203	57	123	21	25	6	0	1	9	19	23	3
Martinez, Edgar, 3b	.281	14	32	0	9	4	0	0	5	4	7	0

Kirby Puckett led the league in both hits (234) and total bases (358).

	AVG	G	AB	R	H	2B	3B	HR	RBI	BB	SO	SB
McGuire, Bill, c	.188	9	16	1	3	0	0	0	2	3	2	0
Presley, Jim, 3b	.230	150	544	50	125	26	0	14	62	36	114	3
Quinones, Rey, ss	.248	140	499	63	124	30	3	12	52	23	71	0
Rabb, John, dh-of	.357	9	14	2	5	2	0	0	4	0	1	0
Renteria, Rich, inf	.205	31	88	6	18	9	0	0	6	2	8	1
#Reynolds, Harold, 2b	.283	158	598	61	169	26	11	4	41	51	51	35
Smith, Brick, 1b	.100	4	10	1	1	0	0	0	1	0	1	0
Valle, Dave, c	.231	93	290	29	67	15	2	10	50	18	38	0
Wilson, Glenn, of	.250	78	284	28	71	10	1	3	17	15	52	1

PITCHING	W	L	ERA	G	GS	CG	SV	IP	H	R	ER	BB	SO
Bankhead, Scott	7	9	3.07	21	21	2	0	135	115	53	46	38	102
Campbell, Mike	6	10	5.89	20	20	2	0	115	128	81	75	43	63
Hanson, Erik	2	3	3.24	6	6	0	0	42	35	17	15	12	36
Jackson, Mike	6	5	2.63	62	0	0	4	99	74	37	29	43	76
*Langston, Mark	15	11	3.34	35	35	9	0	261	222	108	97	110	235
Moore, Mike	9	15	3.78	37	32	9	1	229	196	104	96	63	182
Nunez, Edwin	1	4	7.98	14	3	0	0	29	45	33	26	14	19
*Powell, Dennis	1	3	8.68	12	2	0	0	19	29	20	18	11	15
Reed, Jerry	1	1	3.96	46	0	0	1	86	82	42	38	33	48
Schooler, Mike	5	8	3.54	40	0	0	15	48	45	21	19	24	54
*Scurry, Rod	0	2	4.02	39	0	0	2	31	32	16	14	18	33
Solano, Julio	0	0	4.09	17	0	0	3	22	22	13	10	12	10
Swift, Bill	8	12	4.59	38	24	6	0	175	199	99	89	65	47
Taylor, Terry	0	1	6.26	5	5	0	0	23	26	17	16	11	9
*Trout, Steve	4	7	7.83	15	13	0	0	56	86	53	49	31	14
*Walter, Gene	1	0	5.13	16	0	0	0	26	21	16	15	15	13
*Wilkinson, Bill	2	2	3.48	30	0	0	2	31	28	14	12	15	25

TEXAS

BATTING	AVG	G	AB	R	H	2B	3B	HR	RBI	BB	SO	SB
Brower, Bob, of	.224	82	201	29	45	7	0	1	11	27	38	10
#Browne, Jerry, 2b	.229	73	214	26	49	9	2	1	17	25	33	7
Buechele, Steve, 3b	.251	155	503	68	126	21	4	16	58	65	79	2
#Espy, Cecil, of	.248	123	347	46	86	17	6	2	39	20	83	33
Fletcher, Scott, ss	.276	140	515	59	142	19	4	0	47	62	34	8
Garbey, Barbaro, of-3b	.194	30	62	4	12	2	0	0	5	4	11	0
Incaviglia, Pete, of-dh	.249	116	418	59	104	19	3	22	54	39	153	6
*Kemp, Steve, dh-of	.222	16	36	2	8	0	0	0	2	2	9	1
*Kreuter, Chad, c	.275	16	51	3	14	2	1	1	5	7	13	0
Kunkel, Jeff, 2b	.227	55	154	14	35	9	3	2	15	4	35	0
*McDowell, Oddibe, of	.247	120	437	55	108	19	5	6	37	41	89	33
*O'Brien, Pete, 1b	.272	156	547	57	149	24	1	16	71	72	73	1
#Petralli, Geno, c-3b	.282	129	351	35	99	14	2	7	36	41	52	0
*Reimer, Kevin, dh	.120	12	25	2	3	0	0	1	2	0	6	0
See, Larry, dh-1b	.130	13	23	0	3	0	0	0	0	1	8	0
#Sierra, Ruben, of	.254	156	615	77	156	32	4	23	91	44	91	18
Stanley, Mike, c	.229	94	249	21	57	8	0	3	27	37	62	0
*Steels, James, of	.189	36	53	4	10	1	0	0	5	0	15	2
Sundberg, Jim, c	.286	38	91	13	26	4	0	4	13	15	15	0
#Wilkerson, Curt, 2b-ss	.293	117	338	41	99	12	5	0	28	26	43	9

PITCHING	W	L	ERA	G	GS	CG	SV	IP	H	R	ER	BB	SO
Brown, Kevin	1	1	4.24	4	4	1	0	23	33	15	11	8	12
Cecena, Jose	0	0	4.78	22	0	0	1	26	20	16	14	23	27
*Fossas, Tony	0	0	4.76	5	0	0	0	6	11	3	3	2	2
Guante, Cecilio (56 NY)	5	6	2.82	63	0	0	12	80	67	26	25	26	65
Guzman, Jose	11	13	3.70	30	30	6	0	207	180	99	85	82	157
*Hayward, Ray	4	6	5.46	12	12	1	0	63	63	44	38	35	37
Henry, Dwayne	0	1	8.71	11	0	0	1	10	15	10	10	9	10
*Hoffman, Guy	0	0	5.24	11	0	0	0	22	22	14	13	8	9
Hough, Charlie	15	16	3.32	34	34	10	0	252	202	111	93	126	174
*Jeffcoat, Mike	0	2	11.70	5	2	0	0	10	19	13	13	5	5
*Kilgus, Paul	12	15	4.16	32	32	5	0	203	190	105	94	71	88
Kunkel, Jeff	0	0	0.00	1	0	0	0	1	0	0	0	0	1
May, Scott	0	0	8.59	3	1	0	0	7	8	7	7	4	4
McMurtry, Craig	3	3	2.25	32	0	0	3	60	37	16	15	24	35
Russell, Jeff	10	9	3.82	34	24	5	0	189	183	86	80	66	88
*Vande Berg, Ed	2	2	4.14	26	0	0	2	37	44	19	17	11	18
Vaughn, Dewayne	0	0	7.63	8	0	0	0	15	24	15	13	4	8
*Williams, Mitch	2	7	4.63	67	0	0	18	68	48	38	35	47	61
*Wilson, Steve	0	0	5.87	3	0	0	0	8	7	5	5	4	1
Witt, Bobby	8	10	3.92	22	22	13	0	174	134	83	76	101	148

TORONTO

BATTING	AVG	G	AB	R	H	2B	3B	HR	RBI	BB	SO	SB
Barfield, Jesse, of	.244	136	468	62	114	21	5	18	56	41	108	7
Bell, George, of	.269	156	614	78	165	27	5	24	97	34	66	4
Beniquez, Juan, dh	.293	27	58	9	17	2	0	1	8	8	6	0
Borders, Pat, c	.273	56	154	15	42	6	3	5	21	3	24	0
Butera, Sal, c	.233	23	60	3	14	2	1	1	6	1	9	0
Campusano, Sil, of	.218	73	142	14	31	10	2	2	12	9	33	0
*Ducey, Rob, of	.315	27	54	15	17	4	1	0	6	5	7	1
#Fernandez, Tony, ss	.287	154	648	76	186	41	4	5	70	45	65	15
Fielder, Cecil, dh-1b	.230	74	174	24	40	6	1	9	23	14	53	0
Gruber, Kelly, 3b	.278	158	569	75	158	33	5	16	81	38	92	23
Infante, Alex, 3b	.200	19	15	7	3	0	0	0	0	2	4	0
*Leach, Rick, of-dh	.276	87	199	21	55	13	1	0	23	18	27	0
#Lee, Manny, 2b-ss	.291	117	381	38	111	16	3	2	38	26	64	3
#Liriano, Nelson, 2b	.264	103	276	36	73	6	2	3	23	11	40	12
*McGriff, Fred, 1b	.282	154	536	100	151	35	5	34	82	79	149	6
*Moseby, Lloyd, of	.239	128	472	77	113	17	7	10	42	70	93	31
*Mulliniks, Rance, dh	.300	119	337	49	101	21	1	12	48	56	57	1
*Thornton, Lou, of	.000	11	2	1	0	0	0	0	0	0	0	0
*Whitt, Ernie, c	.251	127	398	63	100	11	2	16	70	61	38	4

PITCHING	W	L	ERA	G	GS	CG	SV	IP	H	R	ER	BB	SO
Bair, Doug	0	0	4.05	10	0	0	0	13	14	6	6	3	8
*Castillo, Tony	1	0	3.00	14	0	0	0	15	10	5	5	2	14
*Cerutti, John	6	7	3.13	46	12	0	1	124	120	56	43	42	65
Clancy, Jim	11	13	4.49	36	31	4	1	196	207	106	98	47	118
Eichhorn, Mark	0	3	4.19	37	0	0	1	67	79	32	31	27	28
*Flanagan, Mike	13	13	4.18	34	34	2	0	211	220	106	98	80	99
Henke, Tom	4	4	2.91	52	0	0	25	68	60	23	22	24	66
*Key, Jimmy	12	5	3.29	21	21	2	0	131	127	53	48	30	65
*Musselman, Jeff	8	5	3.18	15	15	0	0	85	80	34	30	30	39
Nunez, Jose	0	1	3.07	13	2	0	0	29	28	11	10	17	18
Ross, Mark	0	0	4.91	3	0	0	0	7	5	6	4	4	4
Stieb, Dave	16	8	3.04	32	31	8	0	207	157	76	70	79	147
Stottlemyre, Todd	4	8	5.69	28	16	0	0	98	109	70	62	46	67
Ward, Duane	9	3	3.30	64	0	0	15	112	101	46	41	60	91
*Wells, David	3	5	4.62	41	0	0	4	64	65	36	33	31	56
Wills, Frank	0	0	5.23	10	0	0	0	21	22	12	12	6	19

ALCS: Box Scores

Game One: Athletics 2, Red Sox 1

OAKLAND	ab	r	h	bi	bb	so		BOSTON	ab	r	h	bi	bb	so
Lansford 3b	4	1	1	0	0	1		Boggs 3b	4	0	1	1	0	2
Henderson cf	4	0	2	1	0	1		Barrett 2b	4	0	0	0	0	0
Canseco rf	4	1	1	1	0	1		Evans rf	4	0	1	0	0	3
McGwire 1b	4	0	0	0	0	1		Greenwell lf	3	0	0	0	1	0
Steinbach c	2	0	1	0	1	0		Benzinger 1b	4	0	0	0	0	1
Hassey c	1	0	0	0	0	0		Burks cf	4	0	0	0	0	1
Baylor dh	3	0	0	0	1	1		Rice dh	2	0	1	0	1	1
Polonia pr	0	0	0	0	0	0		Romine pr	0	1	0	0	0	0
Phillips lf	3	0	0	0	1	2		Parrish ph	1	0	0	0	0	1
Gallego 2b	4	0	0	0	0	0		Reed ss	2	0	1	0	1	0
Weiss ss	3	0	1	0	0	0		Gedman c	3	0	2	0	1	0
								Romero pr	0	0	0	0	0	0
TOTALS	32	2	6	2	3	7		TOTALS	31	1	6	1	4	9

Oakland . . . . 000 100 010—2
Boston . . . . 000 000 100—1

Game-winning RBI—Henderson.

DP—Oakland 1, Boston 1. LOB—Oakland 6, Boston 9. 2B—Weiss, Evans, Lansford. HR—Canseco. SF—Boggs.

Oakland	IP	H	R	ER	BB	SO
Stewart	6⅓	5	1	1	3	6
Honeycutt W	⅔	0	0	0	0	0
Eckersley S	2	1	0	0	1	3

Boston	IP	H	R	ER	BB	SO
Hurst L	9	6	2	2	3	7

PB—Steinbach. HBP—Reed by Stewart. T—2:55. A—34,104.

Game Two: Athletics 4, Red Sox 3

OAKLAND	ab	r	h	bi	bb	so
Polonia lf	5	0	2	0	0	2
Gallego 2b	0	0	0	0	0	0
Henderson cf	3	1	1	0	1	1
Canseco rf	4	1	1	2	0	0
Parker dh	4	0	1	0	0	0
Lansford 3b	4	1	0	0	0	1
Hassey c	4	1	1	0	0	1
McGwire 1b	4	0	1	1	0	2
Phillips 2b-lf	4	0	2	0	0	1
Weiss ss	4	0	1	1	0	1
TOTALS	36	4	10	4	1	9

BOSTON	ab	r	h	bi	bb	so
Boggs 3b	3	0	0	0	1	1
Barrett 2b	4	0	0	0	0	0
Evans rf	3	1	0	0	1	0
Greenwell lf	2	1	0	0	2	0
Rice dh	4	0	1	0	0	0
Romine pr	0	0	0	0	0	0
Burks cf	4	0	1	1	0	0
Benzinger 1b	3	0	1	0	1	1
Reed ss	2	0	0	0	0	1
Parrish ph	1	0	0	0	0	0
Gedman c	4	1	1	1	0	1
TOTALS	30	3	4	2	5	4

```
Oakland .................... 000 000 301—4
Boston  .................... 000 002 100—3
```

Game-winning RBI—Weiss.
E—Clemens, Henderson. DP—Oakland 1. LOB—Oakland 6, Boston 6. 2B—Phillips. HR—Canseco, Gedman. S—Reed.

Oakland	IP	H	R	ER	BB	SO
Davis	6⅓	2	2	0	5	4
Cadaret	⅓	1	1	1	0	0
Nelson W	1⅓	0	0	0	0	0
Eckersley S	1	0	0	0	0	0

Boston	IP	H	R	ER	BB	SO
Clemens	7	6	3	3	0	8
Stanley	⅓	1	0	0	1	0
Smith L	1⅔	3	1	1	0	1

PB—Gedman. WP—Davis, Clemens. Balk—Clemens. T—3:14. A—34,605.

Game Three: Athletics 10, Red Sox 6

BOSTON	ab	r	h	bi	bb	so
Burks cf	5	2	2	0	0	1
Barrett 2b	4	1	1	0	0	0
Boggs 3b	4	2	3	2	0	0
Greenwell lf	5	1	3	3	0	0
Rice dh	5	0	0	0	0	0
Evans rf	2	0	1	1	2	0
Gedman c	3	0	2	0	1	0
Reed ss	3	0	1	0	1	0
Benzinger 1b	3	0	0	0	0	1
Parrish ph-1b	1	0	0	0	0	1
TOTALS	35	6	12	6	4	5

OAKLAND	ab	r	h	bi	bb	so
Lansford 3b	5	2	3	2	0	0
Henderson cf	5	1	2	2	0	3
Canseco rf	4	0	0	0	1	1
Parker dh	5	1	1	0	0	2
McGwire 1b	4	3	3	1	0	1
Hassey c	3	1	3	3	1	0
Javier lf	3	0	1	1	1	0
Gallego 2b	4	1	1	0	0	2
Weiss ss	4	1	1	1	0	1
TOTALS	37	10	15	10	3	10

```
Boston  .................... 320 000 100— 6
Oakland .................... 042 010 12x—10
```

Game-winning RBI—Hassey.
E—Henderson. DP—Boston 1, Oakland 2. LOB—Boston 8, Oakland 6. 2B—Greenwell, Burks, Weiss, Hassey, Parker. HR—Greenwell, McGwire, Lansford, Hassey, Henderson. S—Barrett. SF—Boggs.

Boston	IP	H	R	ER	BB	SO
Boddicker L	2⅔	8	6	6	1	2
Gardner	4⅔	6	3	3	2	8
Stanley	⅔	1	1	1	0	0

Oakland	IP	H	R	ER	BB	SO
Welch	1⅔	6	5	5	2	0
Nelson W	3⅓	4	0	0	1	0
Young	1⅓	1	1	0	0	2
Plunk	⅓	1	0	0	0	1
Honeycutt	⅓	0	0	0	1	0
Eckersley S	2	0	0	0	0	2

Honeycutt pitched to 1 batter in 8th.
Balk—Welch. T—3:14. A—49,261.

Game Four: Athletics 4, Red Sox 1

BOSTON	ab	r	h	bi	bb	so
Burks cf	4	0	1	0	0	1
Barrett 2b	3	1	0	0	1	0
Boggs 3b	2	0	1	0	2	1
Greenwell lf	4	0	1	0	0	0
Rice dh	2	0	0	1	1	1
Owen dh	0	0	0	0	1	0
Evans rf	3	0	0	0	0	2
Benzinger ph	1	0	0	0	0	0
Gedman c	4	0	0	0	0	0
Reed ss	4	0	1	0	0	0
Parrish 1b	3	0	0	0	0	0
TOTALS	30	1	4	1	5	5

OAKLAND	ab	r	h	bi	bb	so
Lansford 3b	4	0	1	0	0	0
Henderson cf	4	0	1	1	0	2
Canseco rf	4	2	3	1	0	0
McGwire 1b	3	1	1	1	1	1
Parker lf	3	0	1	0	0	2
Javier lf	1	0	1	0	0	0
Steinbach c	2	0	0	0	1	0
Polonia ph	0	0	0	0	1	0
Hassey c	0	0	0	0	0	0
Baylor dh	3	0	1	0	1	0
Gallego 2b	4	0	0	0	0	1
Weiss ss	4	1	2	0	0	2
TOTALS	32	4	10	4	3	9

```
Boston  .................... 000 001 000—1
Oakland .................... 101 000 02X—4
```

Game-winning RBI—Canseco.
E—Parker. DP—Oakland 1. LOB—Boston 7, Oakland 8. 2B—Henderson, Canseco. HR—Canseco. SB—Canseco. SF—Baylor.

Boston	IP	H	R	ER	BB	SO	Oakland	IP	H	R	ER	BB	SO
Hurst L	4	4	2	2	2	5	Stewart W	7	4	1	1	3	5
Smithson	2⅓	3	0	0	0	1	Honeycutt	1	0	0	0	1	0
Smith	1⅔	3	2	2	1	3	Eckersley S	1	0	0	0	1	0

Stewart pitched to 1 batter in 8th.
T—2:55. A—49,406.

ALCS: Composite Box

OAKLAND

Player, Pos.	AVG	G	AB	R	H	2B	3B	HR	RBI	BB	SO	SB
Ron Hassey, c	.500	4	8	2	4	1	0	1	3	1	1	0
Stan Javier, lf	.500	2	4	0	2	0	0	0	1	1	0	0
Luis Polonia, pr-lf-ph	.400	3	5	0	2	0	0	0	0	1	1	0
Dave Henderson, cf	.375	4	16	2	6	1	0	1	4	1	7	0
Mark McGwire, 1b	.333	4	15	4	5	0	0	1	3	1	5	0
Walt Weiss, ss	.333	4	15	2	5	2	0	0	2	0	4	0
Jose Canseco, rf	.313	4	16	4	5	1	0	3	4	1	2	1
Carney Lansford, 3b	.294	4	17	4	5	1	0	1	2	0	2	0
Tony Phillips, lf-2b	.286	2	7	0	2	1	0	0	0	1	4	0
Dave Parker, dh-lf	.250	3	12	1	3	1	0	0	0	0	4	0
Terry Steinbach, c	.250	2	4	0	1	0	0	0	0	2	0	0
Mike Gallego, 2b	.083	4	12	1	1	0	0	0	0	0	3	0
Don Baylor, dh	.000	2	6	0	0	0	0	0	1	1	2	0
TOTALS	.299	4	137	20	41	8	0	7	20	10	35	1

Pitcher	W	L	ERA	G	GS	CG	SV	IP	H	R	ER	BB	SO
Storm Davis	0	0	0.00	1	1	0	0	6⅓	2	2	0	5	4
Dennis Eckersley	0	0	0.00	4	0	0	4	6	1	0	0	2	5
Gene Nelson	2	0	0.00	2	0	0	0	4⅔	5	0	0	1	0
Rick Honeycutt	1	0	0.00	3	0	0	0	2	0	0	0	2	0
Curt Young	0	0	0.00	1	0	0	0	1⅓	1	1	0	0	2
Eric Plunk	0	0	0.00	1	0	0	0	⅓	1	0	0	0	1
Dave Stewart	1	0	1.35	2	2	0	0	13⅓	9	2	2	6	11
Bob Welch	0	0	27.00	1	1	0	0	1⅔	6	5	5	2	0
Greg Cadaret	0	0	27.00	1	0	0	0	⅓	1	1	1	0	0
TOTALS	4	0	2.00	4	4	0	4	36	26	11	8	18	23

BOSTON

Player, Pos.	AVG	G	AB	R	H	2B	3B	HR	RBI	BB	SO	SB
Wade Boggs, 3b	.385	4	13	2	5	0	0	0	3	3	4	0
Rich Gedman, c	.357	4	14	1	5	0	0	1	1	2	1	0
Jody Reed, ss	.273	4	11	0	3	1	0	0	0	2	1	0
Ellis Burks, cf	.214	4	17	2	4	1	0	0	1	0	3	0
Mike Greenwell, lf	.214	4	14	2	3	1	0	1	3	3	0	0
Dwight Evans, rf	.167	4	12	1	2	1	0	0	1	3	5	0
Jim Rice, dh	.154	4	13	0	2	0	0	0	1	2	4	0
Todd Benzinger, 1b-ph	.091	4	11	0	1	0	0	0	0	1	3	0
Marty Barrett, 2b	.067	4	15	2	1	0	0	0	0	1	0	0
Larry Parrish, ph-1b	.000	4	6	0	0	0	0	0	0	0	2	0
Kevin Romine, pr	—	2	0	1	0	0	0	0	0	0	0	0
Spike Owen, ph	—	1	0	0	0	0	0	0	0	1	0	0
Ed Romero, pr	—	1	0	0	0	0	0	0	0	0	0	0
TOTALS	.206	4	126	11	26	4	0	2	10	18	23	0

Pitcher	W	L	ERA	G	GS	CG	SV	IP	H	R	ER	BB	SO
Mike Smithson	0	0	0.00	1	0	0	0	2⅓	3	0	0	0	1
Bruce Hurst	0	2	2.77	2	2	1	0	13	10	4	4	5	12
Roger Clemens	0	0	3.86	1	1	0	0	7	6	3	3	0	8
Wes Gardner	0	0	5.79	1	0	0	0	4⅔	6	3	3	2	8
Lee Smith	0	1	8.10	2	0	0	0	3⅓	6	3	3	1	4
Bob Stanley	0	0	9.00	2	0	0	0	1	2	1	1	1	0
Mike Boddicker	0	1	20.25	1	1	0	0	2⅔	8	6	6	1	2
TOTALS	0	4	5.29	4	4	1	0	34	41	20	20	10	35

Oakland	1	4	3		1	1	0		4	5	1	—	20
Boston	3	2	0		0	0	3		3	0	0	—	11

Game-winning RBIs—Henderson, Weiss, Hassey, Canseco.

E—Clemens, Henderson 2, Parker. DP—Oakland 5, Boston 2. LOB—Oakland 26, Boston 30. S—Reed, Barrett. SF—Boggs 2, Baylor. PB—Steinbach, Gedman. HBP—Reed by Stewart. WP—Davis, Clemens. Balk—Clemens, Welch. Umpires—Denkinger, Hendry, McClelland, Kosc, Kaiser, Shulock. Official Scorers—Charles Scoggins, Lowell Sun; Glenn Schwartz, San Francisco Examiner.

Stuff like the Dodgers isn't easily explained

By JAYSON STARK

History is going to forever show us that the best team in the National League in 1988 was the Los Angeles Dodgers. How that happened, we couldn't tell you.

You definitely can't explain it with facts. That's for sure.

They'd lost 89 games each of the last two years. Then they traded away one of the best starting pitchers in baseball, Bob Welch.

Then the main guy they traded him for, Alfredo Griffin, hit .199 and was out two months with a broken hand.

Besides that, their opening-day starter, that Fernandomaniacal Valenzuela fellow, had a Buenos Noches kind of year. He never won a game after June 14.

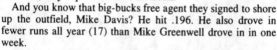

And remember that big slugger in the middle of their lineup, Pedro Guerrero? They were so happy with his work, they deported him to St. Louis.

And you know that big-bucks free agent they signed to shore up the outfield, Mike Davis? He hit .196. He also drove in fewer runs all year (17) than Mike Greenwell drove in in one week.

And you recall that lefthanded bullpen star they got to put

League Champions

(Playoff Champions, Where Applicable)

(Since 1900)

1988—Los Angeles	1958—Milwaukee	1928—St. Louis
1987—St. Louis	1957—Milwaukee	1927—Pittsburgh
1986—New York	1956—Brooklyn	1926—St. Louis
1985—St. Louis	1955—Brooklyn	1925—Pittsburgh
1984—San Diego	1954—New York	1924—New York
1983—Philadelphia	1953—Brooklyn	1923—New York
1982—St. Louis	1952—Brooklyn	1922—New York
1981—Los Angeles	1951—New York	1921—New York
1980—Philadelphia	1950—Philadelphia	1920—Brooklyn
1979—Pittsburgh	1949—Brooklyn	1919—Cincinnati
1978—Los Angeles	1948—Boston	1918—Chicago
1977—Los Angeles	1947—Brooklyn	1917—New York
1976—Cincinnati	1946—St. Louis	1916—Brooklyn
1975—Cincinnati	1945—Chicago	1915—Philadelphia
1974—Los Angeles	1944—St. Louis	1914—Boston
1973—New York	1943—St. Louis	1913—New York
1972—Cincinnati	1942—St. Louis	1912—New York
1971—Pittsburgh	1941—Brooklyn	1911—New York
1970—Cincinnati	1940—Cincinnati	1910—Chicago
1969—New York	1939—Cincinnati	1909—Pittsburgh
1968—St. Louis	1938—Chicago	1908—Chicago
1967—St. Louis	1937—New York	1907—Chicago
1966—Los Angeles	1936—New York	1906—Chicago
1965—Los Angeles	1935—Chicago	1905—New York
1964—St. Louis	1934—St. Louis	1904—New York
1963—Los Angeles	1933—New York	1903—Pittsburgh
1962—San Francisco	1932—Chicago	1902—Pittsburgh
1961—Cincinnati	1931—St. Louis	1901—Pittsburgh
1960—Pittsburgh	1930—St. Louis	1900—Brooklyn
1959—Los Angeles	1929—Chicago	

World Champs

Members of the 1988 World Series Champion Los Angeles Dodgers included Top row, l to r, Tim Crews, Mario Soto, Mike Sharperson, Danny Heep, Mike Devereaux, Jose Gonzalez, Alejandro Pena, Jesse Orosco, Tim Belcher, Mike Marshall, Jeff Hamilton, Jay Howell, Mike Davis, Ramon Martinez, Ken Howell, John Shelby, William Brennan, John Tudor. Middle row, Dr. Ralph Gambardella, Dr. Michael Mellman, Bill DeLury, Chris Gwynn, Tracy Woodson, Mickey Hatcher, Rick Dempsey, Franklin Stubbs, Alfredo Griffin, Tim Leary, Orel Hershiser, Mike Scioscia, Dave Anderson, Ricky Horton, Brian Holton, Pat Screnar. Front row (seated), Bill Buhler, David Wright, Gilberto Reyes, Fernando Valenzuela, Kirk Gibson, Ben Hines, Manny Mota, Joe Amalfitano, Tommy Lasorda, Bill Russell, Mark Cresse, Ron Perranoski, Joe Ferguson, Steve Sax, Todd Maulding, Charlie Strasser. Bottom row, Andrew Cooper, Mark Bossert, Mitch Poole, Shawn Evans, Frank Pinela, Pete Sandoval.

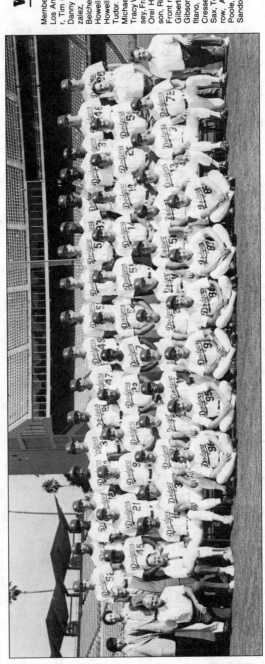

an end to the parade of Ed Vande Bergs? Right, Jesse Orosco. He racked up his fewest saves in six years (nine).

Gibson was the difference

So how did they do it? You tell us.

OK, Kirk Gibson. You've got it. They positively couldn't have done it without Kirk Gibson.

He was only the third prospective National League most valuable player in history who didn't bat .300 *or* hit 30 home runs *or* drive in 100 runs. But just the way he limped around and played Roy Hobbs in October told you all you needed to know about the fire that raged inside him.

And Tim Belcher. Absolutely. Tim Belcher. He went from the player to be named later (from the A's for Rick Honeycutt) to the best rookie pitcher in baseball. Couldn't have done it without him, either.

And Tim Leary. And Jay Howell. And the triumphant return of Alejandro Pena. And Steve Sax. And John Tudor. Yep. They couldn't have done it without them.

And better not forget managing's gift to lasagna, Tommy Lasorda. He might have done his greatest job ever of bear-hugging, motivating and consulting the big Dodger in the sky. They don't get where they got without him. No sir.

Hershiser: too good to be true

Finally, fabulously, there was Orel Leonard Hershiser IV. What a story. He was too good. Too good for the National League. Too good to be true.

He pitched six shutouts in a row. He broke the Record That Would Never Be Broken (Don Drysdale's 58-inning streak of shutout innings).

He started. He relieved. He was unbeatable. He was unflappable. He never lost his stuff. But more important, he never lost his head.

He was just good old Orel Leonard Hershiser IV, regular guy.

"What's happened to me in the last month and a half is unbelievable," he said after beating the New York Mets in Game Seven of the National League playoffs. "But I don't think it's really sunk in yet. I want to stay humble. This game can humble you in a hurry. I want to keep going at it like I'm climbing the mountain."

It's hard enough climbing the mountain by yourself. But Orel Hershiser had to climb it with 23 guys in blue tied to his back.

He never looked down. He never slipped up. And they all reached the top of the mountain together.

They rose above the facts. They rose above the stats. They rose above the National League.

They were the Los Angeles Dodgers. They were the champs.

Tommy Lasorda
. . . motivator

How they did it doesn't matter. All that matters is that they did.

Dodgers subdue Mets

It was a big enough shock to most people that the Dodgers won the NL West. So when they got to the playoffs, they were not what you would call your prohibitive favorites.

When they got there, they had to play those cocky, ferocious Mets. What fun.

The Mets won 100 games. The Mets led the league in pitching. The Mets led the league in home runs. The Mets committed the fewest errors in the league.

And one more thing.

The Mets beat the Dodgers 10 times during the regular season.

Darryl Strawberry slammed his teammates in Esquire magazine, then slammed 39 home runs.

And lost once.

The regular season didn't count once the playoffs started. And there, on the mound, in Game One, was that Orel Hershiser person again.

He spun eight more shutout innings. That made 67 straight. He got to the ninth with a 2-0 lead. Nobody beats Orel Hershiser with a 2-0 lead.

But all year there was Somebody Up There who looked after the Mets. In the ninth, that Somebody showed up.

Single. Double. 2-1. Exit Hershiser. Enter one of the pivotal figures in the postseason soap opera, Jay Howell.

Walk. Blooper to center by Gary Carter. John Shelby, playing Carter in Pasadena, comes tumbling in. Ball hits glove. Ball falls to ground. Mets win. Uh-oh.

But just when you thought the Mets were about to go rolling through the playoffs, along came David Cone, cub reporter.

David Cone spends most of his time pitching for the Mets. He chose the playoffs to begin his spectacular new career in journalism by writing a column for the New York Daily News. Alert the Pulitzer committee.

Before Game Two, he was the best-read columnist around. Especially in the Dodger clubhouse.

He called Hershiser lucky. He called Howell a high school pitcher. Those were the highlights.

The Dodgers almost wore out their Xerox machine running off copies. Then they went out and torched Cone for five runs in two innings. And won easily, 6-3.

That turned the tide in the series. But not for long.

Let us move to the eighth inning of Game Three, the first

playoff game in this decade to be played underwater.

The Dodgers led 4-3. In came Howell again. He threw six pitches. Suddenly, out strolled umpire Harry Wendelstedt for a visit.

Wendelstedt looked at Howell's glove. He found pine tar all over it. Howell got the heave-ho. Later, he got suspended for two games.

The Dodgers bullpen fell apart after he left. The Mets won 8-4. Looked like time to alert the Dodgers' mortician again.

Nope. Game Four. An almost unhittable Dwight Gooden carried a three-hitter and a 4-2 lead into the ninth. The Mets were three outs away from leading the series 3-1.

But Mike Scioscia crashed a stunning home run off Gooden to tie it. Kirk Gibson drilled a series-turning home run in the 12th to win it. Then the new reliever in town, some skinny kid named Hershiser, got the final out to save it. One of the great playoff games ever.

Next day: Not even 12 hours later, in fact. Another Gibson home run powered the Dodgers to a 6-0 lead. They held on to win 7-4. They suddenly had control of the series 3-2.

But they also had a reinjured Gibson, limping around on a bad hamstring he hurt trying to steal a base he really didn't need to steal. He would never be the same again in the postseason. But that is Gibson. His transmission only has one gear.

A terrific game by the now-retired columnist, Cone, evened things up again the next night. So they went to Game Seven. Do you bet on the omnipotent Mets? Or do you bet on Hershiser, pitching on two days' rest?

David Cone went 20-3 during the regular season, but turned sportswriter at an inopportune time.

Danny Jackson of the Reds had a Cy Young-type season, but was overshadowed by the Dodgers' Orel Hershiser.

You bet on Hershiser, of course. The Mets reenacted the glorious 1962 Marv Throneberry era in a disastrous five-run second inning. The amazing Hershiser pitched yet another shutout, a 6-0 five-hitter. On two days' rest. Two.

But even as they sprayed champagne, the victorious Dodgers still were talking about David Cone and the column that changed the series.

"It was as if it represented everyone who doubted us," said Mike Marshall. "We've been in first place almost the whole year, but it seemed like every city we went to, we would beat a club, and then the next day in the paper, that city's manager would be quoted saying we won't be there at the end.

"Well, everybody on this team can read. And here we are."

NL East race

It was supposed to be another round of the NL East's eternal battle of the 80s—Mets vs. Cardinals.

Since 1985, the Mets have won twice, the Cardinals twice. But the difference is that the Mets have finished second in the two years they didn't win.

The Cardinals, on the other hand, have gone from the World Series one year to below .500 the next year three times in this decade. And 1988 was no exception to the pattern.

Before the end of April, they were without John Tudor, Joe Magrane and Ken Dayley. Danny Cox and Greg Mathews wouldn't be far behind.

So they started off 4-12, and got themselves eight games out by April 23. And about all they could do after that was make a couple of charges at Mount .500—and reshape their roster for the future.

Instead of the old familiar faces from St. Louis, it was all those new faces from Pittsburgh who gave the Mets a scare.

Andy Van Slyke had close to an MVP year. Bobby Bonilla, Barry Bonds and Doug Drabek decided they were about ready to be stars. Manager Jim Leyland kept them hungry. And on July 27, the Pirates were two games behind the Mets heading into a huge series at Shea Stadium.

They played three taut pitchers' duels. In the first one, Bob Ojeda pitched a shutout. In the second, Sid Fernandez pitched a shutout. In the third, Ron Darling outdueled Bob Walk 2-1. End of Pirates. End of pennant race.

By season's end, the Pirates had faded to 15 games out. They also had fired the man who rescued them from oblivion, general manager Syd Thrift. He may be gone, but the team he assembled sure isn't. Don't touch that dial in Pittsburgh.

The Expos rode the back of Andres (The Giant) Galarraga long enough to stay in the race until the second week of August. Then the Mets swept them in a doubleheader, jolting them into a suicidal nine-game losing streak. And that was it for them.

So that left the Mets to chase another 100-win season. That's a challenge anywhere. In New York, it's an episode of Wild Kingdom.

Darryl Strawberry hammered his teammates in Esquire magazine. Davey Johnson wasn't sure they wanted him back (they did).

Keith Hernandez went down for two months with hamstring blowouts. They couldn't figure out who was on second, short or third. They played worse-than-.500 baseball (33-35) for nearly 70 games between June 6 and Aug. 21. And only that relentless starting pitching kept them going.

But Hernandez came back. Strawberry bashed 39 home runs. Gregg Jefferies materialized in September to hit .321. Randy Myers became a certifiable bullpen monster. David Cone, the emergency starter, went 20-3.

So despite all their troubles, they still blew away the division. And now they get Jefferies for a *whole* season. Look out.

NL West race

In the beginning, everyone feared the Giants.

Roger Craig and his Humm-Babies still had the incredible split-fingered pitching staff. They finally had found a classic leadoff man in Brett Butler. They were coming off a season in which they'd gone 51-32 after the Fourth of July. Things were all set.

So naturally, they spent the first 80 games of the year bouncing between three games over .500 and three games under. They couldn't hit. They couldn't put a streak together.

They saw their entire rotation—except for Rick Reuschel—go down with various arm woes. And still they were only 2½ games behind the Dodgers at the all-star break.

Then they got swept in a four-game series in Pittsburgh. The same weekend, the Dodgers played a five-game set in Chicago and won all five. The Giants didn't know it, but they were finished right then.

The other big story in the West was the Padres.

By May 28, they were 15 games under .500 (16-31), and Larry Bowa was kicking over everything but the McDLTs. Then he got replaced by GM Jack McKeon, and everything in San Diego changed.

The Padres went 67-47 under McKeon. In the clubhouse, people smiled again, laughed again.

Eric Show, Andy Hawkins and Mark Davis had their best seasons. And the Padres finished third, passing the Giants and Astros on the final weekend of the season.

Amazing. And so was the fact that the NL West became the first NL division in history to have five teams with winning records. The NL East had two.

Hitters

There was Tony Gwynn. He won his second straight batting title, third in five years. That was the good news.

The bad news was that he only had to hit .313 to win it. That was the lowest average by any NL batting champ in history. Laughing Larry Doyle (.320 for the 1915 Giants) is off the hook now.

There was Darryl Strawberry. Love him. Hate him. Cheer him. Boo him. But you can't deny his awesome talent. He led the league in home runs (39). He drove in 101 runs. He scored 101. Only two other men in the league (Will Clark and Andy Van Slyke) kept him company in that 100-100 club.

There was Vince Coleman. He didn't steal 100 bases, for the first time in his career. But he did pass 400 career steals earlier than any player in history. And he did swipe 81, which was enough for him to lead the league for the fourth straight year. Not bad for a guy who has only *played* four years.

There was Jose Oquendo. He may not have had baseball's most spectacular numbers. But he did play nine positions in one year. No National Leaguer could make that claim in the last 70 years.

There was Andres Galarraga. This year was his coming-out party. He hit .300. He led the league in hits (184). He led the league in doubles (42) and total bases (329), too. It's hard to do all that when you're also leading the league in strikeouts (153). But he did it.

Pitchers

There was Danny Jackson. He would have won the Cy Young Award in any league that didn't have a Hershiser in it.

He may not have thrown six straight shutouts. But he went 23-8, same as Hershiser. And he threw 15 complete games, same as Hershiser. And he had six shutouts, second only to you know who. In his case, it sure wasn't embarrassing to finish second.

There was Joe Magrane. The good news was that he won the ERA title (2.18). The bad news was that he only won five games all year. The worst news was that no ERA champ in history ever won fewer games.

There was Tom Browning. He was living in a perfect world Sept. 16. He threw the first perfect game in the National League in 23 years, and just the 12th in either league in this century.

There was Pascual Perez. He threw a no-hitter himself, Sept. 24 against the Phillies. Don't give him a quality start to go with it, though. The game got rained out after five innings.

There was Nolan Ryan, age 41. He led the league in strikeouts. Again. That's only the ninth time he has done that. And the second time since he turned 40. He sure is feeling his age.

There was David Cone. He wasn't even in the Mets' rotation when the season started. He was 20-3 when it ended. Right, 20-3. Nevada-Las Vegas is supposed to go 20-3. Pitchers aren't.

And finally, there was the remarkable Orel Hershiser. He blew away Don Drysdale. He shut down the Mets. He closed out the A's.

In a year of great pitchers, there was no pitcher on earth like this man. He took the mound an exhausting 11 times in the final 41 days. He allowed five earned runs after Aug. 30 (a 0.44 ERA). He was the MVP of the playoffs. He was the MVP of the World Series.

He will always be out there in our minds. Singing hymns to settle himself down. Firing sinkers that looked as though he'd dropped them off a cliff at Malibu. Dropping to one knee as the pandemonium busted loose around him.

What a year for him. What a year for that team he pitched for.

Orel Hershiser and the Dodgers. They were both too good to be true.

1988: General Information

League Championship Series: Los Angeles defeated New York 4-3 in a best-of-7 series for the league pennant.

Regular Season Attendance: New York, 3,047,724; Los Angeles, 2,980,262; St. Louis, 2,892,629; Chicago, 2,089,034; Cincinnati, 2,072,528; Philadelphia, 1,990,041; Houston, 1,933,505; Pittsburgh, 1,865,713; San Francisco, 1,786,482; San Diego, 1,506,896; Montreal, 1,478,659; Atlanta, 848,089.

Managers: Atlanta—Chuck Tanner, Russ Nixon; **Chicago**—Don Zimmer; **Cincinnati**—Pete Rose; **Houston**—Hal Lanier; **Los Angeles**—Tommy Lasorda; **Montreal**—Buck Rodgers; **New York**—Davey Johnson; **Philadelphia**—Lee Elia, John Vukovich; **Pittsburgh**—Jim Leyland; **St. Louis**—Whitey Herzog; **San Diego**—Larry Bowa, Jack McKeon; **San Francisco**—Roger Craig.

1988 All-Star Team (by Baseball America): C—Benito Santiago, San Diego. **1B**—Andres Galarraga, Montreal. **2B**—Steve Sax, Los Angeles. **3B**—Bobby Bonilla, Pittsburgh. **SS**—Ozzie Smith, St. Louis. **OF**—Kevin McReynolds, New York; Darryl Strawberry, New York; Kirk Gibson, Los Angeles. **P**—Orel Hershiser, Los Angeles; Danny Jackson, Cincinnati; David Cone, New York; Dwight Gooden, New York; John Franco, Cincinnati. **Player of the Year**—Darryl Strawberry, New York. **Pitcher of the Year**—Orel Hershiser, Los Angeles. **Rookie of the Year**—Tim Belcher, Los Angeles. **Manager of the Year**—Tommy Lasorda, Los Angeles. **Executive of the Year**—Fred Claire, Los Angeles.

1988: Batting, Pitching Statistics

CLUB BATTING

	AVG	G	AB	R	H	2B	3B	HR	BB	SO	SB
Chicago	.261	163	5675	660	1481	262	46	113	403	910	120
New York	.256	160	5408	703	1387	251	24	152	544	842	140
Montreal	.251	163	5573	628	1400	260	48	107	454	1053	189
St. Louis	.249	162	5518	578	1373	207	33	71	484	827	234
San Francisco	.248	162	5450	670	1353	227	44	113	550	1023	121
Los Angeles	.248	162	5431	628	1346	217	25	99	437	947	131
Pittsburgh	.247	160	5379	651	1327	240	45	110	553	947	119
San Diego	.247	161	5366	594	1325	205	35	94	494	892	123
Cincinnati	.246	161	5426	641	1334	246	25	122	479	922	207
Houston	.244	162	5494	617	1338	239	31	96	474	840	198
Atlanta	.242	160	5440	555	1319	228	28	96	432	848	95
Philadelphia	.240	162	5403	597	1294	246	31	106	489	981	112

CLUB PITCHING

	ERA	G	CG	SHO	SV	IP	H	R	ER	BB	SO
New York	2.91	160	31	22	46	1439	1253	532	465	404	1100
Los Angeles	2.96	162	32	24	49	1463	1291	544	482	473	1029
Montreal	3.08	163	18	12	43	1483	1310	592	508	476	923
San Diego	3.28	161	30	9	39	1449	1332	583	528	439	885
Cincinnati	3.35	161	24	13	43	1455	1271	596	541	504	934
San Francisco	3.39	162	25	13	42	1462	1323	626	550	422	875
Houston	3.41	162	21	15	40	1475	1339	631	558	478	1049
Pittsburgh	3.47	160	12	11	46	1441	1349	616	555	469	790
St. Louis	3.47	162	17	14	42	1471	1387	633	567	486	881
Chicago	3.84	163	30	10	29	1464	1494	694	625	490	897
Atlanta	4.09	160	4	25	1446	1481	741	657	524	810	
Philadelphia	4.14	162	16	6	36	1433	1447	734	659	628	859

INDIVIDUAL BATTING LEADERS
(Minimum 502 Plate Appearances)

	AVG	G	AB	R	H	2B	3B	HR	RBI	BB	SO	SB
*Gwynn, Tony, SD	.313	133	521	64	163	22	5	7	70	51	40	26
*Palmeiro, Rafael, Chi ...	.307	152	580	75	178	41	5	8	53	38	34	12
Dawson, Andre, Chi	.303	157	591	78	179	31	8	24	79	37	73	12

	AVG	G	AB	R	H	2B	3B	HR	RBI	BB	SO	SB
Galarraga, Andres, Mon	.302	157	609	99	184	42	8	29	92	39	153	13
*Perry, Gerald, Atl	.300	141	547	61	164	29	1	8	74	36	49	29
*Grace, Mark, Chi	.296	134	486	65	144	23	4	7	57	60	43	3
Larkin, Barry, Cin	.296	151	588	91	174	32	5	12	56	41	24	40
Law, Vance, Chi	.293	151	556	73	163	29	2	11	78	55	79	1
#McGee, Willie, StL	.292	137	562	73	164	24	6	3	50	32	84	41
*Daniels, Kal, Cin	.291	140	495	95	144	29	1	18	64	87	94	27

* indicates lefthanded batter   # indicates switch hitter

INDIVIDUAL PITCHING LEADERS
(Minimum 162 Innings)

	W	L	ERA	G	GS	CG	SV	IP	H	R	ER	BB	SO
*Magrane, Joe, StL	5	9	2.18	24	24	4	0	165	133	57	40	51	100
Cone, Dave, NY	20	3	2.22	35	28	8	0	231	178	67	57	80	213
Hershiser, Orel, LA	23	8	2.26	35	34	15	1	267	208	73	67	73	178
*Tudor, John, StL-LA	10	8	2.32	30	30	5	0	198	189	60	51	41	87
Rijo, Jose, Cin	13	8	2.39	49	19	0	0	162	120	47	43	63	160
Perez, Pascual, Mon	12	8	2.44	27	27	4	0	188	133	59	51	44	131
Robinson, Don, SF	10	5	2.45	51	19	3	6	177	152	63	48	49	122
Walk, Bob, Pgh	12	10	2.71	32	32	1	0	213	183	75	64	65	81
Martinez, Dennis, Mon	15	13	2.72	34	34	9	0	235	215	94	71	55	120
*Jackson, Danny, Cin	23	8	2.73	35	35	15	0	261	206	86	79	71	161

* indicates lefthanded pitcher

ATLANTA

BATTING	AVG	G	AB	R	H	2B	3B	HR	RBI	BB	SO	SB
Benedict, Bruce, c	.242	90	236	11	57	7	0	0	19	19	26	0
Blauser, Jeff, 2b-ss	.239	18	67	7	16	3	1	2	7	2	11	0
*Blocker, Terry, of	.212	66	198	13	42	4	2	2	10	10	20	1
Davis, Jody, c (88 Chi)	.230	90	257	21	59	9	0	7	36	29	52	0
Gant, Ronnie, 2b-3b	.259	146	563	85	146	28	8	19	60	46	118	19
Garcia, Damaso, 2b	.117	21	60	3	7	1	0	1	4	3	10	1
Gregg, Tommy, of (14 Pitt)	.295	25	44	5	13	4	0	1	7	3	6	0
#Hall, Albert, of	.247	85	231	27	57	7	1	1	15	21	35	15
*James, Dion, of	.256	132	386	46	99	17	5	3	30	58	59	9
*Lemke, Mark, 2b	.224	16	58	8	13	4	0	0	2	4	5	0
Morrison, Jim, 3b-of	.152	51	92	6	14	2	0	2	13	10	13	0
Murphy, Dale, of	.226	156	592	77	134	35	4	24	77	72	125	3
*Perry, Gerald, 1b	.300	141	547	61	164	27	1	8	74	36	49	29
Roenicke, Gary, of	.228	49	114	11	26	5	0	1	7	8	15	0
Royster, Jerry, of-3b	.176	68	102	8	18	3	0	0	1	6	16	0
Runge, Paul, inf	.211	52	76	11	16	5	0	0	7	14	21	0
#Simmons, Ted, ph	.196	78	107	6	21	6	0	2	11	15	9	0
Smith, Lonnie, of	.237	43	114	14	27	3	0	3	9	10	25	4
Thomas, Andres, ss	.252	153	606	54	153	22	2	13	68	14	95	7
Virgil, Ozzie, c	.256	107	320	23	82	10	0	9	31	22	54	2

PITCHING	W	L	ERA	G	GS	CG	SV	IP	H	R	ER	BB	SO
Acker, Jim	0	4	4.71	21	1	0	0	42	45	26	22	14	25
Alvarez, Jose	5	6	2.99	60	0	0	3	102	88	34	34	53	81
*Assenmacher, Paul	8	7	3.06	64	0	0	5	79	72	28	27	32	71
Boever, Joe	0	2	1.77	16	0	0	1	20	12	4	4	1	7
*Cary, Chuck	0	0	6.48	7	0	0	0	8	8	6	6	4	7
Coffman, Kevin	2	6	5.78	18	11	0	0	67	62	52	43	54	24
Eave, Gary	0	0	9.00	5	0	0	0	5	7	5	5	3	0
Eichelberger, Juan	2	0	3.86	20	0	0	0	37	44	19	16	10	13
*Glavine, Tom	7	17	4.56	34	34	1	0	195	201	111	99	63	84
*Jimenez, German	1	6	5.01	15	9	0	0	56	65	39	31	12	26
Mahler, Rick	9	16	3.69	39	34	4	0	249	279	125	102	42	131
Morrison, Jim	0	0	0.00	3	0	0	0	4	3	0	0	2	1
*Olwine, Ed	0	0	6.75	16	0	0	1	19	22	15	14	4	5
Puleo, Charlie	5	5	3.47	53	3	0	1	106	101	46	41	47	70
Smith, Pete	7	15	3.69	32	32	5	0	195	183	89	80	88	124
*Smith, Zane	5	10	4.30	23	22	3	0	140	159	72	67	44	59
Smoltz, John	2	7	5.48	12	12	0	0	64	74	40	39	33	37
Sutter, Bruce	1	4	4.76	38	0	0	14	45	49	26	24	11	40

CHICAGO

BATTING	AVG	G	AB	R	H	2B	3B	HR	RBI	BB	SO	SB
#Berryhill, Damon, c	.259	95	309	19	80	19	1	7	38	17	56	1
#Dascenzo, Doug, of	.213	26	75	9	16	3	0	0	4	9	4	6
Dawson, Andre, of	.303	157	591	78	179	31	8	24	79	37	73	12
Dunston, Shawon, ss	.249	155	575	69	143	23	6	9	56	16	108	30
*Grace, Mark, 1b	.296	134	486	65	144	23	4	7	57	60	43	3
Jackson, Darrin, of	.266	100	188	29	50	10	3	6	20	5	28	4
Law, Vance, 3b	.293	151	556	73	163	29	2	11	78	55	79	1
Meier, Dave, 3b	.400	2	5	0	2	0	0	0	1	0	1	0
#Mumphrey, Jerry, of	.136	63	66	3	9	2	0	0	9	7	16	0
#Palmeiro, Rafael, of	.307	152	580	75	178	41	5	8	53	38	34	12
Roomes, Rolando, of	.188	17	16	3	3	0	0	0	0	0	8	0
Salazar, Angel, ss	.250	34	60	4	15	1	1	0	1	1	11	0
Sandberg, Ryne, 2b	.264	155	618	77	163	23	8	19	69	54	91	25
Sundberg, Jim, c	.241	24	54	8	13	1	0	2	9	8	15	0
Trillo, Manny, inf	.250	76	164	15	41	5	0	1	14	8	32	1
*Varsho, Gary, of	.274	44	73	6	20	3	0	0	5	1	9	5
#Webster, Mitch, of (81 Mtl)	.260	151	523	69	136	16	8	6	39	55	87	22
Wrona, Rick, c	.000	4	6	0	0	0	0	0	0	0	1	0

San Diego's Tony Gwynn had what he considered a subpar year, but still won the batting title.

PITCHING	W	L	ERA	G	GS	CG	SV	IP	H	R	ER	BB	SO
Bielecki, Mike	2	2	3.35	19	5	0	0	48	55	22	18	16	33
Blankenship, Kevin (2 Atl)	1	1	4.60	3	3	0	0	16	14	8	8	8	9
Capel, Mike	2	1	4.91	22	0	0	0	29	34	19	16	13	19
*DiPino, Frank	2	3	4.98	63	0	0	6	90	102	54	50	32	69
Gossage, Rich	4	4	4.33	46	0	0	13	44	50	23	21	15	30
*Hall, Drew	1	1	7.66	19	0	0	1	22	26	20	19	9	22
Harkey, Mike	0	3	2.60	5	5	0	0	35	33	14	10	15	18
Lancaster, Les	4	6	3.78	44	3	1	5	86	89	42	36	34	36
Landrum, Bill	1	0	5.84	7	0	0	0	12	19	8	8	3	6
Maddux, Greg	18	8	3.18	34	34	9	0	249	230	97	88	81	140
*Moyer, Jamie	9	15	3.48	34	30	3	0	202	212	84	78	55	121
Nipper, Al	2	4	3.04	22	12	0	1	80	72	37	27	34	27
*Perry, Pat (12 Cinc)	4	4	4.14	47	0	0	1	59	61	32	27	16	35
Pico, Jeff	6	7	4.15	29	13	3	1	113	108	57	52	37	57
Sanderson, Scott	1	2	5.28	11	0	0	0	15	13	9	9	3	6
Schiraldi, Calvin	9	13	4.38	29	27	2	1	166	166	87	81	63	140
Sutcliffe, Rick	13	14	3.86	32	32	12	0	226	232	97	97	70	144
Tewksbury, Bob	0	0	8.10	1	1	0	0	3	6	5	3	2	1

CINCINNATI

BATTING	AVG	G	AB	R	H	2B	3B	HR	RBI	BB	SO	SB
Brown, Marty, 3b	.188	10	16	0	3	1	0	0	2	1	2	0
#Collins, Dave, of	.236	99	174	12	41	6	2	0	14	11	27	7
Concepcion, Dave, 2b-1b	.198	84	197	11	39	9	0	0	8	18	23	3
*Daniels, Kal, of	.291	140	495	95	144	29	1	18	64	87	94	27
Davis, Eric, of	.273	135	472	81	129	18	3	26	93	65	124	35
Diaz, Bo, c	.219	92	315	26	69	9	0	10	35	7	41	0
*Durham, Leon, 1b (24 Chi)	.218	45	124	14	27	9	1	4	8	14	32	0
Esasky, Nick, 1b	.243	122	391	40	95	17	2	15	62	48	104	7
*Garcia, Leo, of	.143	23	28	2	4	1	0	0	0	4	5	0
*Griffey, Ken, of-1b (69 Atl)	.255	94	243	26	62	6	0	4	23	19	31	1
*Harris, Lenny, 3b	.372	16	43	7	16	1	0	0	8	5	4	4
Larkin, Barry, ss	.296	151	588	91	174	32	5	12	56	41	24	40
McClendon, Lloyd, c-1b	.219	72	137	9	30	4	0	3	14	15	22	4
McGriff, Terry, c	.198	35	96	9	19	3	0	1	4	12	31	1
*Milner, Eddie, of	.176	23	51	3	9	1	0	0	2	4	9	2
*O'Neill, Paul, of-1b	.252	145	485	58	122	25	3	16	73	38	65	8
#Oester, Ron, 2b	.280	54	150	20	42	7	0	0	10	9	24	0
*Quinones, Luis, inf	.231	23	52	4	12	3	0	1	11	2	11	1
*Reed, Jeff, c (43 Mtl)	.226	92	265	20	60	9	2	1	16	28	41	1
#Roenicke, Ron, of	.135	14	37	4	5	1	0	0	5	4	8	0
Sabo, Chris, 3b	.271	137	538	74	146	40	2	11	44	29	52	46
*Snider, Van, of	.214	11	28	4	6	1	0	1	6	0	13	0
*Treadway, Jeff, 2b	.252	103	301	30	76	19	4	2	23	27	30	2
*Winningham, Herm, of (47 Mtl)	.232	100	203	16	47	3	4	0	21	17	45	12

PITCHING	W	L	ERA	G	GS	CG	SV	IP	H	R	ER	BB	SO
Armstrong, Jack	4	7	5.79	14	13	0	0	65	63	44	42	38	45
*Birtsas, Tim	1	3	4.20	36	4	0	0	64	61	34	30	24	38
Brown, Keith	2	1	2.76	4	3	0	0	16	14	5	5	4	6
*Browning, Tom	18	5	3.41	36	36	5	0	251	205	98	95	64	124
*Charlton, Norm	4	5	3.96	10	10	0	0	61	60	27	27	20	39
Concepcion, Dave	0	0	0.00	1	0	0	0	1	2	0	0	0	1
Dibble, Rob	1	1	1.82	37	0	0	0	59	43	12	12	21	59
*Franco, John	6	6	1.57	70	0	0	39	86	60	18	15	27	46

	W	L	ERA	G	GS	CG	SV	IP	H	R	ER	BB	SO
Gray, Jeff	0	0	3.86	5	0	0	0	9	12	4	4	4	5
*Jackson, Danny	23	8	2.73	35	35	15	0	261	206	86	79	71	161
*Murphy, Rob	0	6	3.08	76	0	0	3	85	69	31	29	38	74
Pacillo, Pat	1	0	5.06	6	0	0	0	11	14	7	6	4	11
Rijo, Jose	13	8	2.39	49	19	0	0	162	120	47	43	63	160
Robinson, Ron	3	7	4.12	17	16	0	0	79	88	47	36	26	38
Sierra, Candy (15 SD)	0	1	5.53	16	0	0	0	28	41	17	17	12	24
Soto, Mario	3	7	4.66	14	14	3	0	87	88	49	45	28	34
St. Claire, Randy (6 Mtl)	1	0	3.98	16	0	0	0	20	24	13	9	10	14
Williams, Frank	3	2	2.59	60	0	0	1	63	59	24	18	35	43

HOUSTON

BATTING	AVG	G	AB	R	H	2B	3B	HR	RBI	BB	SO	SB
#Ashby, Alan, c	.238	73	227	19	54	10	0	7	33	29	36	0
#Bailey, Mark, c	.130	8	23	1	3	0	0	0	3	5	6	0
#Bass, Kevin, of	.255	157	541	57	138	27	2	14	72	42	65	31
Bell, Buddy, 3b (21 Cinc)	.241	95	323	27	78	10	1	7	40	26	32	1
Biggio, Craig, c	.211	50	123	14	26	6	1	3	5	7	29	6
#Caminiti, Ken, 3b	.181	30	83	5	15	2	0	1	7	5	18	0
#Candaele, Casey, 2b (36 Mtl)	.170	57	147	11	25	8	1	0	5	11	17	1
Davis, Glenn, 1b	.271	152	561	77	152	26	0	30	99	53	77	4
#Doran, Bill, 2b	.248	132	480	66	119	18	1	7	53	65	60	17
#Drew, Cameron, of	.188	7	16	1	3	0	1	0	1	0	1	0
Fishel, John, of	.231	19	26	1	6	0	0	1	2	3	6	0
Hatcher, Billy, of	.268	145	530	79	142	25	4	7	52	37	56	32
Henderson, Steve, of	.217	42	46	4	10	2	0	0	5	7	14	1
Jackson, Chuck, 3b	.229	45	83	7	19	5	1	1	8	7	16	1
*Meadows, Louie, of	.190	35	42	5	8	0	1	2	3	6	8	4
Pankovits, Jim, 2b-3b	.221	68	140	13	31	7	1	2	12	8	28	2
*Puhl, Terry, of	.303	113	234	42	71	7	2	3	19	35	30	22
Ramirez, Rafael, ss	.276	155	566	51	156	30	5	6	59	18	61	3
Reynolds, Craig, inf	.255	78	161	20	41	7	0	1	14	8	23	3
#Smajstrla, Craig, 2b	.000	8	3	2	0	0	0	0	0	0	1	0
*Spilman, Harry, 1b (40 SF)	.159	46	44	4	7	1	1	1	3	5	9	0
Trevino, Alex, c	.249	78	193	19	48	17	0	2	13	24	29	5
#Young, Gerald, of	.257	149	576	79	148	20	9	0	37	66	66	65

PITCHING	W	L	ERA	G	GS	CG	SV	IP	H	R	ER	BB	SO
*Agosto, Juan	10	2	2.26	75	0	0	4	92	74	27	23	30	33
Andersen, Larry	2	4	2.94	53	0	0	5	83	82	29	27	20	66
Andujar, Joaquin	2	5	4.00	23	10	0	0	79	94	43	35	21	35
Camacho, Ernie	0	3	7.64	13	0	0	1	18	25	15	15	12	13
Childress, Rocky	1	0	6.17	11	0	0	0	23	26	17	16	9	24
Darwin, Danny	8	13	3.84	44	20	3	3	192	189	86	82	48	129
*Deshaies, Jim	11	14	3.00	31	31	3	0	207	164	77	69	72	127
Forsch, Bob (30 StL)	10	8	4.32	36	18	1	0	135	153	73	65	44	54
Heathcock, Jeff	0	5	5.81	17	1	0	0	31	33	25	20	16	12
*Knepper, Bob	14	5	3.14	27	27	3	0	175	156	70	61	67	103
*Meads, Dave	3	1	3.18	22	2	0	0	40	37	20	14	14	27
Meyer, Brian	0	0	1.46	8	0	0	0	12	9	2	2	4	10
Ryan, Nolan	12	11	3.52	33	33	4	0	220	186	98	86	87	228
Scott, Mike	14	8	2.92	32	32	8	0	219	162	74	71	53	190
Smith, Dave	4	5	2.67	51	0	0	27	57	60	26	17	19	38

LOS ANGELES

BATTING	AVG	G	AB	R	H	2B	3B	HR	RBI	BB	SO	SB
Anderson, Dave, ss	.249	116	285	31	71	10	2	2	20	32	45	4
*Davis, Mike, of	.196	108	281	29	55	11	2	2	17	25	59	7
Dempsey, Rick, c	.252	77	167	25	42	13	0	7	30	25	44	1
Devereaux, Mike, of	.116	30	43	4	5	1	0	0	2	2	10	0
*Gibson, Kirk, of	.290	150	542	106	157	28	1	25	76	73	120	31
Gonzalez, Jose, of	.083	37	24	7	2	1	0	0	0	2	10	3
#Griffin, Alfredo, ss	.199	95	316	39	63	8	3	1	27	24	30	7
*Gwynn, Chris, of	.182	12	11	1	2	0	0	0	0	1	2	0
Hamilton, Jeff, 3b	.236	111	309	34	73	14	2	6	33	10	51	0
Hatcher, Mickey, of-1b	.293	87	191	22	56	8	0	1	25	7	7	0
*Heep, Danny, of-1b	.242	95	149	14	36	2	0	0	11	22	13	2
Marshall, Mike, of-1b	.277	144	542	63	150	27	2	20	82	24	93	4
Reyes, Gilberto, c	.111	5	9	1	1	0	0	0	0	0	3	0
Sax, Steve, 2b	.277	160	632	70	175	19	4	5	57	45	51	42
*Scioscia, Mike, c	.257	130	408	29	105	18	0	3	35	38	31	0
Sharperson, Mike, inf	.271	46	59	8	16	1	0	0	4	1	12	0
*Shelby, John, of	.263	140	494	65	130	23	6	10	64	44	128	16
*Stubbs, Franklin, 1b	.223	115	242	30	54	13	0	8	34	23	61	11
Woodson, Tracy, 3b-1b	.249	64	173	15	43	4	1	3	15	7	32	1

PITCHING	W	L	ERA	G	GS	CG	SV	IP	H	R	ER	BB	SO
Belcher, Tim	12	6	2.91	36	27	4	4	180	143	65	58	51	152
Brennan, William	0	1	6.75	4	2	0	0	9	13	7	7	6	7
Crews, Tim	4	0	3.14	42	0	0	0	72	77	29	25	16	45
*Havens, Brad	0	0	4.66	9	0	0	0	10	15	5	5	4	8
*Heep, Danny	0	0	9.00	1	0	0	0	2	2	2	2	0	0
Hershiser, Orel	23	8	2.26	35	34	15	1	267	208	73	67	73	178
Hillegas, Shawn	3	4	4.13	11	10	0	0	57	54	26	26	17	30
Holton, Brian	7	3	1.70	45	0	0	1	85	69	19	16	26	49
*Horton, Ricky	1	1	5.00	12	0	0	0	9	11	7	5	2	8

Departmental Leaders

BATTING

RUNS
Brett Butler, San Francisco 109
Kirk Gibson, Los Angeles 106
Will Clark, San Francisco 102
Darryl Strawberry, New York ... 101
Andy Van Slyke, Pittsburgh 101

HITS
Andres Galarraga, Montreal.... 184
Andre Dawson, Chicago 179
Rafael Palmeiro, Chicago 178
Steve Sax, Los Angeles 175
Barry Larkin, Cincinnati 174

TOTAL BASES
Andres Galarraga, Montreal.... 329
Andre Dawson, Chicago 298
Andy Van Slyke, Pittsburgh 297
Darryl Strawberry, New York ... 296
Will Clark, San Francisco 292

DOUBLES
Andres Galarraga, Montreal 42
Rafael Palmeiro, Chicago 41
Chris Sabo, Cincinnati 40
Sid Bream, Pittsburgh 37
Hubie Brooks, Montreal 35
Dale Murphy, Atlanta............ 35

TRIPLES
Andy Van Slyke, Pittsburgh 15
Vince Coleman, St. Louis 10
Gerald Young, Houston 9
Juan Samuel, Philadelphia 9
Brett Butler, San Francisco 9

HOME RUNS
Darryl Strawberry, New York ... 39
Glenn Davis, Houston........... 30
Will Clark, San Francisco 29
Andres Galarraga, Montreal 29
Kevin McReynolds, New York ... 27

RUNS BATTED IN
Will Clark, San Francisco 109
Darryl Strawberry, New York 101
Andy Van Slyke, Pittsburgh 100
Bobby Bonilla, Pittsburgh 100
Kevin McReynolds, New York ... 99
Glenn Davis, Houston........... 99

GAME-WINNING RBIs
Eric Davis, Cincinnati 21
Kevin McReynolds, New York ... 19
Andres Galarraga, Montreal 16
Andy Van Slyke, Pittsburgh 16
Darryl Strawberry, New York 15

SACRIFICE BUNTS
Orel Hershiser, Los Angeles ... 19
Rick Reuschel, San Francisco ... 19
Roberto Alomar, San Diego 16
Bob Knepper, Houston 14
Rob Thompson, San Francisco .. 14

SACRIFICE FLIES
Andy Van Slyke, Pittsburgh 13
Will Clark, San Francisco 10

Gerald Perry, Atlanta............ 10
Darryl Strawberry, New York 9
Keith Moreland, San Diego 9
Glenn Davis, Houston............ 9

WALKS
Will Clark, San Francisco 100
Brett Butler, San Francisco 97
Kal Daniels, Cincinnati 87
Howard Johnson, New York...... 86
Darryl Strawberry, New York 85
Bobby Bonilla, Pittsburgh........ 85

INTENTIONAL WALKS
Will Clark, San Francisco 27
Howard Johnson, New York..... 25
Darryl Strawberry, New York ... 21
Glenn Davis, Houston........... 20
Bobby Bonilla, Pittsburgh....... 19

HIT BY PITCH
Phil Bradley, Philadelphia 16
Juan Samuel, Philadelphia 12
Glenn Davis, Houston........... 11
Andres Galarraga, Montreal 10
Three tied at 8

STRIKEOUTS
Andres Galarraga, Montreal.... 153
Juan Samuel, Philadelphia 151
Will Clark, San Francisco 129
John Shelby, Los Angeles 128
Darryl Strawberry, New York ... 127

STOLEN BASES
Vince Coleman, St. Louis 81
Gerald Young, Houston 65
Ozzie Smith, St. Louis........... 57
Chris Sabo, Cincinnati 46
Otis Nixon, Montreal 46

CAUGHT STEALING
Vince Coleman, St. Louis 27
Gerald Young, Houston 27
Brett Butler, San Francisco...... 20
Four tied at 14

GIDP
Dale Murphy, Atlanta............ 24
Hubie Brooks, Montreal 21
Tim Wallach, Montreal 19
Gerald Perry, Atlanta............ 18
Benito Santiago, San Diego 18

SLUGGING PERCENTAGE
Darryl Strawberry, New York .. .545
Andres Galarraga, Montreal ... .540
Will Clark, San Francisco ...... .508
Andy Van Slyke, Pittsburgh.... .506
Andre Dawson, Chicago ...... .504

ON-BASE PERCENTAGE
Kal Daniels, Cincinnati .... .397
Brett Butler, San Francisco...... .393
Will Clark, San Francisco ...... .386
Kirk Gibson, Los Angeles ..... .377
Tony Gwynn, San Diego ...... .373

	W	L	ERA	G	GS	CG	SV	IP	H	R	ER	BB	SO
Howell, Jay	5	3	2.08	50	0	0	21	65	44	16	15	21	70
Howell, Ken	0	1	6.39	4	1	0	0	13	16	10	9	4	12
*Krueger, Bill	0	0	11.57	1	1	0	0	2	4	3	3	2	1
Leary, Tim	17	11	2.91	35	34	9	0	229	201	87	74	56	180
Martinez, Ramon	1	3	3.79	9	6	0	0	36	27	17	15	22	23
*Orosco, Jesse	3	2	2.72	55	0	0	9	53	41	18	16	30	43
Pena, Alejandro	6	7	1.91	60	0	0	12	94	75	29	20	27	83
Sutton, Don	3	6	3.92	16	16	0	0	87	91	44	38	30	44
*Tudor, John (21 StL)	10	8	2.32	30	30	5	0	198	189	60	51	41	87
*Valenzuela, Fernando ...	5	8	4.24	23	22	3	1	142	142	71	67	76	64

MONTREAL

BATTING	AVG	G	AB	R	H	2B	3B	HR	RBI	BB	SO	SB
Brooks, Hubie, of	.279	151	588	61	164	35	2	20	90	35	108	7
Engle, Dave, c-of	.216	34	37	4	8	3	0	0	1	5	5	0
Fitzgerald, Mike, c	.271	63	155	17	42	6	1	5	23	19	22	2
*Foley, Tom, 2b-ss	.265	127	377	33	100	21	3	5	43	30	49	2
Galarraga, Andres, 1b	.302	157	609	99	184	42	8	29	92	39	153	13
Hudler, Rex, 2b-ss	.273	77	216	38	59	14	2	4	14	10	34	29
*Huson, Jeff, ss	.310	20	42	7	13	2	0	0	3	4	3	2
#Johnson, Wallace, 1b	.309	86	94	7	29	5	1	0	3	12	15	0

	AVG	G	AB	R	H	2B	3B	HR	RBI	BB	SO	SB
Jones, Tracy, of (37 Cinc)	.295	90	224	30	66	6	1	3	24	20	18	18
*Martinez, Dave, of (75 Chi) .	.255	138	447	51	114	13	6	6	46	38	94	23
*Nettles, Graig, 3b-1b	.172	80	93	5	16	4	0	1	14	9	19	0
#Nixon, Otis, of	.244	90	271	47	66	8	2	0	15	28	42	46
*O'Malley, Tom, 3b	.259	14	27	3	7	0	0	0	2	3	4	0
Paredes, Johnny, 2b	.187	35	91	6	17	2	0	1	10	9	17	5
*Raines, Tim, of	.270	109	429	66	116	19	7	12	48	53	44	33
Rivera, Luis, ss	.224	123	371	35	83	17	3	4	30	24	69	3
Santovenia, Nelson, c	.236	92	309	26	73	20	2	8	41	24	77	2
Tejada, Wil, c	.267	8	15	1	4	2	0	0	2	0	4	0
Wallach, Tim, 3b	.257	159	592	52	152	32	5	12	69	38	88	2

PITCHING	W	L	ERA	G	GS	CG	SV	IP	H	R	ER	BB	SO
Barrett, Tim	0	0	5.79	4	0	0	1	9	10	6	6	2	5
Burke, Tim	3	5	3.40	61	0	0	18	82	84	36	31	25	42
Dopson, John	3	11	3.04	26	26	1	0	169	150	69	57	58	101
*Heaton, Neal	3	10	4.99	32	11	0	2	97	98	54	54	43	43
*Hesketh, Joe	4	3	2.85	60	0	0	9	73	63	30	23	35	64
Holman, Brian	4	8	3.23	18	16	1	0	100	101	39	36	34	58
*Johnson, Randy	3	0	2.42	4	4	1	0	26	23	8	7	7	25
Martinez, Dennis	15	13	2.72	34	34	9	0	235	215	94	71	55	120
McGaffigan, Andy	6	0	2.76	63	0	0	4	91	81	31	28	37	71
Parrett, Jeff	12	4	2.65	61	0	0	6	92	66	29	27	45	62
Perez, Pascual	12	8	2.44	27	27	4	0	188	133	59	51	44	131
*Sauveur, Rich	0	0	6.00	4	0	0	0	3	3	2	2	2	3
Smith, Bryn	12	10	3.00	32	32	1	0	198	179	79	66	32	102
Smith, Mike	0	0	3.12	5	0	0	1	9	6	3	3	5	4
Youmans, Floyd	3	6	3.21	14	13	1	0	84	64	35	30	41	54

NEW YORK

BATTING	AVG	G	AB	R	H	2B	3B	HR	RBI	BB	SO	SB
#Backman, Wally, 2b	.303	99	294	44	89	12	0	0	17	41	49	9
Carreon, Mark, of	.556	7	9	5	5	2	0	1	1	2	1	0
Carter, Gary, c	.241	130	456	39	110	16	2	11	46	34	49	0
*Dykstra, Len, of	.270	126	429	57	116	19	3	8	33	30	43	30
Elster, Kevin, ss	.214	149	406	41	87	12	1	9	37	35	47	2
*Hernandez, Keith, 1b	.276	95	348	43	96	16	0	11	55	31	57	2
#Jefferies, Gregg, 3b-2b	.321	29	109	19	35	8	2	6	17	8	10	5
*Johnson, Howard, 3b-ss	.230	148	495	85	114	21	1	24	68	86	104	23
Lyons, Barry, c	.231	50	91	5	21	7	1	0	11	3	12	0
*Magadan, Dave, 1b-3b	.277	112	314	39	87	15	0	1	35	60	39	0
*Mazzilli, Lee, of-1b	.147	68	116	9	17	2	0	0	12	12	16	4
McReynolds, Kevin, of	.288	147	552	82	159	30	2	27	99	38	56	21
Miller, Keith, inf	.214	40	70	9	15	1	1	1	5	6	10	0
*Sasser, Mackey, c	.285	60	123	9	35	10	1	1	17	6	9	0
*Strawberry, Darryl, of	.269	153	543	101	146	27	3	39	101	85	127	29
Teufel, Tim, 2b	.234	90	273	35	64	20	0	4	31	29	41	0
#Wilson, Mookie, of	.296	112	378	61	112	17	5	8	41	27	63	15

PITCHING	W	L	ERA	G	GS	CG	SV	IP	H	R	ER	BB	SO
Aguilera, Rick	0	4	6.93	11	3	0	0	25	29	20	19	10	16
Cone, Dave	20	3	2.22	35	28	8	0	231	178	67	57	80	213
Darling, Ron	17	9	3.25	34	34	7	0	241	218	97	87	60	161
*Fernandez, Sid	12	10	3.03	31	31	1	0	187	127	69	63	70	189
Gooden, Dwight	18	9	3.19	34	34	10	0	248	242	98	88	57	175
Innis, Jeff	1	1	1.89	12	0	0	0	19	19	6	4	2	14
Leach, Terry	7	2	2.54	52	0	0	3	92	95	32	26	24	51
*McClure, Bob (19 Mtl) ..	2	3	5.40	33	0	0	3	30	35	18	18	8	19
McDowell, Roger	5	5	2.63	62	0	0	16	89	80	31	26	31	46
Mitchell, John	0	0	0.00	1	0	0	0	1	2	0	0	1	1
*Myers, Randy	7	3	1.72	55	0	0	26	68	45	15	13	17	69
Nunez, Edwin	1	0	4.50	10	0	0	0	14	21	7	7	3	8
*Ojeda, Bobby	10	13	2.88	29	29	5	0	190	158	74	61	33	133
*Walter, Gene	0	1	3.78	19	0	0	0	17	21	9	7	11	14
*West, Dave	1	0	3.00	2	1	0	0	6	6	2	2	3	3

PHILADELPHIA

BATTING	AVG	G	AB	R	H	2B	3B	HR	RBI	BB	SO	SB
Aguayo, Luis, ss-3b	.247	49	97	9	24	3	0	3	5	13	17	2
Almon, Bill, 3b-ss	.115	20	26	1	3	2	0	0	1	3	11	0
#Barrett, Tom, 2b	.204	36	54	5	11	1	0	0	3	7	8	0
Bradley, Phil, of	.264	154	569	77	150	30	5	11	56	54	106	11
*Daulton, Darren, c	.208	58	144	13	30	6	0	1	12	17	26	2
*Dernier, Bob, of	.289	68	166	19	48	3	1	1	10	9	19	13
*Gross, Greg, of-1b	.203	98	133	10	27	1	0	0	5	16	3	0
Gutierrez, Jackie, ss-3b ..	.247	33	77	8	19	4	0	0	9	2	9	0
*Hayes, Von, 1b-of	.272	104	367	43	100	28	2	6	45	49	59	20
James, Chris, of-3b	.242	150	566	57	137	24	1	19	66	31	73	7
#Jeltz, Steve, ss	.187	148	379	39	71	11	4	0	27	58	59	3
*Jones, Ron, of	.290	33	124	15	36	6	1	8	26	2	14	0
Jordan, Ricky, 1b	.308	69	273	41	84	15	1	11	43	7	39	1
#Miller, Keith, inf-of	.167	47	48	4	8	3	0	0	6	5	13	0
#Pardo, Al, c	.000	2	2	0	0	0	0	0	0	0	2	0
Parrish, Lance, c	.215	123	424	44	91	17	2	15	60	47	93	0
Russell, John, c	.245	22	49	5	12	1	0	2	4	3	15	0
Samuel, Juan, 2b	.243	157	629	68	153	32	9	12	67	39	151	33
Schmidt, Mike, 3b	.249	108	390	52	97	21	2	12	62	49	42	3

Departmental Leaders

PITCHING

GAMES
Rob Murphy, Cincinnati 76
Jeff Robinson, Pittsburgh 75
Juan Agosto, Houston. 75
Kent Tekulve, Philadelphia 70
John Franco, Cincinnati 70

GAMES STARTED
Tom Browning, Cincinnati 36
Rick Reuschel, San Francisco . . 36
Danny Jackson, Cincinnati 35
Nine tied at 34

COMPLETE GAMES
Orel Hershiser, Los Angeles . . . 15
Danny Jackson, Cincinnati 15
Eric Show, San Diego 13
Rick Sutcliffe, Chicago 12
Dwight Gooden, New York 10

SHUTOUTS
Orel Hershiser, Los Angeles 8
Tim Leary, Los Angeles 6
Danny Jackson, Cincinnati 6
Mike Scott, Houston 5
Bob Ojeda, New York 5

SAVES
John Franco, Cincinnati 39
Jim Gott, Pittsburgh 34
Todd Worrell, St. Louis 32
Mark Davis, San Diego. 28
Steve Bedrosian, Philadelphia . . . 28

WINS
Orel Hershiser, Los Angeles . . . 23
Danny Jackson, Cincinnati 23
David Cone, New York 20
Rick Reuschel, San Francisco . . 19
Three tied at 18

LOSSES
Tom Glavine, Atlanta 17
Rick Mahler, Atlanta. 16
Shane Rawley, Philadelphia 16
Jamie Moyer, Chicago 15
Pete Smith, Atlanta. 15

INNINGS PITCHED
Orel Hershiser, Los Angeles . . . 267
Danny Jackson, Cincinnati 261
Tom Browning, Cincinnati 251
Greg Maddux, Chicago 249
Rick Mahler, Atlanta 249

HITS ALLOWED
Rick Mahler, Atlanta 279

Dwight Gooden, New York 242
Rick Reuschel, San Francisco . 242
Rick Sutcliffe, Chicago 232
Greg Maddux, Chicago 230

RUNS ALLOWED
Rick Mahler, Atlanta 125
Tom Glavine, Atlanta 111
Shane Rawley, Philadelphia 111
Don Carman, Philadelphia 101
Kevin Gross, Philadelphia. 101

HOME RUNS ALLOWED
Tom Browning, Cincinnati 36
Dennis Rasmussen, San Diego . 27
Ron Darling, New York 24
Eric Show, San Diego 22
Dennis Martinez, Montreal 21
Doug Drabek, Pittsburgh 21

WALKS
Kevin Gross, Philadelphia. 89
Mike Dunne, Pittsburgh 88
Pete Smith, Atlanta. 88
Nolan Ryan, Houston 87
Jose DeLeon, St. Louis 86

HIT BATSMEN
Kevin Gross, Philadelphia. 11
Bryn Smith, Montreal. 10
Greg Maddux, Chicago 9
Tom Glavine, Atlanta 8
Rick Mahler, Atlanta. 8
Mike Scott, Houston 8

STRIKEOUTS
Nolan Ryan, Houston 228
David Cone, New York 213
Jose DeLeon, St. Louis 208
Mike Scott, Houston 190
Sid Fernandez, New York. 189

WILD PITCHES
Bob Walk, Pittsburgh. 13
Mike Dunne, Pittsburgh 12
Bruce Ruffin, Philadelphia 12
Kevin Coffman, Atlanta-Chicago. 11
Jeff Robinson, Pittsburgh. 11
Rick Sutcliffe, Chicago 11

BALKS
Pascual Perez, Montreal 10
Dennis Martinez, Montreal 10
David Cone, New York 10
Sid Fernandez, New York 9
Bob Walk, Pittsburgh 9

	AVG	G	AB	R	H	2B	3B	HR	RBI	BB	SO	SB
*Thompson, Milt, of	.288	122	378	53	109	16	2	2	33	39	59	17
*Turner, Shane, 3b-ss . . .	171	18	35	1	6	0	0	1	5	9	0
#Young, Mike, of	.226	75	146	13	33	14	0	1	14	26	43	0

PITCHING	W	L	ERA	G	GS	CG	SV	IP	H	R	ER	BB	SO
Barojas, Salome	0	0	8.31	6	0	0	0	9	7	9	8	8	1
Bedrosian, Steve	6	6	3.75	57	0	0	28	74	75	34	31	27	61
*Calhoun, Jeff	0	0	15.43	3	0	0	0	2	6	4	4	1	1
*Carman, Don	10	14	4.29	36	32	2	0	201	211	101	96	70	116
Clay, Danny	0	1	6.00	17	0	0	0	24	27	17	16	21	12
Dawley, Bill	0	2	13.50	8	0	0	0	9	16	13	13	4	3
Freeman, Marvin	2	3	6.10	11	11	0	0	52	55	36	35	43	37
Frohwirth, Todd	1	2	8.25	12	0	0	0	12	16	11	11	11	11
Gross, Kevin	12	14	3.69	33	33	5	0	232	209	101	95	89	162
Harris, Greg	4	6	2.36	66	1	0	1	107	80	34	28	52	71
Maddux, Mike	4	3	3.76	25	11	0	0	89	91	41	37	34	59
Madrid, Alex	1	1	2.76	5	2	1	0	16	15	5	5	6	2
Moore, Brad	0	0	0.00	5	0	0	0	6	4	0	0	4	2
Palmer, Dave	7	9	4.47	22	22	1	0	129	129	67	64	48	85
*Rawley, Shane	8	16	4.18	32	32	4	0	198	220	111	92	78	87
*Ritchie, Wally	0	0	3.12	19	0	0	0	26	19	14	9	17	8
*Ruffin, Bruce	6	10	4.43	55	15	3	3	144	151	86	71	80	82
*Scherrer, Bill	0	0	5.40	8	0	0	0	7	7	4	4	2	3
Sebra, Bob	1	2	7.94	3	3	0	0	11	15	11	10	10	7
Service, Scott	0	0	1.69	5	0	0	0	5	5	1	1	1	6
Tekulve, Kent	3	7	3.60	70	0	0	4	80	87	34	32	22	43

PITTSBURGH

BATTING	AVG	G	AB	R	H	2B	3B	HR	RBI	BB	SO	SB
Belliard, Rafael, ss	.213	122	286	28	61	0	4	0	11	26	47	7
*Bonds, Barry, of	.283	144	538	97	152	30	5	24	58	72	82	17

BATTING	AVG	G	AB	R	H	2B	3B	HR	RBI	BB	SO	SB
#Bonilla, Bobby, 3b	.274	159	584	87	160	32	7	24	100	85	82	3
*Bream, Sid, 1b	.264	148	462	50	122	37	0	10	65	47	64	9
#Cangelosi, John, of	.254	75	118	18	30	4	1	0	8	17	16	9
Coles, Darnell, of	.232	68	211	20	49	13	1	5	36	20	41	1
#Destrade, Orestes, 1b	.149	36	47	2	7	1	0	1	3	5	17	0
Diaz, Mike, of-1b	.230	47	74	6	17	3	0	0	5	16	13	0
*Distefano, Benny, 1b-of	.345	16	29	6	10	3	1	1	6	3	4	0
Fermin, Felix, ss	.276	43	87	9	24	0	2	0	2	8	10	3
Gonzalez, Denny, inf	.188	24	32	5	6	1	0	0	1	6	10	0
Hostetler, Dave, 1b	.250	6	8	0	2	0	0	0	0	0	3	0
*Lavalliere, Mike, c	.261	120	352	24	92	18	0	2	47	50	34	3
Lind, Jose, 2b	.262	154	611	82	160	24	4	2	49	42	75	15
Milligan, Randy, 1b	.220	40	82	10	18	5	0	3	8	20	24	1
*Oberkfell, Ken, 3b-2b (120 Atl)	.271	140	476	49	129	22	4	3	42	37	34	4
Ortiz, Junior, c	.280	49	118	8	33	6	0	2	18	9	9	1
Pedrique, Al, ss	.180	50	128	7	23	5	0	0	4	8	17	0
Prince, Tom, c	.176	29	74	3	13	2	0	0	6	4	15	0
#Redus, Gary, of	.197	30	71	12	14	2	0	2	4	15	19	5
#Reynolds, R.J., of	.248	130	323	35	80	14	2	6	51	20	62	15
Rodriguez, Ruben, c	.200	2	5	1	1	0	1	0	1	0	2	0
*Van Slyke, Andy, of	.288	154	587	101	169	23	15	25	100	57	126	30
Wilson, Glenn, of	.270	37	126	11	34	8	0	2	15	3	18	0

PITCHING	W	L	ERA	G	GS	CG	SV	IP	H	R	ER	BB	SO
*Cangelosi, John	0	0	0.00	1	0	0	0	2	1	0	0	0	0
Drabek, Doug	15	7	3.08	33	32	3	0	219	194	83	75	50	127
Dunne, Mike	7	11	3.92	30	28	1	0	170	163	88	74	88	70
Fisher, Brian	8	10	4.61	33	22	1	1	146	157	78	75	57	66
*Garcia, Miguel	0	0	4.50	1	0	0	0	2	3	2	1	2	2
Gott, Jim	6	6	3.49	67	0	0	34	77	68	30	30	22	76
Jones, Barry	1	1	3.04	42	0	0	2	56	57	21	19	21	31
*Kipper, Bob	2	6	3.74	50	0	0	0	65	54	33	27	26	39
Kramer, Randy	1	2	5.40	5	1	0	0	10	12	6	6	1	7
*LaPoint, Dave	4	2	2.77	8	8	1	0	52	54	18	16	10	19
*Madden, Morris	0	0	0.00	5	0	0	0	6	5	0	0	7	3
Medvin, Scott	3	0	4.88	17	0	0	0	28	23	16	15	9	16
Palacios, Vicente	1	2	6.66	7	3	0	0	24	28	18	18	15	15
Reed, Rick	1	0	3.00	2	2	0	0	12	10	4	4	2	6
Robinson, Jeff	11	5	3.03	75	0	0	9	125	113	44	42	39	87
*Rucker, Dave	0	2	4.76	31	0	0	0	28	39	19	15	9	16
*Smiley, John	13	11	3.25	34	32	5	0	205	185	81	74	46	129
Walk, Bob	12	10	2.71	32	32	1	0	213	183	75	64	65	81

ST. LOUIS

BATTING	AVG	G	AB	R	H	2B	3B	HR	RBI	BB	SO	SB
#Alicea, Luis, 2b	.212	93	297	20	63	10	4	1	24	25	32	1
*Booker, Rod, 3b	.343	18	35	6	12	3	0	0	3	4	3	2
Brunansky, Tom, of	.245	143	523	69	128	22	4	22	79	79	82	16
#Coleman, Vince, of	.260	153	616	77	160	20	10	3	38	49	111	81
Fitzgerald, Mike, 1b	.196	13	46	4	9	1	0	0	1	0	9	0
*Ford, Curt, of	.195	92	128	11	25	6	0	1	18	8	26	6
Guerrero, Pedro, 1b-3b (59 LA)	.286	103	364	40	104	14	2	10	65	46	59	4
#Herr, Tom, 2b	.260	15	50	4	13	0	0	1	3	11	4	3
Horner, Bob, 1b	.257	60	206	15	53	9	1	3	33	32	23	0
*Jones, Tim, ss	.269	31	52	2	14	0	0	0	3	4	13	0
*Laga, Mike, 1b	.130	40	100	5	13	0	0	1	4	2	21	0
Lake, Steve, c	.278	36	54	5	15	3	0	1	4	3	15	0
Lawless, Tom, 3b-2b	.154	54	65	9	10	2	1	1	3	7	9	6
Lindeman, Jim, of	.209	17	43	3	9	1	0	2	7	2	9	0
#McGee, Willie, of	.292	137	562	73	164	24	6	3	50	32	84	41
*Morris, John, of	.289	20	38	3	11	2	1	0	3	1	7	0
#Oquendo, Jose, 2b-3b	.277	148	451	36	125	10	1	7	46	52	40	4
Pagnozzi, Tom, c-1b	.282	81	195	17	55	9	0	0	15	11	32	0
Pena, Tony, c	.263	149	505	55	133	23	1	10	51	33	60	6
*Pendleton, Terry, 3b	.253	110	391	44	99	20	2	6	53	21	51	3
#Smith, Ozzie, ss	.270	153	575	80	155	27	1	3	51	74	43	57
*Walker, Duane, of-1b	.182	24	22	1	4	1	0	0	3	2	7	0
*Walling, Denny, 3b-of (65 Hou)	.239	84	234	22	56	13	2	1	21	17	25	2

PITCHING	W	L	ERA	G	GS	CG	SV	IP	H	R	ER	BB	SO
*Alba, Gibson	0	0	2.70	3	0	0	0	3	1	2	1	2	3
Arnold, Scott	0	0	5.40	6	0	0	0	7	9	4	4	4	8
Carpenter, Cris	2	3	4.72	8	8	1	0	48	56	27	25	9	24
Costello, John	5	2	1.81	36	0	0	1	50	44	15	10	25	38
Cox, Danny	3	8	3.98	13	13	0	0	86	89	40	38	25	47
*Dayley, Ken	2	7	2.77	54	0	0	5	55	48	20	17	19	38
DeLeon, Jose	13	10	3.67	34	34	3	0	225	198	95	92	86	208
Hill, Ken	0	1	5.14	4	1	0	0	14	16	9	8	6	6
*Magrane, Joe	5	9	2.18	24	24	4	0	165	133	57	40	51	100
Mathews, Greg	4	6	4.24	13	13	1	0	68	61	34	32	33	31
*McWilliams, Larry	6	9	3.90	42	17	2	1	136	130	64	59	45	70
O'Neal, Randy	2	3	4.58	10	8	0	0	53	57	29	27	10	20
Oquendo, Jose	0	1	4.50	1	0	0	0	4	4	2	2	6	1
*Peters, Steve	3	3	6.40	44	0	0	0	45	57	34	32	22	30
Quisenberry, Dan	2	0	6.16	33	0	0	0	38	54	26	26	6	19
Terry, Scott	9	6	2.92	51	11	1	3	129	119	48	42	34	65

	W	L	ERA	G	GS	CG	SV	IP	H	R	ER	BB	SO
Worrell, Todd	5	9	3.00	68	0	0	32	90	69	32	30	34	78

SAN DIEGO

BATTING	AVG	G	AB	R	H	2B	3B	HR	RBI	BB	SO	SB
Abner, Shawn, of	.181	37	83	6	15	3	0	2	5	4	19	0
#Alomar, Roberto, 2b ...	.266	143	545	84	145	24	6	9	41	47	83	24
Alomar, Sandy, ph	.000	1	1	0	0	0	0	0	0	0	1	0
Brown, Chris, 3b	.235	80	247	14	58	6	0	2	19	19	49	0
*Byers, Randy, of	.200	11	10	0	2	1	0	0	0	0	5	0
Clark, Jerald, of	.200	6	15	0	3	1	0	0	3	0	4	0
*Flannery, Tim, 3b	.265	79	170	16	45	5	4	0	19	24	32	3
*Gwynn, Tony, of	.313	133	521	64	163	22	5	7	70	51	40	26
#Jefferson, Stan, of	.144	49	111	16	16	1	2	1	4	9	22	5
*Kruk, John, 1b-of	.241	120	378	54	91	17	1	9	44	80	68	5
Mack, Shane, of	.244	56	119	13	29	3	0	0	12	14	21	5
Martinez, Carmelo, of ..	.236	121	365	48	86	12	0	18	65	35	57	1
Moreland, Keith, 1b-of ...	.256	143	511	39	131	23	0	5	64	40	51	2
*Nelson, Rob, 1b	.190	7	21	4	4	0	0	1	3	2	9	0
Parent, Mark, c	.195	41	118	9	23	3	0	6	15	6	23	0
Ready, Randy, 3b-2b ...	.266	114	331	43	88	16	2	7	39	39	38	6
*Roberts, Bip, 3b-2b	.333	5	9	1	3	0	0	0	0	1	2	0
Santiago, Benito, c	.248	139	492	49	122	22	2	10	46	24	82	15
#Templeton, Garry, ss ..	.249	110	362	35	90	15	7	3	36	20	50	8
Thon, Dickie, ss	.264	95	258	36	68	12	2	1	18	33	49	19
*Wynne, Marvell, of	.264	128	333	37	88	13	4	11	42	31	62	3

PITCHING	W	L	ERA	G	GS	CG	SV	IP	H	R	ER	BB	SO
Booker, Greg	2	2	3.39	34	2	0	0	64	68	31	24	19	43
*Comstock, Keith	0	0	6.75	7	0	0	0	8	8	6	6	3	9
*Davis, Mark	5	10	2.01	62	0	0	28	98	70	24	22	42	102
Grant, Mark	2	8	3.69	33	11	0	0	98	97	41	40	36	61
Harris, Greg W.	2	0	1.50	3	1	1	0	18	13	3	3	3	15
Hawkins, Andy	14	11	3.35	33	33	4	0	218	196	88	81	76	91
Jones, Jimmy	9	14	4.12	29	29	3	0	179	192	98	82	44	82
*Leiper, Dave	3	0	2.17	35	0	0	1	54	45	19	13	14	33
McCullers, Lance	3	6	2.49	60	0	0	10	98	70	29	27	55	81
*Nolte, Eric	0	0	6.00	2	0	0	0	3	3	2	2	2	1
*Rasmussen, Dennis (11 Cin)	16	10	3.43	31	31	7	0	205	199	84	78	58	112
Show, Eric	16	11	3.26	32	32	13	0	235	201	86	85	53	144
Whitson, Ed	13	11	3.77	34	33	3	0	205	202	93	86	45	118

SAN FRANCISCO

BATTING	AVG	G	AB	R	H	2B	3B	HR	RBI	BB	SO	SB
*Aldrete, Mike, of	.267	139	389	44	104	15	0	3	50	56	65	6
Brenly, Bob, c	.189	73	206	13	39	7	0	5	22	20	40	1
*Butler, Brett, of	.287	157	568	109	163	27	9	6	43	97	64	43
*Clark, Will, 1b	.282	162	575	102	162	31	6	29	109	100	129	9
#Escobar, Angel, 3b-ss ..	.333	3	3	1	1	0	0	0	0	0	0	0
Garner, Phil, 3b	.154	15	13	0	2	0	0	0	1	1	3	0
Hayes, Charlie, of-3b ...	.091	7	11	0	1	0	0	0	0	0	3	0
Leonard, Jeffrey, of	.256	44	160	12	41	8	1	2	20	9	24	7
Maldonado, Candy, of ..	.255	142	499	53	127	23	1	12	68	37	89	6
Manwaring, Kirt, c	.250	40	116	12	29	7	0	1	15	2	21	0
*Melendez, Francisco, 1b .	.192	23	26	1	5	0	0	0	3	4	3	0
Melvin, Bob, c	.234	92	273	23	64	13	1	8	27	13	46	0
Mitchell, Kevin, 3b-of ...	.251	148	505	60	127	25	7	19	80	48	85	5
Nixon, Donell, of	.346	59	78	15	27	3	0	0	6	10	12	11
Perezchica, Tony, 2b ...	.125	7	8	1	1	0	0	0	1	2	1	0
*Reid, Jay, ph	.000	2	2	0	0	0	0	0	0	0	1	0
*Riles, Ernest, inf	.294	79	187	26	55	7	2	3	28	10	33	1
Speier, Chris, inf	.216	82	171	26	37	9	1	3	18	23	39	3
Thompson, Rob, 2b	.264	138	477	66	126	24	6	7	48	40	111	14
Tillman, Rusty, of	.250	4	4	1	1	0	0	1	3	2	1	0
#Uribe, Jose, ss	.252	141	493	47	124	10	7	3	35	36	69	14
Wasinger, Mark, 3b	.000	3	2	1	0	0	0	0	0	0	0	0
Williams, Matt, 3b-ss ...	.205	52	156	17	32	6	1	8	19	8	41	0
Youngblood, Joel, of	.252	83	123	12	31	4	0	0	16	10	17	1

PITCHING	W	L	ERA	G	GS	CG	SV	IP	H	R	ER	BB	SO
Bockus, Randy	1	1	4.78	20	0	0	0	32	35	19	17	13	18
Brantley, Jeff	0	1	5.66	9	1	0	1	21	22	13	13	6	11
*Cook, Dennis	2	1	2.86	4	4	1	0	22	9	8	7	11	13
Davis, Ron	1	1	4.67	9	0	0	0	17	15	10	9	6	15
Downs, Kelly	13	9	3.32	27	26	6	0	168	140	67	62	47	118
*Dravecky, Dave	2	2	3.16	7	7	1	0	37	33	19	13	8	19
Garrelts, Scott	5	9	3.58	65	0	0	13	98	80	42	39	46	86
*Hammaker, Atlee	9	9	3.73	43	17	3	5	145	136	68	60	41	65
Krukow, Mike	7	4	3.54	20	20	1	0	125	111	51	49	31	75
LaCoss, Mike	7	7	3.62	19	19	1	0	114	99	55	46	47	70
*Lefferts, Craig	3	8	2.92	64	0	0	11	92	74	33	30	23	58
*Mulholland, Terry	2	1	3.72	9	6	2	0	46	50	20	19	7	18
*Price, Joe	1	6	3.94	38	3	0	4	62	59	33	27	27	49
Reuschel, Rick	19	11	3.12	36	36	7	0	245	242	88	85	42	92
Robinson, Don	10	5	2.45	51	19	3	6	177	152	63	48	49	122
*Samuels, Roger	1	2	3.47	15	0	0	0	23	17	10	9	7	22
Sorensen, Lary	0	0	4.86	12	0	0	2	17	24	13	9	3	9
*Wilson, Trevor	0	2	4.09	4	4	0	0	22	25	14	10	8	15

NLCS: Box Scores

Game One: Mets 3, Dodgers 2

NEW YORK	ab	r	h	bi	bb	so		LOS ANGELES	ab	r	h	bi	bb	so
Wilson cf	4	0	1	0	0	0		Sax 2b	3	1	1	0	0	1
Myers p	0	0	0	0	0	0		Stubbs 1b	3	0	0	0	0	0
Jefferies 3b	4	1	3	0	0	0		Woodson ph-1b	1	0	0	0	0	0
Hernandez 1b	4	0	1	0	0	1		Gibson lf	4	0	0	0	0	2
Strawberry rf	4	1	1	1	0	0		JHowell p	0	0	0	0	0	0
McReynolds lf	3	1	0	0	1	1		Marshall rf	4	0	1	1	0	2
Johnson ss	4	0	0	0	0	1		Shelby cf	4	0	0	0	0	1
Elster ss	0	0	0	0	0	0		Scioscia c	3	1	1	0	0	1
Carter c	4	0	2	2	0	1		Dempsey ph	1	0	0	0	0	0
Backman 2b	3	0	0	0	0	1		Hamilton 3b	3	0	0	0	0	0
Gooden p	2	0	0	0	0	2		Griffin ss	3	0	1	1	0	0
Dykstra ph-cf	0	0	0	0	1	0		Hershiser p	2	0	0	0	1	1
								Gonzalez lf	0	0	0	0	0	0
TOTALS	32	3	8	3	2	7		TOTALS	31	2	4	2	1	10

```
New York . . . . . . . . . . . . . . . . . . . . . . . . . . . . 000   000   003—3
Los Angeles . . . . . . . . . . . . . . . . . . . . . . . . . 100   000   100—2
```

Game-winning RBI—Carter.

E—Backman. DP—Los Angeles 2. LOB—New York 5, Los Angeles 4. 2B—Scioscia, Strawberry, Carter. SB—Sax.

New York	IP	H	R	ER	BB	SO		Los Angeles	IP	H	R	ER	BB	SO
Gooden	7	4	2	2	1	10		Hershiser	8⅓	7	2	2	1	6
Myers W	2	0	0	0	0	0		JHowell L	⅔	1	1	1	1	1

HBP—Sax by Gooden. T—2:45. A—55,582.

Game Two: Dodgers 6, Mets 3

NEW YORK	ab	r	h	bi	bb	so		LOS ANGELES	ab	r	h	bi	bb	so
Dykstra cf	3	1	1	0	1	0		Sax 2b	5	1	1	1	0	0
Jefferies 3b	3	1	1	0	1	0		Hatcher 1b	3	2	1	2	1	0
Hernandez 1b	3	1	2	3	1	1		Gibson lf	2	0	0	0	2	0
Strawberry rf	4	0	2	0	0	2		Marshall rf	4	1	3	2	0	0
McReynolds lf	4	0	0	0	0	2		Shelby cf	4	0	0	0	0	2
Johnson ss	3	0	0	0	1	2		Scioscia c	4	0	1	0	0	0
Carter c	4	0	0	0	0	2		Hamilton 3b	1	1	0	0	2	1
Backman 2b	3	0	0	0	0	0		Griffin ss	4	0	1	0	1	0
Cone p	0	0	0	0	0	0		Belcher p	4	1	1	0	0	1
Sasser ph	1	0	0	0	0	0		Orosco p	0	0	0	0	0	0
Aguilera p	1	0	0	0	0	1		Pena p	0	0	0	0	0	0
Leach p	0	0	0	0	0	0								
Wilson ph	1	0	0	0	0	1								
McDowell p	0	0	0	0	0	0								
TOTALS	30	3	6	3	4	10		TOTALS	31	6	7	6	5	5

```
New York . . . . . . . . . . . . . . . . . . . . . . . . . . . . 000   200   001—3
Los Angeles . . . . . . . . . . . . . . . . . . . . . . . . . 140   010   00X—6
```

Game-winning RBI—Marshall.

DP—Los Angeles 2. LOB—New York 4, Los Angeles 7. 2B—Jefferies, Hatcher, Dykstra. HR—Hernandez. SB—Gibson.

New York	IP	H	R	ER	BB	SO		Los Angeles	IP	H	R	ER	BB	SO
Cone L	2	5	5	5	2	2		Belcher W	8⅓	5	3	3	3	10
Aguilera	3	2	1	1	2	0		Orosco	0	1	0	0	0	0
Leach	2	0	0	0	1	2		Pena	⅔	0	0	0	1	0
McDowell	1	0	0	0	0	0								

Orosco pitched to 1 batter in 9th.

HBP—Hamilton by Cone. Balk—Cone. T—3:10. A—55,780.

Game Three: Mets 8, Dodgers 4

LOS ANGELES	ab	r	h	bi	bb	so		NEW YORK	ab	r	h	bi	bb	so
Sax 2b	5	1	1	0	0	1		Wilson cf	4	2	1	1	1	1
Hatcher 1b	4	0	1	0	0	0		Cone p	0	0	0	0	0	0
Woodson 1b	1	0	0	0	0	0		Jefferies 3b	3	0	1	0	1	0
Gibson lf	5	0	1	0	0	1		Elster pr-ss	0	1	0	0	0	0
Marshall rf	4	1	0	0	1	1		Hernandez 1b	2	0	1	1	3	0
Shelby cf	2	1	1	0	2	1		Strawberry rf	5	1	3	3	0	0
Scioscia c	4	0	2	0	0	0		McReynolds lf	4	0	0	1	1	1
Gonzalez pr	0	1	0	0	0	0		Johnson ss-3b	4	2	0	0	0	0
Dempsey c	0	0	0	0	0	0		Carter c	4	0	1	1	0	0
Hamilton 3b	3	0	1	1	1	0		Backman 2b	4	1	2	2	0	0
Griffin ss	3	0	0	0	0	3		Darling p	2	0	0	0	0	2
Davis ph	0	0	0	0	1	0		Magadan ph	1	0	0	0	0	0
JHowell p	0	0	0	0	0	0		McDowell p	0	0	0	0	0	0
Pena p	0	0	0	0	0	0		Myers p	0	0	0	0	0	0
Orosco p	0	0	0	0	0	0		Dykstra ph-cf	0	1	0	0	1	0
Horton p	0	0	0	0	0	0								
Hershiser p	3	0	0	0	0	1								
Heep ph	0	0	0	0	0	0								
Sharperson ph-ss	0	0	0	1	1	0								
TOTALS	34	4	7	3	6	9		TOTALS	33	8	9	8	7	4

```
Los Angeles . . . . . . . . . . . . . . . . . . . . . . . . . 021   000   010—4
New York . . . . . . . . . . . . . . . . . . . . . . . . . . . . 001   002   05X—8
```

Game-winning RBI—Wilson.

— 54 —

E—Hernandez, Gibson, Hamilton, McDowell. DP—Los Angeles 1. LOB—Los Angeles 9, New York 9. 2B—Strawberry, Backman. SB—Sax, Shelby, Johnson.

Los Angeles	IP	H	R	ER	BB	SO
Hershiser	7	6	3	1	4	4
JHowell	0	0	1	1	0	0
Pena L	⅔	1	2	2	1	0
Orosco	0	1	2	2	1	0
Horton	⅓	1	0	0	0	0

New York	IP	H	R	ER	BB	SO
Darling	6	5	3	2	4	5
McDowell	1⅔	2	1	1	2	3
Myers W	⅓	0	0	0	1	0
Cone	1	0	0	0	0	1

JHowell pitched to 1 batter in 8th; Orosco pitched to 3 batters in 8th.
HBP—Jefferies by Orosco. WP—Hershiser. T—3:44. A—44,672.

Game Four: Dodgers 5, Mets 4

LOS ANGELES	ab	r	h	bi	bb	so	NEW YORK	ab	r	h	bi	bb	so
Sax 2b	5	1	1	0	1	0	Wilson cf	4	0	0	0	1	0
Hatcher 1b	4	1	0	0	1	0	McDowell p	0	0	0	0	0	0
Pena p	0	0	0	0	0	0	Mazzilli ph	1	0	1	0	0	0
Stubbs ph	1	0	0	0	0	1	Jefferies 3b	5	0	0	0	0	1
Leary p	0	0	0	0	0	0	Hernandez 1b	5	1	2	0	1	1
Orosco p	0	0	0	0	0	0	Strawberry rf	6	1	1	2	0	2
Hershiser p	0	0	0	0	0	0	McReynolds lf	5	2	2	1	1	0
Gibson lf	6	1	1	1	0	2	Carter c	4	0	2	1	0	0
Marshall rf	5	0	0	0	1	2	Myers p	0	0	0	0	0	0
Shelby cf	4	1	2	2	1	1	Dykstra cf	1	0	0	0	0	0
Scioscia c	4	1	1	2	0	1	Teufel 2b	3	0	0	0	1	1
Dempsey ph-c	0	0	0	0	1	0	Backman 2b	1	0	0	0	0	0
Hamilton 3b	4	0	0	0	0	1	Elster ss	2	0	0	0	1	0
Sharperson ph-3b	1	0	0	0	0	0	Johnson ph-ss	2	0	0	0	0	0
Griffin ss	4	0	1	0	0	0	Gooden p	3	0	1	0	0	0
Tudor p	2	0	0	0	0	2	Sasser c	2	0	1	0	0	0
Holton p	0	0	0	0	0	0	Darling pr	0	0	0	0	0	0
Heep ph	0	0	0	0	1	0							
Horton p	0	0	0	0	0	0							
Davis ph	0	0	0	0	0	0							
Woodson ph-1b	2	0	1	0	0	0							
TOTALS	42	5	7	5	6	10	TOTALS	44	4	10	4	6	4

Los Angeles . . . . 200 000 002 001—5
New York . . . . 000 301 000 000—4

Game-winning RBI—Gibson.

E—Hatcher, Elster 2. DP—Los Angeles 1, New York 1. LOB—Los Angeles 8, New York 10. 2B—McReynolds. 3B—Carter. HR—Strawberry, McReynolds, Scioscia, Gibson. SB—Sax 3, Shelby, McReynolds. S—Griffin.

Los Angeles	IP	H	R	ER	BB	SO
Tudor	5	8	4	4	1	1
Holton	1	0	0	0	1	1
Horton	2	0	0	0	0	1
Pena W	3	0	0	0	3	1
Leary	⅓	2	0	0	0	0
Orosco	0	0	0	0	1	0
Hershiser S	⅓	0	0	0	0	0

New York	IP	H	R	ER	BB	SO
Gooden	8⅓	5	4	4	5	9
Myers	2	1	0	0	0	0
McDowell L	1⅔	1	1	1	0	1

WP—Gooden 2. Balk—Gooden. T—4:29. A—54,014.

Game Five: Dodgers 7, Mets 4

LOS ANGELES	ab	r	h	bi	bb	so	NEW YORK	ab	r	h	bi	bb	so
Sax 2b	5	1	1	0	0	1	Dykstra cf	3	2	2	3	1	0
Hatcher 1b	3	1	1	0	0	0	Jefferies 3b	4	0	2	1	0	0
Stubbs 1b	2	0	0	0	0	1	Hernandez 1b	4	0	0	0	0	2
Gibson lf	5	1	2	3	0	1	Strawberry rf	4	0	1	0	0	1
Gonzalez pr-lf	0	1	0	0	0	0	McReynolds lf	4	0	1	0	0	0
Marshall rf	5	1	3	1	0	1	Carter c	4	0	1	0	0	1
Shelby cf	3	1	1	0	2	1	Johnson ss	4	1	1	0	0	2
Dempsey c	4	1	2	2	0	0	Backman 2b	4	1	1	0	0	1
Davis ph	1	0	0	0	0	0	Fernandez p	1	0	0	0	0	0
Scioscia c	0	0	0	0	0	0	Leach p	0	0	0	0	0	0
Hamilton 3b	4	0	1	0	0	1	Magadan ph	1	0	0	0	0	1
Griffin ss	4	0	1	1	0	1	Aguilera p	0	0	0	0	0	0
Belcher p	4	0	0	0	0	2	Sasser ph	1	0	0	0	0	0
Horton p	0	0	0	0	0	0	McDowell p	0	0	0	0	0	0
Holton p	0	0	0	0	0	0	Mazzilli ph	1	0	0	0	0	0
TOTALS	40	7	12	7	2	9	TOTALS	35	4	9	4	1	8

Los Angeles . . . . 000 330 001—7
New York . . . . 000 030 010—4

Game-winning RBI—Dempsey.

E—Johnson. LOB—Los Angeles 8, New York 5. 2B—Dempsey 2, Griffin, Marshall, Dykstra. 3B—Marshall. HR—Gibson, Dykstra. SB—Gibson.

Los Angeles	IP	H	R	ER	BB	SO
Belcher W	7	7	4	4	1	6
Horton	⅓	1	0	0	0	1
Holton S	1⅔	1	0	0	0	1

New York	IP	H	R	ER	BB	SO
Fernandez L	4	7	6	6	1	5
Leach	1	1	0	0	0	0
Aguilera	2	1	0	0	0	3
McDowell	2	3	1	1	1	0

Fernandez pitched to 3 batters in 5th; Belcher pitched to 2 batters in 8th.
T—3:07. A—52,069.

Game Six: Mets 5, Dodgers 1

NEW YORK	ab	r	h	bi	bb	so	LOS ANGELES	ab	r	h	bi	bb	so
Dykstra cf	4	2	2	0	0	0	Sax 2b	2	0	0	0	2	0
Backman 2b	4	0	2	0	0	1	Hatcher 1b	3	0	1	1	1	0
Hernandez 1b	5	0	1	1	0	1	Gibson lf	4	0	0	0	0	0
Strawberry rf	3	2	1	0	2	1	Gonzalez lf	0	0	0	0	0	0
McReynolds lf	4	1	4	3	0	0	Marshall rf	4	0	0	0	0	2
Jefferies 3b	4	0	0	0	1	0	Shelby cf	4	0	0	0	0	3
Carter c	4	0	0	0	1	1	Scioscia c	4	0	1	0	0	0
Elster ss	3	0	1	1	2	0	Hamilton 3b	4	0	2	0	0	0
Cone p	4	0	0	0	0	0	Griffin ss	3	0	0	0	0	0
							Davis ph	1	0	0	0	0	0
							Leary p	1	0	0	0	0	0
							Holton p	1	1	1	0	0	0
							Horton p	0	0	0	0	0	0
							Heep ph	1	0	0	0	0	1
							Orosco p	0	0	0	0	0	0
TOTALS	**35**	**5**	**11**	**5**	**6**	**4**	**TOTALS**	**32**	**1**	**5**	**1**	**3**	**6**

New York	101	021	000—5
Los Angeles	000	010	000—1

Game-winning RBI—McReynolds.

E—Hatcher, Hamilton. DP—Los Angeles 2. LOB—New York 13, Los Angeles 7. 2B—Elster, Dykstra, McReynolds. HR—McReynolds. SB—Backman, Hernandez, McReynolds. S—Cone, Backman. SF—McReynolds.

New York	IP	H	R	ER	BB	SO	Los Angeles	IP	H	R	ER	BB	SO
Cone W	9	5	1	1	3	6	Leary L	4	6	4	3	3	3
							Holton	1⅓	1	1	1	0	0
							Horton	1⅔	2	0	0	2	1
							Orosco	2	2	0	0	1	0

Leary pitched to 2 batters in 5th.

PB—Scioscia. HBP—Dykstra by Leary. WP—Cone. T—3:16. A—55,885.

Game Seven: Dodgers 6, Mets 0

NEW YORK	ab	r	h	bi	bb	so	LOS ANGELES	ab	r	h	bi	bb	so
Dykstra cf	3	0	1	0	0	0	Sax 2b	5	2	3	2	0	0
Backman 2b	3	0	1	0	1	0	Hatcher 1b-lf	4	0	1	0	0	0
Hernandez 1b	3	0	0	0	1	1	Gonzalez lf	0	0	0	0	0	0
Strawberry rf	4	0	0	0	0	1	Gibson lf	0	0	0	1	0	0
McReynolds lf	4	0	0	0	0	1	Stubbs 1b	2	0	2	0	1	0
Jefferies 3b	4	0	2	0	0	0	Marshall rf	4	0	1	0	1	1
Carter c	3	0	0	0	0	0	Shelby cf	3	0	0	1	0	3
Aguilera p	0	0	0	0	0	0	Scioscia c	3	1	2	0	0	0
Mazzilli ph	0	0	0	0	0	0	Hamilton 3b	4	1	1	0	0	1
Elster ss	3	0	1	0	0	0	Griffin ss	4	1	0	0	0	0
Johnson ph	1	0	0	0	0	1	Hershiser p	4	1	0	1	0	0
Darling p	1	0	0	0	0	0							
Gooden p	0	0	0	0	0	0							
Magadan ph	1	0	0	0	0	1							
Leach p	0	0	0	0	0	0							
Sasser c	1	0	0	0	0	0							
TOTALS	**31**	**0**	**5**	**0**	**2**	**5**	**TOTALS**	**33**	**6**	**10**	**6**	**2**	**5**

New York	000	000	000—0
Los Angeles	150	000	00x—6

Game-winning RBI—Gibson.

E—Backman, Jefferies. DP—New York 1, Los Angeles 1. LOB—New York 8, Los Angeles 7. 2B—Hatcher, Jefferies. SB—Mazzilli. SF—Gibson, Shelby.

New York	IP	H	R	ER	BB	SO	Los Angeles	IP	H	R	ER	BB	SO
Darling L	1	6	6	4	0	2	Hershiser W	9	5	0	0	2	5
Gooden	3	1	0	0	2	1							
Leach	2	3	0	0	0	1							
Aguilera	2	0	0	0	0	1							

Darling pitched to 5 batters in 2nd.

HBP—Dykstra by Hershiser, Mazzilli by Hershiser. WP—Hershiser. T—2:51. A—55,693.

NLCS: Composite Box

LOS ANGELES

Player, Pos.	AVG	G	AB	R	H	2B	3B	HR	RBI	BB	SO	SB
Brian Holton, p	1.000	3	1	1	1	0	0	0	0	0	0	0
Rick Dempsey, ph-c	.400	4	5	1	2	2	0	0	2	1	0	0
Mike Scioscia, c	.364	7	22	3	8	1	0	1	2	1	2	0
Steve Sax, 2b	.267	7	30	7	8	0	0	0	3	3	3	5
Franklin Stubbs, 1b-ph	.250	4	8	0	2	0	0	0	0	0	4	0
Tracy Woodson, ph-1b	.250	3	4	0	1	0	0	0	0	0	1	0
Mickey Hatcher, 1b-lf	.238	6	21	4	5	2	0	0	3	3	0	0
Mike Marshall, rf	.233	7	30	3	7	1	1	0	5	2	9	0
Jeff Hamilton, 3b	.217	7	23	2	5	0	0	0	1	3	4	0
John Shelby, cf	.167	7	24	3	4	0	0	0	3	5	12	2
Alfredo Griffin, ss	.160	7	25	1	4	1	0	0	3	0	5	0
Kirk Gibson, lf	.154	7	26	2	4	0	0	2	6	3	6	2
Tim Belcher, p	.125	2	8	1	1	0	0	0	0	0	3	0
Orel Hershiser, p	.000	4	9	1	0	0	0	0	0	1	2	0
John Tudor, p	.000	1	2	0	0	0	0	0	0	0	2	0
Mike Davis, ph	.000	4	2	0	0	0	0	0	0	0	1	0
Mike Sharperson, ph-ss-3b	.000	2	1	0	0	0	0	0	0	1	1	0
Danny Heep, ph	.000	3	1	0	0	0	0	0	0	0	1	0
Tim Leary, p	.000	2	1	0	0	0	0	0	0	0	1	0
Jose Gonzalez, lf-pr	—	4	0	2	0	0	0	0	0	0	0	0
TOTALS	.214	7	243	31	52	7	1	3	30	25	54	9

Pitcher	W	L	ERA	G	GS	CG	SV	IP	H	R	ER	BB	SO
Ricky Horton	0	0	0.00	4	0	0	0	4⅓	4	0	0	2	3
Orel Hershiser	1	0	1.10	4	3	0	1	24⅔	18	5	3	7	15
Brian Holton	0	0	2.25	3	0	0	1	4	2	1	1	1	2
Tim Belcher	2	0	4.11	2	2	0	0	15⅓	12	7	7	4	16
Alejandro Pena	1	1	4.15	3	0	0	1	4⅓	1	2	2	5	1
Tim Leary	0	1	6.23	2	1	0	0	4⅓	8	4	3	3	3
John Tudor	0	0	7.20	1	1	0	0	5	8	4	4	1	1
Jesse Orosco	0	0	7.71	4	0	0	0	2⅓	4	2	2	3	0
Jay Howell	0	1	27.00	2	0	0	0	⅔	1	2	2	2	1
TOTALS	4	3	3.32	7	7	0	3	65	58	27	24	28	42

NEW YORK

Player, Pos.	AVG	G	AB	R	H	2B	3B	HR	RBI	BB	SO	SB
Lee Mazzilli, ph	.500	3	2	0	1	0	0	0	1	0	0	1
Len Dykstra, ph-cf	.429	7	14	6	6	3	0	1	3	4	0	0
Gregg Jefferies, 3b	.333	7	27	2	9	2	0	0	1	4	0	0
Darryl Strawberry, rf	.300	7	30	5	9	2	0	1	6	2	5	0
Wally Backman, 2b	.273	7	22	2	6	1	0	0	2	2	5	1
Keith Hernandez, 1b	.269	7	26	2	7	0	0	1	5	6	7	1
Kevin McReynolds, lf	.250	7	28	4	7	2	0	2	4	3	5	2
Kevin Elster, ss-pr	.250	5	8	1	2	1	0	0	1	3	0	0
Gary Carter, c	.222	7	27	0	6	1	1	0	4	1	3	0
Mackey Sasser, c-ph	.200	4	5	0	1	0	0	0	0	0	1	0
Dwight Gooden, p	.200	3	5	1	1	0	0	0	0	0	0	0
Mookie Wilson, cf-ph	.154	4	13	2	2	0	0	0	1	2	2	0
Howard Johnson, ss-ph	.056	6	18	3	1	0	0	0	0	1	6	1
David Cone, p	.000	3	4	0	0	0	0	0	0	0	0	0
Ron Darling, p-pr	.000	3	3	0	0	0	0	0	0	0	0	0
Dave Magadan, ph	.000	3	3	0	0	0	0	0	0	2	0	0
Tim Teufel, 2b	.000	1	3	0	0	0	0	0	0	1	0	0
Rick Aguilera, p	.000	3	1	0	0	0	0	0	0	0	1	0
Sid Fernandez, p	.000	1	1	0	0	0	0	0	0	0	0	0
TOTALS	.242	7	240	27	58	12	1	5	27	28	42	6

Pitcher	W	L	ERA	G	GS	CG	SV	IP	H	R	ER	BB	SO
Randy Myers	2	0	0.00	3	0	0	0	4⅔	1	0	0	2	0
Terry Leach	0	0	0.00	3	0	0	0	5	4	0	0	1	4
Rick Aguilera	0	0	1.29	3	0	0	0	7	3	1	1	2	4
Dwight Gooden	0	0	2.95	3	2	0	0	18⅓	10	6	6	8	20
David Cone	1	1	4.50	3	2	1	0	12	10	6	6	5	9
Roger McDowell	0	1	4.50	4	0	0	0	6	6	3	3	2	5
Ron Darling	0	1	7.71	2	2	0	0	7	11	9	6	4	7
Sid Fernandez	0	1	13.50	1	1	0	0	4	7	6	6	1	5
TOTALS	3	4	3.94	7	7	1	0	64	52	31	28	25	54

Los Angeles	5	11	1		3	5	0		1	1	3		0 0 1 — 31
New York	1	0	2		5	5	4		0	6	4		0 0 0 — 27

Game-winning RBIs—Carter, Marshall, Wilson, Gibson 2, Dempsey, McReynolds.
E—Backman 2, Hernandez, Gibson, Hamilton 2, McDowell, Hatcher 2, Elster 2, Johnson, Jefferies. DP—New York 2, Los Angeles 9. LOB—New York 54, Los Angeles 50. S—Backman 2, Griffin, Cone. SF—McReynolds, Gibson, Shelby. PB—Scioscia. HBP—Sax by Gooden, Hamilton by Cone, Jefferies by Orosco, Dykstra by Leary, Dykstra by Hershiser, Mazzilli by Hershiser. WP—Hershiser 2, Gooden 2, Cone. Balk—Cone, Gooden. Umpires—Wendelstedt, McSherry, West, Rennert, Davidson, Runge. Official Scorers—Red Foley, New York Daily News; Wayne Monroe, Los Angeles scorer.

THE MINOR LEAGUES

Triple-A Leagues

Double-A Leagues

Class A Leagues

Short-Season Class A

Rookie Leagues

Buffalo's Pilot Field drew a minor league-record attendance total of 1,186,651 in 1988, its first year of existence.

Nothing minor about Buffalo success story

By JON SCHER

Incredible. Inconceivable. Incomprehensible.

However you describe it, what happened in Buffalo, N.Y., during the 1988 baseball season was pretty darn amazing.

Eighteen years after Buffalo's International League franchise was revoked for nonsupport, six years after its Eastern League franchise was saved from moving out of town at the last moment, four years after owner Bob Rich purchased an American Association franchise and brought Triple-A baseball back to Buffalo, the impossible happened:

1,186,651.

That's how many tickets were bought at beautiful new Pilot Field in 1988. The total includes sellout crowds of 19,500 for both the National Old-Timers' Baseball Classic and the Triple-A All-Star Game, but even without that windfall the Buffalo Bisons would have broken the all-time minor league attendance record. The Louisville Redbirds were the first minor league team to draw more than a million, with 1,052,438 in 1983, a number that seemed as unbreakable as, well, Don Drysdale's 58 straight scoreless innings.

The Bisons started with solid local ownership, the Rich Products frozen-foods empire. They built attendance with an aggressive promotions and marketing scheme. By 1987, nearly a half-million fans bought tickets at ancient War Memorial Stadium. Then in 1988, the last piece fell into place with the opening of Pilot Field, a $43 million baseball palace. Built to combine the coziness of older parks with the convenience of modern ones, Pilot Field was packed and rocking all season long. A mediocre team didn't prevent Buffalo's fans from demonstrating their support for the Bisons and the city's new downtown stadium.

"It's the culmination of a dream," Rich said. "Buffalo has taken its share of knocks in the past. Now it can show off."

And it isn't stopping now. Pilot Field, built primarily with

Gordon named minors' top player

Tom "Flash" Gordon, a 5-foot-9, 160-pound dynamo, devastated hitters at three levels of the Kansas City Royals' farm system in 1988. Gordon, a 20-year-old righthander, finished the minor league season with a composite 16-5 record and a 1.55 ERA for Class A Appleton, Double-A Memphis and Triple-A Omaha.

Tom Gordon
... Player of Year

Using a hard fastball and sharp-breaking curve, Gordon struck out 263 batters in 186 minor league innings. He walked 75, and allowed just 96 hits and 36 earned runs. After a hard-luck 7-5 stint at Appleton, Gordon won all six of his Southern League starts for Memphis (two shutouts, 0.38 ERA, 62 strikeouts, 16 hits in 47 innings).

Later, after a September promotion to Kansas City, Gordon struck out 18 in 16 innings to finish 1988 with a grand total of 281 strikeouts—second only to Roger Clemens in all of professional baseball.

As a result, Gordon was named Baseball America's 1988 Minor League Player of the Year.

Expos take two honors

Indianapolis won its third straight American Association championship, then topped it off with a victory over Rochester (International) in the first Triple-A Classic.

Other Montreal Expos farm teams in Jacksonville (Southern), West Palm Beach (Florida State), Rockford (Midwest) and Jamestown (New York-Penn) all made the playoffs. And no one may have more overall talent—from pitchers like Brian Holman, John Dopson and Randy Johnson, who finished the season with Montreal; to all-around players like Kevin Dean, Delino DeShields, Tyrone Kingwood and Marquis Grissom. Because of this combination of success, the Expos were named Baseball America's 1988 Organization of the Year.

In addition, Baseball America tabbed Indianapolis manager Joe Sparks as the 1988 Minor League Manager of the Year.

Baseball America's Minor League Players of the Year:

- **1981**—Mike Marshall, of, Albuquerque (Dodgers).
- **1982**—Ron Kittle, of, Edmonton (White Sox).
- **1983**—Dwight Gooden, p, Lynchburg (Mets).
- **1984**—Mike Bielecki, p, Hawaii (Pirates).
- **1985**—Jose Canseco, of, Huntsville/Tacoma (Athletics).
- **1986**—Gregg Jefferies, ss, Columbia/Lynchburg (Mets).
- **1987**—Gregg Jefferies, ss, Jackson (Mets).
- **1988**—Tom Gordon, p, Appleton/Memphis/Omaha (Royals).

Baseball America's Organizations of the Year:

1982—Oakland Athletics.	**1986**—Milwaukee Brewers.
1983—New York Mets.	**1987**—Milwaukee Brewers.
1984—New York Mets.	**1988**—Montreal Expos.
1985—Milwaukee Brewers.	

Baseball America's Minor League Managers of the Year:

- **1981**—Ed Nottle, Tacoma (Athletics).
- **1982**—Eddie Haas, Richmond (Braves).
- **1983**—Bill Dancy, Reading (Phillies).
- **1984**—Sam Perlozzo, Jackson (Mets).
- **1985**—Jim Lefebvre, Phoenix (Giants).
- **1986**—Brad Fischer, Huntsville (Athletics).
- **1987**—Dave Trembley, Harrisburg (Pirates).
- **1988**—Joe Sparks, Indianapolis (Expos).

state and municipal money, can be expanded to 40,000 seats to accommodate major league baseball. Based on the success the Bisons enjoyed in 1988, Buffalo has joined the list of top candidates for a big league expansion team.

"The next goal is the major leagues," Rich said.

Excluding the all-star and old-timers games, Buffalo's attendance goes down in the history books as 1,147,651. That boosted the American Association to a record level: 3,509,465, an increase of 766,288 over 1987.

Pacific Coast League attendance was up 204,858, and the Midwest League, boosted by two expansion teams, attracted 477,785 more fans than in 1987. Overall, minor league attendance reached 21,659,873, the highest level since 1952, according to the National Association of Professional Baseball Leagues. Statistics provided by the National Association, the minors' governing body, indicate an overall increase of 1,444,514 tickets sold, a 7 percent gain over 1987. An average of 2,289 tickets were sold for each of the 9,462 minor league games played in the United States, Canada, Mexico and the Dominican Republic in 1988.

The Triple-A Alliance

The three Triple-A leagues, which had ignored each other since the death of the Triple-A World Series after its first and only year in 1983, got together on two innovative ventures in 1988:

■ They agreed to initiate an annual Triple-A all-star game

Deaths

Johnny Johnson, president of the National Association of Professional Baseball Leagues, died of cancer Jan. 12, 1988. Johnson, 66, had been president of the National Association, the governing body of the minor leagues, since 1979.

Johnson spent 41 years in baseball management. He served in a variety of positions for the New York Yankees, including vice president for minor league operations. In 1970, he was named administrator of Major League Baseball by then-commissioner Bowie Kuhn. He continued in that post until he was elected to the Association presidency.

Johnson's goal as president was to improve the business of minor league baseball. At the time of his death, the minors were in their best-ever financial condition.

Johnny Johnson
... Died in office

"He coined the phrase that we were in a renaissance," said Sal Artiaga, who served Johnson as National Association administrator and was elected to succeed him as president in April. "The value of franchises and the type of operators we have reflects on that. He turned this office around financially."

Other notable deaths during 1988:

■ **Barney Deary,** 62, administrator of baseball's Umpire Development Program since 1969, died Sept. 22 of a heart attack.

■ **Arnold "Jigger" Statz,** 90, perhaps the greatest minor leaguer of all time, died March 16. Statz spent 18 years with the Los Angeles Angels of the Pacific Coast League, compiling a career PCL batting average of .315. He holds PCL records for games (2,790), runs (1,996), hits (3,356), doubles (595) and triples (137).

between American League and National League affiliates. The inaugural game, televised nationally by ESPN, was held in Buffalo July 13 (see box). It was such a success, the three Double-A leagues were beginning to investigate the possibility of setting up a joint all-star game of their own.

■ During the fall of 1987, the American Association and the International League agreed to a de facto merger, creating the Triple-A Alliance. International League president Harold Cooper was named commissioner of the Alliance. Although the leagues nominally maintained their individual identities, they both operated out of Cooper's office near Columbus, Ohio.

The Alliance schedule called for each team to play 40 interleague games. The American Association was the major beneficiary of the arrangement, compiling a 187-131 record in interleague play. Seven of the eight Association clubs had winning records against International League teams. As a result, six Association clubs finished the season above .500, while six of the eight IL clubs wound up below .500.

Jurak leads AL stars to victory

On a night meant to showcase baseball's rising stars before a national television audience, Ed Jurak stole the spotlight. Jurak, 30, a utilityman who had been cast adrift by two major league organizations, tripled and scored the winning run in the ninth inning as the American League farmhands defeated their National League counterparts 2-1 in the first Triple-A All-Star Game.

Jurak, who was hitting .314 for Tacoma of the A's organization, was named the most valuable player. He was the last player off the American League bench.

Until Jurak's triple, Gregg Jefferies' line-drive home run to right had been the game's most exciting moment. The 13 all-star pitchers allowed just 10 hits and struck out 16 batters, 13 of them from the AL team. The game was played July 13 before a sellout crowd of 19,500 at Buffalo's new Pilot Field. Columbus, Ohio, has the 1989 game.

★ ★ ★

American 2, National 1

AMERICAN	ab	r	h	bi	bb	so	NATIONAL	ab	r	h	bi	bb	so
Yelding ss-2b	5	1	1	0	0	1	Brumley ss	3	0	0	0	0	0
Finley cf	3	0	0	0	0	1	Perezchica ss	1	0	0	0	0	0
Quintana cf	2	0	0	0	0	2	DSmith cf-rf	4	0	1	0	0	1
Berroa lf	3	0	1	0	0	0	Daugherty 1b	4	0	0	0	0	0
Freeman lf	2	0	0	0	0	2	Distefano dh	3	0	0	0	1	0
Pyznarski dh	2	0	0	0	0	2	Carreon lf	2	0	0	0	0	0
Ouellette dh	1	0	0	0	1	0	Fishel lf	2	0	1	0	0	1
Medina rf	2	0	0	0	0	0	Gwynn rf	1	0	0	0	0	0
Randall rf	1	0	1	0	1	0	Devereaux cf	2	0	0	0	1	0
O'Malley 3b	4	0	2	0	0	1	Alomar c	2	0	0	0	0	0
Delos Santos 1b	1	0	0	0	1	1	Prince c	2	0	0	0	0	0
Rivera ph-1b	2	0	0	0	0	1	MBrown 3b	1	0	0	0	1	0
Blankenship 2b	3	0	1	0	0	2	Jefferies 3b	2	1	1	1	0	0
Jurak ss	1	1	1	0	0	0	Cora 2b	3	0	0	0	0	0
Palacios c	2	0	0	0	0	0							
Geren c	2	0	0	0	0	1							
TOTALS	36	2	7	1	3	13	**TOTALS**	32	1	3	1	3	3

American	. . . .	001	000	001—2
National	. . . .	000	000	100—1

Game-winning RBI—None.

E—MBrown, O'Malley, Yelding, Perezchica. LOB—American 10, National 7. 2B—Randall. 3B—Jurak. HR—Jefferies. SB—DSmith, Devereaux, Blankenship.

American	IP	H	R	ER	BB	SO	National	IP	H	R	ER	BB	SO
RSmith	2	0	0	0	0	2	West	2	1	0	0	1	2
Nielsen	1	0	0	0	0	0	Sebra	2	2	1	0	0	3
Huismann	1	1	0	0	0	0	Kemp	2	2	0	0	0	1
Milacki	2	1	0	0	2	0	Harris	1	1	0	0	0	3
Lugo W	2	1	1	1	1	1	Bielecki	1	0	0	0	2	2
Pall	⅔	0	0	0	0	0	Boever L	1	1	1	0	0	2
Kinnunen S	⅓	0	0	0	0	0							

WP—West, Harris. T—2:50. A—19,500.

Here's how each team fared in games against the other league:

American Association—Indianapolis, 27-13; Denver, 25-14; Omaha, 25-15; Louisville, 24-16; Nashville, 24-16; Iowa, 23-17; Oklahoma City, 20-19; Buffalo, 19-21.

International League—Rochester, 22-17; Tidewater, 21-19; Syracuse, 16-23; Columbus, 16-24; Richmond, 16-24; Maine, 16-24; Pawtucket, 14-26; Toledo, 10-30.

At the end of the year, the two league champions played in the first Triple-A Classic. Again, the Association was a big winner. Its champion, the Indianapolis Indians, routed the Rochester Red Wings 4-2 in a best-of-7 series.

Originally approved on an experimental basis, the Alliance was extended for three more years in a 14-2 vote at the Triple-A All-Star Game.

Homers hard to come by

Mirroring the decrease in offense at the major league level, home run production dropped drastically in nine of the 11 full-season minor leagues in 1988.

Home runs were up only in the hit-happy Pacific Coast League, which welcomed high-altitude Colorado Springs into the fold. A year after 13 minor leaguers hit 30 or more home runs, no one reached that level in 1988.

Luis Medina of (surprise!) Colorado Springs led the minors with 28 dingers. Medina was able to keep everything in perspective, though: "The only place the ball carries as well as Colorado Springs is the moon," he said.

Meanwhile, pitchers had a field day. There were 32 minor league no-hitters in 1988, up from just 13 in '87. Bill Kazmierczak of Winston-Salem (Carolina) had two, against Salem on April 13 and Virginia on May 20. And Nashville's Herschel Greer Stadium had back-to-back no-hitters: Indianapolis' Randy Johnson and Pat Pacillo held the Sounds hitless Aug. 6, and Nashville's Jack Armstrong no-hit the Indians the next day.

Impatient major league clubs hustled prospects through the minors at an unprecedented pace in 1988. For example, it took the Cubs less than a month to decide first baseman Mark Grace was ready for a promotion from Triple-A Iowa to Wrigley Field. The Yankees convinced Florida State football star Deion Sanders to sign a six-week minor league contract after the June draft, then rushed him from the rookie-level Gulf Coast League, to Class A Fort Lauderdale, to Triple-A Columbus by the time he had to report to fall football practice.

Tom Gordon, Baseball America's Minor League Player of the Year, went on a whirlwind tour of the Kansas City Royals' farm system, striking out 263 batters at three levels (see page xx). Gary Sheffield compiled a .327 batting average at Double-A El Paso and Triple-A Denver of the Brewers' organization.

Ken Griffey Jr. hit .338 in 58 games at Class A San Bernardino (long enough for club management to begin marketing a color poster of the No. 1 pick in the 1987 draft), missed two months with a back injury, then closed the year with the Mariners' Double-A Vermont affiliate.

Pitcher Mike Harkey finished 16-4 with a 2.41 ERA for the Cubs at Double-A Pittsfield and Iowa. Gordon, Sheffield and Harkey, along with Gregg Jefferies—the Minor League Player of the Year in 1986 and '87 who hit .282 for the Mets' Triple-A Tidewater club—all finished the season in the major leagues and will be among the top rookies of 1989.

Among the other stories that made news in 1988:

■ Ronald Sims, an infielder for the Bradenton Braves of the rookie-level Gulf Coast League, was blinded in his left eye when he was hit by a pitch in his first professional game. The accidental beaning occurred June 20, in a game against the Sarasota Dodgers. The eye had to be surgically removed.

■ Four full-season Class A clubs—Fresno and Reno of the

Classification All-Stars

(Selected by Baseball America)

CLASS AAA

C—Sandy Alomar, Las Vegas (Pacific Coast). 1B—Luis delos Santos, Omaha (American Association). 2B—Johnny Paredes, Indianapolis (American Association). 3B—Edgar Martinez, Calgary (Pacific Coast). SS—Mike Brumley, Las Vegas (Pacific Coast). OF—Mike Devereaux, Albuquerque (Pacific Coast); Steve Finley, Rochester (International); Luis Medina, Colorado Springs (Pacific Coast). DH—Rod Allen, Colorado Springs (Pacific Coast). P—Dave West, Tidewater (International); Steve Searcy, Toledo (International); Bill Krueger, Albuquerque (Pacific Coast); Bob Sebra, Indianapolis (American Association); Mark Huismann, Toledo (International).

Player of the Year—Sandy Alomar, Las Vegas (Pacific Coast).

Manager of the Year—Joe Sparks, Indianapolis (American Association).

CLASS AA

C—Todd Zeile, Arkansas (Texas). 1B—Jim McCollom, Midland (Texas). 2B—Mark Lemke, Greenville (Southern). 3B—Jeff Manto, Midland (Texas). SS—Gary Sheffield, El Paso (Texas). OF—Rob Richie, Glens Falls (Eastern); Greg Vaughn, El Paso (Texas); Butch Davis, Charlotte (Southern). DH—Matt Winters, Memphis (Southern). P—Chris Hammond, Chattanooga (Southern); Mike Harkey, Pittsfield (Eastern); Blaine Beatty, Jackson (Texas); Alex Sanchez, Knoxville (Southern); German Gonzalez, Orlando (Southern).

Player of the Year—Gary Sheffield, El Paso (Texas).

Manager of the Year—Buddy Bailey, Greenville (Southern).

CLASS A

C—Tim McIntosh, Stockton (California). 1B—Rich Aldrete, San Jose (California). 2B—Paul Faries, Riverside (California). 3B—Scott Cooper, Lynchburg (Carolina). SS—Luis Sojo, Myrtle Beach (South Atlantic). OF—Derek Bell, Myrtle Beach (South Atlantic); Ken Griffey, San Bernardino (California); Mike White, Vero Beach (Florida State). DH—Mark Leonard, San Jose (California). P—Colin Charland, Palm Springs (California); Kent Mercker, Durham (Carolina); Tom Gordon, Appleton (Midwest); Butch Henry, Cedar Rapids (Midwest); Jimmy Rogers, Myrtle Beach (South Atlantic).

Player of the Year—Ken Griffey, San Bernardino (California).

Manager of the Year—Dick Berardino, Lynchburg (Carolina).

SHORT-SEASON

C—Bert Heffernan, Helena (Pioneer). 1B—Bob Hamelin, Eugene (Northwest). 2B—Kelly Zane, Salt Lake (Pioneer). 3B—Stan Royer, Southern Oregon (Northwest). SS—Jose Oferman, Great Falls (Pioneer). OF—Marquis Grissom, Jamestown (New York-Penn); Trey McCoy, Butte (Pioneer); Derek Lee, Utica (New York-Penn). DH—Rob Maurer, Butte (Pioneer). P—Sean Snedeker, Great Falls (Pioneer); Dan Freed, Jamestown (New York-Penn); Steve Avery, Pulaski (Appalachian); Rusty Meacham, Bristol (Appalachian); Tony Floyd, Southern Oregon (Northwest).

Player of the Year—Jose Oferman, Great Falls (Pioneer).

Manager of the Year—Bobby Floyd, Kingsport (Appalachian).

California League, Miami of the Florida State League and Virginia of the Carolina League—were unable to secure major league affiliations for 1988. Forced to get by with free agents or players on loan from major league farm systems, all four clubs limped to poor records: Fresno, 53-89; Reno, 39-103; Miami, 55-79; Virginia, 41-99.

■ Meanwhile, major league farm directors continued to clamor for more short-season clubs.

The Gulf Coast League expanded from 10 to 12 teams, creating a four-team division based at spring training complexes in central Florida. The Appalachian League, which was down to seven teams a few years ago, expanded from eight to 10 clubs.

And after years of lobbying by the Brewers and Athletics, the National Association allowed a four-team rookie league to form at spring training complexes in Arizona. Organizations involved in the new league had to agree not to drop any of their other short-season farm clubs. At first, the league was named the Arizona State League, but later was shortened to the Arizona League when it was discovered the term "Arizona State" is prohibited for use by corporations in Arizona.

The Padres joined the Brewers and A's in the Arizona League, and the fourth club was comprised of players provided by the Red Sox and Mariners.

■ Continuing a trend that began with the opening of The Ballpark in Maine in 1984 and The Diamond in Richmond in 1985, new ballparks were springing up all over the country.

In addition to Buffalo, new parks opened in Birmingham (Hoover Metropolitan Stadium, a $13 million, 10,000-seat park); South Bend (Stanley Coveleski Regional Stadium, $5.5 million, 5,000 seats); and Colorado Springs (Sky Sox Stadium, $3.4 million, 6,100 seats). And in Charlotte, N.C., plans were announced for a $12 million, 10,000-seat expandable stadium.

■ Minor league baseball went to the movies in 1988. The highlights: "Bull Durham," starring Kevin Costner and Susan Sarandon, a fictional story based at historic Durham Athletic Park in Durham, N.C.; and "Eight Men Out," a dramatization of the 1919 Black Sox scandal, which was filmed at Bush Stadium in Indianapolis. Both movies received good reviews, but "Bull Durham" buried "Eight Men Out" at the box office and became one of the most successful movies of the year. The real-life Durham Bulls weren't complaining—attendance soared to 271,650, a new Class A record, and souvenir sales skyrocketed.

Artiaga named to head minors

Upon the death of National Association president Johnny Johnson on Jan. 12 (see box), Eastern League president Charlie Eshbach, chairman of the National Association's executive committee, took over as acting president of the minors' governing body.

Over the next three months, eight candidates emerged to succeed Johnson: Eshbach; National Association administrator Sal Artiaga; former Reds and Yankees general manager Bill Bergesch; Maine (International) president John McGee; Florida State League president George MacDonald; Albuquerque (Pacific Coast) president Pat MacKernan; former major league and minor league executive Spec Richardson; and Arizona League president Bob Richmond.

Sal Artiaga
... Minors' new boss

Each minor league had one vote in the April 26 election, held at the Airport Hyatt in Dallas. A majority was needed to win on the first ballot, and Artiaga got that. He received nine votes, to six for Richmond. Eshbach and MacDonald got one vote each.

Artiaga, 41, had been administrator of the National Association for six years. He was elected president for a three-year term.

Around the minors

Injury of the year: Reno first baseman Cary Grubb was bitten on the leg by a police dog during a K-9 corps demonstration before a California League game in Modesto ... Ejection of the year, Part One: The El Paso public address announcer was ousted from the ballpark for playing "When Will I Be Loved" over the loudspeakers after a controversial call. The song opens with the lyrics, "I've been cheated, been mistreated." ... Ejection of the year, Part Two: Omaha organist Lambert Bartak was booted for playing the "Mickey Mouse Club" theme song during

Composite Minor League Records

	1988 W	L	Pct.	1987 Pct.	1986 Pct.	1985 Pct.
Los Angeles (7*) .	443	319	.581	.499	.435	.489
Milwaukee (5) ...	347	281	.553	.592	.579	.586
Montreal (6)	384	313	.551	.490	.534	.503
San Diego (5) ...	346	286	.548	.530	.503	.484
Cincinnati (6)	376	320	.540	.501	.533	.553
Cleveland (6)	369	322	.534	.514	.478	.506
Kansas City (6) ..	374	329	.532	.493	.477	.531
Minnesota (5) ...	336	299	.529	.450	.460	.502
Chi. White Sox (6)	366	329	.527	.491	.464	.524
San Francisco (6)	378	330	.527	.537	.521	.544
Detroit (5)	323	302	.517	.461	.456	.462
Baltimore (5)	295	278	.515	.549	.559	.484
NY Mets (7)	393	371	.514	.492	.525	.550
NY Yankees (6) ..	354	338	.512	.524	.538	.596
St. Louis (7)	424	411	.508	.567	.557	.505
Houston (6)	355	346	.506	.549	.526	.529
Pittsburgh (7) ...	382	382	.500	.542	.430	.442
Texas (6)	336	348	.491	.436	.372	.478
Atlanta (8)	438	467	.484	.473	.532	.490
Chicago Cubs (7)	403	441	.477	.533	.525	.484
Toronto (6)	332	375	.468	.511	.496	.512
Seattle (5)	298	341	.466	.472	.508	.496
California (5)	290	343	.458	.464	.503	.472
Philadelphia (6) ..	310	389	.443	.475	.421	.480
Oakland (5)	286	360	.443	.504	.543	.482
Boston (5)	251	383	.396	.445	.539	.469

*Number of farm teams

a rhubarb. "He was playing music derogatory to the profession of umpiring," explained umpire Tony Maners. The next night, about 25 fans showed up wearing Mickey Mouse ears ... The Billy Martin Award: To Columbia Mets manager Butch Hobson, who swiped first base, took it into the clubhouse, painted it orange, then returned it to its rightful place after he was ejected from a South Atlantic League game ... The longest game of the year, a 27-inning affair between the Burlington Indians and the Bluefield Orioles, was played June 24-25 in Burlington, N.C. Bluefield won the eight-hour, 15 minute Appalachian League marathon 3-2. There were about 50 people in the stands when the game ended at 3:27 a.m.

Quotes of the year

THORNTON "BEAN" STRINGFELLOW, Richmond (International) pitcher, describing the difficulty of placing a collect call with a name like that: "If I tell the operator Thornton, she can't understand me. If I tell her Bean, she doesn't believe me."

CLINT HURDLE, St. Lucie (Florida State) manager, after an unruly Father's Day crowd watched the Mets lose 7-1 at the St. Lucie County Sports Complex: "All we had here today is a bunch of repressed, single fathers who didn't have anything better to do than to come out and boo the Mets. It wasn't pretty."

ROCKY BRIDGES, Buffalo manager, after a four-run fifth boosted Maine to a 5-4 victory over the Bisons: "I'm going to propose a new rule in baseball. You should be able to take a mulligan, just like in golf. We'd like to take a mulligan in the fifth. Take that inning away and we win."

TODD PRATT, the Red Sox minor league catcher drafted by the Indians at the Winter Meetings and later returned to the Boston organization, asked about his experiences in the Indians' major league camp: "I've tasted the bitter salt of the minors and the sweet honey of the majors and I don't think I'll ever be out of this game."

Evidence of success: 3 million witnesses

By GEORGE RORRER

Manager Joe Sparks' Indianapolis Indians sipped champagne at the end of a third straight American Association season in 1988, but the big news was the way the turnstiles spun.

Led by Buffalo's all-time minor league home attendance record 1,147,651, the Association became the first minor league to break the 3 million barrier.

Break? Make that crush. Association clubs drew 3,615,678, beating their own record of 2,851,720 (1987). Now even 4 million seems within reach.

In the first year of the Association's alliance with the International League, Buffalo's new Pilot Field was the place to be. Two other Association teams also broke club attendance records—Omaha (308,080) and Iowa (279,091).

Also, Louisville, the only other minor league club to have drawn a million (1983), attracted 574,852; Denver 374,867; Nashville 317,785; Indianapolis 314,016; and Oklahoma City 260,336.

"It was one of those things where you look at the figures after the season and your jaw drops down," said Randy Mobley, administrator of the Triple-A Alliance. "It's a tribute to the caliber of the operators there are in the Association. It's an amazing feat."

League stability

It was such a solid situation that all affiliations for 1989 will remain the same.

Textbook front-office promotions and civic pride helped

League Champions

(Playoff Champions, Where Applicable)

1988—Indianapolis	1956—Indianapolis	1928—Indianapolis
1987—Indianapolis	1955—Minneapolis	1927—Toledo
1986—Indianapolis	1954—Louisville	1926—Louisville
1985—Louisville	1953—Kansas City	1925—Louisville
1984—Louisville	1952—Kansas City	1924—St. Paul
1983—Denver	1951—Milwaukee	1923—Kansas City
1982—Indianapolis	1950—Columbus	1922—St. Paul
1981—Denver	1949—Indianapolis	1921—Louisville
1980—Springfield	1948—St. Paul	1920—St. Paul
1979—Evansville	1947—Milwaukee	1919—St. Paul
1978—Omaha	1946—Louisville	1918—Kansas City
1977—Denver	1945—Louisville	1917—Indianapolis
1976—Denver	1944—Louisville	1916—Louisville
1975—Evansville	1943—Columbus	1915—Minneapolis
1974—Tulsa	1942—Columbus	1914—Milwaukee
1973—Tulsa	1941—Columbus	1913—Milwaukee
1972—Evansville	1940—Louisville	1912—Minneapolis
1971—Denver	1939—Louisville	1911—Minneapolis
1970—Omaha	1938—Kansas City	1910—Minneapolis
1969—Omaha	1937—Columbus	1909—Louisville
1963-68—Did Not	1936—Milwaukee	1908—Indianapolis
Operate	1935—Minneapolis	1907—Columbus
1962—Louisville	1934—Columbus	1906—Columbus
1961—Louisville	1933—Columbus	1905—Columbus
1960—Louisville	1932—Minneapolis	1904—St. Paul
1959—Minneapolis	1931—St. Paul	1903—St. Paul
1958—Minneapolis	1930—Louisville	1902—Indianapolis
1957—Denver	1929—Kansas City	

Alliance Champs

Members of the 1988 Triple-A Alliance Champion Indianapolis Indians included front row, l to r, Mel Houston, Tim Hulett, Johnny Paredes, Rex Hudler, Jack Daugherty, Razor Shines, Mike Smith, clubhouse manager Billy Neely, stadium director Mike Tarrolly. Second row, president and general manager Max Schumacher, manager Joe Sparks, coach Mike Colbern, coach Nelson Norman, Nelson Santovenia, Wilfredo Tejada, Garrett Nago, pitching coach Joe Kerrigan, assistant general manager and publicity director Cal Burleson. Third row, Steve Shirley, Sergio Valdez, Bob Sebra, Jeff Fischer, Brian Holman, Randy Johnson, Gary Wayne, Kurt Kepshire, Joe Hesketh, Tim Barrett. Top row, groundskeeper Eddie Dick, ticket manager Mike Schneider, business manager Dan Stevens, Otis Nixon, Billy Moore, Ron Shepherd, Alonzo Powell, Mike Berger, trainer Tim McCormack, director of special projects Bruce Schmacher.

Top AA Performers

Lavell Freeman
...leading hitter

Luis delos Santos
...MVP

Bob Sebra
...126 K's

Buffalo achieve its attendance goal despite a club that finished third in the Eastern Division, 17 games behind Indianapolis.

Hoping for better numbers on the field, the Pittsburgh organization replaced Buffalo manager Rocky Bridges for 1989 with Terry Collins, the Pacific Coast League's 1988 manager of the year at Albuquerque.

On the field it was an amazing year, too, in its own way. Association clubs had a 187-131 victory margin over IL clubs.

Home runs and hits were down from 1987, and top pitching performances were up. Omaha's Luis Aquino no-hit the Columbus Clippers 2-0 on June 20. Indianapolis' Randy Johnson and Pat Pacillo combined to no-hit Nashville on Aug. 6, but lost 1-0 to the home team. On the next night in the same stadium, Nashville's Jack Armstrong no-hit the Indians and won 4-0.

Three in a row

Indianapolis won its third straight Association pennant. The Indians won their division by 16 games with an 89-53 record, the league's best winning percentage (.672) since Denver went 92-54 (.676) in 1980.

Then Indianapolis beat Omaha in four games in the best-of-5 league championship series. The Indians went on to win the Alliance title by beating International League champion Rochester in six games in a best-of-7 series.

Sparks earned a record fifth Casey Stengel Award as the Association's manager of the year. Named to the league's postseason all-star team were Indianapolis second baseman Johnny Paredes, outfielder Billy Moore and pitcher Bob Sebra.

Late surge nets title

Omaha, managed by Glenn Ezell, surged in the last two weeks to win the Western Division title by three games over Iowa. The Royals' Luis delos Santos was named the league's most valuable player after hitting .307 with a league-leading 87 RBIs.

Nashville, which underwent a number of managerial changes, slipped past Louisville and Buffalo with veteran Frank Lucchesi managing down the stretch, to take second place in the East. The Sounds' Van Snider led the Association in home runs with 23 and in total bases with 259.

Iowa, which never has had a league batting champion, finished with six of the top 10 hitters, led by No. 2 Bill Bathe (.312). The Cubs' Drew Hall was tops in saves with 19, and Dave Meier led in game-winning RBIs with 16.

Denver's Lavell Freeman hit safely in 17 of his last 18 games and won the batting title at .318, the lowest league-leading average since 1909, when Mike O'Neill of Minneapolis hit .196. The Zephyrs' Billy Bates led the Association in triples with 12.

Late in the season, young stars such as Reed, Omaha rookie pitcher Tom Gordon righthander Mike Harkey (Iowa) and infielder Gary Sheffield (Denver) burst onto the big league scene.

East	W	L	Pct.	GB
Indianapolis (Expos) .	89	53	.627	—
Nashville (Reds)	73	69	.514	15
Buffalo (Pirates)	72	70	.507	17
Louisville (Cards)	63	79	.444	26
West				
Omaha (Royals)	81	61	.570	—
Iowa (Cubs)	78	64	.549	3
Denver (Brewers)	72	69	.511	8½
Okla. City (Rangers) .	67	74	.475	13½

1988
Final
Standings

1988: General Information

Playoffs: Indianapolis defeated Omaha 3-1 in best-of-5 final for league championship; Indianapolis defeated Rochester 4-2 in best-of-7 Alliance Series.

Regular Season Attendance: Buffalo, 1,147,651; Louisville, 574,852; Denver, 357,003; Nashville, 317,695; Indianapolis, 293,721; Omaha, 287,096; Iowa, 266,845; Oklahoma City, 260,363.

Managers: Buffalo—Rocky Bridges; **Denver**—Duffy Dyer; **Indianapolis**—Joe Sparks; **Iowa**—Pete Mackanin; **Louisville**—Mike Jorgensen; **Nashville**—Jack Lind, Wayne Garland, Jim Hoff, George Scherger, Frank Lucchesi; **Oklahoma City**—Toby Harrah; **Omaha**—Glenn Ezell.

1988 Official All-Star Team: C—Bill Bathe, Iowa. **1B**—Luis delos Santos, Omaha. **2B**—Johnny Paredes, Indianapolis. **3B**—Tom O'Malley, Oklahoma City. **SS**—Felix Fermin, Buffalo. **OF**—Billy Moore, Indianapolis; Rolando Roomes, Iowa; Van Snider, Nashville. **DH**—German Rivera, Denver. **RHP**—Dorn Taylor, Buffalo; **LHP**—Norm Charlton, Nashville. **Most Valuable Player**—Luis delos Santos, Omaha. **Most Valuable Pitcher**—Bob Sebra, Indianapolis. **Manager of the Year**—Joe Sparks, Indianapolis.

Top 10 Major League Prospects (by Baseball America): 1. Mike Harkey, rhp, Iowa; **2.** Gary Sheffield, 3b, Denver; **3.** Randy Johnson, lhp, Indianapolis; **4.** Brian Holman, rhp, Indianapolis; **5.** Johnny Paredes, 2b, Indianapolis; **6.** Cris Carpenter, rhp, Louisville; **7.** Van Snider, of, Nashville; **8.** Felix Fermin, ss, Buffalo; **9.** Luis delos Santos, 1b, Omaha; **10.** Tom Prince, c, Buffalo.

1988: Batting, Pitching Statistics

CLUB BATTING

	AVG	G	AB	R	H	2B	3B	HR	BB	SO	SB
Iowa	.274	142	4847	661	1330	239	55	108	421	859	118
Denver	.273	141	4744	755	1295	226	55	108	547	809	117
Omaha	.264	142	4746	631	1252	212	50	67	477	785	145
Indianapolis	.260	142	4681	644	1218	241	34	77	439	830	173
Oklahoma City	.257	141	4665	573	1198	212	31	69	473	773	97
Buffalo	.256	142	4692	542	1200	193	31	89	457	766	122
Nashville	.245	142	4736	523	1161	196	39	62	421	797	118
Louisville	.238	142	4660	524	1108	211	36	51	452	779	158

CLUB PITCHING

	ERA	G	CG	SHO	SV	IP	H	R	ER	BB	SO
Indianapolis	2.96	142	13	17	49	1248	1051	486	411	462	966
Buffalo	3.09	142	29	12	34	1248	1145	523	428	424	695
Omaha	3.30	142	20	14	35	1259	1257	524	462	383	800
Nashville	3.51	142	22	9	33	1269	1153	575	495	487	965
Louisville	4.04	142	6	8	39	1241	1239	629	557	484	737
Oklahoma City	4.07	141	19	6	35	1238	1231	618	560	490	835
Denver	4.08	141	34	9	24	1229	1315	641	557	376	734
Iowa	4.12	142	19	9	39	1255	1246	646	574	505	831

INDIVIDUAL BATTING LEADERS
(Minimum 383 Plate Appearances)

	AVG	G	AB	R	H	2B	3B	HR	RBI	BB	SO	SB
*Freeman, Lavell, Den . . .	.318	111	384	54	122	26	7	5	59	44	71	10
Bathe, Bill, Iowa	.312	106	385	48	120	27	2	8	49	27	49	0
Delos Santos, Luis, Oma .	.307	136	535	62	164	25	4	6	87	40	79	2
Meier, Dave, Iowa	.305	125	456	69	139	19	7	20	83	41	74	4
Roomes, Rolando, Iowa . .	.301	112	419	65	126	19	5	16	66	26	134	15
Rivera, German, Den	.300	121	436	76	131	18	4	21	87	47	53	6
#Dascenzo, Doug, Iowa . .	.295	132	505	73	149	22	5	6	49	37	41	30
Paredes, Johnny, Ind . . .	.295	101	400	69	118	17	3	4	46	30	56	43
*Stephenson, Phil, Iowa . .	.293	118	426	69	125	28	11	22	81	50	76	9
*Smith, Dwight, Iowa	.293	129	505	76	148	26	3	9	48	54	90	25

* indicates lefthanded batter   # indicates switch hitter

INDIVIDUAL PITCHING LEADERS
(Minimum 114 Innings)

	W	L	ERA	G	GS	CG	SV	IP	H	R	ER	BB	SO
Taylor, Dorn, Buf	10	8	2.14	22	22	6	0	139	125	45	33	44	65
Fischer, Jeff, Ind	13	8	2.69	28	26	3	0	177	162	63	53	32	110
*Jeffcoat, Mike, OkC	9	5	2.80	22	22	6	0	157	137	53	49	41	95
Aquino, Luis, Omaha	8	3	2.85	25	16	1	0	129	106	43	41	50	93
Sebra, Bob, Ind	12	6	2.94	29	26	4	0	174	154	71	57	59	126
May, Scott, OkC	8	7	2.97	36	17	4	0	152	132	56	50	57	103
Armstrong, Jack, Nvl	5	5	3.00	17	17	4	0	120	84	44	40	38	116
*Charlton, Norm, Nvl	11	10	3.02	27	27	8	0	182	149	69	61	56	161
Kramer, Randy, Buf	10	8	3.13	28	28	6	0	198	161	85	69	50	120
Knudson, Mark, Den	11	8	3.40	24	22	6	0	164	180	67	62	33	66

* indicates lefthanded pitcher

BUFFALO

BATTING	AVG	G	AB	R	H	2B	3B	HR	RBI	BB	SO	SB
#Cangelosi, John, of	.331	37	145	23	48	6	0	0	10	19	19	14
*Destrade, Orestes, 1b ...	.271	77	273	37	74	16	1	12	42	44	67	2
*Distefano, Benny, of	.263	135	482	69	127	26	1	19	63	50	58	6
Fermin, Felix, ss	.261	87	352	38	92	11	1	0	31	17	18	1
Gonzalez, Denny, 3b	.296	75	267	37	79	14	2	8	39	34	62	9
*Gregg, Tommy, of	.294	72	252	34	74	12	0	6	27	25	26	7
Hostetler, Dave, dh-1b ..	.187	84	225	21	42	8	4	4	29	24	67	0
Khalifa, Sammy, 3b	.228	66	215	30	49	9	3	5	21	31	38	3
#Little, Bryan, 2b	.259	46	135	14	35	8	0	1	7	14	11	2
Little, Scott, of	.063	4	16	0	1	0	0	0	1	0	4	1
Milligan, Randy, 1b	.276	63	221	37	61	15	3	2	30	36	40	1
Pedrique, Al, 2b-ss	.307	61	218	23	67	14	2	1	22	13	20	0
Prince, Tom, c	.260	86	304	35	79	16	0	14	42	23	53	3
*Reboulet, Jim, 2b	.280	79	264	29	74	4	0	0	13	25	22	26
Rodriguez, Ruben, c	.256	24	82	4	21	3	1	0	2	3	11	0
Romano, Tom, of	.264	79	280	27	74	9	4	5	19	17	43	11
Rossy, Rico, ss-3b	.246	68	187	12	46	4	0	1	20	13	17	1
Sax, Dave, c	.223	38	103	7	23	3	0	3	11	14	21	1
#Tatis, Bernie, of	.234	124	431	50	101	14	9	6	45	45	88	27

PITCHING	W	L	ERA	G	GS	CG	SV	IP	H	R	ER	BB	SO
*Copp, Bill	0	0	10.38	1	1	0	0	4	8	6	5	2	1
Easley, Logan	1	5	3.93	28	0	0	2	69	69	36	30	28	28
Fansler, Stan	3	7	5.67	15	15	0	0	81	100	58	51	38	28
*Garcia, Miguel	6	2	2.58	25	1	0	2	66	71	26	19	21	34
Gideon, Brett	1	6	3.64	24	0	0	9	42	33	17	17	19	41
Johnson, Dave	15	12	3.51	29	29	9	0	192	213	93	75	55	90
Kramer, Randy	10	8	3.13	28	28	6	0	198	161	85	69	50	120
*Madden, Morris	5	6	3.48	21	14	1	1	109	84	55	42	65	56
Medvin, Scott	5	4	2.41	39	0	0	12	56	38	18	15	25	49
Melton, Larry	1	4	4.36	6	6	0	0	33	29	16	16	18	21
Neidlinger, Jim	0	0	6.23	3	0	0	0	4	7	3	3	1	4
Palacios, Vicente	3	0	1.99	5	5	1	0	32	26	7	7	5	23
*Patterson, Bob	2	0	2.32	4	4	1	0	31	26	12	8	4	20
Reed, Rick	5	2	1.64	10	9	3	0	77	62	15	14	12	50
*Rucker, Dave	0	1	0.88	16	0	0	4	31	16	8	3	18	16
Taylor, Dorn	10	8	2.14	22	22	6	0	139	125	45	33	44	65
Walker, Mike	2	3	2.78	8	8	2	0	55	52	18	17	8	26
Wilmet, Paul	3	2	1.24	19	0	0	4	29	25	5	4	11	19

DENVER

BATTING	AVG	G	AB	R	H	2B	3B	HR	RBI	BB	SO	SB
*Adduci, Jim, of	.265	13	49	3	13	4	0	0	5	0	6	1
#Bates, Billy, 2b	.258	119	472	74	122	16	12	4	44	51	49	29
Brown, Todd, of	.211	24	76	9	16	4	0	1	8	11	6	0
*Cartwright, Alan, 1b-of ..	.250	3	8	1	2	0	0	1	3	0	3	0
Diaz, Kiki, ss	.234	79	278	44	65	7	0	0	21	40	36	8
#Felder, Mike, of	.269	20	78	10	21	4	1	0	5	5	10	8
Freeman, Lavell, of	.318	111	384	54	122	26	7	5	59	44	71	10
*Hamilton, Darryl, of ...	.325	72	277	55	90	11	4	0	32	39	28	23
Kiefer, Steve, 3b-2b	.214	79	294	47	63	11	8	10	45	27	73	6
Komminsk, Brad, of	.239	105	348	55	83	18	3	16	57	49	96	7
O'Brien, Charlie, c	.281	48	153	16	43	5	0	4	25	19	19	1
Pyznarski, Tim, dh-1b ...	.291	102	381	67	111	26	4	10	66	48	105	4
Reynolds, Ronn, c	.240	83	271	36	65	13	1	9	33	24	63	1
Rivera, German, 3b-1b ..	.300	121	436	76	131	18	4	21	87	47	53	6
*Robidoux, Billy Joe, 1b ..	.292	70	240	43	70	24	0	8	42	41	32	1
Rodriguez, Angel, c-1b ...	.241	10	29	7	7	1	0	0	0	1	6	0
Schroeder, Bill, c	.235	6	17	4	4	2	1	0	3	1	6	0
#Scott, Donnie, c	.206	29	68	3	14	2	0	0	3	8	4	0
Sheffield, Gary, 3b-ss ..	.344	57	212	42	73	9	5	9	54	21	22	8
Smith, D.L., ss	.326	15	46	11	15	4	0	1	9	7	13	0
#Smith, Keith, ss-2b	.270	70	211	29	57	8	0	0	22	28	22	1
Stanicek, Steve, of	.304	27	92	18	28	6	0	2	19	10	9	0
Walters, Darryel, of	.247	105	324	51	80	7	5	9	57	26	77	3

PITCHING	W	L	ERA	G	GS	CG	SV	IP	H	R	ER	BB	SO
Aldrich, Jay	3	7	4.63	50	0	0	10	72	83	40	37	20	53
August, Don	4	1	3.52	10	10	3	0	72	79	37	28	14	58

BATTING

R—Billy Moore, Indianapolis 88
H—Luis delos Santos, Omaha 164
TB—Van Snider, Nashville 259
2B—Billy Moore, Indianapolis 34
3B—Billy Bates, Denver 12
HR—Van Snider, Nashville 23
RBI—Luis delos Santos, Omaha 87
—German Rivera, Denver 87
GWRBI—Dave Meier, Iowa 16
SH—Mike Loggins, Omaha 9
SF—Tim Hulett, Indianapolis 9
BB—Dan Rohn, Oklahoma City 81
IBB—Phil Stephenson, Iowa 9
—Van Snider, Nashville 9
HBP—Benny Distefano, Buffalo 12
SO—Rolando Roomes, Iowa 134
SB—Lenny Harris, Nashville 45
CS—Lenny Harris, Nashville 21
Slg. Pct.—Phil Stephenson, Iowa 566
OB Pct.—Lavell Freeman, Denver 385

PITCHING

G—Gibson Alba, Louisville 58
GS—Len Damian, Iowa 29
—Dave Johnson, Buffalo 29
CG—Dave Johnson, Buffalo 9
ShO—Jeff Peterek, Denver 3
Sv—Drew Hall, Iowa 19
W—Dave Johnson, Buffalo 15
L—John Martin, Louisville 13
IP—Randy Kramer, Buffalo 198
H—Dave Johnson, Buffalo 213
R—Dave Masters, Iowa 106
HR—Len Damian, Iowa 16
—Hugh Kemp, Nashville 16
BB—Dave Masters, Iowa 96
HB—Al Hargesheimer, Omaha 12
SO—Norm Charlton, Nashville 161
WP—Norm Charlton, Nashville 13
Bk—Randy Johnson, Indianapolis 20

	W	L	ERA	G	GS	CG	SV	IP	H	R	ER	BB	SO
Birkbeck, Mike	4	1	2.01	5	5	4	0	45	30	10	10	10	30
Bosio, Chris	1	0	3.86	2	2	1	0	14	13	6	6	4	12
Ciardi, Mark	2	4	6.63	8	8	0	0	38	59	30	28	10	17
Clutterbuck, Bryan	9	3	3.44	20	18	5	0	131	133	64	50	32	88
Filer, Tom	4	2	2.10	8	7	3	0	56	40	14	13	9	34
Knudson, Mark	11	8	3.40	24	22	6	0	164	180	67	62	33	66
Madrid, Alex	5	2	4.06	31	4	1	4	89	95	47	40	20	52
Meagher, Adrian	5	7	4.52	17	14	2	0	82	87	48	41	42	55
*Miglio, John	4	6	4.60	46	0	0	1	47	39	26	24	22	38
*Mirabella, Paul	0	0	0.93	8	0	0	1	10	9	3	1	4	7
Mooneyham, Bill	1	3	9.00	5	5	0	0	20	31	24	20	17	4
*Nieves, Juan	0	2	2.29	5	3	0	0	20	11	5	5	7	14
Pacella, John	1	0	8.22	2	1	0	0	8	8	7	7	6	3
Peterek, Jeff	7	6	3.95	19	19	7	0	130	140	62	57	34	76
Romanick, Ron	3	8	5.20	16	14	2	0	88	118	66	51	26	40
*Scarpetta, Dan	2	5	5.58	8	7	0	0	50	62	35	31	18	29
Smith, Keith	0	0	21.00	2	0	0	0	3	10	7	7	1	1
Stoddard, Bob	0	1	5.25	8	2	0	1	24	26	17	14	12	7
Watkins, Tim	6	3	4.10	47	0	0	7	68	62	36	31	35	50

INDIANAPOLIS

BATTING	AVG	G	AB	R	H	2B	3B	HR	RBI	BB	SO	SB
#Bailey, Mark, c	.235	20	51	10	12	2	0	2	6	17	13	0
Berger, Mike, of-dh	.235	40	81	10	19	6	2	0	5	10	14	2
#Candaele, Casey, ss-2b .	.264	60	239	23	63	11	6	2	36	12	20	5
#Daugherty, Jack, 1b-of . .	.285	137	481	82	137	33	2	6	67	56	50	18
Fitzgerald, Mike, c	.250	32	96	12	24	6	1	1	13	9	22	1
*Frobel, Doug, of	.176	8	17	3	3	0	0	0	1	0	10	1
*Hill, Orsino, of	.167	3	6	0	1	0	0	0	1	0	3	0
Houston, Jim, ss	.210	33	81	8	17	4	1	0	5	1	12	3
Hudler, Rex, of-inf	.303	67	234	36	71	11	3	7	25	10	35	14
Hulett, Tim, 3b	.234	126	427	36	100	29	2	7	59	34	106	2
Moore, Billy, of	.285	135	467	88	133	34	2	17	80	65	101	5
Motley, Darryl, of	.329	21	70	13	23	4	0	2	17	7	5	2
#Nago, Garrett, c	.182	6	11	0	2	0	0	0	0	2	6	0
#Nixon, Otis, of	.285	67	235	52	67	6	3	0	19	43	28	40
Noce, Paul, ss-2b (77 Iowa)	.235	106	340	42	80	11	4	4	24	39	70	10
Norman, Nelson, ss	.220	68	159	14	35	1	0	2	18	12	9	0
Paredes, Johnny, 2b	.295	101	400	69	118	17	3	4	46	30	56	43
*Pevey, Marty, c	.227	48	119	16	27	4	1	3	16	8	20	1
Powell, Alonzo, of-c	.262	88	282	31	74	18	3	4	39	28	72	10
*Reed, Jeff, c	.318	8	22	1	7	3	0	0	1	2	2	0
Santovenia, Nelson, c . .	.308	27	91	9	28	5	0	2	13	4	16	0

	AVG	G	AB	R	H	2B	3B	HR	RBI	BB	SO	SB
Shepherd, Ron, of	.227	30	110	8	25	6	0	2	17	4	24	1
#Shines, Razor, dh-1b	.263	118	358	47	94	14	0	12	55	41	56	8
*Taylor, Dwight, of	.254	58	177	29	45	9	1	0	12	10	36	12
Tejada, Wil, c	.233	59	172	16	40	11	1	1	19	7	34	1
*Winningham, Herm, of ...	.200	3	10	2	2	0	1	0	1	0	3	1

PITCHING	W	L	ERA	G	GS	CG	SV	IP	H	R	ER	BB	SO
Barrett, Tim	8	1	1.99	42	0	0	6	72	54	19	16	29	51
Dopson, John	0	0	3.50	3	3	0	0	18	19	7	7	5	15
Fischer, Jeff	13	8	2.69	28	26	3	0	177	162	63	53	32	110
Gardner, Mark	4	2	2.77	13	13	3	0	84	65	30	26	32	71
*Hesketh, Joe	0	0	3.27	8	0	0	2	11	10	5	4	5	16
Holman, Brian	8	1	2.36	14	13	2	0	91	78	26	24	30	70
*Johnson, Randy	8	7	3.26	20	19	0	0	113	85	52	41	72	111
Kepshire, Kurt	8	4	3.45	45	0	0	7	63	64	28	24	30	46
*Livingston, Dennis	0	0	13.50	3	0	0	0	3	6	6	4	5	1
Pacillo, Pat (13 Nvl) ...	3	4	3.86	22	12	0	0	75	76	42	32	30	62
Perez, Pascual	0	0	1.17	2	2	0	0	8	4	1	1	4	7
*Sauveur, Rich	7	4	2.43	43	3	0	10	81	60	26	22	28	58
Sebra, Bob	12	6	2.94	29	26	4	0	174	154	71	57	59	126
*Shirley, Steve	3	6	2.86	35	0	0	9	50	44	18	16	24	56
Smith, Mike	5	1	2.57	32	2	1	5	63	40	22	18	14	55
Valdez, Sergio	5	4	3.43	14	14	0	0	84	80	38	32	28	61
Waddell, Tom	1	1	2.93	10	1	0	1	15	14	5	5	2	9
*Wayne, Gary	0	0	6.14	8	0	0	1	7	9	5	5	3	6
Youmans, Floyd	0	0	3.50	1	1	0	0	3	2	1	1	1	1

IOWA

BATTING	AVG	G	AB	R	H	2B	3B	HR	RBI	BB	SO	SB
Bathe, Bill, c	.312	106	385	48	120	27	2	8	49	27	49	0
#Berryhill, Damon, c	.219	21	73	11	16	5	1	2	11	7	21	0
Crabbe, Bruce, 3b	.253	91	273	31	69	13	1	4	32	34	37	1
#Dascenzo, Doug, of	.295	132	505	73	149	22	5	6	49	37	41	30
*Grace, Mark, 1b	.254	21	67	11	17	4	0	0	14	13	4	1
#Guinn, Brian, ss	.247	116	377	36	93	11	5	7	50	41	53	9
#Lockwood, Rick, 3b (16 Lou)	.186	44	113	10	21	5	0	3	14	6	25	0
Meier, Dave, of	.305	125	456	69	139	19	7	20	83	41	74	4
Roomes, Rolando, of	.301	112	419	65	126	19	5	16	66	26	134	15
*Smith, Dwight, of	.293	129	505	76	148	26	9	9	48	54	90	25
*Stephenson, Phil, 1b	.293	118	426	69	125	28	11	22	81	50	76	9
Tabor, Greg, 2b	.267	130	469	53	125	29	5	5	54	19	85	9
#Valdez, Julio, 2b-ss	.188	8	16	1	3	0	0	0	1	1	1	0
*Varsho, Gary, of	.278	66	234	46	65	16	5	4	26	18	38	8
Wrona, Rick, c	.264	83	193	28	51	9	0	2	23	17	34	0

PITCHING	W	L	ERA	G	GS	CG	SV	IP	H	R	ER	BB	SO
Bielecki, Mike	3	2	2.63	23	3	1	5	55	34	19	16	20	50
Capel, Mike	3	2	3.43	32	2	0	3	58	60	24	23	23	49
Damian, Len	12	11	4.06	29	29	5	0	186	201	91	84	41	100
Danek, Bill	1	2	7.23	4	4	0	0	19	27	16	15	10	11
*Hall, Drew	4	3	2.34	49	0	0	19	65	41	20	17	26	75
Harkey, Mike	7	2	3.55	12	12	3	0	79	55	36	31	33	62
Hirsch, Jeff	2	1	4.14	28	0	0	4	41	56	21	19	18	33
Kopf, Dave	0	1	6.48	11	0	0	0	17	21	12	12	16	8
*Kraemer, Joe	3	3	4.50	20	1	0	1	26	19	14	13	17	26
Landrum, Bill	1	0	2.95	9	0	0	3	21	13	7	7	6	22
Masters, Dave	14	8	5.22	28	28	5	0	167	164	106	97	96	101
*Oelkers, Bryan (14 Ind) ...	6	7	6.02	23	20	0	0	87	91	62	58	54	61
Parmenter, Gary	3	7	4.17	34	7	1	3	86	80	45	40	41	47
*Perry, Pat	0	0	0.00	2	0	0	0	3	0	0	0	4	3
Pico, Jeff	5	2	2.24	10	10	1	0	68	67	28	17	18	40
Renfroe, Laddie	1	3	4.88	16	0	0	0	24	28	13	13	11	12
Sanderson, Scott	1	0	4.73	3	3	0	0	13	13	7	7	2	4
*Scherrer, Bill	1	0	4.91	10	0	0	1	15	23	12	8	7	12
*Strode, Les (6 Lou)	2	3	4.87	24	2	0	0	61	64	35	33	27	35
Surhoff, Rich	0	2	4.76	6	0	0	0	6	8	4	3	1	4
Tewksbury, Bob	4	2	3.76	10	10	2	0	67	73	28	28	10	43
Williams, Roger	10	9	4.20	28	27	1	0	167	176	93	78	75	91
Zarranz, Fernando	1	0	9.64	3	0	0	0	5	8	6	5	2	7

LOUISVILLE

BATTING	AVG	G	AB	R	H	2B	3B	HR	RBI	BB	SO	SB
Agostinelli, Sal, c	.145	27	62	7	9	0	0	0	3	3	7	0
*Alicea, Luis, 2b-ss	.277	49	191	21	53	11	6	1	21	11	21	8
*Booker, Rod, 2b-ss	.259	111	370	50	96	12	1	4	31	45	44	15
*Cole, Alex, of	.232	120	392	44	91	7	8	0	24	42	59	40
Dougherty, Mark, 2b	.224	54	107	15	24	6	2	1	8	12	24	3
Fitzgerald, Mike, 1b	.241	106	382	33	92	14	1	10	50	12	69	1
Green, David, of	.216	59	190	15	41	5	1	1	18	16	39	1
*Hocutt, Mike, 3b	.083	6	12	1	1	0	0	0	0	1	4	0
*Jones, Tim, ss	.257	103	370	63	95	21	2	6	38	36	56	39
*Krenchicki, Wayne, dh-3b	.195	18	41	4	8	1	0	0	2	2	9	1
*Laga, Mike, 1b-dh	.204	13	49	4	10	2	0	1	5	6	5	0
Lindeman, Jim, of-1b	.252	73	262	32	66	18	4	2	30	33	59	2
Lyons, Bill, of-inf	.265	104	268	39	71	11	4	2	30	37	45	7
*Morris, John, of-dh	.100	13	40	3	4	0	0	0	0	2	8	0
Murphy, John, of	.250	119	348	43	87	23	1	4	32	46	58	32

	AVG	G	AB	R	H	2B	3B	HR	RBI	BB	SO	SB
*Puzey, Jim, c	.250	23	60	6	15	1	0	1	4	8	12	0
Robinson, Mike, of	.156	27	32	3	5	1	0	0	0	4	6	0
*Ryal, Mark, of	.256	94	336	35	86	25	1	11	62	19	42	1
#Silver, Roy, of	.237	19	38	3	9	3	1	0	1	0	7	0
Stephens, Carl Ray, c	.189	115	355	26	67	13	2	3	25	45	78	2
*Walker, Duane, of-dh	.276	31	76	7	21	6	0	1	18	8	15	0
Wilson, Craig, 3b	.256	133	497	59	127	27	2	1	46	54	46	6

PITCHING	W	L	ERA	G	GS	CG	SV	IP	H	R	ER	BB	SO
Agostinelli, Sal	0	0	1.93	5	0	0	0	5	3	1	1	1	1
*Alba, Gibson	4	0	3.89	58	0	0	2	81	66	37	35	40	80
Arnold, Scott	0	3	9.72	3	3	0	0	8	12	12	9	12	5
Bargar, Greg	4	2	4.27	9	6	1	0	46	46	26	22	19	29
Botelho, Derek	4	6	4.33	22	8	0	0	69	80	38	33	18	36
Buonantony, Rich	3	5	3.50	10	10	0	0	62	57	31	24	35	31
Carpenter, Cris	6	2	2.87	13	13	1	0	88	81	28	28	26	45
*Conroy, Tim	3	5	5.50	13	12	0	0	52	49	36	32	33	49
Costello, John	1	1	1.84	20	0	0	11	29	17	7	6	7	34
Cox, Danny	0	0	3.09	3	3	0	0	12	11	7	4	6	7
Grapenthin, Dick	3	6	3.63	45	0	0	10	69	67	30	28	21	30
Kinzer, Matt	6	2	3.71	46	0	0	6	80	73	34	33	24	53
Leopold, Jim	0	1	12.42	8	1	0	0	17	34	24	23	6	5
*Magrane, Joe	2	1	3.15	4	4	1	0	20	19	7	7	7	18
Martin, John	7	13	4.32	28	25	1	0	154	158	83	74	49	84
*Mathews, Greg	0	1	7.31	5	4	0	0	16	15	14	13	9	8
*Meridith, Ron	0	0	9.00	4	0	0	0	4	7	4	4	1	0
O'Neal, Randy	3	5	3.71	10	10	1	0	61	59	30	25	21	33
Oyster, Jeff	3	7	4.50	14	12	0	0	76	100	43	38	27	32
*Peters, Steve	1	1	3.67	22	0	0	2	27	25	11	11	16	16
*Rajsich, Dave	6	8	2.86	53	5	1	8	104	98	39	33	40	64
Terry, Scott	0	0	0.00	3	3	0	0	5	2	0	0	1	1
Tunnell, Lee	6	8	3.86	24	20	0	0	135	136	69	58	55	60

NASHVILLE

BATTING	AVG	G	AB	R	H	2B	3B	HR	RBI	BB	SO	SB
Barnes, Sk, 1b-of (21 Buf)	.253	122	379	47	96	16	0	6	39	17	47	15
Boever, Dan, of	.235	117	323	43	76	16	0	3	24	43	38	1
Brown, Marty, 3b	.264	135	484	50	128	15	4	7	55	51	111	15
DeFrancesco, Tony, c	.210	27	62	7	13	1	0	0	2	7	16	1
Earl, Scott, inf-of	.239	113	330	40	79	13	3	0	24	35	64	16
*Finley, Brian, of	.154	4	13	2	2	0	0	0	2	1	4	0
*Garcia, Leo, of	.258	48	178	21	46	5	5	1	17	22	21	4
Gwosdz, Doug, c	.224	30	76	7	17	1	0	2	10	11	20	0
*Harris, Lenny, 2b	.277	107	422	46	117	20	2	0	35	22	36	45
Jones, Tracy, of	.500	2	6	2	3	1	0	0	1	1	0	0
Klipstein, Dave, of	.149	34	94	6	14	1	0	1	3	8	18	1
McClendon, Lloyd, of	.143	2	7	0	1	0	0	0	0	1	1	0
McGriff, Terry, c	.216	35	97	8	21	3	1	1	12	10	15	0
*Milner, Eddie, of	.214	18	70	10	15	2	0	0	3	4	7	1
*Monda, Greg, 1b	.264	54	178	15	47	10	2	0	14	6	28	1
#Oester, Ron, 2b	.189	12	37	4	7	1	0	0	3	3	8	0
Oliver, Joe, c	.205	73	220	19	45	7	2	4	24	18	39	0
Pryor, Buddy, c	.283	25	60	6	17	5	0	2	7	7	20	2
#Quinones, Luis, ss	.276	114	417	42	115	28	6	9	53	29	51	3
*Roenicke, Ron, of	.215	83	237	34	51	7	3	0	16	54	41	8
*Snider, Van, of	.290	135	525	72	152	22	8	23	73	22	96	5
#Tanner, Eddie, 1b-3b	.238	94	256	28	61	15	1	2	29	23	19	0
Vargas, Hedi, 1b-dh	.240	36	121	7	29	6	2	2	12	14	25	0

PITCHING	W	L	ERA	G	GS	CG	SV	IP	H	R	ER	BB	SO
Armstrong, Jack	5	5	3.00	17	17	4	0	120	84	44	40	38	116
*Birtsas, Tim	1	3	3.08	8	8	1	0	50	33	20	17	21	48
Brown, Keith	6	3	1.90	12	12	3	0	85	72	33	18	28	43
*Charlton, Norm	11	10	3.02	27	27	8	0	182	149	69	61	56	161
Dibble, Rob	2	1	2.31	31	0	0	13	35	21	9	9	14	41
Gray, Jeff	8	5	1.97	42	0	0	5	73	59	17	16	18	73
Jefferson, Jim	1	1	6.91	18	0	0	1	27	30	22	21	12	19
*Jones, Mike	5	4	2.54	35	4	1	2	64	46	21	18	32	41
Kemp, Hugh	13	10	4.30	28	27	4	0	176	187	89	84	68	107
Lopez, Rob	3	4	3.95	22	7	0	0	68	62	30	30	26	59
Mitchell, Charlie	4	6	2.18	23	6	0	5	78	66	28	19	31	69
Oliverio, Steve	2	6	5.12	28	8	0	0	84	101	62	48	37	54
Robinson, Ron	0	0	7.36	2	2	0	0	4	4	3	3	3	4
Roesler, Mike	3	2	5.01	32	0	0	1	41	44	25	23	27	31
Sierra, Candy	5	5	4.68	13	13	1	0	73	82	41	38	36	40
Snell, Nate	3	1	3.71	13	4	0	1	51	51	23	21	12	17
St. Claire, Randy (27 Ind)	0	3	2.68	36	0	0	13	40	35	15	12	9	27
Williams, Frank	0	0	9.00	2	0	0	0	3	3	3	3	2	1

OKLAHOMA CITY

BATTING	AVG	G	AB	R	H	2B	3B	HR	RBI	BB	SO	SB
Alyea, Brant, dh	.185	7	27	2	5	1	0	1	4	1	7	0
Bootay, Kevin, of	.280	39	132	17	37	3	0	0	8	7	16	7
#Browne, Jerry, 2b	.252	76	286	45	72	15	2	5	34	37	29	14
*Easler, Mike, dh	.714	2	7	0	5	2	0	0	2	2	0	0
Garbey, Barbaro, of-dh	.308	67	263	30	81	16	0	5	41	8	26	6

	AVG	G	AB	R	H	2B	3B	HR	RBI	BB	SO	SB
Gonzalez, Otto, c	.240	87	246	28	59	8	0	2	19	36	65	1
*Jones, Ruppert, dh-of	.253	50	154	23	39	8	1	7	30	17	23	8
*Kemp, Steve, of-1b	.273	37	121	12	33	6	0	2	19	11	22	1
Klein, Larry, ss-2b	.246	102	224	35	55	9	0	2	25	21	38	6
Kunkel, Jeff, ss-of	.217	56	203	28	44	11	4	5	21	12	50	7
Landrum, Tito, of	.253	69	229	29	58	6	6	3	25	24	44	7
*Marte, Alex, of	.254	39	122	18	31	3	2	0	10	16	13	2
*McDowell, Oddibe, of	.286	18	70	9	20	3	1	1	6	8	10	4
Merrifield, Bill, of-1b	.222	90	261	27	58	10	1	4	26	19	42	0
Millay, Gar, of	.211	18	71	5	15	3	0	2	7	0	11	0
Nichols, Reid, 1b-of	.241	38	133	19	32	6	0	2	19	13	19	3
*O'Malley, Tom, 3b	.291	138	522	68	152	26	4	9	72	62	77	2
*Rohn, Dan, 2b-ss	.257	133	409	60	105	19	6	2	34	81	57	7
Roman, Ray, c	.143	29	70	3	10	0	0	1	4	2	24	0
See, Larry, 1b-c	.261	89	329	34	86	18	2	12	55	19	52	1
*St. Laurent, Jim, of	.263	132	457	51	120	27	0	4	40	41	73	16
Steels, James, of	.313	37	144	21	45	7	2	0	11	10	31	5
*Tolentino, Jose, 1b	.214	48	131	6	28	4	0	0	8	20	20	0
Werner, Don, of	.286	2	7	1	2	0	0	0	1	0	0	0
Wine, Robbie, c	.128	16	47	2	6	1	0	0	1	6	22	0

PITCHING	W	L	ERA	G	GS	CG	SV	IP	H	R	ER	BB	SO
*Alvarez, Wilson	1	1	3.78	5	3	0	0	17	17	8	7	6	9
Anderson, Scott	4	6	4.55	38	10	0	2	97	101	51	49	49	44
Cecena, Jose	0	0	6.00	5	0	0	2	3	6	2	2	0	3
*Fossas, Tony	3	0	2.84	52	0	0	4	67	64	21	21	16	42
*Hayward, Ray	3	2	3.86	8	8	0	0	42	36	21	18	18	31
Henry, Dwayne	5	5	5.59	46	3	0	7	76	57	51	47	54	98
*Hoffman, Guy	3	2	3.07	7	7	0	0	41	40	14	14	11	26
Hurst, Jon	0	0	10.80	1	1	0	0	2	1	2	2	5	2
*Jeffcoat, Mike	9	5	2.80	22	22	6	0	157	137	53	49	41	95
May, Scott	8	7	2.97	36	17	4	0	152	132	56	50	57	103
McMurtry, Craig	2	5	4.35	9	9	2	0	50	55	27	24	21	35
Mielke, Gary	6	5	2.87	38	0	0	13	60	50	21	19	22	42
*Odekirk, Rick	4	8	6.25	19	16	0	0	85	110	69	59	33	38
Pavlas, Dave	3	1	4.47	13	8	0	0	52	59	29	26	28	40
Taylor, Billy	4	8	5.49	20	12	1	1	82	98	55	50	35	42
*Vande Berg, Ed	3	2	3.69	26	0	0	3	46	41	20	19	11	47
Vaughn, Dewayne	4	6	4.81	14	14	3	0	86	105	51	46	22	45
Whitaker, Darrell	1	5	3.99	32	0	0	3	47	53	25	21	14	23
Witt, Bobby	4	6	4.34	11	11	3	0	77	69	42	37	47	70

OMAHA

BATTING	AVG	G	AB	R	H	2B	3B	HR	RBI	BB	SO	SB
#Biancalana, Buddy, ss-2b	.248	91	294	36	73	16	4	1	37	35	66	17
Bilardello, Dann, c	.243	71	235	27	57	14	0	8	45	7	35	0
Capra, Nick, of	.289	93	346	53	100	11	6	1	43	50	49	28
Castro, Jose, 3b	.270	112	385	62	104	17	3	10	44	49	49	0
Citari, Joe, 1b	.189	41	111	16	21	5	0	3	14	17	25	1
Delos Santos, Luis, 1b	.307	136	535	62	164	25	4	6	87	40	79	2
Dodd, Tom, dh-of	.271	82	273	38	74	22	1	7	35	21	47	1
*Eisenreich, Jim, of	.289	36	142	28	41	8	3	4	14	9	20	9
Jirschele, Mike, 3b	.167	7	18	2	3	0	0	0	0	3	3	0
#Johnson, Rondin, 2b	.262	121	465	48	122	13	3	1	41	25	55	13
*Loggins, Mike, of	.245	130	425	44	104	17	8	2	42	54	76	22
Macfarlane, Mike, c	.237	21	76	8	18	7	2	2	8	4	15	0
#Madison, Scotti, of-1b	.240	36	104	14	25	4	3	2	12	17	20	1
Morris, Angel, c	.125	3	8	0	1	0	0	0	0	1	1	0
#Owen, Dave, ss-3b	.267	115	352	44	94	11	4	3	34	59	67	14
Owen, Larry, c	.214	62	196	35	42	10	0	9	30	31	51	1
*Schulz, Jeff, of-dh	.287	101	359	37	103	20	3	5	41	17	47	1
Thurman, Gary, of	.251	106	422	77	106	12	6	3	40	38	80	35

PITCHING	W	L	ERA	G	GS	CG	SV	IP	H	R	ER	BB	SO
*Acker, Larry	0	1	10.38	6	2	0	0	13	22	15	15	2	10
Anderson, Rick	7	4	2.62	14	14	4	0	100	92	37	29	23	54
Aquino, Luis	8	3	2.85	25	16	1	0	129	106	43	41	50	93
*Buchanan, Bob	5	1	2.37	47	0	0	6	76	70	21	20	29	44
DeJesus, Jose	2	3	3.44	7	7	3	0	50	44	22	19	14	57
Fireovid, Steve	11	6	4.27	25	24	2	0	139	169	72	66	30	59
*Gleaton, Jerry Don	4	2	1.45	15	0	0	0	37	30	7	6	14	40
Gordon, Tom	3	0	1.33	3	0	0	0	20	11	3	3	15	29
Hargesheimer, Al	6	9	4.02	24	23	1	0	134	150	68	60	44	78
Luecken, Rick	5	0	2.03	26	0	0	9	40	45	10	9	15	27
Montgomery, Jeff	1	2	1.91	20	0	0	13	28	15	6	6	15	23
Mullen, Tom	2	2	3.88	32	2	0	1	67	71	34	29	23	39
*Sanchez, Zip	7	4	2.91	15	15	3	0	102	102	36	33	36	85
Swaggerty, Bill	10	5	3.43	20	16	2	1	121	123	57	46	27	30
Thompson, Rich	6	7	2.90	17	12	4	2	96	94	36	31	15	46
Vasquez, Aquedo	0	0	9.00	2	0	0	0	4	9	4	4	2	1
Welchel, Don	4	11	3.90	37	8	0	3	97	97	49	42	32	71

Rochester flies high on Wings of Red

By PATTI SINGER

The Baltimore Orioles started the 1988 season with a major league record 21 straight losses, and ended it with a franchise record for defeats. But on the shores of Lake Ontario, the Orioles' future took shape.

The Rochester Red Wings, Baltimore's Triple-A affiliate since 1961 but losers for most of the decade of the '80s, returned to the top of the International League under manager of the year Johnny Oates. They won the IL's Western Division and the pennant, defeating Eastern Division champion Tidewater in a best-of-5 series.

Rochester last won the pennant in 1976, and last won the Governors' Cup, which then went to the winner of the playoffs, in 1974.

It was expected that Baltimore would stake its future on third baseman Craig Worthington, the IL's most valuable player; center fielder Steve Finley, who was rookie of the year and the league's only .300 hitter after beginning the season in Class A; and pitchers Pete Harnisch and Bob Milacki.

A year of change

The Red Wings rise to first place wasn't the only thing new about the league in 1988.

The IL and American Association formed the Triple-A Alliance, and played a number of regular season games against each other. The IL lost the season series decisively, 187-131.

League Champions

(Playoff Champions, Where Applicable)

(Since 1900)

1988—Rochester	1958—Montreal	1928—Rochester
1987—Columbus	1957—Buffalo	1927—Buffalo
1986—Richmond	1956—Rochester	1926—Toronto
1985—Tidewater	1955—Rochester	1925—Baltimore
1984—Pawtucket	1954—Syracuse	1924—Baltimore
1983—Tidewater	1953—Montreal	1923—Baltimore
1982—Richmond	1952—Rochester	1922—Baltimore
1981—Columbus	1951—Montreal	1921—Baltimore
1980—Columbus	1950—Baltimore	1920—Baltimore
1979—Columbus	1949—Montreal	1919—Baltimore
1978—Richmond	1948—Montreal	1918—Toronto
1977—Charleston	1947—Syracuse	1917—Toronto
1976—Syracuse	1946—Montreal	1916—Buffalo
1975—Tidewater	1945—Newark	1915—Buffalo
1974—Rochester	1944—Baltimore	1914—Providence
1973—Pawtucket	1943—Syracuse	1913—Newark
1972—Tidewater	1942—Syracuse	1912—Toronto
1971—Rochester	1941—Montreal	1911—Rochester
1970—Syracuse	1940—Newark	1910—Rochester
1969—Syracuse	1939—Rochester	1909—Rochester
1968—Jacksonville	1938—Newark	1908—Baltimore
1967—Toledo	1937—Newark	1907—Toronto
1966—Toronto	1936—Buffalo	1906—Buffalo
1965—Toronto	1935—Syracuse	1905—Providence
1964—Rochester	1934—Toronto	1904—Buffalo
1963—Indianapolis	1933—Buffalo	1903—Jersey City
1962—Atlanta	1932—Newark	1902—Toronto
1961—Buffalo	1931—Rochester	1901—Rochester
1960—Toronto	1930—Rochester	1900—Providence
1959—Havana	1929—Rochester	

Steve Finley began the season in Class A, but hit his way to Rochester in a big hurry.

Indianapolis also went on to win the Triple-A Classic playoff over Rochester, 4-2, winning the last four games.

Along with the American Association and Pacific Coast League, the IL also participated in the inaugural Triple-A All-Star Game, played in Buffalo.

The IL will have its chance to rally against the Association, as the leagues voted to continue interleague play for at least three more years. Rochester (22-17) and Tidewater (21-19) were the only IL teams with winning records against the Association.

The Guides are gone

Old Orchard Beach, Maine, saw its last Triple-A game for the foreseeable future as the Phillies headed for Scranton/Wilkes-Barre, Pa. and a new ballpark.

Attendance in Maine, after an offseason of haggling in the courtrooms, fell to less than 100,000. The team, born in 1984 at the Maine Guides, couldn't get any respect from anyone—on its last trip home, the airline lost its equipment, and that night's game wasn't played.

The addition of Scranton/Wilkes-Barre led to realignment of the divisions for 1989. Rochester, Syracuse, Scranton and Pawtucket will play in one division, with Toledo, Columbus, Tidewater and Richmond in the other. Division play was added in 1988 as an outgrowth of the Triple-A Alliance.

The Pawtucket Red Sox drew nearly 250,000 fans to McCoy Stadium, a team record. General manager Mike Tamburro was named the league's executive of the year, after wresting $2 million for stadium renovations from the city of Pawtucket.

Syracuse had the biggest turnaround. The Chiefs were 23 games under .500 in mid-June, and rallied to finish second, one game under .500.

Pitchers' year

Eight of the IL's top 10 pitchers compiled ERAs of less than 3.00. The league batting average was .256, and Rochester's Finley was the only player to finish over .300 with enough at-bats to qualify for the batting title.

It seemed IL pitchers threw no-hitters every other day. Actually, there were three: Columbus' Scott Nielsen, June 8 against Maine; Tidewater's John Mitchell, a seven-inning perfect game June 27 against Indianapolis; and Maine's Marvin Freeman, in a seven-inning game July 28 against Richmond. Steve Ellsworth of Pawtucket and Tommy Greene of Richmond barely missed no-hitters.

Dave West
... league ERA champ

Tidewater rookie Dave West led the league with a 1.80 ERA, and was rated the third best prospect in the league by Baseball America in a survey of managers. Nos. 1 and 2 were Richmond's John Smoltz and Toledo's Steve Searcy, also pitchers.

The league graduated several players who made an immediate impact in the majors late in the 1988 season: Maine's Ricky Jordan and Ron Jones in Philadelphia, Tidewater's Gregg Jefferies with the Mets, Rochester's Bob Milacki in Baltimore.

At the other end, several veterans resurrected their careers by spending time in the minors. Richmond resident and longtime major leaguer John Grubb went back to the hometown team, lending some experience to the Richmond Braves. Dale Berra, Ken Landreaux and righthander Dickie Noles contributed to the Red Wings' pennant-winning season. George Vukovich joined Toledo and Rick Langford was one of Columbus' most reliable starters.

East	W	L	Pct.	GB	
Tidewater (Mets)	77	64	.627	—	
Richmond (Braves) ..	66	75	.468	11	**1988**
Pawtucket (Red Sox)	63	79	.444	14½	**Final**
Maine (Phillies)	62	80	.437	15½	**Standings**
West					
Rochester (Orioles) ..	77	64	.546	—	
Syracuse (Blue Jays)	70	71	.496	7	
Columbus (Yankees).	65	77	.458	12½	
Toledo (Tigers)	58	84	.408	19½	

1988: General Information

Playoffs: Rochester defeated Tidewater 3-1 in best-of-5 final for league championship; Indianapolis defeated Rochester 4-2 in best-of-7 Alliance Series.

Regular Season Attendance: Columbus, 377,257; Richmond, 347,645; Rochester, 277,820; Pawtucket, 240,190; Tidewater, 181,667; Syracuse, 181,602; Toledo, 178,203; Maine, 80,064.

Managers: Columbus—Bucky Dent; **Maine**—George Culver; **Pawtucket**—Ed Nottle; **Richmond**—Jim Beauchamp; **Rochester**—Johnny Oates; **Syracuse**—Bob Bailor; **Tidewater**—Mike Cubbage; **Toledo**—Pat Corrales.

1988 Official All-Star Team: C—Bob Geren, Columbus. **1B**—Dave Griffin, Richmond. **2B**—Tom Barrett, Maine. **3B**—Craig Worthington, Rochester. **SS**—Randy Velarde, Columbus. **OF**—Steve Finley, Rochester; Carlos Quintana, Pawtucket; Mark Carreon, Tidewater. **DH**—Lonnie Smith, Richmond. **SP**—Steve Searcy, Toledo. **RP**—Mark Huismann, Toledo. **Most Valuable Player**—Craig Worthington, Rochester. **Most Valuable Pitcher**—Steve Searcy, Toledo. **Rookie of the Year**—Steve Finley, Rochester. **Manager of the Year**—Johnny Oates, Rochester.

Top 10 Major League Prospects (by Baseball America): 1. John Smoltz, rhp, Richmond; **2.** Steve Searcy, lhp, Toledo; **3.** Dave West, lhp,

Tidewater; **4.** Steve Finley, of, Rochester; **5.** Gregg Jefferies, 3b, Tidewater; **6.** Ricky Jordan, 1b, Maine; **7.** Craig Worthington, 3b, Rochester; **8.** Jeff Blauser, ss, Richmond; **9.** Geronimo Berroa, of, Syracuse; **10.** Eric Yelding, 2b, Syracuse.

1988: Batting, Pitching Statistics

CLUB BATTING

	AVG	G	AB	R	H	2B	3B	HR	BB	SO	SB
Tidewater	.256	141	4593	540	1176	218	22	63	442	634	95
Rochester	.250	141	4489	562	1122	224	33	97	419	832	89
Richmond	.248	141	4495	534	1117	204	32	74	474	835	86
Pawtucket	.245	142	4613	519	1128	196	19	93	435	864	99
Columbus	.242	142	4694	498	1138	196	27	70	400	924	93
Maine	.242	142	4419	549	1070	177	25	85	450	870	119
Syracuse	.242	142	4571	523	1105	214	33	64	375	937	180
Toledo	.226	142	4449	433	1005	189	25	75	332	868	90

CLUB PITCHING

	ERA	G	CG	SHO	SV	IP	H	R	ER	BB	SO
Tidewater	3.14	141	27	10	30	1202	1026	496	419	473	796
Rochester	3.31	141	35	13	31	1195	1126	523	439	395	772
Columbus	3.33	142	17	9	31	1245	1138	548	461	430	765
Syracuse	3.35	141	16	11	37	1213	1142	564	452	402	879
Toledo	3.43	142	24	7	28	1209	1118	527	461	441	930
Richmond	3.53	141	17	12	33	1194	1140	525	469	360	812
Pawtucket	3.61	142	22	13	31	1210	1153	557	486	431	859
Maine	4.09	142	14	9	33	1170	1173	629	532	471	786

INDIVIDUAL BATTING LEADERS
(Minimum 383 Plate Appearances)

	AVG	G	AB	R	H	2B	3B	HR	RBI	BB	SO	SB
*Finley, Steve, Roch	.314	120	456	61	143	19	7	5	54	28	55	20
*Morris, Hal, Col	.296	121	452	41	134	19	4	3	38	36	62	8
Griffin, Dave, Rich	.289	128	453	52	131	21	3	21	72	50	82	0
#Barrett, Tom, Maine	.285	114	390	69	111	16	4	1	33	62	42	21
Quintana, Carlos, Paw	.285	131	471	67	134	25	3	16	66	38	72	3
*Jefferies, Gregg, Tide	.282	132	504	62	142	28	4	7	61	32	34	32
Tolman, Tim, Tide	.279	127	426	55	119	22	3	8	55	56	64	4
*Wetherby, Jeff, Rich	.269	137	499	69	134	25	4	6	61	45	74	10
Olson, Greg, Tide	.267	115	344	39	92	19	1	6	48	42	42	0
*Jones, Ron, Maine	.267	125	445	64	119	15	3	16	75	49	53	16

* indicates lefthanded batter   # indicates switch hitter

INDIVIDUAL PITCHING LEADERS
(Minimum 114 Innings)

	W	L	ERA	G	GS	CG	SV	IP	H	R	ER	BB	SO
*West, Dave, Tide	12	4	1.80	23	23	7	0	160	106	42	32	97	143
Nielsen, Scott, Col	13	6	2.40	25	22	8	1	172	142	52	46	42	62
*Searcy, Steve, Tol	13	7	2.59	27	27	3	0	170	131	61	49	79	176
Milacki, Bob, Roch	12	8	2.70	24	24	11	0	177	174	62	53	65	103
*Clements, Pat, Col	6	7	2.75	32	16	0	5	144	136	55	44	34	69
*Guetterman, Lee, Col	9	6	2.76	18	18	6	0	121	109	46	37	26	49
Smoltz, John, Rich	10	5	2.79	20	20	3	0	135	118	49	42	37	115
Mitchell, John, Tide	10	9	2.84	27	27	7	0	190	164	76	60	45	65
Whitehurst, Wally, Tide	10	11	3.05	26	26	3	0	165	145	65	56	32	113
Curry, Steve, Paw	11	9	3.08	23	23	3	0	146	125	56	50	69	110

* indicates lefthanded pitcher

COLUMBUS

BATTING	AVG	G	AB	R	H	2B	3B	HR	RBI	BB	SO	SB
*Alvarez, Chris, 3b	.280	29	100	9	28	3	0	1	12	11	12	1
Buhner, Jay, of	.256	38	129	26	33	5	0	8	18	19	33	1
Close, Casey, of	.188	81	250	24	47	11	4	3	25	23	43	2
*Cruz, Jose, of	.235	5	17	3	4	2	0	1	5	1	4	1
*Dalena, Pete, 1b	.214	123	426	33	91	20	1	7	44	24	59	0
Espinoza, Alvaro, ss-2b	.246	119	435	42	107	10	5	2	30	7	53	4
Geren, Bob, c	.271	95	321	37	87	13	2	8	35	33	69	0
Green, Bob, of	.251	56	207	19	52	9	0	4	30	21	56	7
Jones, Ross, 2b-ss	.234	72	244	26	57	9	3	4	19	48	50	1
Kelly, Roberto, of	.333	30	120	25	40	8	1	3	16	6	29	11
*Krenchicki, Wayne, dh	.241	54	174	18	42	6	0	1	14	20	21	1
Lambert, Rob, dh	.133	8	15	2	2	0	0	0	2	1	6	1
Meulens, Hensley, 3b	.230	55	209	27	48	9	1	6	22	14	61	2
Moronko, Jeff, 3b-of	.201	97	313	32	63	12	0	5	24	17	79	1
*Morris, Hal-of-1b	.296	121	452	41	134	19	4	3	38	36	62	8
Nelson, Jamie, c	.151	28	73	6	11	1	1	0	6	14	22	0
Pena, Bert, dh-2b	.211	47	147	14	31	7	0	1	13	12	33	3
*Sanders, Deion, of	.150	5	20	3	3	1	0	0	0	1	4	1
*Sherlock, Glenn, c	.253	32	95	9	24	4	0	1	6	7	18	0
Stankiewicz, Andy, 2b	.219	29	114	4	25	0	0	0	4	6	25	2
#Tolleson, Wayne, ss-3b	.185	8	27	4	5	0	0	0	1	6	3	1
Velarde, Randy, ss	.270	78	293	39	79	23	4	5	37	25	71	7
#Ward, Turner, of	.251	134	490	55	123	24	1	7	50	48	100	28

PITCHING

PITCHING	W	L	ERA	G	GS	CG	SV	IP	H	R	ER	BB	SO
Allen, Neil	0	1	0.60	2	2	1	0	15	7	2	1	0	7
Carreno, Amalio	0	0	10.80	1	0	0	0	3	8	4	4	0	2
*Clements, Pat	6	7	2.75	32	16	0	5	144	136	55	44	34	69
Davidson, Bobby	0	0	2.37	6	0	0	1	19	19	7	5	8	5
Eiland, Dave	1	1	2.59	4	4	0	0	24	25	8	7	6	13
Fulton, Bill	5	5	3.25	45	1	0	2	80	63	37	29	29	44
*Guetterman, Lee	9	6	2.76	18	18	6	0	121	109	46	37	26	49
*Harrison, Matt	2	3	4.60	8	8	0	0	43	50	29	22	8	25
*Kinnunen, Mike	4	5	3.98	45	5	0	13	81	78	41	36	58	73
Langford, Rick	9	6	3.13	21	21	1	0	127	109	47	44	28	84
Layana, Tim	1	7	6.04	11	9	0	0	48	54	34	32	25	25
*Leiter, Al	0	2	3.46	4	4	0	0	13	5	7	5	14	12
Nielsen, Scott	13	6	2.40	25	22	8	1	172	142	52	46	42	62
Parker, Clay	2	2	3.26	10	10	0	0	50	49	21	18	9	51
*Pena, Hipolito	7	6	3.87	50	3	0	3	105	84	51	45	55	109
Ridenour, Dana	1	2	2.11	14	0	0	0	21	16	9	5	19	24
Schmidt, Eric	2	10	4.31	19	10	0	0	77	82	45	37	25	34
Shields, Steve	0	1	2.52	17	0	0	5	25	28	7	7	6	23
Speck, Cliff	3	7	4.34	32	9	1	1	77	74	46	37	38	54

MAINE

BATTING	AVG	G	AB	R	H	2B	3B	HR	RBI	BB	SO	SB
#Barrett, Tom, 2b-ss	.285	114	390	69	111	16	4	1	33	62	49	21
Berman, Gary, 3b-1b	.294	11	34	3	10	0	0	1	4	1	4	0
*Brown, Tony, of-1b	.299	42	127	12	38	8	1	3	21	11	28	6
*Corcoran, Tim, 1b	.172	14	29	2	5	1	0	0	1	1	2	0
Gutierrez, Jackie, ss-3b	.236	40	144	7	34	4	0	0	11	6	16	2
Henderson, Ramon, of-inf	.190	54	126	8	24	1	1	2	11	14	36	1
Jackson, Ken, ss	.199	72	196	25	39	7	0	0	12	32	53	3
Jelks, Greg, of-3b	.207	88	290	35	60	1	2	9	33	20	52	5
*Jones, Ron, of	.267	125	445	64	119	15	3	16	75	49	53	16
Jordan, Ricky, 1b	.308	87	338	42	104	23	1	7	36	6	30	10
*LeBoeuf, Al, of-1b	.211	7	19	1	4	0	0	0	2	2	3	0
Legg, Greg, 2b-ss	.242	49	149	20	36	7	0	1	9	25	21	3
Leiva, Jose, of	.238	42	126	24	30	3	1	1	8	23	29	16
Lundblade, Rick, c	.298	17	47	3	14	3	0	0	5	1	7	1
#Miller, Keith, of-2b	.280	59	200	38	56	14	1	3	23	27	43	5
Nichols, Howard, 3b	.215	78	237	32	51	6	2	9	32	21	43	3
Olander, Jim, of	.211	25	71	5	15	3	0	0	4	4	18	0
#Pardo, Al, dh-c (32 Tide)	.255	59	153	13	39	8	0	4	21	14	27	1
Russell, John, c-of	.228	110	394	45	90	18	0	13	52	29	108	3
Sullivan, Marc, c-1b	.233	83	257	20	60	16	0	6	20	25	72	3
*Turner, Shane, 3b-ss	.179	38	117	10	21	3	1	0	9	7	21	2
Ward, Kevin, of	.230	134	456	60	105	22	8	11	63	62	118	17
Zayas, Carlos, c	.167	7	18	1	3	0	0	0	0	0	3	0

PITCHING	W	L	ERA	G	GS	CG	SV	IP	H	R	ER	BB	SO
Bedrosian, Steve	0	0	0.00	5	0	0	0	7	6	0	0	2	5
Boudreaux, Eric	2	0	1.93	5	2	0	0	9	7	2	2	0	5
Brink, Brad	5	5	4.29	17	17	3	0	86	100	43	41	21	58
Bystrom, Marty	5	7	4.88	14	14	1	0	72	89	53	39	33	43
*Calhoun, Jeff	1	1	4.66	38	0	0	1	37	32	20	19	24	25
Chambers, Travis	2	3	3.34	29	3	0	0	59	58	33	22	49	44
Clay, Danny	5	1	0.99	25	2	0	10	45	24	7	5	19	41
Dawley, Bill	1	2	2.79	22	1	0	5	39	30	13	12	11	29
*Erickson, Eric	0	0	8.44	4	0	0	0	5	7	5	5	6	7
Freeman, Marvin	5	5	4.62	18	14	2	0	74	62	43	38	46	39
Frohwirth, Todd	7	3	2.44	49	0	0	13	63	52	21	17	19	39
Harris, Greg A.	0	1	1.93	3	0	0	1	5	5	3	1	1	5
Maddux, Mike	0	2	4.18	5	3	1	0	24	25	18	11	10	18
Madrid, Alex	0	0	2.31	2	2	0	0	12	10	3	3	0	9
Malone, Chuck	1	4	6.83	6	6	1	0	28	28	27	21	24	38
McLarnan, John	4	3	3.69	38	1	0	0	78	86	37	32	20	48
Newell, Tom	1	5	6.14	10	8	1	0	44	50	37	30	25	31
*Ritchie, Wally	4	5	4.69	16	14	0	0	79	88	49	41	29	49
Scanlan, Bob	5	18	5.59	28	27	4	0	161	181	110	100	50	79
*Scherrer, Bill (5 Roch)	0	0	0.71	10	0	0	0	5	13	1	1	6	11
Service, Scott	8	8	3.67	19	18	1	0	110	109	51	45	31	87
Shelton, Mike	5	5	3.29	33	7	0	2	98	91	38	36	36	62
Surhoff, Rick	1	2	4.32	6	3	0	0	25	24	15	12	11	24

PAWTUCKET

BATTING	AVG	G	AB	R	H	2B	3B	HR	RBI	BB	SO	SB
*Anderson, Brady, of	.287	49	167	27	48	6	1	4	19	26	33	8
*Birriel, Jose, 1b	.048	6	21	2	1	0	0	0	0	0	3	4
#Cannizzaro, Chris, inf-of	.240	115	409	49	98	15	1	8	39	55	48	7
*Dodson, Pat, 1b	.228	64	197	25	45	7	0	4	28	55	47	3
Gedman, Rich, dh-c	.467	4	15	2	7	1	0	1	1	1	4	0
Gonzalez, Angel, 3b	.202	55	168	15	34	7	1	3	13	21	30	4
Hoffman, Glenn, ss	.240	109	366	38	88	14	0	3	33	36	48	2
Horn, Sam, dh	.233	83	279	33	65	10	0	10	31	44	82	0
Kutcher, Randy, 3b	.233	86	331	40	77	12	2	4	27	24	78	16
Marzano, John, c	.198	33	111	7	22	2	1	0	5	8	17	1
*McInnis, Bill, dh	.000	1	4	0	0	0	0	0	0	0	4	0
Mesh, Mike, of-ss	.236	86	174	15	45	4	3	0	18	20	48	11

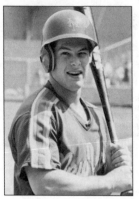

Gregg Jefferies
... big league impact

Dave Griffin
...289-21-72

BATTING	AVG	G	AB	R	H	2B	3B	HR	RBI	BB	SO	SB
#Miller-Jones, Gary, 2b ...	.203	103	335	34	68	10	3	3	24	21	70	2
Quintana, Carlos, of-1b ..	.285	131	471	67	134	25	3	16	66	38	72	3
Romine, Kevin, of	.358	41	148	18	53	6	1	4	26	8	21	3
Sheaffer, Danny, c-1b ...	.274	98	299	30	82	17	1	1	28	18	32	20
Tremblay, Gary, c	.204	74	235	22	48	14	0	8	25	12	54	1
Wade, Scott, of	.237	114	396	42	94	17	2	10	37	24	118	7
Williams, Dana, of	.253	120	470	53	119	29	0	10	47	21	55	11

PITCHING	W	L	ERA	G	GS	CG	SV	IP	H	R	ER	BB	SO
Araujo, Andy	7	4	3.18	41	3	0	3	108	112	43	38	23	64
*Bolton, Tom	3	0	2.79	18	1	0	0	19	17	7	6	10	15
*Crouch, Zach	2	8	4.68	14	14	2	0	85	104	52	44	23	44
Curry, Steve	11	9	3.08	23	23	3	0	146	125	56	50	69	110
Ellsworth, Steve	7	7	3.74	18	16	4	0	108	105	49	45	23	58
Hetzel, Eric	6	10	3.96	22	22	2	0	127	129	67	56	51	122
Johnson, Mitch	4	3	2.92	49	0	0	11	74	61	29	24	19	60
Kiecker, Dana	7	7	3.67	23	22	4	0	132	120	65	54	46	74
Leister, John	6	16	4.31	28	24	5	0	167	161	90	80	75	112
*Rochford, Mike	1	5	3.09	52	0	0	4	82	68	30	28	29	47
Sellers, Jeff	1	1	5.52	3	3	0	0	15	16	9	9	11	9
Smithson, Mike	1	0	0.00	2	1	0	0	7	6	0	0	2	5
Stanley, Bob	1	0	0.82	4	2	0	0	11	7	1	1	5	6
Trautwein, John	0	1	2.00	4	0	0	0	9	4	2	2	6	7
Vasquez, Luis	5	4	3.58	12	11	2	0	75	74	37	30	15	73
Woodward, Rob	1	4	3.86	47	0	0	13	44	44	20	19	24	53

RICHMOND

BATTING	AVG	G	AB	R	H	2B	3B	HR	RBI	BB	SO	SB
#Alicea, Edwin, 2b	.235	50	183	29	43	4	3	5	15	22	37	4
Beauchamp, Kash, of	.222	3	9	1	2	0	0	0	0	0	1	0
Bell, Terry, c	.187	23	75	2	14	2	1	0	6	7	16	0
Blauser, Jeff, ss	.284	69	271	40	77	19	1	5	23	19	53	6
*Blocker, Terry, of	.226	69	266	34	60	3	1	2	9	25	44	12
#Dewey, Todd, c	.150	24	60	5	9	4	2	1	12	5	11	0
*Dunbar, Tommy, of-dh ..	.291	57	189	24	55	8	3	4	33	24	31	4
Espino, Juan, c	.264	51	129	14	34	8	0	2	11	9	22	0
Fischlin, Mike, 2b-ss ...	.181	104	276	20	50	8	1	0	17	30	54	4
Gant, Ronnie, 2b	.311	12	45	3	14	2	2	0	4	2	10	1
Griffin, Dave, 1b	.289	128	453	52	131	21	3	21	72	50	82	0
*Grubb, John, dh-of	.176	34	74	6	13	0	0	0	4	11	18	0
*Jones, Barry, of	.278	35	126	12	35	7	0	3	10	6	12	4
*Justice, Dave, of	.203	70	227	27	46	9	1	8	28	39	55	4
Maldonado, Phil, dh	.333	1	3	1	1	0	0	0	0	0	1	0
*Mizerock, John, c	.218	88	238	21	52	7	0	4	29	18	30	0
Pacho, Juan, 2b-ss	.200	7	25	1	5	1	0	0	1	0	7	0
Rios, Carlos, inf	.257	97	276	27	71	16	1	1	23	24	35	1
#Roby, Ellis, 2b	.000	4	4	0	0	0	0	0	0	0	2	0
Smith, Alex, 3b	.254	125	402	38	102	27	2	1	47	38	90	1
Smith, Lonnie, of-dh	.300	93	290	58	87	13	5	9	51	66	65	26
Tubbs, Greg, of	.246	78	228	43	56	14	2	2	11	28	38	8
*Wetherby, Jeff, of-1b ..	.269	137	499	69	134	25	4	6	61	45	74	10
Wine, Robbie, c (8 Col) ..	.083	16	36	0	3	0	0	0	1	0	15	0

PITCHING	W	L	ERA	G	GS	CG	SV	IP	H	R	ER	BB	SO
Akins, Sid	5	3	3.46	38	0	0	1	88	73	36	34	32	68
Alvarez, Jose	2	1	1.26	10	0	0	3	14	13	2	2	6	10
Boever, Joe	6	3	2.14	48	0	0	22	71	47	17	17	22	71
*Cary, Chuck	0	0	1.42	5	0	0	1	6	4	1	1	2	3
Clary, Marty	6	11	3.38	27	25	2	0	144	142	65	54	37	73
Coffman, Kevin	1	1	4.19	9	2	0	1	19	15	10	9	20	18
Dozier, Tom	0	1	8.44	7	1	0	0	11	14	10	10	7	6
Eave, Gary	5	9	3.56	34	9	2	0	101	100	49	40	31	81

	W	L	ERA	G	GS	CG	SV	IP	H	R	ER	BB	SO
Eichelberger, Juan	2	4	3.14	25	5	0	5	63	58	24	22	13	44
Greene, Tommy	7	17	4.77	29	29	4	0	177	169	98	94	70	130
*Lilliquist, Derek	10	12	3.38	28	28	2	0	171	179	70	64	36	80
Miller, Dave	11	6	4.12	20	20	4	0	116	128	58	53	20	67
*Olwine, Ed	0	0	1.50	8	0	0	0	12	10	2	2	5	9
Smoltz, John	10	5	2.79	20	20	3	0	135	118	49	42	37	115
*Stringfellow, Bean	1	1	2.95	36	1	0	0	43	43	18	14	15	28
Ziem, Steve	0	1	6.35	12	1	0	0	23	27	16	16	7	9

ROCHESTER

BATTING	AVG	G	AB	R	H	2B	3B	HR	RBI	BB	SO	SB
Berra, Dale, ss-2b	.181	69	166	19	30	4	0	3	13	16	31	0
*Cijntje, Sherwin, of	.227	49	185	26	42	8	1	2	12	13	33	6
Cimo, Matt, of	.253	88	265	33	67	14	3	8	20	27	72	3
Davis, Butch, of	.143	8	28	4	4	0	2	0	0	0	2	0
Dulin, Tim, 2b	.333	14	48	7	16	3	0	2	6	6	7	0
*Dwyer, Jim, dh	.296	8	27	7	8	3	1	0	4	6	10	0
*Finley, Steve, of	.314	120	456	61	143	19	7	5	54	28	55	20
*Hughes, Keith, of	.270	77	274	44	74	13	2	7	49	43	57	11
*Landreaux, Ken, of-dh .	.272	64	173	27	47	9	0	7	23	22	21	6
Landrum, Tito, of	.235	5	17	2	4	2	0	1	4	2	2	0
Magrann, Tom, c	.294	7	17	1	5	2	0	0	0	1	6	0
Mata, Vic, dh-1b	.224	69	161	11	36	9	0	1	14	14	26	0
Montgomery, Reg, dh ...	.000	1	2	0	0	0	0	0	0	0	1	0
*Narron, Jerry, c	.250	95	248	31	62	17	0	8	33	31	40	1
Nichols, Carl, c	.228	75	193	20	44	7	1	3	16	21	50	0
*Padget, Chris, 1b-of	.220	120	377	44	83	21	3	10	44	41	73	2
*Pyznarski, Tim, dh	.125	12	32	3	4	0	0	2	5	6	13	1
Rowdon, Wade, 2b-ss ...	.252	86	329	41	83	17	4	7	33	16	58	3
*Salcedo, Ron, 2b	.246	90	236	24	58	14	1	3	27	18	34	2
Smith, D.L., ss	.230	101	304	25	70	10	0	0	19	21	46	2
#Stanicek, Pete, 2b	.174	19	69	13	12	2	1	2	8	10	18	7
*Stone, Jeff, of	.277	71	267	39	74	12	5	3	27	16	50	20
#Tettleton, Mickey, c	.244	19	41	9	10	3	1	1	4	9	15	0
*Traber, Jim, 1b	.285	38	144	17	41	10	0	6	23	13	19	2
Worthington, Craig, 3b ...	.244	121	430	53	105	25	1	16	73	39	93	3

PITCHING	W	L	ERA	G	GS	CG	SV	IP	H	R	ER	BB	SO
Aase, Don	0	0	1.23	7	0	0	3	7	5	1	1	3	6
*Ballard, Jeff	4	3	2.97	9	8	0	0	61	56	26	20	11	32
*Bell, Eric	3	1	1.98	7	7	0	0	36	28	10	8	13	33
*Bowden, Mark	9	5	3.38	24	13	0	0	96	80	40	36	51	94
Brown, Curt	2	0	1.19	10	0	0	2	23	16	4	3	3	10
*Dillard, Gordon	0	2	2.45	5	1	0	0	11	9	5	3	9	6
Gibson, Bob	2	2	1.21	10	0	0	0	22	17	9	3	10	15
Griffin, Mike	4	8	3.85	43	10	0	4	108	102	54	46	30	68
*Habyan, John	9	9	4.46	23	23	8	0	147	161	78	73	46	91
Harnisch, Pete	4	1	2.16	7	7	3	0	58	44	16	14	14	43
*Hickey, Kevin	2	0	1.46	27	0	0	2	37	31	7	6	19	24
Mesa, Jose	0	3	8.62	11	2	0	0	16	21	20	15	14	15
Milacki, Bob	12	8	2.70	24	24	11	0	177	174	62	53	65	103
Morgan, Mike	0	2	4.76	3	3	0	0	17	19	10	9	6	7
Noles, Dickie	10	5	3.12	31	15	5	1	130	124	57	45	31	59
Peraza, Oswald	3	0	2.89	6	1	0	0	44	35	14	14	9	36
*Raczka, Mike	1	5	5.94	41	2	0	10	50	57	38	33	24	35
Sisk, Doug	0	2	5.91	6	1	0	3	11	15	7	7	3	5
Stanhope, Chuck	2	1	4.34	5	4	1	0	29	27	17	14	9	20
*Thurmond, Mark	5	3	2.65	8	8	1	0	54	40	22	16	18	25
Tibbs, Jay	3	1	2.84	4	4	1	0	25	22	12	8	9	18
Williamson, Mark	2	3	3.34	12	3	1	2	30	38	11	11	5	25

SYRACUSE

BATTING	AVG	G	AB	R	H	2B	3B	HR	RBI	BB	SO	SB
Batiste, Kevin, of	.229	34	105	10	24	6	1	1	9	4	39	8
Berroa, Geronimo, of	.260	131	470	55	122	29	1	8	64	38	88	7
Borders, Pat, of	.242	35	120	11	29	8	0	3	14	16	22	0
Butera, Sal, c	.157	42	127	8	20	5	0	0	5	12	12	0
*Campusano, Sil, of	.210	17	62	8	13	3	0	0	3	2	20	1
Dela Cruz, Hector, 3b ...	.202	75	228	25	46	8	0	4	27	29	74	17
Diaz, Carlos, c	.169	27	83	4	14	5	0	1	8	1	23	0
*Ducey, Rob, of	.256	90	317	40	81	14	4	7	42	43	81	7
Escobar, Jose, inf	.210	46	124	8	26	1	1	0	12	9	20	2
*Green, Otis, 1b	.266	109	410	59	109	23	7	10	41	22	68	13
Heath, Kelly, dh-3b	.310	90	287	48	89	22	0	5	41	51	49	5
Hill, Glenallen, of	.233	51	172	21	40	7	0	4	19	15	59	7
Infante, Alex, ss-3b	.300	97	340	48	102	15	4	2	28	19	27	21
#Liriano, Nelson, of	.194	8	31	2	6	1	1	0	1	2	4	2
McElroy, Glen, c	.000	2	3	0	0	0	0	0	0	1	1	0
*Myers, Greg, dh-c	.283	34	120	18	34	7	1	7	21	8	24	1
*Pederson, Stu, of	.278	67	212	30	59	13	3	2	29	35	31	2
Reyna, Luis, 1b	.195	54	200	14	39	8	2	2	15	5	31	14
Rivers, Ken, c	.228	37	123	6	28	4	1	1	14	4	32	0
Shaddy, Chris, 2b	.156	29	90	7	14	3	1	0	5	5	6	30	1
*Thornton, Lou, of-3b	.207	69	246	23	51	12	3	4	22	11	46	11
Tonucci, Norm, 3b	.138	43	145	9	20	5	1	2	15	6	54	2
Yelding, Eric, 2b-ss	.250	138	556	69	139	15	2	1	38	36	102	59

BATTING

PITCHING

Department Leaders

PITCHING

	W	L	ERA	G	GS	CG	SV	IP	H	R	ER	BB	SO
Bair, Doug	3	4	2.34	39	0	0	14	65	41	19	17	20	60
Bencomo, Omar	0	0	3.00	6	0	0	0	9	12	5	3	1	6
*Burgos, Enrique	0	0	7.71	2	0	0	0	2	4	2	2	2	2
*Davis, Steve	10	15	3.29	31	31	4	0	178	166	94	65	66	130
Eichhorn, Mark	4	4	1.17	18	1	0	2	38	35	9	5	15	34
Faulk, Kelly	0	1	13.50	3	0	0	0	3	5	4	4	1	2
McLaughlin, Colin	9	4	2.88	47	1	1	7	69	47	24	22	37	62
*Musselman, Jeff	4	1	2.94	10	1	0	4	49	42	20	16	17	31
Nunez, Jose	5	4	2.90	12	10	0	0	71	62	26	23	16	67
*O'Connor, Jack	2	6	4.11	40	3	0	4	81	86	42	37	28	63
Ross, Mark	3	8	3.61	17	15	2	0	100	101	50	40	19	57
Sanchez, Alex	4	3	3.59	10	10	1	0	58	47	26	23	43	57
*Shirley, Bob	3	6	3.90	36	5	2	3	90	98	50	39	22	45
Stottlemyre, Todd	5	0	2.05	7	7	1	0	48	36	12	11	8	51
*Walsh, Dave	0	1	8.10	3	2	0	0	10	8	9	9	9	10
*Wells, David	0	0	0.00	6	0	0	3	6	7	1	0	2	8
Wills, Frank	6	4	3.24	25	10	0	3	81	70	40	29	25	53
*Yearout, Mike	3	4	4.39	28	18	0	0	107	112	63	52	38	66
*Young, Cliff	9	6	3.42	33	18	4	1	147	133	68	56	32	75

TIDEWATER

BATTING	AVG	G	AB	R	H	2B	3B	HR	RBI	BB	SO	SB
Carreon, Mark, of-dh	.263	102	365	48	96	13	3	14	55	40	53	11
#Contreras, Joaquin, of	.206	32	102	11	21	2	0	2	3	4	15	4
*Cuevas, Angelo, of	.250	3	8	1	2	0	0	0	1	2	0	0
*David, Andre, of	.242	106	359	40	87	16	2	0	35	34	36	2
Dowell, Ken, ss-2b	.206	106	262	19	54	7	2	0	19	31	35	2
*Gardner, Jeff, 2b	.375	2	8	3	3	1	1	0	2	1	1	0
*Hayden, Alan, of	.500	3	12	3	6	1	1	0	0	1	1	1
#Jefferies, Gregg, 3b-ss	.282	132	504	62	142	28	4	7	61	32	34	32
Jones, Geary, c	.125	9	24	5	3	2	0	0	2	3	7	0
#Lawton, Marcus, of	.233	94	335	46	78	16	4	0	17	36	53	25
Lombardi, Phil, of-c	.308	85	292	49	90	14	0	9	44	38	38	2
*McKnight, Jeff, inf-of	.255	113	345	36	88	14	0	2	25	36	32	0
Miller, Keith, 2b-ss	.281	42	171	23	48	11	1	1	15	12	20	8
Olson, Greg, c	.267	115	344	39	92	19	1	6	48	42	42	0
Reed, Darren, of	.241	101	345	31	83	26	0	9	47	32	66	0
Shipley, Craig, ss-3b	.272	40	151	12	41	5	0	1	13	4	15	0
Springer, Steve, 2b-3b	.261	97	337	42	88	15	0	2	25	29	66	4
Tolman, Tim, 1b	.279	127	426	55	119	22	3	8	55	56	64	4

Top IL Performers

C. Worthington
...16 HR's

Steve Searcy
...176 K's

Bob Milacki
...12-8, 2.70

PITCHING	W	L	ERA	G	GS	CG	SV	IP	H	R	ER	BB	SO
Aguilera, Rick	0	0	1.50	1	1	0	0	6	6	1	1	1	4
*Barton, Shawn	2	2	3.06	19	2	0	0	32	34	13	11	11	27
*Conley, Virgil	0	1	5.40	1	1	0	0	5	3	3	3	2	3
Dobie, Reggie	8	5	3.86	20	20	3	0	112	102	51	48	57	78
Drummond, Tim	6	3	3.28	38	2	1	3	82	71	33	30	28	62
Edens, Tom	7	6	3.46	24	21	3	0	135	128	67	52	53	89
*Frey, Steve	6	3	3.13	58	1	0	6	55	38	23	19	25	58
Innis, Jeff	0	5	3.54	34	0	0	4	48	43	22	19	25	43
McCarthy, Tom	8	3	2.67	34	3	0	3	57	49	19	17	29	28
Mitchell, John	10	9	2.84	27	27	7	0	190	164	76	60	45	65
*Niemann, Randy	0	1	10.45	9	1	0	0	10	19	14	12	5	5
Roman, Jose	1	2	7.13	19	0	0	1	24	27	20	19	20	15
Savage, Jack	5	8	3.16	43	9	1	13	88	67	37	31	37	46
*West, Dave	12	4	1.80	23	23	7	0	160	106	42	32	97	143
Weston, Mickey	2	1	1.52	4	4	2	0	30	21	6	5	5	16
Whitehurst, Wally	10	11	3.05	26	26	3	0	165	145	65	56	32	113

TOLEDO

BATTING	AVG	G	AB	R	H	2B	3B	HR	RBI	BB	SO	SB
*Bean, Billy, of-1b	.256	138	484	59	124	19	1	6	40	41	45	12
Beane, Billy, of-dh	.235	110	361	33	85	15	2	9	39	26	112	8
Brown, Mike, of-dh	.279	79	244	22	68	17	2	3	21	22	26	1
Chavez, Pedro, 2b-ss	.222	38	117	8	26	3	0	0	5	8	11	3
DeJesus, Ivan, ss-3b	.235	60	200	16	47	5	1	0	16	13	36	6
Dempsay, Adam, c	.071	11	14	1	1	1	0	0	0	1	5	0
#Felix, Paul, dh-c	.199	71	146	15	29	7	0	6	18	17	45	0
Hoiles, Chris, c-dh	.159	22	69	4	11	1	0	2	6	2	12	1
*Leiper, Tim, of	.167	22	48	6	8	1	0	0	4	6	7	0
#Lovullo, Torey, 2b	.232	57	177	18	41	8	1	5	20	9	24	2
*Lusader, Scott, of	.261	89	329	38	86	11	5	4	46	30	56	22
*Murphy, Dwayne, of	.220	51	173	20	38	9	0	5	15	22	30	2
Palacios, Rey, c	.230	132	409	48	94	26	1	5	27	28	106	4
Reynolds, Jeff, 1b-3b	.204	127	460	38	94	20	1	15	57	23	108	0
Rice, Pete, dh	.163	30	49	3	8	3	0	1	4	5	27	0
Rowland, Donnie, 2b	.175	55	103	9	18	1	1	0	4	10	21	1
Ruiz, Benny, ss-2b	.195	119	293	19	57	8	1	1	15	17	52	2
*Strange, Doug, 3b	.201	82	278	23	56	8	2	6	19	8	38	9
*Vukovich, George, dh-of	.222	89	288	34	64	12	5	5	26	26	52	5
#Walewander, Jim, 2b	.455	4	11	4	5	2	0	0	2	3	3	2
*Wieligman, Rich, 1b	.050	6	20	0	1	0	0	0	1	0	3	0
#Young, Delwyn, of	.251	46	175	25	44	12	2	2	13	15	48	10

PITCHING	W	L	ERA	G	GS	CG	SV	IP	H	R	ER	BB	SO
Beard, Dave	6	7	3.01	21	15	1	0	105	84	37	35	29	76
*Cherry, Paul	0	2	4.64	19	2	0	2	21	21	12	11	13	19
*Clarke, Stan	12	13	3.48	31	29	8	0	189	184	80	73	61	133
Cooper, Dave	2	2	5.05	36	0	0	1	57	61	36	32	31	49
*Duffy, John	0	1	5.60	20	1	0	0	35	42	23	22	10	25
Heinkel, Don	1	0	1.91	8	5	0	1	28	25	7	6	8	30
Huismann, Mark	4	6	1.87	48	0	0	21	58	50	20	12	15	61
King, Eric	3	4	3.26	10	10	2	0	69	54	26	25	23	51
*Lee, Mark	0	1	2.79	22	0	0	0	19	18	7	6	7	13
Pacella, John (1 Roch)	0	3	8.25	10	2	0	0	12	17	17	11	15	9
Pena, Ramon	2	5	3.40	62	1	0	3	90	83	38	34	19	78
Rice, Pete	0	1	3.77	7	0	0	0	14	10	7	6	11	16
Ritter, Reggie	1	9	6.89	15	8	1	0	50	64	43	38	22	33
Schulze, Don	10	13	3.11	27	26	8	0	185	172	72	64	56	107
*Searcy, Steve	13	7	2.59	27	27	3	0	170	131	61	49	79	176
Trujillo, Mike	4	10	3.13	18	16	1	0	106	102	42	37	42	54

— 84 —

Las Vegas' team of Stars lives up to expectations

By BRIAN HILDERBRAND

Before the 1988 season, the Las Vegas Stars were being called one of the most talented teams in the Pacific Coast League since the powerful Albuquerque Dukes of the early 1980s.

In the end, the Stars lived up to their billing by winning their second league championship in three seasons. Las Vegas swept Albuquerque in three games in the Southern Division playoffs, then defeated Vancouver 3-1 in the best-of-5 championship series.

Blessed with a prospect at almost every position, Las Vegas manager Steve Smith responded by winning his second straight league championship. In 1987, Smith led Wichita, the San Diego Padres' Double-A affiliate, to the Texas League title.

Sandy Alomar
. . . PCL's top prospect

"At the beginning of the season, everyone put the hype on us about how good this team was and how much talent we had," Smith said. "The guys did a good job of blocking that out."

Las Vegas also did a respectable job of coming through in the clutch. After winning the first half with a 41-29 record,

League Champions

(Playoff Champions, Where Applicable)

1988—Las Vegas	1960—Spokane	1931—San Fran.
1987—Albuquerque	1959—Salt Lake City	1930—Hollywood
1986—Las Vegas	1958—Phoenix	1929—Hollywood
1985—Vancouver	1957—San Fran.	1928—San Fran.
1984—Edmonton	1956—Los Angeles	1927—Oakland
1983—Portland	1955—Seattle	1926—Los Angeles
1982—Albuquerque	1954—San Diego	1925—San Fran.
1981—Albuquerque	1953—Hollywood	1924—Seattle
1980—Albuquerque	1952—Hollywood	1923—San Fran.
1979—Salt Lake City	1951—Seattle	1922—San Fran.
1978—*Tacoma	1950—Oakland	1921—Los Angeles
*Albuquerque	1949—Hollywood	1920—Vernon
1977—Phoenix	1948—Oakland	1919—Vernon
1976—Hawaii	1947—Los Angeles	1918—Los Angeles
1975—Hawaii	1946—San Fran.	1917—San Fran.
1974—Spokane	1945—San Fran.	1916—Los Angeles
1973—Spokane	1944—San Fran.	1915—San Fran.
1972—Albuquerque	1943—San Fran.	1914—Portland
1971—Salt Lake City	1942—Seattle	1913—Portland
1970—Spokane	1941—Seattle	1912—Oakland
1969—Tacoma	1940—Seattle	1911—Portland
1968—Tulsa	1939—Sacramento	1910—Portland
1967—San Diego	1938—Sacramento	1909—San Fran.
1966—Seattle	1937—San Diego	1908—Los Angeles
1965—Okla. City	1936—Portland	1907—Los Angeles
1964—San Diego	1935—San Fran.	1906—Portland
1963—Okla. City	1934—Los Angeles	1905—Los Angeles
1962—San Diego	1933—Los Angeles	1904—Tacoma
1961—Tacoma	1932—Portland	1903—Los Angeles
		*co-champions

Toasts of the Coast

Edgar Martinez
... top hitter

Erik Hanson
... SO champ

Luis Medina
... HR king

the Stars struggled through the second half at 33-37. But once the playoffs began, the Stars turned it on and won six of seven games. It was their second league title since moving to Las Vegas from Spokane in 1983.

The Stars breezed through the playoffs without the league's top prospect, catcher Sandy Alomar Jr.

Alomar, son of the former major league infielder and current third base coach of the Padres, saw his season cut short by a knee injury sustained in an Aug. 9 collision at home plate.

But Las Vegas had a surplus of talent to pick up the slack. Still, it was the Stars' pitching, which had been inconsistent all season, that carried them in the playoffs.

Collins shuffles off to Buffalo

Less than a month after leading Albuquerque to the best record in the PCL (86-56), and one year after winning the league championship, manager Terry Collins ended his relationship with the Los Angeles Dodgers and took the managing job at Buffalo (American Association) for the 1989 season.

The Pittsburgh Pirates were granted permission to talk to Collins, 39, after the season, and he accepted an offer to manage their Triple-A club. In 5½ seasons in Albuquerque, Collins had a 388-392 record and won three half-pennants. He was named the 1988 PCL manager of the year, and managed the National League all-stars in the Triple-A all-star game.

Collins was one of five managers who left during or immediately after the season. Portland's Jim Mahoney stepped down in midseason, citing personal reasons. Calgary's Bill Plummer became a coach with the parent Seattle Mariners during the all-star break; Steve Swisher of Colorado Springs didn't have his contract renewed by the Cleveland Indians; and Bob Didier of Tucson didn't have his contract renewed by the Houston Astros.

Year of the pitcher

Although the PCL long has been regarded as a hitter's league, several pitchers made their marks in 1988.

Albuquerque had four 10-game winners, including two of the three winningest pitchers in the league. Bill Krueger (15-5), William Brennan (14-8), Dennis Burtt (12-9), and Ken Howell (10-1) all reached double figures in wins. Krueger led the league.

Calgary righthander Erik Hanson led the league in strikeouts with 154, and threw the only no-hitter, a seven-inning gem in the second game of a doubleheader Aug. 21 at home against Las Vegas. Hanson, 23, struck out 10 and allowed only one runner, on a walk. Hanson finished 12-7 after starting the season 0-5.

The hitters were not completely shut out, though. Luis Medina of Colorado Springs had 21 home runs by June 11. He hit only seven the rest of the season, but still led the league. Teammate

Rod Allen drove in 100 runs to lead the league in that category.

Phoenix third baseman Matt Williams showed he was capable of going deep, belting four straight home runs in a game May 25, tying a 25-year-old league record. Williams hit another on his second at-bat the next night, giving him five home runs in six trips to the plate.

Colorado Springs and Phoenix combined for a league-record 13 home runs in a 33-12 Sky Sox victory May 7 at Spurgeon Stadium in Colorado Springs.

Quite a turnaround

Just one season after posting the worst record in Triple-A, the Portland Beavers made it to the playoffs as a wild-card team.

Although Vancouver won both half-pennants in the Northern Division, the Beavers had the best overall record (76-56) of a non-division winner and earned the right to play the Canadians for the division title. In 1987, the Beavers finished 39 games behind first-place Calgary in the North, with a 45-96 record.

After drawing only 359 fans to their first six 'home games' at Desert Sun Stadium in Yuma, Ariz., the Sky Sox rebounded nicely after finally settling into their new stadium in Colorado Springs.

The Sky Sox, who moved from Hawaii, played their first 34 home games in Yuma and in old Spurgeon Stadium before construction on their new park was completed. The franchise drew an average of 3,200 fans a game to new Sky Sox Stadium.

FIRST HALF				
North	W	L	Pct.	GB
Vancouvr (White Sox)	42	29	.592	—
Portland (Twins).....	37	33	.529	4½
Calgary (Mariners) ...	33	38	.465	9
Tacoma (Athletics) ..	31	41	.431	11½
Edmonton (Angels) ..	29	42	.408	13
South				
Las Vegas (Padres) ..	41	29	.586	—
Albuqrque (Dodgers)	38	33	.535	3½
Tucson (Astros)	38	34	.528	4
Phoenix (Giants)	34	38	.472	8
Colo. Spgs. (Indians)	32	38	.457	9
SECOND HALF				
North	W	L	Pct.	GB
Vancouvr (White Sox)	43	28	.606	—
Portland (Twins).....	39	33	.542	4½
Calgary (Mariners) ...	35	36	.493	8
Edmonton (Angels) ..	32	38	.457	10½
Tacoma (Athletics) ..	31	41	.431	12½
South				
Albuqrque (Dodgers)	48	23	.676	—
Las Vegas (Padres) ..	33	37	.471	14½
Phoenix (Giants)	33	38	.465	15
Colo. Spgs. (Indians)	30	39	.435	17
Tucson (Astros)	30	41	.423	18
OVERALL				
	W	L	Pct.	GB
Albuqrque (Dodgers)	86	56	.606	—
Vancouvr (White Sox)	85	57	.599	1
Portland (Twins).....	76	66	.535	10
Las Vegas (Padres) ..	74	66	.529	11
Calgary (Mariners) ...	68	74	.479	18
Tucson (Astros)	68	75	.476	18½
Phoenix (Giants)	67	76	.469	19½
Colo. Spgs. (Indians)	62	77	.446	22½
Edmonton (Angels) ..	61	80	.433	24½
Tacoma (Athletics) ..	62	82	.431	25

1988 Final Standings

1988: General Information

Playoffs: Vancouver defeated Portland 3-0 and Las Vegas defeated Albuquerque 3-0 in best-of-5 semifinals; Las Vegas defeated Vancouver 3-1 in best-of-5 final for league championship.

Regular Season Attendance: Vancouver, 386,220; Calgary, 332,590; Albuquerque, 314,186; Las Vegas, 305,622; Tacoma, 280,168; Edmonton, 243,419; Portland, 207,605; Tucson, 173,889; Phoenix, 171,030; Colorado Springs, 168,248.

Managers: Albuquerque—Terry Collins; **Calgary**—Bill Plummer, Marty Martinez; **Colorado**—Steve Swisher; **Edmonton**—Tom Kotchman; **Las Vegas**—Steve Smith; **Phoenix**—Wendell Kim; **Portland**—Jim Mahoney, Jim Shellenback; **Tacoma**—Brad Fischer; **Tucson**—Bob Didier; **Vancouver**—Terry Bevington.

1988 Official All-Star Team: C—Sandy Alomar Jr., Las Vegas. **1B**—Francisco Melendez, Phoenix. **2B**—Mike Woodard, Vancouver. **3B**—Edgar Martinez, Calgary. **SS**—Mike Brumley, Las Vegas. **OF**—Mike Devereaux, Albuquerque; Luis Medina, Colorado Springs; Cameron Drew, Tucson. **DH**—Rod Allen, Colorado Springs; George Hinshaw, Albuquerque. **RHP**—William Brennan, Albuquerque. **LHP**—Bill Krueger, Albuquerque. **RP**—Karl Best, Portland/Phoenix. **Most Valuable Player**—Sandy Alomar Jr., Las Vegas. **Manager of the Year**—Terry Collins, Albuquerque.

Top 10 Major League Prospects (by Baseball America): 1. Sandy Alomar, c, Las Vegas; **2.** Ramon Martinez, rhp, Albuquerque; **3.** Juan Bell, ss, Albuquerque; **4.** Cameron Drew, of, Tucson; **5.** William Brennan, rhp, Albuquerque; **6.** Greg Harris, rhp, Las Vegas; **7.** Mike Devereaux, of, Albuquerque; **8.** Jerald Clark, of, Las Vegas; **9.** Lance Johnson, of, Vancouver; **10.** Matt Williams, 3b, Phoenix.

1988: Batting, Pitching Statistics

CLUB BATTING

	AVG	G	AB	R	H	2B	3B	HR	BB	SO	SB
Albuquerque	.293	142	4796	794	1405	244	48	106	470	820	182
Calgary	.289	142	4765	737	1377	286	34	122	545	740	126
Las Vegas	.288	140	4900	795	1413	244	52	111	444	879	153
Colorado Springs	.281	139	4714	704	1324	263	46	106	420	745	89
Phoenix	.278	143	4866	696	1351	225	47	87	485	884	71
Portland	.276	142	4713	627	1300	225	54	74	433	622	133
Vancouver	.272	143	4722	661	1285	229	47	67	446	715	153
Edmonton	.271	141	4756	716	1291	264	49	96	423	811	102
Tucson	.267	143	4772	706	1274	251	64	63	526	803	202
Tacoma	.267	144	4741	654	1264	216	37	74	604	832	157

CLUB PITCHING

	ERA	G	CG	SHO	SV	IP	H	R	ER	BB	SO
Vancouver	3.64	142	20	13	43	1233	1197	573	499	448	764
Albuquerque	3.78	142	17	14	34	1234	1242	617	518	451	788
Portland	4.19	142	30	12	37	1213	1251	633	565	483	728
Tacoma	4.20	144	9	8	27	1242	1344	722	579	514	783
Tucson	4.49	143	7	7	35	1238	1424	708	618	415	774
Las Vegas	4.59	140	14	5	30	1220	1380	758	622	528	840
Phoenix	4.82	143	14	7	32	1238	1350	768	663	543	819
Calgary	4.85	142	11	10	34	1206	1324	758	650	521	912
Edmonton	5.04	141	22	10	19	1197	1382	752	671	456	724
Colorado Springs	5.24	139	19	6	22	1189	1391	801	692	437	718

INDIVIDUAL BATTING LEADERS

(Minimum 389 Plate Appearances)

	AVG	G	AB	R	H	2B	3B	HR	RBI	BB	SO	SB
Martinez, Edgar, Cal	.363	95	331	63	120	19	4	8	64	66	40	9
*Melendez, Francisco, Phx	.361	96	368	61	133	26	2	4	58	40	40	5
Hinshaw, George, Alb	.340	120	470	76	160	30	4	13	94	29	71	15
Devereaux, Mike, Alb	.340	109	423	88	144	26	4	13	76	44	46	33
*Woodard, Mike, Van	.332	94	367	63	122	12	10	1	40	37	31	18
Allen, Rod, CS	.324	124	469	84	152	36	4	23	100	44	74	1
#Jose, Felix, Tac	.317	133	504	71	160	28	5	12	83	53	75	16
#Brumley, Mike, LV	.315	113	425	77	134	16	7	3	41	56	84	41
*Briley, Greg, Cal	.313	112	444	74	139	29	9	11	66	40	51	27
Medina, Luis, CS	.310	111	406	81	126	28	6	28	81	42	107	1

* indicates lefthanded batter   # indicates switch hitter

INDIVIDUAL PITCHING LEADERS

(Minimum 115 Innings)

	W	L	ERA	G	GS	CG	SV	IP	H	R	ER	BB	SO
*Krueger, Bill, Alb	15	5	3.01	27	26	7	0	173	167	74	58	69	114
Rodriguez, Rick, CS	8	6	3.06	19	19	5	0	127	112	49	43	43	55
Wojna, Ed, Van	10	6	3.27	21	17	5	1	124	112	55	45	36	73
Peterson, Adam, Van	14	7	3.32	28	28	4	0	171	161	69	63	81	103
Bordi, Rich, Tac	7	7	3.48	40	10	0	3	119	120	61	46	35	81
*Otto, Dave, Tac	4	9	3.52	21	21	2	0	128	123	71	50	63	80
Bitker, Joe, LV	8	10	3.63	28	27	3	0	178	195	98	72	41	106
Galvez, Balvino, Port	11	7	3.77	23	22	3	0	143	149	69	60	63	60
Brennan, William, Alb	14	8	3.82	29	28	5	0	167	177	85	71	51	83
Burtt, Dennis, Alb	12	9	3.83	30	25	1	0	167	185	85	71	56	80

* indicates lefthanded pitcher

ALBUQUERQUE

BATTING	AVG	G	AB	R	H	2B	3B	HR	RBI	BB	SO	SB
Adams, Pat, 1b	.138	11	29	1	4	1	0	0	2	4	5	0
*Amelung, Ed, of	.286	2	7	2	2	1	0	0	0	1	1	0
Asadoor, Randy, 3b-1b	.216	78	204	24	44	8	2	2	19	19	59	1
#Bell, Juan, ss	.300	73	257	42	77	9	3	8	45	16	70	7
*Brown, Jeff D., of	.545	4	11	3	6	4	0	0	2	3	1	0
Debus, Jon, 1b-c	.222	32	90	10	20	4	0	2	13	10	19	0
Devereaux, Mike, of	.340	109	423	88	144	26	4	13	76	44	46	33
*Dugas, Shanie, inf	.288	120	400	60	115	20	1	14	60	42	80	5
Duncan, Mariano, ss-2b	.286	56	227	48	65	4	8	0	25	10	40	33
Garcia, Damaso, 2b	.400	3	5	1	2	1	0	0	1	2	0	0
*Garcia, Steve, 2b-3b	.235	88	306	46	72	12	3	1	33	22	37	7
Gibbons, John, c	.270	76	233	37	63	15	2	3	27	44	52	2
Gonzalez, Jose, of	.306	84	288	57	88	15	2	5	22	36	66	44
Guerrero, Pedro, 1b	.417	5	12	3	5	0	0	1	4	5	5	0
*Gwynn, Chris, of	.299	112	411	57	123	22	10	5	61	39	39	1
Hernandez, Carlos, c	.125	3	8	0	1	0	0	0	1	0	0	0
Hinshaw, George, of-1b	.340	120	470	76	160	30	4	13	94	29	71	15
Huff, Mike, of	.250	2	4	0	1	1	0	0	0	0	0	0
Martinez, Luis, ss	.143	3	7	1	1	1	0	0	0	1	0	0
Michel, Domingo, 1b-of	.375	3	8	3	3	0	0	1	4	0	2	0
#Mota, Jose, 2b	.333	6	15	4	5	0	0	0	1	3	3	1
#Ramsey, Mike, of	.297	124	407	75	121	22	6	7	53	29	50	11
#Ransom, Jeff, 3b	.114	14	35	5	4	1	0	0	5	8	5	0
Reyes, Gilberto, c	.292	98	318	40	93	14	0	12	66	28	63	2
Sharperson, Mike, 2b	.319	56	210	55	67	10	2	0	30	31	25	19
Woodson, Tracy, 1b-3b	.319	85	313	46	100	21	1	17	73	39	48	1

PITCHING	W	L	ERA	G	GS	CG	SV	IP	H	R	ER	BB	SO
Arnold, Tony	2	4	5.67	13	8	1	0	54	60	35	34	11	20
Brennan, William	14	8	3.82	29	28	5	0	167	177	85	71	51	83
Burtt, Dennis	12	9	3.83	30	25	1	0	167	185	85	71	56	80
Crawford, Steve	3	6	3.81	32	2	0	3	54	59	31	23	25	36
Crews, Tim	1	1	2.70	10	0	0	3	13	13	5	4	2	7
*Engel, Steve	0	0	3.86	3	0	0	0	2	2	1	1	1	2
Hartley, Mike	2	2	4.35	18	0	0	3	21	22	11	10	12	16
*Hensley, Chuck	4	3	3.77	52	0	0	4	60	64	34	25	31	39
Heredia, Hector	4	1	2.51	43	0	0	11	72	62	22	20	23	44
Hillegas, Shawn	6	4	3.49	16	15	2	0	101	93	44	39	22	65
Holmes, Darren	0	1	5.06	2	1	0	0	5	6	3	3	1	1
Howell, Jay	10	1	3.27	18	16	0	0	107	92	43	39	42	95
*Krueger, Bill	15	5	3.01	27	26	7	0	173	167	74	58	69	114
Kyles, Stan	4	2	3.41	27	5	0	1	69	66	36	26	27	41
Martinez, Ramon	5	2	2.76	10	10	1	0	59	43	24	18	32	49
Mathis, Ron (8 CS)	2	6	7.29	16	13	0	0	70	106	62	57	24	52
*Searage, Ray	2	3	5.10	51	0	0	8	60	62	39	34	25	58
Torres, Phil	1	1	4.50	8	0	0	1	14	12	7	7	5	13
Zaske, Jeff (7 Tac)	1	1	7.71	11	5	0	0	33	31	31	28	33	28

CALGARY

BATTING	AVG	G	AB	R	H	2B	3B	HR	RBI	BB	SO	SB
*Briley, Greg, of-2b	.313	112	444	74	139	29	9	11	66	40	51	27
#Cochrane, Dave, 1b-3b	.286	120	406	55	116	27	3	15	61	49	96	4
Diaz, Mario, ss	.329	46	164	16	54	18	0	1	30	9	10	1
*Fields, Bruce, of	.321	42	168	31	54	6	1	4	19	10	14	8
*Gibbons, John, of	.107	17	28	3	3	1	0	0	2	6	10	1
Giles, Brian, inf	.272	120	383	76	104	20	2	13	56	70	74	26
Hansen, Roger, c	.250	51	156	16	39	6	0	2	12	4	16	1
Hengel, Dave, of	.230	62	222	29	51	17	1	6	37	20	58	0
*Kingery, Mike, of	.318	47	170	29	54	12	2	1	14	33	23	5
Martinez, Edgar, 3b	.363	95	331	63	120	19	4	8	64	66	40	9
McGuire, Bill, c	.231	37	117	18	27	7	0	2	15	16	25	1
Nixon, Donell, dh-of	.281	40	160	28	45	7	0	3	10	14	20	12
#Ouellette, Phil, c	.285	94	291	38	83	24	2	10	44	36	54	1
Rabb, John, of	.309	48	181	35	56	12	0	13	44	19	20	6
Renteria, Rich, ss-2b	.264	24	87	15	23	6	1	4	10	5	10	3
#Simmons, Nelson, of	.307	128	462	74	142	28	2	14	73	59	66	4
Smith, Brick, 1b	.284	86	306	43	87	18	2	8	50	29	36	4
Vizquel, Omar, ss	.224	33	107	10	24	2	3	1	12	5	14	2
*Watters, Mike, 2b-of	.276	102	344	44	95	12	1	1	31	27	53	6
*Wishnevski, Mike, of	.255	32	94	21	24	6	1	4	16	11	21	2

PITCHING	W	L	ERA	G	GS	CG	SV	IP	H	R	ER	BB	SO
Baller, Jay	10	7	3.75	66	1	0	10	98	91	48	41	33	82
Bankhead, Scott	1	1	7.36	2	2	0	0	11	15	9	9	5	5
*Burroughs, Darren	2	10	5.26	38	14	2	1	115	120	85	67	53	91
Campbell, Mike	4	4	4.48	10	10	3	0	70	80	35	35	26	38
Christ, Mike	0	0	11.57	7	0	0	0	9	17	12	12	7	11
Hanson, Erik	12	7	4.23	27	26	2	0	162	167	92	76	57	154
Hull, Jeff	3	3	3.43	20	7	0	1	58	52	31	22	35	43
*Mendek, Bill	1	1	5.03	8	0	0	1	20	20	12	11	8	14
Nunez, Edwin	2	0	4.70	3	3	0	0	15	15	9	8	4	12
Powell, Dennis	6	4	4.17	21	18	2	1	108	116	57	50	49	81
*Price, Bryan	2	1	6.03	6	5	0	0	31	40	22	21	19	21
Roberts, Scott	0	2	4.23	23	3	0	2	55	63	28	26	18	42

	W	L	ERA	G	GS	CG	SV	IP	H	R	ER	BB	SO
Schooler, Mike	4	4	3.21	26	0	0	8	34	33	19	12	6	47
*Scurry, Rod	2	1	4.07	18	0	0	2	24	26	14	11	16	23
Solano, Julio	3	2	4.89	25	1	0	1	35	32	19	19	17	23
Taylor, Terry	11	9	5.64	24	24	2	0	134	151	89	84	90	97
*Trout, Steve	0	2	1.15	3	3	0	0	16	15	5	2	2	2
Walker, Jim	2	5	5.56	37	9	0	1	100	130	72	62	26	52
*Walter, Gene	0	0	2.08	8	0	0	2	9	9	5	2	1	11
West, Matt	3	7	5.79	12	12	0	0	65	79	47	42	24	38
*Wilkinson, Bill	0	4	9.13	21	4	0	4	24	31	28	24	20	20

COLORADO SPRINGS

BATTING	AVG	G	AB	R	H	2B	3B	HR	RBI	BB	SO	SB
Allen, Rod, dh	.324	124	469	84	152	36	4	23	100	44	74	1
Bell, Jay, ss	.276	49	181	35	50	12	2	7	24	26	27	3
Bennett, Keith, Inf	.214	7	14	4	3	0	0	1	4	4	2	2
*Clark, Dave, of	.297	47	165	27	49	10	2	4	31	27	37	4
Ferretti, Sam, 2b	.196	18	56	6	11	1	0	0	5	3	10	0
Firova, Dan, c	.309	17	55	7	17	2	0	0	4	5	9	0
*Francona, Terry, of	.323	68	235	29	76	15	5	0	32	13	18	0
Higgins, Mark, dh-1b	.200	26	80	9	16	1	0	2	7	10	15	0
#Hinzo, Tom, 2b	.232	119	449	67	104	14	4	1	29	46	76	32
Jimenez, Houston, inf	.293	22	58	11	17	5	1	0	6	4	7	0
*Lampkin, Tom, c	.280	34	107	14	30	6	0	0	7	9	12	0
*Lovell, Don, 1b	.249	121	421	47	105	20	5	3	65	16	31	0
Medina, Luis, of-1b	.310	111	406	81	126	28	6	28	81	42	107	1
Richardson, Tim, 3b	.233	16	43	7	10	1	1	0	2	2	4	0
*Stefero, John, c	.201	62	179	11	36	10	0	3	16	22	46	0
Tingley, Ron, c	.285	44	130	11	37	5	1	3	20	12	23	1
Washington, Randy, of	.285	94	263	43	75	15	2	6	29	31	64	0
Wasinger, Mark, ol-3b (21 Phx) ...	.291	58	196	26	57	12	0	0	15	22	27	4
Whitfield, Ken, of	.284	19	67	8	19	5	0	4	8	3	21	0
Williams, Eddie, 3b	.301	101	365	53	110	24	3	12	58	18	52	0
*Williams, Reggie, of	.294	114	456	72	134	27	5	6	58	40	60	36
Zuvella, Paul, ss	.289	68	232	33	67	11	3	1	28	17	19	6

PITCHING	W	L	ERA	G	GS	CG	SV	IP	H	R	ER	BB	SO
Akerfelds, Darrel	3	7	4.34	49	0	0	6	58	70	43	28	26	49
Brown, Mike	10	9	6.12	26	20	6	1	140	175	101	95	47	95
Codiroli, Chris	5	4	4.86	17	16	0	0	96	104	64	52	42	51
Dedmon, Jeff	2	3	4.35	17	2	0	1	41	56	30	20	11	25
Fowlkes, Alan	4	3	4.76	8	7	1	0	57	58	40	30	18	23
Ghelfi, Tony	4	4	4.52	12	8	1	1	62	67	35	31	27	37
Gordon, Don	3	3	4.24	21	1	1	0	57	62	34	27	13	19
*Havens, Brad	0	0	2.40	9	1	0	0	15	12	4	4	4	7
Hilton, Stan	1	1	5.63	9	5	0	0	40	57	30	25	16	27
*Kaiser, Jeff	3	2	3.74	36	0	0	6	53	56	23	22	19	47
Laskey, Bill	1	1	5.96	12	0	0	2	26	38	22	17	6	15
Murphy, Mike	0	2	7.94	2	2	0	0	11	12	10	10	3	1
Nichols, Rod	2	6	5.68	10	9	2	0	59	69	41	37	17	43
Perlman, Jon	3	1	3.23	22	0	0	5	31	31	16	11	11	19
*Peterson, Rick	0	1	6.75	1	1	0	0	4	7	3	3	2	0
Ritter, Reggie	1	2	11.72	10	0	0	0	18	35	24	23	12	5
Rodriguez, Rick	8	6	3.06	19	19	5	0	127	112	49	43	43	55
Scott, Charles	1	3	6.60	9	9	0	0	46	66	35	34	10	18
Skalski, Joe	10	13	6.55	29	29	3	0	159	186	125	116	64	117
*Wickander, Kevin	0	2	7.16	19	0	0	0	33	44	30	26	27	22
Yett, Rich	0	1	9.00	2	2	0	0	8	10	8	8	3	5

EDMONTON

BATTING	AVG	G	AB	R	H	2B	3B	HR	RBI	BB	SO	SB
Alfaro, Jesus, 3b	.212	18	52	12	11	3	0	2	4	11	9	0
Anderson, Kent, ss	.251	113	374	51	94	22	3	2	39	26	66	10
Bichette, Dante, of	.267	132	509	64	136	29	10	14	81	25	78	7
*Bosley, Thad, of	.308	18	52	13	16	5	1	0	9	7	4	1
*Brady, Brian, of-dh	.273	119	410	68	112	30	5	10	67	29	85	0
Brown, Mike, of	.347	33	118	21	41	6	1	3	21	13	14	1
Coachman, Pete, 2b	.265	129	486	80	129	21	2	6	62	53	63	17
Davis, Doug, c	.257	79	245	28	63	10	0	1	29	28	48	2
Doran, Mark, of	.239	84	255	33	61	9	3	6	20	22	74	4
Dorsett, Brian, c	.262	53	164	21	43	7	0	11	31	28	30	0
*Eppard, Jim, 1b	.262	42	141	18	37	6	1	0	16	16	9	0
Holmes, Stan, 1b-dh	.254	102	331	48	84	17	2	14	62	24	44	1
#King, Kevin, dh	.263	57	213	37	56	12	5	9	35	20	66	4
Marquez, Edwin, c	.395	13	38	8	15	3	2	0	7	5	8	1
#McLemore, Mark, 2b	.267	12	45	7	12	3	0	0	4	4	4	7
Miller, Darrell, of	.317	37	123	14	39	5	3	4	19	10	24	3
Miscik, Bobby, inf	.231	31	104	13	24	6	0	2	11	11	13	1
Noboa, Junior, 2b	.296	50	159	24	47	6	1	0	17	11	12	5
Polidor, Gus, ss	.364	13	33	6	12	4	0	0	7	3	3	0
Ramos, Domingo, 3b (43 CS) ...	.279	50	165	30	46	10	2	2	25	18	18	1
Redfield, Joe, 3b-1b	.290	118	417	67	121	38	1	3	52	36	83	11
#Thomas, Jim, inf-dh	.274	52	164	21	45	4	5	2	20	10	24	2
#Walker, Chico, of	.289	79	304	58	88	17	4	7	39	29	47	25

— 90 —

PITCHING	W	L	ERA	G	GS	CG	SV	IP	H	R	ER	BB	SO
Alicea, Miguel	1	1	6.39	9	0	0	1	13	20	11	9	6	9
Buice, Dewayne	0	0	2.31	9	0	0	0	3	4	3	2		17
Clark, Terry	7	6	4.51	16	16	3	0	114	128	62	57	33	59
Cook, Mike	5	9	4.65	51	5	0	10	91	93	54	47	41	84
Dacus, Barry	0	2	9.85	15	1	0	0	25	41	29	27	12	9
*DiMichele, Frank	0	0	4.05	12	0	0	0	13	16	7	6	6	8
Fetters, Mike	2	0	1.93	2	2	1	0	14	8	3	3	10	11
Harvey, Bryan	0	0	3.18	5	0	0	2	6	7	2	2	4	10
Holmes, Stan	0	0	5.40	4	0	0	0	5	6	3	3	2	0
Johnson, Joe	11	11	5.96	27	27	2	0	156	193	115	103	56	63
Krawczyk, Ray	4	9	4.56	20	13	1	0	95	101	58	48	25	70
Lazorko, Jack	11	8	3.87	21	21	9	0	149	156	72	64	33	59
*Lovelace, Vance	1	3	6.10	46	5	1	1	69	79	48	47	57	58
Lugo, Urbano	9	6	5.26	38	15	2	1	116	148	74	68	47	69
Monteleone, Rich (10 Cal)	4	7	5.08	30	16	3	0	122	141	84	69	27	97
*Reed, Marty	2	7	6.10	11	11	0	0	62	79	47	42	28	13
Venturino, Phil	2	6	6.28	22	7	0	0	62	96	45	43	18	34
Walker, Kurt	0	1	4.41	9	0	0	0	16	20	11	8	5	13
Ward, Colby	0	2	3.77	22	0	0	4	31	23	15	13	16	17
*Young, Shane	2	2	5.40	14	2	0	0	37	39	27	22	32	29

LAS VEGAS

BATTING	AVG	G	AB	R	H	2B	3B	HR	RBI	BB	SO	SB
Abner, Shawn, of	.254	63	252	35	64	16	2	4	34	11	39	0
#Alomar, Roberto, 2b	.270	9	37	5	10	1	0	2	14	1	4	3
Alomar, Sandy, c	.297	93	337	59	100	9	5	16	71	28	35	1
Basso, Mike, c	.197	17	61	8	12	5	0	2	10	5	10	0
Bochy, Mike, c	.231	53	147	17	34	5	0	5	13	17	28	1
Brassil, Tom, 3b-dh	.310	83	239	31	74	10	3	3	34	10	27	3
#Brumley, Mike, ss	.315	113	425	77	134	16	7	3	41	56	84	41
*Byers, Randy, of	.267	100	360	52	96	24	4	6	55	27	89	4
Clark, Jerald, of	.301	107	408	65	123	27	7	9	67	17	66	6
#Cora, Joey, 2b	.296	127	460	73	136	15	3	3	55	44	20	31
Green, Gary, 3b-ss	.272	88	302	39	82	16	2	0	37	16	49	4
#Howard, Tom, of	.251	44	167	29	42	9	1	0	15	12	31	3
#Jefferson, Stan, of	.317	74	278	60	88	14	6	4	33	36	43	19
Mack, Shane, of	.347	55	196	43	68	7	1	10	40	29	44	7
*Nelson, Rob, 1b-dh	.260	116	388	68	101	23	1	23	77	62	131	1
Pounders, Brad, 1b-dh	.279	110	376	47	105	23	1	14	74	33	95	1
#Roberts, Bip, 3b-of	.353	100	343	73	121	21	8	7	51	32	45	29
Wrona, Billy, inf	.375	8	24	8	9	2	0	0	2	4	6	0

PITCHING	W	L	ERA	G	GS	CG	SV	IP	H	R	ER	BB	SO
Bitker, Joe	8	10	3.63	28	27	3	0	178	195	98	72	41	106
*Comstock, Keith	5	4	3.14	50	0	0	17	72	67	32	25	31	78
Costello, Mike	6	5	4.32	17	13	2	0	81	99	57	39	34	44
Gilmore, Terry	1	1	4.76	4	4	1	0	23	26	21	12	8	10
Harris, Greg S.	9	5	4.11	26	25	5	0	160	160	84	73	65	147
Lynch, Joe	6	6	3.27	58	0	0	8	88	93	39	32	39	60
*McKeon, Joel	2	5	6.05	36	10	0	1	100	113	73	67	67	63
Nolte, Eric	8	7	6.03	27	25	1	0	128	168	97	86	53	68
*Roberts, Pete	4	6	6.68	16	13	1	0	69	90	55	51	35	50
Simmons, Todd	12	5	4.29	54	0	0	2	109	127	66	52	39	86
Towers, Kevin	2	5	5.84	27	12	0	0	86	103	69	56	60	53
*Vosberg, Ed	11	7	4.15	45	11	1	2	128	137	67	59	56	75

PHOENIX

BATTING	AVG	G	AB	R	H	2B	3B	HR	RBI	BB	SO	SB
Benjamin, Mike, ss	.170	37	106	13	18	4	1	0	6	13	32	2
*Dabney, Ty, dh-of	.250	68	196	20	49	13	1	2	26	14	37	1
#Escobar, Angel, ss	.200	77	270	32	54	6	6	1	29	29	54	6
Garner, Phil, 2b	.267	17	45	5	12	2	1	1	5	4	4	0
*Graham, Everett, of	.303	44	119	27	36	6	1	3	11	17	17	7
Hayes, Charlie, of-3b	.307	131	492	71	151	26	4	7	71	34	91	4
#Jones, Gary, c	.281	12	32	2	9	1	0	1	4	2	3	0
Manwaring, Kirt, c	.282	81	273	29	77	12	2	2	35	14	32	3
McCue, Deron, of	.200	28	70	12	14	3	0	1	7	10	15	1
*Melendez, Francisco, 1b	.361	96	368	61	133	26	2	4	58	40	40	5
Melvin, Bob, c	.307	21	75	11	23	5	0	2	9	8	13	0
#Meyers, Paul, of	.228	66	215	23	49	7	2	0	21	23	33	2
Perezchica, Tony, 2b-ss	.306	134	517	79	158	18	10	9	64	44	125	10
Ramos, Bobby, c	.181	55	155	11	28	1	0	0	6	20	17	0
*Reid, Jay, of	.276	111	381	62	105	21	6	18	72	59	71	5
Tillman, Rusty, 1b-of	.295	113	421	62	124	25	4	12	71	25	60	7
Williams, Matt, 3b	.271	82	306	45	83	19	1	12	51	13	56	6
Wotus, Ron, 2b-3b	.287	82	261	46	75	8	3	1	33	43	35	7

PITCHING	W	L	ERA	G	GS	CG	SV	IP	H	R	ER	BB	SO
Best, Karl (31 Port)	0	3	4.32	39	0	0	21	42	36	22	20	17	34
Bockus, Randy	4	3	5.96	23	3	0	2	51	63	36	34	22	27
Brantley, Jeff	9	5	4.33	27	19	1	0	123	130	65	59	39	83
Burkett, John	5	11	5.21	21	21	0	0	114	142	79	66	49	74
Bystrom, Marty	3	3	6.14	11	11	0	0	56	68	43	38	26	40
*Cook, Dennis	11	9	3.88	26	25	5	0	141	138	73	61	51	110
Davis, Ron	7	3	2.72	42	0	0	6	43	35	19	13	26	38
*Dravecky, Dave	0	1	16.88	1	1	0	0	3	11	5	5	0	1
*Ferreira, Tony	1	2	3.64	21	0	0	3	30	24	12	12	8	23

	W	L	ERA	G	GS	CG	SV	IP	H	R	ER	BB	SO
Hogan, Mike	0	1	10.80	5	0	0	0	13	22	18	16	8	0
Krukow, Mike	1	0	0.00	1	1	0	0	5	0	0	0	0	5
*Lucas, Gary	1	3	4.52	33	0	0	7	62	75	32	31	13	58
Lynch, Ed	0	1	36.82	1	1	0	0	4	14	15	15	3	2
Mason, Roger	2	9	4.86	19	17	1	0	91	89	62	49	38	62
McCament, Randy	0	1	7.56	19	0	0	1	25	40	26	21	16	7
*Mulholland, Terry	7	3	3.58	19	14	3	0	101	116	45	40	44	49
Ohnoutka, Brian	1	8	5.05	17	15	3	0	89	96	59	50	52	35
*Puikunas, Ed	0	0	6.75	4	0	0	0	5	11	6	4	3	5
*Samuels, Roger	3	2	2.63	30	0	0	8	48	34	16	14	15	33
*Scherrer, Bill	0	0	5.51	12	0	0	1	16	17	10	10	8	11
Sorensen, Lary	4	2	2.76	14	3	1	2	42	42	15	13	12	11
Tate, Stuart	2	4	5.89	27	3	0	2	47	50	38	31	30	46
Villa, Mike	4	1	5.16	25	0	0	0	66	64	40	38	40	35
*Wilson, Trevor	2	3	5.05	11	9	0	0	52	49	35	29	33	49

PORTLAND

BATTING	AVG	G	AB	R	H	2B	3B	HR	RBI	BB	SO	SB
#Baker, Doug, ss	.245	121	417	52	102	17	4	2	41	48	59	17
*Bierley, Brad, of	.246	92	305	44	75	10	1	4	36	36	49	6
*Bullock, Eric, of	.309	117	434	69	134	20	8	2	46	40	43	51
Christensen, John, of (39 Cal)	.304	106	385	57	117	23	3	9	49	42	65	9
Cockrell, Alan, of (102 Phx) ..	.293	120	410	74	120	17	3	10	47	53	118	4
Davidson, Mark, of	.321	15	56	6	18	4	2	0	5	10	8	1
Ficklin, Winston, of-dh ..	.277	123	441	71	122	23	10	5	39	50	85	17
Harper, Brian, c	.353	46	170	34	60	10	1	13	42	14	7	2
Jones, Ricky, 1b-3b	.248	84	278	34	69	15	1	7	39	13	47	1
*Leeper, Dave, dh-p	.280	50	100	7	28	7	0	0	10	5	18	0
Liddle, Steve, c	.200	43	125	17	25	7	3	0	14	14	19	0
*Lowry, Dwight, c	.258	79	244	33	63	13	3	5	33	20	45	2
#Moses, John, of	.348	17	66	13	23	3	1	0	6	5	2	5
Nieto, Tom, c	.278	53	158	11	44	7	2	3	21	21	32	0
*Pittaro, Chris, 2b-ss ...	.241	73	249	21	60	11	3	2	32	21	24	4
Ralston, Bobby, 2b	.286	81	280	26	80	7	1	0	24	18	18	10
Reboulet, Jeff, 2b-ss	.083	4	12	0	1	0	0	0	1	3	2	0
Rodriguez, Victor, 3b-2b ..	.288	139	563	67	162	27	8	9	70	32	48	2
*Torve, Kelvin, 1b	.301	103	385	58	116	28	2	9	46	42	37	5
#Wilson, Phil, of	.192	35	120	16	23	1	0	3	10	11	14	5

PITCHING	W	L	ERA	G	GS	CG	SV	IP	H	R	ER	BB	SO
*Anderson, Allan	1	1	1.26	3	3	1	0	14	11	4	2	5	9
Bryden, T.R.	8	8	4.99	30	13	1	0	114	115	66	63	62	64
Bumgarner, Jeff	2	3	7.71	7	7	0	0	26	33	26	22	32	17
*Casian, Larry	0	1	0.00	1	0	0	0	3	5	3	0	0	0
Davins, Jim	0	5	5.61	41	0	0	7	61	69	39	38	30	55
Galvez, Balvino	11	7	3.77	23	22	3	0	143	149	69	60	63	60
Kepshire, Kurt	2	1	0.61	7	0	0	0	15	11	1	1	6	10
*Leeper, Dave	0	0	8.82	19	0	0	1	34	53	33	33	15	16
*Mason, Mike	2	2	5.81	23	3	0	0	53	62	35	34	33	24
Olivares, Francisco	11	10	4.31	21	21	4	0	134	134	69	64	43	95
Portugal, Mark	2	0	1.37	3	3	1	0	20	15	3	3	8	9
*Schatzeder, Dan	6	4	2.60	13	12	4	0	87	82	26	25	24	55
Smith, Roy	12	9	4.32	22	22	7	0	150	152	82	72	31	110
Soff, Ray	8	5	3.97	28	13	3	0	134	149	66	59	45	61
Straker, Les	0	0	3.20	4	4	0	0	20	19	12	7	8	13
Toliver, Fred	7	2	3.13	13	13	4	0	95	79	42	33	35	54
Trudeau, Kevin	2	2	3.60	8	6	2	0	45	43	24	18	14	24
Winn, Jim	2	3	3.99	22	0	0	7	29	32	14	13	12	21

TACOMA

BATTING	AVG	G	AB	R	H	2B	3B	HR	RBI	BB	SO	SB
Arndt, Larry, 3b	.273	102	326	45	89	10	4	3	37	50	79	18
Blankenship, Lance, 2b ..	.265	131	437	84	116	21	8	9	52	96	75	40
*Brilinski, Tyler, 1b	.257	120	378	41	97	18	1	8	52	30	67	1
*Howitt, Dann, of	.133	4	15	1	2	1	0	0	0	0	4	0
*Jennings, Doug, of	.327	16	49	12	16	1	0	0	9	18	13	5
*Johnson, Roy, dh	.241	99	311	26	75	18	0	7	36	22	47	2
*Jones, Gary, of-dh	.234	116	316	52	74	9	4	2	22	68	63	13
Jones, Jim, c	.256	19	39	5	10	1	0	1	7	10	13	1
Jones, Ross, ss	.111	5	18	0	2	0	0	0	1	2	3	1
#Jose, Felix, of	.317	133	504	71	160	28	5	12	83	53	75	16
Jurak, Ed, ss-3b	.295	126	448	63	132	22	2	7	67	62	55	13
*Krenchicki, Wayne, 3b ..	.278	11	36	4	10	1	1	1	4	8	2	0
McGinnis, Rusty, c-1b ..	.253	63	186	25	47	13	1	2	21	21	38	1
Mercado, Orlando, c	.223	53	148	16	33	6	0	2	19	19	25	0
*Phillips, Tony, inf-of ...	.271	16	59	10	16	1	0	0	2	8	12	0
#Polonia, Luis, of	.335	65	254	58	85	13	5	2	27	29	28	31
Robertson, Andre, ss ...	.258	45	120	16	31	5	3	1	10	5	34	3
Sanchez, Alex, of	.254	130	489	54	124	28	4	10	74	30	77	7
Shaddy, Chris, ss	.223	36	103	15	23	3	1	1	5	8	24	2
Sinatro, Matt, c	.231	77	234	28	54	8	1	2	23	37	41	2
*Sliwinski, Kevin, 1b	.127	21	55	4	7	0	0	1	5	6	14	0
*Xavier, Joe, inf	.282	87	216	23	61	10	1	1	21	18	42	1

PITCHING	W	L	ERA	G	GS	CG	SV	IP	H	R	ER	BB	SO
Bordi, Rich	7	7	3.48	40	10	0	3	119	120	61	46	35	81
Burns, Todd	4	3	3.68	21	5	1	1	73	74	39	30	26	59

BATTING

R—Mike Devereaux, Albuquerque	....	88
H—Vic Rodriguez, Portland	....	162
TB—Rod Allen, Colorado Springs	....	265
2B—Joe Redfield, Edmonton	....	38
3B—Six tied at	....	10
HR—Luis Medina, Colorado Springs	....	28
RBI—Rod Allen, Colorado Springs	....	100
GWRBI—Rob Nelson, Las Vegas	....	14
SH—Larry Arndt, Tacoma	....	9
SF—Ed Jurak, Tacoma	....	10
BB—Lance Blankenship, Tacoma	....	96
IBB—Three tied at	....	9
HBP—Eddie Williams, Colorado Springs	....	12
SO—Rob Nelson, Las Vegas	....	130
SB—Eric Bullock, Portland	....	51
CS—Eric Bullock, Portland	....	18
Slg. Pct.—Luis Medina, Colorado Springs	....	616
OB Pct.—Edgar Martinez, Calgary	....	467

Department Leaders

PITCHING

G—Jay Baller, Calgary	....	66
GS—Reese Lambert, Tacoma	....	30
—Manuel Hernandez, Tucson	....	30
CG—Jack Lazorko, Edmonton	....	10
ShO—Bill Krueger, Albuquerque	....	4
Sv—Karl Best, Portland-Phoenix	....	21
W—Bill Krueger, Albuquerque	....	15
L—Reese Lambert, Tacoma	....	14
IP—Anthony Kelley, Tucson	....	186
H—Manuel Hernandez, Tucson	....	210
—Anthony Kelley, Tucson	....	210
R—Joe Skalski, Colorado Springs	....	125
HR—Joe Skalski, Colorado Springs	....	30
BB—Terry Taylor, Calgary	....	90
HB—T.R. Bryden, Portland	....	10
—Kevin Hagen, Tucson	....	10
SO—Erik Hanson, Calgary	....	154
WP—Joe Skalski, Colorado Springs	....	14
Bk—Mike Loynd, Tucson	....	21

	W	L	ERA	G	GS	CG	SV	IP	H	R	ER	BB	SO
*Clark, Bryan	5	6	3.30	19	14	2	0	93	104	50	34	44	46
Corbell, Charlie	1	4	6.21	6	6	0	0	29	49	26	20	7	6
Corsi, Jim	2	5	2.75	50	0	0	16	59	60	25	18	23	48
Dye, Steve	1	0	0.00	1	0	0	0	3	1	0	0	1	0
Garcia, Apolinar	0	0	9.00	1	1	0	0	5	6	5	5	4	1
*Gorman, Tom	0	0	54.00	1	0	0	0	0	2	2	2	0	0
Jones, Jim	0	0	27.00	1	0	0	0	1	3	3	3	2	1
Killingsworth, Kirk	1	0	3.96	22	0	0	2	36	41	17	16	11	21
*Klink, Joe	2	1	6.05	27	0	0	1	39	48	29	26	17	32
*Lambert, Reese	9	14	4.73	31	30	2	0	160	189	106	84	83	67
Law, Joe	5	3	3.93	12	11	1	0	66	62	31	29	19	46
Meeks, Tim	2	2	6.14	9	8	0	0	37	51	28	25	13	21
*Otto, Dave	4	9	3.52	21	21	2	0	128	123	71	50	63	80
Shaver, Jeff	7	10	4.48	27	27	1	0	147	151	78	73	39	93
*Snyder, Brian	7	8	2.63	54	6	0	0	110	94	37	32	54	86
Stoddard, Bob	0	3	6.68	31	1	0	2	61	76	53	45	32	41
*Von Ohlen, Dave	4	6	4.45	34	0	0	2	57	69	39	28	15	35

TUCSON

BATTING	AVG	G	AB	R	H	2B	3B	HR	RBI	BB	SO	SB
*Allaire, Karl, ss	.273	125	355	61	97	17	5	0	46	69	87	7
#Ashby, Alan, c	.000	2	4	1	0	0	0	0	0	0	0	0
#Bailey, Mark, c-dh	.171	37	111	6	19	7	1	0	9	15	24	1
Biggio, Craig, c	.320	77	281	60	90	21	4	3	39	40	39	19
#Caminiti, Ken, 3b	.272	109	416	54	113	24	7	5	66	29	54	13
#Candaele, Casey, of-2b	.258	17	66	8	17	3	0	0	5	4	6	4
Carpenter, Glenn, 1b	.219	121	361	38	79	20	2	0	30	34	64	7
Datz, Jeff, c	.223	60	148	18	33	7	0	2	11	22	30	2
*Drew, Cameron, of	.356	97	354	50	126	22	7	4	70	23	35	18
Fishel, John, of	.261	102	360	61	94	19	6	18	68	38	68	11
*Gainey, Ty, ph	.250	5	4	0	1	0	0	0	1	0	1	0
Henderson, Steve, of	.278	42	133	17	37	8	0	4	17	23	27	4
Jackson, Chuck, ss-3b	.298	48	151	21	45	8	0	2	11	13	12	6
Keedy, Pat, 3b-of	.269	59	171	24	46	4	0	6	22	23	38	4
*Meadows, Louie, of-1b	.254	85	280	42	71	16	9	5	43	40	68	20
Mikulik, Joe, of	.222	68	176	15	39	6	4	1	17	10	38	6
#Nago, Garrett, c	.239	27	67	11	16	3	0	0	6	11	9	0
Rood, Nelson, 2b-ss	.223	88	197	31	44	5	3	0	18	17	21	21
#Smajstrla, Craig, 2b	.310	134	513	89	159	30	5	4	56	35	40	28
*Spilman, Harry, 1b (9 Phx)	.328	20	64	12	21	4	1	4	17	4	10	0
Trevino, Alex, c	.222	15	45	5	10	3	1	0	3	2	8	0
*Walling, Denny, 3b	.188	5	16	2	3	1	0	0	4	4	4	0
Walters, Dan, c	.000	2	7	0	0	0	0	0	0	0	2	0
*Weaver, Jim, of	.272	130	423	77	115	23	10	8	73	69	82	30

PITCHING	W	L	ERA	G	GS	CG	SV	IP	H	R	ER	BB	SO
Camacho, Ernie	1	6	4.25	36	1	0	5	42	47	24	20	27	27
Cano, Jose	2	1	4.29	4	4	0	0	21	24	11	10	6	11
Childress, Rocky	6	4	3.33	43	6	0	2	97	102	48	36	41	57
Christiansen, Clay	1	4	14.01	14	5	0	0	26	62	44	41	9	7
Crew, Ken	1	1	4.70	17	1	0	0	38	34	21	20	10	34
Deleon, Luis	4	8	5.23	48	3	0	14	65	68	40	38	22	59
*Funk, Tom	0	1	2.04	27	0	0	3	18	15	5	4	10	17
Hagen, Kevin	10	11	4.81	25	23	0	0	131	160	89	70	47	45
Heathcock, Jeff	3	5	5.08	16	13	1	0	80	88	45	45	19	49
Hernandez, Manny	10	9	4.24	31	30	1	0	185	210	99	87	44	122
Kelley, Anthony	13	6	3.96	29	29	4	0	186	210	95	82	43	93
Loynd, Mike	3	12	5.59	29	23	1	0	130	154	96	81	71	97
*Meads, Dave	3	4	1.96	32	0	0	3	46	45	12	10	10	46
Montalvo, Rafael	9	1	4.40	62	4	0	3	117	148	62	57	43	67
*Sambito, Joe	2	2	2.82	34	1	0	5	54	57	17	17	13	43

VANCOUVER

BATTING	AVG	G	AB	R	H	2B	3B	HR	RBI	BB	SO	SB
Alcazar, Jorge, c	.214	40	84	10	18	3	2	0	12	10	21	1
Davis, Mark, of	.212	68	241	24	51	9	2	4	29	28	65	8
Gallagher, Dave, of	.336	34	131	23	44	8	1	4	27	12	21	5
Garcia, Santiago, 2b	.267	74	273	38	73	19	3	4	27	13	42	18
#Hill, Donnie, dh-2b	.346	7	26	5	9	4	0	0	7	3	5	1
Jackson, Ron, dh-1b	.176	18	51	5	9	1	0	1	5	4	5	0
*Johnson, Lance, of	.307	100	411	71	126	12	6	2	36	42	52	49
Karkovice, Ron, c	.250	39	116	12	29	10	0	2	13	8	26	2
Lindsey, Bill, c-dh	.280	95	325	45	91	14	1	6	41	33	47	3
McPhail, Marlin, of-dh ...	.276	91	297	54	82	13	5	5	34	35	52	5
Milholland, Eric, c	.250	4	12	1	3	1	0	0	2	0	3	0
Morman, Russ, 1b-of ...	.300	69	257	40	77	8	1	5	46	32	48	4
Paris, Kelly, 3b	.284	99	359	41	102	32	3	5	52	43	48	9
#Randall, Sap, of	.274	112	402	65	110	24	6	11	61	46	68	7
Schaefer, Jeff, ss	.247	131	450	53	111	30	2	1	59	21	53	7
*Sconiers, Daryl, 1b-dh ..	.262	125	447	59	117	16	2	11	58	40	52	4
Springer, Steve, 3b	.267	27	105	15	28	4	1	2	9	4	17	1
*Thomas, Troy, of	.105	11	19	4	2	1	0	0	0	4	6	1
*Thompson, Tommy, c ...	.433	9	30	5	13	0	0	0	4	2	4	0
Venturini, Pete, inf	.200	31	70	6	14	1	1	0	4	6	11	1
Williams, Ken, of	.250	16	60	8	15	2	1	1	6	2	14	2
*Woodard, Mike, 2b	.332	94	367	63	122	12	10	1	40	37	31	18
#Yastrzemski, Mike, of ...	.211	54	185	13	39	5	0	2	21	21	23	3

PITCHING	W	L	ERA	G	GS	CG	SV	IP	H	R	ER	BB	SO
Bittiger, Jeff	4	1	1.04	7	7	5	0	52	35	9	6	6	49
*Blasucci, Tony	1	0	0.00	2	0	0	0	2	0	0	0	1	2
Chadwick, Ray	2	5	6.51	14	13	0	0	76	94	57	55	42	62
Davis, Joel	7	1	3.75	27	13	1	2	96	101	45	40	27	75
Davis, John	1	0	3.18	15	0	0	5	17	14	7	6	7	9
*Edwards, Wayne	0	0	0.00	2	0	0	0	3	0	0	0	0	2
*Hall, Grady	2	2	4.11	8	8	0	0	46	43	24	21	21	13
Hardy, Jack	9	5	3.42	38	8	1	2	97	94	41	37	19	57
*Hibbard, Greg	11	11	4.12	25	24	4	0	144	155	74	66	44	65
McCarthy, Tom	1	0	1.04	9	0	0	4	19	11	0	0	4	11
Pall, Donn	5	2	2.23	44	0	0	10	73	61	21	18	20	41
*Patterson, Ken	6	5	3.23	55	4	0	12	86	64	37	31	36	89
Pawlowski, John	0	0	4.22	9	0	0	0	21	24	11	10	12	11
Peterson, Adam	14	7	3.32	28	28	4	0	171	161	69	63	81	103
*Rosenberg, Steve	2	0	3.33	20	0	0	3	24	15	9	9	11	17
Segura, Jose	6	6	4.54	20	19	0	0	111	127	69	56	60	39
Thompson, Tommy	0	1	20.25	1	0	0	0	1	5	5	3	2	0
Venturini, Pete	0	1	6.75	3	0	0	0	4	4	4	3	3	2
Willis, Carl	4	4	4.22	40	1	0	4	64	77	36	30	16	44
Wojna, Ed	10	6	3.27	21	17	5	1	124	112	55	45	36	73

Bam Bam goes bye-bye, but Albany wins anyway

By KEVIN IOLE

The Albany Yankees began the 1988 season with the Eastern League's best prospect and ended it as its best team.

Third baseman Hensley "Bam Bam" Meulens spent little more than half the season in Albany, but lived up to his status as one of the top power-hitting prospects in the minor leagues.

Meulens, 20, hit 13 home runs in 278 at-bats before an early July promotion to Triple-A Columbus. Meulens was leading the league in home runs when promoted, and left such an impression that he was voted the top major league prospect in the league by managers in a poll by Baseball America.

The Yankees struggled awhile after losing Meulens, but righted themselves in time to make the

Hensley Meulens
. . . Short stay in EL

playoffs. Once in, there was no denying the Yankees Albany's first title since rejoining the league in 1983.

Albany finished fourth in an oft-turbulent regular season, one in which they had to live through the firing of manager Tommy Jones and the comings and goings of 52 players. But the Yankees had enough to defeat regular season champion Glens Falls, 3-1, in the semifinals, then oust Vermont by the same margin in the finals.

The Yankees had five catchers on their roster at season's end, and often had four of them—Mitch Lyden, John Ramos, Jim Leyritz and Jamie Nelson—in the lineup at the same time.

Jones was fired in June with the Yanks 26-25. They went

League Champions
(Playoff Champions, Where Applicable)

1988—Albany	1965—Pittsfield	1943—Elmira
1987—Harrisburg	1964—Elmira	1942—Scranton
1986—Vermont	1963—Charleston	1941—Elmira
1985—Vermont	1962—Elmira	1940—Binghamton
1984—Vermont	1961—Springfield	1939—Scranton
1983—New Britain	1960—*Williamsport	1938—Elmira
1982—West Haven	—*Springfield	1937—Elmira
1981—Bristol	1959—Springfield	1936—Scranton
1980—Holyoke	1958—Binghamton	1935—Binghamton
1979—West Haven	1957—Reading	1934—Williamsport
1978—Bristol	1956—Schenectady	1933—Binghamton
1977—West Haven	1955—Allentown	1932—Wilkes-Barre
1976—West Haven	1954—Albany	1931—Harrisburg
1975—Bristol	1953—Binghamton	1930—Wilkes-Barre
1974—Thetford Mines	1952—Binghamton	1929—Binghamton
1973—Reading	1951—Scranton	1928—Harrisburg
1972—West Haven	1950—Wilkes-Barre	1927—Harrisburg
1971—Elmira	1949—Binghamton	1926—Scranton
1970—Waterbury	1948—Scranton	1925—*York
1969—York	1947—Utica	—*Williamsport
1968—Reading	1946—Scranton	1924—Williamsport
1967—Binghamton	1945—Albany	1923—Williamsport
1966—Elmira	1944—Binghamton	
		*co-champions

Mike Harkey was Pittsfield's top pitcher, going 9-2 and earning midseason promotion to Triple-A Iowa.

46-41 under new manager Stump Merrill, then played their best ball in the playoffs.

But that wasn't all

The Eastern League was marked as much by its off-the-field news as its play on the field in 1988—all of which led to the EL greatly expanding its boundaries for 1989.

The league announced at midseason that Glens Falls would shift its operation to London, Ontario, for the 1989 season. London is close in proximity to Detroit, its parent club, but not closely aligned to remaining EL teams. After the season came an announcement that the five-year-old Vermont franchise would move to Canton, Ohio, further shifting the league's geographical balance westward.

Meanwhile, Northeastern Baseball Inc., preparing to move

its International League franchise from Maine to Scranton/Wilkes-Barre, Pa., was desperately trying to sell the Williamsport franchise, and initially struck a deal with Burlington, Vt., businessman Ray Pecor Jr.

Pecor's intention was to move the franchise to Vermont, to replace the one that was going to Canton, but EL owners never voted on the sale because of a dispute in the wording of the contract. Later, it appeared the Williamsport franchise would move to Hagerstown, Md.—former home of Baltimore's Class A Carolina League affiliate. A franchise in Hagerstown would shift the league's boundaries to the south.

Harkey working

The league was dominated by pitching in 1988, and no pitcher dominated like Pittsfield's Mike Harkey. Harkey, the No. 1 draft pick of the Chicago Cubs in 1987, was 9-2 with a 1.37 ERA, and earned a midyear promotion to Triple-A Iowa, and eventually to Chicago.

But Harkey wasn't the only top pitching prospect in the league, in a year where batting averages fell off dramatically—from a league-wide .274 in 1987 to .249 in 1988.

Pitcher of the year honors were won by Glens Falls righthander Cesar Mejia, who won his last nine decisions to finish 14-5. Mejia, whom Detroit selected from Toronto in the 1987 minor league draft, pitched one of the league's two no-hitters, zipping the Albany Yankees 3-0 April 17.

On July 8, Pittsfield's Kris Roth pitched a no-hitter against the Harrisburg Senators.

Multitalented outfielder Rob Richie carried Glens Falls to the regular season championship. Richie, who was named the league's most valuable player and its third-best major league prospect by Baseball America, hit .309 with 14 home runs and 82 RBIs.

Richie also led the league in RBIs, hits (155) and total bases (235), was second in games (137) and runs (75) and fourth in average and home runs.

In addition, he made himself a solid outfielder through hard work.

One of the most talked-about players in the league played just 17 games. Outfielder Ken Griffey Jr. joined Vermont in mid-August and hit .279 with two home runs and 10 RBIs. He showed the rounded game which made him the first choice in the 1987 draft, by the Seattle Mariners.

Vermont's Jim Wilson, making a comeback from a serious 1985 hand injury, hit 17 home runs to tie for the league lead with Chris Hoiles of Glens Falls.

Vermont's Rich Morales was named manager of the year for guiding a team short on punch to a 79-60 record and a second-place finish. Vermont, under a new Seattle affiliation, reached the EL championship series for the fifth consecutive year.

	W	L	Pct.	GB	
Glens Falls (Tigers) ..	80	57	.584	—	
Vermont (Mariners) ..	79	60	.568	2	
Pittsfield (Cubs)	75	63	.543	5½	1988
Albany (Yankees)	72	66	.522	8½	Final
Reading (Phillies)	67	69	.493	12½	Standings
Willmsport (Indians) .	66	73	.475	15	
Harrisburg (Pirates) .	65	73	.471	15½	
New Britn (Red Sox) .	47	90	.343	33	

1988: General Information

Playoffs: Vermont defeated Pittsfield 3-1 and Albany defeated Glens Falls 3-1 in best-of-5 semifinals; Albany defeated Vermont 3-1 in best-of-5 final for league championship.

Regular Season Attendance: Harrisburg, 216,940; Albany, 214,663; Reading, 144,007; Williamsport, 100,586; New Britain, 77,964; Vermont, 68,894; Glens Falls, 57,314, Pittsfield, 53,121.

Managers: Albany—Tommy Jones, Stump Merrill; **Glens Falls**—John Wockenfuss; **Harrisburg**—Dave Trembley; **New Britain**—Dave Holt; **Pittsfield**—Jim Essian; **Reading**—Bill Dancy; **Vermont**—Rich Morales; **Williamsport**—Mike Hargrove.

1988 Official All-Star Team: C—Chris Hoiles, Glens Falls. **1B**—Kevin Maas, Albany. **2B**—Andy Stankiewicz, Albany. **3B**—Shane Turner, Reading. **SS**—Omar Vizquel, Vermont. **Util**—Bryan House, Pittsfield. **OF**—Rob Richie, Glens Falls; Jerome Walton, Pittsfield; Oscar Azocar, Albany. **DH**—Jim Wilson, Vermont. **RHP**—Cesar Mejia, Glens Falls. **LHP**—Ken Williams, Glens Falls. **RP**—Dean Wilkins, Pittsfield. **Most Valuable Player**—Rob Richie, Glens Falls. **Pitcher of the Year**—Cesar Mejia, Glens Falls. **Manager of the Year**—Rich Morales, Vermont.

Top 10 Major League Prospects (by Baseball America): 1. Hensley Meulens, 3b, Albany; **2.** Mike Harkey, rhp, Pittsfield; **3.** Rob Richie, of, Glens Falls; **4.** Omar Vizquel, ss, Vermont; **5.** Jerome Walton, of, Pittsfield; **6.** Chuck Malone, rhp, Reading; **7.** Tom Lampkin, c, Williamsport; **8.** Joe Girardi, c, Pittsfield; **9.** Kevin Wickander, lhp, Williamsport; **10.** Bill McGuire, c, Vermont.

1988: Batting, Pitching Statistics

CLUB BATTING

	AVG	G	AB	R	H	2B	3B	HR	BB	SO	SB
Glens Falls	.267	137	4444	660	1186	210	27	83	509	648	172
Pittsfield	.256	140	4467	557	1143	177	31	51	502	699	248
Reading	.254	136	4290	561	1091	160	25	64	475	677	160
Albany	.250	138	4393	563	1100	171	36	71	457	826	111
Harrisburg	.248	139	4549	519	1129	163	28	61	387	734	154
New Britain	.244	138	4305	431	1049	162	23	34	395	679	135
Vermont	.236	139	4261	508	1007	136	27	51	409	770	176
Williamsport	.235	139	4436	505	1042	155	18	60	470	989	135

CLUB PITCHING

	ERA	G	CG	SHO	SV	IP	H	R	ER	BB	SO
Pittsfield	2.95	140	20	18	29	1198	1125	500	393	492	719
Glens Falls	3.08	137	20	9	33	1164	1038	518	398	443	778
Vermont	3.12	139	25	22	39	1164	1049	488	403	392	716
Williamsport	3.19	139	22	9	32	1192	1162	572	423	482	746
Harrisburg	3.29	139	15	10	28	1194	1145	542	437	435	817
New Britain	3.40	138	28	14	15	1144	1048	542	432	435	718
Albany	3.72	138	26	11	36	1157	1121	574	478	412	733
Reading	3.85	136	16	7	30	1138	1059	568	487	513	795

INDIVIDUAL BATTING LEADERS
(Minimum 383 Plate Appearances)

	AVG	G	AB	R	H	2B	3B	HR	RBI	BB	SO	SB
Walton, Jerome, Pitt	.331	120	414	64	137	26	2	3	49	41	69	42
#House, Bryan, Pitt	.316	128	430	61	136	18	5	8	50	58	62	34
Villanueva, Hector, Pitt	.314	127	436	50	137	24	3	10	75	71	58	5
*Richie, Rob, GF	.309	137	501	75	155	24	7	14	82	60	69	24
Estrada, Ed, NB	.303	127	456	42	138	15	6	2	38	18	59	5
Roberts, John, NB	.299	93	335	51	100	12	0	0	26	45	27	39
Austin, Pat, GF	.297	89	337	54	100	13	1	1	30	43	47	24
Little, Scott, Harr	.290	118	410	60	119	14	6	6	52	37	35	21
#Leiper, Dave, GF	.289	91	329	63	95	23	0	2	36	37	33	10
Wilson, James, Vmt	.285	125	439	57	125	18	1	17	73	36	103	11

* indicates lefthanded batter   # indicates switch hitter

INDIVIDUAL PITCHING LEADERS
(Minimum 114 Innings)

	W	L	ERA	G	GS	CG	SV	IP	H	R	ER	BB	SO
Wenson, Paul, GF	8	5	2.04	49	0	0	5	115	112	39	26	34	95
Mejia, Cesar, GF	14	5	2.43	25	25	7	0	163	132	53	44	50	99
Brinkman, Greg, Vmt	11	7	2.46	27	21	6	0	157	136	54	43	38	72
Vasquez, Luis, NB	3	9	2.48	15	15	5	0	112	87	46	31	28	97
Eiland, Dave, Alb	9	5	2.56	18	18	7	0	119	95	39	34	22	66
Neidlinger, Jim, Harr	5	8	2.82	40	11	0	2	125	135	54	39	25	88
Roth, Kris, Pitt	6	5	2.90	27	20	4	0	143	128	52	46	63	77
Davidson, Jackie, Pitt	10	9	2.99	26	20	5	0	145	149	67	48	43	81
McCorkle, Dave, Vmt	7	10	3.00	20	18	3	0	114	117	49	38	24	46
Irvine, Daryl, NB	5	11	3.09	39	14	4	0	125	113	62	43	57	82

* indicates lefthanded pitcher

ALBANY

BATTING	AVG	G	AB	R	H	2B	3B	HR	RBI	BB	SO	SB
*Alvarez, Chris, 3b	.000	4	11	0	0	0	0	0	0	1	3	0
*Arendas, Dan, of	.299	47	144	17	43	2	2	1	15	10	24	2
*Azocar, Oscar, of	.273	138	543	60	148	22	9	6	66	12	48	21
#Becker, Tim, ss	.281	61	217	30	61	7	0	0	16	16	8	14
Calvert, Art, of	.203	21	69	6	14	1	1	2	8	3	21	2
*Cathcart, Gary, of	.173	17	52	7	9	1	0	0	7	10	7	0

Eastern League's Best

Cesar Mejia
... top pitcher

Rob Richie
... RBI leader

Jerome Walton
... top hitter

	AVG	G	AB	R	H	2B	3B	HR	RBI	BB	SO	SB
Close, Casey, of	.169	25	77	8	13	1	0	1	5	2	13	0
Green, Bob, of	.227	66	185	26	42	8	0	0	13	34	43	10
Gwinn, Tony, c	.667	1	3	0	2	1	0	0	2	1	0	0
Hauradou, Yanko, ph	.000	1	1	0	0	0	0	0	0	0	0	0
*Kelley, Dean, 2b	.274	23	84	8	23	5	1	2	7	3	11	0
Lambert, Rob, of	.192	59	151	22	29	3	0	3	16	14	33	3
Leyritz, Jim, c-3b	.241	112	382	40	92	18	5	5	50	43	60	3
Lyden, Mitch, dh	.410	20	78	16	32	7	1	8	21	5	15	0
*Maas, Jason, of-dh	.271	119	369	44	100	12	8	2	34	46	66	15
*Maas, Kevin, 1b	.263	109	372	66	98	14	3	16	55	64	103	5
Meulens, Hensley, 3b	.245	79	278	50	68	9	1	13	40	37	97	3
Nelson, Jamie, c	.242	44	132	20	32	6	0	5	19	25	25	0
Pena, Bert, 3b-ss	.232	23	69	8	16	0	0	0	4	10	14	2
Ramos, John, 3b-of	.222	21	72	11	16	1	3	1	13	12	9	2
Roman, Dan, ss-3b	.227	11	22	2	5	2	0	0	1	2	5	0
Rosario, Mel, c	.136	37	88	3	12	3	0	1	7	6	38	0
Russell, Tony, of	.206	48	155	17	32	7	0	2	18	26	28	11
Scott, Dick, ss	.253	73	229	19	58	9	2	0	19	22	53	1
*Sepanek, Rob, 1b	.212	24	85	6	18	6	0	1	9	8	24	0
Shaw, Scott, dh	.253	28	95	14	24	6	0	1	6	5	20	2
*Sherlock, Glenn, c	.125	6	16	0	2	0	0	0	1	1	5	0
Stankiewicz, Andy, 2b	.268	109	414	63	111	20	2	1	33	39	53	15

PITCHING	W	L	ERA	G	GS	CG	SV	IP	H	R	ER	BB	SO
*Azocar, Oscar	0	0	3.00	3	0	0	0	3	4	1	1	1	1
*Blum, Brent	0	0	10.50	3	0	0	1	6	9	7	7	5	3
Chapin, Darrin	0	0	11.25	3	0	0	0	4	11	7	5	2	4
Christopher, Mike	13	7	3.83	24	24	5	0	153	166	75	65	44	67
Davidson, Bobby	6	3	2.72	34	3	0	6	93	81	36	28	23	62
Eiland, Dave	9	5	2.56	18	18	7	0	119	95	39	34	22	66
Evers, Troy	9	10	4.25	26	26	6	0	159	171	92	75	62	86
*Ferreira, Tony	0	0	7.04	6	0	0	0	8	9	9	6	1	8
Gay, Scott	0	0	4.26	2	0	0	0	6	9	3	3	3	3
Harrison, Matt	5	6	3.71	16	16	4	0	102	117	53	42	26	56
*Howard, Chris	0	0	13.50	2	0	0	0	1	3	2	2	1	1
Imes, Rod	4	1	2.74	7	7	1	0	49	46	21	15	16	24
Knox, Jeff	0	0	7.94	2	2	0	0	6	8	6	5	2	3
Layana, Tim	5	7	4.34	14	14	1	0	87	90	52	42	30	42
*Mmahat, Kevin	2	3	3.99	6	6	0	0	38	30	19	17	24	32
Morrison, Tony	1	1	9.90	3	0	0	0	10	15	11	11	12	6
Ridenour, Dana	5	4	3.92	30	0	0	14	44	29	19	19	26	59
Rodriguez, Gabriel	2	5	3.34	23	8	0	5	62	51	29	23	31	59
Rub, Jerry	1	2	2.11	22	0	0	2	21	18	9	5	4	15
Stanford, Don	1	0	2.53	3	1	0	0	11	8	3	3	3	11
Tirado, Aris	5	5	3.65	34	3	1	7	69	53	31	28	23	54
Torres, Ricky	2	2	3.52	19	0	0	1	61	53	27	24	23	46
*Voeltz, Bill	0	1	4.26	8	0	0	0	6	7	3	3	4	4

GLENS FALLS

BATTING	AVG	G	AB	R	H	2B	3B	HR	RBI	BB	SO	SB
*Anderson, Bernie, of-dh	.215	105	321	51	69	11	1	1	28	45	45	17
Austin, Pat, 2b	.297	89	337	54	100	13	1	0	30	43	47	24
Bradshaw, Kevin, 2b-ss	.232	64	164	18	38	9	1	0	13	15	22	3
Dempsay, Adam, c	.087	16	46	2	4	0	0	0	3	3	11	0
Dimascio, Dan, c	.280	79	211	30	59	8	1	6	31	18	40	1
Hardgrave, Eric, 3b	.214	8	14	1	3	0	0	0	1	1	2	1
*Harris, Lenny, 2b	.338	17	65	9	22	5	1	1	7	9	6	1
Henika, Ron, dh	.185	9	27	2	5	0	0	0	1	1	0	0
Hoiles, Chris, c-dh	.283	103	360	67	102	21	3	17	73	50	57	4
#Housie, Wayne, of	.188	63	202	26	38	4	2	1	16	28	34	9
#Hudson, Lance, of	.289	60	211	27	61	11	3	1	23	12	41	15
#Leiper, Tim, of-1b	.289	91	329	63	95	23	0	2	36	37	33	10

BATTING

R—Ced Landrum, Pittsfield 82
H—Rob Richie, Glens Falls 155
TB—Rob Richie, Glens Falls 235
2B—Mark Howie, Williamsport 28
3B—Oscar Azocar, Albany 9
HR—Chris Hoiles, Glens Falls 17
—Jim Wilson, Vermont 17
RBI—Rob Richie, Glens Falls 82
GWRBI—Jim Wilson, Vermont 18
SH—Jeff Cook, Harrisburg 11
SF—Lance Belen, Harrisburg 11
BB—Hector Villanueva, Pittsfield 71
IBB—Jose Birriel, New Britain 9
HBP—Julius McDougal, Glens Falls 10
SO—Jim Bruske, Williamsport 137
CS—Ced Landrum, Pittsfield 17
SB—Ced Landrum, Pittsfield 69
Slg. Pct.—Chris Hoiles, Glens Falls 500
OB Pct.—Hector Villanueva, Pittsfield 408

PITCHING

G—Dean Wilkins, Pittsfield 59
—Mark Leonette, Pittsfield 59
GS—Three tied at 27
CG—David Eiland, Albany 7
—Cesar Mejia, Glens Falls 7
ShO—Cesar Mejia, Glens Falls 4
Sv—Dean Wilkins, Pittsfield 26
W—Mike Walker, Williamsport 15
L—Jeff Shaw, Williamsport 19
IP—Mike Walker, Williamsport 164
H—Jeff Shaw, Williamsport 173
R—Jeff Shaw, Williamsport 94
HR—Bill Cooper, Glens Falls 15
BB—Chuck Malone, Reading 88
HB—Kris Roth, Pittsfield 14
SO—Mike Walker, Williamsport 145
WP—Mike Walker, Williamsport 17
Bk—Ken Williams, Glens Falls 12

Department Leaders

BATTING	AVG	G	AB	R	H	2B	3B	HR	RBI	BB	SO	SB
#Lovullo, Torey, 3b	.274	78	270	37	74	17	1	9	50	36	44	2
#McDougal, Julius, ss	.241	129	406	55	98	18	2	7	49	52	75	15
*Morhardt, Greg, 1b-of	.232	39	112	11	26	7	0	3	10	10	14	1
*Richie, Rob, of	.309	137	501	75	155	24	7	14	82	60	69	24
*Strange, Doug, 3b	.280	57	218	32	61	11	1	1	36	16	28	11
*Wieligman, Rich, 1b-dh	.235	101	345	42	81	12	1	8	46	45	32	9
#Young, Delwyn, of	.315	80	302	58	95	16	2	11	49	28	47	20

PITCHING	W	L	ERA	G	GS	CG	SV	IP	H	R	ER	BB	SO
Beard, Dave	3	3	1.75	11	6	1	2	46	31	11	9	7	41
*Berrios, Hector	3	0	3.55	25	8	0	1	51	51	25	20	28	36
Cooper, Bill	7	7	3.60	24	21	2	0	130	116	68	52	33	88
*Duffy, John	4	2	3.30	22	1	0	1	46	40	17	17	17	30
*Garces, Robinson	5	2	3.33	14	14	1	0	70	49	37	26	32	54
Gohmann, Ken	0	0	14.54	2	0	0	0	4	7	7	7	1	2
Holman, Shawn	8	3	1.87	52	0	0	10	92	82	36	19	26	44
Lacko, Rich	1	4	5.40	10	10	1	0	47	47	32	28	27	28
*Lee, Mark	3	0	2.42	14	0	0	1	26	27	10	7	4	25
Link, Robert	5	7	2.81	55	0	0	13	83	81	39	26	27	64
Mejia, Cesar	14	5	2.43	25	25	7	0	163	132	53	44	50	99
Ritz, Kevin	8	10	3.82	26	26	4	0	137	115	68	58	70	75
Schwabe, Mike	0	2	3.50	8	0	0	0	18	16	9	7	5	11
Wenson, Paul	8	5	2.04	49	0	0	5	115	112	39	26	34	95
*Williams, Ken	11	7	3.60	26	26	4	0	135	132	67	54	82	86

HARRISBURG

BATTING	AVG	G	AB	R	H	2B	3B	HR	RBI	BB	SO	SB
Banister, Jeff, c	.259	71	205	9	53	6	0	6	26	10	38	0
Belen, Lance, 1b	.231	129	472	51	109	15	1	11	62	30	76	5
Burdick, Kevin, 2b	.281	77	310	40	87	15	1	5	22	23	20	5
*Carter, Steve, of	.286	9	35	7	10	2	0	0	2	1	6	3
Chance, Tony, of	.219	56	196	26	43	8	2	3	10	20	48	9
#Cook, Jeff, of	.257	127	490	55	126	9	2	1	29	45	57	45
#Crowley, Terry, 2b-ss	.241	10	29	2	7	2	0	0	5	3	8	0
Davis, Kevin, 2b-ss	.293	41	133	15	39	8	0	0	9	7	18	5
Gutierrez, Dimas, inf	.229	102	332	37	76	16	1	4	29	28	35	11
*Hill, Orsino, of	.198	25	86	11	17	5	0	1	8	16	18	2
Johns, Ron, 1b-dh	.213	19	61	6	13	3	0	1	8	4	13	0
Khalifa, Sammy, ss	.331	44	142	21	47	4	4	2	15	25	24	5
King, Jeff, 3b	.255	117	411	49	105	21	1	14	66	46	87	5
Little, Scott, of-inf	.290	118	410	60	119	14	6	6	52	37	35	27
#Longmire, Tony, of	.149	32	94	7	14	2	2	0	4	9	12	0
#Molina, Albert, ss	.667	2	3	2	2	0	0	0	0	0	1	0

	AVG	G	AB	R	H	2B	3B	HR	RBI	BB	SO	SB
Perez, Julio, 2b	.222	3	9	2	2	0	1	0	0	0	2	1
Rigos, John, of	.204	45	142	23	29	3	0	1	11	21	27	4
Roca, Gilberto, c	.159	40	126	8	20	2	0	1	7	4	21	1
Rodriguez, Ruben, c	.275	48	160	12	44	7	1	0	19	2	25	2
#Ruskin, Scott, of-1b	.223	90	309	27	69	14	3	3	32	23	99	11
Shields, Tommy, ss	.308	59	198	30	61	4	2	2	21	14	25	7
#Yacopino, Ed, of	.230	34	113	13	26	3	1	0	12	12	13	6

PITCHING	W	L	ERA	G	GS	CG	SV	IP	H	R	ER	BB	SO
Adams, Steve	2	2	5.63	4	4	0	0	24	34	18	15	7	8
*Copp, Bill	5	2	3.71	16	9	1	0	68	54	32	28	19	46
*Curtis, Mike	6	13	3.28	25	25	2	0	143	148	62	52	57	80
*Daniel, Clay	0	0	6.23	2	0	0	0	4	6	6	3	1	1
Fansler, Stan	4	6	3.55	11	11	1	0	66	66	32	26	21	34
Gideon, Brett	3	2	1.36	25	0	0	6	40	27	8	6	21	30
Lind, Orlando	1	2	3.34	39	0	0	3	70	69	33	26	37	48
Melendez, Jose	5	3	2.27	22	4	2	1	71	46	20	18	19	38
Melton, Larry	7	4	3.66	21	21	1	0	120	111	60	49	55	93
Neidlinger, Jim	5	8	2.82	40	11	0	2	125	135	54	39	25	88
Reed, Rick	1	0	1.13	2	2	0	0	16	11	2	2	2	17
Ritter, Chris	4	5	3.39	12	11	1	0	66	60	38	25	25	50
Runge, Scott	1	1	6.91	13	3	0	0	29	39	23	22	13	18
*Russell, Rob	5	7	2.65	51	0	0	10	71	65	23	21	30	61
Sampen, Bill	6	3	3.70	13	12	3	0	83	72	38	34	27	65
Walker, Mike	2	7	3.51	13	13	2	0	74	76	40	29	15	47
Wilmet, Paul	8	3	1.98	28	0	0	6	41	34	10	9	16	32
York, Mike	0	5	3.72	13	13	2	0	82	92	43	34	45	61

NEW BRITAIN

BATTING	AVG	G	AB	R	H	2B	3B	HR	RBI	BB	SO	SB
*Birriel, Jose, 1b-dh	.280	92	289	30	81	21	0	9	43	50	43	0
Bochesa, Greg, dh-c	.196	53	143	9	28	8	0	2	15	15	27	2
Estrada, Ed, 3b-1b	.303	127	456	42	138	15	6	2	38	18	59	5
Gonzalez, Angel, 3b-2b	.202	65	208	13	42	7	2	1	16	29	27	13
Jackson, Laverne, of	.213	97	319	36	68	7	2	1	22	35	57	13
#Jose, Manny, of	.243	109	337	32	82	15	5	1	24	25	74	20
Laseke, Eric, of	.227	31	97	3	22	4	0	0	8	8	7	3
Marzano, John, c	.205	35	112	11	23	6	1	0	5	10	13	1
McGee, Tim, c	.221	69	172	19	38	5	1	0	16	11	14	8
Moritz, Chris, inf	.226	66	221	24	50	8	0	0	12	10	47	7
Palmer, Doug, 2b	.245	121	413	45	101	9	2	0	23	46	28	6
Pratt, Todd, c-1b	.225	124	395	41	89	15	2	8	49	41	110	1
Roberts, John, of	.299	93	335	51	100	12	0	0	26	45	27	39
Rosario, Victor, ss	.259	101	347	28	90	14	1	1	26	11	56	4
Scott, Tary, dh	.000	4	9	1	0	0	0	0	0	3	4	0
Zambrano, Eddie, of	.223	121	381	36	85	13	1	8	30	30	70	10
Zambrano, Roberto, dh-3b	.174	20	69	8	12	3	0	1	7	8	16	1

PITCHING	W	L	ERA	G	GS	CG	SV	IP	H	R	ER	BB	SO
Abril, Odie	1	5	3.67	10	9	2	0	61	58	27	25	34	31
Carista, Mike	8	10	3.45	27	24	3	0	162	147	77	62	48	76
Clarkin, Mike	0	5	5.31	23	0	0	2	42	46	31	25	20	26
*Crouch, Zach	2	3	3.23	8	8	2	0	47	43	19	17	7	40
*Dalton, Mike	6	5	2.24	52	1	1	8	84	65	32	21	39	61
Gabriele, Dan	1	6	8.07	7	7	0	0	29	34	33	26	32	25
Gakeler, Dan	6	13	3.69	26	25	5	0	154	157	74	63	54	110
Irvine, Daryl	5	11	3.09	39	14	4	0	125	113	62	43	57	82
Kiecker, Dana	1	0	0.00	1	1	0	0	6	3	0	0	1	0
Schilling, Curt	8	5	2.97	21	17	4	0	106	91	44	35	40	62
Shikles, Larry	2	5	3.58	36	10	1	2	101	98	44	40	36	44
Skripko, Scott	3	5	2.44	13	7	1	0	48	35	15	13	22	24
*Stewart, Tito	1	8	4.23	50	0	0	3	66	71	34	31	18	39
Vasquez, Luis	3	9	2.48	15	15	5	0	112	87	46	31	28	97

PITTSFIELD

BATTING	AVG	G	AB	R	H	2B	3B	HR	RBI	BB	SO	SB
Amaral, Rich, inf	.277	122	422	66	117	15	4	4	47	56	53	54
Bafia, Bob, 3b-1b	.193	62	176	17	34	7	0	2	11	6	28	1
Bullinger, Jim, ss	.169	88	242	21	41	6	1	3	33	25	53	1
*Chambers, Al, dh-1b	.237	46	156	13	37	5	0	6	22	22	27	2
Cruz, Luis, inf-of	.261	38	111	10	29	3	0	0	6	9	9	5
Girardi, Joe, c	.272	104	357	44	97	14	1	7	41	29	51	7
#House, Bryan, of-2b	.316	128	430	61	136	18	5	8	50	58	62	34
*Landrum, Ced, of	.245	128	445	82	109	15	8	1	39	55	63	69
*LaPenta, Jerry, dh-1b	.205	27	73	4	15	3	0	1	7	8	15	1
*Lewis, John, of	.255	99	306	37	78	12	5	3	23	46	37	9
Mann, Kelly, c	.196	22	51	7	10	3	0	0	3	3	14	0
Small, Jeff, 2b	.235	34	115	4	27	3	0	0	8	5	13	5
*Strickland, Bob, 1b-c	.209	43	86	9	18	3	0	1	14	7	16	0
Thoma, Ray, 3b-ss	.189	104	296	31	56	12	1	1	28	19	56	9
*Tullier, Mike, of	.230	66	135	23	31	6	1	1	8	29	19	2
#Valdez, Julio, inf	.192	25	73	6	14	0	0	0	6	1	15	1
Villanueva, Hector, 1b-c	.314	127	436	50	137	24	3	10	75	71	58	5
Wallace, Tim, 2b-ss	.114	22	35	1	4	0	0	0	3	2	5	0
Walton, Jerome, of	.331	120	414	64	137	26	2	3	49	41	69	42
Wrona, Rick, c	.000	5	6	0	0	0	0	0	1	1	2	0

PITCHING	W	L	ERA	G	GS	CG	SV	IP	H	R	ER	BB	SO
Davidson, Jackie	10	9	2.99	26	20	5	0	145	149	67	48	43	81
Green, John	0	3	5.59	7	2	0	0	19	23	16	12	10	6
Harkey, Mike	9	2	1.37	13	13	3	0	86	66	29	13	35	73
Hirsch, Jeff	2	3	2.43	9	9	0	0	56	49	21	15	22	47
Kazmierczak, Bill	5	3	4.09	12	12	2	0	84	84	39	38	28	54
Kopf, Dave	1	3	5.35	13	6	0	0	37	28	26	22	33	16
*Kraemer, Joe	5	5	2.75	15	15	2	0	95	84	37	29	43	47
Leonette, Mark	8	4	2.30	59	0	0	0	78	89	28	20	33	41
*Parker, Steve	4	4	4.50	51	1	0	1	58	60	31	29	26	25
Parmenter, Gary	4	1	2.18	8	8	1	0	54	45	16	13	19	38
Renfroe, Laddie	9	4	1.96	29	7	1	1	110	102	32	24	24	57
Roth, Kris	6	5	2.90	27	20	4	0	143	128	52	46	63	77
*Scheid, Rich	6	6	3.73	24	20	1	1	118	119	58	49	62	75
Schwarz, Jeff	0	1	5.65	3	3	0	0	14	19	9	9	11	5
Wilkins, Dean	5	7	1.63	59	0	0	26	72	53	25	13	30	59
Zwolensky, Mitch	1	3	4.00	5	4	1	0	27	25	13	12	8	16

READING

BATTING	AVG	G	AB	R	H	2B	3B	HR	RBI	BB	SO	SB
*Bellino, Frank, of	.285	62	214	29	61	9	1	7	37	24	21	2
Berman, Gary, 1b	.221	53	140	14	31	12	0	1	7	11	29	1
*Brown, Tony, of	.281	75	242	32	68	10	1	8	39	31	42	18
Brumfield, Harvey, of	.148	8	27	3	4	0	1	0	1	2	8	2
Calvert, Chris, c	.188	44	112	10	21	0	2	0	11	9	21	4
#Crosby, Todd, 2b	.293	33	92	19	27	0	0	1	8	17	9	4
*DeAngelis, Steve, of	.263	128	434	51	114	21	1	8	58	63	66	12
#Edge, Greg, ss	.254	131	426	55	108	10	3	0	32	59	22	11
Holyfield, Vince, of	.247	116	405	48	100	20	2	7	59	33	82	19
Kaye, Jeff, c	.210	49	143	14	30	4	0	8	22	10	45	0
*LeBoeuf, Al, 1b-dh	.263	83	209	35	55	6	1	4	28	41	33	6
Legg, Greg, 2b	.266	84	312	39	83	8	1	1	33	37	25	6
Leiva, Jose, of	.253	63	198	36	50	9	1	1	14	27	32	28
Lundblade, Rick, c-1b	.220	40	127	13	28	5	0	3	22	11	18	0
*Monda, Greg, 1b	.237	53	177	22	42	10	0	4	26	13	36	1
Nichols, Howard, 3b	.322	33	118	17	38	6	2	4	13	8	22	6
Parker, Rick, inf-of	.257	116	362	50	93	13	3	3	47	36	50	24
Roman, Ray, c	.186	20	59	2	11	2	0	0	6	2	23	0
Schwarz, Tom, 1b	.278	9	18	1	5	0	0	0	1	1	3	0
*Turner, Shane, 3b-2b	.298	78	295	52	88	11	6	3	21	26	53	14
Zayas, Carlos, c	.200	33	95	8	19	3	0	1	7	8	17	1

PITCHING	W	L	ERA	G	GS	CG	SV	IP	H	R	ER	BB	SO
Boudreaux, Eric	5	10	4.23	24	18	3	1	113	130	63	53	32	72
Brantley, Cliff	1	0	6.00	1	1	0	0	6	5	4	4	2	5
*Calhoun, Jeff	0	1	0.75	7	4	0	0	12	6	2	1	4	8
Carreno, Amalio (9 Alb)	3	4	4.07	14	11	1	0	60	60	32	27	32	31
Chambers, Travis	1	2	6.28	9	1	0	0	14	11	10	10	11	10
*Fortugno, Tim	1	4	4.44	29	4	0	0	51	42	29	25	36	48
Grimsley, Jason	1	3	7.17	5	4	0	0	21	20	19	17	13	14
Machado, Julio	6	1	5.43	26	5	0	3	63	69	41	38	34	52
Magee, Warren	6	6	3.73	42	11	2	1	109	88	50	45	52	90
Malone, Chuck	12	7	3.77	22	21	2	0	127	107	63	53	88	117
Mauser, Tim	2	3	3.49	5	5	0	0	28	27	14	11	6	17
*McElroy, Chuck	9	12	4.50	28	26	4	0	160	173	89	80	70	92
Moore, Brad	4	6	3.06	57	0	0	18	71	57	30	24	33	39
Newell, Tom	6	2	3.14	13	11	4	0	80	68	34	28	31	63
Service, Scott	3	4	2.86	10	9	1	0	57	52	25	18	22	39
Sharts, Steve	3	1	2.21	46	0	0	1	61	56	18	15	13	34
Sossamon, Tim	2	5	3.92	27	12	0	3	83	76	45	36	37	48
Surhoff, Rick	4	2	2.44	35	0	0	3	59	49	19	16	15	39
Zayas, Carlos	0	0	3.86	2	0	0	0	2	1	1	1	3	1

VERMONT

BATTING	AVG	G	AB	R	H	2B	3B	HR	RBI	BB	SO	SB
Balelo, Nezi, 2b-ss	.217	122	341	45	74	12	2	1	24	34	49	10
*Brundage, Dave, of-1b	.248	130	435	61	108	15	2	1	50	60	75	19
Carr, Chuck, of	.245	41	159	26	39	4	2	1	13	8	33	21
Foley, Keith, c	.213	32	94	5	20	3	0	0	7	6	11	2
#Fox, Eric, of	.251	129	478	55	120	20	6	3	39	39	69	33
#Fulton, Greg, 1b-3b	.213	119	338	25	72	8	2	1	25	38	44	2
*Gibbons, John, of	.180	47	122	9	22	2	0	0	7	16	16	0
*Goff, Jerry, c	.210	63	195	27	41	7	1	7	23	23	58	2
*Griffey, Ken, of	.279	17	61	10	17	5	1	2	10	5	12	4
Hansen, Roger, c-1b	.301	34	103	12	31	2	1	1	9	5	12	0
Lennon, Patrick, 3b	.259	95	321	44	83	9	3	8	40	21	87	15
McGuire, Bill, c	.206	49	136	16	28	3	0	5	24	23	21	5
Murray, Steve, 2b	.178	72	180	19	32	4	2	3	26	27	34	5
Myers, Dave, 3b	.181	41	138	10	25	2	0	0	8	16	22	4
Uribe, Jorge, of	.216	106	347	33	75	6	1	1	23	18	86	15
Vizquel, Omar, ss	.254	103	374	54	95	18	2	2	35	42	44	30
Wilson, James, dh	.285	125	439	57	125	18	1	17	73	36	103	11

PITCHING	W	L	ERA	G	GS	CG	SV	IP	H	R	ER	BB	SO
Brinkman, Greg	11	7	2.46	27	21	6	0	157	136	54	43	38	72
Christ, Mike	6	6	2.37	17	17	4	0	106	88	34	28	29	52
Doyle, Rich	2	0	0.47	9	0	0	3	19	14	1	1	5	7
Fulton, Greg	0	0	13.50	1	0	0	0	2	3	3	3	0	2
*Helton, Keith	0	1	4.73	7	0	0	0	13	13	7	7	8	9

	W	L	ERA	G	GS	CG	SV	IP	H	R	ER	BB	SO
Hull, Jeff	1	1	1.02	24	0	0	6	44	22	11	5	15	43
Jones, Calvin	7	5	2.65	24	4	0	0	75	52	26	22	47	58
McCorkle, Dave	7	10	3.00	20	18	3	0	114	117	49	38	24	46
*Mendek, Bill	2	2	2.23	34	1	0	9	65	54	19	16	27	42
*Price, Bryan	5	4	3.44	18	14	2	0	81	66	40	31	37	66
Rice, Pat	3	0	1.04	6	3	0	0	26	22	7	3	7	16
Roberts, Scott	0	1	3.60	2	2	0	0	10	7	4	4	2	5
Rojas, Ricky	10	7	4.14	27	27	5	0	152	165	84	70	42	88
Snell, Dave	3	1	5.75	19	0	0	0	41	51	27	26	13	18
*Ward, Colin	4	3	4.00	16	8	3	0	63	64	31	28	28	41
West, Matt	0	0	0.00	3	0	0	0	4	3	0	0	4	1
Wooden, Mark	8	5	3.34	44	0	0	21	59	55	24	22	11	28
Zavaras, Clint	10	7	3.92	24	24	2	0	129	115	67	56	54	120

WILLIAMSPORT

BATTING	AVG	G	AB	R	H	2B	3B	HR	RBI	BB	SO	SB
Bruske, Jim, of	.237	135	443	49	105	12	3	1	44	45	138	16
#Carrasco, Claudio, ss-2b	.200	68	145	13	29	1	1	0	12	23	40	2
Firova, Dan, c	.228	42	127	8	29	3	0	0	11	10	21	2
Gill, Turner, ss	.195	134	411	36	80	10	2	3	22	29	119	11
*Harper, Milt, 1b	.225	122	404	55	91	18	0	12	50	63	78	3
Higgins, Mark, dh-1b	.230	92	335	39	77	10	0	10	42	29	76	1
Howie, Mark, 2b	.257	136	517	53	133	29	0	6	64	41	70	9
Isaacson, Chris, c	.158	12	19	2	3	1	0	1	4	4	9	0
Jordan, Scott, of	.254	129	481	68	122	17	3	4	33	66	93	33
Kent, Lew, c	.234	16	47	5	11	1	0	3	8	4	17	1
*Khoury, Scott, dh	.200	10	20	2	4	1	0	0	0	3	3	0
*Lampkin, Tom, c	.270	80	263	38	71	10	0	3	23	25	20	1
Landrum, Darryl, of	.221	102	326	37	72	15	1	7	35	35	112	10
*Milner, Ted, of	.222	6	9	2	2	0	0	0	2	2	3	1
Richardson, Kerry, dh-of	.210	50	157	16	33	2	1	3	18	17	42	1
Richardson, Tim, of	.245	33	98	8	24	1	0	0	2	1	9	3
Webster, Casey, 3b	.248	137	475	57	118	18	7	7	65	61	100	7
*Westbrook, Mike, of	.259	37	139	18	36	6	0	0	7	11	30	7
Wilson, Doyle, c	.100	8	20	1	2	0	0	0	0	1	9	0

PITCHING	W	L	ERA	G	GS	CG	SV	IP	H	R	ER	BB	SO
*Black, Bud	1	0	0.00	1	1	0	0	5	0	0	0	0	5
Farr, Mike	4	3	3.05	29	8	0	0	94	89	40	32	55	56
Ghelfi, Andy	5	11	4.16	24	18	2	1	134	171	81	62	31	31
Ghelfi, Tony	7	4	2.76	13	13	4	0	88	83	41	27	22	62
Gilles, Mark	0	1	6.23	3	0	0	0	9	16	9	6	4	4
Hilton, Stan	1	1	2.98	18	0	0	0	54	49	22	18	21	40
Keliipuleole, Carl	1	4	2.56	28	0	0	8	32	35	14	9	17	28
Kuzniar, Paul	7	4	1.14	43	0	0	3	63	46	20	8	37	65
*Murphy, Kent	6	5	2.24	32	4	1	4	72	57	34	18	31	58
Murphy, Mike	1	0	4.11	3	2	0	0	15	8	9	7	14	7
Perlman, Jon	0	1	3.38	3	2	0	0	5	5	2	2	0	3
Poehl, Mike	5	2	2.98	9	9	3	0	44	38	17	15	17	27
Scott, Charles	5	4	3.26	15	14	2	0	108	108	45	39	25	46
Shamblin, Bill	0	0	9.45	5	0	0	0	7	12	10	7	2	4
Shaw, Jeff	5	19	3.63	27	27	6	0	164	173	94	66	75	61
Shaw, Theo	2	6	3.28	14	13	1	0	93	83	42	34	47	68
Walker, Mike	15	7	3.72	28	27	3	0	164	162	82	68	74	144
*Wickander, Kevin	1	0	0.63	24	0	0	16	29	14	3	2	9	33
Yett, Rich	0	1	8.10	1	1	0	0	3	6	6	3	3	4

Other teams can't stop Chattanooga choo-choo

By RUBIN GRANT

All signs early in the 1988 Southern League season pointed to a league dominated by pitching.

And that's exactly what transpired during the summer. All 10 teams finished with earned run averages of less than 4.00—with the league champion Chattanooga Lookouts in at a scant 2.79.

Butch Davis
... only .300 hitter

Pitching was so dominant in 1988 that the league batting champion, veteran minor leaguer Butch Davis, was the only player to finish with an average above .300. And he barely did at .301, the second-lowest average for a batting champion in league history.

Chattanooga, appropriately, used strong pitching to win the league championship. In the playoffs, Chattanooga held Memphis and Greenville to a total of 11 runs in seven games. They defeated Memphis 3-1 and swept Greenville, which had the league's best overall record, 3-0.

Lookouts lefthander Chris Hammond broke a club record for victories with a 16-5 record—he won two more in the playoffs—and won the ERA title (1.72).

Righthander Keith Brown helped Chattanooga win the first

League Champions
(Playoff Champions, Where Applicable)

1988—Chattanooga	1961—Asheville	1929—Knoxville
1987—Birmingham	1960—Savannah	1928—Asheville
1986—Columbus	1959—Gastonia	1927—Greenville
1985—Huntsville	1958—Macon	1926—Greenville
1984—Charlotte	1957—Charlotte	1925—Spartanburg
1983—Birmingham	1956—Jacksonville	1924—Augusta
1982—Nashville	1955—Augusta	1923—Charlotte
1981—Orlando	1954—Savannah	1922—Charleston
1980—Charlotte	1953—Savannah	1921—Columbia
1979—Nashville	1952—Montgomery	1920—Columbia
1978—Knoxville	1951—Montgomery	1919—Columbia
1977—Montgomery	1950—Macon	1918—Did Not
1976—Montgomery	1949—Macon	Operate
1975—Montgomery	1948—Greenville	1917—Columbia
1974—Knoxville	1947—Savannah	1916—Augusta
1973—Montgomery	1946—Augusta	1915—Columbus
1972—Montgomery	1943-45—Did Not	1914—Savannah
1971—Did Not	Operate	1913—Savannah
Operate	1942—Macon	1912—Jacksonville
1970—Columbus	1941—Columbia	1911—Columbus
1969—Charlotte	1940—Columbus	1910—Columbus
1968—Asheville	1939—Augusta	1909—Chattanooga
1967—Birmingham	1938—Macon	1908—Jacksonville
1966—Mobile	1937—Savannah	1907—Charleston
1965—Columbus	1936—Columbus	1906—Savannah
1964—Lynchburg	1931-35—Did Not	1905—Macon
1963—Augusta	Operate	1904—Macon
1962—Macon	1930—Greenville	

half with a 9-1 record and 1.42 ERA, before being promoted to Triple-A Nashville and eventually the parent Cincinnati Reds.

Reliever Joe Bruno (7-3, 1.21 ERA, three saves) anchored a strong bullpen.

So dominant was Chattanooga's pitching that the Lookouts won the league title with only one player hitting more than .290 (first baseman Hedi Vargas, .291). No Lookout drove in 70 runs. Their top home run hitters, Vargas and third baseman Keith Lockhart, had 12 each.

"You can't ask any more of the team," Chattanooga manager Tom Runnells said after the Lookouts won the title. "It's nice for the team, and it's nice for the players who worked so hard all season long."

Chattanooga, in its first season of affiliation with Cincinnati, appeared in its first championship series since 1961. The Lookouts had the league's second-best record at 81-62, behind Greenville's 87-57.

Greenville's Braves won both halves in the Eastern Division, and Buddy Bailey was named manager of the year. Bailey began the season at Class A Durham (Carolina), and was promoted to Greenville in late May when Russ Nixon was sent to Atlanta to replace the fired Chuck Tanner. Under Bailey, Greenville was 65-36.

More pitching feats

Orlando reliever German Gonzalez broke the league record for saves with 30, before being promoted to the parent Minnesota Twins in early August. Gonzalez, who had a 1.02 ERA, was named the league's outstanding pitcher.

Columbus reliever Brian Meyer broke a club record for saves with 25.

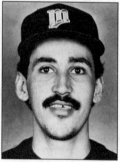

German Gonzalez
... 30 saves

Memphis righthander Jose DeJesus broke a team record for strikeouts with 149. His record might have been obliterated if Tom Gordon had spent the entire season with the Chicks.

Gordon, a 5-foot-9 righthander who was named Baseball America's 1988 Minor League player of the year, made six starts with Memphis after his promotion from Class A Appleton. He was 6-0 with two shutouts, a dazzling 0.38 ERA and 62 strikeouts in 47 innings. Whew!

Gordon went up to Omaha, and eventually to Kansas City.

Knoxville righthander Alex Sanchez led the league in strikeouts with 166, and teammate Steve Cummings finished second behind Chattanooga's Hammond in wins with a 14-11 record.

What happened to the home runs?

Memphis outfielder Matt Winters won the league MVP award by winning the league home run (25) and RBI (91) crowns.

Winters, an 11-year minor league veteran, would have been no better than sixth in home runs in 1987, when three players broke club records for home runs with more than 30. Winters also would have been sixth in RBIs.

Orlando's Bernardo Brito (24) and Knoxville's Francisco Cabrera (20) were the only other players with 20 home runs in '88. Brito, as a Cleveland farmhand, had led his league in homers the previous four seasons.

The lack of power didn't hurt attendance. Birmingham broke a club record and led all Double-A baseball, attracting 269,831 fans in its first year at $14 million Hoover Metropolitan Stadium, which was dubbed The Met. The Barons no doubt would have drawn more if they hadn't had the league's second-worst record.

FIRST HALF

East	W	L	Pct.	GB
Greenville (Braves) ..	43	29	.597	—
Orlando (Twins)	35	36	.493	7½
Jacksonville (Expos).	35	37	.486	8
Charlotte (Orioles)...	30	42	.417	13
Columbus (Astros) ..	26	45	.366	16½

West	W	L	Pct.	GB
Chattanooga (Reds) ..	43	30	.589	—
Knoxville (Blue Jays)	42	31	.575	1
Memphis (Royals) ...	38	34	.528	4½
Huntsville (Athletics)	37	35	.514	5½
Birm. (White Sox)....	31	41	.431	11½

SECOND HALF

East	W	L	Pct.	GB
Greenville (Braves) ..	44	28	.611	—
Columbus (Astros) ..	43	29	.597	1
Charlotte (Orioles)...	39	33	.542	5
Jacksonville (Expos).	34	36	.486	9
Orlando (Twins)	31	39	.443	12

West	W	L	Pct.	GB
Memphis (Royals) ...	41	30	.577	—
Chattanooga (Reds) .	38	32	.543	2½
Knoxville (Blue Jays)	33	38	.465	8
Birm. (White Sox)....	31	41	.431	10½
Huntsville (Athletics)	22	50	.306	19½

OVERALL

	W	L	Pct.	GB
Greenville (Braves) ..	87	57	.604	—
Chattanooga (Reds) .	81	62	.566	5½
Memphis (Royals) ...	79	64	.552	7½
Knoxville (Blue Jays)	75	69	.521	12
Jacksonville (Expos).	69	73	.486	17
Columbus (Astros) ..	69	74	.483	17½
Charlotte (Orioles)...	69	75	.479	18
Orlando (Twins)	66	75	.468	19½
Birm. (White Sox)....	62	82	.431	25
Huntsville (Athletics)	59	85	.410	28

1988
Final
Standings

1988: General Information

Playoffs: Chattanooga defeated Memphis 3-1 and Greenville defeated Jacksonville 3-2 in best-of-5 semifinals; Chattanooga defeated Greenville 3-0 in best-of-5 finals for league championship.

Regular Season Attendance: Birmingham, 269,831; Greenville, 209,791; Memphis, 205,568; Huntsville, 185,811; Jacksonville, 175,396; Chattanooga, 136,921; Columbus, 110,621; Charlotte, 102,467; Knoxville, 87,434; Orlando, 68,904.

Managers: Birmingham—Rico Petrocelli; **Charlotte**—Greg Biagini; **Chattanooga**—Tom Runnells; **Columbus**—Tom Wiedenbauer; **Greenville**—Russ Nixon, Buddy Bailey; **Huntsville**—Tommie Reynolds; **Jacksonville**—Tommy Thompson; **Knoxville**—Barry Foote; **Memphis**—Sal Rende; **Orlando**—Duane Gustavson.

1988 Official All-Star Team: C—Francisco Cabrera, Knoxville. **1B**—Drew Denson, Greenville. **2B**—Mark Lemke, Greenville. **3B**—Carlo Colombino, Columbus. **SS**—Mike Bordick, Huntsville. **Util**—Carlos Martinez, Birmingham. **OF**—Rafael DeLima, Orlando; Barry Jones, Greenville; Bernardo Brito, Orlando; Butch Davis, Charlotte. **DH**—Matt Winters, Memphis. **RHP**—Alex Sanchez, Knoxville. **LHP**—Chris Hammond, Chattanooga. **Most Valuable Player**—Matt Winters, Memphis. **Outstanding Pitcher**—German Gonzalez, Orlando. **Best Hustler**—Jeff Huson, Jacksonville. **Manager of the Year**—Buddy Bailey, Greenville.

Top 10 Major League Prospects (by Baseball America): 1. Pete Harnisch, rhp, Charlotte; **2.** Derek Parks, c, Orlando; **3.** Alex Sanchez, rhp, Knoxville; **4.** Jose DeJesus, rhp, Memphis; **5.** Rafael DeLima, of, Orlando; **6.** Mark Lemke, 2b, Greenville; **7.** Chris Hammond, lhp, Chattanooga; **8.** German Gonzalez, rhp, Orlando; **9.** Dennis Jones, lhp, Knoxville; **10.** Francisco Cabrera, c, Knoxville.

Chattanooga's Chris Hammond was the Southern League's top lefthander, tying for the Double-A lead in wins with 16.

1988: Batting, Pitching Statistics

CLUB BATTING

	AVG	G	AB	R	H	2B	3B	HR	BB	SO	SB
Chattanooga	.254	143	4741	586	1206	203	30	55	519	883	152
Knoxville	.251	144	4634	559	1161	211	36	84	413	917	179
Orlando	.248	141	4545	544	1129	191	21	79	472	760	102
Greenville	.247	144	4738	673	1168	192	39	110	535	887	133
Columbus	.245	143	4614	594	1130	167	43	75	522	877	135
Jacksonville	.244	142	4571	604	1117	217	28	95	558	860	147
Birmingham	.241	144	4702	612	1135	199	22	76	547	867	142
Charlotte	.241	145	4819	601	1163	212	30	81	564	874	161
Huntsville	.234	145	4747	542	1112	185	22	57	592	1031	172
Memphis	.234	143	4551	618	1065	185	33	103	559	969	133

CLUB PITCHING

	ERA	G	CG	SHO	SV	IP	H	R	ER	BB	SO
Chattanooga	2.80	143	19	14	39	1257	1020	485	391	528	913
Knoxville	3.07	144	10	11	38	1239	1048	531	423	547	1024
Greenville	3.15	144	18	12	33	1250	1040	522	437	526	811
Memphis	3.53	143	22	10	42	1219	1149	581	478	464	1017
Charlotte	3.61	145	12	10	31	1283	1246	637	514	489	959
Jacksonville	3.67	142	22	11	27	1211	1073	604	494	586	941
Birmingham	3.86	144	27	11	22	1241	1196	654	533	515	829
Columbus	3.90	143	14	7	37	1217	1172	621	527	539	918
Orlando	3.91	141	18	5	41	1187	1132	621	516	597	835
Huntsville	3.95	145	15	8	26	1272	1310	677	559	490	678

INDIVIDUAL BATTING LEADERS
(Minimum 389 Plate Appearances)

	AVG	G	AB	R	H	2B	3B	HR	RBI	BB	SO	SB
Davis, Butch, Char	.301	101	412	62	124	23	7	13	82	24	40	17
*Delima, Rafael, Orl	.286	137	500	66	143	25	3	3	46	77	87	29
Colombino, Carlo, Col	.285	113	417	61	119	21	8	8	62	23	52	10
Cabrera, Francisco, Knox	.284	119	429	59	122	19	1	20	54	26	75	4
*Braun, Randy, Jax	.284	132	461	62	131	28	2	15	76	53	63	3

BATTING

R—Rafel Skeete, Charlotte 89
H—Mark Lemke, Greenville 153
TB—Mark Lemke, Greenville 238
2B—Kevin Burrell, Memphis 32
3B—Four tied at.............................8
HR—Matt Winters, Memphis...................25
RBI—Matt Winters, Memphis..................91
GWRBI—Domingo Martinez, Knoxville 14
SH—Jeff Richardson, Chattanooga 12
SF—Keith Lockhart, Chattanooga 11
BB—Ed Whited, Greenville 97
IBB—Randy Braun, Jacksonville 8
HBP—Derek Parks, Orlando...................14
SO—Dennis Hood, Greenville 139
SB—Jeff Huson, Jacksonville 55
CS—Kevin Dean, Jacksonville 18
Slg. Pct.—Barry Jones, Greenville 497
OB Pct.—Armando Moreno, Jacksonville 419

PITCHING

G—Paul Thorpe, Charlotte 64
GS—Steve Cummings, Knoxville 33
CG—Gene Harris, Jacksonville 7
ShO—Mark Clemons, Jacksonville 3
Sv—German Gonzalez, Orlando 30
W—Chris Hammond, Chattanooga 16
L—Kirk McDonald, Huntsville 14
IP—Steve Cummings, Knoxville 213
H—Steve Cummings, Knoxville 206
R—Kirk McDonald, Huntsville 119
HR—Jim Daniel, Charlotte 19
BB—Mike Smith, Chattanooga 98
HB—Mike Smith, Chattanooga 10
SO—Alex Sanchez, Knoxville 166
WP—Wayne Edwards, Birmingham 16
Bk—Grady Hall, Birmingham.................11

	AVG	G	AB	R	H	2B	3B	HR	RBI	BB	SO	SB
*Jones, Barry, Grv	.284	101	384	56	109	18	8	16	55	24	56	11
Holtz, Jerry, Char	.281	100	349	59	98	18	8	1	39	82	55	17
Grebeck, Craig, Birm ...	.280	133	450	57	126	21	1	9	53	65	72	5
Martinez, Carlos, Birm ...	.277	133	498	67	138	22	3	14	73	36	82	25
*Winters, Matt, Mem ...	.275	139	488	77	134	21	3	25	91	67	109	1

* indicates lefthanded batter   # indicates switch hitter

INDIVIDUAL PITCHING LEADERS
(Minimum 115 Innings)

	W	L	ERA	G	GS	CG	SV	IP	H	R	ER	BB	SO
*Hammond, Chris, Chat ...	16	5	1.72	26	26	4	0	183	127	48	35	77	127
*Dillard, Gordon, Char ...	7	5	2.19	38	14	2	2	132	97	42	32	67	100
Blankenship, Kevin, Grv ..	13	9	2.34	28	25	4	0	177	132	58	46	83	127
Sanchez, Alex, Knox ...	12	5	2.53	24	24	2	0	149	100	56	42	74	166
Law, Joe, Hunt	9	3	2.56	17	17	4	0	116	100	42	33	33	67
Harnisch, Pete, Char	7	6	2.58	20	20	4	0	132	113	55	38	52	141
Harris, Gene, Jax	9	5	2.63	18	18	7	0	127	95	43	37	45	103
Richards, Rusty, Grv	10	7	2.63	20	20	3	0	147	125	46	43	42	96
Cummings, Steve, Knox ..	14	11	2.75	35	33	3	0	213	206	88	65	64	131
*Drees, Tom, Birm	9	7	2.79	22	21	6	0	158	149	63	49	52	94

* indicates lefthanded pitcher

BIRMINGHAM

BATTING	AVG	G	AB	R	H	2B	3B	HR	RBI	BB	SO	SB
Bertolani, Jerry, ss	.238	133	491	82	117	30	1	5	64	76	64	13
*Cronkright, Dan, 3b	.228	107	359	38	82	11	2	3	42	41	61	6
Davis, Mark, of	.290	66	248	52	72	18	3	6	27	38	55	32
*Eveline, Bill, of	.245	14	49	2	12	1	0	0	9	5	7	1
*Forrester, Tom, dh-of ...	.240	124	446	51	107	18	4	13	72	54	85	4
*Garcia, Cornelio, 1b ...	.284	60	229	37	65	5	3	2	25	29	44	22
Grebeck, Craig, 2b	.280	133	450	57	126	21	1	9	53	65	72	5
Magallanes, Willie, of ...	.193	121	400	48	77	17	1	9	40	42	120	7
Markert, Jim, c	.172	52	151	15	26	1	1	0	7	18	26	0
Martinez, Carlos, of-3b ..	.277	133	498	67	138	22	3	14	73	36	82	25
*Merullo, Matt, c	.261	125	449	58	117	26	0	6	60	40	59	3
*Thomas, Troy, of	.185	97	313	31	58	6	0	0	20	59	65	8
Trafton, Todd, 1b	.212	77	273	35	58	11	0	8	27	16	50	6
Venturini, Pete, ss	.273	38	139	17	38	5	0	0	12	9	29	6
*Waggoner, Aubrey, of-dh .	.200	13	40	6	8	2	2	0	1	11	11	4
Wagner, Dan, of	.206	49	160	16	33	5	1	1	11	8	34	0

PITCHING	W	L	ERA	G	GS	CG	SV	IP	H	R	ER	BB	SO
*Blasucci, Tony	0	2	0.81	22	0	0	3	22	11	6	2	17	25
*Boling, John	1	1	6.58	30	0	0	1	40	47	29	29	11	25
Chadwick, Ray	3	2	3.92	6	6	2	0	39	31	20	17	17	28
*Diaz, Victor	0	1	3.03	18	0	0	0	30	23	11	10	17	21
*Drees, Tom	9	7	2.79	22	21	6	0	158	149	63	49	52	94

	W	L	ERA	G	GS	CG	SV	IP	H	R	ER	BB	SO
*Edwards, Wayne	9	12	4.90	27	27	6	0	167	176	108	91	92	136
Gaynor, Richie	1	5	5.29	12	8	0	1	49	49	38	29	30	31
*Hall, Grady	9	8	2.96	20	20	5	0	137	132	59	45	42	69
Little, Doug	12	13	3.98	27	27	5	0	172	184	95	76	39	98
Menendez, Tony	6	11	3.94	24	24	3	0	153	131	79	67	64	112
Mount, Chuck	7	9	4.01	36	5	0	3	90	81	48	40	53	60
Pawlowski, John	2	3	3.29	23	0	0	7	27	23	14	10	11	28
Renz, Kevin	0	2	5.24	27	1	0	0	46	51	36	27	29	20
Scott, Tim	1	2	3.78	19	5	0	0	52	64	23	22	13	33
Smith, Daryl	1	4	3.23	40	0	0	7	53	42	25	19	27	44

CHARLOTTE

BATTING	AVG	G	AB	R	H	2B	3B	HR	RBI	BB	SO	SB
*Bellino, Frank, dh-of	.235	31	98	11	23	5	0	2	11	20	9	2
*Cijntje, Sherwin, of	.260	78	304	35	79	11	5	1	27	21	45	21
Cusack, Rocky, dh-1b	.221	32	95	17	21	5	0	4	12	23	28	2
Davis, Butch, of-dh	.301	101	412	62	124	23	7	13	82	24	40	17
Dulin, Tim, 2b	.243	110	399	59	97	20	1	11	56	67	47	5
#Farmar, Damon, of	.205	13	44	4	9	0	0	1	1	10	15	2
*Finley, Steve, of	.300	10	40	7	12	4	2	1	6	4	3	2
Gerhart, Ken, of	.154	3	13	2	2	0	0	1	1	2	0	0
Gomez, Leo, 3b	.292	24	89	6	26	5	0	1	10	10	17	1
Holtz, Jerry, of	.281	100	349	59	98	18	8	1	39	82	55	17
Jarrell, Joe, of-3b	.228	88	334	31	76	12	1	16	52	14	89	4
Magrann, Tom, c	.283	20	60	6	17	0	1	1	2	8	3	1
Mims, Larry, of	.162	17	37	8	6	1	0	0	4	4	2	3
Montgomery, Reggie, 1b	.246	43	171	12	42	10	1	3	15	6	18	0
#Nichols, Ty, ss-2b	.201	128	442	49	89	20	3	8	46	30	109	6
*O'Dell, Jim, 1b	.218	91	321	34	70	14	0	6	35	33	54	3
#Perkins, Harold, 3b-of	.306	22	85	10	26	0	0	1	9	5	8	6
Posey, John, c-3b	.206	88	306	30	63	18	0	5	32	39	55	2
Roberts, Norm, of	.111	4	9	0	1	0	0	0	1	1	5	0
*Skeete, Rafel, of	.237	134	494	89	117	18	1	3	29	57	135	53
Smith, Dana, 3b-ss	.245	129	444	46	109	19	0	2	33	61	90	6
Tackett, Jeff, c	.206	81	272	24	56	9	0	0	18	42	46	6

PITCHING	W	L	ERA	G	GS	CG	SV	IP	H	R	ER	BB	SO
Brown, Curt	3	1	4.29	30	0	0	2	57	69	33	27	7	45
Chamberlain, Craig	4	7	5.43	18	8	1	0	65	73	48	39	32	40
Culkar, Steve	0	1	3.00	15	0	0	0	21	16	8	7	7	20
Daniel, Jim	2	7	4.78	31	12	0	3	96	100	67	51	33	52
*Dillard, Gordon	7	5	2.19	38	14	2	2	132	97	42	32	67	100
Harnisch, Pete	7	6	2.58	20	20	4	0	132	113	55	38	52	141
*Hickey, Kevin	1	1	3.72	6	1	0	0	10	10	4	4	8	7
*Householder, Brian	5	8	4.14	20	20	0	0	117	122	70	54	57	76
Milacki, Bob	3	1	2.39	5	5	1	0	38	26	11	10	12	29
*Odekirk, Rick	2	3	2.95	8	5	1	0	37	34	17	12	10	19
Olson, Gregg	0	1	5.87	8	0	0	1	15	24	13	10	6	22
Palermo, Pete	1	0	6.06	8	1	0	0	16	25	15	11	6	16
Price, Kevin	6	8	3.84	46	2	0	11	80	85	40	34	25	45
*Raczka, Mike	0	0	3.94	6	0	0	0	16	17	8	7	10	16
Schilling, Curt	5	2	3.18	7	7	2	0	45	36	19	16	23	32
Sonneberger, Steve	2	7	5.66	13	9	0	0	56	73	39	35	21	40
Stanhope, Chuck	7	8	3.01	21	21	1	0	144	127	58	48	40	97
Thorpe, Paul	6	5	2.67	64	0	0	12	88	80	32	26	45	88
Walton, Rob	7	2	3.50	13	13	0	0	80	73	35	31	12	51
Williams, Bob	1	2	5.40	7	0	0	0	37	43	23	22	14	23

CHATTANOOGA

BATTING	AVG	G	AB	R	H	2B	3B	HR	RBI	BB	SO	SB
DeFrancesco, Tony, c	.143	8	28	2	4	0	0	0	1	3	8	1
*Finley, Brian, of	.273	83	315	48	86	11	2	1	25	51	63	31
Germann, Mark, inf	.269	112	346	34	93	12	0	0	30	63	41	3
Jones, Chris, of	.271	116	410	50	111	20	7	4	61	29	102	11
*Lockhart, Keith, 3b-2b	.266	139	515	74	137	27	3	12	67	61	59	7
*Milner, Eddie, of	.221	17	68	6	15	1	1	0	5	9	8	0
Nunley, Angelo, 2b	.241	100	377	51	91	9	4	1	34	38	67	19
#Oester, Ron, 2b	.304	14	46	5	14	2	0	1	6	6	7	0
Oliver, Joe, c	.248	28	105	9	26	6	0	3	12	5	19	0
Pruitt, Darrell, of-dh	.271	123	425	41	115	18	1	1	30	39	49	20
Pryor, Buddy, of	.230	51	161	26	37	8	1	3	18	25	33	5
*Reyna, Luis, 1b	.272	50	180	16	49	8	0	1	15	10	31	5
Richardson, Jeff, ss	.251	122	399	50	100	17	1	1	37	23	56	8
*Riley, Darren, of	.217	107	368	44	80	16	1	5	39	26	82	22
*Taubensee, Eddie, c	.167	5	12	2	2	0	0	1	1	3	4	0
Vargas, Hedi, 1b	.291	82	309	43	90	26	1	12	61	34	73	1
*Wakamatsu, Don, c-1b	.238	79	235	22	56	9	1	1	26	37	41	0
*Walker, Bernie, of-dh	.249	111	333	53	83	11	7	6	36	49	105	19

PITCHING	W	L	ERA	G	GS	CG	SV	IP	H	R	ER	BB	SO
Brown, Keith	9	1	1.42	10	10	2	0	70	47	11	11	20	34
Bruno, Joe	7	3	1.21	40	1	0	3	74	45	16	10	32	65
Brusky, Brad	2	2	2.10	30	0	0	4	64	51	20	15	18	35
Dale, Philip	4	10	4.30	30	12	5	0	103	117	57	49	30	45
Deitz, Tim	3	5	2.31	56	0	0	12	74	59	25	19	47	75

Mark Lemke
...270-16-80

Pete Harnisch
... 132 IP, 141 K's

	W	L	ERA	G	GS	CG	SV	IP	H	R	ER	BB	SO
*Hammond, Chris	16	5	1.72	26	26	4	0	183	127	48	35	77	127
Jefferson, Jim	3	3	2.92	30	0	0	10	37	31	17	12	22	33
*Lazor, Joe	11	7	3.51	25	25	1	0	161	119	74	63	69	133
*Lono, Joel	0	2	7.64	3	3	0	0	18	24	15	15	5	6
Mead, Timber	9	10	3.09	28	24	2	0	163	141	71	56	62	136
*Minutelli, Gino	0	1	1.59	2	2	0	0	6	6	2	1	4	3
Roesler, Mike	1	1	2.21	16	0	0	9	20	16	5	5	8	13
Scudder, Scott	7	0	2.96	11	11	0	0	70	53	24	23	30	52
Smith, Mike	9	10	3.20	28	28	5	0	194	160	90	69	98	141
Snell, Nate	0	1	18.00	1	0	0	0	1	3	2	2	1	2
Sorensen, Lary	0	1	2.95	7	1	0	1	18	18	7	6	4	12

COLUMBUS

BATTING	AVG	G	AB	R	H	2B	3B	HR	RBI	BB	SO	SB
Afenir, Troy, of-c	.247	137	494	61	122	21	5	16	66	45	131	11
*Baldwin, Jeff, of	.220	39	91	7	20	1	0	0	6	12	19	2
*Brock, Norm, of	.227	87	264	33	60	7	3	2	18	23	41	11
Colombino, Carlo, 3b	.285	113	417	61	119	21	8	8	62	23	52	10
Cooper, Gary, of-3b	.270	140	474	65	128	25	7	7	69	87	87	13
Deiley, Lou, c	.000	1	2	0	0	0	0	0	0	0	1	0
Elliott, John, 2b-ss	.185	33	92	5	17	3	1	0	6	10	29	3
Green, Terry, of	.179	29	95	7	17	2	2	0	5	3	15	6
#Harris, Rusty, ss	.136	10	22	1	3	0	0	0	0	1	4	0
*James, Calvin, of	.232	117	375	55	87	5	4	1	17	49	85	14
Johnson, Richard, 1b-dh	.227	109	343	34	78	15	0	9	40	39	82	2
Lopez, Juan, c	.202	38	109	9	22	3	0	1	8	3	22	1
Mikulik, Joe, of	.275	48	189	33	52	8	4	3	34	16	34	13
Randle, Randy, ss	.239	46	113	18	27	1	1	0	8	11	30	7
Rohde, David, 2b-ss	.267	142	486	76	130	20	2	4	53	81	62	36
Seibert, Gib, ss-of	.247	66	215	37	53	8	0	5	25	31	46	1
Todd, Kyle, 2b-ss	.174	55	172	18	30	6	1	2	14	12	34	2
*Tolentino, Jose, 1b-of	.305	72	259	33	79	10	3	9	53	36	32	1
Walters, Dan, c	.233	98	305	31	71	10	1	7	28	26	42	1

PITCHING	W	L	ERA	G	GS	CG	SV	IP	H	R	ER	BB	SO
*Credeur, Todd	1	3	4.62	15	0	0	4	25	24	13	13	18	34
Crew, Ken	4	5	2.34	21	0	0	1	42	32	17	11	15	45
Deleon, Pedro	2	2	4.50	4	4	0	0	22	23	14	11	8	13
Dunster, Don	9	12	3.51	31	27	5	0	174	181	85	68	25	74
*Edwards, Jeff	0	2	5.40	3	3	0	0	13	11	8	8	9	14
*Funk, Tom	7	3	4.08	38	1	0	4	57	48	28	26	35	30
Givler, Doug	5	5	3.58	35	5	0	2	106	102	49	42	58	104
Graham, Randy (12 Jax)	8	6	3.53	26	12	1	2	89	97	43	35	11	31
*Grovom, Carl	2	0	4.29	5	5	1	0	21	22	10	10	17	19
*Ilsley, Blaise	3	1	5.95	8	8	0	0	39	49	28	26	21	38
Kerfeld, Charlie	2	7	4.50	13	12	1	0	64	63	36	32	21	63
Long, Bruce	0	0	6.57	3	2	0	0	12	15	11	9	9	9
*McCoy, Tim	0	2	5.20	12	4	0	0	36	38	24	21	24	24
Meyer, Brian	4	3	2.27	62	0	0	25	83	61	23	21	36	68
Potts, Dave	0	3	2.88	4	4	1	0	25	19	9	8	8	16
Slowik, Tad	0	0	6.86	13	0	0	0	20	20	18	15	17	15

	W	L	ERA	G	GS	CG	SV	IP	H	R	ER	BB	SO
Spagnola, Glenn	10	10	3.77	28	26	2	0	155	153	86	65	67	111
Vargas, Jose	8	8	3.56	25	25	2	0	154	155	73	61	58	108
*Wells, Terry	5	5	4.57	37	8	1	1	108	92	58	55	85	109

GREENVILLE

BATTING	AVG	G	AB	R	H	2B	3B	HR	RBI	BB	SO	SB
Alva, John, ss	.212	123	481	50	102	17	1	2	43	21	79	7
Beauchamp, Kash, of (8 Knx)	.292	70	226	37	66	16	2	5	33	28	40	6
*Bell, Mike, 1b	.250	4	12	1	3	1	0	0	4	1	1	0
Bell, Terry, c	.212	41	132	17	28	1	1	1	19	20	26	2
*Butts, Dave, 3b	.333	7	24	5	8	1	0	0	4	1	4	1
D'Alessandro, Sal, c	.203	39	118	11	24	3	1	3	18	17	15	0
#Denson, Drew, 1b	.268	140	507	85	136	26	4	13	78	44	116	11
#Dewey, Todd, c	.219	53	160	9	35	3	0	0	11	23	17	4
*Dunbar, Tommy, of	.264	81	261	47	69	19	1	9	44	43	32	10
Fischlin, Mike, ss	.382	11	34	3	13	2	0	0	5	5	3	0
Guerrero, Ino, 1b-dh	.197	61	147	14	29	9	0	5	19	22	32	0
Hood, Dennis, of	.257	141	525	85	135	15	8	14	47	52	139	31
*Jones, Barry, of	.284	101	384	56	109	18	8	16	55	24	56	11
*Justice, Dave, of	.278	58	198	34	55	13	1	9	37	36	43	6
#Lemke, Mark, 2b	.270	143	567	81	153	30	4	16	80	52	92	18
Maldonado, Phil, c	.196	23	51	9	10	0	0	1	6	7	6	0
Pacho, Juan, ss-3b	.212	28	85	14	18	2	0	0	2	9	8	0
Plumb, Dave, c	.000	3	8	0	0	0	0	0	1	0	3	0
#Roby, Ellis, 3b-ss	.153	43	59	6	9	0	1	0	6	7	16	0
*Sabino, Miguel, of	.167	40	126	10	21	4	2	0	5	10	29	4
Tubbs, Greg, of	.238	29	101	13	24	1	1	0	12	13	20	4
Whited, Ed, 3b	.252	132	428	81	108	11	4	16	62	97	84	18
Wine, Robbie, c	.000	6	18	0	0	0	0	0	2	2	5	0

PITCHING	W	L	ERA	G	GS	CG	SV	IP	H	R	ER	BB	SO
Acker, Jim	0	0	1.72	8	4	0	0	16	7	3	3	3	5
Blankenship, Kevin	13	9	2.34	28	25	4	0	177	132	58	46	83	127
Del Rosario, Maximo	6	3	2.97	55	0	0	7	88	67	29	29	40	52
Dozier, Tom	6	4	2.85	28	7	2	0	95	67	35	30	44	73
*Farmer, Bryan	3	2	2.60	51	0	0	7	52	45	22	15	22	24
*Kilner, John	11	7	3.54	27	24	3	0	158	133	71	62	86	80
Marak, Paul	0	0	10.47	12	0	0	0	16	25	19	19	11	9
Mathews, Eddie	10	4	1.72	57	0	0	15	68	56	22	13	28	42
*Mercker, Kent	3	1	3.35	9	9	0	0	48	36	20	18	26	60
Miller, Dave	5	4	2.50	10	10	3	0	72	59	26	20	19	50
Nezelek, Andy	7	8	4.38	26	25	3	0	134	133	77	65	45	89
*Olwine, Ed	1	2	8.16	9	3	0	1	14	17	15	13	6	6
*Polley, Dale	9	6	3.16	36	16	0	2	128	102	56	45	49	67
Richards, Rusty	10	7	2.63	28	20	3	0	147	125	46	43	42	96
Watson, Preston	1	0	5.02	8	1	0	1	14	15	13	8	14	13
Ziem, Steve	2	0	2.86	9	0	0	0	22	18	9	7	8	11

HUNTSVILLE

BATTING	AVG	G	AB	R	H	2B	3B	HR	RBI	BB	SO	SB
Arias, Tony, 1b	.224	29	85	13	19	0	0	3	8	9	29	2
Arndt, Larry, dh-of	.347	19	75	13	26	6	1	1	8	6	22	3
Bordick, Mike, 2b-ss	.270	132	481	48	130	13	2	0	38	87	50	7
Canseco, Ozzie, of	.222	27	99	6	22	7	0	3	12	6	31	3
Dietrick, Pat, of	.268	106	377	42	101	19	2	3	35	47	84	18
Duffy, Darrin, ss	.190	51	163	24	31	6	0	0	8	35	49	2
Hale, DeMarlo, of-1b	.199	44	161	15	32	5	0	1	13	15	24	4
Hemond, Scott, 3b	.220	133	482	51	106	22	4	9	53	48	114	29
Howard, Steve, of-dh	.247	128	461	70	114	19	6	17	78	64	134	29
Jones, Jim, c	.217	57	161	16	35	5	0	0	7	40	33	4
McGinnis, Rusty, c	.260	23	77	9	20	9	0	2	15	7	13	1
Minch, John, c	.255	96	314	30	80	14	0	2	33	28	38	4
#Nelson, Jerome, of	.241	92	353	45	85	6	3	2	25	50	68	17
Peguero, Jerry, 2b-ss	.219	108	324	30	71	13	0	0	28	32	55	18
Robertson, Andre, inf	.182	49	159	15	29	2	1	1	12	14	30	3
Sliwinski, Kevin, of-1b	.171	61	205	21	35	7	0	2	13	27	54	6
*Sparks, Greg, 1b	.233	124	421	47	98	21	0	8	50	48	117	5
*Veras, Camilo, of	.225	99	346	47	78	11	3	3	36	29	84	17

PITCHING	W	L	ERA	G	GS	CG	SV	IP	H	R	ER	BB	SO
Chiamparino, Scott	4	5	3.21	13	13	4	0	84	88	36	30	26	49
Corbell, Charlie	2	2	4.50	5	3	0	0	16	22	9	8	7	8
*Criswell, Brian	1	8	4.14	37	11	1	2	100	113	50	46	42	61
*Holcomb, Scott	4	10	4.78	17	17	0	0	81	79	49	43	49	42
Kent, Bo	5	3	4.09	52	0	0	6	77	83	45	35	29	37
Killingsworth, Kirk	3	1	1.77	26	0	0	8	46	30	12	9	19	42
*Klink, Joe	1	2	0.78	21	0	0	3	35	25	6	3	14	30
Law, Joe	9	3	2.56	17	17	4	0	116	100	42	33	33	67
McDonald, Kirk	6	14	5.00	30	25	2	0	169	195	119	94	65	76
Schock, Will	0	5	3.15	11	11	2	0	69	49	34	24	32	29
Sharpnack, Bob	4	13	6.05	37	13	0	0	119	130	88	80	62	48
Shotkoski, Dave	1	2	4.24	16	0	0	4	23	27	12	11	14	16
*Sparks, Greg	0	0	4.91	2	0	0	0	4	4	2	2	3	0
Tanner, Bruce	7	7	3.23	18	16	2	0	100	104	46	36	25	33
Veres, Dave	3	4	4.15	8	8	0	0	39	50	20	18	15	17
Walton, Bruce	4	5	4.56	42	3	0	3	116	126	64	59	23	82

— 111 —

JACKSONVILLE

BATTING	AVG	G	AB	R	H	2B	3B	HR	RBI	BB	SO	SB
Baker, Bill, 3b-2b	.179	16	28	3	5	0	0	0	1	5	3	2
Beltre, Esteban, ss	.150	35	113	5	17	2	0	0	6	3	28	1
Berger, Mike, of	.232	63	203	29	47	6	3	6	27	30	52	2
Blowers, Mike, 3b	.250	137	460	58	115	20	6	15	60	68	114	6
*Braun, Randy, of-1b	.284	132	461	62	131	28	2	15	76	53	63	3
Caffrey, Bob, c	.228	81	272	30	62	13	3	6	31	14	61	1
Dean, Kevin, of	.256	137	496	81	127	24	4	7	48	88	107	33
Duke, Doug, c	.245	72	229	21	56	12	0	6	27	16	39	1
*Frobel, Doug, dh	.216	16	37	5	8	0	1	3	8	1	6	0
*Hill, Orsino, of	.233	66	202	31	47	8	1	5	28	39	48	6
Houston, Mel, inf-of	.245	80	265	43	65	10	2	1	13	26	36	21
*Huson, Jeff, ss-2b	.248	128	471	72	117	18	1	0	34	59	45	56
Lawrence, Andy, 1b-dh	.242	45	153	12	37	6	1	3	18	10	33	1
Moreno, Armando, 2b	.270	110	352	58	95	22	3	7	57	94	56	6
*Oller, Jeff, c	.000	2	3	0	0	0	0	0	0	0	0	0
Pevey, Marty, dh-c	.261	31	111	21	29	11	0	4	17	8	13	3
Santiago, Norm, of	.167	7	12	1	2	0	0	0	1	2	1	0
*Sipe, Pat, 1b	.244	111	389	45	95	22	1	14	65	15	65	2
Soares, Todd, of	.214	6	14	1	3	1	0	0	2	1	6	0
*Vanderwal, John, of	.260	58	208	22	54	14	0	3	14	17	49	3

PITCHING	W	L	ERA	G	GS	CG	SV	IP	H	R	ER	BB	SO
Alexander, Tommy	5	4	3.66	38	8	0	1	103	81	51	42	47	91
Carriger, Ricky	3	3	3.51	20	0	0	1	26	22	12	10	13	25
Clemons, Mark	5	5	3.69	24	17	5	0	124	125	60	51	32	70
Dixon, Eddie	7	6	2.74	61	0	0	4	92	80	40	28	42	52
Gardner, Mark	6	3	1.60	15	15	4	0	112	72	24	20	36	130
Harris, Gene	9	5	2.63	18	18	7	0	127	95	43	37	45	103
Hoover, John	10	11	4.11	29	28	3	0	160	161	90	73	58	121
Jacobson, Nels	0	4	8.47	5	5	0	0	17	10	19	16	42	12
Jones, Ross	1	0	3.52	7	1	0	0	15	14	6	6	6	5
Lewis, Richie	5	3	3.38	12	12	1	0	61	37	32	23	56	60
*Livingston, Dennis	1	0	2.51	12	0	0	2	14	15	4	4	6	12
Martinez, Art	0	0	1.50	3	0	0	0	6	9	7	1	3	3
*Perez, Yorkis	8	12	5.82	27	25	2	0	130	142	96	84	94	105
Peters, Tim	1	1	1.27	17	0	0	8	28	20	6	4	13	26
*Sauveur, Rich	0	2	4.05	8	0	0	1	7	7	5	3	5	8
Shade, Mike	1	2	4.91	10	0	0	1	15	19	11	8	10	8
*Tabaka, Jeff	1	0	6.55	2	2	0	0	11	14	8	8	5	7
Waddell, Tom	2	1	2.96	25	0	0	3	49	33	22	16	23	29
Weissman, Craig (9 Hunt)	2	5	4.69	38	2	0	4	71	84	46	37	30	53
Welborn, Tony	2	3	6.12	6	6	0	0	25	22	21	17	20	15

KNOXVILLE

BATTING	AVG	G	AB	R	H	2B	3B	HR	RBI	BB	SO	SB
Batiste, Kevin, of	.234	112	363	44	85	14	4	3	22	31	119	31
Bell, Derek, of	.250	14	52	5	13	3	1	0	4	1	14	2
Cabrera, Francisco, c	.284	119	429	59	122	19	1	20	54	26	75	4
Dela Cruz, Hector, of	.181	35	105	15	19	5	0	1	12	10	24	7
Diaz, Carlos, c	.217	7	23	2	5	1	0	0	0	2	4	0
Escobar, Jose, ss	.292	11	24	1	7	1	0	0	2	2	3	0
#Felix, Junior, of	.253	93	360	52	91	16	5	3	25	20	82	40
#Foster, Lindsay, ss	.270	35	89	11	24	3	1	0	11	2	11	2
Garrison, Webster, 2b	.255	138	534	61	136	24	5	0	40	53	74	42
Hill, Glenallen, of	.264	79	269	37	71	13	2	12	38	28	75	10
Infante, Kennedy, 3b	.143	11	28	1	4	0	0	0	0	0	4	0
*Jeter, Shawn, of	.248	80	238	31	59	7	4	3	25	24	46	10
Jones, Mike, of	.192	17	52	6	10	4	0	0	2	1	9	0
Kelly, Jimy, ss	.210	118	352	39	74	17	3	3	30	21	72	9
Malave, Omar, inf-of	.306	66	196	18	60	7	4	3	21	17	28	1
Martinez, Domingo, 1b	.264	143	516	54	136	25	2	13	70	40	88	2
McElroy, Glen, c	.133	14	15	3	2	1	0	0	0	6	2	1
*Pederson, Stu, dh-of	.285	46	144	24	41	8	1	2	18	27	20	7
Quinlan, Tom, 3b	.218	98	326	33	71	19	1	8	47	35	99	4
Rivers, Ken, c	.204	17	49	4	10	3	0	0	3	5	11	0
Stark, Matt, dh-c	.266	97	334	37	89	17	1	11	54	45	28	1
Whiten, Mark, of	.259	28	108	20	28	3	1	2	9	12	20	6

PITCHING	W	L	ERA	G	GS	CG	SV	IP	H	R	ER	BB	SO
Balsley, Darren	4	3	2.35	36	1	0	3	77	55	31	20	25	62
Bencomo, Omar	1	3	6.86	12	0	0	0	20	31	17	15	4	4
Blair, Willie	5	5	3.62	34	9	0	3	102	94	49	41	35	76
Brinson, Hugh	8	6	2.18	25	14	1	1	103	76	31	25	49	79
*Castillo, Tony	1	0	0.00	5	0	0	2	8	2	0	0	1	11
Cummings, Steve	14	11	2.75	35	33	3	0	213	206	88	65	64	131
Guzman, Juan	4	5	2.36	46	2	0	6	84	52	29	22	61	90
Hall, Darren	3	2	2.23	37	0	0	17	40	28	11	10	17	33
Hernandez, Xavier	2	4	2.90	11	11	2	0	68	73	32	22	15	33
*Horsman, Vince	3	2	4.63	20	6	1	0	58	57	34	30	28	40
Jones, Chris	6	9	4.28	35	22	1	1	135	133	74	64	61	119
#Jones, Dennis	8	5	2.62	19	18	0	0	89	57	32	26	64	116
*Mumaw, Steve	1	3	3.00	23	0	0	2	36	26	13	12	19	29
Oliverio, Steve	0	0	10.80	1	0	0	0	2	3	2	2	1	1
Sanchez, Alex	12	5	2.53	24	24	2	0	149	100	56	42	74	166
Sanders, Earl	0	0	1.80	3	0	0	2	5	3	2	1	2	4

	W	L	ERA	G	GS	CG	SV	IP	H	R	ER	BB	SO
Scherer, Doug	0	1	10.13	3	0	0	0	3	2	3	3	3	1
*Shea, John	1	3	5.40	13	0	0	1	18	23	14	11	12	14
Williams, Woody	2	2	3.81	6	4	0	0	28	27	13	12	12	25

MEMPHIS

BATTING	AVG	G	AB	R	H	2B	3B	HR	RBI	BB	SO	SB
#Bowen, Ken, ss-2b	.235	40	115	16	27	2	2	1	12	18	25	5
Brumfield, Jacob, of	.226	128	433	70	98	15	5	6	28	52	104	47
Burrell, Kevin, c-1b	.252	123	453	70	114	32	6	9	69	50	106	6
Citari, Joe, 1b	.239	51	180	21	43	9	2	5	23	17	39	0
Culberson, Charlie, of	.205	45	117	19	24	5	1	1	10	15	40	5
#Gillaspie, Mark, of-dh	.284	62	204	39	58	11	1	10	41	49	40	1
Hunt, Randy, c	.202	78	258	21	52	12	2	6	28	20	43	1
Jackson, Kenny, of	.184	12	38	4	7	4	0	2	5	1	9	0
*Jones, Terry, 1b-dh	.223	60	175	12	39	6	0	2	17	25	21	0
Lozado, Willie, ss	.281	19	64	5	18	2	1	0	7	5	8	0
*Martinez, Chito, of	.227	141	485	67	110	16	4	13	65	66	130	20
#McRae, Brian, 2b	.201	91	288	33	58	13	1	4	15	16	60	13
Miller, Mike, ss-3b	.214	113	345	40	74	9	1	3	26	59	78	5
*Reece, Thad, 3b-2b	.261	117	445	65	116	8	1	1	29	42	43	22
Rivera, Jose, 3b-2b	.207	100	347	36	72	18	2	15	57	31	91	1
Van Blaricom, Mark, ss	.181	34	116	23	21	2	1	0	8	26	23	6
*Winters, Matt, of-1b	.275	139	488	77	134	21	3	25	91	67	109	1

PITCHING	W	L	ERA	G	GS	CG	SV	IP	H	R	ER	BB	SO
*Acker, Larry	2	3	3.68	31	7	2	1	93	92	45	38	30	49
Appier, Kevin	2	0	1.83	3	3	0	0	20	11	5	4	7	18
Blouin, Gary	7	4	2.87	16	16	1	0	94	94	37	30	33	83
*Campbell, Jim	4	3	3.60	53	0	0	8	85	80	39	34	25	81
Crouch, Matt	8	5	2.92	20	20	0	0	114	107	48	37	36	110
DeJesus, Jose	9	9	3.88	20	20	4	0	116	88	56	50	70	149
Encarnacion, Luis	4	3	2.77	49	0	0	22	78	60	27	24	28	64
Gordon, Tom	6	0	0.38	6	6	2	0	47	16	3	2	17	62
Gozzo, Goose	4	9	5.73	33	12	0	3	93	127	64	59	36	48
LeBlanc, Richie	5	6	4.03	14	13	3	0	80	81	50	36	35	51
Luecken, Rick	4	1	2.19	21	0	0	5	25	17	8	6	7	30
McCormack, Brian	1	0	1.23	5	0	0	0	7	6	3	1	3	2
Spratke, Ken	11	9	4.18	34	17	4	4	140	149	77	65	51	105
Stottlemyre, Mel	3	2	2.40	7	7	1	0	45	41	18	12	14	29
Thompson, Rich	3	5	4.15	20	8	3	0	80	87	44	37	17	53
Tresemer, Mike	2	0	2.87	5	1	0	0	16	12	6	5	9	11
Walker, Steve	4	5	3.81	18	13	2	0	83	75	48	35	46	70

ORLANDO

BATTING	AVG	G	AB	R	H	2B	3B	HR	RBI	BB	SO	SB
Aragon, Joey, inf	.230	79	222	28	51	10	2	3	23	27	40	5
*Borg, Gary, 1b	.264	126	386	39	102	17	2	8	50	55	64	4
Brito, Bernardo, of-dh	.240	135	508	55	122	20	4	24	76	20	138	2
Carpenter, Doug, of	.194	11	31	4	6	1	0	0	3	6	8	2
*Delima, Rafael, of	.286	137	500	66	143	25	3	3	46	77	87	29
*Dotzler, Mike, 1b-c	.188	55	154	16	29	8	1	4	13	12	41	1
*Forgione, Chris, of	.221	111	308	31	68	6	1	3	30	22	47	11
*Hale, Chip, 2b	.261	133	482	62	126	20	1	11	65	64	31	8
Jorgensen, Terry, 3b	.246	135	472	53	116	27	4	3	43	40	62	4
Parks, Derek, c	.235	118	400	52	94	15	0	7	42	49	81	1
Reboulet, Jeff, ss	.255	125	439	57	112	24	2	4	41	53	55	18
Williams, Jaime, c-dh	.210	70	214	19	45	6	0	6	25	11	47	1
#Wilson, Phil, of	.289	71	280	42	81	6	0	2	23	24	34	16
Yanes, Eddie, of	.228	49	149	20	34	6	1	1	13	12	25	0

PITCHING	W	L	ERA	G	GS	CG	SV	IP	H	R	ER	BB	SO
Bumgarner, Jeff	3	11	3.84	20	20	3	0	117	129	66	50	56	67
*Casian, Larry	9	9	2.95	27	26	4	0	174	165	72	57	62	104
Cutshall, Bill	1	1	6.86	12	0	0	2	20	30	22	15	15	15
Dyer, Mike	11	13	3.99	27	27	3	0	162	155	84	72	86	125
Galvez, Balvino	2	0	3.04	4	4	0	0	24	23	11	8	8	19
Gasser, Steve	0	1	Inf	1	1	0	0	0	0	5	5	6	0
Gilles, Tom	3	0	3.86	7	3	1	0	26	27	13	11	5	7
Gonzalez, German	2	1	1.02	50	0	0	31	62	41	9	7	19	69
Kibler, Russ (8 Hunt)	5	1	2.14	13	9	0	0	71	65	22	17	18	31
*McKay, Alan	0	0	13.50	4	0	0	0	5	7	9	7	5	5
Nivens, Toby	7	7	3.82	25	21	2	0	139	130	68	59	44	77
*O'Connor, Tim	4	8	4.33	47	1	0	3	73	83	45	35	38	34
Oliveras, Francisco	3	1	4.81	7	4	0	0	43	44	24	23	18	42
Pittman, Park	8	7	3.82	24	18	1	0	104	73	50	44	84	103
Satzinger, Jeff	5	7	5.46	56	3	1	3	117	111	87	71	90	82
Trudeau, Kevin	7	9	4.13	34	9	3	2	109	101	54	50	60	80

Tulsa drills opponents after six losing years

By MIKE KNOBLER

After a six-year wait, what's another hour and nine minutes?

For the Tulsa Drillers, that was the excruciating period between the end of their last regular-season game of 1988 and word that they had made the Texas League playoffs for the first time since 1982.

Tulsa backed into the second-half Eastern Division championship, losing seven of its last nine games. After the last loss, in Jackson, the Drillers sat by the phone to get reports from Little Rock, where first-half champion Shreveport knocked off Arkansas to give Tulsa a half-game victory.

Tulsa (71-65) hadn't even had a winning record since 1982. Now, two seasons after the city's worst pro baseball record (49-86), the Drillers breezed past Shreveport in two games and knocked off El Paso, 4-2 in a best-of-7 final, to claim the league title.

Kevin Reimer
... **21 home runs**

Steve Wilson, a lefthander from Vancouver, British Columbia, went 15-7 for the Drillers during the regular season and 3-0 in the playoffs.

League Champions
(Playoff Champions, Where Applicable)

1988—Tulsa	1959—Austin	1927—Wichita Falls
1987—Wichita	1958—Corp. Christi	1926—Dallas
1986—El Paso	1957—Houston	1925—Ft. Worth
1985—Jackson	1956—Houston	1924—Ft. Worth
1984—Jackson	1955—Shreveport	1923—Ft. Worth
1983—Beaumont	1954—Houston	1922—Ft. Worth
1982—Tulsa	1953—Dallas	1921—Ft. Worth
1981—Jackson	1952—Shreveport	1920—Ft. Worth
1980—Arkansas	1951—Houston	1919—Shreveport
1979—Arkansas	1950—San Antonio	1918—Dallas
1978—El Paso	1949—Tulsa	1917—Dallas
1977—Arkansas	1948—Ft. Worth	1916—Waco
1976—Amarillo	1947—Houston	1915—Waco
1975—*Lafayette	1946—Dallas	1914—*Houston
—*Midland	1943-45—Did Not	—*Waco
1974—Victoria	Operate	1913—Houston
1973—Memphis	1942—Shreveport	1912—Houston
1972—El Paso	1941—Dallas	1911—Austin
1971—Did Not	1940—Houston	1910—*Dallas
Operate	1939—Ft. Worth	—*Houston
1970—Albuquerque	1938—Beaumont	1909—Houston
1969—Memphis	1937—Ft. Worth	1908—San Antonio
1968—El Paso	1936—Tulsa	1907—Austin
1967—Albuquerque	1935—Okla. City	1906—Cleburne
1966—Arkansas	1934—Galveston	1905—Ft. Worth
1965—Albuquerque	1933—San Antonio	1904—Corsicana
1964—San Antonio	1932—Beaumont	1903—Dallas
1963—Tulsa	1931—Houston	1902—Corsicana
1962—Tulsa	1930—Ft. Worth	1900-01—Did Not
1961—San Antonio	1929—Dallas	Operate
1960—Tulsa	1928—Houston	*co-champions

Steve Wilson, a lefthanded pitcher from Vancouver, won 15 games in the regular season and three more in the playoffs.

"This is like the seventh game of the Stanley Cup," Wilson said after winning Game Six.

Righthander Kevin Brown won 10 of his last 13 decisions, and pitched a three-hit shutout in Game One of the championship series.

DH Kevin Reimer, who like Wilson also hails from British Columbia (Enderby), led the team with a .302 average and 21 home runs. First baseman Gary Alexander, in his first full pro season, had a team-high 78 RBIs and a three-run homer to key the Drillers' 7-4 Game Six victory.

"Everybody has had a hand in this," said Jim Skaalen, the Texas League manager of the year. "This has been a fun season. Everybody has contributed. I'm just happy for these guys. It's been a long dry spell in the Rangers organization. This has been the most enjoyable group I've had a chance to work with."

The San Antonio Missions won the first-half Western Division title in their first season after returning to the city's traditional nickname. The Missions had been known as the Dodgers.

Loooonnnnngg game

The Drillers weren't the only team to do a lot of waiting. The Jackson Mets and San Antonio played a league-record, 26-inning game, which San Antonio won 1-0. For 25 innings, it was the longest scoreless tie in the history of professional baseball.

The game was played over two days. After 25 innings, at 2:29 a.m. July 15, the game was suspended. It was resumed before a regularly scheduled game July 16, and lasted just 13 more minutes. Manny Francois singled home Walt McConnell to win it for San Antonio.

The box score's most interesting line belonged to Jackson's Manny Salinas: 10 0 0 0. Mets pitchers struck out 20.

San Antonio righthander Ramon Martinez not only helped the Missions to a first-half title, but eventually wound up in the Los Angeles Dodgers' rotation.

Martinez was the talk of the majors for a while, and earned comparisons to a young Fernando Valenzuela, among others.

He wasn't the only Texas Leaguer playing a key role in a major league pennant race. With Milwaukee stalking Boston in the American League East, Gary Sheffield started at shortstop. Sheffield began the season in El Paso.

Manto most valuable

Midland third baseman Jeff Manto (.301-24-101) was the Texas League's most valuable player. El Paso outfielder Greg Vaughn (.301-28-105) led in home runs and RBIs.

Midland first baseman Jim McCollom shaded El Paso DH Mario Monico, who held a wide lead most of the second half, for the batting title, .343-.342. The margin was actually slightly less than .001.

Jackson lefthander Blaine Beatty (16-8, 2.46 ERA) struck out 103 while walking just 34 in 209 innings to become the league's pitcher of the year. Jackson righthander Mickey Weston went from reliever to starter at midseason, and wound up winning the ERA title at 2.23.

Shreveport lefthander Mike Remlinger was less fortunate. After a brilliant 1987, the 1987 Giants' first-round choice had arm trouble early in his second season.

Arkansas lost its manager, but under happy circumstances. Jim Riggleman moved up to become farm director for the Cardinals when Lee Thomas left St. Louis to become Philadelphia's new general manager. He was replaced by Gaylen Pitts.

Tulsa (188,375) and Jackson (134,967) both broke club attendance records.

FIRST HALF

East	W	L	Pct.	GB
Shreveport (Giants) .	39	28	.582	—
Tulsa (Rangers)	34	34	.500	5½
Arkansas (Cardinals)	30	37	.448	9
Jackson (Mets)......	30	38	.441	9½
West				
San Antnio (Dodgers)	42	26	.618	—
El Paso (Brewers) ...	38	30	.559	4
Wichita (Padres).....	30	38	.441	12
Midland (Angels)	28	40	.412	14

SECOND HALF

East	W	L	Pct.	GB
Tulsa (Rangers)	37	31	.544	—
Arkansas (Cardinals)	37	32	.536	½
Shreveport (Giants) .	35	34	.507	2½
Jackson (Mets)......	31	37	.456	6
West				
El Paso (Brewers) ...	36	30	.545	—
Midland (Angels)	33	34	.493	3½
San Antnio (Dodgers)	31	34	.477	4½
Wichita (Padres).....	30	38	.441	7

1988 Final Standings

OVERALL

East	W	L	Pct.	GB
El Paso (Brewers) ...	74	60	.552	—
San Antnio (Dodgers)	73	60	.549	½
Shreveport (Giants) .	74	62	.544	1
Tulsa (Rangers)	71	65	.522	4
Arkansas (Cardinals)	67	69	.493	8
Midland (Angels)	61	74	.452	13½
Jackson (Mets)......	61	75	.449	14
Wichita (Padres).....	60	76	.441	15

San Antonio righthander Ramon Martinez eventually wound up in the Los Angeles Dodgers' rotation

1988: General Information

Playoffs: Tulsa defeated Shreveport 2-0 and El Paso defeated San Antonio 2-0 in best-of-3 semifinals; Tulsa defeated El Paso 4-2 in best-of-7 finals for league championship.

Regular Season Attendance: Arkansas, 251,892; Shreveport, 234,587; El Paso, 207,236; Tulsa, 188,375; Jackson, 134,967; Midland, 133,105; San Antonio, 130,899; Wichita, 70,525.

Managers: Arkansas—Jim Riggleman, Gaylen Pitts; **El Paso**—Dave Machemer; **Jackson**—Tucker Ashford; **Midland**—Max Oliveras; **San Antonio**—Kevin Kennedy; **Shreveport**—Jack Mull; **Tulsa**—Jim Skaalen; **Wichita**—Pat Kelly.

1988 Official All-Star Team: C—Todd Zeile, Arkansas; Chad Kreuter, Tulsa. **1B**—Jim McCollom, Midland. **2B**—Frank Mattox, El Paso. **3B**—Jeff Manto, Midland. **SS**—Gary Sheffield, El Paso. **Util**— Domingo Michel, San Antonio. **OF**—Greg Vaughn, El Paso; Mike Huff, San Antonio; Jeff Yurtin, Wichita. **DH**—Mario Monico, El Paso. **P**—Blaine Beatty, Jackson; Kevin Brown, Tulsa; Mike Munoz, San Antonio; Joe Olker, Shreveport; Steve Wilson, Tulsa. **Most Valuable Player**—Jeff Manto, Midland. **Pitcher of the Year**—Blaine Beatty, Jackson. **Manager of the Year**—Jim Skaalen, Tulsa.

Top 10 Major League Prospects (by Baseball America): 1. Ramon Martinez, rhp, San Antonio; **2.** Gary Sheffield, 3b, El Paso; **3.** Todd Zeile, c, Arkansas; **4.** Juan Bell, ss, San Antonio; **5.** Greg Vaughn, of, El Paso; **6.** Kevin Brown, rhp, Tulsa; **7.** Mike Munoz, lhp, San Antonio; **8.** Trevor Wilson, lhp, Shreveport; **9.** John Wetteland, rhp, San Antonio; **10.** Jeff Manto, 3b, Midland.

1988: Batting, Pitching Statistics

CLUB BATTING

	AVG	G	AB	R	H	2B	3B	HR	BB	SO	SB
El Paso	.285	134	4661	839	1330	230	31	160	497	939	134
Midland	.281	136	4620	727	1299	214	29	116	499	872	145
San Antonio	.261	133	4494	570	1174	186	28	60	390	685	147
Arkansas	.257	136	4402	566	1130	195	22	57	445	699	69
Wichita	.254	136	4600	639	1170	232	28	100	460	941	63
Tulsa	.252	136	4409	586	1109	189	49	80	459	870	75
Jackson	.249	137	4595	548	1146	212	30	61	451	822	132
Shreveport	.249	136	4518	552	1125	210	43	74	400	885	151

CLUB PITCHING

	ERA	G	CG	SHO	SV	IP	H	R	ER	BB	SO
Shreveport	3.28	136	6	14	45	1200	1080	524	437	434	851
Jackson	3.29	137	24	13	28	1218	1125	552	445	431	815
Tulsa	3.49	136	18	6	31	1164	1100	557	451	433	841
San Antonio	3.60	133	10	12	32	1189	1160	571	476	384	854
Arkansas	3.84	136	19	10	29	1168	1201	605	498	434	882
Wichita	4.33	136	20	12	27	1192	1212	671	574	452	847
Midland	4.99	136	13	3	32	1184	1328	780	657	509	808
El Paso	5.06	134	19	5	35	1169	1277	767	657	524	815

INDIVIDUAL BATTING LEADERS

(Minimum 367 Plate Appearances)

	AVG	G	AB	R	H	2B	3B	HR	RBI	BB	SO	SB
McCollom, Jim, Mid	.343	118	452	95	155	32	3	20	75	37	66	13
*Monico, Mario, EP	.342	111	386	77	132	22	2	8	52	60	45	8
Michel, Domingo, SA	.330	94	352	62	116	21	3	7	50	47	52	15
Baine, Tom, Ark	.307	131	482	69	148	22	2	1	40	60	44	10
Huff, Mike, SA	.304	102	395	68	120	18	10	2	40	37	55	34
*Reimer, Kevin, Tulsa ...	.302	133	486	74	147	30	11	21	76	38	95	4
Manto, Jeff, Mid	.301	120	408	88	123	23	3	24	101	62	76	7
*Skurla, John, Shr	.301	116	392	62	118	16	4	11	51	25	67	12
Vaughn, Greg, EP	.301	131	505	104	152	39	2	28	105	63	120	22
*Carrillo, Matias, EP ...	.298	106	396	76	118	17	2	12	55	26	81	11

* indicates lefthanded batter   # indicates switch hitter

INDIVIDUAL PITCHING LEADERS

(Minimum 109 Innings)

	W	L	ERA	G	GS	CG	SV	IP	H	R	ER	BB	SO
Weston, Mickey, Jack	8	5	2.23	30	14	1	0	125	127	50	31	20	61
*Beatty, Blaine, Jack	16	8	2.46	30	28	12	0	209	191	64	57	34	103
Arnold, Scott, Ark	10	4	2.55	21	21	4	0	131	108	42	37	52	103
*Barfield, John, Tulsa	9	9	2.88	24	24	5	0	169	159	69	54	66	125
*Wilson, Steve, Tulsa	15	7	3.16	25	25	5	0	165	147	72	58	53	132
Hartshorn, Kyle, Jack	11	8	3.29	24	23	4	0	151	135	65	55	58	82
Freeland, Dean, Shr	11	11	3.38	27	27	0	0	176	162	72	66	76	101
*Olker, Joe, Shr	15	2	3.46	26	26	0	0	151	152	67	58	63	94
Osteen, Dave, Ark	9	8	3.46	25	24	8	0	156	153	66	60	22	103
LaFever, Greg, SA	9	7	3.49	26	24	1	0	147	148	69	57	34	82

* indicates lefthanded pitcher

ARKANSAS

BATTING	AVG	G	AB	R	H	2B	3B	HR	RBI	BB	SO	SB
Agostinelli, Sal, c	.300	25	40	8	12	0	0	0	6	8	4	2
Baine, Tom, of	.307	131	482	69	148	22	2	1	40	60	44	10
Figueroa, Bien, ss	.278	126	407	48	113	17	2	0	32	22	49	2
Fregosi, Jim, ss-3b	.216	91	218	24	47	4	1	3	26	25	41	2
*Graham, Everett, of (20 Shr)	.276	54	174	24	48	11	0	5	26	24	25	2
Harrison, Brett, 2b	.249	134	434	52	108	18	2	4	51	51	85	7
*Hocutt, Mike, 1b-3b	.247	64	194	15	48	14	1	6	38	20	52	1
Infante, Kennedy, 3b	.211	12	38	0	8	1	0	0	4	4	4	0
#Lockwood, Rick, 3b	.290	48	186	24	54	12	2	6	32	6	24	0
*Mendez, Jesus, 1b-of ...	.248	126	460	60	114	14	1	5	46	28	44	2
Nunez, Mauricio, of	.225	111	306	32	69	9	4	2	30	19	53	15
*Puzey, Jim, c	.252	49	111	10	28	2	1	1	19	20	12	0
Robertson, Mike, 3b-of ..	.234	113	363	48	85	13	1	3	26	44	69	5
Robinson, Mike, of	.240	69	208	26	50	13	1	2	18	17	54	9
*Schulte, Mark, of	.310	26	29	3	9	4	0	0	4	1	4	0
Senne, Mike, of	.159	14	44	7	7	3	0	0	3	5	10	1
#Silver, Roy, of	.253	57	178	12	45	7	2	1	25	12	23	5
*Thoutsis, Paul, of	.333	7	9	0	3	0	0	0	2	0	0	0
Zeile, Todd, c	.272	129	430	95	117	33	2	19	75	83	64	6

PITCHING	W	L	ERA	G	GS	CG	SV	IP	H	R	ER	BB	SO
Arnold, Scott	10	4	2.55	21	21	4	0	131	108	42	37	52	103
*Engel, Steve	0	2	6.48	5	5	0	0	25	31	20	18	8	20
*Epple, Tom	0	2	15.75	2	2	0	0	4	8	9	7	3	4
Faron, Bob	4	9	4.07	21	21	1	0	122	146	59	55	21	51
*Fassero, Jeff	5	5	3.58	70	1	0	17	78	97	48	31	41	72
Hill, Ken	9	9	4.92	22	22	3	0	115	129	76	63	50	107
*Hill, Steve	3	2	4.12	32	0	0	1	44	51	26	20	24	50
Hilton, Howard	8	7	2.65	66	0	0	7	102	90	39	30	46	90
Hoffman, Dick	0	0	18.00	1	1	0	0	2	5	4	4	1	2
Kinzer, Matt	3	0	3.10	16	0	0	3	29	26	11	10	3	34
*Lepley, John	1	0	6.75	11	0	0	0	9	6	7	7	8	6
Malave, Benito	5	1	4.30	48	1	0	1	82	76	51	39	47	65
Osteen, Dave	9	8	3.46	25	24	8	0	156	153	66	60	22	103
Oyster, Jeff	3	3	3.04	15	13	2	0	83	82	39	28	27	50
Perez, Mike	1	3	11.30	11	0	0	0	14	18	18	18	13	17
Sassone, Mike	3	8	3.79	35	12	0	0	97	102	51	41	36	67
Sontag, Alan	3	6	3.45	19	13	1	0	73	71	37	28	29	40

Top TL Performers

Jeff Manto
...league MVP

Jim McCollom
...bat champ

Blaine Beatty
...16 wins

EL PASO

BATTING	AVG	G	AB	R	H	2B	3B	HR	RBI	BB	SO	SB
Anderson, Roy, c	.237	77	215	31	51	11	2	4	23	28	60	1
Brown, Todd, of	.393	24	89	19	35	9	1	2	16	10	6	5
*Canale, George, 1b	.242	132	496	77	120	23	2	23	93	59	152	9
*Carrillo, Matias, of	.298	106	396	76	118	17	2	12	55	26	81	11
*Cartwright, Alan, dh-of	.302	16	53	11	16	4	0	4	10	3	13	0
*Casey, Tim, of-dh	.230	40	139	19	32	6	0	10	24	8	41	2
*Dewolf, Rob, of	.283	114	428	88	121	20	3	6	52	57	80	16
#Mattox, Frank, 2b	.290	106	379	56	110	9	4	5	51	41	43	24
*McGrew, Charlie, c	.288	23	52	5	15	6	0	0	2	2	15	0
Mitchell, Joe, 3b	.270	131	486	76	131	13	5	18	80	31	108	8
*Monico, Mario, dh-of	.342	111	386	77	132	22	2	8	52	60	45	8
Rodriguez, Angel, c	.239	43	138	28	33	8	1	8	24	7	23	3
#Scott, Donnie, c-3b	.340	13	50	15	17	0	1	1	7	7	7	1
Sheffield, Gary, ss	.314	77	296	70	93	19	3	19	65	35	41	5
*Spiers, Bill, ss	.280	47	168	22	47	5	2	3	21	15	20	1
Torricelli, Tim, c	.429	11	35	7	15	1	0	2	7	3	7	0
Vaughn, Greg, of	.301	131	505	104	152	39	2	28	105	63	120	22
Williams, Fred, inf-of	.263	109	350	58	92	18	1	7	52	42	77	15

PITCHING	W	L	ERA	G	GS	CG	SV	IP	H	R	ER	BB	SO
Ambrose, Mark	2	2	7.11	4	4	0	0	19	26	19	15	9	13
Bass, Barry	9	3	3.99	48	0	0	11	70	77	37	31	37	44
Brisco, Jamie	0	3	4.62	36	0	0	6	49	49	32	25	24	53
Citarella, Ralph	1	0	4.15	8	5	0	0	30	27	17	14	10	22
Fleming, Keith	2	3	4.08	35	0	0	3	68	65	31	31	25	54
Henry, Doug	4	0	3.15	14	3	3	0	46	33	16	16	19	50
Hetrick, Kent	3	3	5.49	10	10	2	0	57	71	41	35	28	31
Hicks, Rob	4	3	6.57	26	0	0	1	51	70	40	37	15	27
Hunter, Jim	8	11	5.67	26	26	2	0	148	163	107	93	77	103
*Kendrick, Pete	0	1	6.75	5	5	0	0	19	30	16	14	6	13
Meagher, Adrian	2	1	3.20	11	4	1	1	39	33	15	14	12	32
Mooneyham, Bill	4	9	6.82	22	17	1	1	99	127	91	75	63	63
Peterek, Jeff	7	1	3.39	9	9	3	0	69	60	32	26	17	54
Price, Kevin	0	0	5.19	3	1	0	0	9	9	8	5	3	5
*Puig, Ed	8	4	4.39	54	0	0	12	92	92	55	45	31	62
Sadler, Alan	4	2	1.93	9	9	2	0	51	44	19	11	26	19
*Scarpetta, Dan	11	6	4.45	18	18	5	0	113	119	70	56	50	81
Serna, Ramon	0	3	9.91	8	6	0	0	26	36	32	29	16	14
*Sonberg, Erik	0	0	10.05	7	0	0	0	14	21	16	16	10	12
Veres, Randy	3	2	3.66	6	6	0	0	39	35	18	16	12	31
*Wheeler, Brad	2	3	8.18	15	11	0	0	58	89	55	53	32	32

JACKSON

BATTING	AVG	G	AB	R	H	2B	3B	HR	RBI	BB	SO	SB
#Contreras, Joaquin, of	.253	95	340	44	86	22	2	6	37	36	62	7
*Cuevas, Angelo, of	.296	106	355	35	105	18	3	8	42	19	69	0
DeButch, Mike, of-inf (59 Wch)	.239	106	373	56	89	11	5	2	30	67	60	40
DeLuca, Kurt, of-c	.202	61	163	15	33	9	0	4	17	16	41	2
*Gardner, Jeff, 2b	.252	134	432	46	109	15	2	0	33	69	52	13
Gelatt, Dave, ss	.000	1	1	0	0	0	0	0	0	0	1	0
*Gideon, Ron, 1b	.225	119	325	38	73	19	0	12	33	35	105	1
*Hayden, Alan, of	.297	135	525	74	156	19	9	1	48	38	56	64
#Jacas, Andre, of	.267	4	15	2	4	0	1	0	1	1	4	1
Jelic, Chris, c	.209	88	273	29	57	13	1	4	25	43	57	3
Jones, Geary, c	.178	41	107	12	19	2	0	1	11	12	33	0
#Lawton, Marcus, of	.298	54	205	42	61	12	0	2	20	26	40	16
Lundblade, Rick, 1b-c	.247	49	162	15	40	6	0	4	19	10	29	1
#Monell, Johnny, of	.250	13	40	4	10	2	0	1	5	2	4	0
Perdomo, Felix, inf	.231	67	143	15	33	11	1	0	16	12	41	0
Roman, Miguel, of-dh	.264	79	227	31	60	12	2	6	41	17	53	0
*Salinas, Manny, 3b-ss	.245	117	421	34	103	17	2	1	51	14	25	0

```
                        BATTING
        R—Greg Vaughn, El Paso .................104
        H—Alan Hayden, Jackson .................156
       TB—Greg Vaughn, El Paso .................279
       2B—Greg Vaughn, El Paso ..................39
       3B—Kevin Reimer, Tulsa ...................11
       HR—Greg Vaughn, El Paso ..................28
      RBI—Greg Vaughn, El Paso .................105
    GWRBI—Kevin Reimer, Tulsa ...................12
       SH—Jeff Gardner, Jackson ..................14
       SF—Scott Coolbaugh, Tulsa ..................8
          —Joaquin Contreras, Jackson ...........8
       BB—Chris Knabenshue, Wichita .............84
      IBB—Three tied at.........................9
      HBP—Luis Lopez, San Antonio ...............13
       SO—George Canale, El Paso ...............152
       SB—Dee Dixon, Shreveport .................72
       CS—C.L. Penigar, Midland .................27
  Slg. Pct.—Jim McCollom, Midland ..............560
   OB Pct.—Mario Monico, El Paso ...............429
                        PITCHING
        G—Jeff Fassero, Arkansas ...............70
       GS—Matt Maysey, Wichita ..................28
          —Blaine Beatty, Jackson ..............28
       CG—Blaine Beatty, Jackson ................12
      ShO—Blaine Beatty, Jackson .................5
       Sv—Jose Dominguez, Shreveport ...........22
        W—Blaine Beatty, Jackson ................16
        L—Brian Givens, Jackson .................14
       IP—Blaine Beatty, Jackson ...............209
        H—Steve McGuire, Midland ...............201
        R—Steve McGuire, Midland ...............117
       HR—Terry Gilmore, Wichita ................20
       BB—John Wetteland, San Antonio ...........77
          —Jim Hunter, El Paso .................77
       HB—Dean Freeland, Shreveport .............11
       SO—Brian Givens, Jackson ...............156
       WP—John Wetteland, San Antonio ...........22
       Bk—Paul McClellan, Shreveport ............22
```

Department Leaders

	AVG	G	AB	R	H	2B	3B	HR	RBI	BB	SO	SB
Sanchez, Zoilo, 3b-1b ...	.227	49	119	25	27	6	1	5	15	19	33	1
Shipley, Craig, ss	.263	89	335	41	88	14	3	6	41	24	40	6
Villanueva, Juan, ss	.226	22	62	8	14	2	0	0	4	5	11	1

PITCHING	W	L	ERA	G	GS	CG	SV	IP	H	R	ER	BB	SO
*Barton, Shawn	2	4	3.27	22	8	0	1	72	74	33	26	26	58
Bayer, Chris	0	2	8.74	4	2	0	0	11	14	12	11	6	6
*Beatty, Blaine	16	8	2.46	30	28	12	0	209	191	64	57	34	103
*Brown, Kevin	1	2	2.20	5	5	1	0	33	24	9	8	11	24
Brown, Rick	1	0	0.00	3	0	0	0	6	5	2	0	3	2
*Conley, Virgil	5	4	3.95	36	8	1	3	107	120	61	47	32	58
Cook, Mitch	1	2	3.93	7	7	0	0	37	37	22	16	9	25
*Givens, Brian	6	14	3.78	26	26	4	0	164	140	78	69	68	156
Hartshorn, Kyle	11	8	3.29	24	23	4	0	151	135	65	55	58	82
*Latham, Bill	1	2	3.58	5	5	0	0	28	35	14	11	10	15
*Rodriguez, Rich	2	7	2.87	47	1	0	6	78	66	35	25	42	68
Roman, Jose	1	4	3.82	22	0	0	4	31	29	14	13	11	22
*Santiago, Mike	1	1	3.50	22	1	0	1	36	29	16	14	14	30
Tapani, Kevin	5	1	2.74	24	5	0	3	62	46	23	19	19	35
Welborn, Todd	0	11	6.00	45	4	1	10	63	49	51	42	63	63
Weston, Mickey	8	5	2.23	30	14	1	0	125	127	50	31	20	61

MIDLAND

BATTING	AVG	G	AB	R	H	2B	3B	HR	RBI	BB	SO	SB
Alfaro, Jesus, 3b-1b	.301	92	309	50	93	20	1	8	60	35	53	1
Alfredson, Tom, of	.254	126	437	70	111	17	3	15	66	65	138	7
#Amaro, Ruben, 2b	.129	13	31	5	4	1	0	0	2	4	5	4
Carrasco, Norm, 2b	.284	68	261	26	74	13	0	2	33	11	23	5
Geivett, Bill, inf	.273	31	77	14	21	0	1	0	7	12	18	3
*Gerber, Craig, ss	.214	91	285	23	61	3	0	0	25	14	26	8
*Grunhard, Dan, of	.286	115	420	69	120	20	2	8	33	40	58	8
Knapp, Mike, c	.263	100	327	34	86	12	1	3	33	35	64	1
*Lee, Wiley, 2b-of	.385	3	13	1	5	0	1	0	0	0	3	2
Manto, Jeff, 3b	.301	120	408	88	123	23	3	24	101	62	76	7
McCollom, Jim, 1b-of ..	.343	118	452	95	155	32	3	20	75	37	66	13
Nunez, Dario, ss	.191	16	47	5	9	0	0	0	6	1	8	0
Opie, Jim, ss-3b	.232	45	151	20	35	5	0	6	23	15	43	3
Pappas, Erik, c-1b	.276	83	275	40	76	17	2	4	38	29	53	16
#Penigar, C.L., of	.269	123	454	63	122	16	5	2	45	46	103	47
*Stevens, Lee, of-dh ..	.297	116	414	79	123	20	2	23	76	58	108	10
#Thomas, Jim, 2b	.318	62	255	45	81	9	5	1	24	35	26	19

PITCHING	W	L	ERA	G	GS	CG	SV	IP	H	R	ER	BB	SO
Alicea, Miguel	1	4	4.64	31	0	0	4	54	53	32	28	20	50
Buckels, Gary	0	0	0.73	7	0	0	1	12	5	2	1	4	9

	W	L	ERA	G	GS	CG	SV	IP	H	R	ER	BB	SO
Burcham, Tim	8	9	5.49	27	27	2	0	143	167	111	87	74	97
Cedeno, Vinicio	1	2	4.48	44	1	0	0	76	72	45	38	38	66
Collins, Chris	5	10	7.31	21	21	1	0	105	143	92	85	54	72
*Corbett, Sherm	3	2	3.40	18	0	0	2	48	48	21	18	11	40
*DiMichele, Frank	1	4	6.57	37	0	0	3	37	48	31	27	29	28
Eggertsen, Todd	6	8	5.67	22	22	1	0	132	173	109	83	52	54
Fetters, Mike	8	8	5.92	20	20	2	0	114	116	78	75	67	101
Geivett, Bill	0	0	3.60	4	0	0	0	5	7	2	2	1	4
Hernandez, Roberto	0	2	6.57	3	3	0	0	12	16	13	9	8	7
McGuire, Steve	8	12	5.37	27	27	5	0	171	201	117	102	58	77
Perry, Jeff	0	1	4.15	5	0	0	2	9	4	4	4	2	8
*Reed, Marty	4	2	2.78	23	4	1	2	58	53	19	18	25	32
Venturino, Phil	3	1	1.11	4	4	1	0	24	18	10	3	4	6
Walker, Kurt	3	5	3.66	47	0	0	12	64	71	31	26	18	60
Ward, Colby	9	2	2.68	26	0	0	2	40	42	17	12	19	32
*Young, Shane	1	2	4.21	29	5	0	4	77	85	43	36	25	62

SAN ANTONIO

BATTING	AVG	G	AB	R	H	2B	3B	HR	RBI	BB	SO	SB
*Amelung, Ed, of	.284	20	67	7	19	3	0	2	7	3	13	0
Batesole, Mike, 3b-1b	.286	53	182	18	52	9	0	4	25	5	24	0
Bell, Juan, ss	.279	61	215	37	60	4	2	5	21	16	37	11
Benitez, Manuel, of	.235	52	119	8	28	9	0	0	4	14	21	0
*Brown, Adam, dh-c	.296	30	98	14	29	5	0	2	13	7	20	0
Bustabad, Juan, ss	.233	97	288	31	67	10	1	1	23	22	36	4
*Fletcher, Darrin, c	.208	89	279	19	58	8	0	1	20	17	42	2
#Francois, Manny, 2b	.245	123	436	48	107	17	1	6	40	55	78	18
Huff, Mike, of	.304	102	395	68	120	18	10	2	40	37	55	34
Kating, Jim, of	.200	16	40	4	8	4	0	0	6	7	4	0
*Kesselmark, Joe, of	.279	66	244	23	68	9	2	2	34	10	23	6
*Kirby, Wayne, of	.240	100	334	50	80	9	2	0	21	21	42	26
Lopez, Luis, 1b-c	.247	123	470	56	116	15	3	7	65	32	33	3
*McConnell, Walt, 3b	.268	93	354	37	95	17	1	11	53	34	57	4
Michel, Domingo, of-1b	.330	94	352	62	116	21	3	7	50	47	52	15
*Mota, Jose, of-2b	.262	82	214	32	56	11	1	1	18	27	35	10
Ortiz, Javier, of-1b	.291	51	182	35	53	13	2	8	33	22	38	6
#Santana, Miguel, of	.245	29	98	11	24	1	0	0	10	5	18	8

PITCHING	W	L	ERA	G	GS	CG	SV	IP	H	R	ER	BB	SO
Crawford, Steve	1	0	0.00	3	0	0	1	6	2	0	0	0	4
Eichhorn, Dave	5	6	3.51	19	16	1	0	105	99	53	41	26	43
Hartley, Mike	5	1	0.80	30	0	0	9	45	25	5	4	18	57
Hickey, Jim	0	2	2.85	17	1	0	0	41	41	19	13	11	15
Humphries, Joe	0	0	3.86	2	0	0	0	2	5	2	1	1	2
LaFever, Greg	9	7	3.49	26	24	1	0	147	148	69	57	34	82
Mack, Tony	6	0	2.95	37	1	0	4	64	57	31	21	26	69
Martinez, Ramon	8	4	2.46	14	14	2	0	95	79	29	26	34	89
Mathis, Ron	5	5	3.86	11	10	0	0	56	47	28	24	17	33
*Munoz, Mike	7	2	1.00	56	0	0	14	72	63	18	8	24	71
Pitz, Mike	3	8	4.80	19	19	2	0	122	142	71	65	21	79
Schweighoffer, Mike	7	8	3.96	43	8	1	2	105	123	57	46	27	42
Tapia, Jose A.	0	0	11.74	8	0	0	0	8	13	12	10	7	6
Torres, Phil	1	3	3.43	36	1	0	2	58	46	30	22	27	56
Wetteland, John	10	8	3.88	25	25	3	0	162	141	74	70	77	140
*Wohler, Barry	6	6	5.96	37	14	0	0	100	128	71	66	32	63

SHREVEPORT

BATTING	AVG	G	AB	R	H	2B	3B	HR	RBI	BB	SO	SB
Benjamin, Mike, ss	.236	89	309	48	73	19	5	6	37	22	63	14
#Carter, Jeff, 2b	.247	124	409	50	101	9	8	3	41	51	52	15
Cucjen, Romy, 3b-1b	.248	123	411	49	102	26	2	11	54	33	91	2
*Dabney, Ty, of	.276	21	76	9	21	5	2	0	10	5	14	3
Davis, Harry, of	.222	113	315	44	70	13	5	5	32	17	83	9
*Dixon, Dee, of	.290	126	455	58	132	4	5	3	36	46	59	72
#Escobar, Angel, ss	.192	22	73	10	14	2	1	0	6	11	15	4
Kmak, Joe, c	.225	71	178	16	40	5	2	1	14	11	19	0
Litton, Greg, 3b-2b	.278	116	432	58	120	35	5	11	64	37	84	2
McCue, Deron, of-1b	.238	65	160	20	38	6	0	5	24	22	31	5
McDonald, T.J., of	.182	76	181	13	33	7	0	0	9	17	40	1
#Meyers, Paul, of	.236	65	220	23	52	8	0	2	17	17	33	1
Nelson, Rick, 1b	.237	54	177	26	42	10	2	7	23	22	67	4
Pena, Jose, c	.245	98	314	29	77	19	1	4	36	15	58	2
Santana, Andres, ss	.167	11	36	3	6	0	0	0	3	4	9	3
*Skurla, John, of-1b	.301	116	392	62	118	16	4	11	51	25	67	12
*Wishnevski, Mike, 1b	.294	44	126	17	37	10	0	4	26	25	35	2

PITCHING	W	L	ERA	G	GS	CG	SV	IP	H	R	ER	BB	SO
*Bonilla, George	4	4	2.65	45	6	0	3	95	86	45	28	31	70
Burkett, John	5	1	2.13	7	7	2	0	51	33	15	12	18	34
Dominguez, Jose	3	6	2.71	59	0	0	22	80	65	31	24	20	67
Freeland, Dean	11	11	3.38	27	27	0	0	176	162	72	66	76	101
*Gunderson, Eric	1	2	5.15	7	6	0	0	37	45	25	21	13	28
Hogan, Mike	3	4	2.50	31	2	0	3	68	52	20	19	21	47
McCament, Randy	3	4	5.36	24	0	0	2	42	56	29	25	14	15
McClellan, Paul	10	12	4.04	27	27	4	0	167	146	89	75	62	128
*McCoy, Tim	1	6	4.58	15	11	0	1	77	78	45	39	34	49
Ohnoutka, Brian	2	2	3.52	9	9	0	0	54	54	25	21	12	40

	W	L	ERA	G	GS	CG	SV	IP	H	R	ER	BB	SO
*Olker, Joe	15	2	3.46	26	26	0	0	151	152	67	58	63	94
*Puikunas, Ed	7	2	2.78	46	0	0	7	78	62	27	24	25	62
*Remlinger, Mike	1	0	0.69	3	3	0	0	13	7	4	1	4	18
Tate, Stuart	3	2	2.03	24	1	0	7	40	27	11	9	18	45
*Wilson, Trevor	5	4	1.86	12	11	0	0	73	55	19	15	23	53

TULSA

BATTING	AVG	G	AB	R	H	2B	3B	HR	RBI	BB	SO	SB
Alexander, Gary, 1b	.265	132	464	71	123	21	6	17	78	70	129	0
Bootay, Kevin, of	.274	83	325	57	89	16	2	3	25	22	51	23
#Cartaya, Joel, ss	.250	54	180	19	45	7	2	0	12	12	27	4
Coolbaugh, Scott, 3b	.270	136	470	52	127	15	4	13	75	76	79	2
Fariss, Monty, ss	.224	49	165	21	37	6	6	3	31	22	39	2
*Glasker, Steve, of	.161	17	62	5	10	0	1	1	2	1	17	1
Jackson, Bubba, c	.144	39	111	10	16	6	0	1	8	12	25	0
#Kreuter, Chad, c	.265	108	358	46	95	24	6	3	51	55	66	2
Millay, Gar, of-dh	.256	109	371	47	95	25	0	8	51	49	71	0
Postier, Paul, 2b-ss	.214	76	224	20	48	5	1	0	16	15	52	0
*Reimer, Kevin, dh-of	.302	133	486	74	147	30	11	21	76	38	95	4
Richardt, Mike, 2b-dh	.255	28	102	15	26	3	0	2	12	7	6	1
Samson, Fred, 2b-ss	.184	14	49	6	9	2	1	0	2	2	17	2
*Scanlin, Mike, of	.177	71	226	23	40	8	3	3	26	25	59	6
Threadgill, George, of	.263	127	476	92	125	13	5	5	34	49	99	23
#Vargas, Jose, 2b	.215	84	279	21	60	6	1	0	17	4	30	5
Wilson, Tack, of	.279	19	61	7	17	2	0	3	0	8	0	

PITCHING	W	L	ERA	G	GS	CG	SV	IP	H	R	ER	BB	SO
*Barfield, John	9	9	2.88	24	24	5	0	169	159	69	54	66	125
Brown, Kevin	12	10	3.51	26	26	5	0	174	174	94	68	61	118
*Cerny, Marty	0	0	2.84	4	0	0	0	6	6	3	2	2	3
Ellis, Rufus	0	1	4.35	7	1	0	0	10	10	5	5	10	5
Harman, Dave	0	0	18.00	1	0	0	0	1	3	2	2	0	1
Lankard, Steve	4	3	3.78	40	0	0	1	69	76	34	29	17	47
Malloy, Bob	1	7	5.17	12	12	0	0	71	93	53	41	24	29
Mays, Jeff	0	1	9.90	6	0	0	0	10	15	11	11	6	7
Pavlas, Dave	5	2	1.98	26	5	1	2	77	52	26	17	18	69
Raether, Rick	4	1	0.96	46	0	0	16	56	35	8	6	28	40
Rockman, Marv	1	0	1.08	6	0	0	0	8	5	1	1	0	5
*Rogers, Kenny	4	6	4.00	13	13	2	0	83	73	43	37	34	76
Thomas, Mitch	6	7	4.35	18	18	0	0	97	89	52	47	69	70
*Valdez, Efrain	6	5	4.55	43	3	0	6	63	63	37	32	24	52
West, Tommy	2	4	4.97	10	9	0	0	51	62	33	28	8	23
Whitaker, Darrell	2	2	2.32	21	0	0	6	50	38	14	13	13	39
*Wilson, Steve	15	7	3.16	25	25	5	0	165	147	72	58	53	132

WICHITA

BATTING	AVG	G	AB	R	H	2B	3B	HR	RBI	BB	SO	SB
#Baerga, Carlos, ss-2b	.273	122	444	67	121	28	1	12	65	31	83	4
Basso, Mike, c	.262	84	279	32	73	15	0	3	35	29	35	0
Cooper, Craig, 1b	.266	99	350	39	93	12	2	7	55	30	77	0
*Hermann, Jeff, of-dh	.232	73	203	27	47	13	3	3	27	22	47	1
#Howard, Tom, of	.301	29	103	15	31	9	2	0	16	13	14	6
Jelks, Pat, of	.227	63	207	34	47	6	2	6	26	19	67	1
*Knabenshue, Chris, of	.245	116	412	68	101	26	2	16	56	84	138	16
Lester, Jimmy, 2b-3b	.252	93	318	45	80	8	2	1	27	40	60	1
Parsons, Scott, of	.231	3	13	3	3	0	0	1	3	1	3	0
*Stevenson, Bill, 1b-dh	.252	99	330	51	83	16	2	16	54	27	77	3
Tatum, Jimmy, 3b	.261	118	402	38	105	26	1	8	54	30	73	2
*Verstandig, Mark, c	.250	4	8	2	2	2	0	0	3	4	1	0
#Wiley, Craig, c	.240	5	208	23	50	10	1	4	21	23	20	1
Wrona, Billy, 2b-ss	.243	120	460	68	112	18	4	4	42	29	59	1
*Yurtin, Jeff, of	.287	132	512	84	147	36	4	16	77	41	106	1

PITCHING	W	L	ERA	G	GS	CG	SV	IP	H	R	ER	BB	SO
Austin, Jim	5	6	4.81	12	12	4	0	73	76	46	39	23	52
*Bauer, Eric	1	4	9.13	5	5	0	0	24	38	24	24	6	15
*Brown, Kevin	1	8	6.38	28	7	0	1	86	88	67	61	51	58
Childers, Jeff	1	3	7.22	6	5	0	0	29	39	23	23	7	14
Costello, Mike	8	4	2.70	15	14	4	0	107	87	40	32	36	70
Ford, Rusty	1	5	4.48	53	1	0	4	74	75	40	37	43	53
Gilmore, Terry	11	7	4.61	25	25	4	0	168	170	94	86	35	112
*Harris, Greg S.	5	10	4.68	33	16	0	3	110	112	74	57	46	86
Luebber, Steve	0	0	1.50	4	0	0	0	6	3	1	1	1	8
Maysey, Matt	9	9	3.71	28	28	4	0	187	180	88	77	68	120
Mills, Mike	7	6	2.47	52	0	0	13	77	76	31	21	25	41
Quinzer, Paul	2	1	3.63	40	0	0	6	89	86	39	36	27	93
*Reece, Jeff	2	2	6.11	15	0	0	0	28	27	21	19	20	28
*Roberts, Pete	3	6	4.65	10	10	2	0	60	70	43	31	28	39
Wood, Brian	4	5	3.63	14	13	2	0	74	85	40	30	36	58

Riverside fields top club in shortest possible time

By JIM ALEXANDER

The final night of the California League's 1988 season provided a healthy dose of optimism for the future in the league's newest city.

Riverside, making its first appearance in the league since 1941—and its first foray into professional baseball of any sort since 1952—found itself with a league championship. The Red Wave, affiliated with the San Diego Padres, swept Stockton in the best-of-5 finals to win the title.

And, significantly, the third game of the series drew the largest crowd of the season in Riverside, 3,684—on the first night of high school football in the area.

That, and the attention generated

Ken Griffey Jr.
... top prospect

by the club's on-field success, will make Riverside's second off-season in the league easier than its first. From the time the club's stadium lease was approved by the Riverside City Council, the club had just 66 days to make $1.2 million worth of improvements in the ballpark, peddle tickets and advertising and, generally, sell a skeptical community on minor league baseball.

Southern migration

The shift of the Salinas franchise to Riverside continued a southward drift of the Cal League, after franchises had relocated in Palm Springs and San Bernardino the two previous seasons.

And, as the 1988 season concluded, there was continuing speculation that one of the league's two troubled clubs, Reno and Fresno, might also shift cities. Both were forced into co-op status in 1988, after having long-time franchise affiliations removed because of stadium problems.

The Fresno Suns, without affiliation with the San Francisco Giants for the first time in 30 years, finished dead last in attendance (34,734) and next to last in winning percentage over

League Champions
(Playoff Champions, Where Applicable)

1988—Riverside	1971—Visalia	1954—Modesto
1987—Fresno	1970—Bakersfield	1953—San Jose
1986—Stockton	1969—Stockton	1952—Fresno
1985—Fresno	1968—Fresno	1951—Santa Barb.
1984—Modesto	1967—San Jose	1950—Modesto
1983—Redwood	1966—Modesto	1949—San Jose
1982—Modesto	1965—Stockton	1948—Santa Barb.
1981—Lodi	1964—Fresno	1947—Stockton
1980—Stockton	1963—Stockton	1946—Stockton
1979—San Jose	1962—San Jose	1943-45—Did Not
1978—Visalia	1961—Reno	Operate
1977—Lodi	1960—Reno	1942—Santa Barb.
1976—Reno	1959—Modesto	1941—Santa Barb.
1975—Reno	1958—Fresno	1916-40—Did Not
1974—Fresno	1957—Salinas	Operate
1973—Lodi	1956—Fresno	1915—Modesto
1972—Modesto	1955—Fresno	1914—Fresno

Cal League's Best

  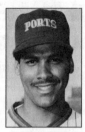

| Paul Faries
...MVP | Adam Brown
...batting champ | Jaime Navarro
...15-5, 3.09 |

the season (53-89). And they played in a makeshift ballpark; the city condemned the grandstand at Euless Park, and after being rebuffed in an attempt to use Fresno State's facilities, the Suns put up portable bleachers, used trailers for clubhouses and used Euless anyway.

Things were a little rosier in Reno, where the Silver Sox finished fourth in the league in attendance—more than 25,000 ahead of Riverside, for whom the Padres jettisoned Reno.

The Silver Sox finished with the league's worst won-loss record, 39-103, and club officials had speculated that the team couldn't continue to operate without a working agreement.

Staved off elimination

Riverside was actually within four outs of elimination in the playoff semifinals. The Red Wave, which won the second-half Southern Division title, lost the first two games to first-half winner Palm Springs—scoring two runs in two games—and trailed 8-7 in Game 3 with two out in the eighth.

But Riverside rallied for five runs in the eighth, won that game 12-8, followed with 13-4 and 10-4 victories to eliminate the Angels, then swept Stockton by scores of 5-2, 3-1 and 7-3.

Star of the future

The league had its share of stars in 1988. The most famous was Ken Griffey Jr., son of veteran major leaguer Ken Griffey. The younger Griffey, an outfielder, was the top player taken in the 1987 draft, by the Seattle Mariners.

Griffey spent a half season with San Bernardino—hitting .338 with 11 homers, 42 RBIs and 32 stolen bases—and that was enough time for him to earn honors as the league's top major league prospect in a Baseball America survey of league managers.

Griffey also provided the Spirit franchise with national publicity before his midseason promotion to Double-A, which turned out to be delayed when a back problem kept him out of action for two months.

Other individual stars, all of whom spent the bulk of the season in the Cal League, included:

■ San Jose pitchers Eric Gunderson (12-5, 2.65), Doug Robertson (7-5, 1.26, 23 saves) and outfielder Mark Leonard (.345 and a league-leading 118 RBIs), who led the Giants into the playoffs

■ Riverside second baseman Paul Faries (.317, 77 RBIs, 65 steals, 108 runs scored), the league's MVP and Rookie of the Year

■ Bakersfield catcher-DH Adam Brown, who led the league in hitting (.352, with 80 RBIs), even though a recovery from elbow surgery limited the amount of time he could catch.

In other league happenings:

Fresno suffered through a 20-game losing streak before a

July 19 victory at San Bernardino. Later in the season, Fresno set a more positive record by turning six double plays in a nine-inning game.

Veteran Alan Fowlkes started the season as pitcher-pitching coach with Reno, but earned a promotion in August when the Cleveland Indians bought his contract and assigned him to Colorado Springs (Pacific Coast).

Riverside and San Jose played the longest uninterrupted game in Cal League history May 22, a six-hour, 19-minutes, 21-inning game finally won by San Jose, 8-5, at Riverside. That game featured the return to active play of Riverside pitching coach Ron Oglesby, who had last pitched professionally in 1973 in the Mexican League but was pressed into duty that night when the Red Wave ran out of pitchers.

And two clubs topped the 100,000 mark in season attendance. San Bernardino, which set a league record in 1987, its first year, fell a little more than 4,000 short of another record-setting season but finished at 154,653. San Jose, enjoying its first year as an affiliate of the Giants, drew 108,386.

FIRST HALF				
North	W	L	Pct.	GB
Stockton (Brewers) ..	47	24	.662	—
San Jose (Giants) ...	43	28	.606	4
Modesto (Athletics) .	29	42	.408	18
Fresno (Co-op)	27	44	.380	20
Reno (Co-op)........	24	47	.338	23
South				
Palm Spr. (Angels)...	40	31	.563	—
San Bern. (Mariners) .	38	33	.535	2
Visalia (Twins)	38	33	.535	2
Riverside (Padres) ...	38	33	.535	2
Bakersfld (Dodgers) .	31	40	.437	9
SECOND HALF				
North	W	L	Pct.	GB
Stockton (Brewers) ..	47	24	.662	—
San Jose (Giants) ...	47	24	.662	—
Modesto (Athletics) .	25	45	.357	21½
Fresno (Co-op)	24	45	.348	22
Reno (Co-op)........	15	55	.214	31½
South				
Riverside (Padres) ...	47	24	.662	—
Visalia (Twins)	42	29	.592	5
Bakersfld (Dodgers) .	40	31	.563	7
San Bern. (Mariners) .	36	35	.507	11
Palm Spr. (Angels)...	30	41	.423	17
OVERALL				
	W	L	Pct.	GB
Stockton (Brewers) ..	94	49	.657	—
San Jose (Giants) ...	91	52	.636	3
Riverside (Padres) ...	85	57	.599	8½
Visalia (Twins)	80	62	.563	13½
San Bern. (Mariners) .	74	68	.521	19½
Bakersfld (Dodgers) .	71	71	.500	22½
Palm Spr. (Angels)...	70	72	.493	23½
Modesto (Athletics) .	54	88	.380	39½
Fresno (Co-op)	53	89	.373	40½
Reno (Co-op)........	39	103	.275	54½

1988
Final
Standings

1988: General Information

Playoffs: Riverside defeated Palm Springs 3-2 and Stockton defeated San Jose 3-2 in best-of-5 semifinals; Riverside defeated Stockton 3-0 in best-of-5 final for league championship.

Regular Season Attendance: San Bernardino, 154,653; San Jose, 108,386; Bakersfield, 92,360; Reno, 85,624; Modesto, 71,500; Riverside, 60,509; Palm Springs, 60,222; Stockton, 58,586; Visalia, 47,593; Fresno,

34,734.

Managers: Bakersfield—Gary LaRocque; **Fresno**—Dean Treanor; **Modesto**—Jeff Newman; **Palm Springs**—Bill Lachemann; **Reno**—Nate Oliver; **Riverside**—Tony Torchia; **San Bernardino**—Ralph Dick; **San Jose**—Duane Espy; **Stockton**—Dave Huppert; **Visalia**—Scott Ullger.

1988 Official All-Star Team: C—Tim McIntosh, Stockton. **1B**—Rich Aldrete, San Jose. **2B**—Paul Faries, Riverside. **3B**—Dave Hollins, Riverside. **SS**—Tommy LeVasseur, Riverside. **OF**—Warren Newson, Riverside; Mark Leonard, San Jose; Ken Griffey, San Bernardino. **DH**—Adam Brown, Bakersfield. **P**—Doug Robertson, San Jose; Eric Gunderson, San Jose; Colin Charland, Palm Springs; Steve Monson, Stockton. **Most Valuable Player**—Paul Faries, Riverside. **Rookie of the Year**—Paul Faries, Riverside. **Pitcher of the Year**—Doug Robertson, San Jose; Colin Charland, Palm Springs. **Manager of the Year**—Dave Huppert, Stockton.

Top 10 Major League Prospects (by Baseball America): 1. Ken Griffey Jr., of, San Bernardino; **2.** Jaime Navarro, rhp, Stockton; **3.** Colin Charland, lhp, Palm Springs; **4.** Paul Faries, 2b, Riverside; **5.** Mark Leonard, of, San Jose; **6.** Doug Robertson, rhp, San Jose; **7.** Bill Spiers, ss, Stockton; **8.** Eric Gunderson, lhp, San Jose; **9.** Dave Hollins, 3b, Riverside; **10.** Adam Brown, c-dh, Bakersfield.

1988: Batting, Pitching Statistics

CLUB BATTING

	AVG	G	AB	R	H	2B	3B	HR	BB	SO	SB
Visalia	.279	142	4777	795	1335	184	21	59	660	850	190
San Jose	.276	143	4754	836	1310	211	38	61	802	900	183
Riverside	.265	142	4713	755	1250	209	29	71	702	888	223
Bakersfield	.262	142	4743	695	1243	209	22	52	606	822	135
Stockton	.260	143	4812	833	1250	215	31	72	773	958	186
San Bernardino	.249	142	4763	686	1186	169	19	85	643	1006	245
Reno	.249	142	4619	613	1150	183	37	68	517	970	160
Palm Springs	.248	142	4672	742	1157	168	43	52	761	1092	122
Fresno	.238	142	4553	596	1083	189	30	57	616	1107	166
Modesto	.235	142	4690	641	1102	177	24	80	750	1063	82

CLUB PITCHING

	ERA	G	CG	SHO	SV	IP	H	R	ER	BB	SO
Stockton	3.24	143	10	7	44	1272	1001	560	458	767	1122
San Jose	3.29	143	33	15	32	1241	1173	563	454	502	1040
Riverside	3.47	142	20	10	45	1264	1129	620	488	616	1052
Bakersfield	3.82	142	16	11	28	1234	1107	660	524	699	958
Visalia	3.88	142	21	13	29	1232	1182	693	531	715	1102
San Bernardino	4.00	142	8	5	37	1262	1164	688	561	638	955
Palm Springs	4.11	142	23	3	29	1239	1302	730	566	658	914
Modesto	4.41	142	17	9	20	1231	1157	771	604	832	928
Fresno	4.80	142	22	1	18	1213	1345	836	647	606	793
Reno	5.90	142	13	1	15	1211	1506	1071	794	797	792

INDIVIDUAL BATTING LEADERS
(Minimum 383 Plate Appearances)

	AVG	G	AB	R	H	2B	3B	HR	RBI	BB	SO	SB
*Brown, Adam, Bak	.352	92	318	66	112	18	3	9	80	54	50	5
*Leonard, Mark, SJ	.345	102	510	102	176	50	6	15	118	118	82	11
*Lanoux, Marty, Vis	.336	138	550	80	185	32	1	5	79	47	61	0
Faries, Paul, Riv	.317	141	578	108	183	39	4	2	77	72	79	65
#Hollins, Dave, Riv	.304	139	517	90	157	32	1	9	92	82	67	13
*Aldrete, Rich, SJ	.301	141	528	85	159	32	4	12	108	74	75	15
*Snyder, Doug, Vis	.300	126	427	90	128	21	3	12	72	98	126	26
*Newson, Warren, Riv	.297	130	438	98	130	23	7	22	91	107	102	36
*Randle, Mike, Vis	.294	113	429	76	126	8	1	2	48	54	41	32
*Bowie, Jim, SB	.293	139	529	76	155	28	0	15	102	58	84	8

* indicates lefthanded batter   # indicates switch hitter

INDIVIDUAL PITCHING LEADERS
(Minimum 114 Innings)

	W	L	ERA	G	GS	CG	SV	IP	H	R	ER	BB	SO
*Holsman, Rich, Riv	8	7	2.38	48	9	2	5	140	100	52	37	94	170
*Charland, Colin, PS	17	5	2.51	27	27	12	0	204	187	76	57	71	183
*Gunderson, Eric, SJ	12	5	2.65	20	20	5	0	149	131	56	44	52	151
Burba, David, SB	5	7	2.68	20	20	0	0	114	106	41	34	54	102
Brooks, Billy, Bak	7	9	2.81	48	9	0	12	122	91	49	38	56	74
Monson, Steve, Sto	14	3	2.87	25	24	1	0	160	122	65	51	73	157
*Elvira, Narciso, Sto	7	6	2.93	25	23	0	0	135	87	49	44	79	161
Marquez, Isidro, Bak	8	3	3.09	20	20	1	0	125	114	54	43	78	106
Navarro, Jaime, Sto	15	5	3.09	26	26	4	0	175	148	70	60	74	151
DeLucia, Rich, SB	7	8	3.10	22	22	0	0	128	110	57	44	58	118

* indicates lefthanded pitcher

BAKERSFIELD

BATTING	AVG	G	AB	R	H	2B	3B	HR	RBI	BB	SO	SB
#Argo, Billy, of	.229	108	328	48	75	6	0	0	25	42	55	13
Barron, Tony, 1b-of	.250	12	20	1	5	2	0	0	4	1	5	0
#Beuder, Jon, of	.192	43	120	20	23	3	2	0	15	21	20	5

Mark Leonard's .345 average and 118 RBIs helped keep San Jose in the pennant race all season long.

	AVG	G	AB	R	H	2B	3B	HR	RBI	BB	SO	SB
*Brown, Adam, dh-c	.352	92	318	66	112	18	3	9	80	54	50	5
*Brown, Jeff L, 1b-dh	.282	133	447	63	126	31	4	8	71	70	80	4
*Dostal, Bruce, of	.251	122	367	59	92	14	2	1	34	58	78	32
Ebel, Dino, ss	.286	3	14	2	4	1	0	0	1	0	0	0
Green, Steve, of	.278	114	407	56	113	25	4	6	56	54	91	19
Henley, Dan, 2b	.240	105	334	52	80	17	0	5	41	52	60	10
Hernandez, Carlos, c	.309	92	333	37	103	15	2	5	52	16	39	3
Hornacek, Jay, c	.186	15	43	4	8	1	0	1	3	10	13	0
*Huebner, John, c	.211	5	19	4	4	0	0	0	2	0	6	0
*Kirby, Wayne, of	.277	12	47	12	13	0	1	0	4	11	4	9
Knapp, John, 3b-p	.197	68	152	13	30	5	1	1	20	13	26	3
*Lewis, Alan, 3b	.249	124	441	79	110	23	1	6	44	68	69	4
#Montgomery, Danny, ss	.156	31	77	5	12	1	0	0	2	7	28	2
Mora, Juan, c	.333	4	12	1	4	1	0	0	0	1	3	0
*Munoz, Jose, 2b-dh	.248	105	347	35	86	6	0	0	24	42	54	7
Santos, Luis, of	.167	3	6	0	1	0	0	0	1	1	2	0
Valdez, Amilcar, 1b-dh	.253	83	312	38	79	21	4	0	6	51	17	46	1
#Vizcaino, Jose, ss	.290	122	434	77	126	11	4	0	38	50	54	13
White, K.G., of	.224	48	165	23	37	8	0	4	21	18	39	5

PITCHING	W	L	ERA	G	GS	CG	SV	IP	H	R	ER	BB	SO
Arnold, Tony	4	3	4.91	12	7	1	0	48	41	31	26	21	23
Brooks, Billy	7	9	2.81	48	9	0	12	122	91	49	38	56	74
Carrasco, Carlos	0	4	4.65	17	7	0	0	60	62	35	31	34	31
*Cerny, Chris	0	0	8.31	2	0	0	0	4	5	4	4	4	4
Gettler, Chris	0	1	7.66	9	1	0	1	22	26	22	19	19	22
Howell, Ken	0	1	1.32	3	3	0	0	14	8	5	2	9	13
Humphries, Joe	7	3	3.62	19	15	1	0	99	106	50	40	37	67
King, Kenny	2	4	4.41	13	5	0	1	35	32	28	17	21	27
Knapp, John	0	1	4.57	11	3	0	0	22	21	11	11	5	12
Kroll, Todd	5	6	5.21	42	1	0	3	85	86	51	49	34	81
*Langley, Lee	5	1	3.75	42	4	0	1	82	66	44	34	72	101
Marquez, Isidro	8	3	3.09	20	20	1	0	125	114	54	43	78	106
*Pena, Dan	0	0	5.59	10	0	0	0	10	8	7	6	10	13
Scott, Tim	4	8	3.64	36	2	0	7	64	52	34	26	26	59
Shinall, Zak	7	8	4.22	28	19	1	0	113	89	65	53	104	63
Soto, Mario	0	1	9.00	1	1	0	0	3	7	6	3	2	2
Springer, Dennis	13	7	3.27	32	20	6	2	154	135	75	56	62	108
Sutton, Don	0	1	4.02	3	3	0	0	16	16	9	7	3	19
Tapia, Jose A.	8	9	3.39	23	22	0	0	138	127	69	52	89	109
Torres, Phil	1	1	0.00	6	0	0	0	5	3	1	0	3	5
Wanish, John	0	0	4.50	9	0	0	0	14	12	10	7	10	19

FRESNO

BATTING	AVG	G	AB	R	H	2B	3B	HR	RBI	BB	SO	SB
Barry, John, ss	.251	94	346	35	87	18	1	0	44	27	72	2
Battaglia, Jeff, of-dh	.188	34	101	15	19	3	0	3	8	12	33	2
Bell, Tom, 3b	1.000	1	1	0	1	0	0	0	0	0	0	0
*Bellino, Frank, of	.360	16	50	11	18	4	1	1	12	11	3	3
*Combs, Marc, of	.128	17	47	6	6	0	0	0	2	4	10	1
#Cruz, Julio, 2b	.199	41	141	14	28	2	0	0	8	22	27	13
*Erickson, Eric, dh-p	.172	10	29	0	5	2	0	0	2	2	6	0
Flowers, Kim, 2b	.183	58	186	20	34	7	3	2	21	20	61	3
Fontes, Brad, c	.119	16	42	5	5	0	0	0	2	4	12	0
Goins, Scott, 3b (7 SJ)	.193	71	228	30	44	10	1	4	28	37	70	9
#Grilione, Dave, of-dh	.162	33	105	6	17	3	0	3	8	10	46	0
Hawkins, Todd, c	.200	52	170	14	34	8	0	1	19	9	22	1
*Hecht, Steve, 2b	.255	52	204	45	52	7	1	1	12	25	32	42
Hobbs, John, 1b-c	.204	26	49	5	10	3	0	0	5	9	16	0
*Mancini, Joe, 3b	.150	15	40	4	6	2	0	0	1	4	12	0
Miyauchi, Hector, of	.211	42	109	17	23	2	0	4	11	16	35	3
Monteiro, Dave, of	.211	4	19	1	4	0	0	0	1	0	5	1
*Murphy, Dwayne, of	.206	13	34	6	7	1	0	1	5	11	11	0
Nash, Dave, of-dh	.249	112	358	57	89	18	3	8	54	78	95	5
Pancoski, Tracey, of	.108	25	65	4	7	2	0	0	3	7	23	1
Richardt, Mike, dh	.331	38	118	14	39	4	1	1	22	25	11	2
Simonds, Dan, c	.252	95	330	28	83	7	2	0	30	18	48	1
Triplett, Tony, of	.266	130	481	78	128	15	7	4	62	50	112	47
*Whitfield, Terry, of	.337	50	184	17	62	13	1	2	25	12	31	0
Yagi, Richard, 3b-ss	.256	122	355	56	91	16	4	7	31	62	92	8
#Young, Ernie, 1b	.230	134	439	67	101	22	6	13	60	87	148	8

PITCHING	W	L	ERA	G	GS	CG	SV	IP	H	R	ER	BB	SO
Banning, Doug	5	8	5.50	27	13	4	2	108	139	81	66	49	84
Billelo, John	0	0	5.59	5	0	0	1	10	8	9	6	11	3
Bowden, Steve	1	0	4.50	6	0	0	1	8	8	4	4	9	8
Bryan, Frank	4	8	4.72	34	14	1	4	101	118	72	53	51	59
Buffolino, Rocco	9	7	4.40	22	21	3	0	119	127	72	58	56	81
Citarella, Ralph	2	4	1.80	24	1	1	6	40	41	17	8	25	45
Comstock, Brad	8	9	4.52	30	19	4	0	151	134	90	76	78	112
Cota, Tim	0	1	3.72	3	1	0	0	10	8	5	4	5	2
*Erickson, Eric	1	0	2.45	5	0	0	2	7	4	2	2	5	8
Geiger, Gary	5	16	3.89	26	26	6	0	169	187	104	73	82	69
Higson, Chuck	4	8	6.75	29	14	2	0	109	148	103	82	63	70
Ingram, Linty	4	4	5.97	13	11	0	0	63	68	51	42	27	63
*Maebe, Kelly	0	1	4.50	2	1	0	0	6	3	5	3	4	1
Manabe, Bullet	2	8	5.75	27	11	1	0	103	118	84	66	56	75
*Montano, Marty	0	0	9.56	9	1	0	0	16	28	17	17	10	9
Rincon, Andy	0	1	5.23	12	0	0	0	31	36	25	18	13	17
*Rowen, Rob	0	5	2.93	8	6	0	0	28	27	24	9	27	21
*Tagi, Antony	8	7	3.67	46	2	0	2	118	117	58	48	24	59
Villasenor, Mike	0	1	3.77	7	0	0	0	14	21	7	6	4	7

MODESTO

BATTING	AVG	G	AB	R	H	2B	3B	HR	RBI	BB	SO	SB
Arias, Tony, 1b	.234	73	261	38	61	11	1	13	42	43	97	4
Barragan, Gerry, ss	.283	30	120	14	34	3	1	0	16	12	18	2
Brito, Jorge, c	.217	96	300	38	65	15	0	5	27	47	104	0
Ciprian, Francis, c	.220	51	132	19	29	6	0	0	8	37	38	3
Clark, Isaiah, 3b-ss	.265	84	310	39	82	16	1	1	25	28	33	6
Coomer, Ron, dh-3b	.279	131	495	67	138	23	2	17	85	60	88	2
*Done, Heriberto, of	.206	11	34	4	7	0	0	0	1	4	6	0
Duffy, Darrin, ss	.256	68	254	47	65	4	3	4	21	69	70	9
Finley, Dave, 3b-dh	.193	81	270	34	52	17	0	2	26	47	50	5
Gilbert, Pat, of	.228	60	193	29	44	7	0	3	19	52	35	3
*Holland, Troy, of	.225	32	89	6	20	2	1	1	9	8	24	1
*Howitt, Dann, of-1b	.252	132	480	75	121	19	3	18	86	81	106	11
Jones, Jim, c	.222	4	18	2	4	1	0	0	2	1	1	0
Martinez, Angel, 2b	.250	41	148	19	37	6	0	2	22	14	38	2
*Martinez, Luis, 2b	.183	58	186	27	34	3	2	1	14	50	51	3
#Pickett, Antoine, of	.236	56	157	28	37	6	2	1	13	20	40	8
Randle, Randy, 2b-ss	.191	60	209	37	40	5	2	2	13	37	53	8
Russell, Dan, 1b-dh	.230	75	257	31	59	11	0	4	36	15	45	4
*Savarino, Bill, dh-c	.132	16	38	3	5	1	0	0	2	5	10	0
#Stratton, Drew, of	.235	134	498	55	117	14	4	5	63	67	102	5
Teixeira, Vince, of	.203	24	69	7	14	3	1	0	7	22	21	3
Watkins, Keith, of	.215	53	172	22	37	4	1	1	14	31	33	5

PITCHING	W	L	ERA	G	GS	CG	SV	IP	H	R	ER	BB	SO
Arias, Tony	0	0	4.32	4	0	0	0	8	8	4	4	6	3
Berg, Rich	2	2	4.39	34	0	0	1	55	59	37	27	25	45
Caraballo, Felix	2	3	4.54	15	0	0	1	42	46	24	21	12	29
Carroll, Jim	1	1	6.35	13	0	0	0	17	17	17	12	16	17
Chiamparino, Scott	5	7	2.70	16	16	5	0	107	89	40	32	56	117
*Dockery, Mike	0	0	1.80	1	1	0	0	5	2	2	1	5	6
Eskew, Dan	1	2	6.15	6	6	0	0	26	30	24	18	21	30
Foley, Jim	3	6	8.55	12	9	0	0	46	54	50	44	48	26
Glover, Jeff	2	7	7.22	12	11	1	0	52	62	53	42	54	26
Gorski, Gary	2	10	3.52	25	23	3	0	143	148	73	56	50	63

	W	L	ERA	G	GS	CG	SV	IP	H	R	ER	BB	SO
Howitt, Dann	0	0	6.43	4	0	0	0	7	13	8	5	3	3
Kopyta, Jeff	3	6	4.61	38	2	1	1	96	87	64	49	76	84
Maye, Steve	2	1	1.68	32	0	0	7	64	45	16	12	24	59
Powers, Tom	1	2	13.89	5	3	0	0	12	13	19	18	16	10
Shotkoski, Dave	4	2	2.14	26	0	0	10	34	31	10	8	12	27
Stancel, Mark	4	12	4.69	35	14	3	0	134	129	85	70	83	84
Veres, Dave	4	11	3.31	19	19	3	0	125	100	61	46	78	91
Weber, Wes	6	7	4.04	17	17	1	0	98	91	59	44	54	81
Williamson, Kevin	1	1	5.65	6	0	0	0	14	19	16	9	9	16
Young, Ray	8	7	5.56	25	19	0	0	99	70	78	61	142	78

PALM SPRINGS

BATTING	AVG	G	AB	R	H	2B	3B	HR	RBI	BB	SO	SB
Alfonzo, Edgar, 3b-ss	.111	4	9	0	1	0	0	0	2	1	3	0
#Amaro, Ruben, 2b-of	.266	115	417	96	111	13	3	4	50	105	61	42
Anderson, Mike, of	.266	83	301	42	80	13	0	1	40	36	76	17
Baca, Mark, of	.254	44	138	23	35	3	1	0	15	20	25	2
Barns, Jeff, ss	.242	103	376	42	91	11	5	2	42	51	65	5
Bell, Bobby, c	.000	6	14	0	0	0	0	0	1	3	5	0
Cerny, Scott, 2b	.260	92	339	63	88	8	3	0	40	62	54	5
Cron, Chris, 3b	.251	127	467	71	117	28	3	14	84	68	147	4
Dominguez, Frank, c	.233	29	103	10	24	5	0	1	9	12	24	0
*Dyson, Ted, 1b-dh	.246	103	349	46	86	16	4	5	52	56	111	1
Gonzales, Larry, c	.200	35	100	11	20	0	0	0	11	22	25	0
*McAnany, Jim, c	.241	29	79	9	19	2	0	2	9	12	19	0
#McLemore, Mark, 2b	.341	11	44	9	15	3	1	0	6	11	7	7
Montero, Jorge, of	.167	10	24	3	4	1	1	0	1	4	9	1
*Musolino, Mike, c	.238	5	21	2	5	0	0	0	1	2	3	1
Nalls, Gary, of	.233	90	313	47	73	14	4	3	40	40	92	5
Neville, Dave, c	.167	20	60	8	10	0	1	0	7	9	13	0
Nunez, Dario, ss	.242	51	161	23	39	4	0	1	20	15	34	0
Orton, John, c-dh	.200	68	230	42	46	6	1	1	28	45	78	5
Peters, Reed, of	.256	73	277	46	71	10	6	2	34	45	54	14
Rose, Bob, dh	.333	1	3	0	1	0	0	0	1	0	1	0
*Sorrento, Paul, 1b-dh	.286	133	465	91	133	27	5	14	99	109	101	3
Washington, Glenn, of	.233	99	343	53	80	3	4	2	39	31	77	10

PITCHING	W	L	ERA	G	GS	CG	SV	IP	H	R	ER	BB	SO
*Bisceglia, Jim	3	1	5.26	33	0	0	1	53	64	35	31	36	57
Butcher, Mike	3	2	5.70	7	7	0	0	43	57	33	27	19	37
*Charland, Colin	17	5	2.51	27	27	12	0	204	187	76	57	71	183
Erb, Mike	10	7	4.40	19	19	3	0	108	102	66	53	62	86
Kannenberg, Scott	8	4	4.76	30	5	2	2	96	123	66	51	38	59
Lewis, Scott	0	1	5.63	2	1	0	0	8	12	5	5	2	7
Long, Jim	6	15	5.43	36	17	1	2	119	112	96	72	93	84
Marino, Mark (51 Reno)	5	8	4.83	54	0	0	3	76	79	63	41	86	92
Merejo, Luis	1	6	3.77	45	0	0	18	60	68	32	25	26	30
Minton, Greg	0	0	0.00	2	0	0	0	4	3	0	0	1	4
Moore, Donnie	0	0	2.25	5	0	0	0	8	4	4	2	4	7
Morehouse, Rich	6	6	3.53	18	18	2	0	110	108	62	43	72	82
Petry, Dan	1	2	6.60	3	3	0	0	15	19	14	11	11	11
Richardson, Jeff	0	4	2.51	44	0	0	5	68	66	24	19	27	56
Tapia, Jose G.	5	8	3.31	30	19	1	1	141	158	77	52	64	91
Vanderwel, Bill	2	7	7.60	25	14	0	0	69	65	67	58	96	45
Ward, Dan	8	4	4.18	35	12	2	1	129	152	71	60	33	71

RENO

BATTING	AVG	G	AB	R	H	2B	3B	HR	RBI	BB	SO	SB
*Allison, Jamie, of-p	.268	129	418	75	112	21	4	8	53	74	72	31
Arias, Pedro, of-inf	.204	36	98	12	20	1	0	0	2	2	35	6
Aylward, Jim, 1b	.271	54	192	27	52	9	1	5	29	22	21	4
Carter, Fred, of	.248	78	282	39	70	9	2	9	37	21	68	8
Childress, Scott, 3b	.328	22	61	9	20	2	0	1	10	10	19	0
*Fernandez, Julio, 2b	.200	62	170	19	34	4	2	0	11	38	40	3
Ferretti, Sam, ss	.279	63	219	30	61	9	0	1	20	14	34	6
Gallardo, Luis, 3b-of	.238	40	105	4	25	4	1	0	6	6	22	0
Garner, Mike, dh-2b	.250	77	268	36	67	5	4	1	15	15	52	16
*Gay, Jeff, c	.263	26	76	3	20	4	0	0	8	3	13	0
Glover, Reggie, 2b-of	.210	30	81	13	17	2	0	0	8	15	15	3
Grubb, Cary, 3b-1b	.224	121	424	49	95	17	4	11	69	30	70	3
Holmes, Chris, c	.125	27	64	8	8	1	0	1	5	4	32	1
Houston, Pete, ss	.247	24	77	10	19	3	1	0	8	15	18	6
Isaacson, Chris, c	.174	16	46	5	8	0	1	0	2	10	18	2
Liddell, Dave, c	.329	26	70	11	23	8	0	0	12	21	13	1
*Milner, Ted, of-dh	.270	58	189	35	51	8	0	2	21	42	37	23
Oliver, Nate, ph	.000	1	1	0	0	0	0	0	0	0	0	0
Ortiz, Joe, c	.235	102	315	34	74	19	2	3	36	20	70	11
Pace, Jim, inf	.237	120	388	49	92	17	1	0	43	57	48	6
Reyes, Giovanny, ss (10 PS)	.264	79	295	32	78	13	3	1	32	12	38	5
Rogers, Robbie, inf	.130	8	23	2	3	0	0	1	1	5	7	1
*Rountree, Mike, dh-of	.215	42	107	15	23	0	0	5	14	23	36	3
*Sims, Kinney, of-dh	.239	75	226	38	54	9	6	1	22	21	69	9
Sloan, Terry, p-of	.250	44	20	2	5	0	1	0	1	1	5	2
#Ward, Gregg, of-p	.189	53	106	8	20	1	0	1	6	19	36	3
Whitfield, Ken, of	.331	84	317	51	105	18	5	18	63	17	78	7

BATTING

R	Greg Ritchie, San Jose	118
H	Marty Lanoux, Visalia	185
TB	Mark Leonard, San Jose	283
2B	Mark Leonard, San Jose	50
3B	Warren Newson, Riverside	7
	Tony Triplett, Fresno	7
HR	Warren Newson, Riverside	22
RBI	Mark Leonard, San Jose	118
GWRBI	Mark Leonard, San Jose	17
SH	Bryan King, San Bernardino	15
SF	Mark Leonard, San Jose	11
BB	Charlie Montoyo, Stockton	156
IBB	Mark Leonard, San Jose	13
HBP	Chris Cron, Palm Springs	26
SO	Ernie Young, Fresno	148
SB	Ted Williams, San Bernardino	71
CS	Mike Brocki, San Bernardino	32
Slg. Pct.	Mark Leonard, San Jose	.555
OB Pct.	Mark Leonard, San Jose	.464

PITCHING

G	Eric Reinholtz, Reno	61
GS	Tom Meagher, San Jose	28
	Paul Abbott, Visalia	28
CG	Colin Charland, Palm Springs	12
ShO	Dennis Springer, Bakersfield	4
Sv	Doug Robertson, San Jose	23
W	Colin Charland, Palm Springs	17
	Tom Meagher, San Jose	17
L	Gary Geiger, Fresno	16
IP	Gil Heredia, San Jose	206
H	Terry Sloan, Reno	216
	Gil Heredia, San Jose	216
R	Terry Sloan, Reno	152
HR	Jim Blueberg, San Bernardino	18
BB	Paul Abbott, Visalia	143
HB	Eric Gunderson, San Jose	17
SO	Paul Abbott, Visalia	205
WP	Ray Young, Modesto	28
Bk	Mike Erb, Palm Springs	12

Department Leaders

PITCHING	W	L	ERA	G	GS	CG	SV	IP	H	R	ER	BB	SO
*Allison, Jamie	0	0	4.61	9	0	0	0	14	20	13	7	5	14
Bobel, Jay	1	4	7.17	14	6	0	0	43	65	46	34	18	11
Fowlkes, Alan	6	10	4.03	24	17	4	3	125	136	73	56	45	102
LaCerra, Tony	1	1	4.40	6	2	0	0	14	20	12	7	10	8
*Madden, Scott	0	8	5.83	25	12	1	0	80	96	70	52	54	33
Mutz, Frank	5	4	4.26	27	8	0	1	80	80	54	38	35	63
Pace, Jim	0	1	9.00	1	1	0	0	1	1	4	1	2	3
Randolph, Scott	0	8	7.64	14	13	0	0	66	88	69	56	53	29
Reinholtz, Eric	2	2	5.06	61	1	0	5	80	115	67	45	32	58
Rivera, Elvin	0	4	7.38	25	4	0	1	57	86	62	47	45	28
Savage, John	2	14	8.21	30	18	1	1	118	175	135	108	74	59
Shamblin, Bill	2	8	6.19	28	9	0	1	68	86	63	47	49	43
Sloan, Terry	8	13	6.75	38	21	4	0	160	216	152	120	136	90
Strong, Joe	4	13	4.79	31	24	2	0	162	168	114	86	96	107
Ward, Gregg	1	2	9.35	16	0	0	0	26	30	46	27	31	15
Warren, Mike	2	3	4.09	7	6	1	0	44	43	25	20	23	41

RIVERSIDE

BATTING	AVG	G	AB	R	H	2B	3B	HR	RBI	BB	SO	SB
*Brooks, Brian, of	.265	128	437	72	116	17	4	9	70	45	78	19
Faries, Paul, 2b	.317	141	578	108	183	39	4	2	77	72	79	65
Farmer, Kevin, c-of	.199	64	166	17	33	5	0	1	17	11	27	2
*Flannery, Tim, dh	.273	4	11	2	3	1	0	0	1	5	3	0
*Garner, Kevin, dh-of	.238	124	446	66	106	18	3	15	72	61	122	4
Hall, Greg, of-1b	.292	110	329	48	96	12	2	2	36	62	44	4
Hendricks, Steve, 1b	.241	122	423	53	102	14	2	5	55	56	92	4
#Hollins, Dave, 3b	.304	139	517	90	157	32	1	9	92	82	67	13
Jelks, Pat, of	.182	34	55	11	10	0	0	2	11	9	17	6
LeVasseur, Tom, ss	.284	133	489	81	139	21	2	1	57	71	64	26
*McDevitt, Terry, inf	.227	64	128	11	29	3	0	0	11	16	25	4
*Newson, Warren, of	.297	130	438	98	130	23	7	22	91	107	102	36
*Skeels, Andy, c	.233	123	395	56	92	19	3	3	57	58	84	8
#Taylor, Will, of	.183	112	295	41	54	5	1	0	16	46	78	31

PITCHING	W	L	ERA	G	GS	CG	SV	IP	H	R	ER	BB	SO
Armstrong, Kevin	8	3	3.84	18	10	0	1	84	81	45	36	31	74
Austin, James	6	2	2.70	12	12	2	0	80	65	31	24	35	73
*Blount, Bill	4	1	2.13	42	0	0	14	72	46	19	17	20	37
Bones, Ricky	15	6	3.64	25	25	5	0	175	162	80	71	64	129
*Cantwell, Robby	0	1	8.04	6	2	0	0	16	24	16	14	9	8
Chavez, Rafael	2	3	2.37	46	0	0	19	65	58	20	17	28	49
Garner, Kevin	0	0	3.38	2	0	0	0	3	0	2	1	4	3
*Harrison, Brian	5	8	4.17	21	20	0	0	101	92	61	47	60	95
*Holsman, Rich	8	7	2.38	48	9	2	5	140	100	52	37	94	170

	W	L	ERA	G	GS	CG	SV	IP	H	R	ER	BB	SO
Lewis, Jim	7	7	3.57	44	1	0	7	98	99	57	39	55	80
Loubier, Steve	8	6	4.04	22	20	2	0	120	118	68	54	63	101
Marx, Bill	5	6	5.70	20	11	0	0	71	76	48	45	49	49
Oglesby, Ron	0	1	9.00	2	0	0	0	3	4	3	2	2	2
Olivares, Omar	3	0	1.16	4	3	1	0	23	18	9	3	9	16
Smithberg, Roger	9	2	3.31	15	15	5	0	103	90	52	38	32	72
Wood, Brian	5	4	3.10	14	14	3	0	99	85	49	34	57	92

SAN BERNARDINO

BATTING	AVG	G	AB	R	H	2B	3B	HR	RBI	BB	SO	SB
*Bowie, Jim, 1b	.293	139	529	76	155	28	0	15	102	58	84	8
Brocki, Mike, 2b	.268	133	477	97	128	12	4	0	49	107	84	48
Diaz, William, 3b	.222	114	388	43	86	12	0	10	43	42	88	4
Disher, Dan, of	.182	40	99	8	18	2	1	0	6	8	40	5
Foley, Keith, c	.200	18	55	5	11	1	0	0	3	2	8	0
*Goff, Jerry, c	.287	65	216	38	62	11	0	13	43	52	59	2
*Griffey, Ken, of	.338	58	219	49	74	13	3	11	42	34	39	32
Gunn, Clay, s	.182	72	187	16	34	4	0	2	19	19	56	2
Hisey, Steve, of-dh	.195	99	282	30	55	9	0	3	27	45	66	0
Hooper, Jeff, c	.204	43	113	11	23	5	0	4	14	10	35	0
*Kemp, Joe, of-dh	.263	109	339	43	89	19	1	8	44	47	80	2
#King, Bryan, ss	.223	134	452	59	101	14	1	1	36	44	59	35
*Kosco, Dru, of	.249	65	209	32	52	7	1	11	32	23	60	1
Murray, Steve, inf	.264	18	53	12	14	0	0	0	6	4	4	3
Rabb, John, of	.261	8	23	5	6	1	1	0	1	4	8	0
Tartabull, Jose, of-dh	.245	112	372	46	91	10	1	0	39	76	54	20
#Williams, Ted, of	.246	135	525	82	129	14	3	6	50	34	137	71
Woods, Anthony, inf	.260	82	223	34	58	7	3	1	20	34	45	12

PITCHING	W	L	ERA	G	GS	CG	SV	IP	H	R	ER	BB	SO
Balabon, Rick	3	2	3.28	7	7	1	0	47	43	19	17	20	29
Bankhead, Scott	0	0	1.64	2	2	0	0	11	6	3	2	4	6
Blueberg, Jim	12	10	4.79	26	26	3	0	162	157	100	86	70	118
Bryant, Erick	0	0	0.00	1	0	0	0	1	0	0	0	0	1
Burba, David	5	7	2.68	20	20	0	0	114	106	41	34	54	102
DeLucia, Rich	7	8	3.10	22	22	0	0	128	110	57	44	58	118
Doyle, Rich	8	3	2.26	43	0	0	9	52	34	15	13	20	39
Eldredge, Ted	2	6	8.78	16	12	0	0	54	50	65	53	65	30
*Felix, Nick	0	0	1.26	9	0	0	4	14	5	4	2	6	15
Goff, Mike	1	0	0.87	7	0	0	2	10	7	3	1	6	4
Hayes, Todd	0	0	7.30	6	0	0	0	12	13	12	10	13	7
*Helton, Keith	8	2	3.04	49	0	0	7	71	59	33	24	54	62
McLain, Tim	0	0	9.00	1	0	0	1	1	1	1	1	2	0
Nelson, Jeff	8	9	5.54	27	27	1	0	149	163	115	92	91	94
Pifer, Gary	0	0	0.00	1	0	0	0	4	0	1	0	3	1
Poissant, Rod	0	1	2.78	11	0	0	2	23	15	8	7	10	31
Rice, Pat	7	7	3.42	33	12	3	3	121	120	56	46	32	114
Ryan, Jody	4	3	4.06	51	3	0	1	109	110	58	49	47	59
Schneider, Paul	1	3	4.70	12	1	0	1	23	15	13	12	13	16
Snell, Dave	1	2	5.98	16	6	0	0	56	69	43	37	29	38
*Townsend, Howard	7	5	2.86	49	2	0	7	88	73	37	28	32	59
*Ward, Colin	0	0	1.86	2	2	0	0	10	6	3	2	4	7

SAN JOSE

BATTING	AVG	G	AB	R	H	2B	3B	HR	RBI	BB	SO	SB
*Aldrete, Rich, 1b	.301	141	528	85	159	32	4	12	108	74	75	15
#Blair, Paul, 2b-ss	.263	138	547	111	144	14	4	1	71	78	90	39
Conner, Greg, of-dh	.282	118	426	60	120	14	2	9	63	48	115	16
*Dabney, Ty, dh	.167	15	54	5	9	1	1	1	6	7	14	0
Decker, Steve, c-dh	.318	47	176	32	56	9	0	4	34	21	21	0
#Hanyuda, Tad, of	.367	70	188	35	69	9	1	1	25	38	38	14
#Johdo, Joe, ss	.235	49	115	27	27	2	0	0	9	19	18	8
Johnson, Erik, 2b	.250	44	160	25	40	3	1	1	16	18	29	4
#Jones, Gary, c-dh	.240	44	129	17	31	4	0	2	18	11	24	1
*Kaiser, Jim, ss	.195	26	87	10	17	2	1	0	5	6	24	1
*Leonard, Mark, of-dh	.345	142	510	102	176	50	6	15	118	118	82	11
Malseed, Jim, of (107 Fres)	.264	118	387	59	102	24	1	2	41	58	84	15
*McNamara, Jim, c	.188	93	314	27	59	9	0	1	41	43	75	2
Mijares, Willie, ss	.221	47	154	23	34	2	1	0	15	13	24	13
Murray, Scott, c	.077	6	13	2	1	0	0	0	0	2	3	0
Patterson, Dave, 3b	.284	140	496	105	141	17	5	8	74	118	69	13
*Ritchie, Greg, of	.286	131	507	118	145	29	5	6	65	116	119	40
*Ronson, Tod, of	.233	83	266	37	62	10	5	0	35	66	62	3
*Suzuki, Ken, 3b	.056	8	18	2	1	0	0	0	1	2	6	0

PITCHING	W	L	ERA	G	GS	CG	SV	IP	H	R	ER	BB	SO
Connelly, Daron	1	1	4.45	30	0	0	1	57	57	28	28	36	51
*Gunderson, Eric	12	5	2.65	20	20	5	0	149	131	56	44	52	151
Heredia, Gil	13	12	3.49	27	27	9	0	206	216	107	80	46	121
Hostetler, Tom	2	0	2.79	6	0	0	0	29	29	11	9	11	27
*Maeda, Koji	10	4	2.36	29	11	3	1	99	79	36	26	48	111
Meagher, Tom	17	8	3.44	28	28	8	0	199	212	94	76	37	165
Meier, Kevin	7	6	4.82	17	17	0	0	99	112	64	53	44	59
Phillips, Montie	11	6	3.49	23	20	5	0	144	127	63	56	64	85
*Pilkington, Eric	1	0	1.59	6	1	1	0	11	9	2	2	11	7
Robertson, Doug	7	5	1.26	57	0	0	23	78	63	18	11	30	103
*Swan, Russ	7	0	2.23	11	11	2	0	77	53	28	19	26	62

	W	L	ERA	G	GS	CG	SV	IP	H	R	ER	BB	SO
Velasquez, Ray	3	3	4.33	38	0	0	4	54	40	31	26	47	61
Villa, Mike	0	0	1.65	7	0	0	3	16	12	4	3	8	13
Yamamoto, Masa	0	2	7.88	12	2	0	0	24	33	21	21	22	24

STOCKTON

BATTING	AVG	G	AB	R	H	2B	3B	HR	RBI	BB	SO	SB
Aguilar, Mark, 3b	.063	7	16	0	1	0	0	0	1	0	7	0
Albers, Rick, 3b	.235	9	17	3	4	0	0	1	1	5	1	0
Ashley, Shon, of-dh	.266	130	497	89	132	30	4	8	80	66	106	12
Brown, Terry, of	.178	13	45	5	8	0	0	0	2	7	15	4
Brown, Todd, of	.263	20	80	11	21	2	0	2	14	7	11	2
*Escalera, Ruben, ss	.257	123	456	71	117	24	3	5	60	70	88	21
Foster, Bryan, ss	.137	15	51	6	7	0	0	0	5	3	20	0
*Guerrero, Sandy, 3b-2b	.278	138	503	101	140	25	3	4	79	80	65	21
Jaha, John, 1b	.255	99	302	58	77	14	6	8	54	69	85	10
Jones, Bobby, of	.264	131	489	71	129	27	1	11	81	50	124	28
*McGrew, Charlie, dh-c	.222	22	63	9	14	2	0	2	9	16	16	0
McIntosh, Tim, c	.283	138	519	81	147	32	6	15	92	57	96	10
Montoyo, Charlie, 2b-ss	.255	134	458	104	117	14	1	3	61	156	96	17
*Raley, Tim, of	.200	2	5	1	1	0	0	0	0	0	2	0
Rodriguez, Angel, dh-c	.250	1	40	7	10	1	0	0	0	8	6	0
Schwarz, Tom, 3b-1b	.271	109	409	58	111	16	1	2	51	50	51	6
Smith, Rob, of	.233	101	313	59	73	6	3	4	38	63	85	22
Sobczyk, Bob, c	.200	14	30	4	6	0	0	0	3	0	5	0
*Spiers, Bill, ss	.269	84	353	68	95	16	3	5	52	42	41	27
Taylor, Dave, c	.234	21	64	8	15	1	0	1	7	11	17	0
Torricelli, Tim, c	.245	34	102	19	25	5	0	2	15	15	21	6

PITCHING	W	L	ERA	G	GS	CG	SV	IP	H	R	ER	BB	SO
*Beavers, Mark (8 Mod)	3	0	4.24	17	1	0	1	34	26	19	16	37	26
Drahman, Brian	4	5	2.02	44	0	0	14	62	57	17	14	27	50
*Elvira, Narciso	7	6	2.93	25	23	0	0	135	87	49	44	79	161
Fitzpatrick, Danny	4	5	3.24	39	2	0	12	94	80	37	34	57	62
Fleming, Keith	2	2	1.37	15	0	0	6	26	17	8	4	11	26
Henry, Doug	7	1	1.78	23	1	1	7	71	46	19	14	31	71
Kolovitz, Mike	0	0	4.50	8	0	0	1	22	21	11	11	10	10
Lane, Heath	0	0	0.00	1	0	0	0	2	1	0	0	0	0
*Miranda, Angel	0	1	7.18	16	0	0	2	26	20	30	21	37	36
Monson, Steve	14	3	2.87	25	24	1	0	160	122	65	51	73	157
Moraw, Carl	11	2	3.92	32	12	0	1	108	86	56	47	68	82
Murphy, Dan	1	4	6.31	12	4	0	2	26	25	22	18	40	26
Navarro, Jaime	15	5	3.09	26	26	4	0	175	148	70	60	74	151
Perez, Leo	0	0	2.57	1	1	0	0	7	7	3	2	3	5
Peters, Dan	1	0	0.00	1	1	0	0	6	2	0	0	2	6
Romanick, Ron	3	0	0.96	4	4	2	0	28	15	4	3	7	17
Sadler, Alan	2	2	3.38	5	5	1	0	24	21	12	9	11	13
Serna, Ramon	4	1	3.51	9	7	0	0	51	39	23	20	22	35
Stone, Brian	7	7	4.58	27	12	0	0	94	86	57	48	86	78
Veres, Randy	8	4	3.35	20	19	1	0	110	94	54	41	77	96
*Villanueva, Gil	3	1	2.25	13	1	0	1	24	8	9	6	36	28

VISALIA

BATTING	AVG	G	AB	R	H	2B	3B	HR	RBI	BB	SO	SB
Arnold, Tim, c	.289	89	325	42	94	12	1	3	55	30	34	3
Blackwell, Larry, of	.268	118	406	75	109	11	1	3	47	71	91	33
*Davis, Kenny, of	.111	6	9	0	1	1	0	0	1	1	1	0
Eccles, John, c-dh	.241	123	431	62	104	20	2	13	85	65	124	2
#Fraticelli, Carl, 2b	.275	35	80	14	22	2	0	0	6	18	18	1
Gilbert, Shawn, ss	.372	14	43	10	16	3	2	0	8	10	7	1
Grant, Kenny, 2b	.224	47	165	38	37	6	0	2	18	38	38	1
Gross, Deryk, of	.259	21	58	7	15	0	0	1	5	2	14	1
*Lanoux, Marty, 3b-dh	.336	138	550	80	185	32	1	5	79	47	61	6
Leius, Scott, ss	.237	93	308	44	73	14	4	3	46	42	50	3
Lexa, Mike, 2b	.260	16	50	3	13	0	0	0	9	5	6	1
Marzan, Jose, 1b	.267	26	60	10	16	2	0	0	8	4	14	1
*Morgan, Kenny, of	.280	115	410	67	115	15	1	7	65	44	83	35
Naveda, Edgar, ss-3b	.282	119	444	71	125	16	2	6	72	33	44	7
*Randle, Mike, of	.294	113	429	76	126	8	1	2	48	54	41	32
*Richardson, A.J., inf	.308	97	321	51	99	11	0	2	39	34	51	3
*Snyder, Doug, 1b	.300	126	427	90	128	21	3	12	72	98	126	26
Zellner, Joey, of	.218	91	261	55	57	10	3	0	29	64	47	40

PITCHING	W	L	ERA	G	GS	CG	SV	IP	H	R	ER	BB	SO
Abbott, Paul	11	9	4.18	28	28	4	0	172	141	95	80	143	205
Bronkey, Jeff	4	6	3.46	43	6	1	9	83	66	44	32	67	58
*Buzzard, Buddy	12	5	3.25	27	17	2	1	127	120	61	46	68	104
Childers, Jeff (8 Mod)	1	1	5.56	12	2	0	0	34	34	24	21	16	22
*Guthrie, Mark	12	9	3.31	25	25	4	0	171	169	81	63	86	182
Heinle, Dana	5	3	4.65	48	4	0	3	99	117	60	51	35	74
James, Troy	1	2	6.23	13	0	0	0	41	38	31	28	28	19
Kline, Doug	8	2	3.65	38	9	1	3	91	83	56	37	58	103
*Leeper, Dave	2	0	3.00	2	2	0	0	12	9	7	4	6	6
Redding, Mike	3	4	4.17	9	8	0	1	50	50	33	23	20	29
Scanlon, Steve	3	2	3.74	36	0	0	0	53	50	27	22	33	37
Simons, Doug	6	5	3.94	17	16	5	0	107	100	59	47	46	123
*Strube, Bob	10	11	4.23	28	27	4	0	175	189	106	82	89	100
*Williams, Jimmy	3	4	3.71	37	0	0	12	51	41	23	21	33	55

Kinston's championship ends 26-year drought

By MARY JO MONNIN

What carried Kinston to first and second half Southern Division titles in 1988 also carried the Indians to the Carolina League championship. Pitching.

The Kinston pitching staff had the CL's lowest team ERA all season and it was pitching that enabled the Indians to top Lynchburg 3-2 to win the league crown.

Kinston pitchers had a 1.77 ERA and held the L-Sox to a collective .195 batting average in the best-of-5 series. During the regular season, the Kinston staff had a combined 3.10 ERA—a half run better than any other team in the league.

Kevin Bearse
...22 saves

The Indians won a franchise record 88 games en route to their first Carolina League title since 1962. The 26-year span between titles was the longest of any active CL franchise.

No pitching ace

The Indians, for all their pitching, had no big winner on their staff. They were led by three 11-game winners: John Githens, Todd Gonzales and Mark Gilles.

Lefthanded reliever Kevin Bearse, meanwhile, won 10 games, had a league-leading 22 saves, and struck out 127 in 103 innings. And his 1.31 ERA was nine innings shy of qualifying for the league lead. In the playoffs, Greg McMichael won two games and had a 1.38 ERA in 13 innings.

Surprisingly, the parent Cleveland Indians fired Kinston manager Glenn Adams following the 1988 season. Adams' emphasis on winning and inability to develop players the way Cleveland wanted were cited as the reasons. Former Waterloo manager Ken Bolek was to replace Adams in Kinston in '89.

Lynchburg was only 25-45 in the first half but reached the playoffs by nipping Hagerstown by one game to win the Northern Division's second half. The L-Sox then topped defending league champion Salem, 2-1, in the semifinals. The Red Sox were forced to compete in the postseason without Jim Orsag, their leading

League Champions

(Playoff Champions, Where Applicable)

1988—Kinston	1973—Win.-Salem	1958—Burlington
1987—Salem	1972—Salem	1957—Durham
1986—Win.-Salem	1971—Peninsula	1956—Fayetteville
1985—Win.-Salem	1970—Win.-Salem	1955—Danville
1984—Lynchburg	1969—Raleigh-Dur.	1954—Fayetteville
1983—Lynchburg	1968—High Pt.-Th.	1953—Danville
1982—Alexandria	1967—Durham	1952—Reidsville
1981—Hagerstown	1966—Rocky Mount	1951—Win.-Salem
1980—Peninsula	1965—Tidewater	1950—Win.-Salem
1979—Win.-Salem	1964—Win.-Salem	1949—Burlington
1978—Lynchburg	1963—Wilson	1948—Martinsville
1977—Peninsula	1962—Kinston	1947—Raleigh
1976—Win.-Salem	1961—Wilson	1946—Raleigh
1975—Rocky Mount	1960—Greensboro	1945—Danville
1974—Salem	1959—Wilson	

Carolina's Best

Mickey Pina
...MVP

Kent Mercker
...ERA leader

Scott Cooper
...45 doubles

hitter (.324), after he pulled a quadricep muscle with six regular season games left.

Red Sox manager Dick Berardino was selected the league's manager of the year. He was later promoted to the Boston Red Sox coaching staff for the 1989 season.

Winners at the gate

The Durham Bulls had a history-making season. Not on the field, but at the gate. The Bulls set a Class A full-season attendance record by drawing 271,650. That bested the previous record of 260,040 set in 1981 by Greensboro.

En route to the record, the Bulls broke their year-old franchise attendance mark of 217,012 and the Carolina League record of 223,507—set in 1947 by Winston-Salem.

In 66 home dates, the Bulls drew an average of 4,116. They outdrew all 26 Double-A teams and 11 Triple-A teams. "Every time you think it would slack off or slow down, something else would pop up," said Bulls general manager Rob Dlugozima. "On a nightly basis for half the year we had to prepare for a full house."

Salem also broke its franchise attendance record by drawing 119,966—bettering the 1987 mark of 111,661.

19-year-old wins title

Prince William's Bernie Williams, 19, earned the Carolina League batting title with a .338 average. Despite a season-ending wrist injury July 14, Williams qualified for the batting title with 18 plate appearances to spare. He fractured his wrist colliding with the outfield wall in Hagerstown.

Williams was a bright spot on a team that had its manager, Wally Moon, fired in mid-season. Moon was replaced by Gene Tenace on June 28, but the Yankees continued to struggle without Williams. The Yanks were 41-51 with the switch-hitter in the lineup and 14-32 without him. Williams was named the league's top major league prospect in a poll of managers by Baseball America.

Other postseason league honors went to lefthanders Kent Mercker of Durham and Bearse, who were named co-pitchers of the year. Although he was promoted to Double-A Greenville (Southern) on July 11, Mercker had enough innings to win the league ERA title (2.68). In 128 innings in the CL, Mercker had 159 strikeouts—missing out on the league strikeout title in the final week of the season.

Lynchburg loaded with prospects

The Boston Red Sox, out of the Carolina League since 1985, made their presence known in Lynchburg. The team came within one game of winning the league title—thanks in large part to the efforts of four top Red Sox prospects.

Left fielder Mickey Pina was named the league most valuable player after a season which included league-leading totals in home runs (21), RBIs (108) and outfield assists (22). Pina was the only batter in the league to drive in more than 100 runs. In eight playoff games, Pina also batted .387 with four home runs and eight RBIs.

Right fielder Bob Zupcic committed just three errors in 135 games. The former Oral Roberts University standout and No. 1 draft pick of the Red Sox batted .297 and had 97 RBIs.

Third baseman Scott Cooper shattered the Lynchburg franchise record with 45 doubles. The previous record of 32 was set by Marshall Brant in 1976. Cooper's .298 average was second best on the team.

History-making no-hitters

Winston-Salem pitcher Bill Kazmierczak became the first pitcher in the 44-year history of the Carolina League to pitch two no-hitters in the same season. Kazmierczak was promoted to Double-A Pittsfield (Eastern) shortly after blanking both Virginia and Salem.

FIRST HALF

North	W	L	Pct.	GB
Salem (Pirates)	40	29	.580	—
Hagerstown (Orioles)	37	33	.529	3½
Pr. William (Yankees)	31	38	.449	9
Lynchburg (Red Sox)	25	45	.357	15½
South				
Kinston (Indians)	45	25	.643	—
Durham (Braves)	44	26	.629	1
Wnstn-Salem (Cubs).	39	31	.557	6
Virginia (Co-op)	18	52	.257	27

SECOND HALF

North	W	L	Pct.	GB
Lynchburg (Red Sox)	43	27	.614	—
Hagerstown (Orioles)	42	28	.600	1
Salem (Pirates)	33	37	.471	10
Pr. William (Yankees)	24	46	.343	19
South				
Kinston (Indians)	43	27	.614	—
Durham (Braves)	38	32	.543	5
Wnstn-Salem (Cubs).	34	36	.486	9
Virginia (Co-op)	23	47	.329	20

OVERALL

	W	L	Pct.	GB
Kinston (Indians)	88	52	.629	—
Durham (Braves)	82	58	.586	6
Hagerstown (Orioles)	79	61	.564	9
Salem (Pirates)	73	66	.525	14½
Wnstn-Salem (Cubs).	73	67	.521	15
Lynchburg (Red Sox)	68	72	.486	20
Pr. William (Yankees)	55	84	.396	32½
Virginia (Co-op)	41	99	.293	47

1988 Final Standings

1988: General Information

Playoffs: Lynchburg defeated Salem 2-1 in best-of-3 semifinals; Kinston defeated Lynchburg 3-2 in best-of-5 final for league championship.

Regular Season Attendance: Durham, 271,650; Hagerstown, 135,380; Salem, 119,966; Prince William, 114,403; Virginia, 91,324; Lynchburg, 81,197; Kinston, 80,623; Winston-Salem, 79,999.

Managers: Durham—Buddy Bailey, Grady Little; **Hagerstown**—Mike Hart; **Kinston**—Glenn Adams; **Lynchburg**—Dick Berardino; **Prince William**—Wally Moon, Gene Tenace; **Salem**—Jay Ward; **Virginia**—Joe Breeden; **Winston-Salem**—Jay Loviglio.

1988 Official All-Star Team: C—Mike Eberle, Hagerstown. **1B**—Jim Orsag, Lynchburg. **2B**—Greg Smith, Winston-Salem. **3B**—Scott Cooper, Lynchburg. **SS**—Ever Magallanes, Kinston. **Util**—Mike Twardoski, Kinston. **OF**—Bernie Williams, Prince William; Mickey Pina, Lynchburg; Bob Zupcic, Lynchburg. **Util OF**—Derrick May, Winston-Salem; Mike Westbrook, Kinston. **DH**—Mitch Lyden, Prince William. **RHP**—Bill Kazmierczak, Winston-Salem; Shawn Boskie, Winston-Salem. **LHP**—Kent Mercker, Durham. **Most Valuable Player**—Mickey Pina, Lynchburg. **Co-pitchers of the Year**—Kent

Mercker, Durham; Kevin Bearse, Kinston. **Manager of the Year**—Dick Berardino, Lynchburg.

Top 10 Major League Prospects (by Baseball America): 1. Bernie Williams, of, Prince William; 2. Scott Cooper, 3b, Lynchburg; 3. Kent Mercker, lhp, Durham; 4. Mickey Pina, of, Lynchburg; 5. Bob Zupcic, of, Lynchburg; 6. Shawn Boskie, rhp, Winston-Salem; 7. Kelly Mann, c, Winston-Salem; 8. Mike Bell, 1b, Durham; 9. Jim Orsag, 1b, Lynchburg; 10. Derrick May, of, Winston-Salem.

1988: Batting, Pitching Statistics

CLUB BATTING

	AVG	G	AB	R	H	2B	3B	HR	BB	SO	SB
Salem	.263	139	4753	708	1251	218	44	109	491	869	190
Durham	.259	140	4610	716	1194	203	21	102	589	777	135
Winston-Salem	.258	140	4621	640	1194	188	36	68	488	741	202
Prince William	.253	139	4649	604	1176	174	29	66	455	867	94
Kinston	.252	140	4580	721	1154	218	30	73	755	978	152
Hagerstown	.250	140	4592	652	1149	216	32	52	558	890	212
Lynchburg	.246	140	4567	689	1122	254	26	83	593	894	85
Virginia	.237	140	4536	511	1077	155	31	39	514	928	117

CLUB PITCHING

	ERA	G	CG	SHO	SV	IP	H	R	ER	BB	SO
Kinston	3.10	140	10	12	44	1225	1074	541	422	509	846
Winston-Salem	3.61	140	26	14	30	1215	1091	600	488	635	1061
Hagerstown	3.65	140	32	12	25	1217	1142	587	494	449	854
Durham	3.77	140	22	10	29	1204	1118	598	504	565	851
Salem	4.04	139	11	6	31	1219	1226	698	548	508	903
Lynchburg	4.12	140	7	4	42	1194	1162	660	547	632	879
Prince William	4.30	139	26	8	22	1188	1237	723	568	547	803
Virginia	4.96	140	22	1	17	1182	1267	834	652	598	747

INDIVIDUAL BATTING LEADERS
(Minimum 378 Plate Appearances)

	AVG	G	AB	R	H	2B	3B	HR	RBI	BB	SO	SB
*Williams, Bernie, PW	.335	92	337	72	113	16	7	7	45	66	66	29
*Bettendorf, Dave, Hag	.327	115	388	51	127	29	5	6	64	50	59	0
*Orsag, Jim, Lyn	.324	112	383	91	124	24	3	12	69	72	99	24
*Twardoski, Mike, Kin	.322	132	450	80	145	26	3	6	87	117	59	21
*May, Derrick, W-S	.305	130	485	76	148	29	9	8	65	37	82	13
Ramos, John, PW	.304	109	391	47	119	18	2	8	57	49	34	8
*Westbrook, Mike, Kin	.299	94	345	76	103	11	4	5	44	60	55	34
*Cooper, Scott, Lyn	.298	130	497	90	148	45	7	9	73	58	74	0
Zupcic, Bob, Lyn	.297	135	482	69	143	33	5	13	97	60	64	10
Faulkner, Craig, Hag	.284	125	440	55	125	25	1	12	76	50	99	1

* indicates lefthanded batter   # indicates switch hitter

INDIVIDUAL PITCHING LEADERS
(Minimum 112 Innings)

	W	L	ERA	G	GS	CG	SHO	SV	IP	H	R	ER	BB	SO
*Mercker, Kent, Dur	11	4	2.68	19	19	5	0	128	102	44	38	47	159	
*Harrison, Phil, W-S	14	4	2.96	28	21	3	0	170	148	73	56	76	169	
Githens, John, Kin	11	6	3.19	32	18	1	1	133	113	59	47	45	74	
*Gonzales, Todd, Kin	11	5	3.26	25	25	2	0	132	111	57	48	75	81	
Murphy, Pete, Sal	9	8	3.29	30	14	1	1	126	127	64	46	38	79	
Weems, Danny, Dur	13	8	3.29	31	27	4	1	191	168	85	70	74	98	
Boskie, Shawn, W-S	12	7	3.39	27	27	4	0	186	176	83	70	89	164	
Rios, Enrique, Lyn	9	8	3.58	27	20	2	0	136	127	69	54	70	95	
Gilles, Mark, Kin	11	8	3.60	26	23	0	1	153	143	74	61	41	73	
Burdick, Stacey, Hag	10	10	3.64	27	22	7	0	166	130	83	67	98	147	

* indicates lefthanded pitcher

DURHAM

BATTING	AVG	G	AB	R	H	2B	3B	HR	RBI	BB	SO	SB
*Bell, Mike, 1b	.257	126	440	72	113	18	3	17	84	58	91	11
Bohlke, Scott, of	.180	24	61	8	11	4	0	0	5	9	13	0
*Butts, Dave, inf	.248	101	335	49	83	17	3	1	35	34	36	6
#Casarotti, Rich, 2b	.323	31	133	26	43	6	0	1	13	6	19	9
*Dodig, Jeff, of-dh	.251	91	231	31	58	6	1	5	28	39	33	6
Fowler, Mike, of	.239	111	327	46	78	21	2	3	40	31	72	12
Guerrero, Inocencio, dh	.235	19	51	10	12	3	0	1	10	15	12	1
*Holcomb, Ted, 2b	.290	65	162	20	47	3	0	2	16	16	19	6
Hunter, Brian, of-1b	.347	13	49	13	17	3	0	3	9	7	8	2
Johnson, Dodd, 1b-3b	.164	74	177	31	29	7	0	7	27	41	42	4
Maldonado, Phil, c	.207	15	29	3	6	0	0	0	2	3	4	0
Maloney, Rich, ss	.228	126	426	54	97	17	1	1	33	52	48	10
Morris, Rick, 3b-2b	.282	100	323	69	91	16	1	11	49	68	53	9
Pennington, Ken, 3b	.316	88	275	49	87	15	0	7	41	20	33	2
*Pfaff, Bob, c	.271	62	188	22	51	6	0	6	29	12	41	3
Plumb, Dave, c	.267	105	360	45	96	15	0	9	69	31	59	2
#Roby, Ellis, ss-of	.231	8	13	5	3	0	0	0	1	4	2	0
*Sabino, Miguel, of	.258	84	318	50	82	13	4	4	31	32	64	24
*Todd, Theron, of	.246	131	455	70	112	17	3	18	66	62	86	12
*Tomberlin, Andy, of	.301	83	256	43	77	16	3	6	35	49	42	16

Bernie Williams was the Carolina League's top prospect, winning the batting title despite an injury.

PITCHING	W	L	ERA	G	GS	CG	SV	IP	H	R	ER	BB	SO
Coffman, Kevin	1	1	4.50	8	0	0	2	10	12	6	5	3	10
Czajkowski, Jim	8	5	3.39	48	0	0	17	58	65	26	22	24	26
Gourlay, Craig	0	0	10.13	2	0	0	0	3	4	3	3	2	2
Greene, Jeff	0	1	4.15	2	0	0	0	4	5	2	2	4	2
Jimenez, Cesar	4	1	4.24	33	0	0	4	74	69	37	35	35	64
LeMasters, Jim	0	2	4.22	11	0	0	3	21	23	11	10	1	16
Longuil, Rich	4	9	5.31	25	19	1	0	115	139	78	68	59	58
Marak, Paul	7	4	2.68	32	7	3	0	101	90	40	30	33	84
*Mercker, Kent	11	4	2.68	19	19	5	0	128	102	44	38	47	159
Reilley, John	1	0	0.00	1	0	0	0	4	2	0	0	1	7
Richards, Rusty	1	0	0.00	1	0	0	0	3	0	0	0	0	3
Siebert, Rick	2	0	7.50	9	1	0	0	12	11	11	10	13	7
*Stanton, Mike	1	0	1.46	2	2	1	0	12	14	3	2	5	14
*Stockam, Doug	8	3	2.52	51	2	0	1	93	80	32	26	41	53
Stoker, Mike	8	6	3.92	26	26	4	0	147	113	75	64	101	111
Tilmon, Pat	1	3	5.35	8	8	0	0	37	45	26	22	19	29
*Upshaw, Lee	7	6	4.17	20	20	4	0	117	109	67	54	46	58
Watson, Preston	2	4	6.12	9	8	0	0	43	41	33	29	33	31
Weems, Danny	13	8	3.29	31	27	4	1	191	168	85	70	74	98
*Williams, Walt	3	1	7.40	12	1	0	0	21	21	19	17	23	14
Ziem, Steve	0	0	0.00	3	0	0	1	8	4	0	0	1	5

HAGERSTOWN

BATTING	AVG	G	AB	R	H	2B	3B	HR	RBI	BB	SO	SB
Ahr, Jeff, of	.211	50	123	13	26	4	1	1	12	18	33	1
*Bettendorf, Dave, dh-1b ..	.327	115	388	51	127	29	5	6	64	50	59	0
*Brown, Terry, of	.152	31	79	15	12	2	2	1	9	15	28	4
#Buford, Don, 2b	.232	137	548	91	127	22	3	2	53	66	87	77
Eberle, Mike, c	.244	123	435	49	106	25	1	5	74	36	88	0
Faulkner, Craig, 1b-c ..	.284	125	440	55	125	25	1	12	76	50	99	1
*Finley, Steve, of	.214	8	28	2	6	2	0	0	3	4	3	4
Harris, Walt, of	.272	127	475	87	129	25	5	1	60	63	89	53
Latmore, Bob, 3b	.245	108	371	32	91	18	1	7	52	22	69	5
*McNees, Kevin, of	.219	45	114	12	25	2	0	0	16	13	21	4
Meadows, Scott, dh-3b ..	.375	8	8	3	3	2	0	0	0	0	2	0
Mims, Larry, of	.264	93	356	72	94	5	2	1	19	60	33	52
Nowak, Matt, 3b	.148	60	149	16	22	8	0	0	8	16	50	0

	AVG	G	AB	R	H	2B	3B	HR	RBI	BB	SO	SB
Paulino, Louie, c	.214	19	56	3	12	2	0	0	7	5	10	0
#Segui, David, 1b-of	.268	60	190	35	51	12	4	3	31	22	23	0
Strijek, Randy, ss	.237	136	465	54	110	15	5	1	39	52	104	6
Voigt, Jack, of	.226	115	367	62	83	18	2	12	42	66	92	5

PITCHING	W	L	ERA	G	GS	CG	SV	IP	H	R	ER	BB	SO
Amarena, Sam	1	0	5.65	13	1	1	1	37	42	25	23	12	15
Borgatti, Mike (15 Vir)	6	11	4.13	30	19	6	0	142	151	78	65	39	102
Bowden, Steve	6	8	3.73	26	17	4	1	130	127	65	54	42	89
Burdick, Stacey	10	10	3.64	27	22	7	0	166	130	83	67	98	147
Culkar, Steve (3 Vir)	5	3	2.91	34	1	0	9	56	50	21	18	26	54
Dela Rosa, Francisco	3	4	4.61	29	1	0	2	41	34	21	21	29	47
*Dubois, Brian (9 Vir)	14	9	4.17	28	28	7	0	184	195	113	85	50	147
Evans, Scott	0	1	6.75	11	0	0	0	15	18	11	11	9	7
Jones, Stacy	3	1	2.87	6	6	3	0	38	35	14	12	12	23
Lopez, Craig	0	1	2.16	2	2	0	0	8	6	2	2	4	10
Miller, Dave	1	2	4.29	3	3	0	0	21	26	12	10	3	7
*Myers, Chris	1	1	2.72	7	7	1	0	40	36	15	12	10	21
Olson, Gregg	1	0	2.00	8	0	0	4	9	5	2	2	2	9
Palermo, Pete	3	1	3.25	14	6	1	0	55	54	24	20	15	31
*Pinder, Chris	5	7	2.77	55	1	0	8	88	73	31	27	30	61
Sander, Mike	14	11	3.65	27	26	4	0	165	174	78	67	53	75
Sonneberger, Steve	3	0	3.72	5	3	1	0	29	27	13	12	4	16
Telford, Anthony	1	0	0.00	1	1	0	0	7	3	0	0	0	10
Williams, Bob	7	3	3.18	16	15	3	0	96	76	46	34	37	54
Wilson, Chaun	0	2	7.25	14	5	0	1	36	48	31	29	23	20

KINSTON

BATTING	AVG	G	AB	R	H	2B	3B	HR	RBI	BB	SO	SB
*Allred, Beau, of	.252	126	397	66	100	23	3	15	74	59	112	6
Baldwin, Chuck, 2b-ss	.236	77	292	31	69	11	4	1	30	28	43	3
Belle, Joey, of	.301	41	153	21	46	16	0	8	39	18	45	2
Bennett, Keith, inf	.232	39	69	9	16	2	0	0	4	13	20	7
Blackwell, Barry, c	.185	26	81	10	15	4	1	2	15	9	15	0
*Epley, Daren, 1b	.290	47	169	22	49	9	1	1	25	21	29	1
#Fairchild, Glenn, ss	.174	46	109	20	19	2	0	0	8	24	34	5
Gamba, T.J., 3b-of	.226	14	53	5	12	1	0	0	2	6	12	1
Isaacson, Chris, c	.268	20	56	13	15	5	0	4	18	8	19	0
Johnson, Brian, dh	.235	5	17	3	4	0	0	0	1	3	4	0
*Johnson, Scott, dh-of	.193	33	57	14	11	1	0	1	5	19	11	0
Kent, Lew, c-1b	.195	49	118	8	23	5	1	0	13	14	35	1
*Khoury, Scott, dh	.187	22	75	7	14	1	0	3	13	6	21	0
Landrum, Darryl, of	.268	25	82	11	22	2	0	2	9	8	29	6
*Liebert, Allen, c	.188	93	298	31	56	14	0	4	34	46	71	1
*Magallanes, Ever, ss-2b	.263	119	396	67	104	13	3	1	45	76	48	12
Maloney, Mark, dh-of	.259	45	139	29	36	9	1	5	24	16	29	2
*Milner, Ted, of	.230	24	74	13	17	0	2	0	7	12	20	10
Pike, Mark, of	.250	3	12	3	3	0	0	0	1	0	3	1
#Richardson, Jim, 3b	.226	122	420	58	95	21	3	3	45	82	88	15
Richardson, Kerry, dh-of	.226	24	84	8	19	4	0	1	9	12	17	0
Seifert, Keith, of-1b	.233	44	116	19	27	5	0	4	20	14	29	1
Swain, Rob, ss-2b	.332	63	190	34	63	9	2	1	29	34	29	7
*Twardoski, Mike, 1b-of	.322	132	450	80	145	26	3	6	87	117	59	21
*Westbrook, Mike, of	.299	94	345	76	103	11	4	5	44	60	55	34
Williamson, Ray, of	.216	123	328	63	71	24	2	6	37	50	101	16

PITCHING	W	L	ERA	G	GS	CG	SV	IP	H	R	ER	BB	SO
*Bearse, Kevin	10	8	1.31	62	0	0	22	103	76	19	15	28	127
Bird, Steven	3	1	3.29	33	0	0	1	63	73	27	23	23	42
Ferlenda, Greg	7	2	3.43	29	7	0	2	89	63	41	34	58	82
Gilles, Mark	11	8	3.60	26	23	0	1	153	143	74	61	41	73
Githens, John	11	6	3.19	32	18	1	1	133	113	59	47	45	74
*Gonzales, Todd	11	5	3.26	25	25	2	0	132	111	57	48	75	81
Harwell, Dave	3	1	2.94	15	15	1	0	64	45	30	21	35	56
Keliipuleole, Carl	1	4	2.72	31	0	0	7	46	39	16	14	28	63
McMichael, Greg	4	2	2.68	11	11	2	0	77	57	31	23	18	35
*Mutis, Jeff	1	0	1.59	1	1	0	0	6	6	1	1	3	2
Nichols, Rod	3	1	4.50	4	4	0	0	24	26	13	12	15	19
Ogden, Charles	9	3	3.63	22	20	1	0	107	115	68	43	47	49
Olin, Steve	5	2	3.02	33	0	0	8	57	49	23	19	15	45
Roscoe, Greg	0	2	6.62	4	4	0	0	18	24	15	13	10	10
Shaw, Theo	6	5	2.96	12	12	3	0	70	52	27	23	36	55
Soos, Charlie	3	2	2.83	41	0	0	2	83	82	40	26	31	32

LYNCHBURG

BATTING	AVG	G	AB	R	H	2B	3B	HR	RBI	BB	SO	SB
*Buheller, Tim, of	.208	95	313	65	65	8	1	1	16	67	52	12
*Cooper, Scott, 3b	.298	130	497	90	148	45	7	9	73	58	74	0
*Devlin, Paul, c	.246	80	224	23	55	11	0	3	42	21	35	4
Gray, Dave, c	.135	23	37	4	5	1	0	0	9	9	10	0
Marchese, Joe, 2b	.268	132	530	71	142	24	0	4	54	24	43	7
Martinez, Gil, ss	.063	11	32	1	2	0	0	0	2	1	7	0
McGee, Tim, c	.500	2	2	0	1	0	0	0	0	0	0	0
Mendenhall, Shannon, ss	.148	83	203	25	30	5	3	0	21	31	79	3
Molero, Juan, 3b	.144	55	153	12	22	4	0	0	8	21	48	2
*Orsag, Jim, 1b-dh	.324	112	383	91	124	24	3	12	69	72	99	24

— 138 —

BATTING

R—Three tied at		91
H—Derrick May, Winston-Salem		148
—Scott Cooper, Lynchburg		148
TB—Scott Cooper, Lynchburg		234
2B—Scott Cooper, Lynchburg		45
3B—Derrick May, Winston-Salem		9
HR—Mickey Pina, Lynchburg		21
RBI—Mickey Pina, Lynchburg		108
GWRBI—Mickey Pina, Lynchburg		17
SH—Mickey Tresh, Prince William		10
SF—Mike Eberle, Hagerstown		11
BB—Mike Twardoski, Kinston		117
IBB—Three tied at		7
HBP—Mark Maloney, Kinston		10
SO—Ondra Ford, Virginia		132
SB—Don Buford, Hagerstown		77
CS—Larry Mims, Hagerstown		14
—Tom Johnson, Virginia		14
Slg. Pct.—Jim Orsag, Lynchburg		.496
OB Pct.—Mike Twardoski, Kinston		.454

Department Leaders

PITCHING

G—Kevin Bearse, Kinston		62
GS—Chip Duncan, Salem		28
—Brian DuBois, Virginia-Hagerstown		28
CG—Four tied at		7
ShO—Bill Kazmierczak, Winston-Salem		3
Sv—Kevin Bearse, Kinston		22
W—Three tied at		14
L—Six tied at		12
IP—Danny Weems, Durham		191
H—Brian DuBois, Virginia-Hagerstown		195
R—Brian DuBois, Virginia-Hagerstown		113
HR—Ben Webb, Salem		20
BB—Jeff Schwarz, Winston-Salem		110
HB—Shawn Boskie, Winston-Salem		17
SO—Phil Harrison, Winston-Salem		169
WP—Heath Slocomb, Winston-Salem		19
Bk—Lee Upshaw, Durham		13

	AVG	G	AB	R	H	2B	3B	HR	RBI	BB	SO	SB
Pina, Mickey, of	.273	136	472	91	129	31	4	21	108	84	118	11
Powers, Scott, ss	.172	90	250	26	43	11	0	1	15	29	65	5
*Sommers, Scott, 1b-2b	.270	94	315	42	85	18	0	6	40	29	25	0
#Weidie, Stuart, of	.194	99	341	52	66	20	2	9	41	64	104	7
Wilson, Craig, c	.187	99	332	27	62	19	1	4	37	23	70	0
Zupcic, Bob, of	.297	135	482	69	143	33	5	13	97	60	64	10

PITCHING	W	L	ERA	G	GS	CG	SV	IP	H	R	ER	BB	SO
*Abbott, John	4	4	3.94	13	13	1	0	75	77	39	33	21	36
Bartels, Billy	6	8	3.40	53	0	0	18	93	88	44	35	56	67
*Brown, Paul	3	3	3.83	10	10	0	0	49	45	28	21	41	42
*Cina, Randy	0	0	6.56	12	0	0	0	23	21	17	17	12	11
Clarkin, Mike	1	1	2.95	9	1	0	2	18	17	10	6	8	10
*Fischer, Tom	7	4	3.52	14	14	2	0	77	72	37	30	25	63
Gabriele, Dan	10	6	2.93	18	18	1	0	107	78	44	35	62	91
*Haley, Bart	2	1	3.43	39	1	0	3	81	70	37	31	35	54
Harris, Reggie	1	8	7.45	17	11	0	0	64	86	60	53	34	48
Kane, Tom	0	0	3.38	10	0	0	2	16	19	9	6	10	10
McCollum, Greg	3	2	4.38	17	0	0	4	39	39	22	19	21	29
Plympton, Jeff	5	4	2.60	41	0	0	12	83	69	30	24	45	105
Richardson, Ronnie	4	10	4.68	29	20	1	1	131	126	83	68	84	78
Rios, Enrique	9	8	3.58	27	20	2	0	136	127	69	54	70	95
Ryan, Ken	2	7	6.18	19	14	0	0	71	79	51	49	45	49
Walters, David	11	6	4.50	34	18	0	0	130	149	80	65	63	91

PRINCE WILLIAM

BATTING	AVG	G	AB	R	H	2B	3B	HR	RBI	BB	SO	SB
#Becker, Tim, ss	.212	27	104	9	22	2	0	0	4	7	5	5
Bishop, Tim, of	.175	56	126	13	22	1	0	1	11	9	20	6
Brow, Dennis, of-dh	.225	111	347	33	78	15	0	2	43	44	90	5
Brown, Ken, of	.176	91	170	31	30	3	3	0	12	24	66	3
Calvert, Art, of	.262	35	141	20	37	12	1	2	21	1	33	3
Crofton, Kevin, c	.169	20	65	6	11	0	0	1	8	6	19	0
*Fernandez, Rey, dh-1b	.178	32	101	9	18	1	3	0	10	4	23	0
Garcia, Santos, dh-c	.056	6	18	0	1	1	0	0	2	0	10	0
Gwinn, Tony, c	.266	19	64	8	17	5	0	2	9	7	12	0
Hauradou, Yanko, of-inf	.290	21	69	12	20	3	0	0	8	9	8	0
*Kelley, Dean, 2b	.274	95	350	41	96	13	1	2	35	32	40	5
*Kraus, Ralph, 1b-of	.246	77	260	33	64	8	3	4	27	21	44	3
Laboy, Jose, 3b	.206	50	141	20	29	5	0	1	13	22	23	1
Lambert, Rob, of-inf	.093	21	54	6	5	2	0	0	2	8	23	3
Lyden, Mitch, of	.282	67	234	42	66	12	2	17	47	19	59	1
*Maas, Kevin, 1b	.296	29	108	24	32	7	0	12	35	17	28	3
*Mitchell, Mark, of-1b	.227	25	97	13	22	2	1	0	12	7	12	0

	AVG	G	AB	R	H	2B	3B	HR	RBI	BB	SO	SB
Morales, William, c	.212	20	33	5	7	0	0	1	3	0	5	1
Ramos, John, c	.304	109	391	47	119	18	2	8	57	49	34	8
Roman, Dan, ss-1b	.311	45	161	15	50	4	0	0	13	2	26	1
*Seeburger, John, 1b	.264	38	144	12	38	4	0	1	18	7	24	1
Sparks, Don, 3b	.247	70	267	22	66	14	0	3	28	8	51	1
Tingle, Darrell, ss-2b	.190	57	137	22	26	6	0	0	12	11	36	2
#Tresh, Mickey, inf	.265	111	381	43	101	12	2	0	29	43	47	1
Williams, Bernie, of	.335	92	337	72	113	16	7	7	45	66	66	29
Williams, Gerald, of	.182	54	159	20	29	3	0	2	18	15	47	6
*Zeihen, Bob, of	.313	44	179	24	56	5	4	0	12	17	14	0

PITCHING	W	L	ERA	G	GS	CG	SV	IP	H	R	ER	BB	SO
*Adkins, Steve	6	4	3.34	31	6	2	0	94	88	44	35	40	92
*Blum, Brent	0	0	3.74	8	0	0	2	22	25	11	9	1	14
Candelaria, Jorge	0	1	6.55	7	0	0	2	11	14	9	8	4	8
Clayton, Royal	5	5	2.36	22	11	3	0	91	81	31	24	25	44
DaCosta, Bill	2	3	6.57	8	7	1	0	37	40	36	27	24	21
Draper, Mike	2	3	3.31	9	5	1	0	35	37	22	13	4	20
Faccio, Luis	0	1	7.56	6	0	0	1	8	16	8	7	7	8
*Foster, Randy	4	9	4.79	27	10	1	0	115	126	75	61	45	71
*Garcia, Victor	9	12	4.29	27	27	3	0	168	183	98	80	77	96
Gogolewski, Doug	1	9	7.71	13	12	2	0	58	60	60	50	53	38
*Howard, Chris	2	2	2.34	31	0	0	3	50	44	18	13	13	40
Imes, Rodney	4	5	4.44	11	11	3	0	77	82	47	38	32	67
Kamieniecki, Scott	6	7	4.40	15	15	7	0	100	115	62	49	50	72
Marris, Mark	3	1	3.82	8	7	1	0	33	34	17	14	13	16
*Michael, Matt	1	0	6.00	5	0	0	0	12	10	11	8	15	9
Mills, Alan	3	8	4.13	42	5	0	4	94	93	56	43	43	59
Popplewell, Tom	4	12	5.56	22	20	1	0	113	127	89	70	63	58
*Rub, Jerry	1	0	1.48	18	0	0	2	24	22	4	4	9	22
Stanford, Don	0	0	5.40	1	0	0	0	2	3	3	1	0	3
Stolenberg, Brad	0	2	8.10	3	3	1	0	13	17	13	12	7	5
Torres, Ricky	2	0	0.32	19	0	0	8	28	17	4	1	10	32

SALEM

BATTING	AVG	G	AB	R	H	2B	3B	HR	RBI	BB	SO	SB
Burdick, Kevin, inf	.321	64	249	42	80	17	2	9	49	26	20	6
*Carter, Steve, of	.286	6	21	4	6	0	0	0	1	0	1	2
Chamberlain, Wes, of	.274	92	365	66	100	15	1	11	50	38	59	14
Chance, Tony, of	.213	54	207	25	44	7	0	5	26	9	51	3
#Crowley, Terry, ss-2b	.215	26	93	10	20	5	2	1	9	14	21	1
Escobar, Oscar, 2b-3b	.226	50	177	20	40	8	3	4	19	8	22	8
#Fortuna, Mike, 2b-3b	.196	15	51	4	10	2	1	0	3	8	17	0
Garcia, Carlos, ss	.275	62	236	21	65	9	3	1	28	10	32	8
Hall, Andy, c	.261	79	283	35	74	12	1	9	32	22	82	0
Hartman, Eddie, 1b	.556	3	9	4	5	0	0	2	6	1	0	0
*Longmire, Tony, of	.275	64	218	46	60	12	2	11	40	36	44	4
Love, John, 3b	.283	59	212	24	60	14	1	2	23	18	29	2
McKinley, Tim, c	.181	64	171	24	31	6	0	1	20	40	44	0
McMillan, Tim, of	.267	12	45	3	12	3	0	1	5	1	19	1
#Merced, Orlando, 3b-2b	.292	80	298	47	87	12	7	7	42	27	64	13
Moser, Steve, dh-2b	.284	68	257	36	73	10	1	3	33	24	26	14
*Peguero, Julio, of	.261	128	517	89	135	17	5	5	50	64	81	43
Perez, Julio, 2b-ss	.216	26	97	13	21	5	0	1	7	3	12	4
Raisanen, Keith, of	.247	49	154	33	38	15	1	5	23	35	35	9
Rigos, John, 1b-of	.258	59	217	36	56	17	4	6	37	33	43	6
Roca, Gilberto, c	.036	7	28	0	1	0	0	0	1	1	1	0
#Ruskin, Scott, of-1b	.292	26	96	16	28	8	2	4	16	10	26	6
Shields, Tommy, ss	.314	45	156	20	49	5	0	3	25	16	14	0
Vizcaino, Junior, 1b	.261	89	333	48	87	8	4	11	58	23	82	20
#Yacopino, Ed, of-dh	.263	66	262	40	69	11	4	7	34	24	34	16

PITCHING	W	L	ERA	G	GS	CG	SV	IP	H	R	ER	BB	SO
Adams, Steve	5	0	4.33	32	3	0	3	89	103	51	43	17	38
Belinda, Stan	6	4	2.76	53	0	0	14	72	54	33	22	32	63
Buckholz, Steve	0	1	4.02	11	0	0	0	16	16	16	7	12	10
Downs, Ron	3	2	2.36	7	7	0	0	46	45	18	12	10	11
Duncan, Chip	8	10	4.54	28	28	0	0	157	168	103	79	70	102
*Forrest, Joel	0	4	9.82	4	4	0	0	18	29	21	20	9	11
Henion, Scott	1	6	5.28	46	3	0	5	73	81	55	43	31	49
*Kirk, Tim	5	5	2.96	57	0	0	8	79	86	36	26	30	66
Lein, Chris	0	0	12.00	1	0	0	0	3	7	4	4	0	2
Melendez, Jose	4	2	4.02	8	8	2	0	54	55	26	24	19	50
Murphy, Pete	9	8	3.29	30	14	1	1	126	127	64	46	38	79
Reed, Rick	6	2	2.74	15	8	4	0	72	56	28	22	17	73
Richardson, Keith	0	0	2.08	2	2	0	0	13	8	4	3	3	13
Rigos, John	0	0	6.00	2	0	0	0	3	2	2	2	4	1
Runge, Scott	0	0	9.00	1	0	0	0	1	1	1	1	0	1
Sampen, Bill	3	3	3.33	8	8	1	0	51	47	22	19	14	59
*Schlopy, Butch	0	0	8.10	2	0	0	0	3	5	4	3	2	3
Shepherd, Keith	2	3	5.83	8	5	0	0	29	26	24	19	29	15
Takach, Dave	1	2	6.75	3	3	0	0	12	12	15	9	7	4
*Torborg, Doug	3	6	4.67	25	11	0	0	89	93	57	46	59	75
Walker, Mike	2	2	3.16	5	5	1	0	37	42	17	13	9	29
Webb, Ben	6	4	6.37	21	15	0	0	82	89	63	58	33	54
York, Mike	9	2	4.68	13	13	2	0	84	65	31	25	52	77

VIRGINIA

BATTING	AVG	G	AB	R	H	2B	3B	HR	RBI	BB	SO	SB
*Alborano, Pete, of	.305	69	210	29	64	6	2	4	32	24	23	2
Anglero, Jose, ss-3b	.172	118	379	28	65	14	2	0	16	34	83	2
Bock, Doug, c	.199	45	161	10	32	3	1	1	19	11	35	0
*Brooks, Kevin, of-dh	.180	57	139	12	25	2	1	0	11	17	32	3
Capello, Pete, 3b	.325	11	40	3	13	3	0	0	3	3	8	1
Cole, Stu, ss	.272	70	257	41	70	10	0	1	22	32	52	10
Corcino, Luis, 3b-2b	.220	105	337	38	74	8	2	1	28	44	82	7
*Ford, Ondra, of	.255	127	459	75	117	12	8	5	38	37	134	17
Gardner, Bill, 3b-1b	.219	13	32	1	7	1	1	0	7	6	9	0
Goff, Tim, dh-c	.204	14	49	2	10	3	0	0	6	4	13	1
#Headley, Kent, of	.219	110	384	53	84	9	1	0	21	50	86	22
*Johnson, Tom, of	.252	133	469	61	118	18	5	6	54	63	76	20
Joslyn, John, 1b	.266	115	379	30	101	22	1	3	58	46	61	0
#Ladnier, Deric, dh-3b	.282	67	255	34	72	12	4	10	46	19	44	8
Laureano, Francisco, 2b	.225	117	387	47	87	9	2	2	37	65	50	21
Morris, Angel, 1b-c	.270	102	345	32	93	13	0	4	35	29	51	1
Papageorge, Greg, c	.000	3	2	0	0	0	0	0	0	1	1	0
Pujols, Ruben, c	.191	45	110	10	21	8	1	1	14	23	37	1
Reese, Kyle, ss	.169	50	142	4	24	2	0	1	8	6	51	1

PITCHING	W	L	ERA	G	GS	CG	SV	IP	H	R	ER	BB	SO
Agar, Jeff	0	1	9.22	8	0	0	0	14	16	17	14	15	7
Boyles, John	3	12	5.14	21	20	4	0	133	145	86	76	54	100
Carballo, Lee	0	1	12.60	4	0	0	0	10	21	19	14	10	5
*Chesna, Jim	0	0	5.19	10	0	0	0	17	18	16	10	19	8
*Duvall, Doug	2	9	5.90	18	16	1	0	76	114	70	50	31	41
Hendrix, Jimi	0	1	6.17	3	1	0	0	12	15	11	8	4	5
Losauro, Carmelo	1	6	6.60	12	10	1	0	44	36	41	32	42	27
Mallea, Luis	2	3	3.96	10	7	0	0	36	35	20	16	28	19
*Marino, John	2	1	4.75	17	0	0	0	30	29	18	16	13	14
Maysonet, Greg	0	2	4.30	14	0	0	2	23	24	12	11	10	7
McKinley, Pat	2	3	4.19	39	1	0	1	77	90	42	36	32	35
Metoyer, Tony	7	12	4.06	26	20	5	0	140	132	81	63	54	90
Meyers, Brian	1	2	4.17	26	0	0	1	45	47	30	21	25	29
Mintz, Doug	1	4	4.70	15	6	1	0	46	43	39	24	34	23
Parnell, Mark	3	2	3.38	24	0	0	8	29	24	13	11	24	32
Powers, Tad	0	1	2.64	23	0	0	3	31	28	11	9	11	17
Prezioso, William	5	9	4.49	18	17	2	0	102	101	61	51	38	54
Price, Phil	3	0	6.52	7	0	0	0	19	24	16	14	10	9
Radcliffe, Ernie	0	8	7.07	13	11	2	0	56	65	55	44	35	43
Reichard, Clyde (2 Sal)	0	0	1.69	9	2	0	1	27	21	12	5	11	23
Willis, Kent	4	8	6.78	29	7	0	0	78	79	69	59	54	66

WINSTON-SALEM

BATTING	AVG	G	AB	R	H	2B	3B	HR	RBI	BB	SO	SB
Adames, Juan, ss-2b	.123	24	57	7	7	0	0	0	5	10	11	2
Bafia, Bob, 1b-3b	.242	55	190	22	46	9	2	3	25	26	30	3
Borders, Todd, c	.000	9	11	0	0	0	0	0	0	3	6	0
Bullinger, Jim, ss	.192	32	104	13	20	4	2	1	11	13	26	4
#Cohoon, Don, 3b-1b	.176	53	159	19	28	6	0	3	16	21	50	5
Cruz, Marlon, of-inf	.293	76	290	43	85	7	4	1	25	22	40	26
Garcia, Butch, 1b-c	.268	134	514	69	138	23	2	14	77	47	72	2
Gatewood, Henry, c	.183	32	82	9	15	2	0	0	6	8	20	0
Grimes, Lee, of	.276	64	239	31	66	12	1	4	36	27	26	13
Hill, Steve, 2b-3b	.250	78	272	35	68	9	4	1	22	31	37	9
*Lewis, John, of	.316	29	95	11	30	4	1	2	16	18	16	9
Mann, Kelly, c	.274	94	307	32	84	11	0	8	40	24	46	5
*May, Derrick, of	.305	130	485	76	148	29	9	8	65	37	82	13
Rivero, Marty, 3b	.190	18	58	9	11	2	0	0	3	1	11	0
#Smith, Greg, 2b	.280	95	361	62	101	12	2	4	29	46	50	52
*Sullivan, Glenn, of-1b	.249	126	489	75	122	25	4	7	63	39	53	12
Tenacen, Francisco, dh	.266	76	256	46	68	12	0	8	46	22	72	12
*Tullier, Mike, of-1b	.286	34	98	14	28	8	1	2	14	15	22	3
#Valdez, Julio, 1b-3b	.154	3	13	0	2	0	0	0	0	0	0	0
Wallace, Tim, ss-3b	.221	107	348	38	77	12	3	2	38	45	39	10
*Woods, Eric, of	.247	58	186	27	46	1	1	0	12	30	30	22

PITCHING	W	L	ERA	G	GS	CG	SV	IP	H	R	ER	BB	SO
Aspray, Mike	2	0	2.28	4	4	2	0	28	24	9	7	12	15
Berringer, John	5	6	3.94	20	14	3	0	91	80	49	40	40	50
Boskie, Shawn	12	7	3.39	27	27	4	0	186	176	83	70	89	164
*Duenas, Tony	0	1	5.40	2	0	0	0	3	4	2	2	1	2
Green, John	5	2	3.38	29	0	0	0	59	58	25	22	19	44
*Harrison, Phil	14	4	2.96	28	21	3	0	170	148	73	56	76	169
Kallevig, Greg	0	3	5.26	4	4	1	0	26	32	19	15	8	12
Kazmierczak, Bill	9	2	1.34	11	11	7	0	87	51	18	13	23	93
Matas, Jim	1	4	5.37	26	3	0	2	60	55	43	36	43	59
Michno, Tom	4	12	2.95	45	2	0	14	82	63	35	27	52	71
Otten, Brian	2	2	5.17	34	0	0	4	54	66	46	36	31	25	50
*Patterson, Gregg	0	1	2.57	1	1	0	0	7	9	2	2	0	7
*Rosario, David	6	5	2.48	27	10	2	0	91	70	38	25	47	94
Schwarz, Jeff	7	12	4.52	24	24	2	0	151	133	93	76	110	153
Slocumb, Heath	6	6	4.96	25	19	2	1	120	122	75	66	90	78

Hurdling 'em all

St. Lucie wins title with rookie manager

By DAVID JONES

Clint Hurdle was a baseball prospect who never quite made it big as a player. But he may have found his niche in the game as a manager.

In his first year as a minor league manager, Hurdle led the expansion St. Lucie Mets to the 1988 Florida State League championship.

Hurdle guided the Mets through the league's three-tiered playoffs with a 2-1 series win over Lakeland in the opening round, past Tampa 2-0 in the semifinals and over West Palm Beach 2-0 in the championship series.

The Mets won the title game 2-1 with a clutch run in the bottom of the eighth inning. It was a microcosm of the way St. Lucie battled back all season from a disappointing start.

Aquedo Vasquez
... MVP

Slow start

The Mets, who only had the sixth-best overall record, started so slowly that Hurdle called a team meeting early in the year and told his players to shape up or ship out. The talk, obviously, worked.

Greg Talamantez, obtained from the Baltimore Orioles organization after being on the O's 40-man roster in 1987, pitched 6⅔ innings in the final game before Dave Trautwein took over and got the win.

Mike White of Vero Beach made a big comeback from a

League Champions

(Playoff Champions, Where Applicable)

1988—St. Lucie	1966—Leesburg	1942-45—Did Not Operate
1987—Ft. Lauderdale	1965—Ft. Lauderdale	1941—Leesburg
1986—St. Petersburg	1964—Ft. Lauderdale	1940—Orlando
1985—Ft. Myers	1963—Sarasota	1939—Sanford
1984—Ft. Lauderdale	1962—Ft. Lauderdale	1938—Gainesville
1983—Vero Beach	1961—Tampa	1937—Gainesville
1982—Ft. Lauderdale	1960—Palatka	1936—St. Augustine
1981—Daytona Bch.	1959—St. Petersburg	1928-35—Did Not Operate
1980—Ft. Lauderdale	1958—St. Petersburg	1927—Orlando
1979—Winter Haven	1957—Tampa	1926—Sanford
1978—Miami	1956—Cocoa	1925—Tampa
1977—Lakeland	1955—Orlando	1924—Lakeland
1976—Lakeland	1954—Lakeland	1923—Orlando
1975—St. Petersburg	1953—Daytona Bch.	1922—St. Petersburg
1974—W. Palm Bch.	1952—Palatka	1921—Orlando
1973—St. Petersburg	1951—Deland	1920—Tampa
1972—Miami	1950—Deland	1919—*Sanford
1971—Miami	1949—St. Augustine	*Orlando
1970—Miami	1948—Daytona Bch.	
1969—Miami	1947—Gainesville	
1968—Orlando	1946—Orlando	*co-champions
1967—St. Petersburg		

Top FSL Performers

Phil Clark
... top catcher

Mike White
... comeback

Lou Frazier
... 87 SB's

disappointing 1987 season, during which he left Bakersfield (California) and went AWOL after being a No. 1 draft pick of the Los Angeles Dodgers a year earlier.

White won the FSL batting title with a .340 average. He far outdistanced the rest of the field. Rey Sanchez of Port Charlotte hit .306 to finish second. There were no other .300 hitters in the league.

White gave credit for his comeback to his new wife and a more mature attitude.

Another Dodger, Chris Nichting, burst onto the scene in his first pro season and became the FSL's top pitching prospect, going 11-3 with a 2.09 ERA.

Nichting's season was all the more remarkable because his father had cancer surgery, and Nichting, a member of the 1987 U.S. Pan American Games team, used part of his 1987 signing bonus to support the family while battling concerns for his father's future.

Baseball City's Aquedo Vasquez became a full-time reliever, and used a new delivery to rack up a league-record 33 saves. He also was named the league's most valuable player. St. Lucie's Kevin Brown won the league ERA title at 1.81.

Marv Foley was named manager of the year after guiding Tampa to the playoffs in the Western Division. But the Chicago White Sox broke off affiliation with the Tarpons after just one season.

Dominating outfielders

The 1988 season definitely was the year of the outfielder. Five of the league's top nine hitters were outfielders. Four of the Top 10 prospects (White, Milt Cuyler of Lakeland, Tyrone Kingwood of West Palm Beach and Karl Rhodes of Osceola), as selected in a poll of managers by Baseball America, were outfielders.

Rhodes finished second in the league in stolen bases, on an Osceola club that shattered the league record for steals (.354). Cuyler hit .298 to finish third in the batting race. Kingwood hit .286, despite missing a month with injuries.

New attendance record

St. Petersburg, boosted by the city's drive to lure the Chicago White Sox to Florida, broke the league attendance record with 170,534 fans.

The league's two expansion teams, St. Lucie and Baseball City, finished fourth and fifth in the 14-team league behind Charlotte (119,385) and Vero Beach (81,831).

The long-suffering Miami Marlins, who shifted their home games to Hialeah midway through the year, were last in attendance (22,197), and may move permanently.

Eight of the 12 clubs returning from 1987 showed a drop in attendance.

FIRST HALF

East	W	L	Pct.	GB
Vero Bch. (Dodgers) .	44	26	.629	—
W. Palm B. (Expos) ..	41	27	.603	2
Ft. Laud. (Yanks)	39	29	.574	4
St. Lucie (Mets)	36	34	.514	9
Miami (Ind.)	27	40	.403	15½
Central				
Osceola (Astros)	44	26	.629	—
Baseball Cty (Royals)	42	28	.600	2
Lakeland (Tigers)	37	33	.529	7
Wtr. Haven (Red Sox)	18	52	.257	26
West				
*Charlotte (Rangers)	35	35	.500	—
Tampa (White Sox) ..	35	35	.500	—
Dunedin (Blue Jays) .	32	38	.457	3
St. Pete. (Cards)	31	39	.443	4
Clearwater (Phillies) .	25	44	.362	9½

SECOND HALF

East	W	L	Pct.	GB
St. Lucie (Mets)	38	31	.551	—
Vero Bch. (Dodgers) .	31	36	.463	6
W. Palm B. (Expos) ..	30	36	.455	6½
Ft. Laud. (Yanks)	30	36	.455	6½
Miami (Ind.)	28	39	.418	9
Central				
Lakeland (Tigers)	40	28	.588	—
Osceola (Astros)	39	28	.582	½
Baseball Cty (Royals)	37	32	.536	3½
Wtr. Haven (Red Sox)	27	42	.391	13½
West				
Tampa (White Sox) ..	36	24	.600	—
St. Pete. (Cards)	37	29	.561	2
Charlotte (Rangers) .	37	30	.552	2½
Dunedin (Blue Jays) .	33	37	.471	8
Clearwater (Phillies) .	27	42	.391	13½

1988 Final Standings

OVERALL

	W	L	Pct.	GB
Osceola (Astros)	83	54	.606	—
Baseball Cty (Royals)	79	60	.568	5
Lakeland (Tigers)	77	61	.558	6½
Vero Bch. (Dodgers) .	75	62	.547	8
Tampa (White Sox) ..	71	59	.546	8½
St. Lucie (Mets)	74	65	.532	10
W. Palm B. (Expos) ..	71	63	.530	10½
Charlotte (Rangers) .	72	65	.526	11
Ft. Laud. (Yanks)	69	65	.515	12½
St. Pete. (Cards)	68	68	.500	14½
Dunedin (Blue Jays) .	65	75	.464	19½
Miami (Ind.)	55	79	.410	26½
Clearwater (Phillies) .	52	86	.377	31½
Wtr. Haven (Red Sox)	45	94	.324	39

*won division on tiebreaker

1988: General Information

Playoffs: West Palm Beach defeated Vero Beach 2-0 and St. Lucie defeated Lakeland 2-1 in best-of-3 quarterfinals; Osceola defeated West Palm Beach 2-0 and St. Lucie defeated Tampa 2-0 in best-of-3 semifinals; St. Lucie defeated Osceola 2-0 for league championship.

Regular Season Attendance: St. Petersburg, 170,534; Charlotte, 117,275; West Palm Beach, 85,733; Vero Beach, 81,831; St. Lucie, 68,150; Baseball City, 63,746; Tampa, 55,900; Lakeland, 53,818; Clearwater, 50,456; Osceola, 44,023; Ft. Lauderdale, 43,620; Dunedin, 33,540; Miami, 28,927; Winter Haven, 27,746.

Managers: Baseball City—Luis Silverio; Charlotte—Bobby Jones; Clearwater—Granny Hamner; Dunedin—Doug Ault; Ft. Lauderdale—Buck

Showalter; **Lakeland**—John Lipon; **Miami**—Jose Santiago; **Osceola**—Keith Bodie; **St. Lucie**—Clint Hurdle; **St. Petersburg**—Dave Bialas; **Tampa**—Marv Foley; **Vero Beach**—John Shoemaker; **West Palm Beach**—Felipe Alou; **Winter Haven**—Doug Camilli.

1988 Official All-Star Team: C—Phil Clark, Lakeland; Carlos Escalera, Baseball City. **1B**—Mike Simms, Osceola. **2B**—Lou Frazier, Osceola. **3B**—Dave Hansen, Vero Beach. **SS**—Rey Sanchez, Charlotte. **Util**—Scott Melvin, St. Petersburg. **OF**—Pedro Munoz, Dunedin; Milt Cuyler, Lakeland; Mike White, Vero Beach. **DH**—Brian Morrison, Miami. **P**—Chris Nichting, Vero Beach; Jerry Kutzler, Tampa; Darren Hursey, Lakeland; Mahiro Yamamoto, Vero Beach. **RHRP**—Aquedo Vasquez, Baseball City. **LHRP**—Greg Everson, Lakeland. **Most Valuable Player**—Aquedo Vasquez, Baseball City. **Manager of the Year**—Marv Foley, Tampa.

Top 10 Major League Prospects (by Baseball America): 1. Chris Nichting, rhp, Vero Beach; **2.** Mike Simms, 1b, Osceola; **3.** Karl Rhodes, of, Osceola; **4.** Geronimo Pena, 2b, St. Petersburg; **5.** Milt Cuyler, of, Lakeland; **6.** Tyrone Kingwood, of, West Palm Beach; **7.** Dave Hansen, 3b, Vero Beach; **8.** Jerry Kutzler, rhp, Tampa; **9.** Mike White, of, Vero Beach; **10.** Eric Milholland, c, Tampa.

1988: Batting, Pitching Statistics

CLUB BATTING

	AVG	G	AB	R	H	2B	3B	HR	BB	SO	SB
Vero Beach	.262	137	4572	585	1199	168	33	46	405	770	135
West Palm Beach	.257	134	4393	566	1130	186	38	47	413	662	92
Lakeland	.257	138	4580	619	1176	142	37	28	410	686	226
Charlotte	.251	137	4556	560	1142	149	47	53	425	781	145
Tampa	.249	130	4166	514	1039	185	45	44	395	694	143
Osceola	.249	137	4422	622	1100	155	45	29	566	897	360
Ft. Lauderdale	.248	134	4423	514	1096	182	20	24	451	687	67
St. Petersburg	.245	136	4487	524	1100	182	41	38	470	838	106
St. Lucie	.244	139	4450	560	1086	173	42	45	552	871	133
Baseball City	.243	139	4503	557	1092	159	49	39	410	830	217
Dunedin	.242	140	4590	523	1110	171	39	81	410	996	113
Miami	.233	134	4151	468	968	160	17	65	409	846	137
Clearwater	.227	138	4444	416	1007	158	26	39	350	791	67
Winter Haven	.225	139	4543	455	1022	142	23	14	399	742	55

CLUB PITCHING

	ERA	G CG	SHO	SV	IP	H	R	ER	BB	SO
West Palm Beach	2.65	134 25	20	22	1144	935	445	337	377	896
Charlotte	2.84	137 17	12	36	1208	1078	487	381	373	785
Lakeland	2.85	138 16	17	35	1226	1098	497	388	426	744
St. Lucie	2.90	139 27	16	32	1206	1084	500	388	383	792
Osceola	2.89	137 22	15	39	1202	1023	495	386	448	803
Vero Beach	2.93	137 27	19	22	1206	1073	482	393	401	909
Baseball City	3.09	139 5	7	50	1225	1096	545	420	491	793
Ft. Lauderdale	3.14	134 30	11	25	1164	1033	507	406	482	819
Dunedin	3.17	140 1	10	40	1217	1094	552	429	515	921
Clearwater	3.25	138 26	10	30	1187	1109	520	428	416	767
Tampa	3.30	130 32	13	29	1111	1009	485	407	351	741
St. Petersburg	3.32	136 15	9	35	1190	1183	556	439	358	739
Miami	4.02	134 26	6	28	1114	1186	639	498	454	696
Winter Haven	4.51	139 28	3	21	1194	1266	773	598	590	686

INDIVIDUAL BATTING LEADERS
(Minimum 389 Plate Appearances)

	AVG	G	AB	R	H	2B	3B	HR	RBI	BB	SO	SB
White, Mike, VB	.340	115	397	54	135	12	11	5	42	29	38	14
Sanchez, Rey, Char	.306	128	418	60	128	6	5	0	38	35	24	29
Clark, Phil, Lake	.298	109	403	60	120	17	4	8	66	15	43	15
Cuyler, Milt, Lake	.296	132	483	100	143	11	3	2	32	71	83	50
Munoz, Pedro, Dun	.293	133	481	59	141	21	7	8	73	52	87	15
Santana, Miguel, VB	.293	85	331	67	97	4	0	0	13	48	44	58
Hansen, Dave, VB	.291	135	512	68	149	28	6	7	81	56	46	2
Mangham, Eric, VB	.289	99	349	53	101	12	2	4	37	36	48	16
Crosby, Todd, Clear	.288	95	354	36	102	14	1	1	30	22	26	3
Kingwood, Tyrone, WPB	.286	110	419	57	120	11	3	0	40	16	61	25

* indicates lefthanded batter   # indicates switch hitter

INDIVIDUAL PITCHING LEADERS
(Minimum 112 Innings)

	W	L	ERA	G	GS	CG	SV	IP	H	R	ER	BB	SO
Brown, Kevin, StL	5	7	1.81	20	20	5	0	134	96	42	27	37	113
Yamamoto, Masahiro, VB	13	7	2.00	25	17	6	0	149	125	42	33	29	105
Nichting, Chris, VB	11	4	2.09	21	19	5	1	138	90	40	32	51	119
Fynan, Kevin, Clear	7	7	2.15	38	12	2	10	122	90	33	29	42	77
Hernandez, Rob, StL	8	7	2.20	30	12	2	0	123	99	39	30	39	64
Shea, John, Dun	4	6	2.20	24	18	1	1	123	115	43	30	25	83
Hursey, Darren, Lake	15	8	2.39	26	26	3	0	166	148	56	44	68	82
Cinnella, Doug, WPB	9	9	2.41	19	19	4	0	127	98	46	34	29	81
Deleon, Pedro, Osc	14	5	2.44	23	22	7	0	166	110	56	45	52	129
Groom, Buddy, Tampa	13	10	2.54	27	27	8	0	195	181	69	55	51	118

* indicates lefthanded pitcher

BASEBALL CITY

BATTING	AVG	G	AB	R	H	2B	3B	HR	RBI	BB	SO	SB
Alcala, Julio, 2b	.250	80	300	35	75	5	3	0	26	14	34	6
Anglero, Jose, ss-2b	.000	2	6	1	0	0	0	0	0	1	2	0
Berry, Sean, 3b	.234	94	304	34	71	6	4	4	30	31	62	24
Clements, Tony, ss	.243	88	288	31	70	9	1	0	25	17	69	11
Cole, Stu, ss-3b	.146	15	41	7	6	0	0	0	4	9	10	2
#Conde, Hector, of-2b	.213	46	127	6	27	4	2	0	16	9	22	5
Conine, Jeff, 1b-dh	.272	117	415	63	113	23	9	10	59	46	77	26
Escalera, Carlos, c	.253	123	411	47	104	20	6	2	48	21	58	13
Goff, Tim, dh-c	.278	12	36	5	10	0	1	0	4	1	8	1
Gonzalez, Carlos, dh	.160	35	100	14	16	3	0	0	7	11	38	6
Hearn, Ed, c-dh	.304	17	56	3	17	4	0	0	5	7	3	0
Jackson, Kenny, of	.238	116	420	59	100	27	1	9	50	38	80	18
*Jones, Terry, dh	.571	2	7	2	4	2	0	0	2	1	0	0
#Koslofski, Kevin, of	.264	108	368	52	97	7	8	3	30	44	71	32
Laureano, Francisco, 2b	.205	20	78	11	16	1	2	1	6	10	12	6
#McRae, Brian, 2b	.308	30	107	18	33	2	0	1	11	9	11	8
Moore, Robert, of	.232	60	224	25	52	4	2	0	10	17	20	12
Pujols, Ruben, c	.172	21	58	5	10	4	0	1	4	3	14	0
Pulliam, Harvey, of	.243	132	457	56	111	19	4	4	42	34	87	21
Rice, Tom, c	.224	34	49	5	11	0	0	0	5	2	12	1
Stombaugh, Chad, c	.222	6	9	1	2	0	0	0	1	3	1	0
Vargas, Trinidad, ss-3b	.213	95	286	25	61	8	1	1	25	17	78	6
Watkins, Darren, of	.222	17	54	9	12	0	1	0	7	2	13	7
*Watson, DeJon, 1b-dh	.245	99	302	43	74	11	4	3	37	63	48	12

PITCHING	W	L	ERA	G	GS	CG	SV	IP	H	R	ER	BB	SO
Adams, Bud	4	8	3.58	22	21	0	0	113	97	63	45	44	54
Adams, Ken	4	2	3.66	29	3	0	0	52	39	30	21	37	25
*Alexander, Jon	9	8	3.16	27	27	0	0	148	122	67	52	81	111
Appier, Kevin	10	9	2.75	24	24	1	0	147	134	58	45	39	111
Balch, Kyle	6	3	3.44	11	11	1	0	65	62	29	25	11	43
Butcher, Mike	1	4	3.86	6	6	0	0	33	32	19	14	10	20
Clark, Dera	5	2	2.71	34	0	0	4	80	73	28	24	31	44
Cole, Victor	5	0	2.06	10	5	0	1	35	27	9	8	21	27
Harlan, Dan	4	3	3.66	32	3	0	1	76	93	43	31	17	33
Jundy, Lorin	1	2	3.18	11	0	0	0	23	22	12	8	10	13
LeBlanc, Richie	8	0	1.89	14	14	1	0	90	88	24	19	21	37
*Magnante, Mike	1	1	4.13	4	4	1	0	24	19	12	11	8	1
Maldonado, Carlos	1	5	5.30	16	7	0	0	53	46	35	31	39	44
Pickens, Kevin	5	6	4.03	24	13	1	1	87	81	44	39	32	66
*Skodny, Joe	1	2	3.60	20	0	0	3	20	22	8	8	8	7
Tresemer, Mike	7	2	2.14	27	1	0	2	67	62	22	16	31	54
Vasquez, Aquedo	3	2	1.67	62	0	0	33	81	54	26	15	30	6
Walker, Steve	4	1	1.55	18	0	0	5	29	20	11	5	18	1

CHARLOTTE

BATTING	AVG	G	AB	R	H	2B	3B	HR	RBI	BB	SO	SB
Asadoor, Randy, of-inf	.215	19	65	12	14	2	0	4	11	10	15	
*Bernardo, Rick, 1b	.244	122	439	38	107	15	1	1	38	36	72	
*Billmeyer, Mickey, dh-c	.266	42	128	11	34	7	0	0	13	11	18	
#Brewer, Omar, c	.273	14	33	8	9	1	2	0	2	11	8	
#Burgos, Paco, 3b-ss	.250	40	116	16	29	9	1	2	16	5	11	
Fontes, Brad, c	.000	2	2	0	0	0	0	0	0	0	1	
Garman, Pat, 3b	.200	6	15	2	3	1	1	1	5	5	2	
Garner, Darrin, 2b	.260	97	319	60	83	7	2	1	23	54	58	3
Gonzalez, Juan, of	.256	77	277	25	71	14	3	8	43	25	64	
Haselman, Bill, dh-c	.245	122	453	56	111	17	2	10	54	45	99	
*Kramer, Mark, of	.226	87	230	31	52	7	2	0	15	29	22	
*Lavender, Robert, of	.238	55	172	15	41	7	3	2	20	15	24	
Loy, Darren, c	.215	93	293	26	63	9	0	3	26	22	42	
*Marte, Alex, of	.280	34	132	16	37	2	5	0	14	12	16	
Niethammer, Darren, 1b-c	.314	35	105	9	33	4	0	1	20	8	21	
Palmer, Dean, 3b	.266	74	305	38	81	12	1	4	35	15	69	
#Paula, Julio, 2b-3b	.188	22	69	8	13	2	0	0	5	8	10	
Samson, Fred, 2b-3b	.206	44	141	19	29	2	3	1	11	13	33	
Sanchez, Rey, ss	.306	128	418	60	128	6	5	0	38	35	24	1
Scruggs, Tony, of	.292	67	240	35	70	11	4	6	42	23	52	
Sosa, Sam, of	.229	131	507	70	116	13	12	9	51	35	106	
Toale, John, dh-1b (55 StL)	.194	66	216	17	42	9	0	1	19	28	44	

PITCHING	W	L	ERA	G	GS	CG	SV	IP	H	R	ER	BB	SO
*Bohanon, Brian	0	1	5.40	2	2	0	0	7	6	4	4	5	
Bryant, Phil	4	2	2.41	35	0	0	10	71	66	20	19	20	4
Castillo, Felipe	2	1	4.76	4	4	0	0	17	24	14	9	2	
Ellis, Rufus	2	7	3.51	16	14	0	0	82	70	35	32	33	45
Hubbard, Jeff	2	4	4.17	22	2	1	2	50	56	28	23	12	4
Hurst, Jon	1	0	1.69	7	2	0	0	16	8	4	3	6	1
*Lamle, Adam	8	13	2.62	27	25	4	0	158	163	65	46	38	4
*Lynch, Dave	6	2	2.02	36	0	0	6	58	43	21	13	22	4
Malloy, Bob	4	6	2.96	13	12	2	0	82	65	30	27	26	6
Manuel, Barry	4	3	2.54	37	0	0	4	60	47	24	17	32	4
Mathews, Terry	13	6	2.80	27	26	2	0	164	141	68	51	49	4
Mays, Jeff	6	4	2.86	27	0	0	3	63	59	30	20	34	4
Morse, Scott	1	1	3.60	3	1	0	0	10	11	4	4	4	

	W	L	ERA	G	GS	CG	SV	IP	H	R	ER	BB	SO
Petkovsek, Mark	10	11	2.97	28	28	7	0	176	156	71	58	42	95
Rivera, Lino	2	1	3.67	25	9	0	2	83	90	40	34	20	52
*Rogers, Kenny	2	0	1.27	8	6	0	1	35	22	8	5	11	26
Rosenthal, Wayne	1	2	2.05	23	0	0	7	26	20	6	6	4	21
West, Tommy	4	1	1.81	12	6	1	1	50	31	15	10	11	26

CLEARWATER

BATTING	AVG	G	AB	R	H	2B	3B	HR	RBI	BB	SO	SB
*Bates, Steve, of-2b	.240	103	333	27	80	13	1	1	32	31	24	0
Berman, Gary, 1b	.267	38	131	13	35	5	0	3	21	9	16	1
*Britt, Bob, of	.172	47	116	7	20	2	1	0	4	6	21	0
Brumfield, Harvey, of	.230	121	473	66	109	15	10	2	25	45	94	37
Brunelle, Rod, of	.214	121	397	37	85	13	3	6	45	45	117	0
Bustamante, Ray, 2b-3b	.155	53	155	8	24	3	0	0	7	5	21	0
*Callas, Pete, dh	.333	3	6	0	2	0	0	0	0	0	4	0
Calvert, Chris, c-3b	.167	29	90	10	15	3	0	1	12	9	15	1
#Crosby, Todd, 2b-3b	.288	95	354	36	102	14	1	1	30	22	26	3
Dantzler, Shawn, c	.255	19	55	1	14	1	0	0	7	2	4	0
Ellison, Paul, c	.200	2	5	0	1	0	0	0	0	0	0	0
*Grotewold, Jeff, 1b-dh	.219	125	442	35	97	23	2	6	39	42	103	2
Howey, Todd, of	.211	29	76	5	16	2	0	0	6	7	22	1
Iglesias, Luis, ss-3b	.224	66	219	18	49	10	0	4	34	21	37	2
*Kirkpatrick, Steve, of	.196	14	56	6	11	0	1	0	2	4	5	0
Maasberg, Gary, 3b	.226	45	159	18	36	6	0	2	16	9	21	2
#Martinez, Nicio, 2b-3b	.190	9	21	2	4	1	0	0	2	2	11	0
McCall, Trey, c	.176	78	222	16	39	5	0	0	13	23	50	1
Reaves, Scott, 3b-of	.179	32	106	7	19	0	0	1	3	9	14	0
#Rosado, Edwin, dh	.000	1	3	0	0	0	0	0	0	0	0	0
Scarsone, Steve, ss-3b	.263	125	456	51	120	21	4	8	46	18	93	14
Stark, Jeff, of	.251	84	267	33	67	13	3	3	22	27	46	3
*White, Gary, c	.148	46	135	8	20	2	0	0	6	4	25	0
Zayas, Carlos, c	.261	49	161	10	42	6	0	1	9	9	20	0

PITCHING	W	L	ERA	G	GS	CG	SV	IP	H	R	ER	BB	SO
Brantley, Cliff	8	11	2.59	24	24	6	0	167	126	55	48	74	124
Caraballo, Ramon	3	0	3.94	24	0	0	0	46	57	23	20	13	19
*Christopher, Fred	9	14	3.98	27	27	5	0	163	169	100	72	58	87
Clark, Garry	6	4	3.57	29	11	3	1	98	112	45	39	28	63
Fagnano, Phil	2	6	4.34	20	10	0	0	64	64	35	31	22	32
*Fortugno, Tim	1	3	2.42	9	3	0	0	26	17	10	7	15	28
Fynan, Kevin	7	7	2.15	38	12	2	10	122	90	33	29	42	77
Grimsley, Jason	4	7	3.73	16	15	2	0	101	80	48	42	37	90
*Limbach, Chris	1	5	2.81	43	1	0	9	83	88	30	26	27	51
Machado, Julio	1	4	2.95	13	3	0	5	37	34	13	12	14	45
Maldonado, Pete	0	4	4.50	14	1	1	1	32	33	18	16	11	22
*Sims, Mark	9	14	2.65	26	26	7	0	176	173	66	52	49	95
Smith, Brad	0	1	1.74	2	2	0	0	10	8	5	2	3	4
Sossamon, Tim	1	1	1.95	11	0	0	2	28	24	8	6	2	15
Thomas, Royal	0	4	9.00	9	2	0	2	19	24	21	19	14	6
*Walden, Travis	0	1	4.91	8	0	0	0	15	10	10	8	7	9

DUNEDIN

BATTING	AVG	G	AB	R	H	2B	3B	HR	RBI	BB	SO	SB
Cabrera, Francisco, c	.400	9	35	2	14	4	0	1	9	1	2	0
Darretta, Dave, 2b	.000	4	4	0	0	0	0	0	0	0	3	0
Davis, Wayne, dh-of	.245	93	282	32	69	13	6	8	32	20	91	16
Diaz, Carlos, c	.196	68	235	20	46	11	0	6	23	20	56	2
Diaz, Jose, ss	.197	138	437	45	86	14	4	9	41	55	89	3
*Etzweiler, Dan, 2b-3b	.268	60	179	14	48	9	0	4	16	14	43	0
#Foster, Lindsay, 3b	.242	65	207	25	50	8	1	2	15	13	35	2
Garcia, Oscar, c	.134	41	97	4	13	0	0	0	2	5	46	0
Infante, Kennedy, 3b-2b	.242	44	161	12	39	9	1	1	14	4	16	1
*Jeter, Shawn, dh	.281	13	32	4	9	1	0	2	3	3	7	0
Jones, Mike, of-dh	.289	72	266	34	77	7	3	5	28	17	40	1
McElroy, Glen, c	.281	12	32	2	9	0	0	0	1	2	5	0
Melisauskas, Todd, c	.233	30	60	5	14	5	0	0	7	6	12	1
Munoz, Pedro, of	.293	133	481	59	141	21	7	8	73	52	87	15
Parese, Billy, 2b-3b	.118	6	17	2	2	0	0	0	1	3	4	0
Rodgers, Paul, of	.223	127	453	70	101	11	5	2	16	56	129	33
Schunk, Jerry, 2b	.257	87	343	36	88	17	2	5	28	19	30	11
Scott, Shawn, inf-of	.194	15	31	4	6	1	1	0	5	4	13	0
#Thompson, Ryan, of	.138	17	29	2	4	0	0	1	2	2	12	0
Tonucci, Norm, 3b	.198	27	96	8	19	0	0	2	9	8	34	5
Townley, Jason, c	.286	2	7	0	2	0	0	0	1	0	1	0
*Wade, Darrin, dh-1b	.238	63	164	21	39	8	2	2	15	25	49	1
Whiten, Mark, of	.252	99	385	61	97	8	5	7	37	41	69	17
Yan, Julian, 1b	.249	136	498	55	124	21	5	16	75	37	115	0
Young, Mark, 2b-3b	.231	23	52	5	12	3	0	0	3	3	8	5

PITCHING	W	L	ERA	G	GS	CG	SV	IP	H	R	ER	BB	SO
Blair, Willie	2	0	2.70	4	0	0	0	7	5	2	2	4	5
*Burgos, Enrique	1	5	4.71	33	4	0	1	50	61	28	26	37	55
*Castillo, Tony	4	3	1.48	30	0	0	12	43	31	9	7	10	46
DePastino, Rich	2	4	4.52	40	4	0	3	80	66	46	40	51	80
Hall, Darren	1	1	1.93	4	0	0	1	9	6	2	2	5	15

	W	L	ERA	G	GS	CG	SV	IP	H	R	ER	BB	SO
Hentgen, Pat	3	12	3.45	31	30	0	0	151	139	80	58	65	125
*Horsman, Vince	3	1	1.36	14	2	0	1	40	28	7	6	13	34
Johnson, Dane	11	6	4.73	32	19	0	0	105	91	73	55	89	73
*Key, Jimmy	2	0	0.00	4	4	0	0	21	15	2	0	1	11
Linton, Doug	2	1	1.63	12	0	0	2	28	19	5	5	9	28
*Mumaw, Steve	2	3	2.76	21	0	0	1	33	34	16	10	17	39
*Musselman, Jeff	0	0	3.18	2	2	0	0	6	6	3	2	1	4
Newcomb, Joe	3	3	2.56	32	0	0	6	60	54	21	17	10	29
Ogliaruso, Mike	2	1	1.08	4	3	0	0	17	10	3	2	11	9
Sanders, Earl	6	7	3.34	28	24	0	0	127	107	63	47	63	86
*Shea, John	4	6	2.20	24	18	1	1	123	115	43	30	25	83
Tracy, Jim	3	5	2.48	42	1	0	4	76	79	25	21	24	49
*Wade, Darrin	0	0	13.50	1	0	0	0	2	7	3	3	1	0
Watts, Bob	3	6	3.07	44	0	0	7	70	63	29	24	18	43
Wishnevski, Bob	11	11	3.89	34	29	0	1	171	158	92	74	61	107

FT. LAUDERDALE

BATTING	AVG	G	AB	R	H	2B	3B	HR	RBI	BB	SO	SB
*Arendas, Dan, of	.274	61	234	29	64	12	5	1	27	19	19	4
#Becker, Tim, ss-2b	.253	20	79	10	20	5	1	0	9	9	3	6
*Berube, Luc, dh	.251	101	343	40	86	18	2	2	41	41	52	5
Bishop, Tim, of	.118	5	17	1	2	1	0	0	1	0	4	1
Calvert, Art, of	.328	40	134	18	44	6	0	6	24	5	31	3
Crofton, Kevin, of	.214	18	56	3	12	2	0	0	6	1	18	0
Dickerson, Bob, 2b	.246	85	305	29	75	21	0	2	42	5	50	1
Ehrhard, Jim, c	.111	3	9	2	1	0	0	0	0	2	4	0
Erickson, Steve, c-of	.257	97	284	45	73	8	3	1	28	91	53	10
Gwinn, Tony, of	.077	8	26	1	2	0	0	0	0	1	10	0
Hailey, Fred, of	.232	35	112	17	26	5	0	0	9	11	18	3
Hauradou, Yanko, 3b-2b	.186	34	102	9	19	4	0	0	15	15	18	1
Hunter, Robert, of	.273	13	44	10	12	1	0	1	3	4	16	4
*Kraus, Ralph, of-1b	.258	60	213	26	55	10	3	0	16	21	27	1
Laboy, Jose, 3b	.281	30	96	8	27	8	1	1	15	8	24	4
Livesey, Jeff, c	.200	9	25	2	5	2	0	0	2	1	11	0
Martin, Mark, c	.143	3	7	0	1	0	0	0	0	0	1	0
Miller, Orlando, ss	.273	3	11	0	3	0	0	0	1	0	1	0
*Mitchell, Mark, of	.284	66	218	25	62	8	0	0	12	17	24	0
Morales, William, c	.121	21	58	2	7	1	0	0	2	3	7	0
*Phillips, Vince, of	.267	106	356	44	95	11	1	1	42	52	43	9
#Rodriguez, Carlos, ss-2b	.239	124	461	39	110	15	1	0	36	23	30	3
Roman, Dan, ss-1b	.293	42	167	25	49	3	0	1	20	18	21	4
Rosario, Mel, c	.067	5	15	1	1	0	0	0	1	3	5	0
*Sanders, Deion, of	.429	6	21	5	9	2	0	0	2	1	3	2
#Tolleson, Wayne, ss	.278	4	18	2	5	0	0	0	5	1	0	0
Turgeon, David, 3b-1b	.254	117	409	44	104	21	0	3	47	41	68	1
#Vargas, Hector, ss	.143	3	14	2	2	0	0	0	3	0	4	0
#Warren, Allen, of	.171	12	35	6	6	1	0	0	2	4	6	0
*Weeks, Tom, 1b	.231	100	342	48	79	10	1	3	28	39	60	1
Williams, Gerald, of	.189	63	212	21	40	7	2	2	17	16	56	4

PITCHING	W	L	ERA	G	GS	CG	SV	IP	H	R	ER	BB	SO
Allen, Neil	0	0	0.00	3	3	0	0	9	2	0	0	1	5
Balabon, Rick	1	1	4.50	7	3	1	1	30	27	17	15	12	22
*Blum, Brent	0	0	5.40	1	0	0	0	2	4	3	1	3	1
*Brill, Todd	0	0	9.00	2	0	0	0	3	7	3	3	0	4
Chapin, Darrin	6	4	0.86	38	0	0	15	63	39	8	6	19	57
Clayton, Jeff	4	2	1.44	6	6	5	0	44	38	10	7	3	16
DaCosta, Bill	0	0	6.48	2	2	0	0	8	16	12	6	9	4
Faccio, Luis	0	2	4.76	20	0	0	1	34	36	22	18	18	33
*Figueroa, Fernando	1	2	3.59	30	0	0	2	48	49	23	19	15	33
Gay, Scott	1	3	6.91	6	5	0	0	27	35	24	21	11	15
Gogolewski, Doug	4	2	3.28	8	8	1	0	49	44	23	18	28	33
*Guidry, Ron	0	0	1.23	4	4	0	0	15	7	2	2	2	17
Imes, Rodney	6	2	1.72	8	7	3	0	58	48	18	11	17	47
Kamieniecki, Scott	3	6	3.62	12	11	1	0	77	71	36	31	40	51
Knox, Jeff	4	2	2.01	10	9	0	0	54	49	15	12	9	20
Manon, Ramon	2	0	2.01	4	4	1	0	22	13	5	5	12	13
Marris, Mark	6	10	3.86	18	16	5	0	112	108	55	48	42	63
*Mmahat, Kevin	7	7	4.13	17	16	3	0	102	96	60	47	57	78
*Morrison, Tony	9	7	2.81	22	16	3	0	128	90	51	40	80	110
Rodriguez, Gabriel	2	1	3.49	12	0	0	0	28	31	15	11	18	23
Stanford, Don	3	1	2.06	22	0	0	1	48	44	17	11	7	25
Stoltenberg, Brad	4	0	3.34	6	5	0	0	32	29	13	12	12	12
Taylor, Wade	4	11	3.45	24	17	7	0	123	109	53	47	57	94
*Voeltz, Bill	2	2	2.85	24	2	0	5	47	42	22	15	10	41

LAKELAND

BATTING	AVG	G	AB	R	H	2B	3B	HR	RBI	BB	SO	SB
Balthazar, Doyle, c-1b	.244	77	242	34	59	6	2	1	16	29	31	10
Beyeler, Arnie, 2b	.234	121	440	43	103	12	3	1	34	36	51	14
Cabrera, Basilio, of	.235	98	336	40	79	13	1	0	31	11	52	30
*Camilli, Kevin, c	.250	7	4	1	1	0	0	0	1	2	0	0
Clark, Phil, c-dh	.298	109	403	60	120	17	4	8	66	15	43	16
#Cuyler, Milt, of-dh	.296	132	483	100	143	11	3	2	32	71	83	50

	AVG	G	AB	R	H	2B	3B	HR	RBI	BB	SO	SB
DeCillis, Dean, ss	.259	122	436	43	113	14	4	5	61	24	64	9
Dempsay, Adam, c	.176	12	34	2	6	0	0	1	2	2	6	0
Estevez, Juan, c	.000	2	4	0	0	0	0	0	0	1	1	0
Foster, Paul, 1b	.143	8	35	1	5	0	1	0	7	2	11	0
*Fox, Blaine, of	.260	103	300	59	78	10	6	3	36	52	42	28
Galindo, Luis, 1b-3b	.263	102	331	35	87	5	1	0	28	45	42	4
*Henika, Ron, 1b	.225	40	142	14	32	2	0	1	14	20	17	2
#Housie, Wayne, of	.269	55	212	31	57	11	3	0	23	13	40	24
#Hudson, Lance, of	.270	69	278	41	75	5	0	2	37	11	45	26
Hufford, Scott, of	.281	42	121	13	34	6	2	0	20	16	26	2
Ingram, Riccardo, dh-of	.205	37	117	10	24	3	1	0	10	10	30	2
Isaac, Richard, dh	.263	6	19	3	5	1	1	0	2	0	7	0
*Livingstone, Scott, 3b	.283	53	180	28	51	8	1	2	25	11	25	1
Marigny, Ron, inf	.212	86	250	34	53	11	2	0	27	31	47	5
*Morhardt, Greg, 1b	.238	38	130	19	31	7	2	2	19	3	14	0
Nieto, Andy, 3b	.277	19	47	3	13	0	0	0	3	1	2	2
Thomson, Rob, c	.000	2	7	0	0	0	0	0	0	0	2	0
#Toney, Andy, of	.241	10	29	5	7	0	0	0	3	4	5	1

PITCHING	W	L	ERA	G	GS	CG	SV	IP	H	R	ER	BB	SO
*Aldred, Scott	8	7	3.56	25	25	1	0	131	122	61	52	72	102
Everson, Greg	7	6	2.02	53	0	0	17	76	58	22	17	29	50
Gohmann, Ken	5	4	3.25	29	2	0	2	72	63	30	26	16	44
Hansen, Mike	12	6	2.73	26	26	6	0	172	142	71	52	49	79
*Hursey, Darren	15	8	2.39	26	26	3	0	166	148	56	44	68	82
Knudsen, Kurt	0	0	0.96	7	0	0	0	9	7	2	1	7	6
Lacko, Rich	1	2	2.84	3	3	0	0	19	13	6	6	9	24
*Lee, Mark	1	0	1.42	10	0	0	1	19	16	7	3	4	15
Nicholson, Keith	1	0	2.17	9	5	0	0	37	24	13	9	22	21
Nosek, Randy	0	4	3.82	8	8	0	0	31	29	17	13	16	11
*O'Neill, Dan	1	6	2.31	38	0	0	5	62	49	17	16	28	49
Phillips, Wade	0	1	12.00	3	2	0	0	6	11	8	8	5	2
Pifer, Gary	3	5	4.66	17	6	0	1	64	78	42	33	21	37
Rightnowar, Ron	2	0	1.46	17	2	0	0	49	41	19	8	11	32
Schwabe, Mike	9	0	1.61	40	5	1	8	112	88	24	20	14	80
*Slavik, Joe	1	3	5.73	14	1	0	1	22	26	15	14	18	12
Terrell, Walt	1	1	6.52	2	2	0	0	10	13	7	7	1	6
*Vesling, Don	10	8	3.14	25	25	5	0	169	170	80	59	36	92

MIAMI

BATTING	AVG	G	AB	R	H	2B	3B	HR	RBI	BB	SO	SB
*Allison, Jeff, of	.266	44	94	6	25	4	0	0	8	4	18	6
Barefoot, Mike, ss-3b	.248	36	109	10	27	0	0	0	5	21	15	6
*Billmeyer, Mickey, c	.206	46	126	7	26	3	0	0	5	16	17	0
#Cotto, Hector, of-ss	.105	11	19	3	2	0	0	0	2	2	5	1
*Diaz, Tony, of-1b	.278	100	284	34	79	9	3	3	25	39	35	8
Evans, Ray, of-c	.063	16	16	2	1	0	0	0	0	1	6	0
Fanizzi, Bill, of	.114	17	35	0	4	2	0	0	1	0	9	0
Gaeta, Bill, of	.000	3	5	1	0	0	0	0	0	2	4	0
Gonzalez, Orlando, ss	.202	34	114	9	23	2	0	0	8	5	8	1
*Hill, Clay, 1b	.179	11	28	3	5	0	0	0	1	2	2	0
*Hoffman, Hunter, 3b	.000	2	4	0	0	0	0	0	0	0	4	0
Hornacek, Jay, c-dh	.224	75	241	29	54	11	1	9	35	18	49	3
Huff, Matt, 1b	.239	90	243	29	58	16	3	4	31	35	70	0
Inagaki, Shuji, 1b-3b	.237	110	241	19	57	6	0	1	20	23	49	7
Martinez, Ricardo, ss-of	.189	68	180	9	34	8	0	0	11	9	42	6
McHugh, Scott, 3b	.213	112	319	36	68	11	0	7	33	38	67	3
McMillan, Tim, of	.209	91	220	27	46	9	1	4	21	12	78	4
Morrison, Brian, of	.260	114	388	48	101	24	2	17	67	41	115	7
Muratti, Rafael, of	.218	118	376	49	82	17	1	9	37	69	68	16
Perez, Julio, 2b-ss	.287	86	328	46	94	12	4	1	21	16	38	31
#Richardi, Rick, 2b-of	.241	125	465	65	112	22	1	8	40	52	95	36
Roca, Gilberto, c	.341	38	138	18	47	3	1	2	21	6	11	1
Sano, Motokuni, c	.105	48	86	6	9	0	0	0	4	14	25	1
*Smith, Bobby Glen, dh-of	.157	33	89	12	14	1	0	0	2	14	16	0

PITCHING	W	L	ERA	G	GS	CG	SV	IP	H	R	ER	BB	SO
Brevell, Ron	0	3	5.40	16	1	0	0	35	41	26	21	18	24
Browning, Mike	9	2	1.61	47	0	0	20	84	70	25	15	30	71
Cangemi, Jamie	4	4	4.39	14	12	1	0	66	66	36	32	55	36
*Clark, Dave	2	0	1.65	3	3	0	0	16	7	4	3	10	5
Giron, Ysidro	0	0	10.69	10	0	0	0	16	24	20	19	17	13
Hatfield, Rob	1	4	4.68	7	7	0	0	33	42	27	17	19	16
*Intorcia, Trent	0	1	4.97	22	0	0	0	25	34	17	14	5	10
Kida, Masao	7	17	3.99	27	27	9	0	162	149	88	72	62	100
*Lono, Joel	7	15	3.77	25	24	5	0	146	154	77	61	27	78
Lynch, Ed	2	2	2.25	4	4	0	0	28	25	7	7	2	21
*Ogiwara, Mitsuru	1	4	6.29	45	1	0	0	49	58	45	34	30	34
Ojeda, Jorge	3	2	5.48	21	3	0	1	44	56	31	27	26	43
Prieto, Arnie	0	2	5.34	41	2	0	4	84	106	60	50	36	50
Rohan, Tony	1	5	3.89	11	8	1	0	42	47	31	18	18	26
Roldan, Sal	0	1	8.00	5	1	0	0	9	15	11	8	5	11
Snell, Nate	0	0	0.00	3	1	0	0	7	5	2	0	1	4
Tarumi, Kanenori	3	5	3.36	35	9	0	3	80	83	46	30	47	45
*Von Ohlen, Dave	3	2	2.66	7	7	0	0	41	46	14	12	10	31

BATTING

R—Milt Cuyler, Lakeland	....	100
H—Dave Hansen, Vero Beach	....	149
TB—Dave Hansen, Vero Beach	....	210
2B—Dan Rohrmeier, Tampa	....	28
—Dave Hansen, Vero Beach	....	28
3B—Sam Sosa, Charlotte	....	12
HR—Brian Morrison, Miami	....	17
RBI—Dave Hansen, Vero Beach	....	81
GWRBI—Dave Hansen, Vero Beach	....	19
SH—Luis Martinez, Vero Beach	....	27
SF—Four tied at	....	9
BB—Steve Erickson, Ft. Lauderdale	....	91
IBB—Jeff Grotewold, Clearwater	....	9
—Dave Turgeon, Ft. Lauderdale	....	9
HBP—Luis Martinez, Vero Beach	....	15
SO—Bert Hunter, Osceola	....	148
SB—Lou Frazier, Osceola	....	87
CS—Milt Cuyler, Lakeland	....	25
Slg. Pct.—Brian Morrison, Miami	....	.464
OB Pct.—Steve Erickson, Ft. Lauderdale	....	.438

PITCHING

G—Aquedo Vasquez, Baseball City	......	62
GS—Pat Hentgen, Dunedin	....	30
CG—Jerry Kutzler, Tampa	....	12
ShO—Pedro DeLeon, Osceola	....	5
—Mark Petkovsek, Charlotte	....	5
Sv—Aquedo Vasquez, Baseball City	....	33
W—Jerry Kutzler, Tampa	....	16
L—Masao Kida, Miami	....	17
IP—Buddy Groom, Tampa	....	195
H—Dale Burgo, Winter Haven	....	192
R—Fred Christopher, Clearwater	....	100
HR—Dale Burgo, Winter Haven	....	12
BB—Dane Johnson, Dunedin	....	89
HB—Bob Wishnevski, Dunedin	....	14
SO—Chris Nichting, Vero Beach	....	151
WP—Cliff Brantley, Clearwater	....	20
Bk—Scott Diez, Miami-West Palm Beach	......	16

OSCEOLA

BATTING	AVG	G	AB	R	H	2B	3B	HR	RBI	BB	SO	SB
Acta, Manny, 3b	.255	107	333	32	85	10	3	0	40	24	62	10
*Baldwin, Jeff, of-dh	.268	55	168	23	45	8	1	1	25	22	23	2
Campos, Rafael, 3b	.000	1	1	0	0	0	0	0	0	0	1	0
Deiley, Lou, c	.163	24	49	3	8	3	0	1	1	6	9	1
Eusebio, Raul, c	.245	118	392	45	96	6	3	0	40	40	69	20
#Frazier, Lou, 2b-ss	.235	130	468	79	110	11	3	0	34	90	104	87
#Harris, Rusty, 3b-ss	.218	75	197	37	43	8	7	1	18	42	40	14
Hithe, Victor, of	.270	127	441	59	119	22	6	1	59	42	99	31
#Hubbard, Trent, 2b-c-of	.260	130	446	68	116	15	11	3	65	61	72	44
Hunter, Bert, of	.233	133	524	86	122	24	4	3	50	39	148	54
Nyssen, Dan, of	.208	34	130	17	27	5	2	0	19	6	17	3
*Rhodes, Karl, of	.283	132	452	69	128	4	2	1	34	81	58	65
#Sanchez, Pedro, ss-2b	.247	122	392	41	97	20	2	2	47	37	64	20
Simms, Mike, 1b	.243	123	428	63	104	19	1	16	73	76	130	9

PITCHING	W	L	ERA	G	GS	CG	SV	IP	H	R	ER	BB	SO
Andujar, Joaquin	1	0	2.70	2	2	0	0	10	8	5	3	3	4
August, Sam	2	0	1.50	5	5	0	0	30	20	9	5	10	28
Bond, Daven	5	7	3.08	32	10	0	1	96	87	46	33	46	43
Bowen, Ryan	1	0	3.95	4	4	0	0	14	12	8	6	10	12
*Credeur, Todd	3	4	1.72	28	0	0	7	47	33	16	9	14	48
Deleon, Pedro	14	5	2.44	23	22	7	0	166	110	56	45	52	129
*Estes, Joel	4	4	2.18	22	0	0	7	41	39	11	10	17	35
*Grovom, Carl	11	6	2.72	23	22	5	0	142	114	52	43	60	117
Hennis, Randy	7	3	2.40	14	14	2	0	83	64	34	22	28	48
McClure, Todd	1	2	2.03	44	1	0	16	58	40	15	13	28	58
Murphy, Gary	1	5	4.44	20	6	1	0	49	43	29	24	29	26
*Normand, Guy	11	5	3.36	29	23	1	0	155	140	69	58	66	95
Novak, Tom	1	0	7.20	2	0	0	0	5	10	6	4	1	2
*Osuna, Al	0	1	6.94	8	0	0	0	12	12	9	9	9	5
Potts, David	10	7	3.24	28	17	3	1	142	141	55	51	14	73
*Rosario, Eliezel	1	0	4.50	3	3	0	0	12	13	6	6	7	10
Sheehan, John	4	3	3.39	41	2	0	7	61	65	36	23	19	32
Simon, Richie	2	2	2.81	6	6	3	0	42	38	18	13	16	19
Van Houten, Jim	4	0	2.19	17	0	0	0	37	34	15	9	13	18

ST. LUCIE

BATTING	AVG	G	AB	R	H	2B	3B	HR	RBI	BB	SO	SB
Bailey, Brandon, 1b	.240	123	396	62	95	16	4	12	55	63	102	3
Bogar, Tim, 2b-ss	.275	76	236	34	65	7	1	2	30	34	57	5
DeLuca, Kurt, of	.184	50	174	11	32	4	2	3	15	15	35	5
#Diaz, Alex, ss	.000	3	6	2	0	0	0	0	1	0	4	0
*Donnels, Chris, 3b	.217	65	198	25	43	14	2	3	22	32	53	4
*Edwards, Jovon, dh-of	.158	21	57	3	9	2	1	0	6	9	7	6

BATTING	AVG	G	AB	R	H	2B	3B	HR	RBI	BB	SO	SB
Gelatt, Dave, 2b-ss	.256	102	313	56	80	18	4	2	27	37	62	18
#Ging, Adam, 3b-2b	.239	119	381	42	91	10	6	5	58	51	62	3
#Hundley, Todd, c	.000	1	1	0	0	0	0	0	0	0	2	1
#Jacas, Andre, of	.243	85	305	40	74	10	1	0	26	37	36	34
Jaster, Scott, of	.179	35	106	13	19	3	0	0	7	12	31	3
Jones, Geary, c	.146	16	48	5	7	3	0	1	10	4	13	1
Liddell, Dave, c	.248	57	165	23	41	5	2	1	13	18	42	0
*Maksudian, Mike, dh (1 Tam)	.244	14	45	8	11	3	1	0	3	8	7	0
Mantrana, Manny, 2b	.217	31	92	11	20	1	0	0	5	15	11	6
McDaniel, Terry, of	.250	4	12	1	3	0	0	0	0	1	3	0
#Monell, Johnny, of	.283	116	441	55	125	18	5	3	48	24	37	16
*Perez, Hector, of-1b	.291	41	141	14	41	7	0	0	14	12	28	1
*Polka, Fritz, c	.216	87	269	33	58	15	0	5	33	31	41	0
Repoz, Craig, of-3b	.256	115	355	44	91	10	4	1	33	58	100	20
Sanchez, Zoilo, ss	.287	51	171	28	49	9	2	5	29	32	39	4
Soper, Mike, 2b	.211	11	19	3	4	1	0	0	1	1	3	0
Villanueva, Juan, ss	.270	90	337	32	91	9	7	1	31	32	63	4

PITCHING	W	L	ERA	G	GS	CG	SV	IP	H	R	ER	BB	SO
Aguilera, Rick	0	0	1.29	2	2	0	0	7	8	1	1	1	5
Anderson, Mike	5	2	3.20	9	9	1	0	51	53	23	18	20	26
Bayer, Chris	3	7	4.70	24	12	0	0	92	96	59	48	28	41
*Brown, Kevin	5	7	1.81	20	20	5	0	134	96	42	27	37	113
Brown, Rick	2	4	3.69	35	0	0	7	39	28	21	16	30	35
Gross, Kip	13	9	2.62	28	27	7	0	178	153	72	52	53	124
*Hernandez, Rob	8	7	2.20	30	12	2	0	123	99	39	30	39	64
*Latham, Bill	1	1	3.79	3	3	0	0	19	13	10	8	6	11
*Meizoso, Gus	8	2	2.48	45	0	0	11	58	44	21	16	26	52
Miller, Mike	0	1	0.00	1	1	0	0	7	2	1	0	2	5
Myres, Doug	2	2	4.08	35	0	0	3	57	67	31	26	19	66
Rauth, Chris	12	9	3.18	25	25	5	0	164	173	73	58	25	79
Stiles, Bill	0	0	7.04	6	0	0	0	8	7	6	6	4	4
Talamantez, Greg	13	9	2.64	25	25	7	0	177	163	65	52	62	110
Tapani, Kevin	1	0	1.42	3	3	0	0	19	17	5	3	4	11
Trautwein, Dave	1	5	3.44	52	0	0	11	71	64	31	27	25	45
*Whitlock, Mike	0	0	0.00	2	0	0	0	2	1	0	0	2	1

ST. PETERSBURG

BATTING	AVG	G	AB	R	H	2B	3B	HR	RBI	BB	SO	SB
*Balfanz, John, 1b-dh	.212	88	293	23	62	8	5	5	43	32	61	0
Carter, Dennis, of	.248	115	403	34	100	22	5	6	50	22	130	7
Cunningham, Joe, 3b-1b	.269	116	402	46	108	15	6	3	35	55	56	0
Elliot, Terry, c	.199	88	301	20	60	7	1	0	29	27	38	0
*Fernandez, Joey, dh	.225	45	160	22	36	7	1	3	25	30	18	0
Green, Terry, dh	.311	21	61	6	19	0	1	0	5	2	4	4
Hewes, Pat, c	.217	57	180	11	39	4	0	0	17	6	20	0
Lara, Crucito, ss	.207	96	334	33	69	12	2	1	20	12	64	7
*Maclin, Lonnie, of	.189	51	175	24	33	3	1	3	12	18	41	9
*Mann, Scott, of (11 WPB)	.277	49	173	27	48	9	1	2	28	15	17	1
Martinez, Julian, of-ss	.251	113	375	54	94	17	1	3	39	46	79	16
Maxey, Kevin, of	.222	70	117	19	26	5	0	1	4	7	39	3
Melvin, Scott, 3b-1b	.279	126	451	50	126	18	5	1	58	59	86	2
Nelson, Darren, of	.246	16	57	7	14	3	0	1	6	8	13	0
#Pena, Geronimo, 2b	.258	130	484	82	125	25	10	4	35	88	103	35
*Schulte, Mark, of	.103	7	29	0	3	0	0	0	0	1	4	0
Senne, Mike, of	.285	109	414	60	118	24	5	6	55	29	58	22
Thomas, Orlando, c	.143	5	14	1	2	0	0	0	3	2	2	0
*Thoutsis, Paul, of-dh	.275	30	91	14	25	4	0	0	8	14	7	0

PITCHING	W	L	ERA	G	GS	CG	SV	IP	H	R	ER	BB	SO
Broadfoot, Scott	1	2	3.98	6	6	0	0	32	33	22	14	7	22
*Daniels, Jerry	5	5	2.39	46	0	0	4	87	70	29	23	30	85
Faron, Bob	3	3	2.97	6	5	1	0	36	41	12	12	11	22
Hamilton, Scott	8	7	3.62	33	18	1	1	129	132	69	52	41	95
Hershman, Bill	1	3	4.59	14	6	0	0	51	55	32	26	24	27
*Hill, Steve	3	1	2.16	11	0	0	3	25	22	6	6	11	25
Hinkle, Mike	3	3	2.13	6	6	2	0	38	33	10	9	5	25
Lawrence, Scott	3	1	3.58	10	5	2	0	38	39	21	15	13	40
*Livchak, Rob	4	6	5.56	18	10	0	0	66	97	53	41	26	42
Mauch, Tom	0	2	4.20	19	7	0	2	56	57	34	26	17	21
North, Jay	8	7	2.67	35	16	4	2	125	112	42	37	40	83
Ozuna, Gabriel	1	0	4.50	5	0	0	0	10	10	5	5	2	9
Perez, Mike	2	2	2.08	35	0	0	17	43	24	12	10	16	45
Picota, Leny	11	10	2.89	23	23	4	0	143	130	57	46	44	65
Pierson, Larry	7	10	3.64	32	18	0	0	143	170	77	58	27	59
Plemel, Lee	1	2	6.97	3	3	0	0	10	19	12	8	4	1
*Sherrill, Tim	2	0	1.54	16	0	0	6	23	14	4	4	8	25
Smith, Ken	2	0	0.00	3	1	0	0	14	10	0	0	3	5
*Zaltsman, Stan	3	4	3.53	35	12	1	0	120	115	59	47	29	73

TAMPA

BATTING	AVG	G	AB	R	H	2B	3B	HR	RBI	BB	SO	SB
Adames, Hernan, inf	.232	26	82	13	19	1	0	0	4	7	14	1
#Baham, Leon, ss	.222	112	378	39	84	21	0	2	32	24	56	4
Brown, Kurt, c	.185	40	119	8	22	3	0	1	10	6	21	2
#Caceres, Edgar, 2b-ss	.203	32	74	5	15	2	0	1	8	10	8	3

BATTING	AVG	G	AB	R	H	2B	3B	HR	RBI	BB	SO	SB
Davis, Brian, of	.147	10	34	3	5	1	0	0	1	0	15	2
*Eveline, Bill, of	.263	86	304	37	80	8	4	1	40	40	38	6
*Garcia, Cornelio, 1b-dh ..	.282	70	213	38	60	7	6	3	28	33	41	23
*Gonzalez, Cliff, of-dh	.296	72	233	31	69	13	2	0	18	20	27	7
*Greene, Jeff, 1b	.236	77	208	30	49	9	0	2	20	23	45	3
Harris, Frank, c	.160	11	25	3	4	0	1	0	1	2	9	0
#Martin, Norberto, 2b	.258	101	360	44	93	10	4	2	33	17	49	24
Milholland, Eric, c	.235	96	298	36	70	13	2	1	24	41	40	6
Murdock, Kevin, dh	.105	9	19	2	2	0	0	0	1	4	10	0
Peel, Jack, 3b-dh	.229	81	266	33	61	18	2	6	39	20	42	2
Rohrmeier, Dan, of	.259	114	421	53	109	28	8	5	50	27	58	11
Sullivan, Carl, of	.285	100	347	44	99	14	4	4	36	36	77	17
Trafton, Todd, 1b	.260	47	154	22	40	9	2	5	24	17	29	0
*Trammell, Marcus, 2b ...	.114	12	35	1	4	0	0	0	3	3	3	3
*Waggoner, Aubrey, of	.222	43	126	19	28	3	6	3	15	21	34	11
Wagner, Dan, of	.278	53	187	21	52	6	1	5	21	14	23	13
Woods, Tony, 3b	.257	85	280	31	72	18	1	3	29	30	54	5

PITCHING	W	L	ERA	G	GS	CG	SV	IP	H	R	ER	BB	SO
*Boling, John	0	0	1.50	3	0	0	1	6	3	2	1	1	4
Cauley, Chris	2	3	2.92	29	0	0	7	52	57	21	17	16	33
Conde, Argenis	1	1	4.56	11	1	0	0	26	21	14	13	13	15
*Groom, Buddy	13	10	2.54	27	27	8	0	195	181	69	55	51	118
*Hall, Todd	1	5	4.15	32	4	0	8	74	69	37	34	29	54
Knackert, Brent	10	8	3.17	23	23	4	0	142	132	58	50	46	78
Kutzler, Jerry	16	7	2.79	26	26	12	0	184	154	73	57	39	100
Lahrman, Tom	2	1	9.00	8	0	0	0	16	16	12	10	5	4
*Manzanillo, Ravelo	10	6	3.04	24	20	2	0	130	93	53	44	49	140
*Mehrtens, Pat	1	0	7.71	7	0	0	0	9	12	9	8	8	11
Ollom, Mike	7	8	3.93	32	15	2	10	124	110	60	54	42	90
Renz, Kevin	0	2	5.40	8	2	0	0	20	16	12	12	12	13
Reynolds, Dave	7	8	3.28	38	12	4	3	121	119	54	44	36	71
*Takach, Dave	1	0	6.08	6	0	0	0	13	22	10	9	3	5
*Wagner, Gerald	0	0	.00	1	0	0	0	4	4	1	0	1	5

VERO BEACH

BATTING	AVG	G	AB	R	H	2B	3B	HR	RBI	BB	SO	SB
Batesole, Mike, dh-3b ...	.237	51	169	22	40	9	0	3	15	17	38	0
Benitez, Manuel, dh-of ...	.242	37	128	13	31	3	0	5	23	15	23	0
Castillo, Braulio, ph	.000	2	1	0	0	0	0	0	0	0	1	0
Demerit, Tom, of	.194	108	350	40	68	8	6	11	43	28	143	9
Esteban, Felipe, 2b	.237	62	131	17	31	1	1	3	9	11	25	1
Floyd, D.J., c	.000	1	2	0	0	0	0	0	0	0	1	0
*Freiling, Howard, 3b	.243	61	239	30	58	10	0	2	40	18	19	3
Gonzalez, Eddie, dh	.207	32	87	9	18	7	0	1	8	4	31	0
Goshay, Henry, of	.222	95	207	22	46	5	1	0	10	26	47	9
*Hansen, Dave, 3b	.291	135	512	68	149	28	6	7	81	56	46	2
Hartman, Jeff, 2b	.194	36	103	14	20	6	0	0	7	12	20	2
*Kesselmark, Joe, of	.353	4	17	6	6	1	0	0	2	4	0	2
Mangham, Eric, of	.289	99	349	53	101	12	2	4	37	36	48	16
Martinez, Luis, ss	.272	127	474	60	129	21	2	0	42	23	62	11
Mons, Jeff, c	.235	70	217	20	51	5	0	0	20	20	45	0
Mustari, Frank, 2b	.194	86	242	32	47	8	3	1	20	18	58	6
Oferman, Jose, ss	.286	4	14	4	4	2	0	0	2	2	0	0
Rojas, Homar, c	.274	91	325	21	89	11	1	3	37	6	45	1
#Santana, Miguel, of	.293	131	331	67	97	4	0	0	13	48	44	58
Spagnuolo, Joe, 2b	.176	7	17	3	3	1	0	1	4	2	1	0
*Traxler, Brian, 1b	.292	72	260	30	76	14	0	2	34	30	35	1
*White, Mike, of	.340	115	397	54	135	12	11	5	42	29	38	14

PITCHING	W	L	ERA	G	GS	CG	SV	IP	H	R	ER	BB	SO
Campbell, Kevin	8	12	2.75	26	26	5	0	164	166	67	50	49	115
Cash, Tim	2	3	2.97	19	0	0	2	36	39	15	12	14	20
*Cox, Carl	9	7	2.99	26	26	4	0	159	161	65	53	48	80
Devine, Kevin	2	2	4.24	18	1	0	3	34	34	17	16	10	35
Humphries, Joe	0	1	5.91	2	2	0	0	11	13	11	7	4	7
Johnson, Carl	3	1	3.92	36	0	0	4	57	49	30	25	29	58
Mayberry, Greg	2	3	2.72	13	4	0	0	43	36	17	13	11	34
Miguel, Tamares	1	0	3.52	8	0	0	0	23	17	13	9	13	18
Nichting, Chris	11	4	2.09	21	19	5	1	138	90	40	32	51	151
*Nina, Rubin	0	0	18.00	1	0	0	0	1	3	2	2	0	1
Nishimura, Hidetsugu	11	3	3.34	23	23	3	0	148	132	63	55	54	124
Noch, Doug	7	7	3.27	19	18	4	1	118	99	47	43	25	67
*Poole, Jim	1	1	3.77	10	0	0	0	14	13	7	6	9	12
Ray, Jay	5	9	2.61	46	0	0	11	76	63	25	22	32	58
Ryan, Kevin	0	2	3.67	14	0	0	0	27	25	17	11	21	20
Springer, Dennis	0	0	4.76	1	1	0	0	6	6	3	3	2	4
*Yamamoto, Masahiro	13	7	2.00	25	17	6	0	149	125	42	33	29	105

WEST PALM BEACH

BATTING	AVG	G	AB	R	H	2B	3B	HR	RBI	BB	SO	SB
Adams, Pat, dh-1b	.214	25	56	9	12	3	0	0	7	21	19	0
Alou, Jose, of	.323	46	133	19	43	3	0	1	20	9	24	1
Beltre, Esteban, ss	.279	69	226	23	63	5	6	0	15	11	38	4
*Clemo, Scott, 2b-3b	.226	88	252	26	57	17	1	0	22	40	37	4
*Dull, Mike, 1b	.268	128	463	60	124	23	6	5	56	49	68	3

	AVG	G	AB	R	H	2B	3B	HR	RBI	BB	SO	SB
Foster, Kevin, 3b	.200	4	10	0	2	0	0	0	1	0	0	0
Gaylor, Bobby, 2b-ss	.276	33	87	18	24	4	0	0	4	5	9	1
Hansen, Terrel, of	.258	58	190	17	49	9	0	4	28	10	38	2
Kingwood, Tyrone, of	.286	110	419	57	120	11	3	0	40	16	61	25
*Mack, Quinn, of	.278	100	349	51	97	10	5	2	25	21	42	10
Mason, Rob, c	.200	25	50	4	10	0	1	0	6	1	9	0
Munoz, Omer, 2b-ss	.257	103	369	36	95	15	1	0	27	14	28	8
#Nago, Garrett, c	.246	41	118	18	29	4	1	4	21	26	18	1
Natal, Rob, c	.240	113	387	47	93	17	0	6	51	29	50	3
*Olier, Jeff, dh-3b	.246	76	203	16	50	8	1	4	23	26	42	0
#Paredes, Jesus, 2b	.211	7	19	4	4	0	0	0	0	0	4	4
Reagans, Javan, of	.000	4	7	0	0	0	0	0	0	1	4	0
*Rodriguez, Boi, 3b	.242	121	425	56	103	22	8	8	54	59	61	6
Santiago, Norm, ss-2b	.220	39	118	14	26	5	0	1	15	8	14	0
Shephard, Kelvin, of	.000	2	4	0	0	0	0	0	2	1	3	0
*Vanderwal, John, of	.277	62	231	50	64	15	2	10	33	32	40	11
Viltz, Corey, of	.240	69	196	30	47	10	3	1	18	29	43	9
Wedvick, Jeff, dh-c	.226	12	31	4	7	2	0	0	4	2	3	0
Zane, Kelly, 2b	.000	2	6	0	0	0	0	0	0	0	1	0

PITCHING	W	L	ERA	G	GS	CG	SV	IP	H	R	ER	BB	SO
Bennett, Chris	0	1	1.73	20	0	0	4	26	19	7	5	11	18
Bottenfield, Kent	10	8	3.33	27	27	9	0	181	165	80	67	47	120
Boyd, Daryl	5	6	2.78	19	18	1	0	97	85	43	30	47	62
Cavalier, Kevin	6	6	1.87	37	3	0	3	87	61	28	18	21	88
Cinnella, Doug	9	9	2.41	19	19	4	0	127	98	46	34	29	81
Collins, Al	6	5	3.75	37	3	1	7	82	79	37	34	29	57
Devlin, Bob	0	1	0.00	8	0	0	1	7	6	2	0	3	7
DeYoung, Rob	5	3	2.22	47	0	0	2	73	52	28	18	34	75
*Diez, Scott (24 Miami)	13	11	3.90	27	27	10	0	159	177	82	69	38	83
*Farwell, Fred	1	0	3.09	6	1	0	0	12	10	5	4	5	9
*Howes, John	5	5	2.99	38	8	0	2	75	78	31	25	22	61
Jacobsen, Nels	9	4	2.74	16	16	7	0	105	71	35	32	40	101
Jones, Ross	4	5	2.03	31	4	0	3	71	59	23	16	11	67
Leon, Danilo	0	0	3.21	6	0	0	0	14	12	6	5	5	15
*Marino, John	0	0	2.19	11	0	0	0	12	11	3	3	1	15
Rojas, Hiti	1	0	3.60	2	2	0	0	5	4	2	2	1	4
*Tabaka, Jeff	7	5	1.71	16	16	2	0	95	71	38	18	34	52
Welborn, Tony	2	4	1.91	14	14	1	0	61	34	18	13	32	53

WINTER HAVEN

BATTING	AVG	G	AB	R	H	2B	3B	HR	RBI	BB	SO	SB
Baker, Mike, 2b	.222	117	436	42	97	10	0	0	28	55	35	17
#Bourne, Kendrick, 1b-of	.155	35	116	14	18	4	1	2	10	20	36	0
*Degifico, Vinnie, dh-1b	.235	99	323	33	76	10	1	5	32	37	65	0
Haggerty, Roger, 3b-1b	.182	88	264	30	48	7	0	5	26	42	56	2
Hill, Tony, of	.199	51	161	14	32	5	2	0	15	10	46	2
Kelly, Michael, of	.229	125	462	41	106	13	2	6	38	29	46	8
Kuilan, Jorge, dh-3b	.176	5	17	1	3	1	0	0	0	2	5	0
Laseke, Eric, of-2b	.250	48	188	26	47	3	3	0	9	24	20	6
Martinez, Gil, of	.269	106	379	40	102	7	3	1	33	31	42	5
Milstien, David, ss-3b	.214	120	429	36	92	15	5	1	26	5	38	2
Monegro, Dave, 2b	.211	6	19	1	4	0	0	1	0	1	4	0
Munoz, Lou, 3b	.067	4	15	0	1	0	0	0	0	1	2	0
Naehring, Tim, ss	.227	42	141	17	32	7	0	0	10	19	24	1
Olson, Warren, 1b-dh	.233	60	172	16	40	3	0	2	16	11	31	0
Padilla, Livio, c	.259	83	286	33	74	10	1	4	23	17	63	3
Paris, Juan, of	.233	45	150	12	35	2	2	0	10	11	11	6
*Plantier, Phil, of-3b	.240	111	337	29	81	13	1	4	32	51	62	0
Rosario, Julio, ss	.087	8	23	3	2	0	1	0	0	0	5	1
*Wallin, Les, 1b	.205	40	132	16	27	7	0	3	16	18	36	1
Warfel, Brian, of	.179	19	67	8	12	3	0	1	6	1	12	1
Williams, Paul, c	.224	91	340	32	76	14	1	7	35	13	83	0
Zambrano, Roberto, of-3b	.198	23	86	11	17	8	0	0	11	2	20	0

PITCHING	W	L	ERA	G	GS	CG	SV	IP	H	R	ER	BB	SO
*Abbott, John	4	8	4.18	14	11	1	0	75	81	48	35	34	44
Abril, Odie	4	9	4.03	17	17	2	0	116	123	65	52	59	95
Burgo, Dale	6	16	3.86	30	26	7	1	193	192	95	83	70	116
*Cina, Randy	0	0	7.94	11	0	0	0	6	9	6	5	7	3
*Diaz, Jhonny	0	0	7.62	11	0	0	0	13	16	17	11	9	9
*Dolan, John	4	4	2.73	8	8	3	0	59	57	26	18	20	15
*Florence, Don	6	8	4.25	27	16	4	0	121	136	72	57	50	56
*Landry, Howard	1	4	5.36	14	4	1	0	49	62	38	29	27	35
Livernois, Derek	3	3	3.15	7	5	3	0	40	39	18	14	12	25
McGowan, Donnie	3	6	5.32	30	2	0	8	69	69	51	41	53	61
*Mosley, Tony	2	8	5.09	33	6	1	3	94	106	75	53	44	37
*Owen, Dave	4	7	4.71	15	14	4	0	94	94	62	49	46	77
Rivera, Carlos	0	1	7.26	13	0	0	0	31	47	36	25	15	13
Skripko, Scott	0	4	3.67	7	4	0	0	27	23	17	11	8	22
Stanley, Bob	0	1	7.20	2	2	0	0	10	13	9	8	3	3
Thompson, Michael	6	7	3.15	16	16	1	0	89	96	49	31	27	22
Treadway, Doug	1	1	10.18	25	0	0	4	41	45	50	46	51	14
Wacha, Chuck	1	7	4.19	22	8	1	5	67	58	39	31	53	39

Three-decade wait ends for Cedar Rapids

By MIKE KOOLBECK

The late August rain of 1988 which revived the parched Midwest also saw an end to a drought of a different sort.

Cedar Rapids, which had qualified for the Midwest League championship series once in its 26 years of membership, ended 30 years of frustration by beating defending champion Kenosha, 3-1, in the 1988 league finals.

Ramon Sambo
...98 steals

Cedar Rapids, in its ninth year of affiliation with the Cincinnati Reds, last won a league title in 1958, when the Al Monchak-managed Braves won the old Three-I League title.

Kenosha, in its fifth year of affiliation with the Midwest League and Minnesota Twins, was bidding for its third title in four years. The Twins won in 1987 and '85.

Little Red Machine

A set of circumstances in the Cincinnati organization the previous winter synergized to create a championship team in Cedar Rapids.

First, Cincinnati withdrew its Florida State League affiliation with Tampa, and moved to Greensboro of the South Atlantic League, considered a slower Class A league.

Then former Tampa manager Marc Bombard, a six-year minor league skipper with three playoff appearances and a Pioneer League title to his credit, was named to manage Cedar Rapids.

Finally, having not put a Cedar Rapids club in the playoffs since 1983, the parent Reds made a commitment to provide a top-notch club.

Leading the 14-team league in both pitching and hitting, Cedar Rapids won the first-half title in the Southern Division. The Reds finished the regular season with a league-leading 87 wins, breaking a 91-year-old club record. And Bombard was named the league's manager of the year in a vote of his peers.

Title time

After losing Game One of the best-of-5 championship series, Cedar Rapids won the next three to take the crown. Pitching paved the way.

Lefthanders Rosario Rodriguez, Butch Henry and Mike Moscrey, with relief help from righthanders Bill Dodd, Mack Jenkins and Milt Hill, limited Kenosha to 11 hits and one run over the final 27 innings of the series. The Reds won 6-0, 15-1 and 6-0.

Cedar Rapids had reached the finals by knocking out the Springfield Cardinals, 2-0, in the Southern Division playoffs. First-half champion Kenosha did likewise to the expansion Rockford Expos in the Northern Division series.

League-al maneuvers

In its first year with 14 members, the league broke its attendance record, drawing nearly 1.65 million.

Peoria, affiliated with the Chicago Cubs, drew a league record 207,294 to Meinen Field. First-year members South Bend (Chicago White Sox) and Rockford were second and third, with South Bend drawing 173,888 and Rockford 158,674.

Best of the Midwest

Reggie Jefferson
... RBI leader

Ruben Gonzalez
... top hitter

Pete Delkus
... 0.26 ERA

Club attendance records also were broken in Cedar Rapids, Springfield, Clinton and Burlington.

Despite a rosy 1988, things took a turn for the worse in mid-September when the Cleveland Indians notified Waterloo owners that they would not be back for the 1989 season. The news was delivered 12 hours before a deadline which would have automatically renewed the working agreement.

Peoria owner Pete Vonachen, who was suspended by league president George Spelius for 20 days in late June for coming onto the playing field to protest a call, sold the Chiefs to a group headed by Chicago real estate developer Clarence Krusinski.

Flashy Gordon

Pitching dominated the league in 1988. Only three hitters managed to finish above .300.

The top pitcher was Appleton's Tom Gordon, voted the league's top prospect in the annual Baseball America poll of managers. Gordon, who finished the season with the parent Kansas City Royals, led the league in strikeouts with 172, despite being promoted to Double-A Memphis with nearly two months left in the season.

Gordon's record was just 7-5, but he had a 2.06 ERA and gave up only 69 hits in 118 innings. His best outing was a 17-strikeout, seven-inning win over Waterloo in which he faced 25 batters.

Kenosha's Lenny Webster, who sat on the Twins' bench in '87 backing up league prospect of the year Derek Parks at catcher, was voted the league's most valuable player in '88. Webster hit .288 with 11 home runs and 87 RBIs, including 13 game-winners.

Wausau's Ruben Gonzalez hit .314 to lead the league—the lowest average for a champion in nearly 20 years. Madison's Scott Brosius (.304) and South Bend's Mike Maksudian (.303) were the only other hitters over .300.

Cedar Rapids' Ramon Sambo broke an eight-year-old league record by stealing 98 bases.

Burlington's Brian Hunter and Cedar Rapids' Steve Davis tied for the home run title with 22 each. That was the lowest total by a league champion since Gary Gaetti had 22 for Wisconsin Rapids in 1980.

Kenosha's Pat Bangtson (17-5) led the league in wins, and the Twins' Pete Delkus was the fireman of the year with 33 saves and a 0.26 ERA.

Four pitchers threw no-hitters. Cedar Rapids' Scott Scudder, voted the league's second-best prospect, blanked Wausau 4-0 May 20; Kenosha's Mike Redding tossed a seven-inning no-hitter in beating Quad City 3-0 in the first game of a June 23 doubleheader; Peoria's Mike Aspray beat Waterloo 5-0 on Aug. 9; and South Bend's Mike Girouard beat Appleton 5-1 on Aug. 22.

The North beat the South 5-2 in the all-star game, played

before 3,537 fans at Clinton's Riverview Stadium. Appleton's Jorge Pedre had a two-run double and scored in the North's three-run seventh inning, and was named the game's MVP.

FIRST HALF				
North	W	L	Pct.	GB
Kenosha (Twins)	41	27	.603	—
Rockford (Expos)....	39	29	.574	2
Madison (Athletics) ...	33	34	.493	7½
Appleton (Royals) ...	28	38	.424	12
So. Bend (White Sox)	29	41	.414	13
Beloit (Brewers)	26	41	.388	14½
Wausau (Mariners) ..	26	41	.388	14½
South				
Cedar Rapids (Reds) .	46	24	.657	—
Clinton (Giants)	42	24	.636	2
Waterloo (Indians) ...	40	26	.606	4
Burlington (Braves)..	37	31	.544	8
Springfield (Cards) ..	32	37	.464	13½
Peoria (Cubs)	29	40	.420	16½
Quad City (Angels) ..	27	42	.391	18½
SECOND HALF				
East	W	L	Pct.	GB
Rockford (Expos)....	45	27	.625	—
Kenosha (Twins)	40	32	.556	5
Beloit (Brewers)	40	33	.548	5½
Madison (Athletics)..	32	41	.438	13½
So. Bend (White Sox)	30	40	.429	14
Appleton (Royals) ...	30	44	.405	16
Wausau (Mariners) ..	26	47	.356	19½
South				
Springfield (Cards) ..	49	21	.700	—
Cedar Rapids (Reds) .	41	29	.586	8
Peoria (Cubs)	41	30	.577	8½
Waterloo (Indians) ...	38	36	.514	13
Clinton (Giants)	36	38	.486	15
Quad City (Angels) ..	33	37	.471	16
Burlington (Braves)..	23	49	.319	27
OVERALL				
	W	L	Pct.	GB
Cedar Rapids (Reds) .	87	53	.621	—
Rockford (Expos)....	84	56	.600	3
Springfield (Cards) ..	81	58	.583	5½
Kenosha (Twins)	81	59	.579	6
Clinton (Giants)	78	62	.557	9
Waterloo (Indians) ...	78	62	.557	9
Peoria (Cubs)	70	70	.500	17
Beloit (Brewers)	66	74	.471	21
Madison (Athletics)..	65	75	.464	22
Quad City (Angels) ..	60	79	.432	26½
Burlington (Braves)..	60	80	.429	27
So. Bend (White Sox)	59	81	.421	28
Appleton (Royals) ...	58	82	.414	29
Wausau (Mariners) ..	52	88	.371	35

1988
Final
Standings

1988: General Information

Playoffs: Kenosha defeated Rockford 2-0 and Cedar Rapids defeated Springfield 2-0 in best-of-3 semifinals; Cedar Rapids defeated Kenosha 3-1 in best-of-5 final for league championship.

Regular Season Attendance: Peoria, 207,294; South Bend, 171,444; Cedar Rapids, 166,121; Rockford 158,674; Springfield, 155,416; Clinton, 127,251; Quad City, 115,459; Beloit, 96,616; Madison, 88,343; Waterloo, 87,819; Appleton, 85,310; Burlington, 78,308; Kenosha, 64,285; Wausau, 55,255.

Managers: Appleton—Brian Poldberg; **Beloit**—Gomer Hodge; **Burlington**—Grady Little, Rick Albert; **Cedar Rapids**—Marc Bombard; **Clinton**—Bill Evers; **Kenosha**—Ron Gardenhire; **Madison**—Jim Nettles; **Peoria**—Jim Tracy; **Quad City**—Eddie Rodriguez; **Rockford**—Alan Bannister; **South**

Kenosha's Lenny Webster was named the Midwest League's most valuable player, after a year that included 87 RBIs.

Bend—Steve Dillard; **Springfield**—Mark DeJohn; **Waterloo**—Ken Bolek; **Wausau**—Rick Sweet.

1988 Official All-Star Team: C—Lenny Webster, Kenosha. **1B**—Reggie Jefferson, Cedar Rapids. **2B**—Rich Casarotti, Burlington. **3B**—Bob Rose, Quad City. **SS**—Shawn Gilbert, Kenosha. **OF**—Jarvis Brown, Kenosha; Jamie Cooper, Clinton; Jeff Forney, Cedar Rapids. **DH**—Bobby Knecht, Appleton. **LHP**—Butch Henry, Cedar Rapids. **RHP**—Tom Gordon, Appleton. **RHRP**—Pete Delkus, Kenosha. **LHRP**—Greg Becker, Springfield. **Most Valuable Player**—Lenny Webster, Kenosha. **Prospect of the Year**—Tom Gordon, Appleton. **Manager of the Year**—Marc Bombard, Cedar Rapids.

Top 10 Major League Prospects (by Baseball America): 1. Tom Gordon, rhp, Appleton; **2.** Scott Scudder, rhp, Cedar Rapids; **3.** Delino DeShields, ss, Rockford; **4.** Butch Henry, lhp, Cedar Rapids; **5.** Andres Santana, ss, Clinton; **6.** Ray Lankford, of, Springfield; **7.** Jarvis Brown, of, Kenosha; **8.** Reggie Jefferson, 1b, Cedar Rapids; **9.** Jamie Cooper, of, Clinton; **10.** Willie Banks, rhp, Kenosha.

1988: Batting, Pitching Statistics

CLUB BATTING

	AVG	G	AB	R	H	2B	3B	HR	BB	SO	SB
Cedar Rapids	.262	140	4817	677	1262	201	21	100	506	912	212
Springfield	.259	139	4608	646	1195	188	48	82	549	730	159
Kenosha	.254	140	4574	680	1161	206	27	45	518	757	247
Clinton	.252	140	4608	587	1159	177	30	63	394	894	240
Madison	.249	140	4652	611	1158	200	27	68	458	773	138
Rockford	.248	140	4669	682	1160	221	28	114	462	993	234
Burlington	.247	140	4539	603	1123	214	19	106	457	1004	132
Appleton	.246	140	4701	585	1157	186	37	40	453	970	188
Waterloo	.246	140	4586	634	1126	203	29	92	538	1061	111
Wausau	.245	140	4599	603	1127	203	17	97	470	895	186
South Bend	.245	140	4625	574	1133	174	27	34	472	863	246
Quad City	.235	139	4526	517	1063	149	29	41	529	992	206
Beloit	.235	140	4590	519	1077	203	30	58	460	959	106
Peoria	.231	140	4653	519	1073	187	34	33	407	997	173

CLUB PITCHING

	ERA	G	CG	SHO	SV	IP	H	R	ER	BB	SO
Cedar Rapids	2.81	140	14	12	35	1244	1020	493	388	440	1051
Peoria	2.86	140	23	11	27	1254	1068	513	398	408	973
Clinton	2.95	140	21	13	35	1216	1082	498	398	422	894
Rockford	3.15	140	19	6	43	1230	1082	544	431	477	933
Springfield	3.18	139	19	11	42	1212	1153	548	428	378	834
Beloit	3.22	140	15	11	43	1237	1130	572	442	458	1081
Waterloo	3.26	140	25	10	33	1231	1118	561	446	470	977
Kenosha	3.29	140	12	8	48	1207	1087	566	441	493	828
Quad City	3.36	139	17	9	22	1209	1123	627	452	508	974
Appleton	3.77	140	11	6	30	1231	1210	658	515	535	983
Madison	3.77	140	23	10	28	1214	1158	637	509	428	779
South Bend	3.89	140	19	3	29	1227	1246	667	531	441	816
Burlington	4.57	140	20	13	22	1185	1218	736	601	577	865
Wausau	4.78	140	14	5	25	1202	1279	817	639	638	812

INDIVIDUAL BATTING LEADERS
(Minimum 378 Plate Appearances)

	AVG	G	AB	R	H	2B	3B	HR	RBI	BB	SO	SB
Gonzalez, Ruben, Wau	.314	115	430	56	135	32	2	9	59	35	50	1
Brosius, Scott, Mad	.304	132	504	82	153	28	2	9	58	56	67	13
*Maksudian, Mike, SB	.303	102	366	51	111	26	3	4	50	60	59	5
*Lee, Wiley, QC	.302	102	348	57	105	17	3	2	46	47	63	53
*Brewer, Rod, Spr	.298	133	457	57	136	25	2	8	64	63	52	6
#Cooper, Jamie, Clin	.297	125	502	75	149	28	2	5	50	19	128	63
Brown, Jarvis, Ken	.294	138	531	108	156	25	7	7	45	71	89	72
Johnson, Chuck, Spr	.292	133	528	65	154	25	5	5	62	27	74	26
*Neel, Troy, Wat	.290	91	331	49	96	20	1	8	57	38	76	0
Azar, Todd, Wau	.288	114	371	46	107	20	2	4	54	33	36	1

* indicates lefthanded batter   # indicates switch hitter

INDIVIDUAL PITCHING LEADERS
(Minimum 112 Innings)

	W	L	ERA	G	GS	CG	SV	IP	H	R	ER	BB	SO
Dewey, Mark, Clin	10	4	1.43	37	7	1	7	119	95	36	19	14	76
Kallevig, Greg, Peo	11	9	1.44	29	18	8	0	175	132	38	28	29	80
Perez, Leo, Bel	10	8	2.05	22	17	5	0	123	96	45	28	31	124
Gordon, Tom, App	7	5	2.06	17	17	5	0	118	69	30	27	43	172
*Henry, Butch, CR	16	2	2.26	27	27	1	0	187	144	59	47	56	163
Farmer, Howard, Rock	15	7	2.51	27	25	8	0	194	153	70	54	58	145
Kramer, Tommy, Wat	14	7	2.54	27	27	9	0	199	173	70	56	60	152
Hostetler, Tom, Clin	11	3	2.54	17	17	4	0	120	85	39	34	37	118
Potestio, Frank, Spr	14	10	2.58	27	27	7	0	182	167	67	52	52	123
Baez, Pedro, Mad	7	9	2.68	32	19	4	2	141	115	50	42	51	81

* indicates lefthanded pitcher

APPLETON

BATTING

	AVG	G	AB	R	H	2B	3B	HR	RBI	BB	SO	SB
*Baum, Jeff, 3b-ss	.236	95	314	46	74	12	3	3	22	40	62	5
*Beall, Mike, 1b	.239	72	255	20	61	10	1	0	23	18	30	5
*Beniquez, Juan, of	.155	23	58	7	9	0	1	0	4	6	32	2
Bock, Doug, c	.241	29	79	11	19	2	2	0	10	13	19	1
Dyer, Linton, of-c	.231	62	160	19	37	7	0	2	19	32	37	2
*Gainous, Trey, of	.256	91	308	49	79	5	3	0	22	35	58	21
Gassman, Mark, of	.179	35	112	12	20	2	0	0	4	6	42	4
Gurchiek, Chris, of	.156	22	77	11	12	2	0	0	1	5	19	2
Halcovich, Frank, dh-of	.176	37	102	7	18	2	0	0	8	8	20	0
Henderson, Frank, of	.203	49	177	18	36	3	0	0	17	19	47	7
#Howard, Dave, ss	.223	114	368	48	82	9	4	1	22	25	80	7
*Knecht, Bobby, dh-util	.280	127	465	65	130	22	8	5	82	62	78	23
Pedre, Jorge, c-dh	.272	111	412	44	112	20	2	6	54	23	76	4
Pujols, Ruben, c	.304	8	23	0	7	1	0	0	2	1	6	0
Robinson, Darryl, 3b-1b	.249	108	393	40	98	16	1	2	33	15	60	4
Shumpert, Terry, 2b	.242	114	422	64	102	37	2	7	39	56	90	36
Spehr, Tim, c	.264	31	110	15	29	3	0	5	22	10	28	3
Watkins, Darren, of	.265	96	366	42	97	8	4	8	46	24	86	33
Wright, Don, of-1b	.270	135	500	67	135	25	2	5	60	55	100	31

PITCHING

	W	L	ERA	G	GS	CG	SV	IP	H	R	ER	BB	SO
Butcher, Mike	0	1	3.00	4	4	0	0	18	17	7	6	5	7
DeLeon, Jesus	6	12	3.25	26	26	1	0	152	148	68	55	77	111
Drezek, Karl	0	7	6.11	19	1	0	2	28	33	23	19	17	15
*Goodenough, Randy	2	1	4.22	28	1	0	2	49	53	27	23	31	23
Gordon, Tom	7	5	2.06	17	17	5	0	118	69	30	27	43	172
Halcovich, Frank	0	0	14.14	5	0	0	0	7	15	11	11	6	3
Hempen, Hal	1	1	7.45	5	0	0	0	10	13	10	8	8	9
Kimbell, Zach	0	0	0.00	6	0	0	0	10	4	0	0	9	9
*Magnante, Mike	3	2	3.21	9	8	0	0	48	48	20	17	15	40
Mallea, Luis	0	6	5.53	12	8	0	0	41	47	42	25	25	24
McCormack, Brian	6	5	2.44	45	0	0	12	81	73	34	22	31	68
Meyers, Brian	1	0	6.94	14	0	0	0	23	27	21	18	14	13
Moeller, Dennis	3	5	3.18	20	18	0	0	99	94	46	35	34	88
Nelson, Doug	5	8	4.27	37	15	1	3	135	140	76	64	49	95
Odom, Tim	2	3	4.21	29	3	0	1	58	64	31	27	26	50

	W	L	ERA	G	GS	CG	SV	IP	H	R	ER	BB	SO
*Pierce, Ben	3	1	2.95	8	7	0	0	40	32	15	13	26	27
Shaw, Kevin	5	4	1.99	18	18	2	0	90	83	40	20	33	40
*Shibata, Keith	2	2	4.91	16	0	0	0	26	27	19	14	13	35
*Smith, Archie	3	10	6.56	24	10	1	1	84	109	66	61	25	68
Stonikas, Bill	7	6	4.73	41	4	1	7	80	85	49	42	29	53
Studeman, Dennis	2	3	2.38	28	0	0	3	34	27	21	9	18	32

BELOIT

BATTING	AVG	G	AB	R	H	2B	3B	HR	RBI	BB	SO	SB
Barragan, Gerry, ss-2b ..	.272	85	316	31	86	11	4	0	28	25	37	9
#Bolick, Frank, 3b	.228	55	180	28	41	14	1	2	16	43	49	3
Brown, Terry, of	.188	10	32	7	6	0	2	0	4	12	8	4
Burrola, Mike, of	1.000	1	1	0	1	0	0	0	0	0	0	0
*Cartwright, Alan, of-dh ..	.256	89	297	42	76	18	4	7	26	30	74	6
Casey, Tim, of-dh	.190	18	63	7	12	2	0	4	11	10	19	1
Cassels, Chris, of	.277	115	393	42	109	16	3	11	60	31	65	5
Clark, Isaiah, ss-3b	.182	24	77	5	14	3	0	1	8	5	11	2
Foster, Bryan, 2b	.186	67	199	22	37	5	2	1	12	21	60	4
#Guerrero, Mike, 2b-ss ...	.176	65	221	20	39	8	1	0	7	14	55	5
*Heffernan, Bert, c	.214	5	14	1	3	0	0	0	0	5	0	0
*Kremer, Ken, 1b	.249	67	229	21	57	11	0	3	23	21	31	1
Listach, Pat, ss	.240	53	200	40	48	5	1	1	18	18	20	20
Littlewood, Mike, 3b	.181	66	210	15	38	5	3	2	16	28	46	8
*Marrero, Oreste, 1b	.173	19	52	5	9	2	0	1	7	3	16	0
*McGrew, Charlie, 1b-c ...	.229	53	179	23	41	14	0	6	27	26	45	2
*Meyett, Don, of	.227	14	44	1	10	2	0	0	0	0	6	0
Moore, Dwayne, of	.146	15	41	2	6	1	0	0	0	4	15	0
*Moore, Randy, of	.209	15	43	4	9	3	0	0	1	1	8	0
*Nilsson, Dave, c-dh	.223	95	332	28	74	15	2	4	41	25	49	2
*Raley, Tim, of	.280	116	418	55	117	17	2	1	36	51	62	8
Rice, Pete, dh	.125	2	8	1	1	0	0	0	0	0	6	0
Rodriguez, Angel, c-1b ..	.140	13	43	4	6	2	0	1	4	2	12	0
Russell, Dan, 1b-2b	.264	25	91	12	24	4	1	2	6	2	16	1
Simonson, Bob, of-dh	.226	91	328	41	74	18	2	6	34	22	119	13
*Snyder, Randy, c	.196	29	92	7	18	4	0	0	6	8	27	3
Sobczyk, Bob, c	.222	6	9	0	2	0	0	0	1	0	4	0
Teixeira, Vince, of-3b	.237	87	283	30	67	10	2	1	16	35	52	7
Torricelli, Tim, c-of	.260	47	154	17	40	11	0	3	23	17	37	1

PITCHING	W	L	ERA	G	GS	CG	SV	IP	H	R	ER	BB	SO
*Adriance, Dan	1	2	5.86	26	2	0	0	55	62	44	36	32	44
*Beavers, Mark	0	2	6.00	2	2	0	0	6	6	6	4	9	3
Chapman, Mark	2	5	1.81	55	0	0	26	95	66	26	19	36	108
George, Chris	7	4	2.95	22	4	0	6	58	52	27	19	14	58
Hetrick, Kent	2	6	2.64	14	10	2	0	82	72	33	24	23	89
Ignasiak, Mike	2	4	2.72	9	9	1	0	56	52	21	17	12	66
Johnson, Chris	8	10	3.95	26	26	0	0	130	137	66	57	42	99
Krippner, Curt	2	5	4.50	16	15	0	0	78	74	52	39	41	95
Perez, Leo	10	8	2.05	22	17	5	0	123	96	45	28	31	124
Peters, Dan	7	9	3.57	27	22	1	0	131	114	60	52	58	103
*Scarpetta, Dan	1	0	0.00	1	1	0	0	8	1	0	0	0	10
Sparks, Steve	9	13	3.79	25	24	5	0	164	162	80	69	51	96
Uribe, Juan	5	1	2.75	28	2	0	1	69	63	31	21	32	68
Voit, Dave	1	1	1.93	6	0	0	0	14	12	7	3	6	15
Wahl, Tim	4	0	2.93	41	0	0	4	80	75	35	26	25	42
*Whitlock, Mike	5	4	2.85	40	6	1	6	88	86	39	28	46	61

BURLINGTON

BATTING	AVG	G	AB	R	H	2B	3B	HR	RBI	BB	SO	SB
Berg, Rick, 3b-c	.195	47	113	17	22	3	0	0	5	23	21	0
Bohlke, Scott, of	.240	73	217	19	52	12	3	4	23	13	36	6
#Casarotti, Rich, 2b	.280	95	361	48	101	23	1	9	53	30	66	11
Champion, Brian, 3b	.240	113	408	57	98	24	0	11	52	41	95	1

League Champions

(Playoff Champions, Where Applicable)

1988—Cedar Rapids	1974—Danville	1960—Waterloo
1987—Kenosha	1973—Wis. Rapids	1959—Waterloo
1986—Waterloo	1972—Appleton	1958—Waterloo
1985—Kenosha	1971—Quad City	1957—Decatur
1984—Appleton	1970—Quincy	1956—Paris
1983—Appleton	1969—Appleton	1955—Dubuque
1982—Appleton	1968—Quad City	1954—Danville
1981—Wausau	1967—Appleton	1953—Decatur
1980—Waterloo	1966—Fox Cities	1952—Decatur
1979—Quad City	1965—Burlington	1951—Danville
1978—Appleton	1964—Fox Cities	1950—Centralia
1977—Burlington	1963—Clinton	1949—Paducah
1976—Waterloo	1962—Dubuque	1948—West Franfort
1975—Waterloo	1961—Quincy	1947—Belleville

	AVG	G	AB	R	H	2B	3B	HR	RBI	BB	SO	SB
*Clark, Jeff, of	.257	11	35	3	9	0	0	0	3	2	6	4
Deak, Brian, c	.246	119	345	58	85	19	1	20	59	79	130	3
Frost, Jerald, ss	.216	119	393	47	85	13	4	0	26	25	97	15
Glass, Steve, inf-of	.250	119	376	41	94	18	1	3	33	40	53	10
#Grilione, Dave, of	.156	28	45	5	7	1	0	2	4	5	15	0
*Holcomb, Ted, 2b	.322	31	121	20	39	5	0	0	8	8	13	3
Hunter, Brian, 1b	.259	117	417	58	108	17	0	22	71	45	90	7
Jones-Pointer, Carl, of ..	.167	81	240	25	40	10	0	6	27	22	81	6
*Martin, Al, of	.279	123	480	69	134	21	3	7	42	30	88	40
Mendoza, Jesus, 1b	.300	22	70	9	21	1	0	2	10	7	15	2
*Mitchell, John, of-1b ...	.225	116	382	46	86	22	1	13	50	38	82	2
Perez, Eduardo, c	.231	64	186	14	43	8	0	4	19	10	33	1
Robinson, Lynn, of	.168	46	95	12	16	3	0	0	7	8	29	5
*Ross, Sean, dh	.306	31	121	31	37	7	2	0	9	9	21	9
*Tomberlin, Andy, of	.343	43	134	24	46	7	3	3	17	22	33	7

PITCHING	W	L	ERA	G	GS	CG	SV	IP	H	R	ER	BB	SO
*Cuesta, Jaime	10	7	4.45	36	12	3	2	129	120	74	64	52	88
Cummings, Brian	5	14	5.11	26	24	6	0	137	154	93	78	64	83
Gourlay, Craig	0	6	6.75	10	9	0	0	45	55	36	34	26	19
Greene, Jeff	0	0	1.42	4	0	0	1	6	3	2	1	1	3
*Karasinski, Dave	5	9	4.09	33	20	3	0	141	156	82	64	50	107
Kurczewski, Tommy (13 Wat)	4	8	4.11	24	11	3	0	85	85	42	39	52	51
LeMasters, Jim	8	2	1.98	37	0	0	11	50	40	13	11	23	42
Maldonado, Johnny	0	2	7.66	11	0	0	0	22	25	21	19	20	16
Murphy, Brian	0	2	6.06	30	1	0	1	52	51	39	35	43	35
Nowlin, Jim	5	5	6.26	34	1	0	6	65	73	57	45	34	45
Scarborough, Stan	0	1	4.15	3	1	0	0	4	3	3	2	4	0
*Smith, Chad	2	5	4.67	31	9	0	0	87	93	58	45	53	46
*Stanton, Mike	11	5	3.62	30	23	1	0	154	154	86	62	69	161
Tilmon, Pat	8	5	3.37	18	18	4	0	118	102	54	44	35	101
Turner, Matt	1	3	6.55	7	6	0	0	34	43	27	25	16	26
*Williams, Walt	0	5	5.15	18	5	0	1	44	50	35	25	36	38
Ziem, Steve	2	2	4.18	16	0	0	0	32	28	21	15	17	21

CEDAR RAPIDS

BATTING	AVG	G	AB	R	H	2B	3B	HR	RBI	BB	SO	SB
Beeler, Pete, c	.242	101	364	39	88	15	0	11	51	31	75	3
Benavides, Freddy, ss ...	.223	88	314	38	70	9	2	1	32	35	75	18
Bishop, Jim, 3b	.240	65	221	35	53	13	0	3	32	37	47	2
*Brock, Norm, of	.291	39	151	15	44	7	1	1	18	17	22	6
Brune, Jim, c	.091	4	11	1	1	0	0	0	1	1	3	0
*Davis, Steve, of	.255	121	424	70	108	20	3	22	77	49	116	15
DeFrancesco, Tony, c ...	.258	28	93	10	24	2	1	2	12	9	14	0
Eastman, Doug, of	.277	90	278	37	77	10	3	4	28	24	36	14
Forney, Jeff, of	.282	135	493	75	139	27	1	12	75	81	108	29
*Jefferson, Reggie, 1b ...	.288	135	517	76	149	26	2	18	90	40	89	2
*Lombardozzi, Chris, 3b ..	.282	59	227	30	64	10	1	7	38	28	37	2
Lonigro, Greg, 2b-ss	.283	117	463	77	131	17	0	3	32	23	31	16
Malinak, Mike, of-dh	.256	109	394	41	101	24	4	14	50	12	97	1
Rush, Eddie, ss-3b	.245	79	208	25	51	6	0	0	13	35	35	6
#Sambo, Ramon, dh-2b ..	.253	139	565	101	143	14	3	1	33	78	116	98
Sapienza, Rich, c	.195	28	82	4	16	1	0	0	10	3	7	0
Sellner, Scott, 2b	.273	4	11	3	3	0	0	1	1	3	4	0

PITCHING	W	L	ERA	G	GS	CG	SV	IP	H	R	ER	BB	SO
Brusky, Brad	1	4	4.40	10	0	0	1	14	12	7	7	9	12
*Chavez, Sam	12	11	3.68	28	27	2	0	169	165	83	69	46	134
Colson, Bruce	1	3	3.17	30	2	0	1	54	44	28	19	23	31
Dodd, Bill	6	4	2.07	46	0	0	10	78	50	19	18	30	103
*Henry, Butch	16	2	2.26	27	27	1	0	187	144	59	47	56	163
Hill, Milt	9	4	2.07	44	0	0	13	78	52	21	18	17	69
Jenkins, Mack	2	0	4.11	17	0	0	0	31	30	16	14	17	16
Moscrey, Mike	11	8	2.74	29	29	7	0	191	163	83	58	80	143
Nordstrom, Carl	0	0	1.96	13	0	0	0	18	16	6	4	7	16
Rodgers, Darrell	14	6	3.01	28	28	3	0	182	161	75	61	60	143
Rodriguez, Rosario	3	4	3.99	13	11	0	0	70	73	41	31	25	47
Scudder, Scott	7	3	2.02	16	15	1	0	102	61	30	23	41	126
*Simpson, Greg	5	4	2.47	44	1	0	10	69	49	25	19	29	48

CLINTON

BATTING	AVG	G	AB	R	H	2B	3B	HR	RBI	BB	SO	SB
Barry, John, ss-3b	.167	24	72	5	12	2	0	0	6	4	15	0
Benoit, Dickens, of	.219	72	247	17	54	9	3	2	29	17	69	8
Carlson, Bill, 1b-dh	.268	128	463	68	124	25	2	11	57	37	66	15
Colbert, Craig, 3b-1b ...	.233	124	455	56	106	19	2	11	64	41	100	8
#Cooper, Jamie, of	.297	125	502	75	149	28	2	5	50	19	128	63
Ealy, Tom, of	.284	72	225	27	64	13	3	2	27	18	49	4
Fernandez, Danny, c	.226	23	53	2	12	1	0	0	3	6	15	2
Goins, Scott, 3b-of	.306	11	36	5	11	2	1	0	4	0	6	1
Guerrero, Juan, 2b-of ...	.275	111	385	57	106	17	3	13	54	13	95	4
Ham, Mike, c	.165	46	115	14	19	3	1	0	13	15	23	4
Johnson, Erik, 2b-3b ...	.224	90	322	29	72	12	3	5	38	28	39	4
Michalak, Tony, 3b-2b ...	.237	92	338	37	80	11	1	0	30	27	28	8
Miller, Todd, of	.188	56	144	15	27	3	2	0	6	10	41	8
*Owens, Mark, c-dh	.262	129	424	63	111	21	2	12	68	99	81	8

	AVG	G	AB	R	H	2B	3B	HR	RBI	BB	SO	SB
*Ronson, Tod, of	.212	17	52	5	11	3	0	1	5	2	6	1
Santana, Andres, ss	.280	118	450	77	126	4	1	0	24	42	83	88
Vuz, John, dh-c	.235	5	17	1	4	0	0	0	1	0	4	0
Westbrooks, Elanis, of	.231	100	308	34	71	4	4	1	18	16	46	11

PITCHING	W	L	ERA	G	GS	CG	SV	IP	H	R	ER	BB	SO
Beck, Rod	12	7	3.00	28	23	5	0	177	177	68	59	27	123
Braukmiller, Ken	0	1	3.97	7	1	0	0	11	11	6	5	5	4
Carter, Larry	2	4	3.10	12	7	0	0	49	48	20	17	14	32
*Connolly, Steve	4	5	1.38	41	1	0	10	65	49	12	10	11	53
Dewey, Mike	10	4	1.43	37	7	1	7	119	95	36	19	14	76
Garcia, Longo	1	2	5.46	9	4	0	0	30	36	19	18	19	25
Hostetler, Tom	11	3	2.54	17	17	4	0	120	85	39	34	37	118
Johnson, Dom	4	8	4.63	24	18	1	0	101	87	63	52	85	67
Lienhard, Steve	12	7	2.93	27	27	6	0	181	169	77	59	36	114
Lucero, Robert	0	3	3.19	13	0	0	0	31	30	14	11	27	19
Meier, Kevin	7	0	1.44	8	8	2	0	56	51	12	9	11	42
*Nelson, Scott	9	9	5.02	23	23	4	0	118	117	74	66	74	90
Phillips, Lonnie	4	6	2.74	35	3	0	6	82	72	30	25	35	70
*Terrill, Jimmy	2	2	1.73	39	1	0	8	62	48	20	12	17	51
Villa, Mike	0	1	2.16	9	0	0	4	8	7	8	2	5	9

KENOSHA

BATTING	AVG	G	AB	R	H	2B	3B	HR	RBI	BB	SO	SB
*Alm, Rick, of	.125	11	24	1	3	0	0	0	3	2	8	0
Brown, Jarvis, of	.294	138	531	108	156	25	7	7	45	71	89	72
*Bruett, J.T., of	.200	3	10	2	2	0	0	0	0	3	0	1
Capellan, Carlos, 2b-of	.244	113	414	48	101	8	2	0	34	10	30	18
Ericson, Mark, dh-c	.268	44	149	13	40	7	0	1	25	7	23	0
Gilbert, Shawn, ss	.279	108	402	80	112	21	2	3	44	63	61	49
*Harter, Andy, 1b	.104	15	48	2	5	0	0	0	3	4	16	0
Jacas, Dave, of	.246	133	495	81	122	24	6	5	77	50	80	49
*Jenny, Shane, 1b-of	.147	43	116	13	17	4	0	1	11	19	40	0
Lexa, Mike, 2b-3b	.255	64	196	28	50	8	1	1	25	25	34	2
Martin, Chris, 1b	.213	26	75	3	16	6	0	0	8	8	20	0
Marzan, Jose, 1b	.267	53	172	42	46	10	1	4	26	38	20	1
Pittman, Doug, c-dh	.167	19	66	7	11	1	0	1	5	11	19	0
*Resetar, Gary, dh-c	.276	40	134	12	37	2	0	0	15	7	16	3
Roskom, Bryan, 2b-ss	.080	10	25	5	2	2	0	0	2	1	6	0
Smith, David, of	.221	120	390	53	86	13	2	2	36	36	74	20
Tatarian, Dean, ss	.208	32	77	11	16	1	0	0	7	14	13	1
Tinkey, Bob, 1b-3b	.241	109	361	40	87	22	2	1	50	54	66	3
Valdez, Frank, 3b	.278	115	424	49	118	29	2	8	60	24	95	25
Webster, Lenny, c-dh	.288	129	465	82	134	23	2	11	87	71	47	3

PITCHING	W	L	ERA	G	GS	CG	SV	IP	H	R	ER	BB	SO
Ard, Johnny	3	0	1.05	4	3	1	0	26	14	3	3	4	16
Bangtson, Pat	17	5	2.87	27	27	3	0	179	171	75	57	69	120
Banks, Willie	10	10	3.73	24	24	0	0	125	109	73	52	107	113
Buzzard, Buddy	1	2	2.33	4	3	0	1	19	15	10	5	9	13
Delkus, Pete	4	2	0.26	61	0	0	33	68	43	13	2	13	57
*Franchi, Kevin	0	0	36.00	3	0	0	0	2	8	8	8	4	4
Gilles, Tom	6	3	3.31	21	11	1	1	90	77	40	33	15	41
Kryzanowski, Rusty	5	3	3.03	43	0	0	4	86	68	35	29	34	59
Marten, Tom	7	4	4.31	22	15	1	0	94	104	54	45	31	40
Meyer, Basil	5	4	2.40	45	3	0	7	79	60	31	21	31	69
*Muh, Steve	2	1	3.72	4	3	0	0	19	14	8	8	13	22
Perez, Alex	0	0	5.14	4	0	0	0	7	11	4	4	5	1
Redding, Mike	6	7	4.28	15	15	4	0	97	89	55	46	24	55
*Stowell, Steve	3	8	5.00	41	12	1	1	90	88	57	50	36	74
Swanson, Chad	6	2	2.74	41	2	0	1	82	75	31	25	31	62
White, Fred	6	8	3.36	26	22	1	0	145	141	69	54	67	82

MADISON

BATTING	AVG	G	AB	R	H	2B	3B	HR	RBI	BB	SO	SB
Britt, Pat, c	.368	5	19	3	7	5	0	0	4	1	5	1
Brosius, Scott, ss-3b	.304	132	504	82	153	28	2	9	58	56	67	13
Canseco, Ozzie, of	.273	99	359	63	98	17	7	12	68	49	84	15
Gavin, Dave, of	.244	106	353	51	86	19	6	9	45	19	90	5
#Gust, Chris, of-2b	.230	94	257	39	59	7	0	0	12	40	31	26
Hale, DeMarlo, 1b-of	.269	66	234	31	63	10	3	2	28	27	39	12
Hanker, Fred, 1b	.251	120	446	43	112	20	1	5	50	22	48	6
*Holland, Troy, dh	.250	2	4	1	1	0	0	0	1	0	1	0
Lewis, Darren, of	.246	60	199	38	49	4	1	0	11	46	37	21
Masters, Frank, c	.210	93	262	22	55	7	0	4	29	33	49	2
Parry, Bob, of	.237	122	451	48	107	27	2	5	53	27	64	6
Reiser, Jamie, ss-2b	.278	83	309	44	86	14	2	2	34	29	44	10
*Reyna, Dion, 1b-dh	.226	17	53	7	12	0	0	0	5	3	13	1
Reynolds, Bill, c	.176	54	153	17	27	6	0	5	17	19	49	0
Robinson, Marteese, 2b	.251	125	499	59	125	21	1	8	49	25	65	17
*Ryser, Mike, c	.212	36	104	12	22	2	0	1	10	15	31	0
Siuda, Matt, 3b-ss	.220	110	382	43	84	11	1	4	40	41	37	2
*Veras, Camilo, dh-of	.188	20	64	8	12	2	1	2	8	6	19	1

PITCHING	W	L	ERA	G	GS	CG	SV	IP	H	R	ER	BB	SO
Alexander, Rob	4	4	3.10	32	2	1	3	87	80	40	30	19	52
Arola, Bruce	0	3	6.13	19	0	0	2	40	49	30	27	18	17

BATTING

R—Jarvis Brown, Kenosha 108
H—Jarvis Brown, Kenosha 156
TB—Ray Lankford, Springfield 242
2B—Terry Shumpert, Appleton 37
3B—Ray Lankford, Springfield 16
HR—Brian Hunter, Burlington 22
　—Steve Davis, Cedar Rapids 22
RBI—Reggie Jefferson, Cedar Rapids 89
GWRBI—Lenny Webster, Kenosha 13
　—Steve Davis, Cedar Rapids 13
SH—Gerry Barragan, Beloit 15
SF—Mark Owens, Clinton 13
　—Dave Jacas, Kenosha..................13
BB—Mark Owens, Clinton 99
IBB—Mark Maksudian, South Bend 9
HBP—Dave Jacas, Kenosha..................15
SO—Troy Ricker, Rockford..................139
SB—Ramon Sambo, Cedar Rapids 98
CS—Andres Santana, Clinton 23
Slg. Pct.—Steve Davis, Cedar Rapids 472
OB Pct.—Mike Maksudian, South Bend 404

PITCHING

G—Pete Delkus, Kenosha 61
GS—Mike Moscrey, Cedar Rapids 29
CG—Tommy Kramer, Waterloo 9
ShO—Five tied at..................3
Sv—Pete Delkus, Kenosha..................33
W—Pat Bangston, Kenosha 17
L—Daryl Green, Quad-City 15
IP—Tommy Kramer, Waterloo 199
H—Curt Hasler, South Bend 206
R—Mike McGuire, Wausau..................102
HR—Kurt Stange, Wausau..................16
　—Ed Caballero, Peoria..................16
BB—Willie Banks, Kenosha..................107
HB—Curt Hasler, South Bend 19
SO—Tom Gordon, Appleton 172
WP—Scott Nelson, Clinton..................27
Bk—Bill Melvin, Peoria 13
　—Frank Potestio, Springfield 13

	W	L	ERA	G	GS	CG	SV	IP	H	R	ER	BB	SO
Baez, Pedro	7	9	2.68	32	19	4	2	141	115	50	42	51	81
Cabrera, Nasusel	3	5	4.99	26	7	0	0	74	82	50	41	28	24
Caraballo, Felix	1	1	7.57	7	6	0	0	27	38	27	23	9	15
Carroll, Jim	1	6	6.13	28	0	0	6	40	33	32	27	29	30
*Chenevey, Jim	11	7	3.36	28	28	6	0	177	156	84	66	84	167
Cundari, Phil	2	6	5.68	19	5	0	0	52	74	45	33	14	37
Dye, Steve	2	3	3.68	20	0	0	5	22	18	13	9	8	8
*Ferguson, Greg	1	1	3.26	11	5	0	0	39	37	15	14	16	34
Garcia, Apolinar	2	4	8.10	10	7	0	0	37	49	39	33	16	17
Schock, Will	10	6	2.71	17	17	3	0	123	96	48	37	37	75
Stocker, Bob	4	8	3.86	38	5	0	10	79	74	42	34	25	61
*Veilleux, Brian	5	6	2.92	16	13	4	0	96	83	41	31	29	56
*Wernig, Pat	11	6	3.02	26	26	5	0	176	168	78	59	41	100

PEORIA

BATTING	AVG	G	AB	R	H	2B	3B	HR	RBI	BB	SO	SB
Andrade, Jose, c	.163	29	80	5	13	3	0	0	3	7	28	0
Arrington, Warren, of	.252	133	488	73	123	20	11	2	41	41	113	47
Bell, Lenny, 3b-1b	.245	64	245	22	60	9	1	1	19	12	67	2
#Bernstine, Pookie, of-dh	.250	63	204	19	51	8	3	0	22	12	30	12
Boswell, Mike, dh-inf	.175	72	200	17	35	7	1	3	18	16	61	4
Canan, Dick, 3b	.287	63	230	32	66	12	1	0	35	19	45	0
Crockett, Rusty, ss-of	.242	63	240	33	58	3	1	1	30	13	32	18
Espinal, Sergio, 2b	.209	53	163	20	34	7	1	3	17	22	57	4
#Hannon, Phil, of	.237	139	562	61	133	21	4	1	49	27	98	34
Hill, Steve, 2b	.208	47	168	15	35	7	1	1	15	15	26	9
*LaPenta, Jerry, dh-1b	.225	79	218	27	49	8	0	4	26	38	47	5
*Paulino, Elvin, 1b	.233	122	404	44	94	19	5	2	40	48	72	3
Rivero, Marty, ss-3b	.209	101	374	36	78	14	1	5	30	15	79	4
Rosario, Jossy, 2b-ss	.188	56	181	12	34	5	0	0	15	11	24	3
*Strickland, Bob, dh	.236	26	72	8	17	2	2	2	11	9	23	1
Tucker, Horace, of	.200	6	10	0	2	0	0	0	0	0	4	0
*Wilkins, Rick, c	.243	137	490	54	119	30	1	8	63	67	110	4
*Williams, Eddie, of	.223	111	323	43	72	12	1	0	24	35	81	23

PITCHING	W	L	ERA	G	GS	CG	SV	IP	H	R	ER	BB	SO
Aspray, Mike	8	14	2.80	25	24	7	0	180	149	73	56	45	116
Caballero, Ed	9	12	3.73	28	28	3	0	166	155	82	69	50	158
Castillo, Frank	6	1	0.71	9	8	2	0	51	25	5	4	10	58
Gardner, John	1	0	5.65	7	1	0	0	14	13	10	9	11	18
Green, John	0	1	2.18	13	0	0	0	21	21	9	5	6	20
*Hamilton, Carl	0	1	3.57	4	4	0	0	18	22	7	7	7	10
Kallevig, Greg	11	9	1.44	29	18	8	0	175	132	38	28	29	80

	W	L	ERA	G	GS	CG	SV	IP	H	R	ER	BB	SO
Massicotte, Jeff	8	12	5.40	41	7	0	1	80	84	66	48	51	74
Matas, Jim	3	0	0.50	3	3	0	0	18	8	1	1	9	19
Melvin, Bill	8	9	3.54	28	27	3	0	181	151	80	71	70	134
*North, Mark	2	0	2.95	32	3	0	0	73	67	40	24	30	68
Robinson, Brett	9	6	3.64	30	16	0	0	131	135	66	53	48	94
*Rodriguez, Gabby	2	2	1.51	53	0	0	5	83	57	23	14	31	62
Sanderson, Scott	0	0	0.00	1	1	0	0	5	4	1	0	0	3
Schulmeister, Dean	0	0	7.71	1	0	0	0	2	3	2	2	2	0
Zarranz, Fernando	3	3	1.15	46	0	0	21	55	42	10	7	9	59

QUAD CITY

BATTING	AVG	G	AB	R	H	2B	3B	HR	RBI	BB	SO	SB
Alfonzo, Edgar, 2b	.204	102	406	36	83	12	2	2	36	23	58	5
Aylward, Jim, 1b	.262	57	202	20	53	9	1	2	26	28	14	2
Baca, Mark, of	.276	23	76	9	21	3	0	0	6	6	9	1
Bell, Bobby, c	.136	9	22	4	3	0	0	0	2	9	6	2
Carr, Terence, of	.156	63	179	31	28	3	0	1	5	34	51	17
Childress, Scott, 3b-of	.222	7	18	4	4	1	0	0	1	2	4	0
#Dela Rosa, Cesar, ss-3b	.221	112	384	31	85	7	3	0	28	33	105	17
Flora, Kevin, ss	.217	48	152	19	33	3	4	0	15	18	33	5
*Gay, Jeff, c	.238	19	63	8	15	1	0	0	6	4	12	2
Giles, Troy, of	.120	9	25	3	3	0	0	0	1	4	13	1
Grant, Kenny, inf-of	.242	45	132	16	32	6	0	0	10	26	32	2
Graves, Chris, of	.192	115	359	45	69	6	3	6	31	50	106	28
Kirwin, Steve, of	.333	5	12	2	4	0	0	0	0	5	0	1
*Lee, Wiley, dh-2b	.302	102	348	57	105	17	3	2	46	47	63	53
Lung, Rodney, c	.169	26	89	7	15	1	0	2	4	7	30	1
Mateo, Hoascar, c	.000	2	8	0	0	0	0	0	0	1	3	0
Molina, Mario, 2b	.236	96	309	18	73	12	0	2	31	22	64	2
*Musolino, Mike, c	.226	53	177	20	40	8	2	4	19	22	27	1
Rasmus, Tony, 2b-1b	.244	13	41	4	10	3	0	1	4	1	11	4
Robinson, Bill, of-dh	.249	117	402	45	100	16	3	6	43	46	121	8
*Rodriguez, Edgar, c	.197	39	137	10	27	6	2	0	10	15	24	1
#Romero, Charlie, of	.253	110	392	45	99	11	2	0	36	32	76	32
Rose, Bob, 3b	.284	135	483	75	137	23	3	13	78	78	92	14
Threadgill, Chris, of	.218	32	110	8	24	1	1	0	9	16	38	8

PITCHING	W	L	ERA	G	GS	CG	SV	IP	H	R	ER	BB	SO
Batista, Miguel	0	1	6.59	7	0	0	0	14	10	12	10	11	11
Buckles, Gary	14	3	3.16	46	0	0	6	80	66	32	28	29	109
Butcher, Mike	0	0	4.50	3	0	0	0	6	6	3	3	4	7
*Dunn, Steve	5	8	3.66	33	19	3	1	130	116	67	53	49	92
Green, Daryl	5	15	3.19	28	28	3	0	155	154	89	55	69	121
Hernandez, Roberto	9	10	3.17	24	24	6	0	165	157	70	58	48	114
Holdridge, Dave	6	12	3.87	28	28	0	0	154	151	92	66	79	110
Lewis, Scott	1	2	4.64	3	3	1	0	21	19	12	11	5	20
McKinnis, Tim	1	2	3.77	39	0	0	0	62	64	35	26	22	49
Mutz, Frank	2	2	3.05	23	0	0	1	41	42	24	14	9	32
Pardo, Larry	0	1	2.56	26	1	0	1	56	49	31	16	33	49
Randolph, Scott	1	1	3.79	7	3	0	0	19	20	12	8	15	9
*Townsend, Jim	4	6	2.48	40	6	0	2	80	75	45	22	37	52
Vann, Brandy	10	11	3.06	27	27	4	0	174	142	73	59	81	146
Wassenaar, Rob	2	5	3.14	48	0	0	11	49	47	24	17	14	50

ROCKFORD

BATTING	AVG	G	AB	R	H	2B	3B	HR	RBI	BB	SO	SB
#Caceras, Edgar, 2b	.265	36	117	25	31	2	0	0	8	12	12	13
Cianfrocco, Archie, 3b	.253	126	455	54	115	34	0	15	66	26	98	6
Colbrunn, Greg, c-dh	.266	115	417	55	111	18	2	7	46	22	60	5
*DeShields, Delino, ss	.252	129	460	97	116	26	6	12	46	95	110	59
*Faulk, Jim, of-dh	.257	113	366	55	94	19	2	6	46	40	69	28
Frye, Paul, of-dh	.280	106	379	49	106	20	1	13	69	30	103	5
#Hernandez, Cesar, of	.246	117	411	71	101	20	4	19	60	25	109	28
Leary, Rob, c	.233	60	176	19	41	7	0	4	16	19	37	1
*Mann, Scott, dh	.239	50	155	27	37	8	1	4	31	41	18	1
Mello, John, inf	.244	109	393	51	96	17	3	10	57	30	82	10
Mitchell, Jorge, of	.185	29	27	4	5	0	0	0	0	2	9	0
#Paredes, Jesus, 2b	.176	21	51	4	9	0	0	0	5	7	6	10
*Pearse, Steve, 2b	.222	20	54	6	12	4	0	0	1	0	5	1
*Penn, Trevor, 1b	.244	130	426	47	104	16	2	5	38	33	51	8
*Piechowski, Tim, of	.133	17	45	5	6	1	0	1	6	4	10	1
Ricker, Troy, of	.240	133	450	63	108	20	5	16	66	27	140	31
Schueler, Russ, 2b-3b	.309	44	136	27	42	4	1	1	18	23	25	15
Shephard, Kelvin, of	.189	42	111	17	21	3	1	1	11	13	32	8
Viltz, Corey, of	.128	13	39	6	5	2	0	0	0	13	17	4

PITCHING	W	L	ERA	G	GS	CG	SV	IP	H	R	ER	BB	SO
Brito, Mario	13	8	3.00	27	27	7	0	186	161	83	62	52	144
Bromby, Scott	4	4	2.63	34	0	0	7	48	51	16	14	9	40
Carter, Jeff	11	5	2.77	39	11	1	3	107	100	38	33	35	91
*Clark, Dave	2	4	4.85	19	0	0	0	30	34	19	16	25	22
Farmer, Howard	15	7	2.51	27	25	8	0	194	153	70	54	58	145
Heiderscheit, Pat	1	0	1.29	1	1	0	0	7	9	1	1	2	4
Kerrigan, Rob	1	2	1.54	15	0	0	5	35	27	8	6	10	20
Lariviere, Chris	0	1	5.06	7	1	0	0	16	15	9	9	8	15
*Marchok, Chris	2	0	3.01	33	3	0	6	69	57	31	23	28	43
*Marino, John	2	1	1.32	8	0	0	0	14	8	2	2	12	12

	W	L	ERA	G	GS	CG	SV	IP	H	R	ER	BB	SO
Minchey, Nate	11	12	4.79	28	27	0	0	150	148	93	80	87	63
Peters, Tim	5	2	0.61	42	0	0	22	59	32	9	4	16	57
*Pollack, Chris	6	4	2.97	20	20	0	0	121	105	58	40	41	101
Rojas, Mel	6	4	2.45	12	12	3	0	73	52	30	20	29	72
Sheary, Kevin	0	1	4.50	19	2	0	0	42	51	26	21	20	43
Shiflett, Matt	5	3	5.46	13	11	0	0	59	57	39	36	37	50
Willis, Kent	1	0	4.43	10	0	0	0	20	22	12	10	8	11

SOUTH BEND

BATTING	AVG	G	AB	R	H	2B	3B	HR	RBI	BB	SO	SB
Adames, Hernan, 2b	.000	2	1	0	0	0	0	0	0	0	0	0
*Allen, Larry, 1b	.228	98	342	37	78	15	0	5	39	27	50	5
Alvarez, Clemente, c	.073	15	41	0	3	0	0	0	1	3	19	0
Bernhardt, Cesar, of-2b ..	.282	124	482	47	136	17	2	1	51	16	32	26
Brown, Kurt, c	.234	44	141	15	33	4	3	1	12	22	25	4
Campbell, Darrin, c	.231	4	13	1	3	1	0	0	0	0	4	0
Cruz, Bernardo, ss	.252	108	377	46	95	7	3	1	35	25	74	52
*Gonzalez, Cliff, of	.250	10	28	5	7	0	0	0	5	2	5	0
Harris, Frank, c	.219	46	146	7	32	3	0	0	15	8	25	1
Hosey, Dwayne, of	.228	95	311	53	71	11	0	2	24	28	55	36
*Maksudian, Mike, 1b-c ..	.303	102	366	51	111	26	3	4	50	60	59	5
McCray, Rod, of	.212	107	306	48	65	10	2	1	24	56	72	55
Murdock, Kevin, c	.193	20	57	7	11	3	1	1	7	9	14	0
Ocasio, Javier, 2b-ss	.272	123	445	65	121	13	2	0	49	55	58	21
Payton, Ray, of-dh	.267	122	480	63	128	29	5	9	69	27	108	12
*Pledger, Kinnis, of	.202	107	371	42	75	13	4	3	34	39	106	19
Sedar, Ed, 1b	.000	4	10	0	0	0	0	0	0	2	7	0
Smith, Ed, 3b	.232	130	462	51	107	14	1	3	46	51	87	5
#Thompson, Rob, c	.125	4	8	0	1	0	0	0	0	0	2	0
#Valera, Wilson, inf	.237	69	198	30	47	7	0	2	21	37	50	5
Warren, Randy, of	.225	13	40	6	9	1	1	1	8	5	11	0

PITCHING	W	L	ERA	G	GS	CG	SV	IP	H	R	ER	BB	SO
Carey, Bill	4	4	5.40	17	12	0	0	65	85	48	39	35	46
Conde, Argenis	3	6	2.99	14	12	1	0	84	78	32	28	32	44
Dela Cruz, Carlos	2	8	6.14	13	12	1	0	63	73	51	43	37	40
*Diaz, Victor	0	3	5.13	22	0	0	1	33	34	20	19	14	42
Felden, Keith	0	1	4.70	17	0	0	1	23	28	16	12	14	14
Girouard, Mike	6	6	4.10	36	9	1	3	108	105	56	49	39	86
Gonzalez, Julian	3	2	2.27	45	0	0	5	71	53	26	18	28	62
Hasler, Curt	7	11	3.44	26	26	6	0	186	206	98	71	27	104
Hudek, John	7	2	1.98	26	0	0	8	55	45	19	12	21	35
Kennedy, Bo	10	8	3.48	27	27	5	0	176	158	81	68	71	109
*Resnikoff, Rob	5	4	2.25	50	1	0	8	56	56	24	14	18	31
Robinson, Randy	6	5	3.13	41	4	1	3	83	76	37	29	22	53
Schrenk, Steve	3	7	5.00	21	18	1	0	90	95	63	50	37	58
*Takach, Dave	0	0	0.00	3	0	0	0	6	4	0	0	2	3
*Tortorice, Mark	3	14	5.70	29	19	3	0	128	150	96	81	44	89

SPRINGFIELD

BATTING	AVG	G	AB	R	H	2B	3B	HR	RBI	BB	SO	SB
#Abreu, Frank, ss	.209	116	359	44	75	10	2	1	42	37	58	13
#Alvarez, Carmelo, ss ...	.100	4	10	0	1	0	0	0	0	3	2	1
*Brewer, Rodney, 1b	.298	133	457	57	136	25	2	8	64	63	52	6
*Fulton, Ed, c	.267	110	374	46	100	20	6	7	55	44	69	0
Gilkey, Bernard, of	.244	125	491	84	120	18	7	6	36	65	53	56
Gonzalez, Orlando, ss ...	.071	6	14	1	1	0	0	0	0	0	2	0
Hall, Joe, 3b	.000	1	1	0	0	0	0	0	0	0	1	0
#Jeffers, Steve, inf	.182	8	11	1	2	0	0	0	0	3	2	0
Johnson, Chuck, of	.292	133	528	65	154	25	5	5	62	27	74	26
*Lankford, Ray, of	.284	135	532	90	151	26	16	11	66	60	92	33
Lara, Crucito, ss	.212	10	33	4	7	1	0	0	2	0	6	0
*Meyer, Steve, dh	.220	21	59	5	13	3	0	1	7	4	6	0
Murphy, John, c	.200	4	5	0	1	0	0	0	0	1	1	0
Nichols, Scott, c	.217	73	184	25	40	6	1	3	13	24	43	5
Ojea, Alex, 2b	.234	135	457	56	107	17	3	5	54	61	92	5
Payton, Dave, dh-3b ...	.254	116	389	57	99	11	1	12	57	55	58	5
Raziano, Scott, 3b	.262	117	405	64	106	15	0	15	60	58	49	1
Roberts, Norm, of-dh ...	.277	66	206	42	57	8	5	9	29	36	60	8
*Thoutsis, Paul, dh-of ...	.272	28	92	5	25	3	0	0	12	8	10	0

PITCHING	W	L	ERA	G	GS	CG	SV	IP	H	R	ER	BB	SO
*Becker, Greg	3	1	1.36	58	0	0	25	66	39	11	10	26	68
Bivens, Bill	11	5	3.79	24	24	3	0	140	112	72	59	55	112
*Epple, Tom	0	2	2.20	3	3	0	0	16	14	7	4	5	17
Gibbs, Jim	3	3	3.91	27	0	0	0	78	89	45	34	17	44
*Glisson, Rob	8	8	3.66	34	21	2	1	138	146	70	56	44	76
Grater, Mark	7	2	1.78	53	0	0	11	81	60	23	16	27	66
Hathaway, Shawn	6	4	2.09	45	0	0	5	82	83	32	19	18	65
Henry, Mike	5	4	4.91	23	10	0	0	70	71	46	38	26	44
Hernandez, Jeremy	12	6	3.54	24	24	3	0	147	133	73	58	34	97
Kisten, Dale	0	0	0.00	1	0	0	0	0	0	0	0	1	0
Potestio, Frank	14	10	2.58	27	27	7	0	182	167	67	52	52	123
*Sala, Dave	2	2	3.06	9	9	0	0	32	39	23	11	21	19
Sudo, Bob	10	9	3.15	24	20	4	0	149	163	58	52	36	77
Taylor, Andy	0	2	5.76	20	1	0	0	30	37	21	19	17	24

WATERLOO

BATTING	AVG	G	AB	R	H	2B	3B	HR	RBI	BB	SO	SB
Arias, Pedro, 3b	.077	5	13	1	1	0	0	0	0	0	4	0
*Baron, Sean, 1b	.217	54	166	25	36	8	0	7	26	32	51	0
Bautista, Ramon, ss	.246	123	452	72	111	14	5	6	38	62	98	23
Baxter, Jim, c	.205	66	190	18	39	5	1	1	13	30	76	0
Belle, Joey, of	.250	9	28	2	7	1	0	1	2	1	9	0
Bennett, Keith, inf	.177	31	79	17	14	5	1	0	7	14	22	6
Butler, Todd, 2b	.227	48	128	18	29	5	0	0	12	15	24	10
Carter, Fred, of	.224	43	143	12	32	9	0	5	18	9	43	0
#Colavito, Steve, of	.155	34	97	10	15	1	0	0	8	9	28	0
Falkner, Rick, of	.273	58	216	30	59	10	1	2	28	23	30	2
Ferretti, Sam, 2b-ss	.105	15	38	2	4	1	0	0	2	5	8	2
Gamba, T.J., of-inf	.258	90	271	38	70	12	5	4	38	29	53	2
Isaacson, Chris, c	.231	19	52	11	12	0	0	4	9	15	23	0
*Johnson, Scott, dh-of	.303	69	195	27	59	11	1	9	29	27	38	0
*Khoury, Scott, dh-of	.290	76	238	37	69	17	4	17	59	39	43	3
Kuld, Pete, c	.223	75	242	31	54	6	1	10	28	20	63	2
Liriano, Julio, of	.239	73	226	23	54	12	1	3	25	7	56	5
Mackie, Scott, of	.241	61	158	22	38	3	0	4	23	20	62	6
McBride, Ivan, 2b-of	.239	31	71	7	17	3	0	0	2	4	10	3
Narleski, Bill, 3b	.247	104	372	47	92	16	1	4	41	50	40	12
*Neel, Troy, 1b	.290	91	331	49	96	20	1	8	57	38	76	0
Pike, Mark, of	.258	132	539	94	139	22	5	4	51	39	109	34
Rogers, Robby, 2b-3b	.249	95	289	37	72	20	2	3	33	46	78	1
Seifert, Keith, 1b-of	.135	21	52	4	7	2	0	0	3	4	17	0

PITCHING	W	L	ERA	G	GS	CG	SV	IP	H	R	ER	BB	SO
Bluhm, Bill	0	1	4.35	7	0	0	1	10	9	5	5	5	10
Casano, Andy	9	8	5.22	33	8	2	1	112	116	76	65	62	86
Compres, Fidel	5	5	4.41	29	3	0	2	67	69	41	33	31	65
Garza, Willie	1	1	3.38	8	1	0	0	16	13	8	6	12	15
*Halle, Andy	0	2	1.86	6	2	0	0	19	12	6	4	7	9
King, Kenny	0	0	4.91	2	0	0	0	4	4	2	2	0	3
Kramer, Tommy	14	7	2.54	27	27	9	0	199	173	70	56	60	152
McBride, Ivan	0	0	7.50	6	0	0	0	12	12	10	10	8	5
McMurtrie, Dan	2	4	2.45	10	6	1	0	44	37	17	12	15	23
Olin, Steve	3	0	1.37	29	0	0	15	39	26	7	6	14	48
*Ortiz, Angel	5	5	2.57	15	15	1	0	98	79	33	28	37	98
Piatt, Doug	2	1	2.21	26	0	0	12	37	33	18	9	11	40
Roscoe, Greg	5	3	3.11	13	13	1	0	81	88	38	28	21	63
Sanchez, Geraldo	10	5	2.54	18	14	5	0	110	97	35	31	31	66
Scaglione, Tony	12	7	3.08	25	25	5	0	167	141	69	57	52	138
Seanez, Rudy	6	6	4.69	22	22	1	0	113	98	69	59	68	93
Stitz, John	3	6	3.15	31	4	0	2	80	93	50	28	18	45

WAUSAU

BATTING	AVG	G	AB	R	H	2B	3B	HR	RBI	BB	SO	SB
Azar, Todd, of-3b	.288	114	371	46	107	20	2	4	54	33	36	1
Brock, Tom, of	.218	48	142	15	31	8	0	1	7	21	34	1
Carr, Chuck, of	.299	82	304	58	91	14	2	6	30	14	49	41
*Colston, Frank, c	.209	67	153	13	32	6	0	2	14	16	32	2
Gonzalez, Ruben, 1b-3b	.314	115	430	56	135	32	2	9	59	35	50	1
Haney, Todd, 2b	.281	132	452	66	127	23	2	7	52	56	54	35
Hoffman, John, c	.244	70	172	17	42	4	0	1	15	19	23	2
Hooper, Jeff, 1b-dh	.204	46	157	21	32	5	0	10	20	11	40	1
Howard, Chris, of	.241	61	187	20	45	10	1	7	20	18	60	1
*Keitges, Jeff, 1b	.234	71	256	22	60	14	0	7	38	16	62	0
*Kosco, Dru, of	.260	49	173	30	45	7	0	9	23	12	39	1
*McDonald, Mike, 3b-dh	.204	123	427	63	87	13	0	18	67	67	102	9
Patrick, Otis, 3b	.220	16	41	3	9	2	0	0	2	4	14	3
*Pritikin, Jim, of	.230	127	435	67	100	19	2	7	40	53	99	40
#Ramirez, Fausto, ss	.176	82	244	18	43	4	2	0	26	19	38	9
Razook, Mark, ss	.199	63	221	22	44	4	2	2	22	14	44	6
Sisney, Lorenzo, c	.196	20	46	5	9	1	0	2	4	4	17	0
Williams, Ray, of	.226	100	323	53	73	11	2	5	35	48	89	31
Woods, Tony, inf	.231	21	65	8	15	6	0	0	1	10	13	2

PITCHING	W	L	ERA	G	GS	CG	SV	IP	H	R	ER	BB	SO
Baldwin, Brian	1	3	8.27	19	4	0	2	37	52	42	34	15	16
Beiras, Mike	2	2	6.75	9	1	0	0	19	26	15	14	13	7
Bieksha, Steve	7	8	5.42	25	21	2	0	116	134	82	70	43	50
*Burlingame, Greg	6	8	3.51	28	19	4	0	131	138	74	51	32	72
*Burnau, Ben	4	3	3.60	11	10	3	0	70	69	32	28	22	44
Collins, Tim	1	1	9.00	13	2	0	0	15	18	17	15	20	14
Colston, Frank	0	0	3.38	5	0	0	0	5	4	2	2	4	4
Doll, Chris	1	3	6.81	12	9	0	0	40	39	39	30	32	34
*Frink, Keith	2	8	5.19	58	1	0	1	118	128	89	68	85	104
Gardiner, Mike	2	1	3.16	11	6	0	1	31	31	16	11	13	24
Goff, Mike	4	6	4.30	51	0	0	16	67	65	36	32	40	67
Hayes, Todd	1	2	4.50	7	0	0	0	16	12	11	8	13	9
McGuire, Mike	2	13	5.31	29	20	0	0	119	119	102	70	106	108
Pifer, Gary	0	5	7.07	7	7	0	0	36	52	33	28	16	19
Stange, Kurt	7	12	3.67	25	25	5	0	157	136	79	64	60	101
Stoerck, Scott	4	3	3.88	29	0	0	0	51	62	31	22	31	33
*Webb, Charlie	4	4	4.43	21	14	0	0	87	100	58	43	40	54
Webster, Rudy	4	6	5.12	41	1	0	5	84	92	58	48	51	50

In a pitchers' year, the Rainbows pitch best

By GENE SAPAKOFF

A baseball axiom says good pitching and good defense will take a team to more than its share of victories, provided Pee Wee Herman isn't batting cleanup.

The Charleston (S.C.) Rainbows did better than pitch well and field splendidly in 1988. They established a South Atlantic League ERA record (2.48), and tied the league record for fielding percentage (.969). Predictably, the Rainbows also broke the club record for wins, finished with the SAL's best overall record (85-53) and won the Southern Division second-half title.

The Rainbows were led by a starting pitching staff that included Darrin Reichle (two no-hitters, 10-3, 2.83), Mike Myers (15-4, 2.51), Omar Olivares (13-6, 2.23) and Rafael Valdez (11-4, 2.25).

Derek Bell
... batting champion

And Charleston wasn't the only team long on quality pitching.

The Myrtle Beach Blue Jays, who finished with the league's second best overall record, featured a fearsome threesome: Jimmy Rogers (18-4, 3.35, 198 Ks), Xavier Hernandez (13-6, 2.49) and Denis Boucher (13-12, 2.64, 169 Ks).

Savannah stopper Tim Sherrill had 16 saves in little more than half a season before being promoted. Sumter's Dennis Burlingame had four shutouts, eight complete games and a 2.55 ERA, but a nonsupport-stained 9-11 record.

Gastonia starter Wilson Alvarez was 4-11, but had a 2.98 ERA and struck out 134 batters in 127 innings before being promoted to Triple-A Oklahoma City.

Spartanburg surprise

Given their 69-69 regular-season record, the Spartanburg Phillies were decided underdogs entering the SAL playoffs.

A stunning five-game winning streak later, the Phillies—and not Charleston or Myrtle Beach—were league champs. Greensboro was eliminated, 2-0, in the divisional playoffs; Charleston, 3-0, in the championship series.

The Phillies allowed just 11 runs in 50 playoff innings. Heroes

League Champions
(Playoff Champions, Where Applicable)

1988—Spartanburg	1976—Greenwood	1964—Salisbury
1987—Myrtle Beach	1975—Spartanburg	1963—Greenville
1986—Columbia	1974—Gastonia	1962—Statesville
1985—Florence	1973—Spartanburg	1961—Shelby
1984—Asheville	1972—Spartanburg	1960—Salisbury
1983—Gastonia	1971—Greenwood	1953-1959-Did Not
1982—Greensboro	1970—Greenville	Operate
1981—Greensboro	1969—Greenwood	1952—Shelby
1980—Greensboro	1968—Greenwood	1951—Shelby
1979—Greenwood	1967—Spartanburg	1950—Lenoir
1978—Greenwood	1966—Spartanburg	1949—Ruthrfrd Co.
1977—Gastonia	1965—Rock Hill	1948—Lincolnton

NOTE: League was known as the Western Carolina League from 1948 through 1962 and as Western Carolinas League through 1979.

South Atlantic Stars

Luis Sojo
. . . all-star

Brant Alyea
. . . .300-25-98

Moises Alou
. . . .313

included lefthanded starter Andy Carter (one earned run in 13 innings), all-star outfielder Jim Vatcher (5-for-14), closer Shelby McDonald (two saves) and second baseman Rod Robertson (game-winning home run in a 1-0, 13-inning suspended-game win over Charleston in Game Two).

First-year manager Mel Roberts was a Spartanburg coach when the club won its last SAL title in 1975, and a player on Spartanburg's 1966 championship team.

Anthony, Alyea blast away

Asheville right fielder Eric Anthony and Gastonia first baseman-DH Brant Alyea were the few exceptions to a Charleston-to-Charleston slugger shortage. Anthony hit 29 home runs (.273, 89 RBIs) and Alyea hit 25 (.300, 98 RBIs).

No other SAL player hit more than 18 home runs.

The Charleston (W.Va.) Wheelers are only two years old, but owner Dennis Bastien already has established the franchise as one of the league's strongest.

Augusta made its SAL debut a successful one with a team led by prospects Moises Alou, Mark Merchant and Wes Chamberlain. Merchant, though, sustained a season-ending shoulder separation July 15—little more than a year after he was the No. 2 pick overall in the 1987 amateur draft.

Myrtle Beach party

Players around the SAL definitely rate Myrtle Beach as their favorite road stop, but not because they have a good time at Coastal Carolina Stadium.

For the second straight season, the Blue Jays had the best mix of talent in the league. Besides the pitching, the roster included league MVP and top prospect Derek Bell (.344-12-60) and all-star shortstop Luis Sojo (.289-5-56).

Bell, in his first full pro season, led the league in hitting—though on a technicality. He was promoted to Class AA Knoxville (Southern) one plate appearance short of the 378 required to qualify for the batting title. But, under scoring rules, one hitless at-bat was added to his total, and since his average was still the league's best by a comfortable margin, he won the title.

In July, Myrtle Beach added the real-life version of Crash Davis.

Like the leading man in "Bull Durham," Jeff Hearron was a catcher with major league experience (brief stints with Toronto in 1985 and '86) sent back to Class A ball. Hearron, 26, was trying to come back from reconstructive shoulder surgery. He hit .218 in 174 at-bats, and was released after the season.

FIRST HALF

North	W	L	Pct.	GB
Spartanburg (Phils) ..	41	28	.594	—
Greensboro (Reds) ..	37	33	.529	4½
Fayetteville (Tigers) .	30	38	.441	10½
Asheville (Astros) ...	29	41	.414	12½
Chrlstn, W.Va. (Cubs)	23	44	.343	17
Gastonia (Rangers) ..	21	48	.304	20

South	W	L	Pct.	GB
Mrtle Bch (Blue Jays)	46	24	.657	—
Augusta (Pirates)....	44	26	.629	2
Chrlstn, S.C. (Padres)	42	27	.609	3½
Columbia (Mets).....	38	32	.543	8
Savannah (Cardinals)	35	34	.507	10½
Sumter (Braves).....	29	40	.420	16½

SECOND HALF

North	W	L	Pct.	GB
Greensboro (Reds) ..	42	27	.609	—
Asheville (Astros) ...	36	34	.514	6½
Fayetteville (Tigers) .	32	35	.478	9
Spartanburg (Phils) ..	28	41	.406	14
Chrlstn, W.Va. (Cubs)	28	42	.400	14½
Gastonia (Rangers) ..	26	42	.382	15½

South	W	L	Pct.	GB
Chrlstn, S.C. (Padres)	43	26	.623	—
Columbia (Mets).....	36	31	.537	6
Mrtle Bch (Blue Jays)	37	32	.536	6
Sumter (Braves).....	35	33	.515	7½
Savannah (Cardinals)	33	33	.500	8½
Augusta (Pirates)....	34	34	.500	8½

OVERALL

	W	L	Pct.	GB
Chrlstn, S.C. (Padres)	85	53	.616	—
Mrtle Bch (Blue Jays)	83	56	.597	2½
Greensboro (Reds) ..	79	60	.568	6½
Augusta (Pirates)....	78	60	.565	7
Columbia (Mets).....	74	63	.540	10½
Savannah (Cardinals)	68	67	.504	15½
Spartanburg (Phils)..	69	69	.500	16
Sumter (Braves).....	64	73	.467	20½
Asheville (Astros) ...	65	75	.464	21
Fayetteville (Tigers) .	62	73	.459	21½
Chrlstn, W.Va. (Cubs)	51	86	.372	33½
Gastonia (Rangers) ..	47	90	.343	37½

1988 Final Standings

1988: General Information

Playoffs: Spartanburg defeated Greensboro 2-0 and Charleston, S.C., defeated Myrtle Beach 2-1 in best-of-3 semifinals; Spartanburg defeated Charleston, S.C., 3-0 in best-of-5 final for league championship.

Regular Season Attendance: Greensboro, 168,675; Charleston, W.Va., 125,998; Augusta, 123,626; Columbia 114,172; Asheville, 95,252; Myrtle Beach, 78,212; Spartanburg, 61,108; Savannah 58,311; Fayetteville, 57,543; Charleston, S.C., 55,909; Gastonia, 50,212; Sumter, 35,067.

Managers: Asheville—Gary Tuck; **Augusta**—Jeff Cox, Woody Huyke; **Charleston, S.C.**—Jack Krol; **Charleston, W.Va.**— Brad Mills; **Columbia**—Butch Hobson; **Fayetteville**—Leon Roberts; **Gastonia**—Orlando Gomez; **Greensboro**—Dave Miley; **Myrtle Beach**—Richie Hebner; **Savannah**—Keith Champion; **Spartanburg**—Mel Roberts; **Sumter**—Ned Yost.

1988 Official All-Star Team: C—Eddie Taubensee, Greensboro. **1B**—

Guillermo Velasquez, Charleston, S.C. **2B**—Williams Suero, Myrtle Beach. **3B**—Brian Lane, Greensboro. **SS**—Luis Sojo, Myrtle Beach. **Util**—Alex Arias, Charleston W.Va. **OF**—Derek Bell, Myrtle Beach; Jim Vatcher, Spartanburg; Moises Alou, Augusta. **Util OF**—Eric Anthony, Asheville. **DH**—Brant Alyea, Gastonia. **RHP**—Jimmy Rogers, Myrtle Beach. **LHP**—Denis Boucher, Myrtle Beach. **Most Valuable Player**—Brant Alyea, Gastonia. **Most Outstanding Pitcher**—Jimmy Rogers, Myrtle Beach. **Manager of the Year**—Richie Hebner, Myrtle Beach. **Coaches of the Year**—Bill Monbouquette, Myrtle Beach; Dave Moharter, Augusta.

Top 10 Major League Prospects (by Baseball America): 1. Derek Bell, of, Myrtle Beach; **2.** Moises Alou, of, Augusta; **3.** Eric Anthony, of, Asheville; **4.** Luis Sojo, ss, Myrtle Beach; **5.** Jimmy Rogers, rhp, Myrtle Beach; **6.** Dennis Burlingame, rhp, Sumter; **7.** Xavier Hernandez, rhp, Myrtle Beach; **8.** Wilson Alvarez, lhp, Gastonia; **9.** Jose Valentin, ss, Charleston, S.C.; **10.** Brian Lane, 3b, Greensboro.

1988: Batting, Pitching Statistics

CLUB BATTING

	AVG	G	AB	R	H	2B	3B	HR	BB	SO	SB
Augusta	.260	138	4499	644	1171	187	49	39	488	982	195
Myrtle Beach	.259	139	4581	674	1186	206	30	105	470	980	98
Spartanburg	.253	138	4509	590	1143	220	20	63	432	853	125
Asheville	.250	140	4524	632	1133	184	21	91	469	912	131
Greensboro	.247	139	4615	576	1141	191	22	60	501	980	176
Gastonia	.245	137	4504	516	1102	174	13	66	422	841	112
Columbia	.244	137	4521	583	1105	169	31	34	517	928	167
Charleston-SC	.239	138	4439	560	1060	178	31	44	550	912	134
Fayetteville	.236	135	4335	495	1024	155	27	40	380	808	133
Savannah	.235	135	4309	488	1011	141	9	43	493	828	90
Sumter	.231	137	4429	516	1023	165	17	66	471	864	129
Charleston-WV	.220	138	4439	413	977	167	15	22	386	804	143

CLUB PITCHING

	ERA	GCG	SHO	SV	IP	H	R	ER	BB	SO
Charleston-SC	2.44	138	40	14	26	1208	1012	435	328	369	881
Greensboro	2.86	139	21	14	40	1220	984	491	388	514	983
Augusta	2.92	138	12	14	40	1189	1080	528	386	471	933
Myrtle Beach	2.96	139	6	17	35	1196	971	495	394	494	1047
Savannah	3.07	135	25	11	26	1167	1118	524	398	335	760
Fayetteville	3.08	135	11	13	28	1168	1044	515	400	460	889
Spartanburg	3.24	138	18	9	28	1179	1088	573	424	497	776
Charleston-WV	3.49	137	20	8	19	1200	1156	576	465	485	842
Columbia	3.52	137	29	8	34	1194	1115	588	467	413	872
Gastonia	3.70	137	10	9	18	1185	1133	662	487	589	972
Asheville	3.77	140	20	9	26	1189	1192	644	498	503	904
Sumter	4.12	137	18	14	31	1174	1183	656	537	449	833

INDIVIDUAL BATTING LEADERS
(Minimum 378 Plate Appearances)

	AVG	G	AB	R	H	2B	3B	HR	RBI	BB	SO	SB
Bell, Derek, MB	.344	91	352	55	121	29	5	12	60	15	67	18
Alou, Moises, Aug	.313	105	358	58	112	23	5	7	62	51	84	24
Vatcher, James, Spar	.302	137	496	90	150	32	2	12	72	89	73	26
Alyea, Brant, Gas	.300	132	504	62	151	22	2	25	98	30	81	3
*Vella, Greg, MB	.290	109	345	53	100	22	0	15	58	45	56	4
Sojo, Luis, MB	.289	135	536	83	155	22	5	5	56	35	35	14
*Velazquez, Guillermo, Char-SC	.287	135	520	55	149	28	3	11	90	34	110	1
Pearson, Kevin, Green	.285	137	512	64	146	29	1	8	72	44	61	6
Hartman, Eddie, Aug	.285	125	446	61	127	16	5	8	72	56	76	8
Suero, Williams, MB	.284	125	493	88	140	21	6	6	52	49	72	21

* indicates lefthanded batter   # indicates switch hitter

INDIVIDUAL PITCHING LEADERS
(Minimum 112 Innings)

	W	L	ERA	G	GS	CG	SV	IP	H	R	ER	BB	SO
Pacholec, Joe, Aug	12	7	2.06	25	25	2	0	148	128	45	34	65	120
Olivares, Omar, Char-SC	13	6	2.23	24	24	10	0	185	166	63	46	43	94
Valdez, Rafael, Char-SC	11	4	2.25	28	17	4	0	152	117	42	38	46	100
*Hansen, Todd, Char-SC	13	11	2.25	28	28	8	0	204	158	69	51	51	138
*Carter, Andy, Spar	11	6	2.30	25	25	4	0	157	110	55	40	75	99
*Duenas, Tony, Char-WV	6	11	2.30	30	19	4	0	164	150	48	42	46	150
Mullino, Ray, Char-WV	7	5	2.31	35	14	1	0	133	124	47	34	44	69
Burlingame, Dennis, Sum	9	11	2.49	24	24	8	0	163	132	59	45	43	89
Myers, Mike, Char-SC	11	4	2.51	27	23	8	0	165	156	67	46	35	97
Kaiser, Keith, Green	11	9	2.52	28	27	7	0	186	135	67	52	101	159

* indicates lefthanded pitcher

ASHEVILLE

BATTING	AVG	G	AB	R	H	2B	3B	HR	RBI	BB	SO	SB
*Anthony, Eric, of-dh	.273	115	439	73	120	36	1	29	89	40	101	10
Beams, Mike, of	.125	11	16	2	2	0	0	0	3	2	5	1
Carver, Billy Paul, c	.259	111	348	43	90	15	1	3	36	19	52	6
Cedeno, Ramon, of	.314	87	338	47	106	19	5	1	46	28	48	18
*Charno, Joe, c	.222	27	54	6	12	1	0	1	3	10	14	4
Cunningham, Dave, 3b-ss	.250	103	304	50	76	8	0	0	29	58	42	14

	AVG	G	AB	R	H	2B	3B	HR	RBI	BB	SO	SB
Delos Santos, Pedro, ss .	.231	73	234	27	54	5	1	2	32	21	59	3
Dickson, Ken, 3b	.245	73	237	23	58	9	1	4	16	10	40	7
*Gonzalez, Luis, 3b	.252	31	115	13	29	7	1	2	14	12	17	2
*Harter, Andy, 1b	.192	13	26	1	5	0	0	0	2	5	12	0
Henry, Carlos, 1b-of	.247	90	275	40	68	6	1	4	34	36	61	5
Horta, Neder, ss	.175	52	120	15	21	3	0	0	9	25	46	5
Laboy, Carlos, of	.206	107	345	44	71	13	4	8	31	27	123	4
Lewis, Dan, dh-of	.239	107	326	52	78	11	0	12	45	47	84	2
*Markley, Scott, dh-of	.200	17	45	5	9	0	0	0	1	7	7	3
Nyssen, Dan, of	.284	50	190	34	54	8	2	10	29	15	40	4
Ortiz, Joe, 1b-c	.270	113	396	49	107	21	1	13	71	24	82	7
*Perez, Gorky, of	.256	97	277	46	71	6	1	2	15	32	39	17
#Renteria, Ed, 2b	.232	132	439	62	102	16	2	0	35	51	40	19

PITCHING	W	L	ERA	G	GS	CG	SV	IP	H	R	ER	BB	SO
*Allen, Harold	11	8	2.83	26	26	4	0	159	152	68	50	69	115
Costello, Fred	6	7	3.55	51	0	0	11	76	76	34	30	31	65
Dovey, Troy	1	0	0.75	9	0	0	0	12	8	7	1	5	9
*Estes, Joel	1	2	3.00	20	1	1	1	63	66	27	21	21	61
*Hartgraves, Dean	5	9	4.49	34	13	2	0	118	131	70	59	47	83
*Hook, Mike	7	6	4.04	25	25	3	0	125	103	69	56	78	126
Johnson, Greg	3	3	4.48	44	0	0	7	62	60	36	31	30	67
Lee, Chris	1	0	2.16	5	0	0	0	8	8	4	2	2	10
Locke, Roger	3	7	6.56	16	16	1	0	59	83	55	43	34	22
*Newman, Danny	6	7	4.17	27	15	2	2	108	110	64	50	47	74
*Osuna, Al	6	1	1.98	31	0	0	3	50	41	19	11	25	41
Royalty, Doug	5	11	4.18	22	19	1	1	123	126	73	57	29	66
Schulte, Joe	1	2	3.08	25	1	0	1	64	62	32	22	27	59
Simon, Richie	9	9	3.32	23	23	6	0	149	144	71	55	53	100
Tafoya, Dennis	0	3	9.00	6	0	0	0	7	15	10	7	4	2

AUGUSTA

BATTING	AVG	G	AB	R	H	2B	3B	HR	RBI	BB	SO	SB
Alou, Moises, of	.313	105	358	58	112	23	5	7	62	51	84	24
Arguellas, Fernando, c	.000	2	4	0	0	0	0	0	0	1	3	0
Barczi, Scott, c	.214	92	285	40	61	4	5	3	30	29	65	16
*Carter, Steve, of	.299	74	278	47	83	18	6	3	43	31	59	22
Chamberlain, Wes, of	.336	27	107	22	36	7	2	1	17	11	11	1
#Crowley, Terry, 2b-ss	.299	75	281	27	84	9	2	1	27	14	42	10
Englett, Todd, c	.146	20	48	6	7	0	1	0	3	6	17	0
Freeman, Pete, c	.234	19	64	9	15	4	0	0	8	5	7	0
Garcia, Carlos, ss	.290	73	269	32	78	13	2	1	45	22	46	11
Garrison, Jimmy, 2b	.255	46	149	31	38	8	1	0	16	18	28	8
Griffith, Jeff, 3b	.228	111	364	48	83	23	3	4	43	47	119	9
Harris, Robert, of-dh	.271	101	410	69	111	6	7	0	29	22	91	30
Hartman, Eddie, 1b	.285	125	446	61	127	16	5	8	72	56	76	8
Jewett, Trent, c	.148	19	54	4	8	0	0	0	3	5	13	1
Love, John, dh-3b	.257	49	183	23	47	12	2	2	27	9	18	2
#Merced, Orlando, 2b-3b	.265	37	136	19	36	6	3	1	17	7	20	2
#Merchant, Mark, of	.242	60	211	36	51	6	0	2	19	41	38	14
#Molina, Albert, ss	.301	56	186	26	56	12	1	0	22	27	23	4
Montejano, Steve, 2b	.203	24	74	8	15	2	0	0	4	3	17	1
Peyton, Mickey, of	.191	21	68	4	13	0	0	0	5	10	17	1
Raisanen, Keith, of	.195	39	123	15	24	9	0	1	17	16	40	4
Shelton, Ben, 1b-dh	.195	38	128	25	25	2	2	5	20	30	72	3
#Valverde, Miguel, ss	.246	65	187	27	46	5	1	0	15	18	48	19
*Velky, Joe, c	.208	11	24	3	5	0	0	0	2	5	8	1
Young, John, of	.161	20	62	4	10	2	1	0	5	4	20	4

PITCHING	W	L	ERA	G	GS	CG	SV	IP	H	R	ER	BB	SO
*Acosta, Jose	3	3	3.86	33	0	0	4	65	82	33	28	25	42
Cohen, Tonny	8	10	4.02	27	26	1	0	139	152	86	62	39	125
Downs, Ron	11	6	3.18	20	20	4	0	125	120	62	44	27	86
Felix, Antonio	0	0	5.00	5	2	0	1	9	11	8	5	6	12
*Forrest, Joel	3	5	3.41	12	12	0	0	66	72	42	25	20	40
Hatfield, Rob	0	1	3.60	2	1	0	0	5	6	7	2	4	3
MaCavage, Joe	6	3	3.01	41	0	0	6	78	54	30	26	40	73
Mercedes, Guillermo	0	3	5.45	19	1	0	1	40	47	30	24	12	28
Miller, Paul	6	5	2.89	15	15	2	0	90	80	34	29	28	51
Pacholec, Joe	12	7	2.06	25	25	2	0	148	128	45	34	65	120
Richardson, Keith	3	1	0.31	4	4	1	0	29	18	3	1	4	17
Runge, Scott	5	0	0.83	24	2	0	8	54	32	12	5	22	59
*Schlopy, Butch	7	4	1.90	38	0	0	9	76	52	22	16	38	81
Shepherd, Keith	7	3	4.02	16	16	1	0	85	71	45	38	50	49
Smith, Willie	1	4	2.98	30	1	0	6	48	35	20	16	29	48
Toy, Tracy	4	5	2.13	31	10	1	5	110	97	40	26	47	80
*West, Darin	1	0	3.75	4	1	0	0	12	12	6	5	7	11
Wurm, Garry	1	0	1.74	2	0	0	0	10	11	3	2	8	9

CHARLESTON, S.C.

BATTING	AVG	G	AB	R	H	2B	3B	HR	RBI	BB	SO	SB
Barker, Tim, 2b	.261	15	46	3	12	2	1	1	5	7	7	3
Brooks, Monte, of-2b	.174	89	281	33	49	8	1	0	22	36	53	19
*Cisarik, Brian, of	.303	65	221	35	67	14	3	0	28	56	37	19
*Farmer, Reggie, of	.261	125	360	42	94	16	6	2	35	61	106	26
*Harrison, Keith, of	.197	64	117	23	23	2	1	0	7	13	31	11
Hillemann, Charles, of	.250	118	444	75	111	22	4	5	41	39	102	28

	AVG	G	AB	R	H	2B	3B	HR	RBI	BB	SO	SB
*King, Michael, c-dh	.222	105	333	27	74	10	1	5	28	27	69	0
#Kleven, Mark, 2b-3b	.000	8	14	0	0	0	0	0	0	1	6	0
Lutticken, Bob, c	.199	91	271	30	54	3	1	3	27	17	65	0
Pellegrino, Tony, 3b	.258	134	497	66	128	18	6	5	62	71	73	2
*Sanchez, Osvaldo, dh-of	.190	37	105	12	20	3	0	4	12	13	34	1
Silverio, Nelson, dh	.245	83	261	25	64	15	2	1	36	28	49	0
Torchia, Todd, of	.185	49	124	8	23	2	1	0	8	22	35	0
#Valentin, Jose, ss	.232	133	444	56	103	20	1	6	44	45	83	11
*Velazquez, Guillermo, 1b	.287	135	520	55	149	28	3	11	90	34	110	1
Wasem, Jim, 2b	.222	114	401	70	89	15	0	1	40	80	52	16

PITCHING	W	L	ERA	G	GS	CG	SV	IP	H	R	ER	BB	SO
*Bond, David	1	6	3.22	24	8	1	3	81	63	41	29	36	75
Brocail, Doug	8	6	2.69	22	13	5	2	107	107	40	32	25	107
Estrada, Jay	7	5	2.26	45	0	0	12	68	56	21	17	19	51
*Forbes, Willie	0	0	0.00	2	0	0	0	3	1	0	0	3	2
*Hansen, Todd	13	11	2.25	28	28	8	0	204	158	69	51	51	138
Lewis, Tony	2	5	3.34	23	5	1	0	67	69	37	25	27	48
Myers, Mike	15	4	2.51	27	23	8	0	165	156	67	46	35	97
Olivares, Omar	13	6	2.23	24	24	10	0	185	166	63	46	43	94
Reichle, Darrin	10	3	2.84	20	20	3	0	108	62	38	34	61	115
Soltero, Saul	5	3	1.32	36	0	0	9	68	57	17	10	23	54
Valdez, Rafael	11	4	2.25	28	17	4	0	152	117	42	38	46	100

CHARLESTON, W.V.

BATTING	AVG	G	AB	R	H	2B	3B	HR	RBI	BB	SO	SB
Arias, Alex, ss	.258	127	472	57	122	12	1	0	33	54	44	41
Bell, Lenny, 3b-1b	.199	54	196	11	39	9	2	2	18	12	44	0
Borders, Todd, dh	.000	3	4	0	0	0	0	0	0	1	1	0
Canan, Dick, inf	.211	28	95	9	20	5	0	1	8	10	13	0
#Cohoon, Don, 2b-of	.167	24	78	9	13	3	0	1	7	13	20	0
Eggleston, Skip, 2b	.108	45	102	6	11	4	0	0	3	12	32	4
Espinal, Sergio, 2b-3b	.194	44	129	15	25	4	0	0	5	17	23	3
Gatewood, Henry, dh-c	.235	45	166	9	39	10	0	1	19	11	23	0
Grimes, Lee, of	.221	74	272	22	60	16	0	1	28	21	32	7
*Jensen, John, of	.266	61	214	23	57	16	2	6	29	25	52	1
Jose, Elio, dh-of	.149	55	161	13	24	7	1	0	4	6	58	3
Owens, Steve, 3b-dh	.215	120	377	36	81	11	0	0	32	39	70	17
*Perry, Eric, 1b-dh	.230	55	183	15	42	9	0	3	22	18	41	0
Ramirez, Nick, 2b-ss	.095	11	21	4	2	0	0	0	2	1	6	2
Ramsey, Fernando, of	.241	121	381	36	92	5	1	0	15	14	68	15
*Reeder, Mike, 1b-dh	.220	114	376	36	83	14	2	1	29	37	89	11
Rosario, Jossy, 2b	.189	44	148	12	28	4	0	0	9	5	20	2

	AVG	G	AB	R	H	2B	3B	HR	RBI	BB	SO	SB
Santana, Reuben, 2b ...	.036	13	28	4	1	1	0	0	2	3	13	0
*Shelton, Harry, of	.242	131	480	56	116	17	6	1	28	46	75	28
*Strickland, Bob, of-1b ...	.245	27	98	6	24	5	0	2	12	6	19	0
Taylor, Scott, c	.212	39	104	3	22	3	0	0	10	2	11	1
Walbeck, Matt, c	.218	104	312	28	68	9	0	2	24	30	44	7
Wentz, Keith, ss	.216	11	37	3	8	3	0	1	5	3	6	0
Wilder, Dave, pr	.000	3	0	0	0	0	0	0	0	0	0	0

PITCHING	W	L	ERA	G	GS	CG	SV	IP	H	R	ER	BB	SO
*Cakora, Matt	1	1	4.13	39	4	0	2	72	71	34	33	25	48
Campos, Frank	9	13	4.86	39	14	1	2	113	119	71	61	87	87
Coleman, Dewayne	2	4	3.12	39	0	0	8	52	45	31	18	20	30
Davis, Braz	7	12	3.18	23	23	3	0	147	120	67	52	76	119
*Duenas, Tony	6	11	2.30	30	19	4	0	164	150	48	42	64	150
Eddings, Jay	2	4	2.87	38	1	0	2	88	98	41	28	21	27
Gardner, John	0	2	5.63	10	0	0	0	16	18	10	10	8	13
Gomez, Henry	6	14	3.98	27	27	7	0	172	150	82	76	68	137
*Gomez, Pat	2	7	5.38	36	9	0	5	79	75	53	47	52	97
Lopez, Marcos	9	13	3.52	26	26	4	0	164	184	91	64	37	65
Mullino, Ray	7	5	2.31	35	14	1	0	133	124	47	34	44	69

COLUMBIA

BATTING	AVG	G	AB	R	H	2B	3B	HR	RBI	BB	SO	SB
Bogar, Tim, 2b-ss	.282	45	142	19	40	4	2	3	21	22	29	5
#Diaz, Alex, ss	.262	123	481	82	126	14	11	0	37	21	49	28
*Donnels, Chris, 3b	.241	42	133	19	32	6	0	2	13	30	25	5
Gonzalez, Javier, c	.200	79	250	21	50	4	2	3	21	15	58	0
Jaster, Scott, of	.218	72	234	35	51	6	1	3	26	31	41	11
*Jimenez, Alex, 1b	.216	103	343	40	74	12	1	4	35	40	69	1
Joiner, Dave, inf	.237	61	177	17	42	8	1	0	13	12	26	3
Lau, Dave, c	.211	78	209	19	44	6	0	0	19	29	38	2
Lemle, Rob, of	.235	71	213	34	50	5	0	0	16	40	56	16
Mantrana, Manny, 2b ...	.303	80	320	47	97	23	0	2	35	28	34	9
McDaniel, Terry, of	.247	127	449	76	111	16	6	5	43	74	73	41
*Murrell, Rodney, 3b-dh ..	.233	110	335	36	78	14	0	5	46	51	57	10
Natera, Luis, inf	.189	37	95	10	18	2	0	0	9	7	26	1
Naughton, Danny, of ...	.253	70	182	17	46	6	2	0	14	18	47	2
Polanco, Radhames, 3b	.143	34	91	10	13	1	0	1	7	10	31	1
Roseboro, Jaime, of	.272	125	486	53	132	24	4	2	72	23	74	27
*Spoolstra, Scott, dh-1b ...	.277	110	314	41	87	15	1	4	45	57	71	4
*Turtletaub, Greg, of	.226	23	62	4	14	3	0	0	5	9	20	1

PITCHING	W	L	ERA	G	GS	CG	SV	IP	H	R	ER	BB	SO
Anderson, Mike	7	5	4.01	18	18	4	0	114	94	62	51	45	114
Bauer, Pete	4	5	3.71	40	0	0	12	68	64	33	28	23	55
Durant, Rick	3	4	3.95	29	4	0	2	66	77	40	29	25	73
*Elli, Rocky	13	8	3.47	27	27	4	0	169	147	87	65	65	104
*Hillman, Eric	1	6	3.95	17	13	0	1	73	54	45	32	43	60
Larose, Steve	4	4	3.95	32	0	0	10	41	52	28	18	18	33
Marina, Juan	11	8	3.07	26	26	5	0	173	167	74	59	61	83
McAnarney, Jim	0	3	6.52	22	1	0	0	50	59	40	36	35	33
Miller, Mike	14	8	2.76	31	20	8	3	163	146	64	50	28	98
Ponder, Kevin	2	1	3.39	30	1	0	5	82	80	36	31	19	71
Valera, Julio	15	11	3.20	30	27	8	1	191	171	77	68	51	144
*Whitlock, Mike	0	0	0.00	4	0	0	0	4	4	2	0	0	4

FAYETTEVILLE

BATTING	AVG	G	AB	R	H	2B	3B	HR	RBI	BB	SO	SB
Adler, Marc, 3b-2b	.216	116	422	51	91	11	2	8	49	40	49	11
*Bello, Duben, 1b	.170	35	47	6	8	0	0	0	3	8	12	4
*Camilli, Kevin, dh-1b	.202	41	109	14	22	5	0	2	19	17	20	0
Castillo, Benny, of	.204	37	93	12	19	3	0	4	8	12	30	1
Castro, Liliano, 2b-ss	.228	99	289	21	66	2	1	0	24	6	39	9
Doster, Zack, of	.239	104	293	43	70	12	3	1	30	33	87	8
Fryman, Travis, ss	.234	123	411	44	96	17	4	0	47	24	83	18
Henderson, Bill, c-1b	.243	97	292	23	71	8	0	3	27	26	37	4
Ingram, Riccardo, of	.180	17	50	7	9	2	1	0	3	2	15	0
Isaac, Richard, dh-of	.241	11	29	0	7	2	0	0	0	0	8	1
Luciani, Randy, 1b	.211	46	123	16	26	7	1	2	13	19	40	0
Martin, Darryl, of-dh	.223	70	229	19	51	9	1	1	12	20	35	1
Melendez, Luis, c	.216	73	194	21	42	8	2	2	20	14	52	3
Nieto, Andy, 2b	.264	69	227	21	60	6	1	0	18	13	27	1
#Pegues, Steve, of	.256	118	437	50	112	17	5	6	46	21	90	21
*Raley, Dan, 1b-3b	.259	55	166	18	43	12	0	3	20	28	21	2
Shebelut, Lance, 1b	.200	28	100	11	20	5	0	2	9	15	12	2
#Toney, Andy, of	.282	94	347	54	98	15	1	4	35	45	51	37

PITCHING	W	L	ERA	G	GS	CG	SV	IP	H	R	ER	BB	SO
Belcher, Glenn	3	4	3.56	47	2	0	6	81	81	47	32	46	42
*Coker, Larry	0	2	3.78	17	0	0	0	33	34	20	14	10	19
*Cook, Ron	9	6	3.07	25	25	2	0	141	112	51	48	59	114
Duquette, Chuck	4	3	3.40	42	0	0	10	50	46	23	19	22	41
*Garces, Robinson	3	4	2.27	12	12	1	0	67	49	28	17	26	58
Haas, Rob	4	3	1.81	11	11	0	0	55	59	20	11	19	46
Knudsen, Kurt	3	1	1.35	12	0	0	1	20	8	4	3	9	22
Liriano, Felix	1	3	5.09	31	8	0	1	69	75	50	39	40	38

	W	L	ERA	G	GS	CG	SV	IP	H	R	ER	BB	SO
Lumley, Mike	3	3	2.91	10	9	1	0	59	38	23	19	25	56
Meacham, Rusty	0	3	6.20	6	5	0	0	25	37	19	17	6	16
Nicholson, Keith	2	5	2.09	16	15	0	0	90	80	40	21	34	60
*Parascand, Steve	3	4	5.08	18	4	0	0	39	38	24	22	21	41
*Ramos, Jose	5	5	3.74	46	0	0	4	65	69	36	27	32	55
*Richards, Dave	3	9	1.97	47	0	0	6	69	49	17	15	29	86
Steward, Chuck	5	4	2.05	30	11	0	0	110	87	30	25	46	76
Stone, Eric	0	5	7.23	7	7	0	0	19	16	15	15	11	14
Wilkins, Mike	14	9	2.91	26	26	7	0	176	166	68	57	25	105

GASTONIA

BATTING	AVG	G	AB	R	H	2B	3B	HR	RBI	BB	SO	SB
Alyea, Brant, of-dh	.300	132	504	62	151	22	2	25	98	30	81	3
*Baker, Jay, of-3b	.218	90	239	20	52	7	0	1	16	30	57	3
Barretto, Saul, c	.227	92	277	22	63	10	0	2	23	19	39	0
Belcher, Kevin, of	.245	105	392	56	96	13	1	8	44	40	81	22
#Brewer, Omar, of	.237	82	262	25	62	14	1	5	22	41	80	1
#Burgos, Paco, 3b-ss . . .	.276	75	290	37	80	19	1	5	28	14	34	4
#Cartaya, Joel, ss	.322	44	143	19	46	4	0	1	12	21	7	5
#Colon, Cris, ss	.198	75	232	23	46	12	0	1	11	12	46	6
Garman, Pat, dh-3b	.232	67	237	41	55	7	1	8	30	36	52	8
*Glasker, Steve, of	.257	38	144	23	37	5	3	0	6	11	30	8
*Hainline, Jeff, 1b	.115	12	26	1	3	0	0	0	1	6	16	0
*Lavender, Robert, of . . .	.208	30	53	7	11	1	0	0	2	6	12	1
Law, Travis, of	.100	3	10	3	1	0	0	0	1	3	1	1
Losa, Bill, c	.138	38	94	9	13	2	0	0	4	9	41	5
McCutchen, Jim, of	.211	55	175	15	37	7	2	1	19	23	39	6
*Meyer, Brad, 3b-1b	.196	96	270	25	53	6	1	2	19	47	47	8
Murphy, Miguel, of (64 Fay)	.237	98	287	33	68	12	3	1	24	10	69	11
*Patrick, Mike, dh-c	.274	25	73	5	20	2	0	0	4	8	6	0
Pearn, Joe, c	.236	62	140	15	33	9	0	1	8	16	25	0
Sable, Luke, 2b	.251	134	491	58	123	13	1	0	30	37	54	24
Velez, Jose, 1b	.273	100	366	42	100	18	0	6	48	14	69	2

PITCHING	W	L	ERA	G	GS	CG	SV	IP	H	R	ER	BB	SO
*Alvarez, Wilson	4	11	2.98	23	23	1	0	127	113	63	42	49	134
*Burgos, John	4	1	2.95	28	2	0	2	58	54	28	19	28	52
Castillo, Felipe	5	10	2.78	23	23	3	0	139	122	67	43	48	69
*Cerny, Marty	9	7	3.02	23	21	3	0	146	125	59	49	46	103
Evans, Brian	2	2	2.64	20	0	0	0	31	23	9	9	17	15
*Findlay, Bill	2	4	3.97	22	0	0	1	48	39	24	21	31	51
Kopczynski, Todd	0	0	3.38	3	0	0	0	3	3	1	1	0	1
Lipscomb, Bruce	1	1	3.03	12	0	0	0	30	32	14	10	7	17
Moore, Greg	1	1	6.35	4	0	0	0	6	10	4	4	2	4
Nen, Robb	0	5	7.45	14	10	0	0	48	69	57	40	45	36
Patterson, Glenn	0	0	10.38	4	0	0	0	4	6	6	5	7	7
Pavlik, Roger	2	12	4.59	18	16	0	0	84	94	65	43	58	89
*Penland, Ken	0	1	7.94	3	1	0	0	11	16	11	10	7	13
*Reitzel, Mike	4	3	3.81	19	4	1	0	54	54	30	23	23	17
Rockman, Marv	2	7	2.44	43	0	0	5	85	76	29	23	27	87
Shiflett, Chris	0	1	8.57	9	3	0	0	21	25	23	20	19	12
*Sipple, John	2	2	2.63	16	8	1	1	68	50	23	20	31	66
*Steiner, Brian	1	2	4.26	10	7	0	0	32	34	24	15	22	32
Taylor, Mike	8	9	3.44	47	4	1	7	102	117	60	39	49	78
Wilkinson, Spencer	0	11	4.86	31	15	0	2	83	65	58	45	68	89

GREENSBORO

BATTING	AVG	G	AB	R	H	2B	3B	HR	RBI	BB	SO	SB
Berry, Mark, dh	.222	47	158	21	35	12	1	0	16	24	25	5
Brown, Don, of	.243	132	448	72	109	20	2	9	39	78	102	51
Brune, Jim, c	.227	16	44	4	10	0	0	0	1	3	12	1
*Casillas, Adam, 1b-dh . . .	.285	96	316	33	90	14	1	4	48	36	16	1
Colvard, Benny, dh	.250	2	8	0	2	0	0	0	0	0	3	1
Lane, Brian, 3b	.282	115	451	55	127	17	3	3	52	32	68	9
Lee, Terry, dh-1b	.321	25	56	8	18	5	0	2	9	11	11	0
Letterio, Shane, 2b	.223	92	287	32	64	12	1	0	23	27	45	14
#Martinez, Luis, 1b	.219	25	64	4	14	0	0	0	7	2	15	1
Mealy, Tony, of	.240	85	288	44	69	14	2	5	27	28	100	25
Mee, Jimmy, c	.243	39	115	14	28	4	0	1	17	11	26	0
Pearson, Kevin, 1b-of . . .	.285	137	512	64	146	29	1	8	72	44	61	6
#Rickman, Andy, 2b-ss . . .	.235	59	166	18	39	4	0	1	11	39	36	4
Robinson, Brad, of-dh . . .	.217	77	240	28	52	10	3	5	25	24	68	1
Schnurbusch, Chris, inf (67 Fay)	.256	118	391	55	100	8	2	1	35	37	60	11
Silverio, Francisco, of . . .	.164	25	61	2	10	1	0	0	4	2	21	1
Smith, Jack, ss	.196	136	439	52	86	17	1	7	44	62	126	12
*Taubensee, Eddie, c	.258	103	330	36	85	16	1	10	41	44	93	8
#Thomas, Keith, of	.240	108	438	63	105	12	4	4	26	17	122	30
*Wolfer, Jim, c	.231	8	13	3	3	0	1	0	1	3	8	0

PITCHING	W	L	ERA	G	GS	CG	SV	IP	H	R	ER	BB	SO
Hester, Steve	12	5	2.92	20	20	4	0	139	131	55	45	34	78
Huseby, Ken	7	11	3.73	26	26	5	0	157	148	87	65	57	79
Jeffery, Scott	8	3	1.30	38	0	0	6	90	55	14	13	32	70
Jenkins, Mack	0	4	3.31	18	3	0	2	52	49	29	19	18	50
Kaiser, Keith	11	9	2.52	28	27	7	0	186	135	67	52	101	159
Marsh, Quinn	2	3	3.63	33	1	0	3	74	65	34	30	28	49

	W	L	ERA	G	GS	CG	SV	IP	H	R	ER	BB	SO
Mullins, Ron	4	5	3.14	39	0	0	19	43	34	18	15	32	45
Risley, Bill	8	4	4.11	23	23	3	0	120	82	60	55	84	135
*Rodriguez, Rosario	6	4	1.52	23	3	0	2	65	49	15	11	24	53
*Rogers, Dusty	7	6	2.57	20	19	1	0	112	99	48	32	55	97
Stading, Greg	2	2	1.84	15	0	0	1	29	16	7	6	9	35
Turek, Joe	10	3	2.75	19	17	0	0	111	91	44	34	32	91
*Vierra, Joey	2	1	2.40	34	0	0	7	41	30	13	11	8	42

MYRTLE BEACH

BATTING	AVG	G	AB	R	H	2B	3B	HR	RBI	BB	SO	SB
Bell, Derek, of	.344	91	352	55	121	29	5	12	60	15	67	18
*David, Greg, 3b	.225	122	423	64	95	12	1	15	57	56	104	5
DeLa Rosa, Juan, of	.229	134	477	54	109	12	5	7	66	31	108	11
Dixon, Bryan, of	.174	12	23	2	4	0	0	0	1	10	1	1
*Etzweiler, Dan, dh	.294	17	34	7	10	0	0	1	8	11	9	1
Floyd, Chris, c	.500	5	10	0	5	0	0	0	2	1	1	0
Harding, Greg, dh	.000	1	3	0	0	0	0	0	0	0	1	0
Hearron, Jeff, dh	.218	47	174	22	38	5	1	9	34	18	53	0
Knorr, Randy, c	.234	117	364	43	85	13	0	9	42	41	91	0
Kolecki, Roy, ss-2b	.139	21	36	2	5	1	0	0	2	2	13	0
Malave, Omar, inf	.450	8	20	3	9	3	0	0	1	2	3	0
Marquez, Edgar, of	.200	16	45	4	9	2	0	0	5	5	16	1
Martinez, Rafael, 2b-ss	.171	12	35	3	6	1	0	0	4	3	9	1
Nunez, Bernie, of	.260	130	484	69	126	22	3	11	60	22	108	6
Pilkinton, Lem, c	.270	26	63	11	17	5	0	3	11	11	19	0
Pino, Rolando, dh-3b	.246	70	211	33	52	14	0	3	23	52	53	1
Provence, Todd, 1b	.204	92	270	50	55	15	2	5	22	34	114	5
Sojo, Luis, ss	.289	135	536	83	155	22	5	5	56	35	35	14
Suero, Williams, 2b	.284	125	493	88	140	21	6	6	52	49	72	21
Taveras, Marcos, of	.174	18	23	3	4	0	0	1	5	1	10	3
Townley, Jason, c	.400	5	15	4	6	2	0	1	3	1	4	0
*Vella, Greg, 1b-of	.290	109	345	53	100	22	0	15	58	45	56	4
Young, Mark, of	.241	46	145	21	35	5	2	3	14	21	33	6

PITCHING	W	L	ERA	G	GS	CG	SV	IP	H	R	ER	BB	SO
*Boucher, Denis	13	12	2.84	33	32	1	0	197	161	81	62	63	169
*Cromwell, Nate	8	8	2.90	21	20	1	0	124	88	47	40	67	86
Dodd, Dan	0	0	3.60	6	0	0	0	10	13	4	4	2	9
Hernandez, Xavier	13	6	2.55	23	22	2	0	148	116	52	42	28	111
Johnson, Curtis	0	0	7.36	5	0	0	0	7	5	6	6	4	10
*Lloyd, Graeme	3	2	3.62	41	0	0	2	60	71	33	24	30	43
*MacDonald, Robert	3	4	1.69	52	0	0	15	53	42	13	10	18	43
Rogers, Jimmy	18	4	3.35	33	32	2	0	188	145	84	70	95	198
Silverstein, Al	7	7	3.55	39	9	0	3	117	105	55	46	37	106
Timlin, Michael	10	6	2.86	35	22	0	0	151	119	68	48	77	106
Towey, Steve	0	2	7.15	6	2	0	0	11	12	11	9	19	17
Wapnick, Steve	4	3	2.24	54	0	0	12	60	44	18	15	31	69
*Woide, Steve	4	2	2.34	44	0	0	3	69	50	23	18	23	80

SAVANNAH

BATTING	AVG	G	AB	R	H	2B	3B	HR	RBI	BB	SO	SB
#Alvarez, Mike, of	.230	72	196	34	45	2	0	0	17	27	14	19
Barrs, Stan, inf	.253	69	257	27	65	5	0	2	19	11	46	1
#Carmona, Greg, ss	.160	33	100	11	16	1	0	0	4	11	29	2
*Carter, Ed, of	.256	126	390	50	100	9	0	0	28	50	46	18
Colescott, Rob, dh-c	.231	93	308	34	71	15	0	6	32	33	105	2
Doss, Greg, dh	.167	6	12	0	2	0	0	0	3	0	4	0
Ferguson, Jim, 2b-3b	.223	103	319	54	71	11	1	0	25	72	48	10
Gentleman, Jean-Paul, 2b	.179	14	39	2	7	3	0	0	1	2	5	0
Grier, Antron, of	.225	32	80	13	18	3	1	0	6	4	19	6
#Huffman, Kris, ss	.237	89	283	40	67	3	0	1	21	45	46	4
Johnston, Ryan, of	.167	37	84	9	14	2	1	1	14	10	14	0
*Kroeger, J.T., c	.100	5	10	0	1	0	0	0	0	2	1	0
Looper, Ed, 3b	.242	104	355	34	86	13	1	7	40	40	54	6
*MacLin, Lonnie, of	.235	46	119	10	28	3	0	0	9	12	19	8
Nelson, Darren, of-dh	.231	99	329	27	76	16	1	1	37	24	87	4
*Olmsted, Reed, 1b	.228	127	452	39	103	17	2	4	53	43	82	1
Pettengill, Tim, c	.220	29	91	9	20	2	0	1	4	8	11	0
Rosario, Francisco, c	.212	42	137	10	29	1	0	0	8	12	21	2
Ross, Mike, 2b	.233	48	172	18	40	7	0	3	18	12	23	1
Sellick, John, of-1b	.267	126	450	53	120	25	1	17	68	52	113	3
Thomas, Orlando, c	.260	45	123	9	32	3	1	0	13	19	40	2

PITCHING	W	L	ERA	G	GS	CG	SV	IP	H	R	ER	BB	SO
Behny, Mark	2	5	4.73	18	5	0	0	53	54	41	28	27	39
Broadfoot, Scott	6	8	2.74	20	20	5	0	125	127	54	38	21	77
*Harvick, Brad	3	8	3.80	25	14	0	1	104	106	60	44	27	48
Hempen, Hal	1	1	4.95	8	1	0	0	20	23	15	11	8	16
Hershman, Bill	2	1	5.26	7	5	1	0	26	32	23	15	16	15
Hinkle, Mike	7	9	2.89	22	22	8	0	150	158	68	48	25	103
Hoffman, Dick	3	1	1.45	4	4	1	0	31	27	7	5	6	15
Horsley, Clint	0	1	8.10	6	0	0	0	7	9	9	6	8	3
Lawrence, Scott	9	4	2.74	16	16	4	0	105	108	38	32	26	56
*Lepley, John	1	1	1.69	12	0	0	3	21	20	4	4	7	19
*Livchak, Rob	1	1	2.61	5	5	1	0	31	30	11	9	6	22
Marte, Roberto	4	5	4.16	42	0	0	4	63	54	36	29	31	49
Meamber, Tim	4	7	3.21	25	16	1	0	112	114	47	40	36	63

	W	L	ERA	G	GS	CG	SV	IP	H	R	ER	BB	SO
Plemel, Lee	1	1	2.59	5	5	1	0	31	23	11	9	7	24
Russo, Tony	10	5	1.35	45	0	0	2	73	48	21	11	27	58
*Sherrill, Tim	3	2	1.79	31	0	0	16	45	26	12	9	13	62
Smith, Ken	10	6	3.15	26	21	3	0	154	145	61	54	36	79
Taylor, Andy	1	1	3.60	9	1	0	0	15	14	6	6	8	12

SPARTANBURG

BATTING	AVG	G	AB	R	H	2B	3B	HR	RBI	BB	SO	SB
*Barragan, Jimmy, 1b	.261	125	468	56	122	27	2	7	53	50	66	2
Batiste, Kim, ss	.249	122	430	51	107	19	6	6	52	14	101	16
*Britt, Bob, of	.181	22	72	8	13	3	0	0	2	8	13	0
Cobb, Mark, of	.296	92	321	39	95	15	3	4	44	28	83	5
Ellison, Paul, c	.152	23	66	6	10	2	0	0	1	9	14	0
Felton, Fred, of	.118	13	34	4	4	0	0	0	2	3	10	1
Foley, Martin, 3b-2b	.249	85	293	34	73	17	1	5	28	16	78	3
*Kirkpatrick, Steve, of	.249	121	457	68	114	18	2	1	36	63	41	33
Lindsey, Doug, c	.235	90	324	29	76	19	0	4	46	29	68	4
Maasberg, Gary, 3b	.253	52	190	27	48	16	1	1	25	13	37	2
Reaves, Scott, 3b-ss	.268	99	347	54	93	11	1	5	42	54	67	1
#Robertson, Rod, 2b	.242	124	430	54	104	12	1	8	39	13	83	29
#Rosado, Edwin, c	.267	6	15	0	4	0	0	0	1	0	5	0
Ruckman, Scott, 3b-1b	.234	79	274	32	64	14	0	7	29	16	53	1
Stark, Jeff, of	.241	25	83	10	20	1	0	0	6	12	17	0
Trevino, Tony, dh-2b	.071	7	14	3	1	1	0	0	2	2	5	0
Vatcher, James, of	.302	137	496	90	150	32	2	12	72	89	73	26
*White, Gary, c	.226	51	190	23	43	12	1	4	31	11	39	2
Zayas, Carlos, c	.400	2	5	2	2	1	0	0	0	2	0	0

PITCHING	W	L	ERA	G	GS	CG	SV	IP	H	R	ER	BB	SO
Ashby, Andy	1	1	2.70	3	3	0	0	17	13	7	5	7	16
*Carter, Andy	11	6	2.30	25	25	4	0	157	110	55	40	75	99
Coulter, Darrell	6	11	3.66	26	15	1	0	116	126	63	47	58	92
Elam, Todd	0	4	4.98	7	7	0	0	34	35	25	19	23	17
Fagnano, Phil	1	1	3.55	8	3	0	1	33	28	13	13	10	23
*Hurta, Bob	7	8	4.60	23	23	0	0	117	124	69	60	68	61
*LaRosa, John	3	2	1.78	30	1	0	3	76	53	28	15	30	63
Maldonado, Pete	1	0	8.36	6	0	0	0	14	26	13	13	4	8
Mauser, Tim	2	1	1.96	4	3	0	0	23	15	6	5	5	18
*McCarthy, Greg	4	2	4.04	34	1	0	2	65	52	36	29	52	65
McDonald, Shelby	6	6	2.52	47	0	0	13	75	70	33	21	27	46
Peek, Tim	6	3	1.87	37	4	0	9	106	77	26	22	30	80
*Rambo, Matt	12	10	3.73	26	26	6	0	166	180	98	69	54	105
Thomas, Royal	6	13	3.03	22	22	7	0	146	134	74	49	47	67
Tracy, Richard	3	1	5.14	9	5	0	0	35	45	27	20	7	16

SUMTER

BATTING	AVG	G	AB	R	H	2B	3B	HR	RBI	BB	SO	SB
Baldwin, Tony, of-dh	.245	114	392	65	96	17	4	9	45	66	125	38
#Carrion, Junior, ss	.181	65	221	18	40	5	0	0	9	9	55	2
*Cloninger, Greg, 2b-ss	.254	116	389	51	99	9	0	5	39	45	48	4
Cole, Popeye, of	.252	120	413	74	104	19	3	1	30	58	60	38
Colon, David, of	.195	74	251	25	49	6	1	0	18	13	43	4
Cuevas, John, c	.252	95	329	37	83	16	0	6	31	22	64	3
Davis, Mark, 1b	.240	127	463	47	111	20	1	18	61	19	78	2
Fredymond, Juan, ss	.235	10	34	7	8	1	0	1	4	6	12	0
Gilbert, Greg, 2b-3b	.213	62	202	22	43	12	0	4	22	26	45	7
Harper, Greg, c	.170	16	47	4	8	0	0	0	3	6	18	0
Johnson, Dodd, of	.225	28	102	10	23	3	0	0	4	14	18	1
*Kremers, Jimmy, dh-c	.266	72	256	30	68	12	3	5	42	39	53	1
Mendoza, Jesus, 1b	.198	38	106	4	21	2	1	1	8	4	34	0
Mitchell, Keith, of	.249	98	341	35	85	16	1	5	33	41	50	9
Redington, Tom, 3b	.196	129	429	45	84	13	1	11	60	75	71	4
#Relaford, Winnie, of	.211	45	166	23	35	4	1	0	9	8	33	13
Saccomanno, Joe, ss	.258	51	190	12	49	5	1	0	17	11	30	3
*Stuart, Rob, of	.259	9	27	2	7	3	0	0	1	3	5	0
Williams, Ted, c	.145	27	69	5	10	2	0	0	8	6	21	0

PITCHING	W	L	ERA	G	GS	CG	SV	IP	H	R	ER	BB	SO
Burlingame, Dennis	9	11	2.49	24	24	8	0	163	132	59	45	43	89
Clark, Mark	0	0	9.39	7	2	0	0	15	25	16	16	15	12
*Currin, Wes	7	4	2.17	49	0	0	5	87	77	33	21	24	80
Gourlay, Craig	0	1	4.00	7	1	0	0	18	20	11	8	6	13
Meister, Ralph	2	9	5.92	17	17	2	0	79	97	61	52	28	54
Mitchell, Glenn	0	2	9.31	10	2	0	0	19	18	26	20	23	13
Nied, David	12	9	3.76	27	27	3	0	165	156	78	69	53	133
Reilley, John	3	3	5.89	36	2	0	1	73	88	53	48	30	52
Rivera, Ben	9	11	3.17	27	27	3	0	173	167	77	61	52	99
Siebert, Rick	0	0	9.00	1	0	0	0	1	1	1	1	2	0
Turner, Matt	1	0	4.60	7	0	0	0	16	17	8	8	3	7
Valencia, Jose	1	0	4.98	22	3	0	1	60	57	34	33	33	42
Vazquez, Mark	7	11	5.35	32	18	1	0	133	145	93	79	76	74
*Waznik, Allan	5	5	5.15	28	12	1	0	93	115	75	53	39	89
Wright, Skipper	8	5	1.95	45	0	0	24	65	55	19	14	16	69
Ziegler, Greg	0	2	9.90	2	2	0	0	10	11	12	11	6	6

Oneonta owns title after torrid pennant race

By GARY PICCIRILLO

Look back on the 1988 New York-Penn League season, and you will find nothing extraordinary about the Oneonta Yankees.

They simply went about their business day after day, lacking flash and power and pizzazz. It was easy not to notice them.

"If I had to categorize us," Oneonta manager Gary Allenson said, "I'd say we were a blue-collar team. We worked hard and battled back."

And never stopped until the NY-P championship was won. After surviving a wicked pennant race that went down to the final night of the regular season, Oneonta swept Jamestown in the best-of-3 playoffs for its fourth league crown this decade, 10th overall.

The playoff victory capped a torrid run for the title that found the McNamara Division champions winning 11 of their last 13 games.

Oneonta rallied to take the series

Marquis Grissom
... No. 1 prospect

opener against Jamestown 5-3 by scoring twice in the 13th inning. The Yankees clinched the championship with a 2-1 decision in Game Two. Eighth-inning doubles by Skip Nelloms and Rod Ehrhard tied the game and set the stage for a Rey Fernandez sacrifice fly.

Oneonta trailed in each of its last eight games, including the two in the playoffs.

"We just had the mental makeup to come back," Allenson said. "During the season, everybody seemed to get hot except us. We didn't get hot until we had to."

A race to the finish

The Yankees didn't put together impressive winning streaks. The secret to their success was consistency and perseverance.

Oneonta finished with the league's best record (48-28), but fought off challenges from three, sometimes four, division rivals.

League Champions
(Playoff Champions, Where Applicable)

1988—Oneonta	1971—Oneonta	1954—Corning
1987—Geneva	1970—Auburn	1953—Jamestown
1986—St. Catharines	1969—Oneonta	1952—Jamestown
1985—Oneonta	1968—Oneonta	1951—Hornell
1984—Little Falls	1967—Auburn	1950—Olean
1983—Utica	1966—Auburn	1949—Bradford
1982—Niagara Falls	1965—Binghamton	1948—Lockport
1981—Oneonta	1964—Auburn	1947—Jamestown
1980—Oneonta	1963—Batavia	1946—*Jamestown
1979—Oneonta	1962—Auburn	—*Batavia
1978—Geneva	1961—Olean	1945—Batavia
1977—Oneonta	1960—Wellsville	1944—Jamestown
1976—Elmira	1959—Wellsville	1943—Wellsville
1975—Newark	1958—Geneva	1942—Jamestown
1974—Oneonta	1957—Erie	1941—Bradford
1973—Auburn	1956—Wellsville	1940—Olean
1972—Niagara Falls	1955—Hamilton	1939—Olean
		*co-champions

Top NY-P Performers

Dan Freed
... 13-1, 0.67

Andy Mota
... batting champ

Derek Lee
....341, 54 steals

The Stedler Division race was a bit more simple, but no less intense. Jamestown led by four games on Aug. 21, and seemed poised to put away the title. But Erie won nine of 10 and closed to 1½ games out with two to play, both against the Expos.

When the Orioles scored a 7-4 victory on Sept. 1, the season came down to one game, winner take all. Jamestown righthander Dan Freed scattered nine hits over 10 innings, and the Expos advanced to the playoffs with a 2-1 win.

Shining stars of the NY-P

It was fitting that Freed got the call in Jamestown's most important regular-season game.

A 17th-round draft pick out of Illinois State, Freed was the league's top pitcher, winning 13 of 14 decisions to go with a sterling 0.67 ERA.

Because he started the last game of the regular season, Freed was unavailable for the playoffs. So was teammate Danilo Leon, who had pitched the night before.

Leon, who was 10-3 with a 1.16 ERA, combined with Freed to give the Expos a formidable 1-2 punch. Leon pitched four shutouts, tying Erie's Dave Miller for the league high.

Leading the offense for Jamestown was outfielder Marquis Grissom, voted the league's top prospect by a Baseball America poll of NY-P managers.

Grissom struggled early, but wound up with a .323 average. He led the league in runs (69), at-bats (291) and total bases (146), and his 94 hits were second only to Auburn's Andy Mota, who had 95 and led the league in hitting.

A number of other players also had superb seasons:

Derek Lee of Utica stole a league-high 54 bases, drove in 47 runs and was second to Mota in batting with a .341 average. Lee helped the Blue Sox establish a league record with 271 stolen bases.

Utica reliever Ron Stephens went 8-0, had eight saves and finished with a 0.92 ERA, helped along by a streak of 36⅔ scoreless innings.

No joke in Geneva

The national media zeroed in on Geneva, where the Cubs lost 18 straight to tie a league record set by Watertown in 1985.

After Geneva lost five in a row, general manager Ken Shepard vowed to sleep on a cot in the McDonough Park press box until the team won. Shepard returned to his double bed two weeks later.

To the Cubs' credit, they went 27-51, winning as many games as St. Catharines and only one fewer than Elmira.

Looking ahead to 1989

The NY-P made postseason news off the field when the league granted conditional approval for the Watertown Pirates to move to Welland, Ontario, for 1989. Welland would be the league's third Canadian team, joining St. Catharines and Hamilton.

The league also accepted Olean, N.Y., as an expansion franchise and planned to add another club, making 14 .teams. All moves were pending the approval of the National Association.

McNamara	W	L	Pct.	GB	
Oneonta (Yankees) ..	48	28	.632	—	
Utica (White Sox)....	47	29	.618	1	
Auburn (Astros)	42	33	.560	5½	
Little Falls (Mets)....	39	36	.520	8½	1988 Final Standings
Watertown (Pirates) .	35	39	.473	12	
Elmira (Red Sox)	28	48	.368	20	
Stedler					
Jamestown (Expos) .	47	29	.618	—	
Erie (Orioles)	46	31	.597	1½	
Hamilton (Cards)	36	39	.480	10½	
Batavia (Phillies)	31	44	.413	15½	
St. Cthrns (B. Jays)..	27	46	.370	18½	
Geneva (Cubs)	27	51	.346	21	

1988: General Information

Playoffs: Oneonta defeated Jamestown 2-0 in best-of-3 final for league championship.

Regular Season Attendance: Utica, 65,384; Hamilton, 60,380; Oneonta, 53,187; Jamestown, 52,177; Elmira, 48,978; Erie, 47,589; Auburn, 37,973; St. Catharines, 34,786; Batavia, 31,230; Little Falls, 30,126; Geneva, 24,654; Watertown, 19,649.

Managers: Auburn—Frank Cacciatore; **Batavia**—Don McCormack; **Elmira**—Bill Limoncelli; **Erie**—Bobby Tolan; **Geneva**—Bill Hayes; **Hamilton**—Dan Radison; **Jamestown**—Roger LaFrancois; **Little Falls**—Bill Stein; **Oneonta**—Gary Allenson; **St. Catharines**—Eddie Dennis; **Utica**—Rick Patterson; **Watertown**—Stan Cliburn.

1988 All-Star Team: C— Luis Paulino, Erie. **1B**— Andy Mota, Aurburn. **2B**—Pat Kelly, Oneonta. **3B**—Radhames Polanco, Little Falls. **SS**—Bob DeJardin, Oneonta. **Util**—Opie Moran, Hamilton. **OF**—Marquis Grissom, Jamestown; Derek Lee, Utica; Darwin Pennye, Watertown; Titi Roche, Little Falls. **RHP**—Dan Freed, Jamestown; Woody Williams, St. Catharines. **LHP**—Wally Trice, Aurburn; Chris Hill, Little Falls. **DH**—John Furch, Utica. **Manager of the Year**—Roger LaFrancois, Jamestown.

Top 10 Major League Prospects (by Baseball America): 1. Marquis Grissom, of, Jamestown; **2.** Derek Lee, of, Utica; **3.** Dan Freed, rhp, Jamestown; **4.** Luis Gonzalez, 3b, Auburn; **5.** Woody Williams, rhp, St. Catharines; **6.** David Proctor, rhp, Little Falls; **7.** Stacy Jones, rhp, Erie; **8.** Andy Mota, 1b-3b, Auburn; **9.** Radhames Polanco, 3b, Little Falls; **10.** Dave Miller, rhp, Erie.

1988: Batting, Pitching Statistics

CLUB BATTING

	AVG	G	AB	R	H	2B	3B	HR	BB	SO	SB
Jamestown	.270	76	2570	370	695	104	24	44	242	461	94
Oneonta	.259	76	2655	387	687	105	39	20	324	512	96
Auburn	.259	75	2475	427	640	110	16	35	383	583	186
Utica	.254	76	2398	397	608	75	37	20	322	512	270
Little Falls	.253	76	2511	323	635	99	16	31	219	463	92
Erie	.245	77	2526	370	619	112	7	45	312	501	136
Watertown	.240	74	2435	348	584	78	21	32	262	525	141
Geneva	.232	78	2581	272	598	78	10	20	235	518	91
Batavia	.230	75	2444	314	561	102	8	49	241	577	83
Hamilton	.225	75	2448	300	551	85	6	30	293	544	116
St. Catharines	.217	73	2291	261	498	72	12	24	284	530	78
Elmira	.215	77	2548	258	549	76	14	26	276	587	44

CLUB PITCHING

	ERA	G	CG	SHO	SV	IP	H	R	ER	BB	SO
Jamestown	2.68	76	21	9	13	671	546	265	200	260	540
Erie	2.83	77	23	10	23	680	602	268	214	211	501
Oneonta	2.86	76	6	3	17	688	644	294	219	230	552
Hamilton	3.34	75	6	2	17	658	577	311	244	247	606
Geneva	3.41	78	14	4	9	683	636	353	259	282	547
Utica	3.50	76	9	3	18	658	599	352	256	346	532
Little Falls	3.53	76	14	7	14	649	563	339	255	313	516
St. Catharines	3.71	73	3	6	11	636	577	359	262	303	495
Elmira	3.73	77	16	1	8	677	646	372	281	293	460
Watertown	3.84	74	8	3	19	641	570	352	273	329	555
Auburn	3.85	75	11	3	11	644	622	368	275	276	537
Batavia	4.33	75	6	4	14	642	643	394	309	303	472

INDIVIDUAL BATTING LEADERS
(Minimum 211 Plate Appearances)

	AVG	G	AB	R	H	2B	3B	HR	RBI	BB	SO	SB
Mota, Andy, Aub	.351	72	271	56	95	15	3	3	47	38	34	31
*Lee, Derek, Utica	.341	76	252	51	86	7	5	2	47	50	48	54
Kelly, Pat, One	.329	71	280	49	92	11	6	2	34	16	45	25
Grissom, Marquis, Jam	.323	74	291	69	94	14	7	8	39	35	39	23
*Brown, Terry, Erie	.319	60	207	42	66	14	2	13	49	31	58	11
Pennye, Darwin, Wtn	.314	72	274	41	86	10	3	3	30	27	41	22
Polanco, Radhames, LF	.313	75	284	41	89	13	4	6	42	23	59	4
#Boddie, Rod, Jam	.312	59	205	35	64	5	7	1	22	27	19	8
Trevino, Tony, Bat	.306	67	245	48	75	13	3	5	36	33	52	12
*Piechowski, Tim, Jam	.303	63	201	38	61	11	4	1	23	25	17	15

* indicates lefthanded batter   # indicates switch hitter

INDIVIDUAL PITCHING LEADERS
(Minimum 62 Innings)

	W	L	ERA	G	GS	CG	SV	IP	H	R	ER	BB	SO
Freed, Dan, Jam	13	1	0.67	15	15	9	0	121	80	16	9	18	82
Leon, Danilo, Jam	10	3	1.16	15	15	7	0	116	75	29	15	48	100
Miller, Dave, Erie	8	3	1.37	11	11	7	0	86	49	17	13	23	61
Williams, Woody, StC	8	2	1.54	12	12	2	0	76	48	22	13	21	58
*Trice, Wally, Aub	8	4	1.90	14	13	6	0	104	83	34	22	24	107
*Sodders, Mike, Gen	7	3	2.15	14	14	7	0	117	87	33	28	28	119
*Tomlin, Randy, Wtn	7	5	2.18	15	15	5	0	103	75	31	25	25	87
Young, Anthony, LF	3	5	2.20	15	10	4	0	74	51	33	18	34	75
*Bradford, Mark, Bat	2	2	2.31	16	4	2	0	70	43	21	18	41	40
Greer, Ken, One	5	5	2.40	15	15	4	0	112	109	46	30	18	60

* indicates lefthanded pitcher

AUBURN

BATTING	AVG	G	AB	R	H	2B	3B	HR	RBI	BB	SO	SB
Beams, Mike, of-dh	.282	51	174	30	49	10	2	5	43	21	52	5
Campos, Rafael, inf	.000	4	2	0	0	0	0	0	0	0	1	0
*Charno, Joe, c-dh	.218	40	133	20	29	5	2	4	31	21	40	0
Crockum, Ken, of	.204	20	54	5	11	1	0	0	5	5	7	8
*Fuller, Harry, of	.264	63	220	48	58	7	1	0	22	43	40	25
*Gonzalez, Luis, 3b	.312	39	157	30	49	10	3	5	27	12	19	2
Horta, Neder, 2b-ss	.193	54	150	28	29	2	0	1	10	36	44	5
Jenkins, Bernard, of	.244	58	201	35	49	11	0	6	46	30	61	9
#Lamphere, Larry, 2b	.212	54	170	29	36	6	0	0	15	18	43	17
Lewis, Mica, ss	.280	58	193	32	54	10	3	3	22	42	48	15
*Lofton, Kenny, of	.214	48	187	23	40	6	1	1	14	19	51	26
Massarelli, John, c	.302	59	179	29	54	8	1	0	26	32	31	25
Mota, Andy, 1b-3b	.351	72	271	56	95	15	3	4	47	38	34	31
Shermet, Dave, of-3b	.248	63	214	37	53	11	0	3	26	44	53	15
Spurgeon, Scott, 1b	.201	53	169	23	34	8	0	4	24	22	58	3

PITCHING	W	L	ERA	G	GS	CG	SV	IP	H	R	ER	BB	SO
*Desapio, Jim	3	2	3.80	14	12	0	0	73	79	39	31	32	44
Dunnum, Rick	7	0	3.66	18	10	1	1	86	88	45	35	38	81
Farmer, Gordy	8	4	3.60	15	15	3	0	95	75	47	38	38	93
Gonzales, Ben	0	2	4.97	6	0	0	0	13	12	7	7	3	13
*Klinefelter, David	2	3	4.42	8	7	0	0	37	42	30	18	21	18
Morris, Ken	5	5	4.52	17	8	1	0	72	79	46	36	43	38
Scheckla, Rod	1	1	4.44	13	1	0	1	26	25	16	13	16	25
Small, Chris	2	6	6.96	15	9	0	0	53	66	56	41	30	41
Tafoya, Dennis	2	2	2.78	21	0	0	6	32	28	20	10	12	22
*Trice, Wally	8	4	1.90	14	13	6	0	104	83	34	22	24	107
*Windes, Rod	4	4	4.10	25	0	0	3	53	45	28	24	19	55

BATAVIA

BATTING	AVG	G	AB	R	H	2B	3B	HR	RBI	BB	SO	SB
Barrick, Andy, 3b-1b	.200	52	165	19	33	8	0	2	20	25	23	1
Carlin, Mike, 2b	.255	16	47	5	12	0	0	0	4	1	8	3
*Cummings, Brian, 1b	.231	61	242	24	56	7	0	13	41	6	59	1
Donahoe, Jim, c	.250	31	96	9	24	4	0	2	13	4	13	0
Drury, Scott, c	.167	10	24	2	4	0	0	0	4	4	12	0
Ellison, Paul, c	.296	8	27	3	8	0	0	1	4	4	8	0
Enos, Eric, c	.192	32	99	10	19	1	0	1	6	7	17	1
Felton, Fred, of	.228	36	101	12	23	3	0	0	7	14	34	8
Galloway, Isaac, of	.197	43	157	17	31	5	0	3	10	6	44	0
#Keller, Steve, 3b	.186	42	145	9	27	6	0	2	19	10	20	1
Lozinski, Tony, c	.270	12	37	4	10	1	0	0	4	4	8	0
Marsh, Tom, of	.255	62	216	35	55	14	1	8	27	18	54	6
#Martinez, Nicio, ss	.145	42	124	11	18	6	0	1	8	16	43	1
Santa Cruz, Nick, ss	.215	59	205	31	44	8	0	0	18	30	43	11
Taft, Tim, c	.000	1	2	0	0	0	0	0	0	0	1	0
Tenhunfield, Joe, dh-of	.134	29	82	9	11	2	1	1	8	1	23	4
Trevino, Tony, 2b-of	.306	67	245	48	75	13	3	5	36	33	52	12
Ventress, Leroy, of	.251	70	271	45	68	14	2	3	19	35	58	36
*Walker, Chris, dh	.311	48	135	20	42	10	1	6	24	23	41	0
Zerb, Troy, 2b	.042	7	24	1	1	0	0	0	2	0	16	0

PITCHING	W	L	ERA	G	GS	CG	SV	IP	H	R	ER	BB	SO
Allen, Dave	0	0	108.00	2	0	0	0	1	3	10	8	6	1
Ashby, Andy	3	1	1.61	6	6	2	0	45	25	11	8	16	32

	W	L	ERA	G	GS	CG	SV	IP	H	R	ER	BB	SO
Backs, Jason	0	2	9.00	4	0	0	1	4	9	6	4	3	5
*Bradford, Mark	2	2	2.31	16	4	2	0	70	43	21	18	41	40
Bratlien, Eric	2	5	4.28	24	0	0	8	40	44	22	19	13	36
Dell, Tim	1	0	1.21	22	1	1	2	52	39	14	7	12	43
Douty, Dean	0	4	6.24	14	7	1	0	49	52	41	34	24	35
Elam, Todd	7	6	3.82	15	15	3	0	94	97	47	40	36	84
Maldonado, Pete	3	2	5.63	15	0	0	2	24	35	17	15	4	14
*Owens, Mike	1	7	7.07	13	12	1	0	56	69	58	44	44	45
*Shade, Tony	0	0	5.79	6	0	0	0	14	16	11	9	4	10
Taft, Tim	0	0	5.40	1	0	0	0	2	3	2	1	2	1
Tracy, Richard	1	0	2.77	6	0	0	1	13	9	5	4	2	6
Trlicek, Rick	2	3	7.39	8	8	0	0	32	27	32	26	31	26
Viggiano, Matt	5	3	5.88	14	7	1	0	57	70	45	37	29	31
Wilson, Gary	4	9	3.60	15	15	2	0	90	102	52	36	35	60

ELMIRA

BATTING	AVG	G	AB	R	H	2B	3B	HR	RBI	BB	SO	SB
Dorante, Luis, dh-of	.197	31	76	14	15	6	0	0	2	15	16	1
Flaherty, John, c	.235	46	162	17	38	3	0	3	16	12	23	2
Hanks, Chris, dh	.200	40	120	14	24	3	0	1	11	17	21	0
Marrs, Terry, of	.113	44	97	7	11	2	1	0	5	9	30	4
*Matilla, Pedro, of	.154	39	117	9	18	2	1	1	4	10	24	1
Michael, Steve, of-p	.262	34	84	11	22	5	0	2	11	4	29	2
Monegro, Miguel, 2b	.244	40	135	12	33	2	0	1	12	2	23	1
Moore, Bart, 2b	.231	43	143	18	33	0	1	1	8	18	35	2
Munoz, Lou, of-2b	.217	52	152	10	33	5	0	1	14	9	33	3
Naehring, Tim, ss	.305	19	59	6	18	3	0	1	13	8	11	0
#Rivers, Mickey, of	.201	63	199	22	40	9	1	2	15	14	66	10
Rosario, Julio, 3b-ss	.176	34	91	7	16	1	1	0	4	2	14	0
Scannell, Larry, of	.100	15	40	4	4	1	0	0	3	4	8	0
Spencer, John, of	.196	70	219	16	43	5	2	1	23	14	61	5
#Tatum, Willie, 1b-dh	.286	58	192	30	55	8	2	4	22	32	52	1
Thornton, Al, 1b-dh	.189	61	201	17	38	6	2	4	21	17	51	0
Valentin, John, ss	.217	60	207	18	45	5	1	2	16	36	35	5
Warfel, Brian, of	.250	29	48	5	12	2	0	0	2	11	4	2
Whitehead, Chris, 3b	.248	70	206	21	51	6	2	2	21	42	51	5

PITCHING	W	L	ERA	G	GS	CG	SV	IP	H	R	ER	BB	SO
*Dolan, John	3	2	2.42	6	6	1	0	45	38	21	12	12	17
Dzafic, Bernie	3	5	4.18	17	8	0	0	71	89	42	33	11	44
Estrada, Pete	6	8	2.50	17	16	10	0	119	106	44	33	24	73
Harris, Reggie	3	6	5.30	10	10	0	0	54	56	37	32	28	46
Kite, Dan	3	3	3.18	12	5	1	0	40	24	24	14	33	47
Michael, Steve	0	1	10.13	6	2	0	0	11	15	16	12	17	3
Morrison, Jim	1	4	5.36	17	5	1	0	50	51	37	30	26	37
Pratts, Alberto	3	1	2.04	17	0	0	6	40	28	12	9	20	15
Rivera, Carlos	0	2	4.81	18	0	0	2	43	41	26	23	28	33
Rush, Andy	3	8	4.15	14	13	2	0	78	71	47	36	46	66
Sanders, Al	2	6	2.90	17	11	1	0	84	79	41	27	28	66
Stange, Tim	0	1	4.55	11	0	0	0	28	29	19	14	14	14
*Taylor, Scott	1	0	0.00	2	1	0	0	4	2	0	0	3	8
Warfel, Brian	0	1	4.50	8	0	0	0	12	17	6	6	3	7

ERIE

BATTING	AVG	G	AB	R	H	2B	3B	HR	RBI	BB	SO	SB
Ahalt, Dell, 3b-1b	.200	58	160	22	32	7	1	4	16	24	59	5
*Bautista, Hector, of	.191	13	47	3	9	1	0	0	1	2	3	0
Block, Bob, of	.204	22	54	9	11	0	0	1	5	9	15	3
*Brown, Terry, of-dh	.319	60	207	42	66	14	2	13	49	31	58	11
Browning, Steve, c	.151	29	86	7	13	4	0	1	6	6	22	0
*Fleita, Oneri, 1b	.222	32	90	15	20	3	0	5	16	17	14	1
#Gilbert, Roy, of	.254	73	287	53	73	19	0	1	32	33	35	30
Gordon, John, 2b-3b	.245	62	192	27	47	8	0	7	36	32	36	6
Hayden, Paris, dh-of	.240	50	171	29	41	8	0	5	25	12	35	2
Holland, Tim, inf	.198	69	242	23	48	6	1	0	12	11	54	5
*Lee, Keith, of	.250	67	248	43	62	8	2	3	16	41	66	29
Lofton, Rodney, ss-2b	.300	72	250	49	75	12	1	0	37	35	29	37
McNaney, Scott, 2b	.233	30	86	7	20	3	0	1	10	14	17	1
Pancoski, Tracey, dh	.200	2	5	0	1	0	0	0	0	2	2	0
Paulino, Luis, c	.276	61	210	28	58	9	0	2	29	23	25	0
Soto, Jose, 1b-c	.161	20	56	6	9	2	0	0	3	4	13	0
Withers, Mark, of-3b	.252	46	135	16	34	8	0	2	14	16	18	4

PITCHING	W	L	ERA	G	GS	CG	SV	IP	H	R	ER	BB	SO
Amarena, Sam	3	0	0.41	7	0	0	0	22	12	1	1	4	12
Blohm, Pete	4	5	4.27	13	10	3	0	72	75	39	34	22	49
Burgin, Chris	6	4	3.52	15	15	5	0	100	94	45	39	28	70
*Cavers, Mike	5	1	2.83	18	8	0	0	57	54	28	18	30	49
Constant, Andres	1	1	4.61	15	0	0	4	27	21	14	14	10	25
Deutsch, Mike	7	1	2.98	14	14	3	0	94	94	38	31	27	71
Evans, Scott	1	1	6.67	8	4	0	1	30	32	24	22	7	23
Jones, Stacy	3	3	1.33	7	7	3	0	54	51	12	8	15	40
*Linskey, Mike	3	3	3.11	10	8	2	1	55	46	24	19	18	50
Miller, Dave	8	3	1.37	11	11	7	0	86	49	17	13	23	61
Mondile, Steve	2	2	1.07	27	0	0	12	42	31	10	5	11	30
Powers, Tad	3	7	2.21	25	0	0	5	41	42	16	10	15	30

GENEVA

BATTING	AVG	G	AB	R	H	2B	3B	HR	RBI	BB	SO	SB
Canino, Carlos, c	.000	5	11	0	0	0	0	0	0	0	8	0
Eggleston, Skip, 2b	.199	51	176	18	35	5	1	0	12	17	45	3
Fairey, Jim, of	.198	49	162	15	32	7	1	0	8	16	28	2
#Figueroa, Juan, of	.263	35	99	14	26	4	2	0	11	7	27	1
*Franco, Matt, 3b-1b	.256	44	164	19	42	2	0	3	21	19	13	2
Jose, Clemente, of	.077	9	26	0	2	0	0	0	0	0	15	0
Jose, Elio, dh	.288	47	184	25	53	13	0	4	23	9	32	5
*Leonard, Matt, dh-3b	.211	20	57	2	12	2	0	0	8	8	7	1
Mundy, Rick, c	.151	41	126	9	19	0	0	1	8	6	41	1
Murphy, Jim, of	.229	67	223	21	51	5	1	4	24	14	61	9
*Perry, Eric, 1b	.280	68	236	26	66	7	0	4	22	29	44	4
Ramirez, Nick, ss	.196	34	92	11	18	2	0	0	1	10	23	5
*Shreve, Ben, 2b	.196	17	56	2	11	0	1	0	1	6	9	1
Smith, Tracy, ss-p	.193	52	135	9	26	3	0	0	11	14	31	5
St.Peter, Bill, 3b-ss	.224	67	241	27	54	13	0	1	23	24	46	4
Taylor, Scott, c	.259	50	158	14	41	3	0	0	14	5	15	3
Washington, Kraig, 2b-of	.268	44	168	22	45	3	0	0	11	6	16	15
*Williams, Eric, of	.243	73	267	38	65	9	4	3	22	45	57	30

PITCHING	W	L	ERA	G	GS	CG	SV	IP	H	R	ER	BB	SO
*Ellis, Tim	1	1	4.28	16	2	0	0	34	33	20	16	27	35
Espino, Francisco	2	5	2.63	17	6	0	0	62	60	27	18	19	45
Gardner, John	1	7	3.21	14	13	2	0	84	76	42	30	49	61
Goodwin, Dave	4	8	4.87	17	13	0	0	81	94	56	44	33	36
Johnston, Dan	1	2	2.98	24	0	0	4	45	37	22	15	17	37
Knight, Darrin	2	3	2.17	18	2	0	3	46	21	12	11	29	40
Lutz, Chris	5	8	2.64	13	13	3	0	82	79	38	24	21	55
Rodriguez, Eligio	0	2	6.91	15	1	0	0	27	37	27	21	12	23
Salles, John	0	0	11.57	1	1	0	0	2	7	3	3	3	1
Smith, Tracy	0	4	6.20	15	1	0	0	20	20	18	14	12	21
*Sodders, Mike	7	3	2.15	16	14	7	0	117	87	33	28	28	119
*Stroud, Derrick	4	8	3.81	16	12	2	2	83	85	55	35	32	74

HAMILTON

BATTING	AVG	G	AB	R	H	2B	3B	HR	RBI	BB	SO	SB
Battell, Mark, c	.203	52	143	9	29	4	0	2	14	13	43	1
*Brown, Winston, of	.400	5	15	3	6	3	0	0	1	3	2	0
*Butts, Randy, dh-1b	.135	18	37	3	5	1	0	1	3	8	6	0
Christian, Rick, of	.202	65	238	29	48	7	1	0	8	14	57	21
Elci, Lee, c-dh	.225	43	151	15	34	9	0	3	19	11	25	5

	AVG	G	AB	R	H	2B	3B	HR	RBI	BB	SO	SB
Fanning, Steve, ss	.223	60	175	22	39	8	0	0	2	28	58	5
*Federico, Joe, 1b-dh	.233	73	262	38	61	8	0	9	40	41	58	6
Gentleman, Jean-Paul, 2b	.235	40	115	8	27	3	0	0	10	8	19	3
*Graham, Steve, of	.227	61	194	18	44	3	0	0	15	20	30	8
Grier, Antron, of	.333	5	9	2	3	0	0	0	0	1	4	0
Hall, Joe, of-1b	.285	70	274	46	78	9	1	2	37	30	37	30
#Jordan, Brian, of	.310	19	71	12	22	3	1	4	12	6	15	3
*Lampe, Ed, of	.150	59	173	28	26	7	1	1	9	32	61	21
Malchesky, Tom, 3b	.171	65	205	10	35	3	0	2	18	11	65	3
Moran, Opie, 2b-ss	.259	75	259	42	67	11	1	5	28	46	43	8
Redman, Tim, c	.184	22	49	5	9	0	1	0	3	9	7	0
#Robinson, Kevin, of	.220	14	41	5	9	3	0	0	1	6	7	1
Ross, Mike, 2b	.243	10	37	5	9	3	0	1	11	6	7	1

PITCHING	W	L	ERA	G	GS	CG	SV	IP	H	R	ER	BB	SO
Brooks, Rod	3	2	5.81	13	7	0	0	48	53	33	31	26	43
*Cebuhar, John	3	3	3.35	22	3	0	0	38	37	20	14	20	45
*Chadwick, Bob	0	0	4.91	7	0	0	1	11	10	6	6	6	8
Clark, Mark	6	7	3.05	15	15	2	0	94	88	39	32	32	60
Duvall, Brad	3	3	3.54	13	13	0	0	76	63	39	30	40	58
Halama, Scott	2	0	1.55	14	0	0	1	29	24	7	5	14	22
Houser, Chris	0	3	4.24	10	2	0	0	17	14	14	8	13	12
Kisten, Dale	1	4	1.88	23	0	0	10	53	31	16	11	14	66
*Lepley, John	3	0	0.00	6	0	0	1	14	6	4	0	5	17
Majer, Steffen	2	4	3.32	12	10	2	0	65	56	32	24	24	61
Plemel, Lee	1	0	0.00	1	1	0	0	5	3	0	0	0	8
*Richardson, Dave	5	9	4.15	17	13	1	0	87	93	49	40	24	91
Satterfield, Cory	5	4	3.28	18	11	1	4	82	70	36	30	14	80
Weese, Dean	2	0	3.00	24	0	0	0	39	29	16	13	15	37

JAMESTOWN

BATTING	AVG	G	AB	R	H	2B	3B	HR	RBI	BB	SO	SB
*Atha, Jeff, 2b-3b	.208	63	202	33	42	8	0	2	30	19	26	6
#Boddie, Rod, of	.312	59	205	35	64	5	7	1	22	27	19	8
Cordero, Wilfredo, ss	.258	52	190	18	49	3	0	2	22	15	44	3
Echemendia, Idaiberto, 1b-3b	.333	33	90	12	30	1	0	3	16	11	18	1
Grissom, Marquis, of	.323	74	291	69	94	14	7	8	39	35	39	23
Kaub, Keith, 1b-dh	.273	61	209	27	57	4	0	8	37	27	51	2
#Kosco, Bryn, 3b-ss	.284	63	229	26	65	19	2	8	42	18	48	1
Laker, Tim, c	.224	47	152	14	34	9	0	0	17	8	30	2
Mitchell, Jorge, of-3b	.234	40	128	22	30	4	0	5	9	9	34	6
#Paredes, Jesus, ss-2b	.290	24	62	9	18	1	0	0	9	8	8	11
*Piechowski, Tim, of	.303	63	201	38	61	11	4	1	23	25	17	15
Reagans, Javan, of-dh	.240	35	125	15	30	4	0	3	17	4	33	4
*Robitaille, Martin, 1b	.231	52	134	10	31	8	1	1	12	10	39	0
Shephard, Kelvin, of	.313	21	67	7	21	3	0	0	5	4	14	2
*Siddall, Joe, c	.213	53	178	18	38	5	3	1	16	14	29	5
*Stanley, Tim, 2b	.290	36	107	16	31	5	0	1	5	8	12	2

PITCHING	W	L	ERA	G	GS	CG	SV	IP	H	R	ER	BB	SO
*Alleyne, Issac	5	5	2.72	14	14	4	0	79	70	34	24	32	80
Archibald, Dan	1	5	4.58	18	7	0	4	53	61	30	27	28	36
Davis, Bret	3	1	2.87	18	0	0	3	38	26	14	12	14	50
Finigan, Kevin	3	2	2.37	15	4	0	0	49	43	20	13	15	37
Freed, Dan	13	1	0.67	15	15	9	0	121	80	16	9	18	82
Heiderscheit, Pat	1	2	4.26	3	3	0	0	19	15	9	9	9	11
Kerrigan, Rob	3	1	0.90	6	0	0	1	20	12	4	2	5	21
Klancnik, Joe	0	0	37.80	2	0	0	0	2	4	7	7	8	1
Leon, Danilo	10	3	1.16	15	15	7	0	116	75	29	15	48	100
Oropeza, Dave	4	1	2.28	6	6	1	0	43	28	13	11	14	40
Overeem, Steve	0	1	4.66	12	0	0	1	19	18	13	10	9	17
Rivera, Angel	0	0	6.35	4	0	0	0	6	4	8	4	14	1
*Sajonia, Brian	0	1	4.71	13	4	0	0	29	30	18	15	12	16
Solarte, Jose	2	2	4.96	13	1	0	2	33	33	22	18	15	19
*Winston, Darrin	2	4	4.91	14	7	0	2	44	47	28	24	19	29

LITTLE FALLS

BATTING	AVG	G	AB	R	H	2B	3B	HR	RBI	BB	SO	SB
Baez, Kevin, ss	.266	70	218	23	58	7	1	1	19	32	30	7
*Bales, Tom, dh-c	.182	16	44	4	8	2	0	0	2	2	10	0
Becker, Tom, 2b	.255	27	98	11	25	4	0	0	9	11	14	1
#Harris, Vince, of (42 Uti)	.200	69	225	46	45	4	2	0	17	53	33	53
Height, Ron, 2b-ss	.108	29	74	11	8	2	0	1	6	7	27	1
#Hundley, Todd, c	.188	52	176	23	33	8	0	2	18	16	31	1
May, Lee, of	.211	64	213	31	45	12	2	1	21	11	68	13
Noelke, Mike, 2b	.271	31	96	11	26	2	1	0	10	9	6	2
Olah, Bob, 1b	.285	70	260	21	74	6	0	7	43	15	50	1
Piskor, Steve, c	.276	28	87	14	24	3	0	5	14	7	15	1
Polanco, Radhames, 3b	.313	75	284	41	89	13	4	6	42	23	59	4
*Roche, Titi, of-dh	.303	68	284	45	86	17	2	2	25	14	24	30
Sanchez, Sammye, of	.237	43	156	15	37	6	0	2	15	8	21	3
Saunders, Doug, 2b	.300	29	100	10	30	6	1	0	11	6	15	1
*Turtletaub, Greg, of-1b	.219	64	178	21	39	8	0	2	21	29	44	2
Walker, Lonnie, of	.248	51	145	24	36	6	4	2	15	11	39	7

PITCHING	W	L	ERA	G	GS	CG	SV	IP	H	R	ER	BB	SO
Bross, Terry	2	1	3.09	20	6	0	1	55	43	25	19	38	59
Fine, Tom	4	4	4.15	10	8	0	0	43	43	27	20	32	27
Griffin, Terry	5	7	3.39	14	13	2	0	98	79	46	37	27	62
*Hill, Chris	5	5	3.06	13	13	2	0	79	56	32	27	35	66
*Lott, Hank	0	0	0.00	4	0	0	0	6	6	3	0	10	6
Newton, Steve	1	3	6.03	17	1	0	1	31	36	29	21	20	29
Perez, Vladimir	6	5	4.62	17	12	4	0	76	78	46	39	25	53
Plummer, Dale	5	1	1.33	25	0	0	10	41	27	7	6	7	37
Proctor, David	5	3	4.21	12	12	2	0	68	57	43	32	45	53
Wenrick, John	2	1	3.30	23	0	0	2	46	53	22	17	17	30
Young, Anthony	3	5	2.20	15	10	4	0	74	51	33	18	34	75
*Zimmerman, Brian	1	1	5.76	17	1	0	0	30	33	26	19	22	19

ONEONTA

BATTING	AVG	G	AB	R	H	2B	3B	HR	RBI	BB	SO	SB
Ausmus, Brad, c	.250	2	8	0	1	0	0	0	0	0	2	0
Bridges, Jason, of	.225	68	249	40	56	10	3	3	32	43	53	5
#DeJardin, Bob, ss	.295	69	288	45	85	8	4	1	27	33	47	15
Ehrhard, Rod, c-of	.243	67	243	37	59	14	7	3	29	42	72	2
*Erhardt, Herb, 1b-3b	.203	72	266	27	54	12	0	3	30	24	46	1
*Fernandez, Rey, of-dh	.278	53	198	15	55	9	4	3	41	8	44	0
Hunter, Robert, of	.269	28	108	21	29	5	1	1	12	23	24	10
Kelly, Pat, 2b	.329	71	280	49	92	11	6	2	34	16	45	25
Knoblauh, Jay, of	.173	40	133	18	23	3	2	0	9	20	33	5
Livesey, Jeff, c-dh	.222	37	126	15	28	3	1	2	9	17	30	0
Martin, Mark, c	.278	6	18	0	5	0	0	0	3	1	2	0
*Nelloms, Skip, of	.273	59	205	29	56	8	3	2	30	25	33	5
*Seeburger, John, 1b	.333	22	90	14	30	5	1	0	14	12	19	0
Torres, Miguel, 3b-2b	.259	59	189	31	49	7	1	0	24	22	26	16
Vargas, Hector, 3b-ss	.259	46	143	24	37	5	2	0	16	13	23	11
#Warren, Allen, of	.000	4	3	0	0	0	0	0	0	0	0	0
*Zeihen, Bob, of	.273	27	99	20	27	5	4	0	15	24	9	1
Zeratsky, Mark, c	.077	5	13	2	1	0	0	0	1	1	4	0

PITCHING	W	L	ERA	G	GS	CG	SV	IP	H	R	ER	BB	SO
*Brill, Todd	4	0	2.72	13	0	0	0	36	29	12	11	10	27
Brink, Craig	0	1	4.13	9	0	0	0	24	25	11	11	5	12
Broxton, Cliff	1	1	1.69	10	0	0	4	16	11	3	3	4	18
Candaleria, Jorge	3	0	.93	9	0	0	0	19	9	2	2	12	23
*Canestro, Art	2	1	2.43	16	0	0	1	41	32	16	11	16	44
Cook, Andy	8	4	3.62	16	16	2	0	102	116	50	41	21	65
Draper, Mike	2	1	.84	8	0	0	3	11	10	4	1	3	16
Greer, Ken	5	5	2.40	15	15	4	0	112	109	46	30	18	60
Hoffman, Jeff	0	0	3.55	9	0	0	0	13	15	9	5	9	10
*Johnson, Jeff	6	1	2.98	14	14	0	0	88	67	35	29	39	91
Makemson, Jay	4	1	3.38	9	0	0	0	45	44	28	17	27	40
Martel, Ed	2	2	3.02	9	8	0	0	42	53	20	14	8	24
*Nielsen, Jerry	6	2	.71	19	1	0	0	38	27	6	3	18	35
Prybylinski, Bruce	1	2	1.17	19	0	0	8	23	11	3	3	7	27
Seminara, Frank	4	7	4.37	16	13	0	1	78	86	49	38	33	60

ST. CATHARINES

BATTING	AVG	G	AB	R	H	2B	3B	HR	RBI	BB	SO	SB
Barry, Jose, of	.260	38	123	16	32	4	1	0	9	14	28	11
Brooks, Eric, dh-c	.224	47	152	10	34	3	1	1	9	29	49	2
Dixon, Bryan, of	.228	28	101	16	23	2	1	1	10	13	8	0
Eliopolis, Jim, c	.500	2	2	0	1	0	0	0	1	0	0	0
Garcia, Anastacio, c	.300	4	10	0	3	1	0	0	2	1	1	0
Guarache, Jose, 1b	.111	4	18	3	2	1	0	0	2	2	7	0
Harding, Greg, 1b	.260	56	208	21	54	13	0	6	32	14	28	5
*Hodge, Tim, dh	.000	2	3	0	0	0	0	0	0	0	1	0
Marquez, Edgar, of	.226	55	190	32	43	7	2	2	17	23	64	8
Martinez, Jose, 2b-3b	.211	51	147	14	31	4	0	2	15	17	31	8
Martinez, Rafael, 2b-ss	.216	55	194	22	42	8	2	1	18	17	39	9
Montalvo, Rob, ss	.168	62	190	34	32	4	0	0	18	25	48	4
Salazar, Luis, 3b	.208	62	216	19	45	6	1	1	26	16	22	1
Serra, Armando, dh-3b	.154	10	26	2	4	0	0	0	0	1	8	1
Taveras, Marcos, of	.209	64	206	26	43	6	1	1	15	25	54	7
Taylor, Mike, ss	.250	2	4	1	1	0	0	0	0	5	2	1
*Thompson, Ryan, of	.175	23	57	13	10	4	0	0	2	24	21	2
Townley, Jason, c	.218	64	225	19	49	4	0	5	18	30	65	4
Vaughan, Rick, c	.154	5	13	2	2	0	0	0	3	4	3	1
*Wade, Darrin, dh-1b	.255	29	102	11	26	4	1	2	8	12	18	0
*Wilson, Nigel, of	.204	40	103	12	21	1	2	2	11	12	32	8

PITCHING	W	L	ERA	G	GS	CG	SV	IP	H	R	ER	BB	SO
Brown, Timothy	1	3	3.00	15	8	1	0	72	58	33	24	22	37
*Castro, Pablo	0	0	31.50	3	0	0	0	2	1	7	7	8	0
Dodd, Dan	1	9	3.41	18	16	0	0	98	79	51	37	37	79
Evaschuk, Brad	1	2	7.27	16	1	0	0	26	31	23	21	19	12
*Jockish, Mike	0	0	3.73	17	0	0	4	31	32	19	13	24	36
Johnson, Curtis	1	8	4.59	17	6	0	4	51	47	32	26	27	44
McCutcheon, Greg	0	1	5.06	4	1	0	0	11	12	9	6	7	8
Nowak, Rick	1	3	2.88	4	4	0	0	25	21	14	8	10	24
*Olivares, Jose	3	2	3.69	17	0	0	1	39	42	24	16	22	37
Placeres, Ben	0	0	22.50	2	0	0	0	2	5	5	5	1	1

	W	L	ERA	G	GS	CG	SV	IP	H	R	ER	BB	SO
*Seal, Mike	2	2	1.93	15	0	0	1	33	25	12	7	18	34
Villa, Jose	0	1	6.00	3	0	0	0	6	7	5	4	4	4
*Ward, Anthony	2	8	4.48	18	12	0	0	72	75	50	36	41	64
Weathers, David	4	4	3.02	15	12	0	0	63	58	30	21	26	36
Williams, Woody	8	2	1.54	12	12	2	0	76	48	22	13	21	58
Wolfe, Donn	3	1	5.40	17	1	0	1	30	36	23	18	16	21

UTICA

BATTING	AVG	G	AB	R	H	2B	3B	HR	RBI	BB	SO	SB
Alvarez, Clemente, c ..	.235	53	132	15	31	5	1	0	14	11	36	5
*Bargman, Todd, dh-of ...	.118	27	68	5	8	0	0	2	4	5	22	0
Bedoya, Raul, inf	.254	47	63	14	16	4	0	0	4	7	13	1
Berry, Brett, of	.238	32	63	12	15	1	1	0	3	8	13	7
*Chasey, Mark, 1b	.231	75	225	38	52	3	2	1	29	46	60	21
Fuller, Paul, c	.306	48	144	21	44	7	1	0	20	21	27	6
Furch, John, dh	.337	30	104	18	35	10	1	5	25	8	16	7
Harris, Keith, of	.273	23	66	10	18	2	1	0	9	4	15	8
Hosey, Dwayne, of	.143	3	7	0	1	0	0	0	0	0	2	1
*Lee, Derek, of	.341	76	252	51	86	7	5	2	47	50	48	54
*Lukachyk, Rob, 3b	.282	71	227	42	64	10	8	7	48	31	48	9
#Mehl, Steve, of	.274	68	226	50	62	9	3	2	24	25	40	40
Merejo, Jesus, ss-3b ...	.222	16	27	2	6	0	0	0	3	1	6	0
Murdock, Kevin, dh-c ...	.200	20	65	4	13	1	1	0	5	7	16	1
Tejada, Eugenio, ss	.247	71	223	28	55	7	3	0	19	13	47	16
*Trammell, Marcus, 2b ..	.204	66	221	35	45	2	4	0	21	25	30	33
*Walsh, Ed, 1b	.125	3	8	1	1	1	0	0	1	1	4	0
Warren, Randy, 2b-of ...	.212	42	104	15	22	3	3	1	11	17	29	19
*Zaksek, John, of	.172	17	29	6	5	0	1	0	2	5	10	6

PITCHING	W	L	ERA	G	GS	CG	SV	IP	H	R	ER	BB	SO
Carey, Bill	7	2	3.80	17	1	0	1	47	43	26	20	20	45
Chaffin, John	0	0	0.00	2	0	0	0	1	1	2	0	2	2
Cooper, Virgil	3	3	3.84	15	15	3	0	84	86	49	36	38	60
*Dabney, Fred	9	4	2.67	19	13	1	0	88	83	40	26	41	69
Dela Cruz, Carlos	7	3	2.96	15	13	4	0	91	70	34	30	52	77
Felden, Keith	6	3	4.61	17	10	0	1	66	72	43	34	37	37
Fuller, Scott	4	3	4.61	17	8	1	0	57	54	37	29	41	44
*Galvan, Mike	0	0	4.76	5	3	0	0	17	14	11	9	12	11
Marshall, Brett	0	1	6.35	2	1	0	0	6	10	9	4	0	3
*Mehrtens, Pat	0	4	4.68	16	9	0	1	65	60	46	34	44	59
Merigliano, Frank	1	4	1.60	24	0	0	7	45	36	15	8	19	53
Mitchener, Mike	1	1	1.35	7	0	0	0	7	5	1	1	5	6
*Parascand, Steve	1	0	1.80	4	2	0	0	10	10	3	2	8	9
*Pena, Jose	0	1	10.67	11	1	0	0	14	21	26	17	17	9
Stephens, Ron	8	0	0.92	22	0	0	8	59	34	10	6	10	48

WATERTOWN

BATTING	AVG	G	AB	R	H	2B	3B	HR	RBI	BB	SO	SB
Arguellas, Fernando, c ..	.235	30	68	6	16	2	0	0	7	8	17	2
#Arnold, Bryan, c	.181	37	94	13	17	1	2	2	16	9	36	3
*Bluthardt, Jay, dh-of ..	.308	15	39	3	12	3	0	0	4	4	5	1
Buksa, Ken, c	.265	44	136	11	36	6	1	0	12	7	19	4
Cowley, Scott, of	.228	20	57	13	13	2	0	0	8	14	18	1
*Denkenberger, Ralph, 1b-dh	.266	60	199	26	53	9	3	1	30	11	43	10
Estep, Chris, of	.237	71	232	50	55	7	3	9	34	42	72	25
Huyler, Mike, 2b	.161	42	87	6	14	2	0	0	4	3	12	3
Johnson, Deron, of	.045	8	22	3	1	0	0	0	2	3	4	0
*Merejo, Domingo, of ...	.249	67	257	44	64	9	7	9	33	16	52	16
Montejano, Steve, 2b-ss .	.071	6	14	2	1	0	0	0	0	0	1	0
Pennye, Darwin, of	.314	72	274	45	86	10	3	3	30	27	41	22
Peyton, Mickey, of-2b ..	.203	28	69	8	14	0	0	0	4	1	21	6
Spalt, Paul, ss	.192	59	182	23	35	6	0	0	10	42	34	15
Stone, Dave, dh-3b	.245	19	49	6	12	2	0	1	11	5	15	0
Valla, Mike, c	.000	16	20	3	0	0	0	0	0	1	5	2
Wakefield, Tim, 1b	.189	54	159	24	30	6	2	3	20	25	57	3
Wehner, John, 3b	.275	70	265	41	73	6	0	3	31	21	39	18
Williams, Flavio, 2b-ss ..	.274	59	168	19	46	6	0	0	22	20	17	3
Young, John, of	.140	16	43	5	6	1	0	1	3	3	17	1

PITCHING	W	L	ERA	G	GS	CG	SV	IP	H	R	ER	BB	SO
Ausanio, Joe	2	4	1.32	28	0	0	13	48	29	10	7	27	56
Buckholz, Steve	2	1	1.96	18	0	0	3	37	27	17	8	28	33
*Byerly, Rod	1	1	3.60	2	2	0	0	10	14	5	4	1	8
Castner, Rodger	1	5	6.03	9	8	1	0	37	47	36	25	25	39
*Forrest, Joel	5	4	4.89	10	10	1	0	57	55	35	31	33	35
Holmes, Tim	2	3	5.29	16	7	0	2	49	54	37	29	17	51
Koller, Mark	2	2	5.16	11	8	0	0	45	49	32	26	30	20
Lewis, Craig	1	3	6.91	11	4	0	0	29	31	28	22	20	30
Nielsen, Dan	0	2	6.00	14	1	0	0	27	29	22	18	24	29
Richardson, Keith	6	1	1.21	8	6	0	0	45	29	11	6	8	35
Santana, Ernie	2	1	6.10	12	3	0	0	21	19	18	14	25	20
Stevanus, Mike	2	1	2.55	23	0	0	0	42	28	12	12	15	41
Studstill, Thomas	2	4	3.69	8	8	1	0	54	50	27	22	22	30
*Tomlin, Randy	7	5	2.18	15	15	5	0	103	75	31	25	25	87
*Underwood, Bobby	0	2	5.84	19	2	0	1	37	34	31	24	29	41

View from Spokane looks like a winner

By VINCE BRUUN

Asking Spokane Indians general manager Tom Leip about the state of the Northwest League is like asking Los Angeles Dodgers GM Fred Claire to assess the state of Major League Baseball.

"Having won our second consecutive championship, I'd be a fool if I thought the state of the Northwest League was anything but wonderful," Leip said.

Leip, a Northwest League executive since 1982, removed his rose-colored glasses and took a more objective look at the 34-year-old NWL.

"If you want to state it in financial terms, the league is in better shape now than at any time since I've been involved with it," he said. "We are very solid."

The 1988 season provided ample evidence to support his claim. There were no offseason franchise shifts, and the league landed an additional player development contract when the Dodgers swooped into Salem to fill the vacancy created when the California Angels moved their PDC to Bend.

New look for Boise?

Bend's acquisition of a PDC left the Boise Hawks as the only team without a major league affiliation, and that was by Boise's design.

Boise, which began operation in 1987, plays its home games at Wigle Field, a substandard high school park on the outskirts of town. Despite two losing seasons, residents of Idaho's largest city have supported the team well. The Hawks drew 65,634 in '88, down about 5,000 from the first season.

League attendance continued to prosper in 1988. The total of 540,464 was down, barely, from the record 542,075 in 1987.

League Champions

(Playoff Champions, Where Applicable)

1988—Spokane	1963—Yakima	1923-36—Did Not Operate
1987—Spokane	1962—Wenatchee	
1986—Bellingham	1961—Lewiston	1922—Calgary
1985—Everett	1960—Yakima	1921—Yakima
1984—Tri-Cities	1959—Yakima	1920—Victoria
1983—Medford	1958—Yakima	1919—Seattle
1982—Salem	1957—Wenatchee	1918—Seattle
1981—Medford	1956—Yakima	1917—Great Falls
1980—*Bellingham	1955—Eugene	1916—Spokane
—*Eugene	1954—Vancouver	1915—Seattle
1979—Central Ore.	1953—Spokane	1914—Vancouver
1978—Grays Harbor	1952—Victoria	1913—Vancouver
1977—Bellingham	1951—Spokane	1912—Seattle
1976—Walla Walla	1950—Yakima	1911—Vancouver
1975—Eugene	1949—Vancouver	1910—Spokane
1974—Eugene	1948—Spokane	1909—Seattle
1973—Walla Walla	1947—Vancouver	1908—Vancouver
1972—Lewiston	1946—Wenatchee	1907—Aberdeen
1971—Tri-City	1943-45—Did Not Operate	1906—Tacoma
1970—Lewiston		1905—Everett
1969—Rogue Valley	1942—Vancouver	1904—Boise
1968—Tri-City	1941—Spokane	1903—Butte
1967—Medford	1940—Tacoma	1902—Butte
1966—Tri-City	1939—Tacoma	1901—Portland
1965—Tri-City	1938—Bellingham	
1964—Yakima	1937—Tacoma	*co-champions

Everett's Royce Clayton was one of two first-round draft picks playing in the Northwest League in 1988.

"Attendance wise, I couldn't be disappointed," said league president Jack Cain. "We couldn't continue to grow every year. We averaged 1,813 per game, and there's a lot of leagues in the country that don't do that."

The Eugene Emeralds again led the league in attendance. The Emeralds attracted 137,372 to Civic Stadium, breaking their own record of 132,824, set in '87.

Bend (40,442) and Everett (63,894) also established franchise attendance records, while Spokane just missed. The Indians drew the league's second-best total, 113,143, just 1,522 off the team record set in '87.

Spokane, again

The Spokane Indians became the first team in 13 years to win back-to-back NWL championships, and the Indians did it in dramatic fashion.

Spokane, which waited until the final day of the regular season to clinch the Northern Division title, defeated Southern Oregon two games to one in the best-of-3 championship series.

In the deciding game, played Sept. 5 before 3,752 at Spokane's Interstate Fairgrounds, Mike Humphreys stole home with two out in the bottom of the eighth inning to give the Indians a come-from-behind 3-2 victory.

The Indians were near .500 for most of the season, and had to win eight of their last nine to qualify for the playoffs.

Spokane and Everett actually tied for the Northern Division title, both with 42-34 records, but the Indians won on the second tiebreaker—runs scored in head-to-head play. The teams tied their season series at five wins each—the first tiebreaking criterion—but Spokane edged Everett 66-65 in runs scored.

It was an odd way to win a division championship, but the Indians made the most of it. Spokane lost Game One 5-0 before rallying for 4-0 and 3-2 wins.

Numbers game

A number of NWL players had noteworthy seasons from an individual standpoint.

Offensively, Spokane's Scott Bigham hit .334 to win the batting title, and led the league with 105 hits. Teammate John Kuehl finished second in hitting (.325), and led in doubles (25) and RBIs (65).

Eugene's Bob Hamelin hit 17 home runs to lead the NWL in that department, and also finished third with 61 RBIs.

For overall numbers, Boise DH and coach Jeff Mace was difficult to top. Mace finished eighth in hitting (.310), third in home runs (13), third in RBIs (62) and first in total bases (158) and at-bats (316).

Southern Oregon's Stan Royer, one of two 1988 first-round draft choices playing regularly in the NWL (Everett's Royce Clayton was the other), had a fine first season in pro ball. Royer finished fifth in batting (.318) and added six homers and 48 RBIs.

Southern Oregon's Lee Tinsley edged Bellingham's Ellerton Maynard 41-40 for the stolen base title. Both were caught stealing 10 times.

From a pitching standpoint, where does one begin?

Though several pitchers performed spectacularly, perhaps the best place was Southern Oregon.

The 1-2 starting punch of lefthanders Kevin MacLeod (9-1, 2.89) and Tony Ariola (8-3, 2.63), and stalwart relief work from Tony Floyd (3-2, 0.94), played a large role in the Athletics' march to the Southern Division title.

Ariola led the league with 107 strikeouts, while MacLeod was fourth with 99. Floyd broke a league record with 17 saves.

Everett lefthander Doug Messer (11-3, 2.81) led the league in wins and finished third in strikeouts (100). He was the glue in the Giants' drive for the Northern Division title.

Another pitcher with fine numbers was Eugene's Bill Drohan (7-1, 2.10), who helped keep the Emeralds in the Southern Division race for most of the season.

And although he didn't pitch enough to qualify for the Top 10 in ERA, Salem's Gordie Hershiser had numbers (7-0, 2.31) that might even impress his older brother. Surely you've heard of Orel Hershiser.

North	W	L	Pct.	GB
*Spokane (Padres) ..	42	34	.553	—
Everett (Giants)	42	34	.553	—
Boise (Ind.)	30	46	.395	12
Bellinghm (Mariners)	25	51	.329	17
South				
So. Oregon (A's).....	46	30	.605	—
Salem (Dodgers)	43	33	.566	3
Eugene (Royals).....	38	38	.500	8
Bend (Angels)	38	38	.500	8
*won division on tiebreaker				

1988 Final Standings

1988: General Information

Playoffs: Spokane defeated Southern Oregon 2-1 in best-of-3 series for league championship.

Managers: Bellingham—P.J. Carey; **Bend**—Don Long; **Boise**—Mal Fichman; **Eugene**—Paul Kirsch; **Everett**—Joe Strain; **Southern Oregon**—Lenn Sakata; **Salem**—Tom Beyers; **Spokane**—Steve Lubratich.

Regular Season Attendance: Eugene, 137,372; Spokane, 113,143; Boise, 67,559; Southern Oregon, 64,974; Everett, 63,887; Bend, 43,587; Salem, 34,927; Bellingham, 15,015.

1988 Official All-Star Team: C—Eddie Tucker, Everett. **1B**—Bob Hamelin, Eugene. **2B**—Scott Bigham, Spokane. **3B**—Stan Royer, Southern Oregon. **SS**—Rafael Bournigal, Salem. **OF**—Shannon Coppell, Everett; Jeff Mace, Boise; Brauilio Castillo, Salem. **DH**—John Kuehl, Spokane. **LHP**—Kevin MacLeod, Southern Oregon. **RHP**—Tony Floyd, Southern Oregon.

Player of the Year—Stan Royer, Southern Oregon. **Manager of the Year**—Lenn Sakata, Southern Oregon.

Top 10 Major League Prospects (by Baseball America): 1. Stan Royer, 3b, Southern Oregon; **2.** Royce Clayton, ss, Everett; **3.** Victor Cole, rhp, Eugene; **4.** Luis Lopez, ss, Spokane; **5.** Bob Hamelin, 1b, Eugene; **6.** Greg Pirkl, c, Bellingham; **7.** Kevin MacLeod, lhp, Southern Oregon; **8.** Lee Hancock, lhp, Bellingham; **9.** Kelly Lifgren, rhp, Spokane; **10.** Lee Tinsley, of, Southern Oregon.

1988: Batting, Pitching Statistics

CLUB BATTING

	AVG	G	AB	R	H	2B	3B	HR	BB	SO	SB
Boise	.274	76	2655	442	728	141	14	40	318	530	32
Spokane	.265	76	2634	446	697	118	20	27	326	598	109
Southern Oregon	.258	76	2592	391	669	101	20	25	316	618	132
Everett	.257	76	2595	449	666	104	15	33	395	556	115
Salem	.255	76	2626	428	670	111	25	43	286	610	130
Eugene	.237	76	2506	340	595	107	8	29	349	629	118
Bellingham	.226	76	2531	287	571	77	10	34	291	685	103
Bend	.223	76	2567	328	573	85	19	29	296	693	70

CLUB PITCHING

	ERA	G	CG	SHO	SV	IP	H	R	ER	BB	SO
Southern Oregon	3.28	76	4	8	25	678	588	343	247	308	633
Eugene	3.45	76	0	7	22	678	597	358	260	327	720
Bend	3.49	76	10	4	19	681	619	349	264	286	639
Salem	3.58	76	1	5	24	679	603	337	270	329	609
Everett	3.95	76	4	3	11	679	680	396	298	312	611
Spokane	4.22	76	9	2	16	676	686	392	317	277	519
Boise	4.97	76	6	4	10	661	730	450	365	335	565
Bellingham	4.98	76	2	1	11	657	666	486	364	403	623

INDIVIDUAL BATTING LEADERS
(Minimum 205 Plate Appearances)

	AVG	G	AB	R	H	2B	3B	HR	RBI	BB	SO	SB
Bigham, Scott, Spo	.334	76	314	65	105	18	3	0	38	38	41	12
#Kuehl, John, Spo	.325	76	302	55	98	25	1	5	65	29	72	13
#Krumback, Mark, Boise	.324	69	262	50	85	18	1	5	51	33	41	9
Royer, Stan, SO	.321	73	287	48	92	19	3	6	48	33	71	1
Coppell, Shannon, Ever	.320	67	259	47	83	13	2	0	39	28	56	20
Bournigal, Rafael, Salem	.313	70	275	54	86	10	1	0	25	38	32	11
Hillman, Joe, SO	.310	50	187	33	58	9	1	1	27	25	26	2
Mace, Jeff, Boise	.310	76	316	54	98	21	0	13	62	26	57	0
Humphreys, Mike, Spo	.307	76	303	67	93	16	5	6	59	46	57	21
Disarcina, Gary, Bend	.305	71	295	40	90	11	5	2	39	27	34	7

INDIVIDUAL PITCHING LEADERS
(Minimum 61 innings)

	W	L	ERA	G	GS	CG	SV	IP	H	R	ER	BB	SO
Bliven, Wes, Bend	6	3	2.04	12	8	2	0	71	54	24	16	13	60
Vidmar, Don, Bend	3	4	2.08	25	5	2	3	78	65	32	18	22	90
Drohan, Bill, Eug	7	1	2.10	17	9	0	0	73	54	30	17	32	71
*James, Todd, Bend	4	3	2.32	13	13	2	0	89	69	28	23	28	84
*Bryand, Renay, Spo	6	3	2.48	18	6	2	2	80	71	29	22	23	74
*Hancock, Lee, Bell	6	5	2.60	16	16	2	0	100	83	37	29	31	102
*Ariola, Tony, SO	8	3	2.63	15	15	2	0	96	73	30	28	29	107
Vaughn, Randy, Eug	4	4	2.82	15	15	0	0	80	62	37	25	37	75
*MacLeod, Kevin, SO	9	1	2.89	15	15	0	0	84	52	31	27	43	99
*Messer, Doug, Ever	11	3	2.90	15	15	3	0	102	96	42	33	22	100

BELLINGHAM

BATTING	AVG	G	AB	R	H	2B	3B	HR	RBI	BB	SO	SB
Barrett, Keith, 3b-1b	.183	61	202	20	37	10	0	4	17	28	77	2
Brock, Tom, of	.438	4	16	6	7	2	0	0	4	3	1	0
Candelari, Ricky, of	.242	61	219	26	53	8	1	2	13	26	53	1
Cayson, Tony, of	.151	44	119	11	18	1	0	0	2	9	36	4
Daughtry, Dorian, of	.210	30	100	7	21	2	0	0	4	3	26	3
Del Pozo, Roberto, 3b	.103	14	39	1	4	1	0	0	0	3	22	1
Howard, Chris, c	.333	2	9	3	3	0	0	1	3	1	2	0
Maynard, Ellerton, of	.265	67	249	53	66	8	3	3	27	44	61	40
McLaughlin, Mike, ss	.225	44	160	12	36	3	0	0	12	17	44	11
McNamara, Tom, ss	.224	50	143	13	32	3	0	0	7	21	17	4
*Miller, Johan, c	.188	43	138	10	26	1	0	0	12	22	48	1
Patrick, Otis, 2b-dh	.210	55	181	27	38	6	2	2	13	31	58	12
Pirkl, Greg, dh-c	.240	65	246	22	59	6	0	6	35	12	59	1
Reyan, Julio, of	.258	57	209	18	54	10	2	7	34	17	53	1
*Schmidt, Pete, 1b	.188	69	240	21	45	8	0	3	24	30	64	0
Stargell, Tim, 2b-3b	.279	69	258	37	72	8	2	6	35	24	61	22

PITCHING	W	L	ERA	G	GS	CG	SV	IP	H	R	ER	BB	SO
Beiras, Mike	1	4	7.29	7	7	0	0	33	41	30	27	22	29
Bryant, Erick	3	1	5.31	19	1	0	2	42	42	31	25	20	39
Doll, Chris	2	1	5.63	17	2	0	0	38	41	27	24	34	42
Eldredge, Ted	0	5	9.00	6	6	0	0	29	39	40	29	26	13
*Felix, Nick	4	1	1.15	22	0	0	5	39	27	8	5	16	54
*Hancock, Lee	6	5	2.60	16	16	2	0	100	83	37	29	31	102

Top NWL Performers

Stan Royer
... top prospect

John Kuehl
... all-star DH

Bob Hamelin
... 70 G, 17 HR

	W	L	ERA	G	GS	CG	SV	IP	H	R	ER	BB	SO
*Kohli, John	1	0	5.30	17	0	0	0	36	39	33	21	33	35
*Kosnik, Jim	1	7	6.36	15	10	0	0	47	64	56	33	40	40
*Liss, Tom	2	9	4.03	16	15	0	0	80	79	48	36	35	82
Mangual, Victor	1	4	5.54	15	5	0	0	52	34	38	32	41	48
Pitcher, Scott	2	4	5.19	32	1	0	4	50	49	37	29	26	46
Schula, Mike	0	1	14.21	5	0	0	0	6	16	12	10	6	3
Stoerck, Scott	1	1	5.26	13	1	0	0	26	34	24	15	11	25
Webb, Scott	0	0	5.40	2	0	0	0	3	3	4	2	5	2
White, Joe	1	5	5.84	11	6	0	0	37	39	31	24	25	30
Wilkinson, Brian	0	3	5.75	12	6	0	0	36	35	30	23	31	31

BEND

BATTING	AVG	G	AB	R	H	2B	3B	HR	RBI	BB	SO	SB
Brito, Francisco, 3b	.185	23	81	9	15	2	0	0	7	5	14	1
*Carrasquillo, Angel, dh-1b	.182	7	22	1	4	0	0	0	3	2	10	0
Cooper, Gary, 3b	.234	13	47	6	11	3	1	1	9	5	8	1
#Cunningham, Shawn, 2b .	.000	2	2	1	0	0	0	0	0	0	1	0
DiSarcina, Gary, ss`	.305	71	295	40	90	11	5	2	39	27	34	7
*Edmonds, Jim, of	.221	35	122	23	27	4	0	0	13	20	44	4
Eldridge, Rodney, dh	.333	12	45	10	15	5	1	1	5	7	11	1
Jones, Bill, c	.000	1	3	1	0	0	0	0	0	1	2	0
Kelso, Jeff, of	.136	32	103	10	14	3	2	2	7	10	46	0
Kipila, Jeff, 1b	.206	69	253	34	52	12	2	9	42	40	71	2
Kirwin, Steve, dh	.236	33	127	30	30	4	3	1	6	23	36	13
Martinez, Ramon, 3b	.230	61	226	28	52	9	2	2	19	25	51	2
Mateo, Huascar, c	.140	12	43	4	6	1	0	0	1	1	7	0
Neville, Dave, c	.269	8	26	1	7	1	0	0	2	4	6	0
Oberdank, Jeff, 2b	.246	71	284	28	70	5	2	1	27	27	58	12
Partrick, Dave, of	.225	58	204	21	46	7	1	4	24	7	85	14
Pesce, John, of	.308	5	13	2	4	0	0	0	2	1	0	0
*Phillips, J.R., of-1b	.190	56	210	24	40	8	0	4	24	21	71	3
Sheehy, Tom, of	.059	6	17	0	1	1	0	0	2	2	7	0
*Sturdivant, Dave, c	.188	50	176	19	33	3	0	2	19	28	49	0
Taft, Tim, c	.133	12	45	1	6	0	0	0	4	2	7	0
Threadgill, Chris, of	.224	65	223	35	50	6	0	0	15	38	75	10

PITCHING	W	L	ERA	G	GS	CG	SV	IP	H	R	ER	BB	SO
Batista, Miguel	2	2	4.98	14	0	0	0	22	31	21	12	11	16
Bliven, Wes	6	3	2.04	12	8	2	0	71	54	24	16	13	60
Carter, Glenn	3	4	4.60	9	9	1	0	45	46	25	23	15	47
Fritz, John	0	0	3.65	14	7	0	0	44	46	25	18	23	30
*Holzemer, Mark	4	6	5.24	13	13	1	0	69	59	51	40	47	73
*James, Todd	4	3	2.32	13	13	2	0	89	69	28	23	28	84
Lewis, Scott	5	3	3.50	9	9	2	0	62	63	33	24	12	53
Marchese, John	2	2	1.29	32	0	0	16	35	16	7	5	11	58
Martin, Justin	6	1	4.22	31	0	0	0	64	54	33	30	33	49
Murphy, Gary	1	1	0.96	6	0	0	0	9	6	2	1	5	9
*Neal, Dave	1	6	7.52	11	11	0	0	41	58	42	34	39	29
*Tejeda, Enrique	0	1	5.79	7	0	0	0	9	13	7	6	10	6
*Vegely, Bruce	1	2	2.93	18	1	0	0	43	39	19	14	17	35
Vidmar, Don	3	4	2.08	25	5	2	3	78	65	32	18	22	90

BOISE

BATTING	AVG	G	AB	R	H	2B	3B	HR	RBI	BB	SO	SB
*Bakke, Paul, of	.191	34	68	12	13	0	0	0	3	7	18	1
#Beuder, Jon, of	.265	41	117	20	31	8	0	2	13	12	20	1
Bolar, Wendell, 3b-2b ...	.225	64	187	43	42	11	3	2	18	25	48	5
Bottenfield, Kevin, dh-1b .	.338	36	77	10	26	3	0	2	10	16	15	0
Depew, Darren, c	.272	47	103	16	28	6	2	0	14	10	28	0
*Douglas, Brad, of	.171	14	41	3	7	2	0	0	4	4	8	1
Gurchiek, Chris, of	.264	53	163	28	43	4	1	4	15	13	41	5
#Krumback, Mark, of	.324	69	262	50	85	18	1	5	51	33	41	9
Mace, Jeff, of	.310	76	316	54	98	21	6	13	62	26	57	0
Malone, Jack, 2b	.290	66	241	40	70	14	2	2	41	39	38	3

BATTING

```
        R—Mike Humphreys, Spokane ..............67
        H—Scott Bigham, Spokane..................105
       TB—Jeff Mace, Boise ......................158
       2B—John Kuehl, Spokane....................25
       3B—Four tied at ............................5
       HR—Bob Hamelin, Eugene ...................17
      RBI—John Kuehl, Spokane....................65
    GWRBI—Mike Humphreys, Spokane...............9
       SH—Three tied at ...........................7
       SF—Scott Marabell, Salem ..................9
       BB—Lee Tinsley, Southern Oregon ..........66
      IBB—Joe Mancini, Boise ......................4
      HBP—Joel Smith, Southern Oregon ...........13
       SO—Lee Tinsley, Southern Oregon ..........106
       SB—Lee Tinsley, Southern Oregon ..........41
       CS—Three tied at ..........................10
 Slg. Pct.—Bob Hamelin, Eugene ................. .604
  OB Pct.—Scott Bigham, Spokane ............... .412
```

PITCHING

```
        G—John Marchese, Bend ....................32
       GS—Lee Hancock, Bellingham................16
          —John Bilello, Boise....................16
       CG—John Bilello, Boise .....................3
          —Doug Messer, Everett...................3
      ShO—Eight tied at ...........................1
       Sv—Tony Floyd, Southern Oregon ...........17
        W—Doug Messer, Everett ...................11
        L—Tom Liss, Bellingham.....................9
          —Hector Wagner, Eugene...................9
       IP—John Bilello, Boise ...................111
        H—A.J. Sager, Spokane ...................123
        R—A.J. Sager, Spokane ....................67
       HR—Bill Gibbons, Everett ..................10
       BB—Greg Harvey, Eugene ....................57
       HB—Todd James, Bend .........................8
       SO—Tony Ariola, Southern Oregon ..........107
       WP—Justin Martin, Bend.....................13
          —Bob Brucato, Spokane...................13
       Bk—Vic Mangual, Bellingham.................14
          —Tony Ariola, Southern Oregon .........14
```

Department Leaders

BATTING	AVG	G	AB	R	H	2B	3B	HR	RBI	BB	SO	SB
*Mancini, Joe, dh-3b	.278	64	209	30	58	9	1	4	37	26	27	1
#Moore, Mike, of	.143	6	7	3	1	0	0	0	0	0	5	0
Myers, Pat, 2b-ss	.263	28	80	10	21	5	0	0	5	11	26	1
*Qualls, Mike, 2b	.271	23	70	15	19	7	0	0	15	13	15	1
*Shambaugh, Mike, 1b ...	.235	75	285	35	67	13	2	2	33	25	72	1
*Shultis, Chris, ss-3b ...	.294	76	299	48	88	16	2	2	36	26	40	2
Winterburn, Scott, c	.238	56	130	25	31	4	0	2	18	32	31	1

PITCHING	W	L	ERA	G	GS	CG	SV	IP	H	R	ER	BB	SO
*Backus, Todd	3	5	5.15	14	13	1	0	73	84	52	42	44	75
Bilello, John	8	5	3.49	16	16	3	0	111	97	53	43	44	86
*Griffin, Barry	4	7	5.82	15	15	0	0	73	72	55	47	49	69
*Holub, Ed	2	3	4.97	18	8	0	0	54	61	38	30	24	41
Janikowski, Randy	2	2	6.70	19	1	0	0	43	52	37	32	18	27
Larson, Mike	0	5	3.26	27	0	0	2	39	34	25	14	23	30
*Lavrusky, Chuck	1	2	4.54	20	0	0	0	38	43	22	19	23	30
Lomeli, Mike	3	6	4.19	31	2	1	3	69	71	41	32	33	61
*Lundeen, Larry	4	3	6.23	15	13	0	0	56	80	47	39	29	37
*Pavelka, Mike	0	0	13.50	1	0	0	0	2	6	4	3	2	1
Ramirez, Ed	1	1	4.14	23	0	0	0	37	39	24	17	22	32
Tate, Mike	2	4	5.29	27	4	1	5	51	62	35	30	19	63
*Wenrick, Bill	0	3	9.98	4	4	0	0	15	29	17	17	5	13

EUGENE

BATTING	AVG	G	AB	R	H	2B	3B	HR	RBI	BB	SO	SB
Buchanan, Rob, c	.145	24	55	7	8	2	0	0	6	26	17	2
Collins, Ron, dh-3b	.206	41	141	14	29	6	1	0	13	17	39	8
Davis, Kelvin, 3b	.171	13	35	7	6	1	0	0	3	8	15	0
Garber, Jeff, 2b-3b	.251	65	243	31	61	14	2	1	25	30	45	12
Gardner, Bill, 3b	.250	21	60	10	15	3	0	0	5	12	24	1
Gilcrist, John, of	.193	38	109	12	21	1	1	0	4	13	33	3
*Hamelin, Bob, 1b	.298	70	235	42	70	19	1	17	61	56	67	9
Henderson, Francisco, of .	.214	44	140	14	30	1	0	0	13	10	42	4
Holley, Bobby, 3b-ss	.241	46	170	28	41	7	0	1	16	25	32	3
Hulse, Jeff, c	.265	55	204	30	54	10	0	5	28	22	53	4
Ingram, Gerald, of	.228	59	219	25	50	8	2	2	19	15	41	8
#Preston, Steve, 2b-dh ..	.273	64	238	38	65	8	1	0	25	57	36	34
Richardson, Milt, of	.241	46	162	21	39	8	0	0	16	14	43	11
Rolls, David, c-dh	.171	35	111	14	19	5	0	3	10	19	44	2
#Russell, Fred, ss	.272	46	162	19	44	7	0	0	13	15	38	9
Sholl, Derek, of	.200	17	60	6	12	1	0	0	7	1	18	2
*Watson, Frankie, of	.191	46	162	22	31	6	0	0	13	9	42	6

PITCHING	W	L	ERA	G	GS	CG	SV	IP	H	R	ER	BB	SO
Balch, Kyle	1	0	1.23	3	0	0	0	7	5	4	1	2	9
Cole, Victor	1	0	1.52	15	0	0	9	24	16	6	4	8	39
Drezek, Karl	1	0	3.86	7	0	0	0	12	7	5	5	8	8
Drohan, Bill	7	1	2.10	17	9	0	0	73	54	30	17	32	71
Harvey, Greg	4	4	4.26	15	15	0	0	63	60	38	30	57	63
Hoeme, Steve	0	1	4.10	23	1	0	1	37	25	17	17	24	32
Hopper, Brad	2	4	2.44	32	0	0	5	59	60	28	16	18	72
Irvin, Kyle	3	2	1.84	26	1	0	4	44	29	17	9	19	73
Johnston, Joel	4	7	5.20	14	14	0	0	64	64	49	37	34	64
*Magnante, Mike	1	1	0.56	3	3	0	0	16	10	6	1	2	26
Otto, Steve	1	3	5.03	21	2	0	0	48	58	29	27	19	36
*Shibata, Keith	1	1	7.45	16	1	0	0	29	38	28	24	14	40
Sholl, Derek	0	0	20.25	2	0	0	0	1	3	5	3	5	1
Smith, Jim	4	1	2.86	23	0	0	3	35	30	13	11	20	44
Vaughn, Randy	4	4	2.82	15	15	0	0	80	62	37	25	37	75
Wagner, Hector	4	9	3.68	15	15	0	0	86	76	46	35	28	67

EVERETT

BATTING	AVG	G	AB	R	H	2B	3B	HR	RBI	BB	SO	SB
Brady, Pat, of-1b	.235	63	221	38	52	10	0	7	38	57	52	9
Clayton, Royce, ss	.259	60	212	35	55	4	0	3	30	27	54	10
Coppell, Shannon, of	.320	67	259	47	83	13	2	0	39	28	56	20
Davenport, Adell, 1b	.236	61	229	40	54	14	1	5	29	31	65	0
Decker, Steve, dh-c	.524	13	42	11	22	2	0	2	13	7	5	0
Gray, Steve, ss	.300	6	20	4	6	0	1	0	1	3	5	1
Greenwood, Mike, of	.176	21	51	5	9	0	1	1	10	1	17	0
Hall, Kevin, of	.300	4	10	2	3	1	0	0	1	0	3	0
*Hecht, Steve, 2b	.159	13	44	8	7	1	0	0	4	6	7	6
Hilpert, Adam, dh	.000	1	3	0	0	0	0	0	0	1	2	0
Lee, Greg, ss-2b	.220	20	41	6	9	2	0	0	2	0	8	1
Minier, Johnny, 3b	.296	40	142	22	42	2	3	1	30	14	22	1
Patterson, John, 2b	.250	58	232	37	58	10	4	0	26	18	27	21
Pratt, Steve, c	.180	22	61	8	11	1	1	1	11	13	14	0
*Sanderson, Mike, of	.206	39	126	22	26	6	0	1	19	32	31	1
Standiford, Mark, 2b-dh	.272	57	206	39	56	13	1	5	37	42	44	0
Tucker, Scooter, c-dh	.261	45	153	24	40	5	0	3	23	30	34	0
Wandler, Mike, 3b	.254	40	114	19	29	4	0	0	24	23	17	2
Warren, Glen, c	.224	40	98	21	22	6	0	1	10	11	27	7
Williams, Matt, c	.231	32	104	9	24	2	0	0	10	4	23	0
#Williams, Reggie, of	.256	61	227	52	58	8	1	3	30	47	43	36

PITCHING	W	L	ERA	G	GS	CG	SV	IP	H	R	ER	BB	SO
*Berry, Bill	0	3	3.93	21	1	0	2	34	36	20	15	15	34
Brauckmiller, James	0	1	5.68	11	0	0	0	19	29	19	12	9	14
Breitenbucher, Karl	2	6	6.62	17	8	0	0	52	70	47	38	26	51
Cantrell, Dave	1	2	6.05	21	2	0	0	39	44	30	26	22	26
Carter, Larry	1	3	5.57	4	4	0	0	21	17	14	13	14	27
Dela Rosa, Domingo	0	0	4.91	12	0	0	0	15	19	8	8	10	14
*Durham, Shane	4	1	1.71	7	7	0	0	47	30	13	9	9	49
Fye, Chris	3	2	3.19	27	2	0	0	48	36	20	17	34	42
Gibbons, Bill	5	4	3.48	15	14	1	0	83	78	46	32	31	63
Horan, Dave	3	3	4.12	12	12	0	0	63	70	44	29	41	33
Lucero, Robert	5	3	5.43	15	11	0	0	68	81	47	41	34	61
*Messer, Doug	11	3	2.90	15	15	3	0	102	96	42	33	22	100
Sharko, Gary	3	3	3.14	31	0	0	5	43	41	26	15	16	39
Vuz, John	4	0	2.22	28	0	0	4	45	33	20	11	29	58

SOUTHERN OREGON

BATTING	AVG	G	AB	R	H	2B	3B	HR	RBI	BB	SO	SB
Borelli, Dean, c	.200	43	140	9	28	7	1	0	6	10	19	0
Buccheri, James, of-dh	.286	58	231	42	66	8	1	0	17	20	35	25
Carcione, Tom, c	.187	43	139	13	26	3	0	1	21	19	59	1
Chimelis, Joel, ss	.276	61	225	40	62	8	0	1	27	30	36	14
Correia, Ron, 2b-ss	.251	56	207	23	52	7	3	1	19	18	41	6
Espinal, Josue, 2b	.187	47	134	18	25	1	1	0	9	15	26	12
Hillman, Joe, 1b	.310	50	187	33	58	9	1	1	27	25	26	2
Jones, Dewayne, 2b	.193	18	57	10	11	2	2	0	2	11	5	14
Messerly, Mike, dh-1b	.242	67	240	34	58	12	3	6	52	19	66	3
*Reyna, Dion, dh-1b	.200	3	10	1	2	0	0	0	1	0	2	0
Ritter, Ken, dh-of	.222	5	9	2	2	1	0	0	0	4	0	0
Royer, Stan, 3b	.321	73	287	48	92	19	3	6	48	33	71	1
*Savarino, Bill, 1b	.271	13	48	6	13	2	0	1	13	6	10	0
#Smith, Joel, of	.254	68	244	39	62	6	5	3	28	20	66	21
#Tinsley, Lee, of	.249	72	257	56	64	8	2	3	28	66	106	41
Vannaman, Tim, of	.271	55	177	17	48	8	0	0	17	26	37	4

PITCHING	W	L	ERA	G	GS	CG	SV	IP	H	R	ER	BB	SO
*Ariola, Tony	8	3	2.63	15	15	2	0	96	73	30	28	29	107
Arola, Bruce	1	1	2.20	19	0	0	2	33	35	11	8	12	30
Eskew, Dan	4	2	2.40	9	9	0	0	49	29	20	13	21	61
*Ferguson, Greg	3	0	1.16	4	4	1	0	23	14	5	3	9	24
Floyd, Tony	3	2	0.94	30	0	0	17	48	30	13	5	15	55
*Harris, Ray	4	4	3.01	16	8	0	3	75	65	33	25	27	60
Lawson, Jim	2	3	3.40	24	6	0	2	53	47	29	20	36	38
*MacLeod, Kevin	9	1	2.89	15	15	0	0	84	52	31	27	43	99
Messerly, Mike	0	1	12.00	2	0	0	0	3	5	4	4	2	2
Mungin, Mike	4	1	4.11	19	7	0	0	57	52	36	26	42	36

	W	L	ERA	G	GS	CG	SV	IP	H	R	ER	BB	SO
Powers, Tom	1	2	3.86	10	3	0	0	23	14	13	10	18	21
Rizza, Gerard	2	2	3.60	14	0	0	0	25	31	19	10	8	20
Rozman, Rick	1	3	3.97	12	6	1	1	48	49	27	21	12	39
Venuto, Nick	3	4	8.41	16	2	0	0	41	67	58	38	22	28
Wilson, Steve	1	1	2.79	11	1	0	0	19	21	10	6	9	13

SALEM

BATTING	AVG	G	AB	R	H	2B	3B	HR	RBI	BB	SO	SB
Barron, Tony, of	.303	73	261	54	79	6	3	9	38	24	75	36
Bournigal, Rafael, ss	.313	70	275	54	86	10	1	0	25	38	32	11
Cardenas, Daniel, of	.222	41	135	15	30	5	0	3	17	9	53	7
Castillo, Braulio, of	.281	73	306	51	86	20	5	8	41	22	72	16
Finkin, Steve, 3b-2b	.254	57	205	43	52	9	1	9	38	40	51	13
Fujioh, Yasuhara, of-dh	.200	19	40	4	8	3	1	0	8	6	9	0
Hartman, Jeff, 2b-dh	.248	67	234	42	58	12	1	0	32	40	35	14
Hermann, Jeff, of	.117	23	60	5	7	2	0	0	4	6	21	1
Maehara, Hiroyoki, 3b	.196	54	168	26	33	6	2	1	12	18	59	1
Marabell, Scott, dh-of	.247	75	271	47	67	13	3	8	53	35	74	9
McMurray, Brock, of	.174	8	23	4	4	0	0	1	2	5	9	0
#Montgomery, Danny, ss	.268	12	41	5	11	3	0	0	3	3	10	6
Mora, Juan, c	.233	64	223	26	52	7	4	2	35	12	47	2
Ortiz, Hector, c	.143	32	77	5	11	1	0	0	4	5	16	0
*Rodriguez, Henry, 1b	.289	72	291	47	84	14	4	2	38	21	42	14
Santos, Luis, of	.250	2	4	0	1	0	0	0	2	0	0	0
Zink, Wendall, 3b	.100	3	10	0	1	0	0	0	0	1	4	0

PITCHING	W	L	ERA	G	GS	CG	SV	IP	H	R	ER	BB	SO
Calderon, Ed	0	2	2.70	11	0	0	0	17	14	7	5	13	13
*Currie, Brian	1	4	2.47	29	1	0	12	47	44	19	13	21	53
Gastelum, Macario	2	2	6.23	11	7	0	0	30	24	26	21	31	25
Gettler, Chris	4	1	1.54	22	0	0	5	53	38	13	9	14	48
Gonzalez, Larry	5	5	4.74	14	14	1	0	76	84	45	40	32	46
Hershiser, Gordie	7	0	2.31	10	10	0	0	58	46	20	15	10	58
Luckham, Kenny	7	2	3.67	16	11	0	0	69	63	39	28	39	47
Miguel, Tamares	2	4	6.75	15	5	0	1	44	50	39	33	28	51
Olson, Dan	0	0	2.36	19	0	0	1	53	35	20	14	24	53
Parham, Bill	4	2	4.54	8	8	0	0	42	36	22	21	20	28
Piscetta, Rob	2	4	2.68	20	1	0	4	57	47	19	17	29	55
Van Zytveld, Jeff	4	4	3.29	12	8	0	0	55	49	28	20	27	38
Wanish, John	5	3	4.03	19	11	0	1	76	71	40	34	41	92

SPOKANE

BATTING	AVG	G	AB	R	H	2B	3B	HR	RBI	BB	SO	SB
Bigham, Scott, 2b	.334	76	314	65	105	18	3	0	38	38	41	12
Briggs, Dave, of	.230	71	270	40	62	9	3	1	32	9	61	8
*Cisarik, Brian, of	.000	2	6	0	0	0	0	0	1	1	1	0
Conley, Greg, c	.196	49	163	22	32	4	0	1	18	18	55	10
Curnow, Bob, c-dh	.214	32	112	12	24	3	1	0	9	9	21	3
Humphreys, Mike, of	.307	76	303	67	93	16	5	6	59	46	57	21
#Kuehl, John, 3b	.325	76	302	55	98	25	1	5	65	29	72	13
*Kuhn, Chad, 1b-dh	.150	47	147	23	22	6	0	2	14	34	58	5
#Lopez, Luis, ss	.304	70	312	50	95	13	1	0	35	18	59	3
Proctor, Craig, of-dh	.162	38	111	14	18	3	1	0	10	19	37	2
Riesgo, Nikco, of	.251	65	219	45	55	8	3	7	51	44	59	24
*Smith, Greg, 1b	.266	71	278	36	74	12	1	4	44	29	53	6
*Verstandig, Mark, c	.196	32	97	16	19	1	1	1	10	32	24	1
Witkowski, Matt, pr	.000	1	0	1	0	0	0	0	0	0	0	0

PITCHING	W	L	ERA	G	GS	CG	SV	IP	H	R	ER	BB	SO
*Aquino, Pedro	8	3	4.24	15	15	1	0	100	108	55	47	32	88
Brucato, Bob	4	7	4.07	14	14	2	0	86	80	47	39	44	66
*Bryand, Renay	6	3	2.48	18	6	2	2	80	71	29	22	23	74
*Cantwell, Robby	0	4	4.54	9	3	0	0	36	37	26	18	15	12
Hart, Jeff	0	0	6.75	1	0	0	0	3	5	4	2	1	4
Haslock, Chris	5	3	3.99	23	0	0	8	38	40	20	17	24	29
*Hightower, Barry	0	0	7.59	6	0	0	0	11	10	9	9	9	4
*Hoyer, Brad	4	1	2.36	23	0	0	5	42	31	13	11	15	36
Lebron, Jose	0	0	4.50	1	0	0	0	2	0	1	1	0	0
Leslie, Reggie	0	0	8.10	4	0	0	1	7	7	6	6	6	8
Lifgren, Kelly	6	3	3.69	13	13	2	0	76	65	40	31	37	61
Morton, Ron	0	4	3.88	23	0	0	0	51	52	29	22	12	24
*Murdock, Joe	0	0	3.60	1	1	0	0	5	3	4	2	3	2
*Reed, William	0	0	9.00	1	0	0	0	1	2	3	1	0	2
Sager, A.J.	8	3	5.11	15	15	2	0	99	123	67	56	27	74
Thompson, Squeezer	1	3	7.43	12	9	0	0	40	52	39	33	28	30

Amazin' Kingsport Mets are doormats no more

By JON SCHER

In Kingsport's first seven seasons as a New York Mets affiliate, the club compiled an overall record of 185-299. That's a .382 winning percentage, math fans. The Mets' *best* record was 35-35 in 1980.

Then came 1988. Just like the Amazin' Mets of 1969, Kingsport rose from the bottom to win a championship. The K-Mets trounced Burlington 2-0 in the best-of-three playoff, and the Tennessee city celebrated its first Appalachian League title since 1977, when Kingsport was affiliated with the Atlanta Braves.

The turnaround may have been helped by the New York Mets' decision to add a club in the Gulf Coast League, where they were able to send their youngest prospects. While the GCL Mets staggered to 21-42, Kingsport rolled to a 46-26 regular season record, tying Bristol for first place in the Southern Division.

The Mets and Tigers staged a one-game playoff Aug. 30. Kingsport won the afternoon game 4-2, then played Northern Division winner Burlington in the first game of the championship series that night.

The Amazin' K-Mets defeated the defending league champs 5-1 to open the final series. Greg Langbehn pitched a four-hit complete game, striking out 15 Indians and walking one.

Pitching carried the Mets again in Game Two, played in Burlington. Denny Harriger held the Tribe to three hits in the decisive 3-1 victory. Burlington went ahead 1-0 in the second inning, but the Mets answered with three in the third. Jim Morrisette's single scored Rodolfo Hernandez with the go-ahead run.

Loaded with prospects

Six first-round picks were assigned to Appy League clubs: pitchers Steve Avery (Pulaski), Johnny Ard (Elizabethton) and John Ericks (Johnson City); shortstops Mark Lewis (Burlington) and Austin Manahan (Princeton); and first baseman Rico Brogna (Bristol). League managers considered Avery and Lewis the

League Champions

(Playoff Champions, Where Applicable)

1988—Kingsport	1968—Marion	1949—Bluefield
1987—Burlington	1967—Bluefield	1948—Pulaski
1986—Pulaski	1966—Marion	1947—New River
1985—Bristol	1965—Salem	1946—New River
1984—Elizabethton	1964—Johnson City	1945—Kingsport
1983—Paintsville	1963—Bluefield	1944—Kingsport
1982—Bluefield	1962—Bluefield	1943—Bristol
1981—Paintsville	1961—Middlesboro	1942—Bristol
1980—Paintsville	1960—Wytheville	1941—Elizabethton
1979—Paintsville	1959—Morristown	1940—Johnson City
1978—Elizabethton	1958—Johnson City	1939—Elizabethton
1977—Kingsport	1957—Bluefield	1938—Greenville
1976—Johnson City	1956—Did Not	1937—Penning. Gap
1975—Johnson City	Operate	1926-36—Did Not
1974—Bristol	1955—Salem	Operate
1973—Kingsport	1954—Bluefield	1925—Greenville
1972—Bristol	1953—Welch	1924—Knoxville
1971—Bluefield	1952—Welch	1923—Knoxville
1970—Bluefield	1951—Kingsport	1922—Bristol
1969—Pulaski	1950—Bluefield	1921—Johnson City

Pulaski's Steve Avery (7-1, 1.50) was one of six No. 1 draft picks in the Appalachian League.

cream of the crop.

Burlington may have lost the championship on the field, but the Indians remained first at the gate. They improved on their own league record, reporting a season attendance of 71,375. Martinsville, one of two expansion teams, was second at 48,930. The other expansion club, Princeton (W.Va.), reported 31,366.

The Indians and Bluefield Orioles made national headlines June 24, with a 27-inning marathon that lasted until 3:27 a.m. The Orioles wound up winning the eight hour, 15 minute endurance contest 3-2.

Burlington also was involved in the year's worst beanball war in the second game of an Aug. 16 doubleheader in Wytheville. Manager Mike Bucci and pitcher David Oliveras were ejected and the Indians forfeited the game. Bucci said he pulled his team off the field despite a 1-0 lead because a Wytheville coach threatened Indians shortstop Lewis, saying Lewis would not "walk off the field under his own power."

North	W	L	Pct.	GB
Burlington (Indians) .	37	32	.536	—
Pulaski (Braves)	35	35	.500	2½
Princeton (Pirates) ..	33	37	.471	4½
Martinsville (Phillies)	29	41	.414	8½
Bluefield (Orioles) ...	24	47	.338	14
South				
Kingsport (Mets)	47	26	.644	—
Bristol (Tigers)	46	27	.630	1
Johnson City (Cards)	41	31	.569	5½
Elizabethton (Twins).	33	37	.471	12½
Wytheville (Cubs) ...	28	40	.412	16½

1988
Final
Standings

1988: General Information

Playoffs: Kingsport defeated Burlington 2-0 in best-of-3 final for league championship.

Regular Season Attendance: Burlington, 71,466; Martinsville, 48,980; Kingsport, 41,044; Princeton, 31,275; Bluefield, 25,683; Johnson City, 21,549; Wytheville, 20,331; Bristol, 20,224; Pulaski, 15,209; Elizabethton, 14,670.

Managers: Bluefield—Glenn Gulliver; **Bristol**—Rick Magnante; **Burlington**—Mike Bucci; **Elizabethton**—Ray Smith; **Johnson City**—Jorge Aranzamendi; **Kingsport**—Bobby Floyd; **Martinsville**—Rollie DeArmas; **Princeton**—Jim Thrift; **Pulaski**—Cloyd Boyer; **Wytheville**—Steve Roadcap.

1988 Official All-Star Team: C—Jeff Champ, Bluefield. **1B**—Vince Zawaski, Kingsport. **2B**—Rodolfo Hernandez, Kingsport. **3B**—Jim Morrisette, Kingsport. **SS**—Mark Lewis, Burlington. **OF**—Wayne Weinheimer, Wytheville; Glen Gardner, Pulaski; Curtis Pride, Kingsport. **DH**—Tom Aldrich, Bristol. **Util. INF.**—Nick Macaluso, Martinsville. **Util. OF.**—Charlie White, Johnson City. **RHP**—Rusty Meacham, Bristol; **LHP**—Steve Avery, Pulaski. **Most Valuable Player**—Vince Zawaski, Kingsport. **Manager of the Year**—Bobby Floyd, Kingsport.

Top 10 Major League Prospects (by Baseball America): 1. Steve Avery, lhp, Pulaski; **2.** Mark Lewis, ss, Burlington; **3.** Johnny Ard, rhp, Elizabethton; **4.** Rico Brogna, 1b, Bristol; **5.** Roberto Smalls, rhp, Wytheville; **6.** Julian Vasquez, rhp, Kingsport; **7.** Toby Borland, rhp, Martinsville; **8.** Curtis Pride, of, Kingsport; **9.** Matt Murray, rhp, Pulaski; **10.** Alan Newman, lhp, Elizabethton.

1988: Batting, Pitching Statistics

CLUB BATTING

	AVG	G	AB	R	H	2B	3B	HR	BB	SO	SB
Kingsport	.274	73	2405	434	659	111	20	47	327	464	99
Johnson City	.271	72	2305	372	625	108	17	46	247	456	96
Bristol	.261	73	2388	456	623	109	11	62	364	514	67
Wytheville	.256	68	2290	365	587	98	15	30	278	534	42
Pulaski	.253	70	2248	368	568	90	14	43	293	455	134
Bluefield	.248	71	2380	331	590	79	15	24	276	552	77
Princeton	.245	70	2277	330	558	92	24	38	290	683	170
Burlington	.236	69	2262	322	533	89	15	27	316	496	121
Martinsville	.229	70	2327	304	534	89	7	51	245	624	42
Elizabethton	.229	70	2304	301	528	89	18	34	234	529	66

CLUB PITCHING

	ERA	G	CG	SHO	SV	IP	H	R	ER	BB	SO
Burlington	3.15	69	5	7	17	608	543	283	213	246	512
Kingsport	3.40	73	10	5	23	617	518	301	233	243	507
Bristol	3.42	73	9	6	17	615	534	311	234	305	610
Pulaski	3.63	70	11	4	6	592	498	331	239	309	508
Johnson City	3.81	72	3	3	18	594	572	324	251	261	532
Martinsville	4.35	70	2	2	18	598	626	378	289	247	517
Elizabethton	4.52	70	11	3	13	603	528	377	303	401	609
Princeton	4.85	70	3	3	13	593	626	400	320	298	525
Bluefield	4.98	71	3	3	8	611	696	443	338	271	520
Wytheville	5.35	68	3	2	11	575	664	435	342	289	467

INDIVIDUAL BATTING LEADERS

(Minimum 194 Plate Appearances)

	AVG	G	AB	R	H	2B	3B	HR	RBI	BB	SO	SB
Weinheimer, Wayne, Wvl	.355	67	211	54	75	20	0	4	53	56	41	3
#Shireman, Jeff, JC	.339	52	189	41	64	8	1	2	19	23	15	4
Aldrich, Tom, Bris	.338	63	219	50	74	17	1	10	49	24	42	10
Mendez, Julio, JC	.325	63	206	43	67	14	1	4	45	31	24	6
*Gardner, Glen, Pul	.316	68	256	44	81	14	1	10	51	27	22	15
Culberson, Calvain, Pul	.313	54	182	39	57	11	1	6	26	29	34	13
*Martinez, Luis, JC	.313	55	195	35	61	14	3	7	35	14	29	5
Davidson, Mike, Bris	.305	58	187	43	57	5	3	1	27	38	32	7
Hernandez, Rodolfo, Kpt	.296	72	284	52	84	14	3	1	54	44	38	15
McBride, Loy, Eliz	.288	62	233	37	67	14	3	4	39	21	40	11

* indicates lefthanded batter   # indicates switch hitter

INDIVIDUAL PITCHING LEADERS

(Minimum 58 Innings)

	W	L	ERA	G	GS	CG	SV	IP	H	R	ER	BB	SO
Meacham, Rusty, Bris	9	1	1.43	13	9	2	0	75	55	14	12	22	85
*Avery, Steve, Pul	7	1	1.50	10	10	3	0	66	38	16	11	19	80
Corbin, Archie, King	7	2	1.56	11	10	4	0	69	47	23	12	17	47
Kairis, Bob, Bur	7	5	1.89	14	13	1	0	81	69	24	17	18	85
Ard, Johnny, Eliz	4	1	1.97	9	8	1	0	59	40	17	13	26	71
Harriger, Denny, King	7	2	2.14	13	12	2	0	92	83	35	22	24	59
Garces, Richard, Eliz	5	4	2.29	17	3	1	5	59	51	22	15	27	69
Furmanik, Dan, King	9	1	2.30	13	11	4	0	78	54	26	20	28	52
Jones, Mike, Bris	7	4	2.56	15	15	4	0	95	75	33	27	33	100
Koller, Mike, Bris	8	2	2.60	13	13	2	0	80	73	35	23	24	88

* indicates lefthanded pitcher

BLUEFIELD

BATTING

BATTING	AVG	G	AB	R	H	2B	3B	HR	RBI	BB	SO	SB
*Bautista, Hector, of-dh	.288	46	163	28	47	2	1	0	20	17	22	6
Champ, Jeff, c	.287	42	150	19	43	9	0	0	26	17	34	10
#Fowler, John, 3b-1b	.206	60	218	22	45	10	1	3	25	16	60	3
Frias, Israel, c	.600	2	5	3	3	0	0	2	1	1	1	0
Gutierrez, Ricky, ss	.245	62	208	35	51	8	2	2	19	44	40	5
*Hicks, Aman, of	.226	50	186	22	42	5	0	0	14	18	43	6
Janutolo, Brian, inf	.146	31	89	10	13	2	2	0	5	5	31	1
Lafollette, Chris, dh-of	.297	29	101	14	30	3	0	2	17	10	29	0
Marsham, Fritsroy, of	.121	15	33	4	4	0	0	0	1	7	15	0
Mercedes, Luis, 2b	.274	59	215	36	59	8	4	0	20	32	39	16
#Meredith, Steve, 3b	.267	40	116	27	31	2	1	5	14	25	31	6
Metts, Carey, c	.302	48	172	20	52	9	3	4	32	8	28	3
Nicosia, Steve, of	.266	50	192	20	51	5	0	0	14	10	38	10
Perez, John, of	.188	6	16	2	3	0	0	0	2	4	4	1
Ramirez, Juan, of	.205	53	190	24	39	4	0	5	24	21	61	4
Redman, Joe, 2b-3b	.175	24	63	5	11	1	0	0	2	14	16	1
*Richardson, Mike, 1b	.279	44	154	25	43	8	0	1	25	19	26	5
Twenty, Mark, of	.218	26	78	8	17	2	1	0	5	3	25	0

PITCHING

PITCHING	W	L	ERA	G	GS	CG	SV	IP	H	R	ER	BB	SO
Bell, Brent	1	4	5.89	15	4	0	1	37	44	33	24	21	24
*Bretwisch, Bob	3	5	4.10	12	12	0	0	75	74	41	34	33	64
Brown, Charlie	2	3	6.20	19	0	0	2	45	56	39	31	17	37
Fowler, Don	0	3	4.21	20	1	0	2	36	43	25	17	17	35
Holmes, Wes	0	1	5.40	8	0	0	0	8	9	5	5	8	12
Kerr, Zachary	1	4	7.69	17	7	0	0	55	76	53	47	23	56
Marett, John	0	2	2.89	16	1	0	0	37	44	27	12	22	26
*Rhodes, Arthur	3	4	3.31	11	7	0	0	35	29	17	13	15	44
Ricci, Chuck	4	6	6.66	14	14	1	0	73	92	61	54	48	73
Shebby, Chris	3	3	4.76	12	6	0	0	45	56	38	24	13	26
Slomkowski, Rich	2	6	5.26	13	9	1	0	65	79	51	38	17	40
Somerville, Robbie	0	1	3.68	13	3	0	2	37	35	19	15	16	39
*Williams, Steve	5	5	3.48	18	7	1	1	62	59	34	24	21	44

BRISTOL

BATTING

BATTING	AVG	G	AB	R	H	2B	3B	HR	RBI	BB	SO	SB
Aldrich, Tom, 1b-3b	.338	63	219	50	74	17	1	10	49	24	42	10
*Biggs, Doug, of	.286	25	49	10	14	5	0	0	9	20	16	1
*Brogna, Rico, 1b-of	.254	60	209	37	53	11	2	7	33	25	42	3
Castillo, Ben, of	.268	21	71	16	19	1	0	4	17	12	17	0
Davidson, Mike, of	.305	58	187	43	57	5	3	1	27	38	32	7
Delas, Mickey, c-dh	.284	56	169	28	48	8	0	10	41	25	38	3
Estevez, Juan, c	.238	29	42	2	10	1	0	0	2	2	12	0
Frassa, Bob, of	.122	33	49	11	6	0	0	1	4	11	15	0
Henriquez, Francisco, 2b	1.000	4	1	0	1	0	0	0	0	0	0	0
#Hill, Beau, 2b-ss	.222	17	36	7	8	1	0	0	4	11	5	0
#Howard, Ron, 2b	.235	62	213	40	50	8	0	2	22	29	43	13
#Maldonado, Carlos, ss-2b	.125	23	40	8	5	0	0	0	2	8	4	1
Padilla, Freddy, 3b	.323	26	62	10	20	4	0	1	12	2	9	0
Pemberton, Rudy, of	.000	6	5	2	0	0	0	0	0	1	3	0
*Rendina, Mike, 1b	.200	39	75	12	15	3	0	3	16	9	18	0
Roach, Brett, 3b	.278	57	187	30	52	10	2	4	37	14	41	2
*Rojas, Jose, 2b-ss	.200	5	5	1	1	0	0	0	0	2	3	0
Rosa, Julio, ss	.219	70	201	39	44	7	1	0	22	36	39	6
Rowland, Rich, c-dh	.274	56	186	29	51	10	1	4	41	27	39	1
Spann, Tookie, of	.267	61	191	43	51	13	0	9	24	47	54	7
Walker, Duane, of	.230	59	191	38	44	5	1	6	27	21	42	6

PITCHING

PITCHING	W	L	ERA	G	GS	CG	SV	IP	H	R	ER	BB	SO
Betances, Marcos	5	3	4.24	13	13	1	0	64	48	37	30	50	57
*Brader, Tim	2	2	2.21	29	0	0	11	41	27	12	10	13	45
Ferm, Ed	1	2	6.51	16	0	0	0	28	39	25	20	15	25
Gollehon, Chris	0	1	9.58	8	1	0	0	10	9	14	11	12	15
Hayes, Jimmy	3	6	4.05	12	12	0	0	53	35	31	24	55	55
Jones, Mike	7	4	2.56	15	15	4	0	95	75	33	27	33	100
Kiley, John	2	2	6.17	8	0	0	1	12	9	9	8	7	14
Knudsen, Kurt	0	0	0.00	2	0	0	0	2	4	3	0	1	0
Koller, Mike	8	2	2.60	13	13	2	0	80	73	35	23	24	88
Meacham, Rusty	9	1	1.43	13	9	2	0	75	55	14	12	22	85
*Nozling, Paul	0	0	6.92	5	0	0	0	13	19	12	10	1	11
Rudolph, Blaine	4	1	2.11	17	5	0	2	55	44	25	13	29	59
Shea, Kurt	1	2	5.52	14	5	0	1	46	50	32	28	26	28
Shoup, Lee	1	1	3.60	14	0	0	1	20	25	11	8	7	19
Thomas, Rob	3	0	4.22	13	0	0	1	21	22	18	10	10	9

BURLINGTON

BATTING

BATTING	AVG	G	AB	R	H	2B	3B	HR	RBI	BB	SO	SB
Arias, Pedro, 2b-ss	.000	6	10	2	0	0	0	0	0	1	5	1
*Baron, Sean, 1b	.458	9	24	5	11	2	0	2	7	7	4	0
*Barranco, Vince, of	.228	63	158	46	36	6	1	0	13	71	34	34
#Bonchek, Jeff, 3b-1b	.273	54	139	20	38	6	0	1	18	34	33	2
Butler, Todd, 2b	.282	13	39	10	11	1	0	1	3	7	12	7
Castillo, Axel, of	.183	44	142	10	26	5	0	0	9	14	29	2
Delbene, John, c	.118	23	34	3	4	0	0	0	1	6	6	0
*Eddy, Martin, of-dh	.216	52	116	11	25	5	1	0	13	19	33	4

```
            R—Curtis Pride, Kingsport ......................59
            H—Rodolfo Hernandez, Kingsport ...........84
           TB—Vince Zawaski, Kingsport................138
           2B—Jim Morrisette, Kingsport..................21
           3B—Ben Shreve, Wytheville ......................5
             —Juan Belbru, Johnson City ..................5
           HR—Vince Zawaski, Kingsport..................16
          RBI—Vince Zawaski, Kingsport..................67
       GWRBI—Vince Zawaski, Kingsport...................9
           SH—Charlie White, Johnson City ...............6
           SF—Tim Howard, Kingsport..........................6
             —Glen Gardner, Pulaski..........................6
           BB—Vincent Barranco, Burlington .............71
          IBB—Five tied at........................................3
         HBP—Mike Mathiot, Elizabethton ................7
             —Nick Macaluso, Martinsville ..................7
           SO—Mark Thomas, Princeton ..................102
           SB—Gregory Sims, Princeton ..................39
           CS—Gregory Sims, Princeton ..................13
    Slg. Pct.—Tom Aldrich, Bristol ......................562
     OB Pct.—Wayne Weinheimer, Wytheville ........491
```

Department Leaders

PITCHING

```
            G—Toby Borland, Martinsville .................34
           GS—Mike Jones, Bristol ..........................15
           CG—Steve Wendell, Pulaski .......................5
          ShO—Four tied at ........................................2
           Sv—Toby Borland, Martinsville .................12
            W—Three tied at .......................................9
            L—Alan Newman, Elizabethton ..............8
             —Steve Wendell, Pulaski.........................8
           IP—Steve Wendell, Pulaski ....................101
            H—Tony Whitson, Wytheville .................118
            R—Tony Whitson, Wytheville ...................68
           HR—Tony Whitson, Wytheville ..................13
           BB—Antonio Felix, Princeton...................59
           HB—Andy Reich, Kingsport ........................9
           SO—Mike Jones, Bristol.........................100
           WP—Alan Newman, Elizabethton ..............17
           Bk—Don Elliott, Martinsville ......................9
```

	AVG	G	AB	R	H	2B	3B	HR	RBI	BB	SO	SB
Falkner, Rick, of	.385	7	26	5	10	5	0	2	9	2	3	1
#Gilmore, Lenny, of	.261	60	184	23	48	12	2	3	29	13	26	4
Gomez, Fabio, 3b	.202	57	188	18	38	3	1	4	22	11	46	7
Johnson, Brian, dh	.444	8	27	5	12	3	0	1	3	2	5	2
Lewis, Mark, ss	.264	61	227	39	60	13	1	7	43	25	44	14
#Mazey, Randy, of	.217	39	83	16	18	4	1	1	9	14	23	3
Mota, Carlos, c	.236	55	178	26	42	6	4	0	13	22	48	6
Odor, Rouglas, 2b-ss	.248	63	222	39	55	3	2	1	39	32	32	13
Roberts, Brent, 1b	.217	59	198	16	43	6	1	3	28	14	31	3
*Smith, Lawrence, of-inf	.132	22	38	5	5	1	0	0	0	3	18	5
Williams, Dan, c-1b	.210	39	100	9	21	4	1	1	8	8	23	1
#Young, Don, of	.233	45	129	14	30	4	0	0	4	11	41	12

PITCHING	W	L	ERA	G	GS	CG	SV	IP	H	R	ER	BB	SO
Alexander, Charles	0	1	2.35	6	0	0	1	8	8	5	2	6	6
*Allen, Scott	3	1	2.59	17	3	0	2	49	44	19	14	17	50
Ashworth, Mike	2	2	4.15	14	4	0	1	52	58	30	24	10	24
Baez, Angel	4	1	2.18	10	9	0	0	54	40	18	13	22	33
Blundin, Barry	3	4	4.82	23	2	0	3	62	73	43	33	32	35
*Halle, Andy	5	3	3.96	12	6	2	1	52	46	24	23	17	48
Kairis, Bob	7	5	1.89	14	13	1	0	81	69	24	17	18	85
*Kiser, Garland	2	2	2.03	7	5	1	0	31	22	11	7	9	29
McMichael, Greg	2	0	2.57	3	3	1	0	21	17	9	6	4	20
*Merriman, Brett	0	4	2.58	8	8	0	0	45	39	20	13	13	45
*Mutis, Jeff	3	0	0.41	3	3	0	0	22	8	1	1	6	20
Oliveras, David	2	1	2.11	10	3	0	2	21	9	14	5	22	35
Pettiford, Cecil	0	1	2.19	4	1	0	1	12	9	4	3	11	15
Piatt, Doug	0	0	13.50	2	0	0	1	1	4	2	2	1	1
Richardson, Dave	0	1	4.97	4	0	0	0	13	16	9	7	1	7
Roberts, Brent	0	0	3.86	6	0	0	0	7	7	3	3	3	1
Terpinas, Bill	2	3	3.82	22	0	0	5	31	31	19	13	17	22
*Woodfin, Olonzo	2	2	4.91	11	9	0	0	44	37	25	24	36	32

ELIZABETHTON

BATTING	AVG	G	AB	R	H	2B	3B	HR	RBI	BB	SO	SB
*Bruett, J.T., of	.297	28	91	23	27	3	0	0	3	19	15	17
*Dunn, Steve, 1b	.284	26	95	9	27	4	0	2	14	8	22	0
Freeman, Rick, c	.130	45	131	11	17	4	0	2	13	20	55	0
Garcia, Amadeo, of	.190	36	126	12	24	3	4	0	9	6	24	2
#Garcia, Cheo, of-2b	.259	59	228	31	59	9	3	2	27	15	46	9
Leon, Jose, c	.098	17	41	2	4	0	0	0	2	6	5	0
Lugo, Angel, ss	.194	12	31	3	6	1	1	0	2	4	9	1
Martin, Chris, 1b	.239	29	109	14	26	7	0	1	16	14	30	1

	AVG	G	AB	R	H	2B	3B	HR	RBI	BB	SO	SB
Mathiot, Mike, of-c	.278	41	144	25	40	8	1	4	22	17	30	10
McBride, Loy, of	.288	62	233	37	67	14	3	4	39	21	40	11
McKinnon, Willie, of	.063	10	16	0	1	0	0	0	0	0	7	0
Milene, Jeff, c	.111	8	18	3	2	0	0	0	0	4	8	0
#Mota, Willie, 3b	.271	34	118	13	32	8	2	0	13	4	15	0
#Nunez, Alejandro, ss	.151	31	53	8	8	0	0	0	1	3	16	3
*Oliva, Pedro, dh	.253	51	150	16	38	4	0	7	29	12	42	0
Pichardo, Francisco, of-2b	.140	18	50	3	7	0	0	0	1	2	17	2
Rivera, David, 2b	.235	25	51	8	12	0	0	0	3	1	7	1
Roskom, Bryan, 2b	.154	33	91	12	14	2	0	1	4	11	28	1
Santana, Hector, of	.167	16	30	1	5	0	0	0	0	1	11	0
#Shipman, Bob, of	.211	25	57	4	12	3	0	0	4	12	20	2
Tatarian, Dean, ss-3b	.200	57	170	21	34	6	2	1	15	24	26	1
Wacker, Wade, 3b-ss	.247	45	154	26	38	5	2	3	15	19	27	4
Wright, J.P., of-dh	.239	36	117	19	28	8	0	7	18	11	29	1

PITCHING	W	L	ERA	G	GS	CG	SV	IP	H	R	ER	BB	SO
Abel, Jack	0	0	8.80	13	1	0	2	15	16	15	15	11	13
Ard, Johnny	4	1	1.97	9	8	1	0	59	40	17	13	26	71
Garces, Richard	5	4	2.29	17	3	1	5	59	51	22	15	27	69
Garcia, Franklin	0	0	6.27	9	0	0	1	19	17	13	13	18	9
*Harrington, Jody	1	0	5.68	4	0	0	0	6	6	5	4	6	12
Mahomes, Pat	6	3	3.69	13	13	3	0	78	66	45	32	51	93
*Muh, Steve	2	3	3.75	9	9	0	0	58	43	29	24	41	62
*Newman, Alan	2	8	8.13	13	12	2	0	55	57	62	50	56	51
Perez, Alex	0	0	12.08	6	0	0	0	13	23	19	17	11	7
*Pomeranz, Mike	2	6	5.07	17	4	1	1	50	39	29	28	33	39
Reyes, Elvis	0	0	10.13	7	0	0	0	8	11	9	9	13	9
*Richardson, David	3	4	3.36	15	7	0	1	56	50	29	21	27	54
Rovasio, Dom	3	3	3.35	24	0	0	3	38	34	26	14	29	53
Sutton, Doug	5	5	3.49	13	13	3	0	85	68	42	33	36	63
Watts, Walter	0	0	33.75	5	0	0	0	4	7	15	15	16	4

JOHNSON CITY

BATTING	AVG	G	AB	R	H	2B	3B	HR	RBI	BB	SO	SB
Belbru, Juan, of	.230	64	200	29	46	12	5	7	30	11	57	8
Berlin, Randy, 1b	.209	45	129	13	27	3	0	3	16	14	44	2
Biggers, Al, ss-3b	.262	49	141	21	37	5	1	0	12	16	19	4
Calzado, Johnny, 1b-3b	.213	53	141	18	30	6	3	3	15	13	54	7
#Carmona, Greg, ss	.328	21	64	15	21	1	1	1	8	17	7	8
Davis, Jerry, of	.179	35	78	6	14	5	0	0	5	10	29	2
Decker, Bill, of	.281	69	221	29	62	7	2	4	35	11	41	4
Edwards, Calvin, ss	.000	8	12	0	0	0	0	0	0	0	4	0
#Huffman, Kris, ss-3b	.370	9	27	8	10	0	0	0	5	5	0	3
*Kroeger, J.T., c	.326	17	43	13	14	3	0	3	9	9	11	1
Langiotti, Freddy, c	.186	27	59	7	11	1	0	0	5	4	11	0
Maack, Jeff, inf	.194	13	36	5	7	2	0	1	3	7	6	0
#Martinez, Luis, c-of	.313	55	195	35	61	14	3	7	35	14	29	5
Mendez, Julio, inf	.325	63	206	43	67	14	1	4	45	31	24	6
Pettengill, Tim, c	.288	20	66	14	19	7	0	2	12	6	11	1
*Shannon, Dan, dh	.289	47	142	17	41	11	0	3	22	8	38	1
#Shireman, Jeff, 2b	.339	52	189	41	64	8	1	2	19	23	15	4
Stephens, John, 3b	.258	46	93	14	24	1	0	1	11	23	15	7
White, Charlie, of	.272	69	257	44	70	8	0	5	27	25	37	33

PITCHING	W	L	ERA	G	GS	CG	SV	IP	H	R	ER	BB	SO
Corry, Steve	3	4	5.26	15	9	0	0	51	54	34	30	29	51
Ericks, John	3	2	3.73	9	9	1	0	41	27	20	17	27	41
Goguen, Phil	1	1	6.10	17	1	0	0	31	33	26	21	19	40
Golden, Brian	1	2	4.57	17	3	0	0	41	39	23	21	31	52
Grimes, David	6	0	2.73	26	0	0	2	59	64	21	18	14	56
Grubb, Sean	6	3	3.55	13	12	1	0	66	68	39	26	24	57
Halama, Scott	1	1	2.36	6	4	0	0	27	22	12	7	12	17
Hensley, Mike	4	3	3.91	14	10	1	0	69	65	41	30	36	74
*Hitt, Dan	5	2	1.35	30	0	0	7	40	37	11	6	6	48
Hoffman, Richard	7	2	3.19	11	9	0	0	59	59	25	21	18	47
Martinez, Frankie	2	5	5.15	12	10	0	0	44	41	33	25	23	19
Ozuna, Gabriel	0	4	1.07	21	0	0	9	25	18	6	3	9	29
Suero, Rafael	2	2	5.87	15	5	0	0	38	45	32	25	12	20

KINGSPORT

BATTING	AVG	G	AB	R	H	2B	3B	HR	RBI	BB	SO	SB
Castillo, Berto, c	.293	24	75	7	22	3	0	1	14	15	14	0
Harris, James, dh	.167	2	6	0	1	0	0	0	0	1	1	0
Hernandez, Rodolfo, 2b	.296	72	284	52	84	14	3	1	54	44	38	15
*Hines, Tim, c	.280	31	107	24	30	9	1	2	22	12	17	0
#Howard, Tim, dh-ss	.280	68	243	39	68	14	4	3	46	27	43	7
Howell, Pat, of	.267	66	251	43	67	6	3	0	16	12	52	27
Morrisette, Jim, 3b	.283	71	258	45	73	21	2	10	36	28	52	12
Navarro, Tito, ss	.244	54	172	26	42	3	2	0	23	30	27	13
Ostopowicz, Rich, of-dh	.186	39	102	22	19	2	0	2	15	28	26	4
Parouse, Daniel, c	.258	20	66	11	17	1	0	1	5	9	20	1
*Pride, Curtis, of	.284	70	268	59	76	13	1	8	27	50	48	23
Tesmer, Jim, dh-of	.237	15	38	5	9	2	0	0	6	5	3	1
Young, Derrick, of	.280	72	271	45	76	12	2	3	42	20	46	5
Zawaski, Vince, 1b	.284	72	264	56	75	11	2	16	67	46	77	1

PITCHING	W	L	ERA	G	GS	CG	SV	IP	H	R	ER	BB	SO
Corbin, Archie	7	2	1.56	11	10	4	0	69	47	23	12	17	47
*Fidler, Andy	0	0	6.75	5	1	0	0	9	6	7	7	6	12
Fine, Tom	0	3	3.06	3	3	0	0	18	17	13	6	9	12
Furmanik, Dan	9	1	2.30	13	11	4	0	78	54	26	20	28	52
Harriger, Denny	7	2	2.14	13	13	2	0	92	83	35	22	24	59
*Hudson, Jon	0	1	4.08	17	0	0	3	18	15	10	8	13	14
Johnson, Paul	2	2	6.10	24	0	0	5	31	33	22	21	16	32
Krogman, Monte	0	1	9.00	7	0	0	1	12	8	13	12	11	6
*Langbehn, Greg	3	3	3.49	7	4	0	0	28	26	15	11	11	29
Medina, Luciano	2	3	3.86	18	2	0	4	40	35	21	17	12	43
Reich, Andy	9	2	2.64	13	13	0	0	89	77	36	26	32	71
Richmond, Ryan	6	2	4.84	13	12	0	0	71	68	44	38	37	65
Rogers, Bryan	2	3	6.32	15	2	0	0	31	30	23	22	14	35
Vasquez, Julian	0	1	3.19	14	2	0	10	31	19	13	11	13	30

MARTINSVILLE

BATTING	AVG	G	AB	R	H	2B	3B	HR	RBI	BB	SO	SB
Bean, Kenneth, of	.148	27	81	7	12	0	0	0	2	6	32	1
Bennett, Al, of	.284	52	201	22	57	8	1	4	24	6	57	9
Breaux, Greg, 2b	.154	14	26	2	4	2	0	0	1	1	12	0
Churchill, Tim, 1b	.239	42	159	19	38	8	1	4	21	8	31	2
*Current, Matt, c	.109	19	55	5	6	0	0	0	2	5	13	0
*Doyle, Tom, 1b	.197	22	71	8	14	3	0	1	7	8	19	1
Escobar, John, ss	.216	43	139	13	30	2	0	0	11	13	28	2
#Etheridge, Jeff, of	.163	22	86	17	14	1	0	1	6	13	34	8
*Johnson, Lute, of	.188	48	165	22	31	7	1	1	12	24	61	2
Linares, Antonio, of	.284	43	148	22	42	7	0	4	23	6	19	5
#Llanos, Aurelio, of	.102	19	59	5	6	1	0	1	3	10	33	0
Lowe, Chris, of	.253	25	75	13	19	6	1	1	3	13	28	3
Luzinski, Anthony, c	.250	2	4	0	1	0	0	0	0	0	1	1
*Macaluso, Nick, 2b	.278	68	223	51	62	9	1	12	44	55	53	3
Maracara, Oswaldo, 2b-3b	.185	14	27	3	5	0	0	0	1	3	6	0
*Marshall, John, 3b-1b	.277	66	253	29	70	11	1	10	45	24	33	0
Perez, Eulogio, ss	.176	14	51	6	9	5	1	0	1	5	16	1
#Rosado, Edwin, c	.258	57	194	27	50	8	0	4	24	12	35	0
Rosario, Victor, 1b-dh	.288	17	52	6	15	2	0	1	6	5	7	0
Talford, Calvin, of	.375	13	24	2	9	0	0	1	3	0	6	1
Tejada, Francisco, c	.138	16	29	3	4	0	0	2	4	4	13	0
Toney, Chris, 3b	.190	45	163	17	31	9	0	4	19	13	67	4
Walker, Ray, ss	.119	16	42	5	5	0	0	1	3	11	20	3

PITCHING	W	L	ERA	G	GS	CG	SV	IP	H	R	ER	BB	SO
Backs, Jason	2	1	1.87	25	0	0	3	34	24	11	7	16	36
Borland, Toby	2	3	4.04	34	0	0	12	49	42	26	22	29	43
Coccia, Dan	0	0	6.75	10	0	0	0	19	24	14	14	13	13
Dafforn, Mike	4	2	5.73	19	1	0	0	38	46	28	24	21	25
Elliott, Don	4	2	3.66	15	10	0	1	59	47	37	24	31	77
Fletcher, Ed	1	3	4.67	15	14	1	1	69	81	44	36	33	61
Garcia, Reggie	2	1	3.83	17	3	0	0	52	48	28	22	23	58
Goergen, Todd	1	5	6.69	14	6	0	0	39	62	40	29	15	18
*Harper, Brian	4	8	4.75	14	14	0	0	66	83	51	35	17	45
*Johnston, Craig	2	4	5.77	11	8	0	4	44	57	37	28	13	36
Kent, Troy	1	7	4.27	23	1	0	1	46	43	27	22	14	26
Lindsey, Darrell	6	5	2.80	13	13	1	0	84	69	35	26	22	79

PRINCETON

BATTING	AVG	G	AB	R	H	2B	3B	HR	RBI	BB	SO	SB
Antigua, Felix, c	.282	20	39	2	11	3	0	0	6	2	5	1
Cowley, Scott, of	.246	23	57	8	14	0	1	1	10	10	17	1
Feliz, Felix, 3b	.111	14	27	1	3	0	0	0	1	1	7	3
#Fortuna, Mike, 3b-2b	.264	43	129	19	34	3	2	3	16	21	30	5
Garcia, Tomas, 2b	.231	30	39	13	9	1	0	0	2	3	10	11
Jerich, Bill, of	.245	16	49	4	12	5	1	1	7	11	8	0
Jewett, Trent, c	.161	24	62	6	10	3	0	1	7	10	23	1
Johnson, Deron, of	.269	20	78	16	21	7	1	2	6	6	24	8
Kerekes, Kevin, of-dh	.271	36	118	13	32	3	1	1	13	9	26	7
Manahan, Austin, ss	.181	64	227	31	41	4	4	6	33	24	102	12
McNabb, Glen, 2b	.247	46	154	21	38	4	0	0	15	20	27	13
Nelson, Erik, c	.250	12	32	6	8	1	2	1	4	4	10	3
*Osborne, Jeff, dh-c	.262	17	42	3	11	1	0	0	3	2	13	1
Pennyfeather, William, of	.333	16	57	11	19	2	0	1	5	6	15	1
#Romero, Mandy, c	.310	30	71	7	22	6	0	2	11	13	15	1
*Seymour, Winston, dh-1b	.258	52	159	18	41	10	1	1	24	11	40	5
Shelton, Ben, 1b	.221	63	204	34	45	7	3	4	20	42	82	8
Sims, Gregory, of	.270	60	204	40	55	13	2	0	12	51	38	42
Spriggs, George, 3b	.216	53	162	24	35	4	2	0	15	17	53	13
Stout, Jeff, 2b-ss	.342	21	73	15	25	3	3	0	8	4	7	11
Thomas, Mark, of	.236	67	258	36	61	11	1	13	46	16	122	16
*Velky, Joe, c	.281	14	32	3	9	1	0	1	5	5	8	1

PITCHING	W	L	ERA	G	GS	CG	SV	IP	H	R	ER	BB	SO
Dooley, Marvin	3	7	5.68	12	10	1	0	44	49	38	28	25	23
Doss, Ray	1	0	6.38	17	0	0	1	24	21	21	17	16	24
Felix, Antonio	3	5	3.32	13	13	1	0	76	60	38	28	59	92
*Honeywell, Brent	1	0	4.11	6	0	0	1	15	16	7	7	4	22
*Juran, Craig	2	1	5.67	25	0	0	0	46	44	30	29	23	50

	W	L	ERA	G	GS	CG	SV	IP	H	R	ER	BB	SO
*Kuder, Jeff	4	3	5.09	14	11	0	0	64	70	40	36	24	68
*Latham, John	0	3	10.19	9	4	0	1	18	24	25	20	12	9
Martinez, Ramon	1	3	6.75	16	0	0	1	23	26	20	17	15	24
Mays, Keith	1	1	6.27	12	1	0	0	19	26	21	13	21	16
Maysonet, Greg	0	0	3.18	5	0	0	0	6	6	5	2	6	3
McDowell, Tim	3	5	3.69	14	9	0	0	61	67	35	25	19	49
McKinney, Tony	2	0	1.10	2	2	0	0	16	10	2	2	3	8
Minor, Blas	0	1	4.41	15	0	0	7	16	18	10	8	5	23
*Payne, Jeff	1	1	6.75	2	2	0	0	7	6	5	5	5	5
Slaughter, Garland	4	1	5.19	14	3	0	0	35	40	22	20	19	22
Tunall, Steve	3	5	4.16	14	14	1	0	89	105	53	41	18	54
*Wilson, Richard	4	1	5.68	23	1	0	2	32	37	26	20	20	33

PULASKI

BATTING	AVG	G	AB	R	H	2B	3B	HR	RBI	BB	SO	SB
Carter, Garrett, of	.215	38	93	9	20	3	0	4	15	5	26	2
Culberson, Calvain, of-dh	.313	54	182	39	57	11	1	6	26	29	34	13
*Gardner, Glen, of-dh	.316	68	256	44	81	14	1	10	51	27	22	15
Gonzalez, Wallace, c	.045	11	22	1	1	0	0	0	1	1	13	0
Goselin, Scott, inf	.281	52	146	25	41	2	0	1	17	25	27	7
*Greenwood, John, 1b	.247	61	186	29	46	10	0	6	26	16	51	2
#McCoy, Brent, ss	.283	21	60	11	17	6	0	0	9	11	6	4
Minaya, Roberto, of	.286	61	210	33	60	10	1	0	31	13	29	20
Mitta, Christopher, 3b	.231	59	212	34	49	9	1	5	28	24	44	5
Piela, Dave, c-1b	.207	38	92	9	19	3	0	1	13	16	32	0
Reis, Paul, 2b	.234	58	175	40	41	3	4	0	15	17	21	18
#Relaford, Winnie, of	.223	49	166	28	37	3	1	0	14	34	36	28
Rigsby, Rick, c	.282	32	78	8	22	2	1	1	15	4	20	5
Rizzo, Tom, ss	.199	50	141	23	28	5	0	2	13	33	31	5
*Simmons, Randy, dh-of	.242	55	161	29	39	8	4	7	31	28	42	10
Urman, Mike, c	.147	25	68	6	10	1	0	0	6	10	21	0

PITCHING	W	L	ERA	G	GS	CG	SV	IP	H	R	ER	BB	SO
*Arnold, Greg	0	0	4.50	1	0	0	0	2	3	3	1	2	0
*Avery, Steve	7	1	1.50	10	10	3	0	66	38	16	11	19	80
Dickman, Dave	4	2	2.88	16	1	0	1	34	23	17	11	20	35
*Flynn, Erroll	4	3	4.03	14	0	0	2	22	19	14	10	23	24
Grove, Scott	4	3	3.59	14	9	0	1	58	42	34	23	36	32
*Hailey, Roger	0	0	11.25	1	1	0	0	4	4	6	5	3	6
*Lange, Bill	1	1	10.80	7	0	0	0	10	19	14	12	12	8
Lowery, Phil	2	1	3.52	15	3	0	1	38	35	22	15	12	29
Murray, Matt	2	4	4.17	13	8	0	1	54	48	32	25	26	76
Reis, Dave	2	5	4.97	13	12	1	0	71	81	54	39	34	36
*Thomas, Ron	0	1	4.74	11	3	0	0	25	28	18	13	13	17
Wendell, Steve	3	8	3.83	14	14	6	0	101	85	50	43	30	87
Wohlers, Mark	5	3	3.32	13	9	1	0	60	47	37	22	50	49
Zona, Jeff	1	2	1.55	17	0	1	0	46	25	13	8	28	23

WYTHEVILLE

BATTING	AVG	G	AB	R	H	2B	3B	HR	RBI	BB	SO	SB
Adames, Juan, ss-2b	.270	38	141	29	38	3	0	0	18	27	29	5
*Bailey, Troy, of	.252	38	119	19	30	3	1	0	10	14	37	4
Bonneau, Rob, ss-2b	.205	26	83	18	17	2	0	2	13	12	23	2
Borders, Todd, 1b	.400	4	5	0	2	1	0	0	1	1	1	0
Browder, Bubba, c	.196	23	51	9	10	2	0	1	10	8	16	0
Cancel, Danny, of	.333	3	6	0	2	0	0	0	1	0	3	0
Canino, Carlos, dh	.139	14	36	4	5	0	0	1	4	8	22	0
Carosielli, Marc, 2b	.190	28	63	3	12	2	0	0	6	2	18	1
Cole, Marvin, ss-2b	.315	51	184	24	58	6	2	0	18	7	12	7
*Franco, Matt, 3b	.392	20	79	14	31	9	1	0	16	7	5	0
Huff, Brad, c	.231	12	26	1	6	0	0	0	0	3	11	1
*Leonard, Matt, 1b	.256	29	78	5	20	2	1	1	15	16	21	0
Paynter, Bill, c	.190	50	174	20	33	3	0	3	13	12	48	2
#Roberson, Kevin, of	.209	63	225	39	47	12	2	3	29	40	86	3
*Shreve, Ben, 2b-3b	.264	35	121	23	32	4	5	2	12	15	21	1
Sierra, Louie, of	.217	21	60	12	13	2	1	1	11	5	10	1
Smith, Woody, 3b	.267	53	206	33	55	11	1	7	29	10	57	2
*Uribe, Milieiades, 1b	.210	47	186	28	39	8	0	2	22	19	28	3
Washington, Kraig, 2b-of	.328	15	61	14	20	2	0	0	9	8	5	1
*Weinheimer, Wayne, of	.355	67	211	54	75	20	0	4	53	56	41	3
Wentz, Keith, c	.256	10	39	4	10	2	0	0	3	3	6	1
*Williams, Jerome, of	.239	38	134	12	32	4	1	3	10	5	33	5

PITCHING	W	L	ERA	G	GS	CG	SV	IP	H	R	ER	BB	SO
Burns, Daren	2	5	5.68	9	9	1	0	52	67	46	33	20	44
Doss, Jason	0	2	6.54	18	3	0	1	52	61	45	38	38	45
*Gamble, Billy	0	2	7.62	12	0	0	2	13	16	11	11	9	12
*Gladu, Mike	6	4	5.67	14	10	0	1	60	57	46	38	49	66
Martinez, Juan	0	0	4.18	18	1	0	0	28	25	15	13	18	15
Rasp, Ronnie	5	6	4.14	22	5	1	2	63	64	39	29	27	53
*Reed, Sean	5	4	4.70	13	8	0	0	59	61	34	31	28	56
Rodriguez, Eligio	0	1	7.36	5	0	0	0	7	11	6	6	0	6
Schulmeister, Dean	0	1	4.38	16	0	0	5	12	12	7	6	5	15
Smalls, Roberto	3	6	4.36	13	13	0	0	76	81	52	37	45	68
*Thobe, Tom	3	3	8.95	18	5	0	0	57	90	66	57	30	31
Whitson, Tony	4	6	4.22	14	14	1	0	92	118	68	43	20	66

Rich Dodger draft benefits Great Falls

By DANNY KNOBLER

The Great Falls Dodgers capped off one of the Pioneer League's best seasons ever in 1988 by beating Butte, 3-2, in the league championship series. The Dodgers finished off the Copper Kings with a 4-3 win Sept. 3 in Great Falls.

Great Falls broke a league record with a 2.93 team ERA and hit .319, just .001 off the league record. The club's 52-17 record was just 1½ games behind Great Falls' record 54-16 season in 1985.

The parent Los Angeles Dodgers believed their 1988 draft was among their best ever—and 19 drafted players played at Great Falls. Pioneer League managers, in a survey by Baseball America, agreed that Great Falls was loaded with prospects, but the league's top player didn't even come out of the draft.

Shortstop Jose Oferman, a switch-hitting 19-year-old Dominican, broke a league record with 57 steals, and hit .335. Managers said he was even more impressive defensively, and one called him "a franchise player."

Record for ineptitude

At the other end of the Pioneer League standings were the Medicine Hat Blue Jays. The Jays finished 12-58—four games worse than any Pioneer League team in history. Only the 16-54 Helena Phillies of 1983 came close.

The overmatched Jays were the league's youngest team, and they featured the youngest general manager in baseball, 20-year-old Dean Linden. When Medicine Hat lost its first eight games of the year, Linden vowed to sleep in a tent at Medicine Hat Athletic Park until the Jays won. He waited through tornado warnings, and the streak ended at 16.

Between the Dodgers and Blue Jays were the independently-operated Salt Lake Trappers, the minor leagues' cult team. The Trappers won 29 straight games in 1987 en route to their third straight title. They finished three games behind Southern Division champ Butte in 1988, and broke records only for attendance. Salt Lake drew 176,217, more than the city's last Triple-A team attracted in twice as many home dates.

Butte made the league's biggest turnaround after signing a

League Champions

(Playoff Champions, Where Applicable)

1988—Great Falls	1971—Great Falls	1954—Great Falls
1987—Salt Lake	1970—Idaho Falls	1953—Salt Lake City
1986—Salt Lake	1969—Ogden	1952—Idaho Falls
1985—Salt Lake	1968—Ogden	1951—Great Falls
1984—Helena	1967—Ogden	1950—Billings
1983—Billings	1966—Ogden	1949—Pocatello
1982—Medicine Hat	1965—Treasure Valley	1948—Twin Falls
1981—Butte	1964—Treasure Valley	1947—Twin Falls
1980—Lethbridge	1963—Magic Valley	1946—Salt Lake City
1979—Lethbridge	1962—Billings	1943-45—Did Not
1978—Billings	1961—Great Falls	Operate
1977—Lethbridge	1960—Boise	1942—Pocatello
1976—Great Falls	1959—Billings	1941—Ogden
1975—Great Falls	1958—Boise	1940—Ogden
1974—Idaho Falls	1957—Billings	1939—Twin Falls
1973—Billings	1956—Boise	
1972—Billings	1955—Magic Valley	

Top Performers

Jose Oferman
...No. 1 prospect

Kelly Zane
....379 average

Trey McCoy
...14 home runs

player development contract with the Texas Rangers. As a co-op in 1987, the Copper Kings finished 19-50. The Ranger prospects finished 44-26 in 1988.

Getting nasty

In addition to winning the league title, Great Falls did some fighting. The Dodgers and Pocatello Giants were involved in an Aug. 18 brawl that PL president Ralph Nelles said was the worst he'd seen in 13 years in office. Great Falls manager Tim Johnson ended up with a collapsed lung and spike wounds on his back, but returned in time for the playoffs.

The Dodgers' dominant pitching finished off the playoff series with Butte. Righthander Sean Snedeker, who went 8-2 and led the league with a 2.20 ERA, took a perfect game into the eighth inning before Dominic Pierce lined a one-out single over first baseman Eric Karros' head.

Butte put three singles and three errors together for three runs in the inning, and the Copper Kings had the tying run on second when Johnson summoned lefty James Wray, who had five wins, three saves and a 2.04 ERA during the year.

Wray, who also saved Game One for Snedeker, got Joe Wardlow to fly out to end the inning, then retired the Copper Kings in the ninth.

Wardlow was Butte's hitting star in the series, starting 10-for-16 before going hitless in the final game. Karros had two hits in Great Falls' 13-6 opening-game win, and four more in Butte's 6-5 win in Game Two.

Great Falls took the lead in the series with a 9-2 win in Game Three, as Jeff Hartsock scattered eight hits and struck out 11.

North	W	L	Pct.	GB	
Great Falls (Dodgers)	52	17	.754	—	
Helena (Brewers)	41	29	.586	11½	
Billings (Reds)	35	34	.507	17	1988
Med. Hat (Blue Jays) .	12	58	.171	40½	Final
South					Standings
Butte (Rangers)	44	26	.629	—	
Salt Lake (Ind.)	41	29	.586	3	
Idaho Falls (Braves) .	28	42	.400	16	
Pocatello (Giants) ...	26	44	.371	18	

1988: General Information

Playoffs: Great Falls defeated Butte 3-2 in best-of-5 final for league championship.

Regular Season Attendance: Salt Lake, 176,217; Billings, 87,762; Great Falls, 71,497; Idaho Falls, 64,672; Butte, 28,338; Helena, 26,892; Pocatello, 20,785, Medicine Hat, 10,553.

Managers: Billings—Dave Keller; **Butte**—Bump Wills; **Great Falls**—Tim Johnson; **Helena**—Dusty Rhodes; **Idaho Falls**—Jim Procopio; **Medicine Hat**—Rocket Wheeler; **Pocatello**—Jack Hiatt; **Salt Lake**—Barry Moss.

1988 All-Star Team: C—Bert Heffernan, Helena. **1B**—Rob Maurer, Butte. **2B**—Kelly Zane, Salt Lake. **3B**—Michael Songini, Billings. **SS**—Jose Oferman, Great Falls. **OF**—Trey McCoy, Butte; Ben Colvard, Billings; Donovan Campbell, Idaho Falls. **DH**—Mando Verdugo, Salt Lake. **P**—Sean Snedeker, Great Falls; Richard Nowak, Medicine Hat; Steve Reed, Pocatello. **Manager of the Year**—Tim Johnson, Great Falls.

Top 10 Major League Prospects (by Baseball America): 1. Jose Oferman, ss, Great Falls; **2.** Bill Bene, rhp, Great Falls; **3.** Donovan Campbell, of, Idaho; **4.** Ramser Correa, rhp, Helena; **5.** Ben Colvard, of, Billings; **6.** Thayer Swain, of, Butte; **7.** Robb Maurer, 1b, Butte; **8.** Chris Morrow, of, Great Falls; **9.** Sean Snedeker, rhp, Great Falls; **10.** Rod Morris, of, Butte.

1988: Batting, Pitching Statistics

CLUB BATTING

	AVG	G	AB	R	H	2B	3B	HR	BB	SO	SB
Great Falls	.319	69	2422	534	772	135	31	50	332	422	162
Butte	.307	70	2539	551	780	125	30	58	320	421	95
Salt Lake City	.297	70	2480	487	737	104	17	47	362	447	65
Billings	.274	69	2381	402	653	93	27	25	283	474	156
Idaho Falls	.271	70	2458	400	667	96	25	39	261	530	131
Helena	.268	70	2340	402	628	117	11	49	341	439	80
Pocatello	.247	70	2371	358	585	80	30	26	282	564	49
Medicine Hat	.212	70	2293	253	485	70	18	24	282	657	60

CLUB PITCHING

	ERA	G	CG	SHO	SV	IP	H	R	ER	BB	SO
Great Falls	2.93	69	6	6	13	602	483	257	196	245	628
Helena	4.05	70	10	5	8	604	617	347	272	332	542
Salt Lake City	4.35	70	10	4	13	610	665	379	295	229	496
Billings	4.53	69	3	3	18	602	624	399	303	267	420
Butte	5.45	70	2	1	19	608	676	437	368	355	487
Pocatello	5.49	70	2	1	14	605	714	521	369	371	522
Idaho Falls	5.67	70	2	1	12	615	752	503	387	311	422
Medicine Hat	5.75	70	3	2	6	601	776	544	384	352	437

INDIVIDUAL BATTING LEADERS
(Minimum 189 Plate Appearances)

	AVG	G	AB	R	H	2B	3B	HR	RBI	BB	SO	SB
*Maurer, Rob, Butte	.391	63	233	65	91	18	3	8	59	35	34	0
Colvard, Benny, Bill	.387	51	199	39	77	10	5	7	47	22	31	18
Zane, Kelly, SLC	.379	63	261	56	99	11	4	3	38	40	30	8
Karros, Eric, GF	.366	66	268	68	98	12	1	12	55	32	35	8
McCoy, Trey, Butte	.357	68	252	68	90	21	2	14	78	47	47	2
*Slavin, David, Poc	.356	64	216	34	77	11	0	2	48	37	32	2
*Marrero, Oreste, Hel	.354	67	240	52	85	15	0	16	44	41	48	2
Shaw, Kerry, SLC	.353	54	201	54	71	8	2	2	44	37	13	6
Brooks, Jerry, GF	.347	68	285	63	99	21	3	8	61	24	25	7
*Songini, Mike, Bill	.347	56	196	40	68	6	5	3	32	29	13	10

INDIVIDUAL PITCHING LEADERS
(Minimum 56 Innings)

	W	L	ERA	G	GS	CG	SV	IP	H	R	ER	BB	SO
Snedeker, Sean, GF	8	2	2.20	13	12	5	0	86	64	29	21	16	102
Kiefer, Mark, Hel	4	4	2.65	15	9	2	0	68	76	30	20	17	51
Hartsock, Jeff, GF	7	2	2.67	14	13	1	0	81	62	30	24	26	108
Nowak, Rick, MH	2	5	3.09	12	11	0	0	64	63	24	22	27	68
Lane, Heath, Hel	8	4	3.38	15	8	4	0	75	72	29	28	17	63
*Riscen, Fred, SLC	6	1	3.53	10	10	3	0	64	56	28	25	20	67
Kandalaft, Kevin, MH	2	6	3.72	16	11	2	0	73	83	51	30	36	48
*Wenrick, Bill, SLC	7	4	3.72	13	12	2	0	77	74	40	32	23	69
Groennert, John, Bill	6	3	3.74	13	13	1	0	75	76	44	31	15	43
James, Mike, GF	7	1	3.76	14	12	0	0	67	61	36	28	41	59

BILLINGS

BATTING	AVG	G	AB	R	H	2B	3B	HR	RBI	BB	SO	SB
Bond, Doug, 1b	.244	50	176	27	43	4	0	3	30	11	25	4
Brune, Jim, c	.226	10	31	5	7	3	1	0	7	7	7	3
*Clark, Tim, 2b	.290	53	169	27	49	3	2	1	19	33	21	19
Colvard, Benny, of-dh	.387	51	199	39	77	10	5	7	47	22	31	18
Davis, Alton, of-dh	.238	33	105	21	25	9	2	0	8	19	29	6
Fuller, Jon, dh-c	.281	31	96	11	27	2	0	0	11	10	22	2
Hamilton, Dave, 3b	.100	5	10	0	1	0	0	0	0	2	1	2
Javier, Vicente, ss	.210	31	100	16	21	3	0	0	17	9	21	4
Johnson, Dante, of	.133	10	30	3	4	1	0	0	3	1	9	0
Mulvaney, Mike, 1b-dh	.302	51	202	32	61	11	0	2	38	15	25	4
Mulville, Duane, c	.286	37	126	19	36	6	0	0	13	20	25	4
*Parrotte, Brian, 3b	.333	7	18	3	6	1	1	2	6	2	5	0
Perozo, Danny, of	.265	42	155	26	41	6	2	0	9	9	43	15
Reyes, Steve, of	.215	52	163	27	35	10	0	3	16	22	46	11
#Rickman, Andy, ss	.333	5	15	7	5	0	0	0	1	6	1	1
Sanders, Reggie, ss	.234	17	64	11	15	1	1	0	3	6	4	9
Sellner, Scott, 2b-ss	.315	58	216	40	68	11	3	2	38	23	27	9
*Songini, Mike, 3b	.347	56	196	40	68	6	5	3	32	29	13	10
Sutko, Glenn, c	.153	30	85	3	13	2	1	1	7	14	38	3
Terzarial, Tony, of	.227	61	225	45	51	4	4	1	23	23	81	30

PITCHING	W	L	ERA	G	GS	CG	SV	IP	H	R	ER	BB	SO
Almaraz, Johnny	5	5	5.04	13	9	0	0	55	55	35	31	25	54
Anderson, Mike	3	1	3.25	17	4	0	2	44	36	17	16	21	52
Dempster, Kurt	0	1	14.49	12	1	0	0	14	17	34	22	29	7
Economy, Scott	1	3	4.90	14	10	0	1	64	72	47	35	31	37
Foster, Steve	2	3	1.19	18	0	0	7	30	15	5	4	7	26
Groennert, John	6	3	3.74	13	13	1	0	75	76	44	31	15	43
*Landy, Brian	6	5	4.66	14	13	0	0	75	92	53	39	22	25
McAuliffe, Dave	3	2	2.27	16	0	0	2	32	26	9	8	7	27
*McCarthy, Steve	0	1	5.94	10	1	0	1	17	23	14	11	6	12
Nichols, Brian	1	2	6.87	17	0	0	3	37	43	32	28	24	37
Nordstrom, Carl	3	6	5.20	14	13	2	0	73	72	47	42	36	48
*Rodriguez, Tomas	0	1	4.50	19	0	0	2	34	46	33	17	25	25
Spradlin, Jerry	4	1	3.21	17	5	0	0	48	45	25	17	14	25
Stewart, Carl	0	0	0.00	1	0	0	0	1	2	1	0	1	1
Thomas, C.L.	1	0	5.40	2	0	0	0	3	4	3	2	4	1

BUTTE

BATTING	AVG	G	AB	R	H	2B	3B	HR	RBI	BB	SO	SB
#Colon, Cris, ss	.195	49	190	21	37	3	4	1	19	3	34	3
Fariss, Monty, ss	.396	17	53	16	21	1	0	4	22	20	7	2
Fontes, Brad, c	.056	7	18	0	1	0	0	0	0	1	6	0
Frye, Jeff, 2b	.286	55	185	47	53	7	1	0	14	35	25	16
*Hainline, Jeff, dh	.000	1	3	0	0	0	0	0	0	0	1	0
Hamilton, Mike, c	.250	23	60	4	15	1	0	0	6	2	9	0
Izzo, Darryn, 3b	.185	15	27	4	5	0	0	1	4	3	8	2
Law, Travis, of	.200	3	10	6	2	0	0	0	0	5	1	1
*Lewis, Joe, c	.238	34	101	14	24	3	0	0	9	11	13	0
Losa, Bill, c-dh	.279	62	222	46	62	7	1	6	52	24	63	8
*Maurer, Rob, 1b	.391	63	233	65	91	18	3	8	59	35	34	0
McCoy, Trey, of	.357	68	252	68	90	21	2	14	78	47	47	2
*Morris, Rod, of	.327	69	281	77	92	20	3	4	41	35	31	33
Pierce, Dominic, 3b-dh	.332	65	259	35	86	14	6	1	48	20	40	2
Spear, Mike, of	.296	58	206	35	61	13	2	7	37	13	40	1
*Swain, Thayer, of-dh	.297	53	212	59	63	9	4	7	36	28	35	18
*Wardlow, Joe, 2b-3b	.339	62	227	53	77	8	4	5	45	38	27	7

PITCHING	W	L	ERA	G	GS	CG	SV	IP	H	R	ER	BB	SO
Allen, Steve	2	2	9.32	17	6	0	1	46	74	53	48	14	30
Cunningham, Everett	6	4	6.01	14	14	0	0	79	103	61	53	24	51
Hvizda, Jim	2	2	4.50	26	0	0	5	42	43	24	21	10	43
*Kuzma, Greg	1	2	8.79	11	5	0	0	29	44	33	28	25	14
MacNeil, Tim	2	2	3.00	24	0	0	9	39	33	15	13	32	35
Nen, Robb	4	5	8.75	14	13	0	0	48	65	55	47	45	28
Pavlik, Roger	3	0	4.59	8	8	1	0	49	46	29	25	34	56
*Penland, Ken	1	1	3.48	11	0	0	0	21	24	12	8	12	15
Randle, Carl	4	2	6.25	19	3	0	0	45	45	44	31	55	41
*Saavedra, Francisco	0	0	15.00	3	0	0	0	3	6	5	5	4	5
Schorr, Bill	1	0	9.82	9	0	0	0	7	13	12	8	9	4
*Shaw, Cedric	5	2	3.99	12	12	0	0	56	54	28	25	32	50
Shiozaki, Kenny	1	0	3.32	17	0	0	2	38	37	19	14	7	36
Spencer, Kyle	7	4	4.14	18	9	1	1	72	65	36	33	37	43
Tomori, Denny	5	0	2.51	13	0	0	1	32	24	11	9	14	27

GREAT FALLS

BATTING	AVG	G	AB	R	H	2B	3B	HR	RBI	BB	SO	SB
#Beals, Bryan, of-2b	.256	31	90	17	23	1	1	0	9	11	25	8
Boddie, Erik, of	.333	51	204	41	68	14	2	4	45	27	54	8
Brooks, Jerry, of-3b	.347	68	285	63	99	21	3	8	61	24	25	7
*Carr, Ernie, 3b-2b	.333	64	255	49	85	20	3	4	62	29	35	11
*Carroll, Don, of	.280	48	164	29	46	3	0	1	25	25	33	20
Finkin, Steve, ss-2b	.267	7	15	1	4	2	0	0	0	1	5	0
Hermann, Jeff, of	.346	12	26	5	9	2	2	1	3	6	6	1
*Huebner, John, c	.357	14	42	2	15	3	0	0	7	3	8	0
Karros, Eric, 1b	.366	66	268	68	98	12	1	12	55	32	35	8
McMurray, Brock, of	.200	10	25	4	5	0	1	1	5	4	4	2
*Morrow, Chris, of	.286	60	217	48	62	11	3	8	40	28	50	13
#Oferman, Jose, ss	.335	60	251	75	84	11	5	2	28	38	42	57
Pye, Eddie, 2b	.300	61	237	50	71	8	4	2	30	29	28	19
#Rice, Lance, c	.283	47	159	30	45	8	2	0	27	31	29	4
White, K.G., of	.167	2	6	0	1	0	0	0	1	0	0	0

PITCHING	W	L	ERA	G	GS	CG	SV	IP	H	R	ER	BB	SO
Bene, Bill	5	0	4.55	13	12	0	0	65	53	43	33	45	56
Biberdorf, Cam	2	2	2.59	27	0	0	8	31	25	12	9	11	36
Braase, John	4	0	3.09	17	7	0	0	55	59	22	19	12	44
Castillo, Jeff	1	2	4.04	15	1	0	2	36	35	18	16	15	24
Dawson, David	5	2	2.06	25	1	0	0	48	29	16	11	25	52
Hartsock, Jeff	7	2	2.67	14	13	1	0	81	62	30	24	26	108
James, Mike	7	1	3.76	14	12	0	0	67	61	36	28	41	59
*McHugh, Mike	1	0	2.00	5	4	0	0	18	9	6	4	13	14
Snedeker, Sean	8	2	2.20	13	12	5	0	86	64	29	21	16	102
*Valdes, Ramon	4	1	1.20	12	1	0	0	30	15	8	4	11	37
Wengert, Bill	3	3	3.60	14	6	0	0	45	44	28	18	23	42
*Wray, James	5	2	2.04	27	0	0	3	40	27	9	9	7	54

BATTING

R—Rod Morris, Butte		77
H—Jerry Brooks, Great Falls		99
TB—Trey McCoy, Butte		160
2B—Trey McCoy, Butte		21
—Jerry Brooks, Great Falls		21
3B—Donovan Campbell, Idaho Falls		9
HR—Oreste Marrero, Helena		16
—Mando Verdugo, Salt Lake		16
RBI—Trey McCoy, Butte		80
GWRBI—Bill Losa, Butte		10
SH—Don Meyett, Helena		7
SF—Ernie Carr, Great Falls		13
BB—Tommy Boyce, Salt Lake		64
IBB—Mike Songini, Billings		3
—Reuben Smiley, Pocatello		3
HBP—Scott Sellner, Billings		6
—Kerry Shaw, Salt Lake		6
SO—Ed Smith, Medicine Hat		93
SB—Jose Oferman, Great Falls		57
CS—Tim Clark, Billings		10
—Jose Oferman, Great Falls		10
Slg. Pct.—Trey McCoy, Butte		.635
OB Pct.—Kerry Shaw, Salt Lake		.467

PITCHING

G—Sean Johnson, Salt Lake		33
GS—Mike Brady, Medicine Hat		17
CG—Sean Snedeker, Great Falls		5
ShO—Sean Snedeker, Great Falls		2
—Bill Wenrick, Salt Lake		2
Sv—Steve Reed, Pocatello		13
W—Willie Ambos, Salt Lake		9
L—Mike Brady, Medicine Hat		9
IP—Terry Glover, Salt Lake		92
H—Willie Ambos, Salt Lake		114
R—Mike Brady, Medicine Hat		80
HR—Carl Hanselman, Pocatello		11
BB—Scott Ebert, Pocatello		60
HB—Three tied at		8
SO—Jeff Hartsock, Great Falls		108
WP—Mike Brady, Medicine Hat		18
Bk—Scott Economy, Billings		11
—Mark Eskins, Idaho Falls		11

Department Leaders

HELENA

BATTING	AVG	G	AB	R	H	2B	3B	HR	RBI	BB	SO	SB
#Bolick, Frank, 3b	.298	40	131	35	39	10	1	10	28	32	31	5
Diaz, Angel, ss	.224	55	152	19	34	6	2	1	16	9	26	6
Erickson, Don, ss-2b	.236	46	106	14	25	2	1	1	17	20	17	1
Guerrero, Jaime, ss	.205	45	117	21	24	5	1	0	10	17	29	5
#Guerrero, Mike, ss	.286	7	28	4	8	0	0	0	5	2	1	1
*Heffernan, Bert, c	.281	65	196	47	55	13	0	4	31	61	40	14
*Hutson, Tim, dh-1b	.263	58	167	22	44	17	0	5	26	26	35	5
Lee, Stewart, 3b-dh	.224	40	107	17	24	1	0	6	12	17	23	0
*Marrero, Oreste, 1b	.354	67	240	52	85	15	0	16	44	41	48	2
Marrero, Vilato, 2b	.270	68	267	41	72	14	2	3	36	22	35	8
*Meyett, Don, of	.276	41	127	25	35	3	0	0	11	14	19	10
Moore, Dwayne, of-dh	.205	25	83	10	17	1	0	1	11	7	13	1
Muhammad, Robert, of	.186	17	43	7	8	3	0	0	7	5	14	0
*O'Leary, Troy, of	.347	67	202	40	70	11	1	0	27	30	32	10
Odewaldt, Larry, c	.182	33	55	8	10	3	0	0	8	12	10	2
Rodriguez, Ruben, of	.229	52	109	13	25	2	3	0	17	17	28	5
Roebuck, Joe, of	.258	60	190	24	49	11	0	2	28	10	34	4
Tilly, Brad, 2b	.200	7	20	3	4	0	0	0	2	0	4	1

PITCHING	W	L	ERA	G	GS	CG	SV	IP	H	R	ER	BB	SO
Andrzejewski, Joe	0	0	0.00	1	0	0	0	1	0	0	0	1	1
Correa, Ramser	2	2	3.95	13	7	0	0	43	38	22	19	24	34
*Fitzgerald, Dave	2	2	4.34	9	8	1	0	46	44	29	22	20	36
Grayson, Mike	3	0	3.80	21	0	0	2	47	44	26	20	22	45
Ignasiak, Mike	2	0	3.09	7	0	0	1	12	10	5	4	7	18
Jefferson, Ron	3	4	6.28	11	8	0	0	43	51	33	30	22	23
Kiefer, Mark	4	4	2.65	15	9	2	0	68	76	30	20	17	51
Kostichka, Steve	3	1	5.19	16	0	0	0	35	48	26	20	21	27
Krippner, Curt	3	4	3.88	11	11	2	0	67	73	35	29	43	72
Landry, Greg	1	2	6.62	13	5	1	0	34	38	31	25	41	27
Lane, Heath	8	4	3.38	15	8	4	0	75	72	29	28	17	63
Meyer, Mike	0	0	0.00	2	0	0	0	2	4	3	0	0	3
*Miranda, Angel	5	2	3.86	14	11	0	0	61	54	32	26	58	75
Sandoval, Memo	1	1	4.78	20	3	0	2	43	45	35	23	30	33
Voit, Dave	4	3	1.95	17	0	0	3	28	20	11	6	9	34

IDAHO FALLS

BATTING	AVG	G	AB	R	H	2B	3B	HR	RBI	BB	SO	SB
Albertson, John, c	.229	30	83	10	19	4	1	1	9	12	25	1
*Blanks, Daryl, of	.305	67	226	54	69	8	4	1	34	31	22	32

	AVG	G	AB	R	H	2B	3B	HR	RBI	BB	SO	SB
*Campbell, Donovan, of	.341	69	276	49	94	8	9	3	28	25	47	35
Guerrero, Ramces, 2b	.226	56	168	29	38	9	1	5	23	28	49	7
Hall, Lamar, ss	.206	59	204	28	42	5	1	0	14	8	30	10
Harper, Greg, c	.227	48	150	22	34	5	2	2	23	19	47	0
*Henry, Kevin, 3b	.324	21	74	13	24	5	1	2	12	7	19	3
Hutchinson, Sean, c	.281	15	32	2	9	3	0	0	6	2	11	1
*Jones, Chris, 1b	.278	60	187	28	52	9	1	4	26	16	27	7
Koenig, Eric, of	.286	20	42	2	12	1	0	1	8	2	10	0
Kuhlman, Eric, of-p	.174	19	23	2	4	0	0	0	1	5	8	0
*LeClair, Keith, of	.264	59	208	34	55	9	2	1	18	24	46	9
Lopez, Steve, of-1b	.313	66	243	41	76	11	1	9	55	23	80	8
*Monteiro, Dave, of	.000	2	5	1	0	0	0	0	0	0	2	0
Paddy, Marco, 1b-c	.276	41	105	15	29	5	0	0	16	19	1	
*Schoonover, Gary, ss-2b	.379	43	145	23	55	6	1	0	25	9	10	5
Stivers, Pat, 3b	.191	62	220	37	42	6	0	10	35	25	61	8
*Stuart, Rob, dh	.241	24	54	8	13	2	1	0	5	4	15	3
*Tarasco, Tony, of	.000	8	11	1	0	0	0	0	1	5	2	1

PITCHING	W	L	ERA	G	GS	CG	SV	IP	H	R	ER	BB	SO
Bacosa, Al	5	2	4.35	21	0	0	6	39	43	24	19	15	49
Czarnik, Chris	4	5	4.92	14	14	1	0	75	99	57	41	19	33
Eskins, Mark	2	5	5.35	14	12	1	0	69	90	57	41	21	40
Gardey, Rudy	2	4	6.21	15	14	0	0	67	75	52	46	39	43
Greene, Russ	0	1	8.75	12	0	0	0	24	45	34	23	10	23
*Johnson, Judd	1	4	4.60	15	2	0	0	31	45	23	16	5	21
Karlan, Dennis	0	0	0.00	1	0	0	0	1	1	0	0	0	0
Kortright, Jim	6	3	4.71	18	0	0	1	50	51	32	26	26	35
Kuhlman, Eric	0	0	5.14	7	0	0	0	28	25	17	16	19	10
Lehnerz, Dan	1	2	8.26	12	5	0	0	28	32	31	26	34	15
Meier, Jeff	2	4	5.29	18	0	0	3	32	39	27	19	10	26
Mitchell, Glenn	1	6	7.79	13	13	0	0	54	70	53	47	47	38
Opdyke, Paul	1	1	8.23	13	0	0	0	27	36	38	25	28	32
Richey, Rod	3	3	4.71	18	0	0	2	50	52	34	26	22	37
Shrewsbury, Mark	0	1	3.90	10	3	0	0	30	41	21	13	12	14
Yochum, Ken	0	1	2.89	5	1	0	0	9	8	3	3	3	4

MEDICINE HAT

BATTING	AVG	G	AB	R	H	2B	3B	HR	RBI	BB	SO	SB
Barry, Jose, of	.241	8	29	5	7	1	1	0	2	5	9	3
*Giannelli, Ray, 3b-c	.244	47	123	17	30	8	3	4	28	19	22	0
Guarache, Jose, 3b-1b	.232	53	181	17	42	8	0	6	23	9	26	2
Hernandez, Johnny, 3b	.181	38	83	9	15	1	0	1	9	10	32	3
*Hodge, Tim, dh-of	.186	30	97	10	18	3	0	2	9	20	38	1
Holifield, Rich, of	.271	31	96	16	26	4	1	1	6	9	27	6
*Jaime, Juan, c	.213	61	230	23	49	4	1	0	13	14	38	3
Jones, Terry, 2b	.162	23	68	12	11	1	1	1	5	14	17	4
Mendez, Eddy, of	.307	62	228	24	70	11	5	0	27	25	43	4
*Olibris, Bernardo, 1b	.194	56	175	22	34	5	2	2	19	25	66	9
Parese, Billy, 2b	.209	46	158	18	33	2	0	0	12	33	50	2
#Reed, Marcileno, of	.089	29	56	8	5	0	0	0	0	12	24	4
Rollins, Brian, ss-dh	.217	36	106	15	23	2	1	0	9	19	23	3
Scott, Shawn, of	.199	42	141	13	28	6	1	0	14	14	51	7
Smith, Ed, of	.162	64	229	22	37	0	1	5	24	16	94	8
Uribe, Relito, ss	.150	52	160	7	24	6	0	1	9	16	66	1
Vaughan, Rick, c	.240	39	129	14	31	8	1	1	12	22	31	0

PITCHING	W	L	ERA	G	GS	CG	SV	IP	H	R	ER	BB	SO
Batista, Gabriel	0	1	9.72	5	0	0	0	8	13	12	9	4	7
Bradley, Eric	1	3	5.45	15	1	0	0	33	41	29	20	17	20
Brady, Jim	0	9	5.26	18	17	0	0	89	103	85	52	44	66
*Bruzdewicz, Tim	2	5	4.91	21	2	0	1	33	41	30	18	17	27
Carter, Eric	0	2	8.53	15	0	0	0	19	34	31	18	17	6
Embry, Todd	0	5	8.84	18	7	0	0	39	68	56	38	33	18
Hutson, Scott	2	2	5.61	20	0	0	1	43	64	36	27	20	26
Kandalaft, Kevin	2	6	3.72	16	11	2	0	73	83	51	30	36	48
Kerr, Chris	0	0	6.97	6	0	0	0	10	17	9	8	6	5
Mooney, Jeff	0	1	5.24	19	0	0	0	34	53	24	20	11	16
Nowak, Rick	2	5	3.09	12	11	0	0	64	63	24	22	27	68
Ogliaruso, Mike	0	6	9.17	10	10	0	0	35	53	45	36	33	18
*Olivares, Jose	0	1	3.24	3	0	0	0	8	8	7	3	7	11
Placeres, Ben	1	4	7.89	7	6	0	0	22	27	24	19	25	14
*Seal, Mike	0	0	11.81	4	0	0	0	5	12	12	7	5	6
Villa, Jose	0	3	4.97	22	0	0	4	29	31	20	16	19	30
Wilson, Terry	2	5	6.67	23	5	1	0	55	65	49	41	31	38

POCATELLO

BATTING	AVG	G	AB	R	H	2B	3B	HR	RBI	BB	SO	SB
Booth, David, of	.255	51	149	26	38	6	3	0	12	20	47	5
Burnett, Lance, of	.000	10	18	1	0	0	0	0	0	2	9	0
Cruz, Victor, ss	.182	35	88	8	16	4	2	1	12	8	33	1
#George, Andre, 2b	.236	39	106	17	25	0	3	0	9	22	20	3
Gray, Steve, ss	.245	47	143	28	35	7	2	2	10	12	45	7
Hall, Kevin, of	.167	22	66	8	11	0	2	0	6	10	25	2
Hewatt, Brett, of	.089	25	56	5	5	1	1	0	1	5	31	1
Hilpert, Adam, 3b-1b	.263	62	232	38	61	9	5	1	36	9	29	3
#Kaiser, Jeff, 2b	.224	32	107	13	24	4	0	2	8	9	23	2
Laya, Jesus, c	.298	43	131	16	39	5	1	0	24	10	24	1

BATTING	AVG	G	AB	R	H	2B	3B	HR	RBI	BB	SO	SB
#Lee, Greg, 3b	.167	8	18	3	3	0	0	0	0	3	6	0
Penrod, Jack, 1b-of	.265	57	200	20	53	7	1	5	39	19	33	5
*Rosso, Pasqual, 1b	.217	6	23	5	5	1	0	2	5	2	9	0
*Slavin, David, c-1b	.356	64	216	34	77	11	0	2	48	37	32	2
*Smiley, Rueben, of	.286	50	185	39	53	3	3	1	16	31	33	7
*Smith, Adam, dh-c	.281	52	146	32	41	9	2	6	29	30	28	2
Speakes, Joey, of	.244	51	168	28	41	8	3	1	19	30	35	4
#Thompson, Sean, 2b	.253	34	95	12	24	1	0	0	3	9	23	1
Torgeson, Brad, of	.116	31	69	10	8	1	0	2	10	8	37	2
#Toussaint, Daris, of	.127	31	63	8	8	1	1	1	5	4	21	0
Welch, Bryce, 3b	.207	25	87	7	18	2	1	0	10	2	19	1

PITCHING	W	L	ERA	G	GS	CG	SV	IP	H	R	ER	BB	SO
Arias, Francisco	1	1	4.60	23	0	0	0	45	55	31	23	30	22
Brock, Don	1	1	4.50	27	0	0	0	54	57	34	27	32	54
Dela Rosa, Domingo	2	1	2.25	10	0	0	0	20	18	11	5	4	17
Ebert, Scott	1	4	4.75	12	12	0	0	53	48	52	28	60	52
Ferrick, Mitchell	3	5	4.92	14	10	1	0	57	73	52	31	24	39
*Hancock, Chris	2	5	8.86	12	11	0	0	43	60	54	42	43	31
Hanselman, Carl	1	8	8.34	12	11	0	0	45	78	66	42	31	37
*Hernandez, Marino	0	0	5.16	19	0	0	0	23	30	19	13	16	29
Horan, Dave	0	0	5.14	3	1	0	0	7	10	5	4	3	5
Myers, Jimmy	4	5	5.40	12	12	0	0	58	72	50	35	32	39
Page, Greg	1	3	7.62	19	0	0	0	39	57	47	33	27	36
Reed, Steve	4	1	2.54	31	0	0	14	46	42	20	13	8	47
*Rogers, Kevin	2	8	6.20	13	13	1	0	70	73	51	48	35	70
Sanchez, Carlos	0	0	13.50	3	0	0	0	3	4	4	4	6	1
*Wuthrich, David	4	2	4.46	22	0	0	0	42	36	24	21	17	43

SALT LAKE CITY

BATTING	AVG	G	AB	R	H	2B	3B	HR	RBI	BB	SO	SB
*Allison, Jeff, of	.293	50	164	31	48	10	2	0	23	18	25	11
Boyce, Tommy, of	.282	64	213	42	60	11	2	2	41	64	45	3
Edward, John, of	.130	6	23	1	3	0	0	0	1	1	10	0
Ehmig, Greg, 1b	.262	61	248	46	65	11	2	13	49	32	82	0
Fellows, Bill, c	.222	3	9	0	2	1	0	0	1	3	1	0
Hurni, Rick, of	.286	49	161	28	46	3	0	1	17	19	28	10
Karczewski, Ray, ss	.244	45	160	21	39	3	0	3	26	24	36	1
McKercher, Tim, c-1b	.371	37	132	24	49	6	2	1	17	17	9	4
*Moore, Randy, of	.269	19	52	10	14	4	0	0	9	3	10	3
Ohama, Kevin, ss	.239	13	46	8	11	1	0	0	6	4	8	2
Peralta, Marty, dh-1b	.255	47	184	26	47	5	1	4	36	16	42	2
Shaw, Kerry, 3b-dh	.353	54	201	54	71	8	2	2	44	37	13	6
Sloniger, Chris, 3b-ss	.250	49	160	30	40	7	0	1	18	19	21	2
Verdugo, Mando, c-dh	.335	66	257	62	86	17	0	17	62	35	43	1
Waid, Pat, of	.273	52	209	48	57	6	2	0	22	30	44	12
Zane, Kelly, 2b	.379	63	261	56	99	11	4	3	38	40	30	8

PITCHING	W	L	ERA	G	GS	CG	SV	IP	H	R	ER	BB	SO
Ambos, Willie	9	2	4.58	15	14	2	0	90	114	60	46	22	50
Carballo, Lee	1	3	4.61	20	0	0	3	27	29	18	14	9	23
Edwards, Bobby	1	0	4.56	10	0	0	0	26	35	17	13	0	19
Gardner, Myron	4	8	5.18	15	13	1	0	80	94	62	46	44	66
Gibbons, Mike	1	3	0.82	26	0	0	8	33	24	5	3	4	28
Glover, Terry	6	4	4.58	17	15	2	0	92	104	60	47	31	64
*Johnson, Sean	2	2	3.08	33	0	0	1	50	52	23	17	14	46
Ramirez, Ed	0	2	7.11	4	0	0	0	6	5	9	5	5	5
*Reber, Blaine	3	0	2.73	9	2	0	1	26	25	9	8	19	24
*Riscen, Fred	6	1	3.53	10	10	3	0	64	56	28	25	20	67
Roldan, Sal	1	0	4.76	6	1	0	0	11	6	6	6	11	10
St. John, Anthony	0	0	4.91	9	0	0	0	11	15	12	6	10	15
Tanner, Dean	0	0	9.49	3	3	0	0	12	19	16	13	12	7
*Titchener, Mark	0	0	37.80	3	0	0	0	3	13	14	14	5	2
*Wenrick, Bill	7	4	3.72	13	12	2	0	77	74	40	32	23	69

Complex Baseball

GULF COAST LEAGUE

Youthful Yankees win it all down south

By JOHN ROYSTER

Someone once said it's great to be young and a Yankee . . . or something like that.

At any rate, the youngest Yankees, those on New York's farm team in the rookie class Gulf Coast League, lost only 18 games in 1988 and won the league championship.

The Yankees played .714 baseball (45-18) but still went to the final weekend before edging the Dodgers and White Sox for the South Division title in a league that expanded by two teams and was realigned in 1988.

Ken Juarbe then struck out 12 batters in 6⅓ innings as the Yankees edged the North Division-champion Royals 3-2 in a one-game playoff for the GCL title. Reliever Mark Ohlms finished up for Juarbe and earned a save.

Walker No. 1 prospect

The two division championship clubs were the only teams to have their parent clubs' top draft picks. Pitcher Todd Malone was the Yankees top selection, even though he was only a fourth round pick overall. Outfielder Hugh Walker of the Royals was Kansas City's No. 1 selection. Walker was rated the No. 1 major league prospect in a Baseball America survey of managers in the two complex-based minor leagues, the Gulf Coast and Arizona,

Walker hit just .240, but stole 27 bases in a short season.

Malone wasn't included among the top 10 prospects, but had a fine season statistically. He went 6-1 with a 1.64 ERA and 81 strikeouts in 66 innings.

The Gulf Coast League expanded to accomodate Cleveland and the New York Mets. Resulting realignment created a smaller North Division (Royals, Indians, Astros, Reds) based at complexes in Baseball City and Osceola County.

The South Division had eight teams—based in the traditional complexes at Bradenton and Sarasota. There was no interdivisional play until the playoff.

North	W	L	Pct.	GB
Royals	39	24	.619	—
Indians.............	38	25	.603	1
Astros	28	35	.444	11
Reds...............	21	42	.333	18
South				
Yankees	45	18	.714	—
Dodgers	43	20	.683	2
White Sox.........	42	21	.667	3
Rangers............	35	28	.556	10
Pirates.............	26	37	.413	19
Expos..............	24	39	.381	21
Mets	21	42	.333	24
Braves	16	47	.254	29

1988 Final Standings

1988: General Information

Playoffs: Yankees defeated Royals in one-game playoff for league championship.

Managers: Astros—Julio Linares; **Braves**—Pedro Gonzalez; **Dodgers**—Jose Alvarez; **Expos**—David Jauss; **Indians**—Billy Williams; **Mets**—John

Tamargo; **Pirates**—Julio Garcia; **Rangers**—Chino Cadahia; **Reds**—Sam Mejias; **Royals**—Carlos Tosca; **White Sox**—Art Kusnyer; **Yankees**—Brian Butterfield.

1988 All-Star Team: C—James Harris, Mets. **1B**—Marc Tepper, Indians. **2B**—Javier Murillo, Indians. **3B**—Dennis Walker, White Sox. **SS**—Dino Ebel, Dodgers. **OF**—Scott Tedder, White Sox; Brian Davis, White Sox; Mike Rhodes, Yankees. **SP**—Lenny Brutcher, White Sox. **RP**—Brett Marshall, White Sox. **Manager of the Year**—Brian Butterfield, Yankees.

Top 10 Major League Prospects, combined Gulf Coast League and Arizona League (by Baseball America): 1. Hugh Walker, of, Royals; **2.** Alex Tejada, ss, Expos; **3.** Manny Garcia, 2b, Rangers; **4.** Eliziel Rosario, lhp, Astros; **5.** Ed Ricks, of, Athletics (Arizona League); **6.** Ricky Rhodes, rhp, Yankees; **7.** Darren Oliver, lhp, Rangers; **8.** Ben Howze, rhp, Expos; **9.** Angel Martinez, ss, Athletics (Arizona League); **10.** Melvin Nieves, of, Braves.

1988: Batting, Pitching Statistics

CLUB BATTING

	AVG	G	AB	R	H	2B	3B	HR	BB	SO	SB
Dodgers	.265	63	2037	326	540	83	15	11	225	355	73
White Sox	.261	63	2133	317	556	85	24	15	212	393	104
Yankees	.251	63	2098	323	527	79	24	12	175	414	95
Indians	.240	63	2119	345	508	101	17	13	305	423	89
Royals	.230	64	2148	301	494	81	14	6	317	380	114
Rangers	.229	63	2043	261	467	82	21	17	224	446	74
Reds	.224	64	2082	242	466	74	15	7	244	467	64
Mets	.224	63	2065	242	462	67	16	10	242	458	68
Braves	.220	63	2030	193	446	71	4	4	159	390	59
Astros	.218	63	2085	253	455	67	21	13	203	485	91
Pirates	.214	63	2073	222	443	70	10	12	230	431	99
Expos	.204	64	2015	218	412	72	10	22	208	570	131

CLUB PITCHING

	ERA	G	CG	SHO	SV	IP	H	R	ER	BB	SO
Dodgers	2.16	63	7	11	17	534	380	169	128	204	488
Yankees	2.30	63	6	10	19	563	444	202	144	194	578
Astros	2.74	64	4	2	13	555	469	259	169	248	436
Pirates	2.74	64	1	3	17	564	489	269	172	215	433
Rangers	2.76	63	0	8	19	544	444	214	167	175	402
White Sox	2.83	64	4	20	553	440	247	174	166	384	
Royals	3.15	64	9	18	580	509	256	203	211	439	
Indians	3.47	63	8	8	15	562	454	281	217	272	452
Expos	3.74	64	3	3	12	547	560	318	227	252	387
Braves	3.77	64	4	2	9	527	556	327	221	231	348
Mets	4.03	65	9	5	8	549	540	356	246	238	432
Reds	4.16	64	0	4	11	551	491	345	255	338	428

INDIVIDUAL BATTING LEADERS
(Minimum 170 Plate Appearances)

	AVG	G	AB	R	H	2B	3B	HR	RBI	BB	SO	SB
*Tedder, Scott, White Sox	.341	58	214	30	73	13	0	0	25	28	16	8
Ebel, Dino, Dodgers	.337	63	208	42	70	8	1	4	36	29	21	6
Rhodes, Mike, Yankees	.318	57	195	29	62	9	2	2	41	19	42	14
Kohyama, Kazuyoshi, Dodgers	.311	61	196	40	61	12	5	0	25	26	31	5
Murillo, Javier, Indians	.300	58	207	39	62	11	3	0	29	31	36	7
Alvarez, Jorge, Dodgers	.293	55	167	23	49	13	2	0	24	17	25	5
Harris, James, Mets	.291	58	206	28	60	7	1	4	34	31	36	6
Benitez, Luis, Rangers	.286	63	220	38	63	8	4	2	19	38	38	14
Cedeno, Andujar, Astros	.285	46	165	25	47	5	2	1	20	11	34	10
Garcia, Manuel, Rangers	.280	56	211	28	59	16	1	0	24	9	41	16

* indicates lefthanded batter   # indicates switch hitter

INDIVIDUAL PITCHING LEADERS
(Minimum 50 Innings)

	W	L	ERA	G	GS	CG	SV	IP	H	R	ER	BB	SO
*Kiser, Garland, Indians	5	1	1.29	7	7	2	0	56	31	12	8	17	45
*Rosario, Eliezel, Astros	8	2	1.34	12	12	4	0	87	67	22	13	14	57
*McCray, Eric, Rangers	3	2	1.44	12	11	0	0	56	39	15	9	27	42
Bustillos, Albert, Dodgers	6	3	1.46	17	6	1	2	68	46	13	11	12	65
Gardner, Chris, Astros	4	3	1.46	12	9	0	0	55	37	18	9	23	41
*Malone, Todd, Yankees	6	1	1.64	12	12	2	0	66	55	17	12	21	81
*Nina, Robin, Dodgers	10	2	1.85	13	13	2	0	78	55	21	16	15	66
Hudson, Jim, Royals	5	2	1.95	13	12	3	0	88	70	25	19	11	79
McKinney, Tony, Pirates	2	3	1.96	11	9	1	0	55	64	24	12	14	31
Hartzog, Cullen, Yankees	5	2	2.00	13	13	1	0	76	65	24	17	23	82

* indicates lefthanded pitcher

ASTROS

BATTING	AVG	G	AB	R	H	2B	3B	HR	RBI	BB	SO	SB
Alvarez, Tomas, 3b-ss	.180	33	100	7	18	5	0	0	7	1	10	4
Anglada, Raymundo, 2b-3b	.143	6	14	3	2	0	0	1	2	0	2	0
Bennett, Brian, c	.193	43	150	17	29	5	1	2	14	11	47	0
Campos, Rafael, 2b-ss	.150	31	107	13	16	2	1	0	6	11	23	0
Cedeno, Andujar, ss	.285	46	165	25	47	5	2	1	20	11	34	10
Crockom, Ken, of	.256	31	117	21	30	3	2	0	8	17	17	16

BATTING	AVG	G	AB	R	H	2B	3B	HR	RBI	BB	SO	SB
*Echevarria, Juan, 1b-dh	.217	43	143	20	31	5	3	2	14	23	29	3
Encarnacion, Juan, of ...	.219	54	201	22	44	12	3	2	33	14	59	9
*Given, Eric, c	.203	24	59	10	12	1	0	0	5	21	10	0
Henderson, Dave, dh ...	.273	18	55	11	15	2	0	2	11	5	13	2
*Holum, Brett, 3b	.222	6	18	1	4	0	0	0	2	1	6	0
Hudgins, Mark, 2b	.164	21	61	4	10	0	0	0	3	5	11	0
Jones, Marty, of	.179	32	112	9	20	2	1	1	16	8	45	1
Quijada, Ed, 3b	.222	44	153	17	34	3	2	1	12	7	45	3
#Reed, Toncie, of	.262	51	195	18	51	12	2	1	15	7	33	11
*Ruscitto, Andy, 1b	.150	41	127	15	19	2	0	0	11	29	39	1
#Santana, Jose, of	.255	53	192	29	49	6	3	0	17	23	39	22
#Valentin, Ed, dh	.292	9	24	0	7	1	0	0	5	1	1	1
Washington, Dave, 2b ...	.185	29	92	11	17	1	1	0	12	8	22	2

PITCHING	W	L	ERA	G	GS	CG	SV	IP	H	R	ER	BB	SO
Amick, Pat	0	0	2.08	3	0	0	0	9	10	6	2	7	9
*Campusano, Teo	2	4	3.07	22	1	0	2	44	44	28	15	24	21
Dovey, Troy	1	1	1.48	12	1	0	4	24	16	8	4	11	28
Emm, Artie	1	4	3.51	9	6	0	0	33	35	17	13	16	22
Fascher, Stan	0	2	8.64	3	3	0	0	8	11	12	8	4	3
Gardner, Chris	4	3	1.46	12	9	0	0	55	37	18	9	23	41
Gonzales, Ben	1	2	0.66	17	0	0	6	27	23	5	2	6	28
Griffiths, Brian	2	6	2.95	14	7	0	0	55	46	26	18	16	43
*Gutierrez, Anthony	1	2	3.66	17	0	0	0	39	31	20	16	16	15
Kile, Darryl	5	3	3.17	12	12	0	0	60	48	34	21	33	54
*Marrero, Roger	0	0	7.71	3	0	0	0	2	2	3	2	3	0
*Navarro, Luis	0	2	5.03	15	0	0	0	20	20	18	11	23	11
Perez, Francisco	3	4	4.02	12	12	0	0	65	61	34	29	22	56
Ponte, Edward	0	0	1.20	5	0	0	1	15	8	2	2	4	22
*Rosario, Eliezel	8	2	1.34	12	12	4	0	87	67	22	13	14	57
Van Houten, Jim	0	0	3.38	5	0	0	0	11	10	6	4	4	8

BRAVES

BATTING	AVG	G	AB	R	H	2B	3B	HR	RBI	BB	SO	SB
#Apolonario, Oswaldo, 2b-ss .	.257	41	113	5	29	0	0	0	2	6	16	5
Berroa, Fabricio, 2b	.231	49	156	21	36	6	1	0	5	9	33	2
#Carrion, Junior, ss	.204	16	49	3	10	0	0	0	3	4	7	0
*Clark, Jeff, of	.254	27	71	8	18	5	0	0	5	9	12	4
*Crowson, Dave, c	.074	11	27	0	2	0	0	0	4	1	1	0
Doyle, Steve, ss	.245	16	49	2	12	4	0	0	6	1	10	1
#Hall, Albert, of	.250	2	8	1	2	0	0	0	1	0	0	0
*Heath, Lee, of	.201	48	139	10	28	3	0	0	5	5	38	7
Hendricks, Rivelino, of ..	.222	17	54	7	12	0	0	0	4	4	8	1
*Johnson, Jeff, 1b-dh ...	.202	57	173	16	35	5	0	1	15	31	28	1
#Kupsey, John, 3b-ss	.217	44	138	18	30	5	0	0	16	12	25	5
Lopez, Javier, c	.191	31	94	8	18	4	0	1	9	3	19	1
#Nieves, Melvin, of	.170	56	176	16	30	6	0	1	12	20	53	5
Petit, Rolando, dh-util ..	.255	56	188	24	48	9	1	0	24	8	25	9
Polo, Andres, of	.230	44	113	11	26	2	1	0	5	5	18	8
Pullins, Jimmie, of	.125	11	24	0	3	1	0	0	0	2	12	0
*Roble, Josman, 1b-dh ...	.273	48	143	14	39	4	0	1	13	12	31	4
Saccomanno, Joe, ss	.280	12	50	6	14	3	0	1	2	1	1	1
Simms, Ron, dh	.000	1	3	0	0	0	0	0	0	0	0	0
*Tarasco, Tony, of	.234	21	64	10	15	6	1	0	4	7	7	3
Thomas, Colovito, of	.000	4	4	1	0	0	0	0	1	1	2	0
Tyson, Kevin, c	.200	24	65	7	13	1	0	0	2	10	22	0
Waldenbelger, Dave, 3b .	.231	29	91	5	21	6	0	0	10	4	21	1
*Wright, Brian, c	.132	15	38	0	5	1	0	0	2	3	1	1

PITCHING	W	L	ERA	G	GS	CG	SV	IP	H	R	ER	BB	SO
Bond, Mark	0	1	1.59	3	0	0	0	6	5	4	1	2	2
*Cary, Chuck	0	2	3.75	4	4	0	0	12	15	5	2	18	—
Chmielewski, Shon	0	0	8.14	10	0	0	0	21	31	21	19	10	9
Clark, Mark	1	1	1.64	2	2	0	0	11	11	3	2	5	7
Close, Bill	0	0	13.50	1	0	0	0	2	3	3	3	2	0
Clouse, David	0	4	2.96	10	6	0	1	49	55	24	16	8	21
Crowson, Dave	0	0	13.50	1	0	0	0	1	5	4	2	0	0
DeJaynes, Paul	2	5	5.80	10	5	0	0	45	55	32	29	15	36
Deushane, Mark	4	7	2.51	13	13	1	0	75	76	36	21	22	53

	W	L	ERA	G	GS	CG	SV	IP	H	R	ER	BB	SO
Duncan, Rob	2	4	2.25	11	8	1	0	52	45	28	13	17	33
Hopson, Dan	2	2	2.27	17	0	0	4	40	38	15	10	19	33
*Kelly, Kevin	0	3	4.55	10	6	0	0	28	27	23	14	33	26
Keshock, Chris	0	0	3.38	3	0	0	1	8	8	5	3	7	5
Maldonado, Johnny	2	1	2.41	14	1	0	2	34	31	12	9	11	33
Naveda, Yonny	0	3	5.01	15	0	0	0	32	34	25	18	28	17
Parker, Jarrod	0	4	7.66	5	5	0	0	22	37	28	19	13	7
Yankovich, Eric	1	5	5.91	12	5	0	1	35	40	31	23	20	19
Ziegler, Greg	2	5	2.30	9	8	2	0	55	44	23	14	17	29

DODGERS

BATTING	AVG	G	AB	R	H	2B	3B	HR	RBI	BB	SO	SB
Alvarez, Jorge, 2b	.293	55	167	23	49	13	2	0	24	17	25	5
Ashley, Billy, of	.154	9	26	3	4	0	0	0	0	1	9	1
*Cepero, Ismael, 1b-of	.219	58	151	22	33	6	0	1	23	26	21	3
Chiusano, Mike, c	.143	11	21	2	3	0	0	0	3	5	10	0
*Collier, Anthony, of-dh	.273	50	161	28	44	9	0	2	20	15	28	1
Ebel, Dino, ss	.337	63	208	42	70	8	1	4	36	29	21	6
Floyd, D.J., c	.164	27	55	3	9	2	0	0	4	6	18	0
Fujioh, Yasuhara, of	.375	16	40	7	15	5	0	1	15	7	3	0
Ganino, Eric, c	.161	26	56	7	9	0	0	0	6	7	21	0
Gonzalez, Freddy, 1b-3b	.292	47	137	21	40	6	1	2	24	9	22	5
Gonzalez, Jesus, c-1b	.208	45	120	23	25	2	3	0	12	10	15	4
*Harvell, Rod, of-dh	.249	61	209	37	52	5	1	0	12	13	31	21
Kohyama, Kazuyoshi, of	.311	61	196	40	61	12	5	0	25	26	31	5
Manfredonia, Doug, inf	.271	32	96	18	26	3	0	1	10	13	26	4
Miller, Bill, 3b-2b	.268	49	149	14	40	4	0	0	18	23	16	5
Rijo, Rafael, of	.262	59	172	23	45	5	0	0	13	5	36	13
Rios, Felix, dh	.000	1	2	0	0	0	0	0	0	0	0	0
Virgo, Ryan, of	.000	7	6	1	0	0	0	0	0	2	1	0
Zink, Wendall, 3b	.233	26	60	10	14	2	2	0	8	9	19	0

PITCHING	W	L	ERA	G	GS	CG	SV	IP	H	R	ER	BB	SO
Branconier, Paul	6	1	2.70	10	10	2	0	47	36	20	14	15	21
Bustillos, Albert	6	3	1.46	17	6	1	2	68	46	13	11	12	65
Calderon, Ed	1	1	3.77	10	1	0	0	31	28	19	13	18	21
Cantres, Jorge	4	2	2.70	12	7	0	1	40	30	16	12	22	30
Coleman, Dale	3	1	1.12	19	0	0	3	40	19	7	5	11	29
*Enno, Clayton	4	2	1.77	16	3	1	0	41	23	8	8	23	52
Hershiser, Gordie	1	1	2.16	4	0	0	0	8	4	3	2	4	6
*Nina, Robin	10	2	1.85	13	13	3	2	78	55	21	16	15	66
Parham, Bill	1	0	1.98	9	0	0	0	14	7	5	3	4	21
Pascual, Jorge	1	0	2.35	9	2	0	1	23	23	9	6	11	24
Robinson, Napoleon	0	2	1.36	24	1	0	9	40	32	10	6	11	49
Sampson, Mike	2	2	3.33	10	10	0	0	46	30	19	17	30	57
*St. Esteban, Mike	0	0	1.86	5	0	0	1	10	8	3	2	5	6
Taveras, Ramon	4	3	2.37	10	10	1	0	49	39	16	13	23	41

EXPOS

BATTING	AVG	G	AB	R	H	2B	3B	HR	RBI	BB	SO	SB
#Cartwright, Ricardo, of	.094	29	53	9	5	0	1	0	3	2	26	5
#Correa, Marlon, 2b-3b	.233	30	43	4	10	2	0	0	4	5	8	0
Davison, Scotty, 2b-ss	.194	30	98	11	19	3	0	0	8	9	21	8
#Elder, Isaac, of	.152	52	132	24	20	3	0	0	2	24	64	34
Foster, Kevin, 3b-2b	.256	49	164	21	42	10	1	2	21	21	33	16
#Gonzalez, Frank, c	.182	28	66	1	12	0	0	0	2	2	13	2
Johnson, Kevin, of	.168	50	113	13	19	5	1	0	5	19	54	11
Lake, Ken, of-1b	.269	58	193	30	52	7	4	3	16	43	53	9
*LeMuth, Steve, 1b	.214	53	182	20	39	8	0	8	30	20	60	8
Maldonado, Ricardo, c	.178	46	135	12	24	6	0	3	12	9	40	1
Mason, Robbie, c	.138	30	94	2	13	3	0	0	8	9	12	0
Polemil, Juan, of	.191	53	157	15	30	7	2	1	11	5	47	6
Reagans, Javan, of	.294	20	68	8	20	2	0	3	14	5	13	6
Tejada, Alex, ss	.255	57	200	23	51	8	0	0	15	16	32	17
#Walker, Roosevelt, 2b	.226	54	168	13	38	6	1	0	9	12	47	12
Woods, Tyrone, 3b	.121	43	149	12	18	2	0	2	12	7	47	2

PITCHING	W	L	ERA	G	GS	CG	SV	IP	H	R	ER	BB	SO
Bennett, Chris	0	0	0.00	4	0	0	2	5	5	2	0	0	4
Clisanchez, Gil	2	1	3.46	7	1	0	0	13	16	9	5	6	6
Espinosa, Carlos	1	2	3.97	17	0	0	0	34	39	19	15	13	23
Farrell, Mike	1	1	11.88	9	1	0	0	17	28	23	22	12	8
*Gogos, Keith	1	2	4.39	19	0	0	0	27	32	17	13	14	19
Heiderscheit, Pat	3	4	3.18	9	9	0	0	51	64	27	18	12	36
Howze, Ben	2	5	4.87	13	12	0	0	61	55	43	33	55	32
Klancnik, Joe	1	2	3.57	6	3	0	0	18	18	14	7	9	14
Lane, Kevin	1	2	6.65	15	0	0	1	23	34	20	17	6	25
Lariviere, Chris	3	1	0.00	14	0	0	4	25	15	2	0	8	24
Nelson, Eric	2	0	3.63	13	0	0	0	17	25	8	7	6	11
Oropeza, Dave	2	2	2.12	8	8	2	0	51	37	17	12	9	63
Ramirez, Juan	1	4	3.15	20	4	0	2	46	45	28	16	17	32
Solarte, Jose	0	1	2.31	6	1	0	2	12	11	3	3	5	6
St. Claire, Steve	1	5	3.77	11	11	0	0	57	49	30	24	29	30
Tuss, Jeff	1	3	2.60	9	7	1	0	45	36	19	13	15	25
Wessel, Troy	0	1	9.00	7	0	0	0	9	13	14	9	8	6
Whitehead, Steve	2	3	3.19	9	7	0	1	37	38	23	13	28	23

BATTING

R—Darin Campbell, Indians 45
H—Scott Tedder, White Sox 73
TB—Deno Ebel, Dodgers 92
2B—Manuel Garcia, Rangers 16
—Doug Cronk, Rangers 16
3B—Dan Segui, Mets.............................7
HR—Steve Lemuth, Expos 8
RBI—Marc Tepper, Indians 45
GWRBI—Anthony Berry, Rangers 8
SH—Jose Herrera, Yankees 7
SF—Mike Rhodes, Yankees 7
BB—Pedro Vasquez, Royals 49
IBB—Hugh Walker, Royals........................5
—Robert Fletcher, White Sox 5
HBP—Hugh Walker, Royals......................11
SO—Lew Hill, Yankees 69
SB—Isaac Elder, Expos 34
CS—Alex Tejada, Royals 13
Slg. Pct.—Deno Ebel, Dodgers 442
OB Pct.—Deno Ebel, Dodgers 427

PITCHING

G—Ed Ohman, Rangers 27
GS—Victor Garcia, Reds 14
CG—Eliezel Rosario, Astros 4
ShO—Paul Branconier, Dodgers 2
—Dave Oropeza, Expos 2
Sv—Ed Ohman, Rangers 11
—Brett Marshall, White Sox 11
W—Robin Nina, Dodgers 10
L—Mark Deushane, Braves......................7
IP—Jim Hudson, Royals..........................88
H—Mark Deushane, Braves.....................76
R—Chris Butler, Mets 49
HR—Meredith Sanford, Reds 6
BB—Ben Howze, Expos 55
HB—Three tied at..................................7
SO—Cullen Hartzog, Yankees...................82
WP—Teryl Morrison, Indians 13
—Dwayne Van Horn, Reds 13
Bk—Pedro Borbon, White Sox 14

Department Leaders

INDIANS

BATTING	AVG	G	AB	R	H	2B	3B	HR	RBI	BB	SO	SB
#Alvarado, Jeffrey, of	.219	22	32	6	7	1	0	0	2	4	11	1
Blackwell, Barry, c	.303	23	76	12	23	3	0	1	12	9	8	0
*Brown, Stacy, of	.189	51	159	28	30	4	2	0	17	27	49	4
Campbell, Darin, 3b	.175	58	160	45	35	8	1	2	21	27	28	11
Cofer, Brian, ss-3b	.259	45	147	23	38	5	1	0	18	17	27	16
#Dariah, Bruce, 2b	.143	8	7	2	1	0	0	0	0	2	2	0
#Felton, Lawrence, of	.111	9	9	1	1	0	0	0	1	0	7	0
*Ferran, Alex, of	.238	60	206	25	49	8	5	0	24	20	39	5
*Harrell, Steve, of	.257	26	35	8	9	0	0	0	5	2	12	4
Kull, Bill, of-3b	.253	58	198	36	50	13	2	1	27	47	22	16
*Meddaugh, Dean, of-2b	.174	45	115	15	20	4	1	0	16	15	25	3
Mraz, Todd, c	.246	44	118	14	29	7	0	1	9	10	16	4
Murillo, Javier, 2b	.300	58	207	39	62	11	3	0	29	31	36	7
Ortiz, Ramon, of	.173	39	81	8	14	1	1	0	5	13	18	2
Pough, Clyde, ss-dh	.260	52	173	28	45	11	0	3	21	24	52	1
Smith, Lawrence, of-inf	.252	28	103	15	26	6	0	1	13	7	26	6
*Tepper, Marc, 1b	.275	58	207	30	57	15	1	4	45	39	36	1
*Wallman, Scott, c	.267	27	45	10	12	4	0	0	2	11	9	1

PITCHING	W	L	ERA	G	GS	CG	SV	IP	H	R	ER	BB	SO
Baez, Angel	2	1	3.55	3	2	0	1	25	22	13	10	11	21
Baker, Andy	0	2	9.85	14	0	0	1	25	25	30	27	20	15
*Bevenour, Keith	2	2	2.44	12	9	1	1	66	55	22	18	19	67
Hebets, Brad	3	1	2.30	23	0	0	6	31	23	14	8	16	27
*Kiser, Garland	5	1	1.29	7	7	2	0	56	31	12	8	17	45
Leger, Ed	1	1	5.14	10	0	0	2	14	14	13	8	15	18
McElfish, Shawn	0	0	5.50	12	0	0	1	18	20	12	11	14	9
Morrison, Teryl	3	4	2.47	14	11	1	1	69	52	29	19	45	58
Neill, Scott	4	3	4.22	10	8	1	0	53	46	37	25	26	50
Richardson, Dave	3	1	3.43	7	7	2	0	39	29	15	15	12	31
*Rivera, Roberto	6	5	3.25	14	12	1	0	69	64	32	25	21	38
Scarborough, Bill	6	4	4.24	18	2	0	1	57	40	33	27	37	42
Shepherd, Matt	2	0	3.67	11	3	0	1	34	30	17	14	15	29

METS

BATTING	AVG	G	AB	R	H	2B	3B	HR	RBI	BB	SO	SB
Bonini, Mark, 1b-c	.000	2	1	0	0	0	0	0	0	0	0	0
Cameron, Stanton, of	.234	51	171	24	40	10	1	1	15	25	33	10
Castillo, Berto, c	.265	22	68	7	18	4	0	0	10	4	4	2
*Davis, Nicky, 1b	.212	62	212	18	45	8	1	1	25	30	54	2
Diaz, Alberto, 2b-ss	.307	23	88	11	27	2	1	0	2	3	11	12
Echoles, Jamie, of	.125	5	16	1	2	0	0	0	1	1	9	1

	AVG	G	AB	R	H	2B	3B	HR	RBI	BB	SO	SB
Geronimo, Angel, 2b-3b	.571	3	7	3	4	0	0	0	1	0	1	0
Harris, James, dh-c	.291	58	206	28	60	7	1	4	34	31	36	6
#Hartmann, Reid, 2b	.239	34	109	15	26	4	0	0	5	14	20	3
Minnifield, Wallace, of	.173	45	127	9	22	3	1	1	11	6	48	3
Moore, Devren, of	.181	50	155	13	28	4	1	1	10	13	46	4
Reyes, Fred, c	.133	11	15	1	2	0	0	0	0	2	6	0
Rudolph, Mason, c	.170	31	106	8	18	4	0	0	13	5	28	2
Saunders, Doug, ss-2b	.250	16	64	8	16	4	1	0	10	9	14	2
Segui, Dan, 3b-2b	.223	63	215	35	48	9	7	1	19	37	35	5
Tesmer, Jim, of-1b	.297	38	158	20	47	3	1	0	16	3	9	5
#Thompson, Jeff, ss	.151	50	166	25	25	1	1	0	11	31	45	6
Washington, Kyle, of	.202	52	129	14	26	3	0	1	6	22	43	4
Wiese, Marc, 3b	.240	11	25	2	6	1	0	0	1	5	7	1
Yan, Tito, 2b-ss	.074	13	27	0	2	0	0	0	0	2	1	0

PITCHING	W	L	ERA	G	GS	CG	SV	IP	H	R	ER	BB	SO
Bristow, Rich	2	3	8.31	13	1	0	0	17	29	27	16	6	10
Brown, Fred	2	2	4.19	7	7	1	0	39	37	21	18	10	25
Butler, Chris	1	4	4.76	13	11	1	0	57	67	49	30	18	46
Carrasco, Hector	0	2	4.17	14	2	0	0	37	37	29	17	13	21
Castillo, Juan	0	2	6.41	9	3	0	0	20	28	19	14	9	16
Dorn, Chris	1	6	4.50	26	0	0	3	36	36	24	18	15	22
*Fidler, Andy	2	1	1.47	9	6	1	0	43	26	14	7	22	56
Johnstone, John	3	4	2.68	12	12	3	0	74	65	29	22	25	57
Lehnerz, Mike	0	2	7.71	12	5	0	0	28	26	28	24	35	21
*Lott, Hank	0	2	3.32	15	0	0	4	19	20	9	7	5	24
Medina, Luciano	0	0	1.00	3	1	0	1	9	3	1	1	1	7
Polanco, Nicolas	4	5	3.40	12	9	2	0	53	48	33	20	18	39
Sample, Deron	4	4	3.15	21	3	1	0	46	45	20	16	18	29
Scott, Craig	1	1	2.86	11	0	0	0	22	19	10	7	14	20
Torres, Jose	1	2	5.52	13	4	0	0	31	37	25	19	17	24
*Willoughby, Mark	0	2	5.95	12	1	0	0	20	17	18	13	12	15

PIRATES

BATTING	AVG	G	AB	R	H	2B	3B	HR	RBI	BB	SO	SB
Antigua, Felix, c	.341	13	44	6	15	2	0	2	9	2	3	0
Beltran, Angel, c	.154	19	65	4	10	1	0	0	3	3	9	2
#Bullett, Scott, of	.180	21	61	6	11	1	0	0	8	7	9	2
*Clemens, Troy, c	.135	15	37	1	5	0	0	0	5	4	5	1
*Datcher, Ron, 2b	.188	9	16	2	3	0	0	0	0	1	1	0
Delos Santos, Alberto, dh	.170	12	47	6	8	0	0	0	3	0	11	3
Denard, Kevin, 3b	.208	14	48	4	10	1	0	1	3	4	10	0
Feliz, Felix, 2b-ss	.278	5	18	4	5	1	0	0	1	1	3	2
Feliz, Janeiro, ss-2b	.094	24	53	3	5	0	0	0	1	10	25	1
Green, Darryl, c	.108	12	37	1	4	0	1	0	5	4	12	0
Hays, Kevin, c-1b	.125	19	48	4	6	1	0	0	4	9	5	0
Henderson, Val, of	.264	49	193	26	51	7	1	0	12	19	31	23
Lytle, Wade, 3b	.213	52	169	22	36	7	0	3	15	25	42	3
Martin, Jon of	.309	16	55	3	17	4	1	0	7	7	10	3
*McGhay, Paul, 1b	.119	15	42	3	5	0	0	0	3	1	15	2
#Molina, Albert, ss	.348	6	23	2	8	2	0	0	2	1	3	2
Nelson, Erik, c	.179	13	39	5	7	2	0	0	1	5	11	3
*Osborne, Jeff, 1b	.377	21	69	10	26	5	1	0	10	13	9	3
Pennyfeather, William, of	.243	17	74	6	18	2	1	1	7	2	18	3
Redmond, Andre, of	.159	45	145	18	23	5	0	2	13	19	40	19
Robles, Roberto, of	.154	4	13	1	2	0	0	0	0	0	6	0
Rodriguez, Roman, ss-3b	.208	50	168	21	35	7	1	0	12	13	21	5
Schmitt, Gary, of	.000	2	4	2	0	0	0	0	0	0	1	0
Solarte, Nollys, of	.135	34	96	14	13	2	0	3	10	23	39	7
Stout, Jeff, 2b-ss	.333	3	15	2	5	1	0	0	1	2	1	1
Thompson, Mike, 1b	.221	26	86	5	19	3	1	0	12	7	17	0
Tinnin, Derek, 2b	.215	50	163	17	35	2	2	0	11	22	36	13
*Wall, Mike, dh-1b	.300	40	140	13	42	8	1	0	13	16	18	0
West, Robert, of	.181	31	105	10	19	6	0	0	5	8	20	1

PITCHING	W	L	ERA	G	GS	CG	SV	IP	H	R	ER	BB	SO
Broadwater, Tom	0	0	6.75	4	0	0	0	5	7	6	4	5	3
*Byerly, Rod	2	2	1.95	8	6	0	0	37	34	12	8	10	41
Ellis, Doug	2	1	1.17	6	1	0	0	23	22	6	3	4	15
Grantges, Terence	1	5	5.76	13	2	0	1	25	24	23	16	18	16
*Haupt, Rich	0	0	2.08	6	0	0	1	9	8	3	2	6	10
*Honeywell, Brent	1	4	2.06	8	4	0	0	35	29	17	8	6	36
Lunsford, Greg	0	1	3.68	10	1	0	2	22	22	10	9	7	18
Magria, Javier	2	3	3.14	12	8	0	0	49	38	27	17	32	47
McKinney, Tony	2	3	1.96	11	9	1	0	55	64	24	12	14	31
Neeley, Jeff	4	3	2.55	14	0	0	3	35	29	15	10	4	29
Pagan, Joe	1	2	3.45	11	2	0	0	29	23	19	11	17	17
*Payne, Jeff	1	1	2.25	5	0	0	2	8	5	4	2	3	8
Roeder, Steve	0	0	1.42	6	1	0	0	13	10	4	2	11	3
Santiago, Delvy	0	2	5.70	9	3	0	1	24	26	18	15	11	12
Skyrd, Chris	0	2	3.54	6	4	0	1	20	22	13	8	9	14
Smith, Todd	0	0	8.31	3	0	0	0	4	5	6	4	7	3
Studstill, Thomas	3	2	1.52	7	7	0	0	41	26	15	7	5	34
Udell, Matt	1	1	2.93	11	3	0	2	28	30	12	9	12	11
*Way, Ron	3	1	1.72	13	5	0	2	37	22	11	7	20	35
*West, Darin	2	2	2.17	7	4	0	0	29	17	8	7	5	32
Wurm, Garry	1	2	2.57	10	4	0	2	35	25	15	10	8	22

RANGERS

BATTING	AVG	G	AB	R	H	2B	3B	HR	RBI	BB	SO	SB
Benitez, Luis, ss-2b	.286	63	220	38	63	8	4	2	19	38	38	14
*Berry, Anthony, of	.250	62	236	36	59	6	6	1	23	29	57	17
Bruckner, Glen, dh-1b	.207	10	29	3	6	1	0	1	5	0	8	1
Cole, Lucius, of	.172	46	93	17	16	4	1	0	7	21	24	6
Colon, Tony, c	.400	8	10	1	4	1	0	0	1	3	2	0
*Cronk, Doug, 1b	.221	62	222	21	49	16	2	3	34	21	49	2
Delgado, Pablo, dh-of	.198	36	116	15	23	1	0	1	12	13	24	0
Galvez, Jose, ss	.214	27	70	5	15	3	0	1	11	3	14	0
*Gamez, Bob, of	.170	31	88	13	15	1	1	0	4	9	16	0
Garcia, Manuel, 2b	.280	56	211	28	59	16	1	0	24	9	41	16
Hernandez, Jose, 3b	.160	55	162	19	26	7	1	1	13	12	36	4
Mendazona, Mike, c	.183	26	71	10	13	1	0	1	6	10	4	0
Morrow, Timmy, of	.248	32	113	15	28	2	4	2	9	9	30	3
Robinson, Lindsey, 3b	.213	35	94	9	20	4	0	1	10	13	19	0
Rodriguez, Jorge, of	.250	6	20	2	5	0	0	0	1	2	3	0
Scruggs, Tony, of	.083	5	12	1	1	0	0	0	0	3	4	1
Shore, Jeff, of-c	.261	53	176	21	46	9	0	2	31	26	43	9
#Torres, Carmelo, ss-2b	.000	4	6	0	0	0	0	0	0	0	0	0
Williams, Cliff, c	.202	31	94	7	19	2	1	1	7	3	34	1

PITCHING	W	L	ERA	G	GS	CG	SV	IP	H	R	ER	BB	SO
Barreiro, Fernando	1	1	2.57	8	1	0	0	21	17	9	6	3	17
Castro, Confesor	2	4	3.08	12	11	0	0	64	60	27	22	15	35
DeVaughan, Todd	0	0	0.00	1	0	0	0	2	3	0	0	0	1
Ebarb, Wayne	1	1	3.90	14	0	0	1	28	29	17	12	11	18
Hurst, Jon	1	0	0.59	5	1	0	0	15	5	1	1	4	13
Huth, Jon	6	2	5.46	15	3	0	0	28	20	20	17	18	24
Lipscomb, Bruce	2	1	1.71	13	0	0	5	21	17	7	4	3	10
*Lynch, Dave	0	0	0.00	1	0	0	0	2	0	0	0	0	3
*McCray, Eric	3	2	1.44	12	11	0	0	56	39	15	9	27	42
Mileski, Tom	1	0	2.31	5	1	0	0	12	9	3	3	6	6
Molina, Manny	0	4	3.48	15	0	0	1	34	34	16	13	7	23
Morse, Scott	0	1	1.00	6	4	0	0	18	9	2	2	3	17
Ohman, Ed	1	1	0.99	27	0	0	11	36	26	5	4	5	39
*Oliver, Darren	5	1	2.15	12	9	0	0	54	39	16	13	18	59
Olsson, Dan	0	0	54.00	1	0	0	0	0	2	2	2	0	0
Romero, Ronaldo	3	5	3.05	12	10	0	0	59	45	25	20	14	30
*Saavedra, Francisco	0	0	1.35	2	0	0	0	7	5	1	1	2	11
Simmons, Jeff	1	1	4.97	8	0	0	0	13	15	12	7	9	13
*Valarezo, Pedro	0	0	7.36	6	0	0	1	7	8	6	6	4	7
Valdez, Francisco	7	4	3.55	13	12	0	0	63	62	30	25	22	33

REDS

BATTING	AVG	G	AB	R	H	2B	3B	HR	RBI	BB	SO	SB
Arland, Mark, of	.197	47	142	12	28	7	0	1	17	20	54	6
Baez, Igor, c-dh	.261	36	111	11	29	3	0	1	12	9	16	0
Coker, Shane, of	.166	49	181	12	30	7	0	0	10	10	43	6
Cudjo, Lavell, of	.258	55	182	29	47	8	1	1	12	26	32	9
Davis, Alton, of	.377	20	69	8	26	8	1	2	21	5	9	2
Gianni, Gaetano, c	.175	27	80	4	14	2	0	0	6	10	30	1
*Gillum, K.C., 3b	.242	49	165	24	40	9	3	0	12	21	37	6
Jones, Eugene, of	.242	55	194	24	47	7	0	0	18	16	23	19
Kovarick, Paul, 1b-dh	.268	47	153	27	41	4	1	1	21	34	42	3
Kroell, Rob, ss	.210	55	157	18	33	4	0	0	8	19	22	1
Lora, Julio, 2b-3b	.143	23	56	4	8	1	1	0	6	2	24	0
Mathews, Jeremy, ss-3b	.242	30	91	7	22	3	3	0	16	7	22	0
Moore, Cary, 2b	.159	27	63	9	10	0	0	1	2	7	20	0
#Moore, Larry, 2b	.160	26	81	9	13	1	0	0	3	7	12	5
*Parrotte, Brian, 2b-3b	.285	38	130	16	37	2	4	0	14	18	18	2
*Reagan, Kyle, 1b-dh	.212	39	132	16	28	8	0	0	13	17	29	2
*Tucker, Bob, c	.063	11	16	0	1	0	0	0	1	2	10	1
Weeks, Trevor, c	.131	26	61	9	8	0	0	0	6	11	17	1
Williams, Rosie, of	.200	5	15	1	3	0	0	0	1	3	6	0
*Wolfer, Jim, dh	.333	1	3	1	1	0	1	0	0	0	1	0

PITCHING	W	L	ERA	G	GS	CG	SV	IP	H	R	ER	BB	SO
*Abugherir, Amer	0	3	7.30	16	1	0	0	25	31	25	20	16	16
Anderson, Mike	0	1	4.91	2	2	0	0	7	6	7	4	5	11
Ayala, Bobby	0	4	3.82	20	0	0	3	33	34	23	14	12	24
*Edward, John	0	1	7.56	5	2	0	0	8	4	13	7	14	8
*Fermin, Nilson	2	3	3.73	13	13	0	0	70	71	33	29	27	32
Garcia, Victor	4	4	2.27	13	13	0	0	71	60	27	18	30	47
Linares, Yfrain	1	5	6.68	19	0	0	0	34	39	33	25	19	25
*Malley, Mike	3	2	3.22	11	2	0	0	22	16	18	8	15	20
Manon, Ramon	2	1	2.51	16	0	0	2	32	32	11	9	8	14
McDaniel, Joel	0	2	2.92	9	0	0	1	12	7	7	4	16	11
Munoz, Francisco	0	0	6.75	1	0	0	0	3	5	2	2	1	5
Peters, Mike	2	0	1.42	15	0	0	3	25	19	6	4	10	29
Sanford, Meredith	3	4	3.23	14	11	0	1	53	34	24	19	25	64
Satre, Jason	0	3	2.49	11	10	0	0	47	31	16	13	29	44
Stewart, Carl	0	0	13.50	2	0	0	0	2	2	3	3	2	2
Susana, Jacinto	2	3	6.17	16	0	0	0	23	34	21	16	14	14
Thomas, C.L.	1	4	2.94	11	11	0	0	49	36	25	16	25	47
Van Horne, Dwayne	0	0	24.43	11	0	0	0	7	4	22	19	33	3
Wilburn, Trey	1	2	7.50	15	0	0	1	24	25	24	20	29	19
*Williams, Dwayne	0	0	16.88	3	0	0	0	3	1	5	5	4	2

ROYALS

BATTING	AVG	G	AB	R	H	2B	3B	HR	RBI	BB	SO	SB
*Beniquez, Juan, of	.200	23	40	4	8	3	0	0	1	1	6	4
Byrnes, Tim, ss-3b	.252	52	147	31	37	3	0	0	16	41	21	10
#Conde, Hector, of	.240	6	25	4	6	0	1	0	4	5	6	3
Davis, Kelvin, 3b	.212	18	52	13	11	1	1	0	9	15	5	3
Deleon, Huascar, c	.209	46	148	13	31	5	1	0	17	10	22	0
Garibaldo, Christobal, ss ...	.228	35	123	15	28	4	1	0	12	8	18	7
Guanchez, Harry, 1b ..	.262	27	61	10	16	5	0	0	4	9	9	0
Johnson, Darron, 1b-dh ..	.250	54	176	18	44	6	0	1	25	22	23	4
Mayberry, Marvin, c	.308	10	13	0	4	1	0	0	3	2	2	1
Melendez, Hector, 1b-2b ..	.224	36	116	13	26	6	0	0	15	21	23	2
Miranda, Giovanni, 3b-2b ..	.231	44	117	20	27	1	0	0	4	9	14	9
Moore, Kerwin, of	.176	53	165	19	29	5	0	0	14	19	49	20
#Nunez, Dimerson, c	.236	34	89	9	21	4	1	1	14	9	11	0
*Perry, Scott, of-dh	.236	57	161	24	38	10	2	0	15	44	37	7
Prusia, Greg, of-dh	.263	58	209	22	55	12	1	4	30	9	39	7
Stombaugh, Chad, c	.174	21	46	6	8	1	0	0	6	10	10	0
#Vasquez, Pedro, 2b	.216	63	218	39	47	5	0	0	23	49	35	10
*Walker, Hugh, of	.240	63	242	41	58	9	6	0	24	34	50	27

PITCHING	W	L	ERA	G	GS	CG	SV	IP	H	R	ER	BB	SO
*Alicano, Albert	0	0	2.00	7	0	0	1	18	10	7	4	9	9
*Aranguren, Ismael	6	3	2.70	12	12	0	0	67	53	23	20	15	43
Bowling, Stan	0	0	3.86	14	0	0	0	26	17	16	11	28	20
Connor, John	5	1	7.36	17	2	0	1	29	41	28	24	24	17
Hempen, Hal	3	2	4.65	16	0	0	0	31	34	17	16	12	27
Hofer, John	3	0	0.51	22	0	0	9	35	17	5	2	11	27
Holshouser, Jeff	3	3	3.12	12	10	0	1	61	61	25	21	11	24
Hudson, Jim	5	2	1.95	13	12	3	0	88	70	25	19	11	79
Jundy, Lorin	1	0	5.12	10	0	0	3	19	16	12	11	11	25
Karklins, Greg	4	6	2.22	13	12	0	0	69	63	24	17	16	56
Kimbell, Zach	3	2	5.48	16	0	0	2	23	19	19	14	16	19
*Lee, Ben	0	1	7.20	4	0	0	0	5	7	5	4	5	5
*McCormick, John	3	3	3.60	12	12	0	0	65	58	34	26	20	46
Nocas, Luke	0	0	0.00	2	0	0	1	4	2	0	0	1	6
Pichardo, Hipolito	0	0	13.50	1	0	0	0	1	3	2	2	1	3
*Pierce, Ben	1	1	2.57	4	4	1	0	21	19	7	6	12	26
Rodriguez, Sammy	1	0	3.68	6	0	0	0	15	17	7	6	4	6
Wellington, Rob	1	0	0.00	2	0	0	0	3	2	0	0	2	1

WHITE SOX

BATTING	AVG	G	AB	R	H	2B	3B	HR	RBI	BB	SO	SB
Abbatinozzi, Paul, c	.253	29	83	11	21	7	1	1	18	11	20	0
*Bargman, Todd, 1b-of ...	.323	9	31	5	10	2	0	0	2	1	10	0
Bedoya, Raul, 2b	.000	3	11	0	0	0	0	0	1	0	3	0
*Braxton, Glen, dh	.258	28	89	17	23	2	2	1	14	14	24	7
Busby, Mike, ss	.276	51	185	22	51	8	1	1	22	19	27	4
Colontino, Paul, of	.053	7	19	1	1	0	0	0	0	0	5	1
Cruz, Jose, 2b	.095	13	21	2	2	1	0	0	1	4	5	1
Davis, Brian, of	.267	52	202	43	54	6	6	2	20	9	38	13
Egan, Scott, c	.148	20	54	4	8	0	0	0	2	6	15	1
*Fletcher, Robert, 2b	.250	57	212	36	53	9	1	1	20	28	19	20
Furch, John, dh-1b	.500	3	10	1	5	2	1	0	3	3	1	0
Harris, Keith, of	.324	23	68	14	22	1	3	1	15	7	13	4
*James, Steve, of	.083	18	36	2	3	0	0	0	1	8	18	0
Martinez, Angel, c	.250	3	8	0	2	0	0	0	0	1	1	0
*Moye, Wayne, of	.211	32	71	15	15	3	0	0	9	6	12	9
Ramos, Jorge, ss-3b	.306	26	72	13	22	2	0	0	7	6	20	3
Silva, Mario, 3b	.094	15	32	2	3	0	1	0	0	4	13	0
Singley, Joe, dh-c	.259	19	58	5	15	4	2	0	3	6	14	1
*Tedder, Scott, of-1b	.341	58	214	30	73	13	0	0	25	28	16	8
Teter, Craig, dh-of	.286	4	14	2	4	1	0	0	1	0	5	0
Thomas, Dwight, 1b	.201	46	169	25	34	8	4	2	24	19	47	4
#Thompson, Rob, c	.290	22	69	13	20	2	2	1	12	10	13	4
Walker, Dennis, 3b	.238	50	181	28	43	4	0	4	31	10	23	8
*Zaksek, John, of	.329	27	79	8	26	4	1	1	11	5	14	6

PITCHING	W	L	ERA	G	GS	CG	SV	IP	H	R	ER	BB	SO
Borbon, Pedro	5	3	2.41	16	11	1	1	75	52	28	20	17	67
Brutcher, Lenny	9	1	2.55	14	9	0	1	60	52	22	17	8	31
Burroughs, Ken	1	0	1.71	17	0	0	6	21	8	4	4	12	29
Davis, Freddie	2	2	3.86	17	0	0	0	35	32	17	15	11	19
Garcia, Ramon	2	1	2.45	13	0	0	0	22	15	9	6	4	17
Garrett, James	3	2	7.25	11	1	0	0	22	21	21	18	13	15
Harvey, Dwayne	1	0	1.69	3	0	0	0	5	5	3	1	3	1
Hulme, Pat	3	0	2.83	11	9	0	0	48	38	22	15	14	23
Mallett, Lane	0	0	18.00	1	0	0	0	1	2	3	2	1	2
Marshall, Brett	4	1	0.87	25	0	0	11	41	24	6	4	4	29
Martinez, Gabriel	0	0	5.40	2	0	0	0	5	3	5	3	6	2
Middaugh, Scott	3	3	2.45	11	10	1	0	59	50	31	16	7	41
Mitchener, Mike	0	0	0.00	2	0	0	0	1	2	1	0	1	5
*Radinsky, Scott	0	0	5.40	5	0	0	0	3	2	2	2	4	7
Ruffin, Johnny	4	2	2.30	13	11	1	0	59	43	27	15	22	31
Thigpen, Arthur	2	3	6.63	16	0	0	0	19	25	16	14	16	19
Ventura, Jose	3	3	2.62	12	12	1	0	76	67	31	22	23	46

YANKEES

BATTING	AVG	G	AB	R	H	2B	3B	HR	RBI	BB	SO	SB
Ausmus, Brad, c	.256	43	133	22	34	2	0	0	15	11	25	5
#Castillo, Manuel, 2b-3b	.254	32	71	14	18	1	1	0	9	9	18	5
*Cortes, Hernan, 1b-dh	.257	43	148	33	38	10	6	1	17	23	28	6
Davis, Russell, 2b-3b	.230	58	213	33	49	11	3	2	30	16	39	6
Garcia, Santos, c	.182	13	33	8	6	0	0	1	5	5	8	0
Hernandez, Enrique, c	.160	9	25	2	4	1	0	0	2	1	7	0
Herrera, Jose, 3b-ss	.251	58	211	26	53	8	0	0	24	3	28	3
#Hill, Lew, of	.249	54	201	31	50	4	4	2	19	13	69	7
*Howell, David, 1b-dh	.250	59	204	28	51	9	1	0	29	19	28	9
Miller, Orlando, 2b-ss	.182	14	44	5	8	1	0	0	5	3	10	1
Obando, Sherman, of-dh	.256	49	172	26	44	10	2	4	27	16	32	8
*Perez, Beban, of	.241	30	112	20	27	3	2	0	11	10	30	7
Reyes, Rolando, c	.100	4	10	1	1	0	0	0	1	1	2	0
Rhodes, Mike, of-1b	.318	57	195	29	62	9	2	2	41	19	42	14
*Sanders, Deion, of	.280	17	75	7	21	4	2	0	6	2	10	11
Thigpen, Leonard, of-3b	.234	27	64	7	15	1	0	0	4	6	15	1
Tingle, Darrell, ss-2b	.241	39	141	19	34	5	1	0	11	12	19	8
Torres, Miguel, 2b	.286	2	7	2	2	0	0	0	1	1	1	1
#Warren, Allen, of	.400	6	15	8	6	0	0	0	1	3	1	2
Zeratsky, Mark, c	.100	4	10	1	1	0	0	0	3	0	1	0

PITCHING	W	L	ERA	G	GS	CG	SV	IP	H	R	ER	BB	SO
Broxton, John	3	1	2.04	22	0	0	5	40	24	12	9	12	48
*Eckert, Mike	3	0	2.10	15	1	0	3	30	28	16	7	9	24
*Filson, Pete	0	0	0.00	1	0	0	0	1	0	0	0	0	1
Hartzog, Cullen	5	2	2.00	13	13	1	0	76	65	24	17	23	82
*Howell, David	0	0	1.80	7	0	0	0	10	6	3	2	2	9
*Juarbe, Ken	7	0	2.08	12	10	0	0	65	44	19	15	23	67
*Malone, Todd	6	1	1.64	12	12	2	0	66	55	17	12	21	81
*Michael, Matt	0	0	3.86	10	0	0	0	14	11	8	6	8	14
Ohlms, Mark	4	3	0.74	24	0	0	10	37	19	4	3	16	64
Ortiz, Jose	0	0	1.74	9	0	0	0	10	9	3	2	1	9
Perez, Cesar	0	1	2.57	6	0	0	0	7	5	3	2	2	6
*Perry, Steve	0	0	6.00	2	0	0	0	3	3	3	2	5	5
Persia, Lauriano	2	6	4.14	19	0	0	1	37	40	19	17	7	30
Pickrell, Jesse	2	1	2.35	12	1	0	0	23	18	11	6	12	16
Ralph, Curtis	6	0	2.64	12	12	0	0	65	62	26	19	22	37
Rhodes, Ricky	6	3	2.33	12	12	1	0	70	43	26	18	27	76
Stoltenberg, Brad	1	0	2.45	2	2	0	0	7	7	3	2	2	9

ARIZONA LEAGUE

Milwaukee famous as new league's winner

By JOHN ROYSTER

The Milwaukee Brewers fielded the first champion of the Arizona League in 1988, which is only fitting since that organization was instrumental in creating the new rookie complex league.

The Milwaukee and Oakland organizations had pushed for an Arizona-based rookie league for years, and finally got it approved in February of 1988. They each fielded a team, as did the San Diego Padres.

But most of the national headlines were for the league's fourth team—the co-op fielded with little cooperation between the Boston Red Sox and Seattle Mariners.

Seattle's players would play one day, and Boston's the next. Each side wore its own uniforms, and each usually suited up about 12 players for a game. Collectively (?), they went 12-47.

Like the Gulf Coast League in Florida, Arizona League games were played during the day, at spring training complexes in Scottsdale and Peoria.

	W	L	Pct.	GB	
Brewers	40	18	.690	—	1988 Final Standings
Athletics	34	24	.586	6	
Padres	31	28	.525	9½	
Red Sox/Mariners	12	47	.203	28½	

1988: General Information

Managers: Athletics—Dave Hudgens; **Brewers**—Alex Taveras; **Padres**—Jaime Moreno; **Red Sox/Mariners**—Mike Verdi (Boston), Myron Pines (Seattle).

1988 All-Star Team: C—Gerald Cifarelli, Padres. **1B**—Leon Glenn, Brewers. **2B**—Matt Witkowski, Padres. **3B**—Frank Bolick, Brewers. **SS**—Luis Mateo, A's. **OF**—Tim McWilliam, Padres; Ed Ricks, A's; Osvaldo Sanchez, Padres. **LHP**—Joe Murdock, Padres. **RHP**—Jeff Hart, Padres. **DH**—Robert Muhammed, Brewers. **LHRP**—Will Love, A's. **RHRP**—Marty Willis, Brewers. **Most Valuable Player**—Ed Ricks, A's. **Manager of the Year**—Alex Taveras, Brewers.

Top 10 Major League Prospects (by Baseball America): See Gulf Coast League, Page 209.

1988: Batting, Pitching Statistics

CLUB BATTING

	AVG	G	AB	R	H	2B	3B	HR	BB	SO	SB
Peoria Brewers	.292	58	1981	423	578	97	41	28	285	350	98
Scottsdale Padres	.287	59	2002	383	575	67	30	27	247	405	110
Red Sox/Mariners	.278	59	2013	298	559	98	22	19	164	373	82
Scottsdale Athletics	.266	58	1940	392	516	84	25	30	350	397	73

CLUB PITCHING

	ERA	G	CG	SHO	SV	IP	H	R	ER	BB	SO
Peoria Brewers	4.01	58	10	2	14	512	498	282	228	178	383
Scottsdale Athletics	4.72	58	7	1	11	509	568	323	267	163	377
Scottsdale Padres	5.64	59	3	2	9	515	559	377	323	305	411
Red Sox/Mariners ...	7.19	59	8	0	3	502	604	511	401	400	354

INDIVIDUAL BATTING LEADERS
(Minimum 162 Plate Appearances)

	AVG	G	AB	R	H	2B	3B	HR	RBI	BB	SO	SB
McWilliam, Tim, Padres ..	.451	48	182	50	82	8	7	4	47	25	6	8
Cifarelli, Gerard, Padres ..	.350	51	183	34	64	9	2	3	31	25	19	10
Aguilar, Mark, Brewers ..	.349	51	195	36	68	5	3	0	32	21	23	4
*Glenn, Leon, Brewers ..	.340	55	212	54	72	13	10	8	53	24	29	5
*Love, Will, Athletics ..	.327	50	153	30	50	13	4	5	38	18	28	0
Witkowski, Matt, Padres ..	.323	51	201	37	65	5	3	0	25	16	32	17
*Love, Sylvester, Brewers ..	.323	57	229	72	74	13	9	5	30	45	26	32
Simmons, Enoch, Athletics ..	.307	42	150	41	46	9	3	1	23	40	26	18

* indicates lefthanded batter   # indicates switch hitter

INDIVIDUAL PITCHING LEADERS
(Minimum 48 Innings)

	W	L	ERA	G	GS	CG	SV	IP	H	R	ER	BB	SO
Hart, Jeff, Padres	5	0	2.07	10	8	1	0	61	35	16	14	22	42
Saldana, Dan, RS-M	2	2	2.39	8	7	2	0	49	40	22	13	24	44
*Carmody, Kevin, Brewers ..	3	0	2.94	13	4	1	0	49	36	22	16	23	51
Patrick, Bronswell, Ath ...	8	3	2.99	14	13	2	0	96	99	37	32	16	64
Carter, Larry, Brewers ..	6	2	3.19	14	12	3	1	85	81	40	30	13	65
Wegman, Bruce, Brewers ..	9	1	3.51	12	11	1	0	67	69	33	26	14	59
Tucker, Vance, Padres ...	4	5	4.04	12	11	1	0	76	69	43	34	39	58
Federico, Gustavo, Brw ..	3	4	4.86	12	12	3	0	70	77	43	38	30	44

* indicates lefthanded pitcher

ATHLETICS

BATTING	AVG	G	AB	R	H	2B	3B	HR	RBI	BB	SO	SB
Armas, Marcos, 1b-3b ...	.293	17	58	14	17	2	1	0	10	5	17	0
*Beck, Wynn, c	.221	36	113	16	25	3	0	4	19	16	18	0
Figuero, Tito, c-inf	.234	42	137	20	32	4	3	4	18	22	44	1
Furcal, Lorenzo, 2b	.190	8	21	5	4	1	0	0	3	8	7	0
Heck, Bob, c	.269	19	52	8	14	2	0	0	8	8	14	1
*Holland, Troy, of	.385	4	13	3	5	1	0	0	3	4	0	2
Jones, Dewayne, 2b	.300	3	10	0	3	2	0	0	3	0	4	0
Lewis, Darren, of	.333	5	15	8	5	3	0	0	4	6	5	4
*Love, Will, dh-lhp	.327	50	153	30	50	13	4	5	38	18	28	0
Martinez, Angel, ss	.406	17	69	17	28	6	0	2	10	7	13	3
#Mateo, Luis, ss	.256	54	215	41	55	5	2	0	20	31	42	5
McCormick, Glenn, 3b-ss ..	.223	45	166	32	37	6	1	0	19	33	37	5
Mercedes, Henry, c	.400	2	5	1	2	0	0	0	0	0	0	0
*Nina, Julio, 1b-of	.269	47	167	39	45	7	1	4	27	34	33	6
Ricks, Ed, of	.272	55	184	50	50	7	7	8	41	51	49	14
Ritter, Ken, of-dh	.234	38	124	22	29	6	1	2	14	30	29	1
Simmons, Enoch, of	.307	42	150	41	46	9	3	1	23	40	26	18
#Vargas, Jose, 2b	.228	46	162	29	37	2	2	0	11	25	19	6
Watkins, Keith, of	.333	1	3	0	1	0	0	1	1	1	0	0
Webber, Jeff, of	.264	35	121	15	32	3	0	0	18	11	14	5

PITCHING	W	L	ERA	G	GS	CG	SV	IP	H	R	ER	BB	SO
Briscoe, John	1	1	3.51	7	6	0	0	26	26	14	10	6	23
Caraballo, Felix	0	1	1.80	2	2	1	0	10	7	3	2	4	9
Coccia, Joe	0	0	7.30	6	1	0	0	12	17	10	10	1	7
*Dockery, Mike	4	0	3.38	8	7	2	0	45	37	19	17	12	32

BATTING

R—Sylvester Love, Brewers 72
H—Tim McWilliam, Padres 82
TB—Leon Glenn, Brewers 129
2B—Will Love, Athletics 13
　—Leon Glenn, Brewers 13
3B—Leon Glenn, Brewers 10
HR—Leon Glenn, Brewers 8
　—Ed Ricks, Athletics 8
RBI—Leon Glenn, Brewers 53
GWRBI—Will Love, Athletics 9
SH—Three tied at 4
SF—Tim McWilliam, Padres 7
BB—Ed Ricks, Athletics 51
IBB—Four tied at 2
HBP—Scot Welish, Padres 8
SO—Brian Span, Padres 58
SB—Sylvester Love, Brewers 32
CS—Gerald Cifarelli, Brewers 8
Slg. Pct.—Tim McWilliam, Padres 632
OB Pct.—Tim McWilliam, Padres 507

PITCHING

G—Jose Lebron, Padres 24
GS—Bronswell Patrick, Athletics 13
CG—Larry Carter, Brewers 3
　—Gustavo Federico, Brewers 3
ShO—Five tied at 1
Sv—Marty Willis, Brewers 8
W—Bruce Wegman, Brewers 9
L—Richard Delgado, Co-op 10
IP—Bronswell Patrick, Athletics 96
H—Bronswell Patrick, Athletics 99
R—Bill Reed, Padres 64
　—Richard Delgado, Co-op 64
HR—Bronswell Patrick, Athletics 7
BB—Jim Magill, Co-op 51
HB—Four tied at 6
SO—Larry Carter, Brewers 65
WP—Joaquin Tejada, Co-op 8
Bk—Will Love, Athletics 10

	W	L	ERA	G	GS	CG	SV	IP	H	R	ER	BB	SO
Dye, Steve	0	0	0.00	5	0	0	1	8	7	2	0	3	2
Foley, Jim	1	0	4.00	3	1	0	0	9	11	5	4	4	8
Fuson, Robin	0	0	0.00	1	0	0	0	3	2	0	0	2	4
Garcia, Apolinar	1	1	8.31	2	2	0	0	13	19	14	12	4	8
Golmont, Van	2	3	7.02	7	6	1	0	33	44	27	26	6	35
Guzman, Dionny	0	2	8.61	16	1	0	1	23	36	27	22	8	18
Holmes, Chad	3	5	8.44	18	1	0	2	37	61	43	35	6	21
Hosinski, Steve	1	0	5.23	4	2	0	0	10	13	7	6	7	8
*Love, Will	4	1	5.54	11	4	0	0	37	41	27	23	20	30
Mejia, Leandro	0	0	0.00	1	0	0	0	1	1	0	0	0	0
Miller, Graham	2	0	3.64	13	1	0	1	30	34	21	12	13	16
Patrick, Bronswell	8	3	2.99	14	13	2	0	96	99	37	32	16	64
Peck, Steve	1	0	4.03	6	4	1	0	29	26	14	13	7	27
Sanchez, Manolo	2	1	5.29	5	3	0	0	17	17	12	10	13	10
Seda, Dave	2	2	6.28	13	1	0	1	29	37	21	20	13	25
Taylor, Bill	2	4	3.44	17	2	0	4	37	29	20	14	16	29
Wilson, Steve	0	0	6.00	1	1	0	0	3	3	3	2	1	1

BREWERS

BATTING	AVG	G	AB	R	H	2B	3B	HR	RBI	BB	SO	SB
Aguilar, Mark, 3b	.349	51	195	36	68	5	3	0	32	21	23	4
#Bolick, Frank, 3b	.375	23	80	20	30	9	3	1	20	22	8	1
Brown, Javier, 2b	.242	38	132	22	32	6	0	1	15	9	27	2
Burrola, Mike, 2b-of	.440	6	25	8	11	0	2	0	6	6	4	4
Diez, Steve, c	.272	27	81	16	22	1	1	0	9	15	18	2
Garcia, Librado, of	.255	51	196	42	50	12	3	4	39	20	53	26
*Glenn, Leon, 1b	.340	55	212	54	72	13	10	8	53	24	29	5
#Guerrero, Mike, ss	.276	8	29	9	8	1	0	0	7	5	5	0
Hernandez, Arned, c	.375	3	8	2	3	0	0	0	0	1	0	1
Hill, Beau, ss	.218	32	110	17	24	6	0	0	10	12	12	2
*Love, Sylvester, of	.323	57	229	72	74	13	9	5	30	45	26	32
Montalvo, Nelson, of	.222	13	36	7	8	2	0	1	6	6	12	2
Moore, Dwayne, dh	.429	3	7	1	3	2	0	0	1	1	1	1
Muhammad, Robert, dh-of	.356	35	132	24	47	10	4	5	30	16	20	3
Parks, Bryan, c	.292	33	113	11	33	6	4	0	16	5	19	0
Pfaff, Rich, of	.296	49	169	39	50	6	2	3	40	34	33	5
Rodriguez, Francisco, c	.125	35	80	9	10	2	0	0	6	8	22	0
Scott, Bob, dh-of	.160	20	50	10	8	2	0	0	2	14	16	3
Snow, Tim, 2b-ss	.266	37	94	22	25	2	0	0	12	21	21	5

PITCHING	W	L	ERA	G	GS	CG	SV	IP	H	R	ER	BB	SO
Barton, John	3	0	3.32	16	0	0	2	38	46	24	14	11	32
*Carmody, Kevin	3	0	2.94	13	4	1	0	49	36	22	16	23	51
Carter, Larry	6	2	3.19	14	12	3	1	85	81	40	30	13	65

	W	L	ERA	G	GS	CG	SV	IP	H	R	ER	BB	SO
Federico, Gustavo	3	4	4.86	12	12	3	0	70	77	43	38	30	44
Hitt, Jimmy	4	3	4.85	11	10	0	0	59	60	38	32	29	42
*Kapea, Danny	1	1	5.65	8	0	0	1	14	19	12	9	2	7
Kiley, John	3	2	4.56	9	5	1	1	47	42	25	24	12	50
Kinder, Jeff	4	3	4.76	12	0	0	3	28	24	16	15	17	18
Kostichka, Steve	0	0	0.00	2	0	0	0	2	2	0	0	3	1
Reyes, Juan	1	0	3.00	2	2	0	0	9	7	4	3	6	3
Wegman, Bruce	9	1	3.51	12	11	1	0	67	69	33	26	14	29
Willis, Marty	3	2	4.33	20	2	1	8	44	36	25	21	19	41

PADRES

BATTING	AVG	G	AB	R	H	2B	3B	HR	RBI	BB	SO	SB
Cifarelli, Gerard, c	.350	51	183	34	64	9	2	3	31	25	19	10
*Cioffi, Michael, 1b-dh	.168	38	113	20	19	3	0	1	10	24	38	4
Figueroa, Alex, rhp-dh	.321	20	28	6	9	0	0	0	5	1	8	0
Harris, Eric, of	.184	45	147	24	27	1	0	0	2	8	52	15
Hart, Darrin, of	.280	35	118	26	33	6	1	3	17	19	27	6
Holbert, Ray, ss	.259	49	170	38	44	1	0	3	19	37	32	20
Lebron, Jose, p-3b	.176	28	17	2	3	0	0	0	0	1	4	0
Leslie, Reggie, p-inf	.263	20	19	3	5	0	1	0	3	1	4	1
Lopez, Pedro, c	.284	42	156	18	44	4	6	1	22	12	24	9
McWilliam, Tim, of	.451	48	182	50	82	8	7	4	47	25	6	8
Peacock, Richard, of	.168	38	119	9	20	4	0	0	5	9	43	5
Reed, Bill, p-of	.200	23	15	2	3	2	0	0	1	1	4	0
*Sanchez, Osvaldo, of	.339	34	124	28	42	10	3	5	20	12	26	1
Span, Brian, 3b	.271	55	210	39	57	4	6	5	30	17	58	13
*Welish, Scott, 1b-of	.299	58	194	45	58	10	1	2	27	37	28	6
Witkowski, Matt, 2b-ss	.323	51	201	37	65	5	3	0	25	16	32	17

PITCHING	W	L	ERA	G	GS	CG	SV	IP	H	R	ER	BB	SO
Figueroa, Alex	2	0	6.25	16	3	0	2	45	60	36	31	24	31
Florie, Bryce	4	5	7.98	11	6	0	0	38	52	44	34	22	29
Hart, Jeff	5	0	2.07	10	8	1	0	61	35	16	14	22	42
*Hightower, Barry	0	0	4.09	5	0	0	0	11	6	6	5	11	6
Lebron, Jose	3	2	5.66	24	0	0	0	49	63	37	31	24	38
Leslie, Reggie	4	0	4.76	17	2	0	5	40	38	23	21	19	47
*Murdock, Joe	4	4	5.98	10	10	0	0	62	80	44	41	29	47
*Reed, William	1	7	8.39	17	8	0	1	59	75	64	55	45	50
Thompson, Squeezer	1	1	3.72	2	2	0	0	10	12	5	4	13	12
Tucker, Vance	4	5	4.04	12	11	1	0	76	69	43	34	39	58
Tukes, Stan	3	4	6.34	11	9	1	1	55	56	43	39	40	43
*Welish, Scott	0	0	8.10	2	0	0	0	3	5	4	3	1	3
Wilkerson, Walter	0	0	15.88	5	0	0	0	6	9	11	10	13	5

RED SOX/MARINERS

BATTING	AVG	G	AB	R	H	2B	3B	HR	RBI	BB	SO	SB
*Alvarez, David, 1b	.330	26	97	15	32	4	2	1	21	2	14	0
Amparo, Nelson, of-1b	.204	31	98	8	20	3	0	2	15	2	31	1
Barbara, Dan, c	.253	30	91	15	23	5	0	0	15	19	16	3
*Burrus, Daryl, 1b-c	.188	36	80	11	15	3	0	1	15	19	21	2
Byrd, James, ss-2b	.298	33	121	18	36	7	2	2	13	6	19	7
*Chevalier, Boneel, ss	.319	30	113	18	36	2	1	0	4	9	12	12
Crowder, Kevin, 3b	.252	31	107	13	27	6	1	0	15	4	21	1
Davis, Doug, of-1b	.220	32	118	18	26	7	2	4	18	12	30	0
Delgado, Alex, c-inf	.351	34	111	11	39	10	0	0	22	6	5	2
Del Pozo, Roberto, 3b	.222	15	45	7	10	0	1	0	6	8	13	2
*Doyle, Bernie, of-dh	.275	28	80	14	22	6	0	0	8	13	15	2
Guzman, Eddy, 2b	.350	25	80	9	28	2	0	0	4	1	12	0
*Higgins, Steve, of-p	.386	17	44	9	17	3	2	0	5	1	4	2
Jenkins, Garrett, of-c	.248	33	121	17	30	6	0	0	12	2	20	5
Moore, Meredith, of-1b	.276	28	87	12	24	2	2	0	5	10	20	6
Roas, Pedro, 2b	.322	31	115	12	37	7	0	0	13	5	15	3
*Thomas, Delvin, of-inf	.275	31	120	25	33	7	1	2	12	11	18	11
*Thomas, Kelvin, of	.248	33	129	21	32	5	3	3	16	12	29	9
Webb, Scott, dh-p	.267	17	30	4	8	2	0	0	3	3	9	2
Witherspoon, Richard, of	.274	33	113	24	31	6	5	0	18	14	24	3
Zambrano, Jose, of-c	.313	28	99	15	31	5	0	4	14	4	16	6

PITCHING	W	L	ERA	G	GS	CG	SV	IP	H	R	ER	BB	SO
*Bennett, Jim	2	1	4.33	6	4	1	0	27	23	15	13	6	17
*Burnau, Ben	1	1	7.13	3	3	1	0	18	21	15	14	11	10
Delgado, Richard	1	10	6.64	13	11	1	1	61	83	64	45	34	31
*Diaz, Jhonny	1	3	11.10	14	5	0	1	41	59	57	51	30	19
*Fajaldo, Albergio	0	1	10.98	13	0	0	0	20	26	26	24	21	12
*Gordon, Little Anthony	1	6	9.30	15	5	0	0	40	52	52	41	36	33
*Higgins, Steve	0	1	19.06	4	0	0	0	6	17	14	12	5	3
Magill, James	1	6	5.27	15	9	0	0	55	54	38	32	51	47
Nunez, Ramon	0	3	8.55	12	1	0	0	20	26	24	19	28	10
Pemberton, Jose	0	1	11.40	10	1	0	0	15	26	32	19	30	15
Poissant, Rod	0	0	3.86	3	0	0	0	5	4	2	2	2	2
*Riley, Ed	1	4	4.06	9	6	2	1	44	39	29	20	34	41
Saldana, Dan	2	2	2.39	8	7	2	0	49	40	22	13	24	44
Santana, Eleuterio	0	1	11.57	10	0	0	0	9	12	16	12	14	6
Schula, Mike	1	2	7.59	7	0	0	0	11	10	13	9	5	9
Tejada, Joaquin	1	4	7.77	12	6	1	0	49	72	53	42	36	29
Webb, Scott	0	1	5.31	8	1	0	1	20	15	13	12	17	19

AND THERE'S MORE . . .

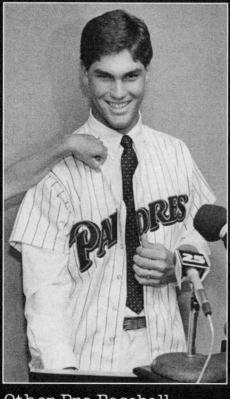

Other Pro Baseball

College Baseball

Amateur Baseball

The 1988 Draft

These Reds are finishing in first every season

By KEN LEIKER

The Mexico City Reds won their second straight league championship in 1988 and third in the last four seasons.

The Reds captured the South Zone title with the best record in the league (82-45), then cruised through three best-of-7 playoff series with a 12-2 record.

Jesus Rios
...21 wins

The Reds defeated Saltillo in five games in the championship series. Former major leaguers Fernando Arroyo and Salome Barojas pitched a combined 1-0 shutout in the decisive game.

Barojas then left to join the Philadelphia Phillies. He had 17 saves during the season and five in the playoffs.

Saltillo finished fourth in the North Zone with a 59-68 record, qualifying for the playoffs by one-half game. The Sarape Makers eliminated champion Laredo in six games and second-place Monterrey in five to advance to the championship series.

Fifth title for Reyes

The championship was the fifth for Reds manager Cananea Reyes, a league record. Reyes, in his 14th year as a manager in the league, recorded his 1,000th victory during the season. He also was criticized heavily by media and fans when the Reds lost a doubleheader while he was attending a political rally, although the club had approved his absence.

The Reds' best offensive player was long-time star third baseman Nelson Barrera. He led the league in RBIs (124), was third in home runs (31) and batting average (.372) and was indirectly responsible for a 1 million pesos ($455) fine levied against the Mexico City Tigers.

The Tigers accused Barrera of using an illegal bat, but the umpires did not agree. The league fined the Tigers for "defaming" Barrera and the Reds.

Laredo was the host for the all-star game, which was played on the American side of the border towns which share the Owls' home games.

The North scored an 8-0 victory. Enrique Aguilar of

League Champions

(Playoff Champions, Where Applicable)

1988—M.C. Reds	1977—Nuevo Laredo	1965—M.C. Tigers
1987—M.C. Reds	1976—M.C. Reds	1964—M.C. Reds
1986—Puebla	1975—Tampico	1963—Puebla
1985—M.C. Reds	1974—M.C. Reds	1962—Monterrey
1984—Yucatan	1973—M.C. Reds	1961—Veracruz
1983—Campeche	1972—Cordoba	1960—M.C. Tigers
1982—Ciudad Juarez	1971—Jalisco	1959—M.C. Reds
1981—*M.C. Reds	1970—Aguila	1958—Nuevo Laredo
—*Reynosa	1969—Reynosa	1957—M.C. Reds
1980—No champion	1968—M.C. Reds	1956—M.C. Reds
1979—Puebla	1967—Jalisco	1955—M.C. Tigers
1978—Aguascalientes	1966—M.C. Tigers	*co-champions

Aguascalientes, who hit a three-run homer, was selected the game's most valuable player.

Close race for bat crown

For the first time in five years, it did not take a plus-.400 batting average to lead the league.

Nick Castaneda, who never escaped Class A in five seasons in the Pittsburgh Pirates organization, won the title with a .374 average in one of the closest races ever. Five points separated the top five hitters.

The home run champion with 36 was Leo Hernandez of Union Laguna, who later joined Milwaukee's Double-A team in El Paso. Former Atlanta Braves farmhand Mike Cole led the league with 80 stolen bases.

Lefthander Dave Walsh of Laredo, on loan from the Toronto Blue Jays organization, was the ERA champion (1.73) and had a 14-1 record and a 17-strikeout game. But Walsh, 27, faltered in the playoffs, giving up seven runs in 2⅔ innings.

The dominant pitcher in the league was righthander Jesus "Chito" Rios of the Tigers, who led in victories (21-6), strikeouts (195) and innings (234), and was second in ERA (2.31). Rios, 24, has had brief minor league trials with the Phillies, Yankees and Angels.

Hanging 'em up

Jack Pierce, the most prolific American power hitter in league history, retired during the 1988 season to become a scout with the Braves, his original team in the States. Pierce hit 294 homers in Mexico, including a record 54 in 1986.

Derek Bryant, who hit 123 home runs from 1984-87, also retired. Bryant, who played in the major leagues with the Athletics, took a position as a scout for the Brewers, which led to him becoming the manager at Monterrey, which has a working agreement with Milwaukee.

Former major leaguers Cesar Cedeno, Al Chambers and Doug Frobel joined the league in 1988, but Cedeno's stay was short. He left Saltillo after a week, saying he could not adjust to the 5,000-feet altitude.

Willie Aikens, who set league records in 1986 for average (.454) and RBIs (154), returned for his third season, but no longer had the small park and light air of Puebla to aid his offense. The franchise was moved to Guadalajara, Mexico's second-largest city, and renamed Jalisco. The park was much bigger, and Aikens hit the first 18 of his 30 homers on the road.

Attendance in Guadalajara was 270,000, compared to 125,000 in Puebla in 1987. It might have been higher, but Jalisco fans boycotted several games after the team's best pitcher, German Jimenez (14-2, 2.72 ERA), was sold to the Atlanta Braves in late June.

North	W	L	Pct.	GB		
Laredo	77	51	.602	—		
San Luis Potosi	64	62	.508	12		
Monterrey	62	69	.473	16½		
Saltillo	59	68	.465	17½		
Union Laguna	59	69	.461	18		
Aguascalientes	54	72	.429	22		
Monclova	47	84	.359	31½	1988	
South					Final	
Mexico City Reds	82	45	.646	—	Standings	
Jalisco	75	55	.577	8½		
Mexico City Tigers	72	56	.563	10½		
Yucatan	70	56	.556	11½		
Leon	68	63	.519	16		
Campeche	62	65	.488	20		
Tabasco	46	82	.359	36½		

1988: General Information

Playoffs: Saltillo defeated Laredo 4-2, Monterrey defeated San Luis Potosi 4-1, Mexico City Reds defeated Yucatan 4-1 and Jalisco defeated Mexico City Tigers 4-2 in best-of-7 quarterfinals; Saltillo defeated Monterrey 4-1 and Mexico City Reds defeated Jalisco 4-0 in best-of-7 semifinals; Mexico City Reds defeated Saltillo 4-1 in best-of-7 final for league championship.

Regular Season Attendance: Yucatan, 285,869; Jalisco, 270,500; San Luis Potosi, 220,843; Union Laguna, 178,831; Nuevo Laredo 160,253; Mexico City Tigers, 155,580; Mexico City Reds, 153,460; Saltillo, 152,580; Leon, 151,635; Monclova, 145,980; Campeche, 144,321; Monterrey, 141,258; Aguascalientes, 120,000; Tabasco, 115,148.

Managers: Aguascalientes—Sergio Robles; **Campeche**—Francisco Estrada; **Jalisco**—Carlos Paz; **Laredo**—Jose Guerrero; **Leon**—Obed Placencia; **Mexico City Reds**—Ben Reyes; **Mexico City Tigers**—Alfredo Ortiz; **Monclova**—Miguel Sotelo, Aurelio Monteagudo; **Monterrey**—Lee Sigman, Derek Bryant; **Saltillo**—Victor Fabela, Sergio Robles; **San Luis Potosi**—Gregorio Luque; **Tabasco**—Miguel Solis; **Union Laguna**—Alfredo Rios, Mark Weidemaier; **Yucatan**—Roberto Castellon.

1988: Batting, Pitching Statistics

INDIVIDUAL BATTING LEADERS

(Minimum 356 Plate Appearances)

	AVG	G	AB	R	H	2B	3B	HR	RBI	BB	SO	SB
Nick Castaneda, Yuc	.374	94	321	76	120	25	0	23	78	72	52	1
Nelson Barrera, MCR	.372	129	460	90	171	26	0	31	124	50	51	7
Trench Davis, Mty	.371	127	472	81	175	23	5	2	51	43	46	34
Darryl Motley, UL	.370	87	324	67	120	14	1	17	61	31	52	14
David Villagomez, Ags	.369	119	439	65	162	35	5	8	65	38	55	2
David Stockstill, Jal	.356	130	472	121	168	30	2	18	89	82	39	4
Willie Aikens, Jal	.352	126	412	96	145	27	1	30	119	112	60	0
Greg Smith, Sal	.351	105	387	77	136	28	3	19	66	40	54	23
Harold Perkins, Leon	.351	132	524	101	184	33	15	7	70	60	93	43
Juan Reyes, SLP	.347	121	455	80	158	34	1	23	96	46	94	0
Daniel Fernandez, MCR	.347	119	427	108	148	24	2	9	39	84	50	52
Leo Hernandez, UL	.345	127	455	88	157	19	0	36	125	63	35	10
Enrique Aguilar, Ags	.343	122	452	104	155	27	2	35	115	43	50	8
Donald Cosey, Mva-Leo	.340	132	514	92	175	42	5	17	111	54	51	8
Marco Antonio Guzman, Cam	.336	129	446	73	150	31	3	18	94	65	52	2
Armando Sanchez, MCR	.334	117	461	77	154	25	6	8	67	44	33	6

INDIVIDUAL BATTING

(U.S. Players and Players with 300 At-Bats)

	AVG	G	AB	R	H	2B	3B	HR	RBI	BB	SO	SB
Derek Bryant, Mty	.357	46	126	26	45	9	0	5	26	29	18	3
Darryl Rector, Sal	.356	16	59	7	21	1	1	0	2	3	10	1
Lemmie Miller, Sal	.344	17	64	12	22	4	0	0	7	9	8	2
Wes Clements, Yuc	.340	66	235	39	80	15	1	15	54	35	59	0
Orlando Sanchez, Jal	.332	127	443	84	147	22	2	24	98	69	52	0
Mike Cole, Cam	.331	124	480	109	159	17	14	2	42	59	20	80
Francisco Guerrero, UL	.327	129	495	101	162	23	2	3	37	68	66	45
Leonardo Valenzuela, Mva	.327	128	443	91	145	23	6	20	83	75	80	24
Luis Fernando Diaz, Lar	.325	124	495	74	161	28	5	7	46	35	83	14
Juan Pacho, Yuc	.324	89	361	58	117	14	2	0	33	27	35	5
Eddie Castro, Leon	.321	131	421	105	135	29	1	33	106	117	93	2
Manuel Cazarin, Leon	.321	116	390	66	125	35	2	6	55	38	42	1
Sergio Vizcarra, SLP	.321	92	386	68	124	22	7	4	38	27	14	16
Jesus Sommers, Leon	.319	124	457	68	146	26	1	10	75	57	54	0
Max Venable, Yuc	.319	13	47	14	15	0	1	1	8	7	5	1
Joel Serna, Mva	.318	123	469	87	149	22	1	15	73	59	64	9
Lorenzo Bundy, MCR	.317	89	315	60	100	20	2	11	60	52	31	5
Jeff Brown, MCT	.317	37	123	23	39	13	0	6	20	6	21	0
Antonio Lopez, Tab-Ags	.313	127	483	65	151	20	2	22	82	27	58	10
Juan Navarrete, Sal	.313	104	419	58	131	12	3	1	44	18	21	0
Gerardo Sanchez, Lar	.311	129	483	85	150	25	1	12	55	41	48	14
Francisco Javier Arce, SLP	.310	123	436	87	135	22	2	22	95	64	74	0
Felix Garzon, Cam	.310	123	442	58	137	19	1	14	81	33	60	1
Victor Quintero, Tab	.310	97	361	36	112	16	2	2	29	24	14	4
Alonso Tellez, MCR	.310	127	500	86	155	25	1	17	95	34	53	8
Roberto Vizcarra, Leon	.310	124	471	85	146	24	3	3	60	47	42	29
Andres Mora, Lar	.308	85	299	51	92	13	1	21	67	40	35	2
Carlos Villela, Ags	.306	116	461	78	141	17	11	4	52	23	62	3
Alejandro Cruz, Lar	.305	116	413	84	126	18	0	31	86	71	53	11
Guadalupe Quintero, Leon	.305	103	308	47	94	14	4	6	49	23	36	3
Fernando Villaescusa, Yuc	.304	104	391	51	119	11	2	1	31	26	14	12
Jose Perez, Tab	.303	110	356	44	108	19	1	5	36	52	58	3
Marco Antonio Romero, Jal	.301	96	329	38	99	9	6	3	44	19	49	5
Juan Rodriguez, Yuc	.301	127	469	82	141	15	1	3	47	57	14	11
Carlos Valencia, Ags	.301	118	422	58	127	23	5	10	67	27	44	1
Tony Walker, Lar	.301	105	366	57	110	11	7	2	38	48	54	28
Doug Frobel, MCR	.299	58	197	29	59	11	0	10	38	25	55	3
Luis Alfonso Cruz, SLP	.299	104	384	69	115	18	5	14	54	26	46	4
Pablo Machiria, MCT	.298	107	372	52	111	21	2	14	57	25	46	2
Ossie Olivares, Tab-MCT-Sal	.298	114	406	70	121	18	8	0	35	60	32	8

	AVG	G	AB	R	H	2B	3B	HR	RBI	BB	SO	SB
Guillermo Rodriguez, Jal . . .	.298	129	493	70	147	27	3	22	95	22	83	3
Cesar Cedeno, Sal	.297	11	37	4	11	1	0	0	5	8	8	0
David Dominguez, SLP	.296	123	453	83	134	25	3	22	101	59	74	0
Ruben Navarro, UL	.296	118	385	46	114	21	2	3	33	46	61	6
Martin Morones, Mva	.295	106	356	67	105	13	6	5	43	28	48	22
Andres Sanchez, MCR	.295	110	312	42	92	8	2	3	33	31	51	8
Baltazar Valdes, Mva-Mty . .	.295	128	438	59	129	17	1	17	84	44	67	1
Eduardo Torres, Sal	.294	120	405	66	119	20	4	17	82	57	83	5
Ed Amelung, MCT	.293	16	58	7	17	3	0	1	7	5	8	0
Alejandro Lizarraga, Jal	.291	88	309	30	90	12	2	4	34	20	26	1
Martin Arzate, Jal	.290	113	396	75	115	6	7	1	25	62	34	10
Julian Wong, Sal	.289	82	256	25	74	10	6	0	24	23	23	2
Jose Juan Bellazetin, MCT . .	.288	126	423	67	122	17	2	9	56	103	43	15
Eddie Bronson, Yuc	.288	67	233	33	67	12	0	4	25	24	25	4
Ricardo Saenz, Sal	.288	120	417	75	120	21	6	2	53	37	43	10
Luis Alberto Valdez, Mty . . .	.287	118	411	63	118	15	3	0	43	34	37	2
Al Chambers, MCT-Ags-Mty .	.285	70	228	28	65	19	0	7	38	41	50	4
Manuel Baca, MCR	.284	114	402	54	114	16	2	16	67	27	49	3
Jose Quiroz, MCT	.284	106	348	37	99	21	1	7	44	28	58	0
Miguel Serratos, Cam	.284	104	356	39	101	11	1	15	48	18	57	0
Ricardo Valenzuela, Sal	.283	92	300	29	85	8	0	4	31	20	44	3
Felipe Gutierrez, Mcr	.282	122	443	53	125	23	2	10	59	15	46	5
Alfonso Rosario, Mva-Cam . .	.282	127	447	71	126	19	3	19	79	65	61	9
Jesus Gonzalez, Jal	.281	130	524	85	147	26	2	5	68	41	29	1
Raymundo Torres, Yuc	.280	121	436	78	122	24	1	25	93	54	87	2
Fernando Elizondo, Tab-Yuc .	.279	114	430	55	120	25	1	4	43	29	31	6
Antonio Aguilera, Mty	.277	128	466	80	129	17	12	8	47	39	77	25
Glen Walker, Cam-Mva	.277	77	267	45	74	14	1	14	60	39	51	3
Guadalupe Leal, UL	.276	116	373	49	103	18	3	11	47	34	60	5

INDIVIDUAL PITCHING LEADERS
(Minimum 106 Innings)

	W	L	ERA	G	GS	CG	SV	IP	H	R	ER	BB	SO
Dave Walsh, Lar	14	1	1.73	18	18	9	0	125	82	28	24	77	141
Jesus Rios, MCT	21	6	2.31	30	28	19	0	234	192	69	60	63	195
Mercedes Esquer, Yuc	14	6	2.45	28	27	15	0	217	201	69	59	55	127
Alfonso Pulido, MCR	11	4	2.52	19	19	12	0	139	150	41	39	23	60
Jesus Moreno, Lar	17	6	2.59	25	25	19	0	205	164	70	59	47	105
Ricardo Solis, Sal	17	11	2.60	32	30	21	0	231	238	77	67	49	152
Angel Moreno, MCT	13	10	2.68	27	27	12	0	201	198	73	60	60	119
Herminio Dominguez, Cam . .	9	7	2.71	25	25	5	0	160	159	72	48	62	93
German Jimenez, Jal	14	2	2.72	18	18	12	0	149	173	55	45	32	95
Roberto Osuna, Mty	8	7	2.85	49	6	1	0	123	99	44	39	49	105
Miguel Solis, Tab	7	7	2.95	20	19	7	0	122	128	50	40	37	47
Ben Morrow, MCR	11	2	2.96	24	20	5	0	140	135	52	46	50	77
Jeff Perry, UL	10	6	3.15	59	1	0	12	109	96	41	38	43	108
Ildefonso Velazquez, Cam . .	12	13	3.22	27	27	14	0	179	189	78	64	48	72

INDIVIDUAL PITCHING
(U.S. Players and Players with 100 innings)

	W	L	ERA	G	GS	CG	SV	IP	H	R	ER	BB	SO
Robert Moore, Leon	1	0	2.25	11	0	0	0	15	17	4	4	5	5
Jeff Zaske, SLP	0	3	2.63	20	1	0	5	27	21	10	8	18	24
Salome Barrojas, MCR	14	4	3.14	51	0	0	17	103	89	40	36	54	60
Jeff Perry, UL	10	6	3.15	59	1	0	12	109	96	41	38	43	108
Freddie Arroyo, MCR	2	2	3.31	5	5	1	0	33	30	12	12	6	13
Arturo Gonzalez, Mty	13	12	3.35	26	26	15	0	191	191	93	71	47	133
Adolfo Navarro, Mty	4	13	3.40	25	25	7	0	151	137	64	57	52	137
Isaac Jimenez, MCT	11	9	3.41	32	21	5	1	142	140	67	54	78	89
Jim Hickey, Mty	4	2	3.51	18	1	0	5	33	32	14	13	11	12
Eleazar Beltran, Sal-Cam . .	9	6	3.51	23	23	4	0	123	139	58	48	68	57
Luis Fernando Mendez, MCR	14	5	3.61	24	24	6	0	152	132	68	61	71	83
Jaime Orozco, Lar	16	13	3.71	30	26	16	1	201	200	94	83	43	118
Martin Raygoza, Cam	12	13	3.73	28	27	9	0	188	186	91	78	68	83
Luis Alfonso Velazquez, Leon	11	9	3.76	27	26	10	0	175	191	106	73	86	136
Julio Cesar Miranda, Sal . . .	9	11	3.83	38	20	4	5	148	158	74	63	87	125
Francisco Sombra, UL	11	11	3.88	33	28	8	0	169	179	83	73	56	93
Luis Enrique Huerta, Cam . .	5	6	3.90	29	16	3	0	127	134	62	55	48	53
Ramon Villegas, Yuc	9	8	3.90	41	9	2	6	111	120	67	48	32	44
Mark Torrence, Tab	1	2	3.91	16	2	0	3	25	29	12	11	11	13
Juan Ontiveros, SLP	11	4	3.91	49	1	1	2	104	116	56	45	36	43
Andres Cruz, Yuc	13	9	3.92	26	25	8	0	172	150	82	75	88	106
Aurelio Zamudio, MCT	13	10	3.93	27	25	7	0	172	183	81	75	65	68
Javier Carranza, Lar	12	11	3.94	25	24	16	0	185	197	96	81	72	102
Guadalupe Chavez, Leon . . .	10	10	4.00	31	20	6	3	133	146	64	59	47	59
Hilario Renteria, UL	13	10	4.03	27	27	5	0	181	200	104	81	53	70
Encarnacion Hernandez, UL .	10	9	4.14	33	22	6	0	163	182	87	75	41	68
Martin Torres, Jal-Tab	7	14	4.22	29	24	7	0	171	207	94	80	59	77
Martin Hernandez, MCR . . .	12	7	4.23	30	28	10	1	192	179	101	90	87	100
John Ludy, Mty	7	6	4.27	23	22	4	0	137	129	72	65	42	85
Armando Reynoso, Sal	11	11	4.30	32	29	10	0	180	176	98	86	85	92
Francisco Montano, Ags-Yuc	11	5	4.34	29	21	6	0	141	140	75	68	49	81
Mario Alberto Rodriguez, Sal .	7	9	4.35	42	10	4	5	114	130	67	55	49	52
Gustavo Delgadillo, Ags . . .	9	8	4.39	27	26	7	0	150	201	95	73	38	43
Kevin Devine, MCT	5	5	4.48	17	12	4	0	84	94	50	42	37	47
Rafael Garcia, Ags	11	10	4.53	27	26	10	1	183	176	111	92	78	152

Lions roar through series for third straight year

By WAYNE GRACZYK

The Pacific League champion Seibu Lions won their third straight Japan Series title by defeating the Central League champ Chunichi Dragons, 4-1, extending their dominance in the Japanese pro baseball world.

The Lions had won the P.L. pennant on the final day of the year, when the rival Kintetsu Buffaloes tied their season-ending game with the Lotte Orions. Because of the Japanese system of counting tie games, the Buffaloes finished second despite having more wins than Seibu. Chunichi coasted to the C.L. crown by 12 games over the Yomiuri Giants.

While the Lions continued their run of success, it was a season of change in Japan.

The change started before the season, with the opening of the 50,000-seat Tokyo Dome, Japan's first domed stadium. The Dome, nicknamed "The Big Egg," was the site of the Mike Tyson-Tony Tubbs heavyweight title fight in March, then opened for baseball with a 12-

Bill Gullickson
... 14-9, 3.10

team preseason tournament. The Dome was the home field for the Yomiuri Giants and the Nippon Ham Fighters.

Several newcomers were among the 21 U.S. players who opened the season in Japan, including ex-big leaguers Bill Gullickson, Bill Madlock and Doug DeCinces.

Ponce top slugger

Puerto Rico native Carlos Ponce, formerly of the Milwaukee Brewers, won the home run and RBI titles in the Central League with totals of 33 and 102, respectively. His Taiyo Whales teammate Jim Paciorek was runner-up in the batting race with a .332 average.

Former California Angels farmhand Ty Van Burkleo of the Seibu Lions was second in the Pacific League home-run derby with 38. Ralph Bryant, a one-time Los Angeles Dodger, socked 34 homers and drove in 73 runs in a little more than half a season in leading the Buffaloes to P.L. flag contention.

Times weren't so happy for two other U.S. players. Kintetsu Buffaloes first baseman Dick Davis was arrested June 7 for possession of marijuana. Davis, who had played in Japan since 1984, was immediately suspended by the team, and later was released.

Less than a month later, the Hanshin Tigers made the most controversial move of the year, releasing popular American Randy Bass. Bass told the Tigers June 27 that he would stay with his hospitalized eight-year-old son, rather than return to the team. Then on July 19, Tigers general manager Shingo Furuya leaped to his death from the eighth floor of a Tokyo hotel. Furuya was believed to be under pressure from management to get an agreement with Bass.

Another controversial move came after the season, when Japanese home run king Sadaharu Oh resigned as the Giants' manager. While the move was announced as a resignation, it was widely believed Oh was fired.

The year also saw the end of Masayuki Kakefu's playing

career. Kakefu, the Hanshin Tigers' third baseman, was one of the most popular players in Japan.

Dragons relief ace Genji Kaku (Kuo Yuan-tzu of Taiwan) was named Central League MVP with a 7-6 record, 1.95 ERA and a Japan-record 37 saves in 61 appearances. The Pacific League player of the year was Nankai Hawks DH Hiromitsu Kadota, 40, who had 44 home runs with 125 RBIs while batting .310.

Like U.S. baseball, Japanese baseball will welcome a new commissioner in 1989. Juhei Takeuchi, 79, stepped down in June after two years on the job, citing ill health. A replacement was scheduled to be named in the spring.

Central League

	W	L	T	Pct.	GB
Chunichi Dragons..	79	46	5	.632	—
Yomiuri Giants	68	59	3	.535	12
Hiroshima Carp	65	62	3	.512	15
Taiyo Whales	59	67	4	.468	20½
Yakult Swallows ...	58	69	3	.457	22
Hanshin Tigers	51	77	2	.398	29½

Pacific League

	W	L	T	Pct.	GB
Seibu Lions	73	51	6	.589	—
Kintetsu Buffaloes .	74	52	4	.587	—
Nippon Ham Fighters .	62	65	3	.488	12½
Hankyu Braves	60	68	2	.469	15
Nankai Hawks	58	71	1	.450	17½
Lotte Orions	54	74	2	.422	21

1988 Final Standings

1988: General Information

Playoffs: Seibu defeated Chunichi 4-1 in best-of-7 Japan Series.
Managers: Chunichi—Senichi Hoshino; **Hanshin**—Minoru Murayama; **Hiroshima**—Junro Anan; **Taiyo**—Takeshi Koba; **Yakult**—Junzo Sekine; **Yomiuri**—Sadaharu Oh; **Hankyu**—Toshiharu Ueda; **Kintetsu**—Akira Ogi; **Lotte**—Michiyo Arito; **Nippon Ham**—Shigeru Takada; **Nankai**—Tadashi Sugiura; **Seibu**—Masaaki Mori.

1988: Batting, Pitching Statistics

INDIVIDUAL BATTING LEADERS
(U.S. players only)

	AVG	G	AB	R	H	HR	RBI
Warren Cromartie, Giants, of	.333	49	186	31	62	10	36
Jim Paciorek, Whales, 1b-of	.332	130	497	58	165	17	76
Randy Bass, Tigers, 1b	.321	22	78	9	25	2	8
Tony Bernazard, Hawks, 2b	.315	111	438	71	138	20	60
Ben Oglivie, Buffaloes, of	.311	114	392	61	122	22	65
Ralph Bryant, Buffaloes, of	.307	74	267	50	82	34	73
Mike Easler, Fighters, dh	.304	97	355	47	108	19	58
Dick Davis, Buffaloes, 1b	.303	42	152	16	46	7	22
Gary Rajsich, Dragons, 1b-of	.293	101	358	56	105	16	53
Carlos Ponce, Whales, of	.292	130	497	79	145	33	102
Boomer Wells, Braves, 1b	.289	88	339	48	98	14	46
Randy Johnson, Carp, 3b	.285	41	144	16	41	3	12
Ty Van Burkleo, Lions, of	.268	118	366	67	98	38	90
George Wright, Hawks, of	.263	89	300	31	79	11	27
Bill Madlock, Orions, dh	.263	123	437	47	115	19	61
Ruppert Jones, Tigers, 1b-of	.254	52	169	19	43	8	27
Doug DeCinces, Swallows, 1b-3b	.244	84	291	39	71	19	44
Brian Dayett, Fighters, of	.243	35	115	11	28	4	13
Dallas Williams, Braves, of	.242	100	363	38	88	10	30
Rick Lancellotti, Carp, of	.189	79	264	33	50	19	50
Terry Harper, Swallows, of	.143	10	35	5	5	2	6

INDIVIDUAL PITCHING LEADERS
(U.S. Players only)

	W	L	ERA	G	CG	SV	IP	ER	BB	SO
Matt Keough, Tigers	12	12	2.76	28	7	0	180	55	45	97
Bill Gullickson, Giants	14	9	3.10	26	14	0	203	70	51	134
Bob Gibson, Swallows	7	11	4.87	23	4	0	140	76	70	76

Escogido players, including MVP Rufino Linares (center) celebrate their Caribbean World Series championship.

Regan managerial debut a tough act to follow

By KEN LEIKER

The Dominican Republic, buoyed by a strong pitching staff, cruised to the championship of the 18th Caribbean World Series, the culmination of winter league seasons in four nations.

The tournament was held Feb. 4-9 in Santo Domingo, the capital of the Dominican Republic. Each team played six games, two each against the other nations.

Host Escogido clinched the championship in its fifth game with a 2-1 victory over Venezuela, represented by Caracas.

Escogido finished with a 4-2 record. Mexico (Tijuana) and Puerto Rico (Mayaguez) had 3-3 records, and Venezuela was 2-4.

It was the sixth title for a Dominican entry since the Series resumed—without Cuba—in 1970,

Phil Regan
... successful debut

but the first for a Dominican team other than Licey, the capital city's other team.

Regan engineered triumph

The architect of Escogido's championship was former major league pitcher Phil Regan, 50 years old and managing for the first time in his professional career.

Regan set his pitching rotation so that major leaguers Jose DeLeon (Cardinals) and Jose Nunez (Blue Jays) would face Puerto Rico, the pretournament favorite.

DeLeon and Royals farmhand Luis Encarnacion limited Puerto Rico to four hits in a 3-2 victory that was decided by Stan Javier's single in the 11th inning.

Puerto Rico beat the Dominicans 5-1 in the final game—a day after the title had been decided. Expos farmhand Hiti Rojas pitched instead of Nunez, and most of the Dominican regulars were on the bench, recovering from the celebration.

The Dominican staff compiled a 1.80 ERA—more than half a run lower than any other team. One of the key contributors was former major leaguer Ramon de los Santos, a lefthanded

— 227 —

reliever who faced six batters and recorded seven outs.

The Dominican team batting average of .207 was the lowest in the tournament. The only players to hit more than .200 were Javier (.421, four RBIs) and former big leaguer Rufino Linares (.389, five RBIs), who was selected the most valuable player in the tournament.

Tom Pagnozzi (Cardinals) of Puerto Rico was the leading hitter in the Series with a .474 average, two home runs and four RBIs. The pitching leaders were DeLeon and Encarnacion, who each worked seven shutout innings.

Only seven home runs were hit in the 12 games, compared to 30, a Series record, a year earlier in Hermosillo, Mexico.

The 1989 Series was awarded to Mazatlan, Mexico.

Economic woes in all four nations continued to threaten the existence of the winter leagues. Many clubs employed fewer U.S. players than the allotted limit because natives can be hired more cheaply.

The Escogido club was taken over by the league during the season and, according to Dominican sources, was able to play in the Series only because of financial help from the Licey ownership.

Dominican Republic

Don McMahon had agreed to be the pitching coach for Escogido during the 1987-88 Dominican season, but he had a fatal heart attack while pitching batting practice for the Los Angeles Dodgers in the summer.

The Dodgers asked special assignment scout Phil Regan to replace McMahon in Escogido. With the club's record at 11-15, Manny Mota, despite his status as a national hero, was fired as manager and replaced by Regan.

Under Regan, Escogido won 20 of its last 32 games, finishing 32-28 and in a third-place tie with Estrellas, behind Licey (38-22) and Aguilas (35-25).

Licey and Aguilas were eliminated in the playoff tournament. Then Escogido beat Estrellas in a best-of-7 series to qualify for the Caribbean World Series.

Stan Javier
... batting titlist

The league's most valuable player was Estrellas catcher Mark Parent (Padres), the home run leader with 10. Javier (Athletics) won the batting title (.363) for the second straight year. Nunez led the league in wins (8-2) and strikeouts (86). Jim Lefebvre (Athletics coach) of Licey was manager of the year.

REGULAR SEASON				
	W	L	Pct.	GB
Licey	38	22	.633	—
Aguilas	35	25	.583	3
Escogido	32	28	.533	6
Estrellas	32	28	.533	6
Azucareros........	27	33	.450	11
Caimanes	16	44	.267	22
PLAYOFFS				
	W	L	Pct.	GB
Escogido	6	3	.667	—
Estrellas	5	4	.556	1
Licey	4	5	.444	2
Aguilas	3	6	.333	3

1987-88 Final Standings

Playoffs: Escogido defeated Estrellas 4-3 in best-of-7 final for league championship.

INDIVIDUAL BATTING LEADERS

(Minimum 100 At-bats)

	AVG	AB	R	H	2B	3B	HR	RBI	BB	SO	SB
Sanchez, Alejandro, Azu ..	.366	101	16	37	3	0	4	25	6	16	2
#Javier, Stanley, Agu	.363	146	30	53	7	2	1	25	32	18	19
Fermin, Felix, Agu	.354	198	37	70	5	4	0	18	25	8	11
*Polonia, Luis, Agu	.339	180	42	61	8	6	1	23	27	29	15
*James, Dion, Est	.333	126	15	42	7	0	0	18	15	9	2
*Orsulak, Joe, Est	.325	237	40	77	10	2	0	26	39	19	11
*Sabino, Miguel, Est	.324	145	22	47	6	3	2	19	16	32	2
Jurak, Ed, Lic	.324	176	18	57	9	2	0	22	25	23	1
#Felix, Junior, Esc	.322	180	25	58	5	4	2	18	24	39	6
*Hamilton, Darryl, Cai	.314	169	24	53	8	1	2	12	18	14	5
Rodriguez, Ruben, Agu ...	.307	179	26	55	8	4	2	37	11	31	0
*Sasser, Mackey, Esc	.305	167	19	51	6	1	2	18	6	5	1
Linares, Rufino, Esc	.304	214	31	65	8	2	6	41	16	28	8
Carreon, Mark, Est	.296	233	38	69	8	1	6	39	15	22	11
Parent, Mark, Cai	.294	221	32	65	11	1	10	37	19	30	4
Borders, Pat, Cai	.290	217	15	63	10	1	1	25	19	32	1
Ramirez, Rafael, Est	.288	191	22	55	9	0	0	19	17	21	3
Cabrera, Francisco, Cai ...	.287	115	12	33	7	0	1	10	4	13	2
Ramos, Domingo, Azu	.286	220	24	63	5	2	0	19	26	11	6
Velarde, Randy, Azu	.285	193	32	55	15	0	6	23	21	40	4
#Dilone, Miguel, Azu	.282	220	37	62	10	3	1	27	38	27	15
Delos Santos, Luis, Esc ...	.276	123	15	34	12	1	1	16	16	16	0
*Sanchez, Pedro, Est	.276	116	19	32	6	0	0	12	13	11	6
Laureano, Francisco, Cai ..	.275	102	17	28	6	2	2	10	21	12	1
Gonzalez, Angel, Agu	.273	132	30	36	5	1	3	17	15	18	1
Bichette, Dante, Azu	.273	216	26	59	6	2	0	12	12	36	3
Castillo, Carmelo, Lic	.266	139	16	37	6	0	2	13	11	22	2
Noboa, Junior, Azu	.264	227	22	60	9	2	1	18	15	20	4
#Destrade, Orestes, Azu ..	.263	137	25	36	3	1	7	24	31	36	0
Garcia, Santiago, Cai	.261	157	15	41	7	1	1	23	6	19	4
Thomas, Andres, Esc	.261	176	21	46	6	0	3	22	6	24	5
*Garcia, Leo, Agu	.260	223	24	58	10	0	1	22	19	21	9
#Castillo, Juan, Agu	.258	132	24	34	9	1	1	13	28	20	3
Mata, Victor, Agu	.258	128	13	33	11	0	0	24	10	15	0
#Lee, Manny, Azu	.254	169	22	43	7	2	1	14	33	24	6
Belliard, Rafael, Lic	.252	163	17	41	5	1	0	17	4	24	1
Yan, Julian, Cai	.251	175	23	44	5	2	6	14	13	51	1
*Steels, James, Est	.251	207	26	52	3	1	1	21	21	18	11
*Cijntje, Sherwin, Est	.250	144	22	36	8	0	0	11	12	26	11
Campusano, Silvestre, Lic .	.250	160	23	40	8	2	4	21	16	31	7
Vargas, Leonel, Est	.248	105	7	26	5	0	0	16	8	16	1
#Liriano, Nelson, Esc	.246	195	26	48	7	2	1	17	25	20	7
Berroa, Geronimo, Esc ...	.243	144	10	35	7	0	0	13	10	20	0
*Marte, Alexis, Azu	.231	134	13	31	2	2	0	8	15	15	7
Norman, Nelson, Cai	.230	139	15	32	4	0	0	10	17	8	5
Roman, Miguel, Cai	.224	134	12	30	5	0	3	18	4	25	1
*Bryant, Ralph, Esc	.216	167	21	36	5	1	4	14	21	40	2

INDIVIDUAL PITCHING LEADERS

(Minimum 35 Innings)

	W	L	ERA	G	GS	CG	SV	IP	H	BB	SO
*Otto, Dave, Lic	5	1	1.27	10	10	0	0	57	49	15	39
Vargas, Jose, Est	5	3	1.57	11	6	2	0	52	41	21	19
Tapia, Jose, Lic	3	1	1.64	20	1	0	3	55	41	21	34
Vaughn, Dwayne, Agu	3	1	1.75	10	9	2	0	62	56	16	42
*Vande Berg, Ed, Esc	2	2	2.02	8	5	0	0	36	34	11	20
Encarnacion, Luis, Esc ...	3	5	2.09	31	0	0	8	52	45	17	30
Nunez, Jose, Esc	8	2	2.26	15	14	3	0	100	78	29	85
Clark, Terry, Azu	4	6	2.32	14	14	2	0	97	91	20	46
Mejia, Cesar, Esc	1	1	2.41	13	4	0	0	37	33	19	17
Rijo, Jose, Lic	4	3	2.55	11	11	1	0	60	47	13	43
Weston, Mickey, Agu	4	2	2.66	26	0	0	2	41	45	10	16
Perez, Melido, Cai	3	5	2.75	14	12	0	0	72	67	22	54
Cano, Jose, Azu	4	4	2.79	12	12	1	0	68	61	26	40
*Finley, Chuck, Azu	3	4	2.80	13	12	2	0	74	64	31	44
Vasquez, Aquedo, Cai	0	3	2.86	18	4	0	0	50	56	22	23
Bautista, Jose, Agu	8	3	2.95	13	13	2	0	85	84	22	30
Araujo, Andy, Lic	5	3	2.95	20	3	0	2	40	35	11	19
*Valdez, Efrain, Lic	5	0	2.96	16	6	0	0	55	45	24	28
*Acker, Larry, Agu	3	3	2.97	25	0	0	0	39	47	11	18
Pawlowski, John, Est	5	3	3.02	24	0	0	8	42	39	18	25
Caraballo, Felix, Lic	3	2	3.18	19	3	2	1	57	57	22	37
Perez, Pascual, Lic	2	5	3.32	10	10	1	0	65	61	11	42
Deleon, Jose, Esc	3	4	3.34	10	10	0	0	57	56	20	53
Peterson, Adam, Est	5	4	3.38	15	15	2	0	88	92	23	39
Mesa, Jose, Lic	5	1	3.39	11	11	0	0	64	59	34	37
*Hall, Grady, Est	7	6	3.40	16	15	3	0	103	109	24	49
Cook, Mike, Azu	6	3	3.42	13	13	0	0	79	78	31	36
Barrett, Tim, Esc	5	3	3.42	28	3	1	0	50	43	23	22
Pena, Ramon, Agu	6	5	3.46	24	0	0	4	52	51	14	31
Rivas, Martin, Azu	5	5	3.66	32	0	0	7	47	50	14	30
*Alba, Gibson, Azu	1	3	3.89	28	1	0	0	42	38	24	22
Danek, Bill, Agu	2	3	3.95	14	13	1	0	73	78	31	36

Puerto Rico

Mayaguez finished second in the Puerto Rican League regular season, three games behind Santurce. The clubs also were the playoff finalists, and Mayaguez won a best-of-7 series to advance to the Caribbean World Series.

Mayaguez was managed by Jim Riggleman, who was the Cardinals manager at Double-A Arkansas in 1988, and will be on St. Louis' coaching staff in 1989.

Angels reliever Bryan Harvey, who had 16 saves and a 2.05 ERA for San Juan, was a unanimous selection as the league's most valuable player.

Randy Milligan of Ponce, who was traded from the Mets to the Pirates before the 1988 season, won the batting championship with a .354 average. Ivan Calderon (White Sox) of Ponce was the home run leader (eight), and Francisco Melendez (Giants) the RBI leader (33).

Bryan Harvey
. . . league MVP

Kevin Kennedy (Dodgers) of Santurce was voted manager of the year.

REGULAR SEASON

	W	L	Pct.	GB
Santurce	31	21	.596	—
Mayaguez	29	25	.537	3
Ponce.	27	27	.500	5
San Juan.	25	26	.490	5½
Caguas	24	30	.444	8
Arecibo	23	30	.434	8½

1987-88 Final Standings

PLAYOFFS

	W	L	Pct.	GB
Mayaguez	9	3	.750	—
Santurce	8	4	.667	1
Ponce.	4	8	.333	5
San Juan.	3	9	.250	6

Playoffs: Mayaguez defeated Santurce 4-3 in best-of-7 final for league championship.

INDIVIDUAL BATTING LEADERS
(Minimum 100 At-bats)

	AVG	AB	R	H	2B	3B	HR	RBI	BB	SO	SB
Milligan, Randy, Pon	.347	147	27	51	7	3	4	23	39	37	1
#Cora, Joey, Pon	.328	122	22	40	5	2	0	12	16	11	5
#Quinones, Luis, May	.327	113	17	37	9	1	3	19	6	15	1
Martinez, Carmelo, Cag	.327	101	13	33	9	0	2	18	14	12	1
Perez, Julian, Pon	.320	103	12	33	5	1	3	14	24	9	0
*Johnson, Lance, May	.314	140	19	44	3	2	0	4	2	8	16
Rodriguez, Edwin, Are	.303	175	22	53	4	1	1	24	11	26	3
#Alomar, Roberto, Cag	.302	199	31	60	13	2	3	10	13	16	14
#Alicea, Luis, Are	.297	175	22	52	8	2	0	15	19	11	5
Ortiz, Javier, SJ	.294	160	15	47	11	2	4	19	27	42	0
Romine, Kevin, May	.292	144	12	42	9	0	1	14	12	19	3
Thurman, Gary, Are	.288	160	35	46	8	3	1	8	17	26	14
Howard, Tom, May	.284	116	28	33	10	3	4	19	12	24	2
Hinshaw, George, Sant . . .	.284	102	8	29	2	2	1	10	3	16	2
*Eppard, Jim, SJ	.282	142	8	40	3	0	0	8	13	10	2
Lind, Jose, Sant	.281	160	23	45	7	1	1	9	16	14	9
Palacios, Rey, May	.280	175	28	49	9	0	6	24	26	36	0
Mack, Shane, Pon	.279	183	28	51	6	4	2	8	10	31	14
Diaz, Mario, Cag	.279	147	17	41	4	1	3	17	5	8	0
Cotto, Henry, Cag	.277	195	19	54	12	1	1	21	17	28	12
Kelly, Roberto, Cag	.276	116	23	32	5	2	4	10	13	20	6
Rivera, Luis, May	.276	116	12	32	9	1	0	10	7	10	2
*Cuevas, Angelo, Cag	.274	106	13	29	11	0	0	11	11	15	0
*Weaver, Jim, Are	.273	110	16	30	4	1	2	16	19	25	3
Pagnozzi, Tom, May	.273	143	12	39	6	1	0	20	7	21	0
*Melendez, Francisco, Are .	.268	190	26	51	12	1	6	33	22	19	2

	AVG	AB	R	H	2B	3B	HR	RBI	BB	SO	SB
Pankovits, Jim, May	.266	188	23	50	9	2	5	30	15	29	3
Devereaux, Mike, Sant	.259	166	18	43	8	1	4	21	7	15	6
Beniquez, Juan, Sant	.258	132	24	34	10	2	4	20	15	23	0
Sharperson, Mike, Sant	.256	172	28	44	8	1	1	22	28	21	7
Ortiz, Junior, Pon	.255	157	11	40	5	0	3	18	11	16	1
Abner, Shawn, Pon	.254	181	21	46	8	2	6	27	12	28	3
*Rodriguez, Ferdinand, Are	.250	112	13	28	5	1	1	6	9	8	1
Rossy, Elam, SJ	.250	104	11	26	2	1	0	5	13	9	1
*Sanchez, Orlando, Sant	.250	128	15	32	6	1	4	18	22	25	0
Rivera, Jesus, Are	.248	129	16	32	5	0	4	27	21	26	0
Mercado, Orlando, Cag	.248	165	12	41	8	0	6	26	9	22	1
Bilardello, Dann, Are	.246	167	21	41	10	2	2	15	6	19	1
#Cangelosi, John, May	.246	187	31	46	9	2	4	22	35	19	19
Calderon, Ivan, Pon	.242	161	23	39	9	1	8	24	16	25	4
Bell, Jay, Sant	.241	141	22	34	7	0	4	20	30	25	4
*Jennings, Doug, SJ	.234	145	14	34	15	0	3	18	23	33	0
#Sierra, Ruben, Sant	.231	160	23	37	10	1	6	22	20	33	4
Rodriguez, Victor, Pon	.220	150	8	33	7	0	0	5	13	14	0
#Brumley, Mike, SJ	.218	142	10	31	3	1	1	12	13	24	13
Gutierrez, Jackie, Pon	.217	115	12	25	3	1	1	7	5	15	1
#Nixon, Otis, SJ	.211	109	14	23	5	0	0	11	14	20	12
*Willard, Jerry, Sant	.209	129	16	27	3	0	1	8	28	21	0
Kiefer, Steve, Cag	.207	179	27	37	7	1	6	19	26	37	5

INDIVIDUAL PITCHING LEADERS
(Minimum 35 Innings)

	W	L	ERA	G	GS	CG	SV	IP	H	BB	SO
Alicea, Miguel, SJ	1	1	0.93	20	0	0	0	39	24	6	24
Frohwirth, Todd, Are	6	2	1.30	31	0	0	7	55	44	16	31
*Nieves, Juan, SJ	3	2	1.53	6	6	0	0	35	23	14	37
Heinkel, Don, May	5	3	1.69	13	11	2	0	80	61	17	50
Mathis, Ron, Sant	3	2	2.01	8	8	1	0	40	32	8	27
*Agosto, Juan, May	3	4	2.05	29	0	0	5	44	30	12	37
*Kinnunen, Mike, Cag	5	3	2.22	17	7	3	0	65	51	28	54
Filer, Tom, Cag	2	4	2.31	12	10	1	0	62	61	8	29
Harris, Greg, Pon	3	5	2.32	10	10	1	0	62	50	21	38
Perez, Mike, Sant	6	2	2.45	22	0	0	6	37	26	16	26
Meeks, Tim, May	1	2	2.52	10	5	0	1	36	25	13	21
*Kaiser, Jeff, Sant	4	1	2.73	13	9	0	1	53	52	20	29
Ritter, Reggie, Sant	1	2	2.75	8	6	0	0	39	37	9	20
*Birtsas, Tim, Pon	6	3	2.76	10	10	2	0	65	64	20	37
*Nolte, Eric, Pon	1	3	2.80	6	6	0	0	35	30	10	19
Deleon, Luis, May	6	3	3.07	12	12	2	0	73	64	14	53
*Reed, Marty, SJ	4	2	3.10	11	11	0	0	61	52	28	20
*Krueger, Bill, Sant	6	3	3.17	11	11	2	0	71	77	22	44
*Leeper, Dave, Are	4	5	3.24	10	9	1	0	50	61	14	14
Krawczyk, Ray, Pon	2	4	3.32	10	9	0	0	65	67	20	44
Corbell, Charlie, SJ	4	5	3.36	12	12	0	0	64	58	26	37
*Jeffcoat, Mike, Pon	3	4	3.47	11	9	3	0	60	61	17	33
Davis, Joel, SJ	3	1	3.75	10	10	1	0	50	60	26	33
Oliveras, Francisco, Cag	4	8	3.78	13	13	2	0	83	80	29	44
Buonantony, Rich, May	4	3	4.14	13	13	0	0	72	69	41	25

Venezuela

Lara, heavily stocked with prospects from the Blue Jays, won the Venezuelan League regular season title for the second straight season, but was eliminated in the 12-game playoff round.

Caracas, which tied for second with Magallanes during the regular season, defeated Aragua in the best-of-7 championship series.

Mets coach Bill Robinson, seeking his first experience as a manager, guided Caracas.

A year after leading the league in home runs and RBIs, Cecil Fielder (Blue Jays) of Lara won the batting title with a .389 average.

Leo Hernandez (Brewers) of Aragua led the league in home runs (11) and RBIs (45).

Oswald Peraza (Orioles) of Lara was the ERA champion (1.16), and

Cecil Fielder
... batting champ

Magallanes reliever Jose Villa led the league in wins (9-1). The dominant reliever was Mike Schooler (Mariners) of Caracas, who had 11 saves, a 0.59 ERA and struck out 50 in 46 innings.

Schooler and Andres Galarraga, Caracas' best hitter, did not participate in the Caribbean World Series.

REGULAR SEASON

	W	L	Pct.	GB
Lara	37	23	.617	—
Magallanes	33	27	.550	4
Caracas	33	27	.550	4
Aragua	29	31	.483	8
La Guaira	25	35	.417	12
Zulia	23	37	.383	14

1987-88
Final
Standings

PLAYOFFS

	W	L	Pct.	GB
Caracas	7	5	.583	—
Aragua	7	5	.583	—
Lara	5	7	.417	2
Magallanes	5	7	.417	2

Playoffs: Caracas defeated Aragua 4-2 in best-of-7 final for league championship.

INDIVIDUAL BATTING LEADERS
(Minimum 100 At-bats)

	AVG	AB	R	H	2B	3B	HR	RBI	BB	SO	SB
Fielder, Cecil, Lar	.389	131	25	51	11	0	7	32	32	27	0
Salazar, Luis, LG	.371	197	35	73	11	1	10	39	19	32	7
Galarraga, Andres, Car	.343	102	20	35	6	2	4	21	12	27	2
*Delima, Rafael, Ara	.333	168	29	56	6	5	1	13	29	14	4
#Vizquel, Omar, Car	.332	199	28	66	7	5	1	21	20	16	6
Chavez, Pedro, Mag	.329	216	27	71	14	1	1	18	13	20	7
*Bean, Billy, Mag	.321	193	28	62	15	2	0	19	31	29	4
Paredes, Johnny, Zul	.321	109	26	35	6	1	0	15	12	13	11
Espinoza, Alvaro, Ara	.317	183	25	58	4	2	3	20	4	18	2
Nixon, Donell, Car	.316	133	19	42	7	1	3	16	16	19	10
Manrique, Fred, Lara	.311	190	39	59	12	2	2	32	19	33	1
Sojo, Luis, Lara	.310	197	26	61	8	3	0	30	11	12	1
*Gregg, Tommy, Mag	.308	169	25	52	9	5	0	17	28	17	5
Polidor, Gus, Car	.305	128	11	39	3	0	0	15	8	16	3
Tovar, Raul, LG	.303	152	24	46	6	2	1	20	7	19	3
Hill, Glenallen, Lara	.303	198	32	60	9	2	8	39	20	43	6
Infante, Alexis, Lara	.301	209	34	63	6	2	0	28	28	19	11
*Smith, Dwight, Zul	.301	196	41	59	13	3	2	11	48	38	29
Escobar, Oscar, Lara	.300	100	8	30	5	1	0	13	7	15	1
Gutierrez, Dimas, Mag	.293	198	26	58	13	4	0	22	14	11	5
*Azocar, Oscar, Car	.289	190	10	55	11	3	0	16	6	16	4
Hernandez, Leo, Ara	.286	217	32	62	11	0	11	45	25	18	3
*Mendez, Jesus, Ara	.283	180	21	51	2	3	0	16	17	14	1
*Olivares, Ossie, Ara	.282	142	19	40	7	1	0	9	16	11	0
Naveda, Edgar, Mag	.280	161	9	45	6	0	2	13	11	20	0
*Laya, Ricardo, LG	.277	141	21	39	3	0	0	9	12	16	4
Armas, Tony, Car	.276	123	16	34	5	2	3	21	9	28	3
Oliver, Joe, Ara	.275	189	16	52	8	1	5	32	13	34	0
Santovenia, Nelson, LG . . .	.273	132	9	36	8	0	2	18	9	23	0
Quintana, Carlos, Zul	.273	198	25	54	7	2	3	28	44	31	2
Trillo, Manny, Zul	.268	112	9	30	4	0	2	20	14	13	1
#Caceres, Edgar, Car	.265	226	27	60	7	2	0	16	28	19	7
*Guillen, Ozzie, LG	.263	137	22	36	4	0	0	10	4	11	2
*Ducey, Rob, Lara	.261	226	43	59	15	3	4	36	33	51	3
*Soto, Fernando, Zul	.257	148	16	38	2	1	0	10	15	26	2
#Cartaya, Joel, LG	.253	150	16	38	1	0	0	5	11	13	2
Leiva, Jose, Zul	.252	111	14	28	2	1	1	7	17	18	15
Uribe, Jorge, Car	.247	170	14	42	9	3	1	13	11	45	3
Martinez, Carlos, LG	.246	122	13	30	6	1	3	14	7	34	2
Estrada, Asdrubal, Mag . . .	.245	155	14	38	2	0	0	20	11	19	1
Rincones, Hector, Ara . . .	.238	160	17	38	4	1	0	12	17	8	0
Monasterio, Juan, LG	.236	123	7	29	2	1	0	10	5	18	0
*Justice, Dave, Lara	.234	184	27	43	12	1	4	24	32	36	4
#Berryhill, Damon, Zul	.234	175	15	41	5	1	5	30	19	27	0
Williams, Reggie, Ara . . .	.231	147	20	34	7	1	1	11	15	21	6
Munoz, Omer, Zul	.227	203	19	46	7	1	0	14	3	17	2
Malave, Omar, Lara	.224	125	13	28	3	1	0	8	10	16	2
Zambrano, Eduardo, Zul . . .	.224	152	20	34	9	2	0	14	16	29	6

INDIVIDUAL PITCHING LEADERS
(Minimum 35 Innings)

	W	L	ERA	G	GS	CG	SV	IP	H	BB	SO
Schooler, Mike, Car	4	2	0.59	26	0	0	11	46	27	11	50
Peraza, Oswald, Lar	6	1	1.16	16	7	1	0	62	47	15	42
Maddux, Greg, Zul	7	4	1.49	12	12	4	0	96	82	21	66
Placeres, Ben, Lara	4	0	1.70	17	6	0	0	53	50	26	25
*Wells, Dave, Lara	3	1	1.77	11	0	0	3	20	13	3	25
Heredia, Ubaldo, Car	5	2	1.92	12	12	1	0	80	63	17	38
Lunar, Luis, LG	3	4	1.93	14	7	3	0	61	51	36	36
Clary, Marty, Lara	4	2	1.98	16	9	1	2	77	65	24	39

	W	L	ERA	G	GS	CG	SV	IP	H	BB	SO
*Alvarez, Wilson, Zul	3	3	2.19	10	8	0	0	49	38	33	21
Eichelberger, Juan, Lara . .	5	4	2.20	13	12	1	0	82	66	36	45
*Sanchez, Israel, LG	6	6	2.51	14	12	5	1	90	87	26	53
Bencomo, Omar, Mag	4	3	2.60	11	10	0	0	55	53	15	21
*Sauveur, Rich, Mag	5	3	2.60	14	13	1	0	87	86	27	55
Jones, Barry, Car	6	3	2.79	26	0	0	4	42	38	16	25
*Castillo, Antonio, Lara . . .	6	4	3.00	15	13	0	0	69	70	22	48
*Wyatt, Dave, Car	3	1	3.11	7	7	0	0	38	35	17	16
Hernandez, Angel, LG	4	3	3.11	13	12	0	0	67	72	18	28
Lugo, Urbano, Car	2	1	3.15	9	7	0	0	40	44	17	9
*Charlton, Norm, Ara	6	4	3.35	13	13	1	0	81	75	25	53
Tapia, Jose, Car	3	4	3.80	21	7	0	1	66	46	26	29
Carreno, Amalio, Car	3	7	3.89	14	13	0	0	72	76	37	38
Gonzalez, German, Ara . . .	2	4	4.00	32	0	0	6	36	33	16	35
Nevada, Yonny, Ara	1	2	4.07	13	8	0	0	42	38	23	11
Jones, Odell, LG	2	4	4.17	7	7	2	0	37	40	15	13
Cepeda, Rafael, Zul	1	2	4.17	15	8	0	1	58	62	13	19
Leal, Luis, Lara	6	4	4.18	12	11	0	1	60	63	16	43
Kemp, Hugh, Ara	5	7	4.20	14	14	3	0	86	103	27	62
Espinoza, Roberto, Mag . . .	2	7	4.31	16	13	1	0	77	98	33	34

Mexico

Tijuana had the best record during the regular season (38-19), then eliminated Guaymas, Hermosillo and Navojoa in the playoffs to win its first league title in 30 years.

Tim Leary
. . . developed split-finger

Tijuana, however, was later banished from the Mexican Pacific League for reportedly enticing players from opposing teams to not play their competitive best in games against Tijuana. They sat out the 1988-89 winter league season, reducing the number of clubs to nine.

Tim Leary of the Dodgers, commuting from his home in Santa Monica, Calif., had a 9-0 record and 1.24 ERA for Tijuana. He used the work to develop a split-finger pitch, which helped improve his record with the Dodgers from 3-11 in 1987 to 17-11 in 1988.

Tijuana's best offensive player, outfielder Brady Anderson, also was a commuter from the Los Angeles area. Anderson hit .350 but did not have enough plate appearances to qualify for the batting title. He opened the major league season as Boston's center fielder, and later was traded to the Orioles.

Leary and Anderson did not participate in the Caribbean World Series, where Tijuana got only five extra-base hits and 10 RBIs in 73 at bats from its 3-4-5 hitters, Chris Knabenshue (Padres), Kevin Ward (Phillies) and Nelson Barrera.

Barrera, playing for Culiacan during the regular season, led the league in home runs (16). Knabenshue, playing for Mexicali, was the RBI leader (48) and had 15 homers.

North	W	L	Pct.	GB	
Tijuana	38	19	.667	—	
Mexicali	37	23	.617	2½	
Hermosillo	33	25	.569	5½	
Guaymas	26	33	.441	13	1987-88 Final Standings
Obregon	26	36	.419	14½	
South					
Culiacan	31	27	.534	—	
Navojoa	31	29	.517	1	
Mazatlan	29	28	.509	1½	
Los Mochis	25	35	.417	7	
Guasave	20	41	.328	12½	

Playoffs: Tijuana defeated Hermosillo 5-3 and Navojoa defeated Mazatlan 5-4 in best-of-9 semifinals; Tijuana defeated Navojoa 4-0 in best-of-7 final for league championship.

Stanford hits hot streak just in time to repeat

By DANNY KNOBLER

Not since the University of Southern California won five straight titles from 1970-74 had a team won back-to-back College World Series championships. Many of those champions didn't even return to Omaha to defend their titles.

Stanford, its season marked by inconsistent play, almost fell into the same trap in 1988.

The defending champion Cardinal finished a distant second to Arizona State in the Pacific-10 Conference Southern Division. They also lost their regional opener to St. John's, and had to fight back through the losers' bracket, beating Kentucky twice to advance to the College World Series.

**Lee Plemel
... series MVP**

An early loss and lack of hitting at Omaha almost ended Stanford's season prematurely, but in the end the Cardinal turned back Arizona State, 9-4, in an all-Pac 10 final to win the NCAA title for the second year in a row.

They struggled early

Stanford arrived in Omaha as the nation's seventh-ranked team, and opened with a 10-3 win over No. 2-ranked Fresno State. But the Cardinal fell into the losers' bracket with a sloppy loss to Cal State Fullerton, and risked elimination when they went to the ninth inning tied 1-1 with Miami. A costly Hurricane error kept the Cardinal alive.

Because of the Series' new two-division format used to guarantee a one-game final for CBS television, Stanford needed two straight wins over Cal State Fullerton, which had won three of four previous games between the teams in 1988, to advance to the championship game.

College World Series
All Time Champions

1988—Stanford	46-23	1967—Arizona State	53-12
1987—Stanford	53-17	1966—Ohio State	27- 6
1986—Arizona	49-19	1965—Arizona State	54- 8
1985—Miami, Fla.	64-16	1964—Minnesota	31-12
1984—Cal St. Fullerton	66-20	1963—USC	35-10
1983—Texas	66-14	1962—Michigan	34-15
1982—Miami, Fla.	54-18	1961—USC	36- 7
1981—Arizona State	55-13	1960—Minnesota	34- 7
1980—Arizona	43-25	1959—Oklahoma State	27- 5
1979—Cal St. Fullerton	60-14	1958—USC	29- 3
1978—USC	54- 9	1957—California	35-10
1977—Arizona State	57-12	1956—Minnesota	33- 9
1976—Arizona	56-17	1955—Wake Forest	29- 7
1975—Texas	59- 6	1954—Missouri	22- 4
1974—USC	50-20	1953—Michigan	21- 9
1973—USC	51-11	1952—Holy Cross	23- 6
1972—USC	47-13	1951—Oklahoma	19- 9
1971—USC	46-11	1950—Texas	27- 6
1970—USC	45-13	1949—Texas	23- 7
1969—Arizona State	56-11	1948—USC	26- 4
1968—USC	39-12	1947—California	31-10

Stanford coach Mark Marquess hoists the trophy after the Cardinal's second straight NCAA championship.

Senior Lee Plemel, who worked Stanford's opening-game win over Fresno State, pitched the Cardinal to a 4-1 win over the Titans, then gave way to freshmen Mike Mussina and Stan Spencer, who were handed the task of winning Stanford's two biggest games of the year. Coincidentally, Stanford's dormant offense came to life.

After scoring only 19 runs on 25 hits in their first four games, Stanford supported Mussina with a 9-5 win on 10 hits in the semifinal against Cal State Fullerton, and 13 more hits, to back Spencer, in the championship game against Arizona State.

"With this team," said coach Mark Marquess, who would go on to win a gold medal with Team USA at the Olympics, "you don't really know what you're going to get. And it doesn't really matter who's pitching."

Experience wins out

Plemel won the College World Series most valuable player award for his two victories, but Stanford won without individual stars. Plemel, who played in three College World Series, said this group of players might not have been as talented as Stanford's 1985 CWS team, when he was a freshman.

"That was a great group talent-wise," Plemel said of the team that was eliminated in three games. "This isn't any better. It's just a group that works well together. I guess you could call the players we have winners."

They also had the advantage of experience.

"They had an advantage there was no way we could overcome," said losing Arizona State coach Jim Brock. "They had been in the final with the same players, and they won. They came into the park and it was deja vu."

Arizona State won the opposite side of the CWS bracket, whipping Wichita State 19-1 in the other semifinal. But Stanford put the championship game away early, scoring five runs in the first inning off ASU's Rusty Kilgo.

The series attracted a tournament-record 132,698 fans, plus network TV coverage for the title game for the first time.

College Champs

Members of the 1988 College World Series Champion Stanford Cardinal included Top row, l to r, assistant coach Tom Dunton, Mike Mussina, Stan Spencer, Ryan Turner, Jeff Light, Jeff Saenger, Mike Eicher, Ron Witmeyer, Mark Carper, Paul Carey, Ed Sprague, assistant coach Kirk Mason. Middle row, head coach Mark Marquess, Todd French, Brian Johnson, Jack Hollis, Lee Plemel, Doug Robbins, Steve Chitren, Brian Keyser, Eric Cox, Mike Zuercher, Brad Brown, assistant coach Dean Stotz. Bottom row, Scott Weiss, Troy Paulsen, Eric DeGraw, Rob Robbins, team manager Scott Schaeffer, Glenn Stevenson, Tim Griffin, Frank Carey, David Verduzco, Robbie Kamerschen.

Brock named coach of year

Arizona State's loss in the championship game finished an otherwise outstanding season for the Sun Devils, who 3½ years earlier were slapped with a conference probation for abuses in their work-study program. By 1987, they returned to the College World Series, but didn't win a game. In 1988, they won their conference, handily—and nearly won the national title.

Brock, who at times during the probation period wondered if he'd keep his job, was selected Baseball America's 1988 coach of the year for bringing the Sun Devils, five-time CWS champions, back to national prominence.

Stanford became the 22nd Pac-10 South team to win the College World Series. In fact, winning the Pac-10 Southern Division race in 1988 was no easier than winning the national

John Olerud, Washington State's two-way star, was Baseball America's college player of the year.

title. The Six-Pac, as the league calls itself, sent three of its six teams (Stanford, Arizona State and California) to Omaha. A fourth (USC) lost in a regional final.

Two-way performer

Good as the Pac-10 South was in 1988, the division didn't provide college baseball with the top individual performance of 1988. That honor went to the Pac-10's Northern Division, where Washington State sophomore John Olerud put together the most amazing two-way performance in college annals.

As a lefthanded pitcher, Olerud went a perfect 15-0 with a 2.49 ERA. At the plate, he led the Pac-10 North in six of nine offensive categories, running away with the Triple Crown (.449, 22 home runs, 75 RBIs). Baseball America named him a first-team All-American at both pitcher and designated hitter, and presented him with its college player of the year award.

"I'm not real sure," Olerud said when asked whether his professional future is as a pitcher or first baseman. "My freshman year I felt real confident out there pitching. This year I had

1988 All-America Team

John Olerud
Player of Year

Andy Benes
Pitcher of Year

K. Dressendorfer
Freshman of Year

Ben McDonald

Mike Fiore

Jim Campanis

FIRST TEAM

Pos.	Player, School	Yr.	Avg	AB	R	H	2B	3B	HR	RBI	SB
C	Jim Campanis, USC	Jr.	.392	222	57	87	18	2	23	92	0
1B	Lance Shebelut, Fresno State	Sr.	.401	279	97	112	14	2	32	94	1
2B	Kevin Higgins, Arizona State	Jr.	.361	299	88	108	21	3	10	68	11
3B	Robin Ventura, Oklahoma St.	Jr.	.391	230	89	90	16	1	24	88	2
SS	Monty Fariss, Oklahoma St.	Jr.	.397	242	95	96	14	4	30	114	6
OF	Mike Fiore, Miami (Fla.)	Sr.	.397	224	81	89	23	6	15	83	30
	Billy Masse, Wake Forest	Sr.	.422	223	83	94	23	4	24	77	35
	Tom Goodwin, Fresno State	So.	.347	323	87	112	11	4	0	42	62
DH	John Olerud, Washington St.	So.	.464	233	83	108	21	3	23	81	1

Pos.	Player, School	Yr.	W	L	ERA	G	Sv	IP	H	BB	SO
P	Andy Benes, Evansville	Jr.	16	3	1.42	24	2	146	87	36	188
	Ben McDonald, Louisiana St.	So.	13	7	2.65	22	1	119	96	27	144
	Gregg Olson, Auburn	Jr.	7	3	2.00	36	10	72	43	27	113
	John Olerud, Washington St.	So.	15	0	2.49	19	1	123	100	39	113
	Kirk Dressendorfer, Texas	Fr.	15	2	2.26	23	2	136	103	36	134

SECOND TEAM

Pos.	Player, School	Yr.	Avg	AB	R	H	2B	3B	HR	RBI	SB
C	Troy Buckley, Santa Clara	So.	.442	217	54	96	21	0	16	82	0
1B	Turtle Zaun, N.C. State	Sr.	.399	228	74	91	19	0	29	87	0
2B	Mark Standiford, Wichita St.	Sr.	.374	254	81	95	26	1	28	97	3
3B	Ed Sprague, Stanford	Jr.	.339	257	62	87	16	0	22	81	5
SS	Dave Silvestri, Missouri	Jr.	.406	219	89	89	18	8	21	79	17
OF	Tookie Spann, Tulane	Jr.	.376	178	59	67	14	0	21	73	7
	Trey McCoy, Virginia Tech	Jr.	.381	194	70	74	20	2	24	69	3
	Ernie Carr, Jacksonville	Sr.	.440	216	53	95	32	1	9	75	13
DH	Mike Willes, Brigham Young	Sr.	.416	219	86	91	11	0	35	100	4

Pos.	Player, School	Yr.	W	L	ERA	G	Sv	IP	H	BB	SO
P	Eric Stone, Texas	Jr.	15	3	2.85	24	3	133	89	72	140
	Linty Ingram, Arizona St.	Sr.	17	5	3.82	29	2	181	185	52	153
	John Salles, Fresno St.	Jr.	15	2	3.45	25	0	177	168	43	152
	Brian Barnes, Clemson	Jr.	13	2	3.33	22	1	138	124	62	140
	Tim McDonald, C. Michigan	Sr.	16	1	1.83	17	0	108	79	54	87

THIRD TEAM

C—Brian Johnson, Texas. **1B**—Eric Karros, UCLA. **2B**—Ty Griffin, Georgia Tech. **3B**—Don Sparks, Loyola Marymount. **SS**—Bret Barberie, USC. **OF**—Steve Hosey, Fresno State; Ted Wood, New Orleans; Jay Knoblauh, Rice. **DH**—Oneri Fleita, Creighton. **P**—Rich Crane, Fresno State; Dana Allison, James Madison; Scott Erwin, Georgia Tech; Jeff Gidcumb, Florida; Joe Grahe, Miami (Fla.).

Evansville righthander Andy Benes won Baseball America's pitcher-of-the-year award.

a little trouble with my control, and I was hitting well. This year, I'd say hitting. It just depends on whichever I'm doing better at the time."

Florida A&M sophomore Marquis Grissom also turned in a solid two-way season, going 9-3 with a 2.40 ERA as a pitcher, and hitting .448 with 12 homers in his role as an outfielder. He was picked in the third round of the June draft by Montreal—and became a full-time outfielder with the Expos.

Benes: top pitcher

There was little question what Evansville's Andy Benes did best in 1988.

A 6-6, 235-pound former college football and basketball player, Benes specialized in throwing a 95 mph fastball. Overall, he went 16-3 with a 1.42 ERA and led the nation with eight shutouts and 188 strikeouts.

His marked improvement over his first two college seasons earned him Baseball America's 1988 pitcher of the year award. It also earned him the biggest bonus ever given a drafted player ($235,000) when the San Diego Padres chose him No. 1 overall in the June draft.

Benes was just 11-11 with a 5.13 ERA in his first two years at Evansville, but started concentrating only on baseball in the fall of 1987. He struck out 14 in seven innings of a fall game, then caught scouts' attention by fanning 21 in a win over North Carolina Wilmington on March 6. He sewed up the top spot in the draft when he threw a 1-0, eight-hit win against host Arizona State in the NCAA West II Regional.

Benes and most of college baseball's other top players combined to win a gold medal at the 1988 Olympics in Seoul, South Korea.

Texas pitcher Kirk Dressendorfer, meanwhile, earned first-team All-American honors and was named Baseball America's freshman of the year after he went 15-2 with a 2.26 ERA. He became the first freshman since former Longhorn Greg Swindell to win the Southwest Conference player of the year

The Top 25
(Final 1988 Ranking, by Baseball America)

1. Stanford	46-23	14. Washington State	52-14
2. Arizona State	60-13	15. Clemson	53-14
3. Wichita State	56-16	16. Pepperdine	37-24
4. Oklahoma State	61- 8	17. Florida State	50-18
5. Fresno State	56-12	18. USC	36-26
6. Cal State Fullerton	43-18	19. Kentucky	38-25
7. Florida	48-19	20. South Carolina	43-21
8. Miami, Fla.	52-14	21. Santa Clara	43-18
9. California	40-25	22. Nevada-Las Vegas	40-22
10. Texas	58-11	23. Georgia Tech	45-24
11. Texas A&M	52-15	24. Michigan	48-19
12. Mississippi State	44-20	25. Central Michigan	47-15
13. Loyola Marymount	48-18		

award.

But Dressendorfer's Longhorns failed to make the College World Series for the second time in three years. In the previous three-year period, Texas had appeared in the CWS title game each year.

Auburn's Gregg Olson battled mononucleosis over the final half of the college season, but had another solid season as a relief pitcher for the Tigers, winning first-team All-America honors for the second year in a row. He became the fourth player picked in the June draft, and was pitching for the Baltimore Orioles by September.

Cowboys were missing

The biggest surprise of 1988 was that Oklahoma State was missing from the College World Series. The Cowboys had made seven straight trips to Omaha, and were ranked No. 1 by Baseball America for all but one week during the regular season. But Wichita State blasted their hosts 15-5 in the title game of the Midwest regional to earn the trip instead.

Robin Ventura and Monty Fariss, who anchored the left side of the Oklahoma State infield for three years, had All-American seasons for the Cowboys. Ventura hit .391 with 26 home runs and 96 RBIs, while Fariss had an even more productive campaign with a .397 average, 30 home runs and a national-high 114 RBIs. Both were No. 1 draft picks.

Fresno State, despite being eliminated in two straight games at the College World Series, also had a memorable 1988 season. The Bulldogs were ranked No. 1 briefly after winning a school record 32 games—two short of the national record.

Fresno State had three pitchers win at least 14 games, and on offense broke a number of school records—including home runs (Lance Shebelut, 32) and stolen bases (Tom Goodwin, 61). A school record 159,205 fans (47 dates) saw the Bulldogs play at home.

For the second year in a row, Brigham Young's Mike Willes led the nation in homers, with 35. BYU also set a national record by blasting 161 home runs.

Coaching changes

The end of the 1988 season saw several major coaching changes.

Dave Snow, a former Baseball America coach of the year at Loyola Marymount, moved to perennial West Coast doormat Long Beach State. Former Snow assistant Chris Smith was hired at Loyola Marymount. Also in southern California, Dave Gorrie retired at Pepperdine after 29 years of college coaching, and was replaced by former Cal State Dominguez Hills coach Andy Lopez.

Winners again

Lewis Clark State won its fourth championship in five years by beating Grand Canyon 9-3 in the final game of the NAIA

Lance Shebelut broke the Fresno State school record with 32 home runs.

World Series, played on the Warriors' home field in Lewiston, Idaho.

Pitcher Steve Callahan won the final game and the Series MVP award, after going 2-0 with a 1.80 ERA and 17 strikeouts in 15 innings. Washburn outfielder J.P. Wright was selected NAIA player of the year, hitting .483 with 22 home runs and 77 RBIs.

Back in winner's circle

Florida Southern swept through the six-team NCAA Division II World Series in Montgomery, Ala., beating Cal State Sacramento 5-4 in 12 innings in the final game. The Moccasins won their seventh national title, and first since 1985. Outfielder Chris Leach, who was 11-for-16 with six runs scored, was named the tournament MVP.

Tampa first baseman Tino Martinez, meanwhile, was the Division II player. Martinez, the Seattle Mariners' No. 1 draft pick and a U.S. Olympian, hit .453 with 22 home runs and 58 RBIs.

Ithaca wins Division III title

In the NCAA Division III World Series at Bristol, Conn., Ithaca College rallied from a 5-2, seventh-inning deficit to beat Wisconsin-Oshkosh in the final game. The Bombers scored the tying and winning runs on bases-loaded walks in the eighth. Pitcher Joe Sottolano, who threw 2⅓ scoreless innings of relief in the title game, earned MVP honors.

JUCO champs

Florida's Hillsborough Community College ended a three-year title run by Texas' San Jacinto JC by beating the top-ranked Gators twice in the Junior College World Series in Grand Junction, Colo.

The Hawks, unranked entering the 10-team double-elimination tournament, beat San Jacinto 7-2, then 11-4 in the title game. Southern Idaho first baseman Chris Hanks, who went 8-for-17, had four home runs and 12 RBIs and was walked intentionally six times, was named the tournament MVP.

In the California junior college ranks, top-ranked Rancho Santiago JC was upset twice in the state tournament. Sacramento City College won its first championship in 35 years by beating Rancho Santiago twice on the final day. Rancho Santiago's Bob Hamelin, a second-round draft pick of Kansas City, was the state JUCO player of the year. Hamelin batted .521 and broke state records with 31 home runs and 107 RBIs.

NCAA Division I

American South

	Conf.		Overall	
	W	L	W	L
New Orleans	14	1	42	23
La. Tech	10	4	42	19
Pan American	8	7	33	25
*SW Louisiana	6	8	41	23
Lamar	4	11	20	31
Arkansas St.	2	13	15	26

*Won conference tournament

Atlantic Coast

	Conf.		Overall	
	W	L	W	L
Clemson	18	2	54	14
N.C. State	13	6	45	16
*Georgia Tech	12	8	45	24
Virginia	11	10	32	19
North Carolina	10	11	34	27
Wake Forest	7	12	32	26
Maryland	5	14	20	26
Duke	3	16	10	35

*Won conference tournament

Atlantic-10

	Conf.		Overall	
East	W	L	W	L
*Rutgers	14	2	38	21
Massachusetts	9	7	36	16
Temple	8	8	27	27
Rhode Island	5	11	10	28
St. Joseph's	4	12	16	23
West				
West Virginia	12	4	33	17
G. Washington	11	5	30	26
Penn State	8	8	24	26
St. Bonaventure	7	9	26	21
Duquesne	2	14	17	16

*Won conference tournament

Big East

	Conf.		Overall	
North	W	L	W	L
Providence	12	6	22	27
*St. John's	9	9	25	18
Boston College	8	10	15	16
Connecticut	7	11	24	18
South				
Villanova	16	2	32	22
Seton Hall	12	6	39	16
Georgetown	4	13	12	31
Pittsburgh	3	14	9	20

*Won conference tournament

Big Eight

	Conf.		Overall	
	W	L	W	L
*Oklahoma State	21	3	61	8
Oklahoma	16	8	45	21
Missouri	14	10	42	22
Nebraska	12	12	48	23
Kansas State	8	16	34	24
Iowa State	8	16	27	31
Kansas	5	19	25	34

*Won conference tournament

Big South

	Conf.		Overall	
	W	L	W	L
Coastal Carolina	15	0	35	12
Baptist	10	5	27	16
*Campbell	10	8	32	16
Winthrop	8	8	22	15
Augusta	8	10	16	27
Radford	4	10	13	26
UNC Asheville	1	15	9	32

*Won conference tournament

Big Ten

	Conf.		Overall	
	W	L	W	L
Michigan	20	8	48	19
*Minnesota	17	11	38	28
Michigan State	16	12	41	20
Ohio State	16	12	32	28
Wisconsin	15	13	28	27
Iowa	14	14	29	25
Illinois	12	16	26	20
Indiana	11	17	39	19
Northwestern	11	17	28	28
Purdue	8	20	26	34

*Won conference tournament

Colonial Athletic Assn.

	Conf.		Overall	
	W	L	W	L
James Madison	13	1	43	11
*George Mason	8	6	34	27
East Carolina	8	6	33	14
William & Mary	5	9	17	28
UNC Wilmington	4	10	11	42
Richmond	4	10	26	33

*Won conference tournament

East Coast

	Conf.		Overall	
	W	L	W	L
*Towson State	12	2	31	17
Delaware	11	3	35	12
Rider	9	5	21	19
Hofstra	8	6	12	22
Lehigh	6	8	12	16
Lafayette	6	8	14	21
Bucknell	3	11	8	22
Drexel	1	13	6	27

*Won conference tournament

ECAC

	Conf.		Overall	
New England	W	L	W	L
Maine	11	2	33	24
Hartford	9	5	29	12
C. Connecticut	8	7	21	12
Vermont	5	9	10	21
Northeastern	7	8	19	23
New Hampshire	2	11	11	28
Diamond				
C.W. Post	9	3	26	14
N.Y. Tech	8	4	27	25
West Chester	7	5	22	23
Pace	5	7	23	21
Brooklyn	1	11	6	31
Metro N.Y.				
F. Dickinson	9	3	26	13
Long Island	7	5	20	14
St. Francis	5	7	10	17
Monmouth	5	7	10	22
Wagner	4	8	12	28
Upstate N.Y.				
LeMoyne	12	2	26	11
Siena	9	6	16	17
Canisius	7	7	11	17
Utica	7	8	12	14
Niagara	6	9	12	26
Colgate	3	12	9	21

MAAC

	Conf.		Overall	
	W	L	W	L
*Fordham	13	2	36	15
LaSalle	9	5	24	19
St. Peter's	7	8	16	20
Fairfield	6	9	13	25
Iona	5	9	15	21
Holy Cross	3	10	6	20

*Won conference tournament

EIBL

	Conf.		Overall	
	W	L	W	L
Pennsylvania	14	4	28	11
Navy	12	6	23	16
Yale	11	7	22	18
Dartmouth	10	8	18	22
Princeton	9	9	21	17
Harvard	9	9	16	18
Army	7	11	15	22
Brown	7	11	22	19
Columbia	6	12	17	22
Cornell	5	13	18	26

Metro

	Conf.		Overall	
	W	L	W	L
South Carolina	14	3	43	21
*Florida State	12	6	50	18
Virginia Tech	11	7	40	20
S. Mississippi	9	6	36	26
Memphis State	6	8	27	22
Cincinnati	7	10	28	21
Louisville	3	15	18	35
*Won conference tournament				

Mid-American

	Conf.		Overall	
	W	L	W	L
C. Michigan	24	8	47	15
E. Michigan	21	11	35	22
Miami, Ohio	18	13	37	25
W. Michigan	18	14	33	22
Toledo	15	17	30	25
Kent	14	18	27	25
Bowling Green ...	13	18	27	30
Ohio	11	21	22	35
Ball State	9	23	21	39

Mid-Continent Universities

	Conf.		Overall	
	W	L	W	L
Blue				
Valparaiso	6	5	14	40
Illinois-Chicago ...	6	6	27	29
Cleveland State ...	5	6	16	32
Gray				
*SW Missouri St. ..	12	0	41	17
E. Illinois	6	6	27	23
W. Illinois	4	8	17	19
N. Iowa	2	10	11	43
*Won conference tournament				

Midwestern Collegiate

	Conf.		Overall	
	W	L	W	L
East				
Notre Dame	9	3	39	22
Detroit...........	6	6	31	24
Xavier...........	5	7	19	37
Dayton	4	8	20	29
West				
*Evansville	7	1	44	20
Butler	3	5	15	26
St. Louis	2	6	11	29
*Won conference tournament				

Missouri Valley

	Conf.		Overall	
	W	L	W	L
*Wichita State.....	16	4	56	16
Creighton	12	8	43	21
S. Illinois	11	9	40	22
Bradley	8	12	34	25
Illinois State	7	13	21	25
Indiana State	6	14	31	28
*Won conference tournament				

Ohio Valley

	Conf.		Overall	
	W	L	W	L
North				
E. Kentucky	9	1	34	22
Morehead St......	5	6	18	24
Youngstown St. ..	2	9	24	25
South				
Tennessee Tech ..	19	4	35	17
*M. Tenn. St.......	14	7	33	26
Austin Peay	10	12	23	27
Murray State	10	14	13	24
Tennessee State ..	3	19	12	31
*Won conference tournament				

Pacific-10

	Conf.		Overall	
	W	L	W	L
South				
Arizona State	21	9	60	13
Stanford	18	12	46	23
California	16	14	40	25
USC	13	17	36	26
UCLA	12	18	31	28
Arizona..........	10	20	33	26
North				
*Washington State .	18	4	52	14
Oregon State	14	10	30	19

Portland State (Pacific-10 North cont.)

	Conf.		Overall	
Portland State	12	9	33	25
Gonzaga	12	11	28	28
Portland	11	13	28	27
Washington	8	16	17	28
E. Washington ...	6	18	25	34
*Won division tournament				

PCAA

	Conf.		Overall	
	W	L	W	L
Fresno State......	20	1	56	12
Nevada-Las Vegas	14	7	40	22
Cal St Fullerton ...	12	8	43	18
San Jose State....	9	11	31	30
UC Irvine	9	12	30	28
Pacific	9	12	19	32
UC Santa Barbara	6	15	23	39
CS Long Beach ...	4	17	14	45

Southeastern

	Conf.		Overall	
	W	L	W	L
*Florida..........	21	6	48	19
Kentucky	18	9	38	25
Mississippi St.	17	10	44	20
Auburn	16	10	39	16
Louisiana St......	16	11	39	21
Georgia	11	16	29	28
Vanderbilt	11	16	30	23
Alabama	9	17	27	26
Tennessee	9	18	21	29
Mississippi	6	21	24	29
*Won conference tournament				

Southern

	Conf.		Overall	
	W	L	W	L
North				
Va. Military	11	7	20	20
Appalachian St. ...	9	7	29	17
Marshall	7	9	23	17
E. Tenn. St.......	7	11	16	35
South				
*W. Carolina	14	3	38	24
The Citadel	12	16	33	20
Davidson	7	11	28	26
Furman..........	2	15	8	29
*Won conference tournament				

Southland

	Conf.		Overall	
	W	L	W	L
McNeese State ...	13	7	31	31
NE Louisiana	11	8	19	26
Texas-Arlington ...	10	9	33	22
Stephen F. Austin ..	11	10	22	29
Sam Houston St. ..	11	10	32	25
NW Louisiana.....	9	12	23	28
SW Texas St.	7	11	31	27
North Texas St. ...	8	13	14	38

Southwest

	Conf.		Overall	
	W	L	W	L
*Texas	18	2	58	11
Texas A&M	17	4	52	15
Arkansas	12	9	39	23
Baylor	9	12	25	31
Texas Christian ...	8	13	27	32
Texas Tech	7	14	34	25
Houston	6	14	33	22
Rice	6	15	31	28
*Won conference tournament				

Southwest Athletic

	Conf.		Overall	
	W	L	W	L
East				
Alcorn State	18	6	20	21
Jackson State	15	9	24	25
Miss. Vall. St.	11	11	13	32
Alabama State ...	2	19	11	26
West				
Grambling	18	5	31	21
*Southern	16	8	28	21
Texas Southern ...	9	15	16	36
Prairie View	3	19	4	40
*Won conference tournament				

Sun Belt

	Conf.		Overall	
East	W	L	W	L
*Va. Cmmnwlth.	11	5	45	16
Jacksonville	11	6	39	24
UNC Charlotte	7	10	28	27
Old Dominion	5	13	24	31
West				
Western Kentucky	14	4	43	21
South Alabama	11	7	41	22
South Florida	5	11	26	33
Ala-Birmingham	4	12	22	28

*Won conference tournament

Trans-America

	Conf.		Overall	
East	W	L	W	L
Ga. Southern	13	4	30	27
*Stetson	9	8	35	25
Mercer	7	10	24	25
Samford	5	12	8	49
West				
Centenary	11	5	30	20
Ark.-Little Rock	8	8	27	29
Hardin-Simmons	5	11	30	30

*Won conference tournament

West Coast Athletic

	Conf.		Overall	
	W	L	W	L
Pepperdine	19	4	37	24
Santa Clara	18	5	43	18
Loyola Mrymnt.	18	6	48	18
San Diego	9	14	28	28
St. Mary's	8	15	24	35
Nevada-Reno	5	17	27	29
San Francisco	4	20	16	34

Western Athletic

	Conf.		Overall	
	W	L	W	L
San Diego State	21	5	47	18
*Brigham Young	20	5	41	18
Hawaii	21	6	40	21
Wyoming	14	13	25	27
New Mexico	11	17	23	31
Utah	8	17	10	32
Air Force	7	21	25	33
Colorado State	4	22	17	36

*Won conference tournament

Independents

	Overall	
	W	L
Miami, Fla.	52	14
Delaware State	25	11
New Mexico St.	38	18
Fla. International	40	19
Central Florida	40	20
Florida A&M	26	13
Tulane	32	18
SE Louisiana	30	18
Md-Balto County	25	16
Nicholls State	28	21
Oral Roberts	30	29
Akron	28	31
U.S. International	18	26
N. Colorado	19	28
Chicago State	18	29
Liberty	18	32
Bethune-Cookman	9	23
Boston U.	7	17
Md-Eastern Shore	7	24

DIVISION I LEADERS

TEAM BATTING
BATTING AVERAGE

	G	AVG
Brigham Young	60	.379
Indiana	58	.355
New Mexico State	56	.355
Fresno State	68	.350
Oklahoma State	69	.350
Wyoming	52	.350
James Madison	56	.347
North Carolina State	61	.346
Loyola Marymount	66	.344
Hartford	41	.344
Bethune-Cookman	32	.344
Florida A&M	39	.344
Minnesota	66	.342
LeMoyne	38	.342
Maryland-Balt. Co.	41	.342

RUNS SCORED

	G	R
Oklahoma State	69	778
Fresno State	68	670
Nebraska	71	658
Brigham Young	60	649
Arizona State	73	647
Texas	70	614
Loyola Marymount	66	606
Wichita State	73	586
Missouri	64	573
North Carolina State	61	571

HOME RUNS

	G	HR
Brigham Young	60	161
Oklahoma State	69	154
Virginia Tech	60	140
North Carolina State	61	123
Fresno State	68	120
Western Carolina	62	116
Georgia Tech	69	107
Louisiana Tech	61	102
Arizona State	73	100
So. Mississippi	62	89
Wichita State	73	86
UCLA	59	85
Washington State	66	85

STOLEN BASES

	G	SB	ATT
Va. Commonwealth	62	197	239
Florida State	69	197	241
Clemson	68	188	228
Wichita State	73	186	212
Miami (Fla.)	67	186	264
Ill.-Chicago	56	177	241
San Diego State	66	168	236
Nicholls State	51	166	210
Eastern Kentucky	56	162	219
Bethune-Cookman	32	161	177
Central Michigan	62	161	204

TEAM PITCHING
EARNED RUN AVERAGE

	G	ERA
Penn	39	2.97
Evansville	64	2.99
Central Michigan	62	3.09
Auburn	55	3.13
Va. Commonwealth	62	3.23
Navy	39	3.28
Fla. International	59	3.34
Florida State	69	3.35
Miami (Fla.)	67	3.45
SW Louisiana	64	3.46
Florida	68	3.47
Texas	70	3.49
Texas A&M	67	3.50
Massachusetts	52	3.56

TEAM FIELDING
FIELDING AVERAGE

	G	PCT
Loyola Marymount	66	.9699
Arkansas	62	.9695
Southern Illinois	62	.969
Towson State	48	.969
Pan American	58	.969
Florida	68	.968
Miami (Fla.)	67	.968
Santa Clara	62	.967
Texas A&M	67	.967
UCLA	59	.967
Cal St. Fullerton	61	.967
Evansville	64	.966

INDIVIDUAL BATTING
(Minimum 125 At-Bats)

	AVG	G	AB	R	H	2B	3B	HR	RBI	BB	SO	SB
Scott Baerns, Tenn. Tech .	.476	53	187	76	89	14	3	8	42	33	20	33
John Olerud, Wash. State .	.464	66	233	83	108	21	3	23	81	50	22	1
Maurice Vaughn, S. Hall . .	.463	49	162	49	75	16	0	14	70	47	17	9
Darron Healey, Appy St. . .	.462	42	145	44	67	14	1	6	35	22	10	1
Paul Cluff, BYU	.453	59	214	64	97	14	1	13	58	30	13	2
Marquis Grissom, Fla. A&M	.448	39	143	63	64	10	10	12	48	34	5	15
Troy Buckley, Santa Clara .	.442	62	217	54	96	21	0	16	82	34	23	0
Ernie Carr, Jacksonville . .	.440	63	216	53	95	32	1	9	75	44	11	13
Rod Boddie, Jas. Madison .	.436	56	218	65	95	16	5	9	60	32	24	15
Mario Moccia, N. Mexico St.	.434	56	198	63	86	20	3	19	90	32	16	0
Brett Roach, E. Mich.	.434	58	182	58	79	17	1	14	53	22	25	18
Mark Frankenberg, Air Frce	.434	57	198	55	86	11	1	21	83	27	21	0
Mike Mulvaney, Wyoming .	.431	52	197	63	85	15	2	13	52	20	16	2
Greg Harding, Richmond . .	.425	59	233	61	99	17	1	19	67	24	13	3
Keith LeClair, W. Car.	.423	62	239	65	101	15	4	18	67	24	31	12
Billy Masse, Wake Forest .	.422	58	223	83	94	23	4	24	77	55	20	35
James Mouton, St. Mary's .	.420	39	143	34	60	7	6	2	21	15	15	26
Ron Pezzoni, East. Ky	.420	51	188	47	79	7	4	5	38	23	11	23
Steve Meredith, ETSU	.419	51	167	42	70	10	2	3	29	24	19	15
Lee Sammons, Augusta . . .	.418	40	153	34	64	11	3	6	23	17	16	13
David Chadd, Kansas State .	.418	49	201	66	84	18	0	11	54	37	22	4
Mike Willes, BYU	.416	60	219	86	91	11	0	35	100	47	17	4
Steve Sada, Akron	.416	59	226	59	94	10	10	6	49	24	12	30
Mike Davidson, Mich. St. . .	.415	61	195	63	81	12	3	11	57	29	24	15
Eric Karros, UCLA	.415	58	241	53	100	14	2	17	54	33	28	11
Jeff Nesci, LeMoyne	.415	38	130	42	54	15	0	8	41	22	8	4
Brent Carrier, Tenn. Tech .	.414	53	181	46	75	15	1	6	60	26	6	12
Dan Peltier, Notre Dame . .	.414	60	215	62	89	21	3	7	70	36	17	9
John Beckwith, Akron	.413	59	218	43	90	21	1	10	69	19	30	2
Fred Hinojosa, Houston . . .	.412	58	177	47	73	19	3	5	46	39	11	3
Tommy Green, Appy St. . . .	.411	44	168	36	69	15	0	7	43	8	15	1
Donovan Campbell, Tx. So.	.411	52	175	39	72	15	1	6	36	20	14	12
Jeff Bagwell, Hartford	.410	41	161	49	66	12	1	14	58	26	10	1
Dan A'Alonzo, Md.-Balt. Co.	.409	40	171	44	70	9	7	7	38	6	6	2
Ron DiGiacopo, Pace	.408	44	191	43	78	17	2	11	63	8	11	10
Oneri Fleita, Creighton . . .	.408	60	240	61	98	30	2	15	69	25	20	3
Mike Humphreys, Tx. Tech	.407	60	214	77	87	13	2	18	73	45	38	7
Mickey Morandini, Indiana .	.407	58	214	70	87	15	5	9	55	41	15	35
Dave Silvestri, Missouri . . .	.406	64	219	89	89	18	8	21	79	58	30	17
Pat Kelly, West Chester . . .	.406	44	160	35	65	16	5	2	30	20	19	13
Don Sparks, Loyola Mrymnt	.405	63	259	74	105	23	2	13	79	13	19	6
Steve Finken, Michigan . . .	.404	63	193	52	78	14	1	13	41	45	38	25
Julio Morales, C.W. Post . .	.404	43	166	47	67	11	1	13	48	18	12	11
Jeromy Burnitz, Okla. St. . .	.403	55	159	61	64	13	3	15	57	36	36	2
Lenny Richardson, Dela. . .	.402	47	184	67	74	15	6	5	28	35	15	20
Scott Meadows, Ohio St . .	.402	59	199	53	80	14	2	10	55	28	14	9
Lance Shebelut, Fresno St.	.401	68	279	97	112	16	2	32	94	52	19	1
Barry Petrachenko, LaSalle	.401	43	177	61	71	10	5	0	39	37	14	35
Jeff Jetel, E. Ill.	.401	48	137	33	55	10	0	4	26	38	16	6
Chris Ebright, Oklahoma . .	.400	66	240	74	96	16	6	18	87	44	34	3
Chuck Graham, San Diego .	.400	52	205	41	82	20	3	4	52	16	24	0

RUNS SCORED

	G	R
Ken Ramos, Nebraska	71	100
Lance Shebelut, Fresno St. . .	68	97
Robin Ventura, Okla. St.	69	96
Monty Fariss, Okla. St.	69	95
Mike Mordecai, USA	62	94
Bert Heffernan, Clemson	68	93
Dave Silvestri, Missouri	64	89
Kevin Higgins, Ariz. St.	73	88
Tom Goodwin, Fresno St. . . .	68	87
Mike Willes, BYU	60	86
Edwin Alicea, Fla. St.	69	86
Travis Law, Okla. St.	58	85
Brandon Mitchell, Fresno St. .	68	85
Billy Masse, Wake Forest . . .	58	83
Brian Bark, N.C. State	61	83
Ted Wood, New Orleans	64	83
John Olerud, Wash. St.	66	83
Jeff Garber, Jas. Madison . . .	56	82
Pat Pesavento, Notre Dame . .	61	81
Mike Fiore, Miami (Fla.)	67	81
Ty Griffin, Ga. Tech	68	81
Brian Cisarik, Texas	69	81
Mark Standiford, Wich. St. . .	73	81
Brad Beanblossom, Okla. St. .	66	79

	G	H
John Olerud, Wash. St.	66	108
Steve Hosey, Fresno St.	68	108
Kevin Higgins, Ariz. St.	73	108
Jerry Brooks, Clemson	68	106
Mike Patrick, Texas	69	106
Don Sparks, Loy. Mary.	63	105
Troy Paulsen, Stanford	69	104
Steve Willis, Ariz. St.	72	104
Travis Tarchione, Loy. Mary. .	66	102
Keith LeClair, W. Car.	62	101
Eric Karros, UCLA	58	100
Brian Bark, N.C. State	61	100
Robin Ventura, Okla. St.	69	100
Greg Harding, Richmond	59	99
Oneri Fleita, Creighton	60	98
Eddie Zosky, Fresno St.	62	98
Paul Cluff, BYU	59	97
Brandon Mitchell, Fresno St. .	68	97
Ricky Candelari, Ariz. St. . . .	73	97

HITS

	G	H
Lance Shebelut, Fresno St. .	68	112
Tom Goodwin, Fresno St. . .	68	112
Steve Pearse, Fresno St. . . .	68	112

TOTAL BASES

	G	TB
Lance Shebelut, Fresno St. . .	68	226
Monty Fariss, Okla. St.	69	208
Mike Willes, BYU	60	207
Mark Standiford, Wich. St. . .	72	207
John Olerud, Wash. State . . .	66	204
Billy Masse, Wake Forest . . .	58	197
Robin Ventura, Okla. St.	69	196
Dave Silvestri, Missouri	64	186
Turtle Zaun, N.C. State	60	185

	G	TB
Dan Rumsey, Ariz. St.	73	181
Keith LeClair, Appy St.	62	179
Jerry Brooks, Clemson	68	179
Steve Hosey, Fresno St.	68	179
Jim Campanis, USC	62	178
Chris Ebright, Okla.	66	178
Greg Harding, Richmond	59	177
Oneri Fleita, Creighton	60	177
Ricky Candelari, Ariz. St.	73	173
Don Sparks, Loy. Mary.	63	171
Trey McCoy, Va. Tech	60	170

DOUBLES

	G	2B
Ernie Carr, Jacksonville	63	32
Oneri Fleita, Creighton	60	30
Steve Willis, Ariz. St.	72	29
Vince Castaldo, Kentucky	63	27
Mike Patrick, Texas	69	27
Dewayne Jones, USA	62	26
Steve Hosey, Fresno St.	68	26
Mark Standiford, Wich. St.	72	26
Dan Rumsey, Arizona St.	73	25
Jon Pittenger, Missouri	64	24
Brad Beanblossom, Okla. St.	66	24
Brandon Mitchell, Fresno St.	68	24
Donnie Poplin, UNC-Charlotte	56	23
Billy Masse, Wake Forest	58	23
Rob Maurer, Evansville	63	23
Don Sparks, Loy. Mary.	63	23
Matt Anderson, Oklahoma	65	23
Mike Fiore, Miami (Fla.)	67	23
Ricky Candelari, Ariz. St.	73	23

TRIPLES

	G	3B
Marquis Grissom, Fla. A&M	39	10
Bob Zeihen, Ind. St.	55	10
Steve Sada, Akron	59	10
Rob Katzaroff, UCLA	59	10
Tony Fair, Portland St.	46	9
Kevin Long, Arizona	56	9
Mike Sabo, Indiana	58	9
Rob Maurer, Evansville	63	9

HOME RUNS

	G	HR
Mike Willes, BYU	60	35
Lance Shebelut, Fresno St.	68	32
Monty Fariss, Okla. St.	69	30
Mark Standiford, Wich. St.	72	28
Robin Ventura, Okla. St.	69	26
Clint Fairey, W. Car.	59	25
Turtle Zaun, N.C. State	60	25
Billy Masse, Wake Forest	58	24
Trey McCoy, Va. Tech	60	24
Jim Campanis, USC	62	23
John Olerud, Wash. St.	66	23
Rick Vaughn, ORU	59	22
Skip Nelloms, W. Car.	60	22
Ed Sprague, Stanford	68	22
Tookie Spann, Tulane	50	21
Brian Mahaffey, SW Mo. St.	55	21
Rick Falkner, Portland	56	21
Ed Beuerlein, La. Tech	56	21
Mark Frankenberg, Air Force	57	21
Ken Shamburg, La. Tech	61	21
Dave Silvestri, Missouri	64	21
Bobby Benjamin, Nebraska	71	21
Keith Kaub, CS Fullerton	60	20
Sedgwick McCollum, So. Miss	62	20
Billy Parham, Ga. Tech	68	20
Tim Spehr, Ariz. St.	69	20

RUNS BATTED IN

	G	RBI
Monty Fariss, Okla. St.	69	114
Mike Willes, BYU	60	100
Mark Standiford, Wich. St.	72	97
Robin Ventura, Okla. St.	69	96
Lance Shebelut, Fresno St.	68	94
Jim Campanis, USC	62	92
Dan Rumsey, Ariz. St.	73	91
Mario Moccia, New Mex. St.	56	90
Turtle Zaun, N.C. State	60	87
Chris Ebright, Oklahoma	66	87
Ricky Candelari, Ariz. St.	73	84
Mark Frankenberg, Air Force	57	83

Tom Goodwin
... 62 steals

	G	RBI
Troy Buckley, Santa Clara	62	82
Jon Pittenger, Missouri	64	81
John Olerud, Wash. St.	66	81
Ed Sprague, Stanford	68	81
Luis Gonzalez, USA	62	80
Jerry Brooks, Clemson	68	80
Don Sparks, Loy. Mary.	63	79
Dave Silvestri, Missouri	64	79
Bobby Benjamin, Nebraska	71	78
Billy Masse, Wake Forest	58	77
Mark Brockell, Jas. Madison	56	75
Craig Cala, LSU	60	75
Eddie Zosky, Fresno St.	62	75
Ernie Carr, Jacksonville	63	75
Tim Hutson, Notre Dame	61	74
Pat Mooney, Creighton	64	74

BASES ON BALLS

	G	BB
Bobby Benjamin, Nebraska	71	91
Brian Cisarik, Texas	69	83
Edwin Alicea, Fla. St.	69	71
Mark Standiford, Wich. St.	72	70
Mike Fiore, Miami (Fla.)	67	69
Ken Ramos, Nebraska	71	68
Dan Raley, Wichita St.	72	68
Ted Wood, New Orleans	64	66
Bill Meier, Creighton	64	66
Tim Boyce, NY Tech	53	63
Bert Heffernan, Clemson	68	62
Robin Ventura, Okla. St.	69	61

STRIKEOUTS

	G	SO
Bobby Benjamin, Nebraska	71	70
Rich Bielski, Georgia	56	68
Chris Estep, Kentucky	59	67
Garrett Carter, So. Car.	64	65
Brett Hendley, Ga. Southern	57	64
Mario Linares, Florida	68	64
Ricky Candelari, Ariz. St.	73	63
Monte Gibbs, Mississippi	44	61
Billy Parham, Ga. Tech	68	61

TOUGHEST TO STRIKE OUT
(Minimum 70 At-Bats)

	AB	SO	Ratio
Ken Herring, LeMoyne	157	2	78.5
Al Kolesar, Yale	128	2	64.0
Brian Bark, NC State	258	5	51.6
Steve Pearse, Fresno St.	291	8	36.4
Jeff Solis, No. Colo.	132	4	33.0
Brent Carrier, Tenn Tech	181	6	30.2
George Lopez, Ark.-LR	178	6	29.7
Joe Markulike, Bucknell	116	4	29.0

STOLEN BASES

	G	SB	ATT
Tom Goodwin, Fresno St.	68	62	73
Lawrence Smith, Bth-Ck.	30	58	61
Edwin Alicea, Fla. St.	69	51	57
Mike Lansing, Wich. St.	66	51	58
Larry Lamphere, C. Mich	61	50	58
Todd Butler, Oklahoma	66	46	50
Wayne Rose, Beth-Cook.	30	44	45
Tony Krupski, St. Bona.	46	43	49
Tim Barker, VCU	62	42	47
Scooter Love, So. Miss	62	42	50

	G	SB	ATT
Ross Kagawa, Hawaii ...	62	41	47
J.T. Bruett, Minnesota	66	41	49
Mike Palys, Temple	53	40	47
Jeff Stout, Indiana	55	40	51
Billy Wright, VCU	62	40	54
Adam Knicely, VCU	62	39	46
Jack Allen, Fordham ...	48	39	51
Pat Pesavento, N. Dame .	61	38	50
Travis Law, Okla. St.	58	37	42
Steve Soto, N. Mexico St.	56	37	48
Rick Gaebe, So. Ill.......	62	36	38
Ruben Rodriguez, SW La.	55	36	41
Bruce Stephens, Butler .	39	36	43

HIT BY PITCH

	G	HBP
Mike Weimerskirch, Iowa St. .	58	22
Logan Collins, USA	56	18
Dave Sturdivant, UNLV	59	17
Brian Turang, Loy. Mary. .	64	16
Terrance Batiste, Nebraska .	49	15
Gary Scott, Villanova	48	14
Paul Johnson, Rutgers	59	14
Mike Couture, Clemson	62	14
Jim Conner, Wash. St.	64	14
Rusty Crockett, Texas	58	13
Jim Campanis, USC	62	13
Chris Gadsden, Creighton ...	64	13

INDIVIDUAL PITCHING
(Minimum 60 Innings)

PITCHING	W	L	ERA	G	GS	CG	SV	IP	H	R	ER	BB	SO
Brian Evans, Jacksonville .	8	1	1.19	33	0	0	6	68	55	21	9	17	65
Andy Benes, Evansville .	16	3	1.42	24	16	13	2	146	87	28	23	36	188
Dana Allison, Jas. Madison .	12	2	1.53	14	14	12	0	100	64	22	17	15	91
Tim McDonald, C. Mich .	16	1	1.83	17	17	13	0	108	79	36	22	54	87
Gregg Olson, Auburn .	7	3	2.00	36	1	0	10	72	43	23	16	27	113
Jim Poole, Ga. Tech .	4	4	2.03	45	0	0	9	71	62	33	16	40	113
Tom McGraw, Wash. St. .	7	1	2.11	14	8	4	1	60	47	20	14	22	46
Bob Aylmer, Fordham .	3	3	2.12	33	1	0	13	64	48	23	15	21	53
Chris Nabholz, Towson St. .	6	3	2.12	12	11	7	0	76	67	30	18	25	72
Pat Combs, Baylor .	7	2	2.16	19	14	9	2	100	77	39	24	46	97
David Krol, Toledo .	6	7	2.20	16	15	9	1	102	80	34	25	17	90
Jerry Dipoto, VCU .	7	4	2.23	20	16	10	3	117	89	35	29	37	96
Brian Dodd, Ariz. St. .	6	1	2.25	17	12	1	1	76	65	24	19	30	39
Kirk Dressendorfer, Texas .	15	2	2.26	23	18	12	2	136	103	46	34	36	134
Bill Prezioso, Wm & Mary .	7	5	2.32	12	11	8	0	89	87	39	23	24	50
Mark Dunford, VCU .	9	0	2.33	13	11	4	0	70	58	26	18	33	35
Todd Bibza, Navy .	6	5	2.35	14	12	6	1	77	68	25	20	18	47
Marquis Grissom, Fla. A&M .	9	3	2.40	12	12	12	0	86	94	57	23	44	93
Erik Schullstrom, Fresno St.	14	2	2.40	25	15	11	2	146	142	56	39	29	146
Kevin Griffin, Dartmouth .	5	3	2.40	14	11	5	1	60	62	20	16	22	34
Charles Nagy, Connecticut .	6	4	2.40	15	12	8	1	86	51	32	23	37	113
Ben Burnau, Miami (Ohio) .	11	3	2.41	15	11	5	1	97	82	33	26	41	65
Doug Simons, Pepperdine .	11	3	2.42	18	15	11	1	130	116	48	35	33	83
Mark Czarkowski, Hartford .	6	1	2.43	21	5	1	3	74	60	25	20	28	31
Mike Mongiello, Fair. D'son .	8	2	2.44	16	7	7	1	74	55	25	20	31	85
Ricky Kimball, Fla. St. .	7	2	2.44	30	5	2	8	77	55	26	21	30	77
Michael Nau, S. Houston St. .	5	2	2.45	14	13	5	0	67	63	34	18	29	35
Jeff Zona, VCU .	14	3	2.46	19	13	8	1	102	67	33	28	38	69
Bret Davis, Fla. St. .	7	4	2.46	23	0	0	2	80	78	37	22	29	77
Dave Voit, Kentucky	8	2	2.48	34	0	0	7	65	48	20	18	27	66
Steve Foster, Tex.-Arlington .	11	7	2.49	23	15	12	1	123	105	49	34	38	96
John Olerud, Wash. St. .	15	0	2.49	19	16	5	1	123	100	46	34	39	113
Dave Bauer, Rutgers	7	2	2.50	12	10	4	0	68	59	28	19	16	34
Jim Hvizda, Old Dominion .	9	6	2.52	32	8	6	7	121	105	49	34	24	107
Dan Freed, Ill. St. .	5	3	2.52	10	10	8	0	82	78	35	23	15	67
Rob Brown, San Diego St. .	9	3	2.53	17	17	6	0	110	107	46	31	34	99
Steve Wieman, Navy	6	3	2.53	13	9	5	1	68	54	29	19	11	61
Brad Hebets, SW La.	7	2	2.54	11	10	0	0	60	59	33	17	29	28
Brian Ahern, C. Fla.	6	3	2.54	9	9	5	0	71	66	26	20	16	60
Tim Dobos, Akron	8	3	2.55	15	13	10	0	95	77	42	27	42	95
Joel Shapiro, Jacksonville .	7	5	2.58	19	15	2	1	98	92	46	28	42	81
Todd Kemp, Tenn. Tech .	9	2	2.58	16	10	8	2	87	76	33	25	35	132
Scott Renner, Auburn	4	2	2.58	23	12	2	0	87	79	34	25	30	64
Jim McCauley, C.W. Post .	8	4	2.59	13	10	5	0	83	73	37	24	28	61
Scott Erwin, Ga. Tech	13	0	2.61	17	16	4	0	114	84	46	33	55	106
Ed Rayburg, Duquesne .	6	3	2.64	12	9	6	2	68	44	21	20	51	89
David Goins, C. Fla.	7	3	2.64	15	7	2	0	75	67	26	22	22	31
Keith Richardson, Ga. South .	8	5	2.65	20	16	10	2	122	102	49	36	26	114
Ben McDonald, LSU	13	7	2.65	22	14	10	1	119	96	46	35	27	144

WINS

	W	L
Linty Ingram, Ariz. St.	17	5
Tim McDonald, C. Mich	16	1
Andy Benes, Evansville	16	3
Jeff Gidcumb, Florida	16	7
John Olerud, Wash. St.	15	0
Rich Crane, Fresno St.	15	2
Kirk Dressendorfer, Texas ...	15	2
John Salles, Fresno St.	15	2
Eric Stone, Texas	15	3
Tim Pugh, Okla. St.	14	1
Wes Bliven, Santa Clara ...	14	2
Erik Schullstrom, Fresno St. .	14	2
Jeff Zona, Va. Comm.	14	3
Mike Magnante, UCLA	14	4
Dave Richardson, MTSU ...	14	5
David Haas, Wichita St.	14	5
Scott Erwin, Ga. Tech	13	0

	W	L
Brian Barnes, Clemson	13	2
Joe Grahe, Miami (Fla.)	13	5
Joe Slusarski, New Orleans ..	13	6
Ben McDonald, LSU	13	7
Dana Allison, Jas. Madison .	12	2
Steve Surico, Loy. Mary. ...	12	2
Rusty Kilgo, Ariz. St.	12	3
Victor Cole, Santa Clara ...	12	6
Lee Plemel, Stanford	12	8
Brad Rhodes, N.C. State ...	11	1
Pat Hope, Okla. St.	11	1
Tom Keffury, Okla. St.	11	1
John Marshall, San Diego St. .	11	2
Dennis Burbank, Pepperdine .	11	2
Doug Simons, Pepperdine ..	11	3
Ben Burnau, Miami (Ohio) ...	11	3
Johnny Wiggs, Florida	11	3
Brad DuVall, Va. Tech	11	3

Name	W	L
Jeff Hartsock, N.C. State	11	3
Gerald Alexander, Tulane	11	4
Wally Trice, USIU	11	4
Randy Powers, USC	11	5
Greg Wilcox, Davidson	11	5
Daren Kizziah, W. Kentucky	11	6
Steve Foster, UTA	11	7
Scott Lewis, UNLV	11	7
Bobby Edwards, Arkansas	11	7
Howard Landry, SW La.	11	8

LOSSES

Name	W	L
Chad Holmes, CSLB	3	13
Tim Carroll, Samford	2	11
Chris Mosley, No. Tex. St	2	11
Jerome Hunt, UNC-W	3	11
Troy Taylor, Ala.-Birm.	4	11
Don Fowler, Duke	3	10
Dennis Scully, St. Mary's	4	10
Todd Deck, Pacific	4	10
Mike Shebek, Ball State	5	10

APPEARANCES

Name	G
Jim Poole, Ga. Tech	45
Tom Hickox, Stetson	43
Gregg Olson, Auburn	36
Jess Feathers, CSLB	36
Dave Voit, Kentucky	34
Marc Lipson, Georgia	34
Darryl Scott, Loy. Mary.	33
Mike Martin, Miss. St.	33
Brian Evans, Jacksonville	33
Bob Aylmer, Fordham	33
Steve Chitren, Stanford	33

COMPLETE GAMES

Name	GS	CG
John Salles, Fresno St.	23	15
Mike Lumley, E. Mich.	14	13
Andy Benes, Evansville	16	13
Tim McDonald, C. Mich.	17	13
Dave Richardson, MTSU	17	13
Linty Ingram, Ariz. St.	21	13
Marquis Grissom, Fla. A&M	12	12
Gerald Alexander, Tulane	14	12
Dana Allison, Jas. Madison	14	12
Steve Foster, UT Arlington	15	12
Kirk Dressendorfer, Texas	18	12
Robert Jackson, Fla. A&M	13	11
Erik Schullstrom, Fresno St.	15	11
Doug Simons, Pepperdine	15	11
Ben Burnau, Miami (O.)	15	11
Mike Draper, Ga. Mason	16	11
Dave Kandra, Pan Am	16	11
Howard Landry, SW La.	16	11
Joe Grahe, Miami (Fla.)	21	11

SAVES

Name	G	SV
Tom Hickox, Stetson	43	14
Darryl Scott, Loy. Mary.	33	13
Bob Aylmer, Fordham	33	13
Brian Beatson, So. Car.	27	12
Brad Wanzenberg, Davidson	26	11
Scott Centala, Texas A&M	26	11
Jamie McAndrew, Florida	24	10
Steve Chitren, Stanford	33	10
Gregg Olson, Auburn	36	10

INNINGS PITCHED

Name	G	IP
Linty Ingram, Ariz. St.	29	181
John Salles, Fresno St.	25	177
Joe Grahe, Miami (Fla.)	24	167
Rich Crane, Fresno St.	22	161
Joe Slusarski, New Orleans	22	160
David Haas, Wichita St.	22	158
Scott Lewis, UNLV	21	152
Jeff Gidcumb, Florida	21	150
Longo Garcia, CS Fullerton	20	148
Wes Bliven, Santa Clara	22	142
Dan Archibald, San Jose St.	21	147

BASE ON BALLS

Name	IP	BB
Victor Cole, Santa Clara	137	89
Jeff Lynch, UCSB	54	82
Steve Muh, Georgia	122	82
Dan Kite, LSU	105	79
John Pope, Rice	67	77
Mike McNary, Loy. Mary.	103	77
Russ Springer, LSU	119	73

Mark Beck
...162 K's

STRIKEOUTS

Name	IP	SO
Andy Benes, Evansville	146	188
Mark Beck, CS Fullerton	135	162
Russ Springer, LSU	119	156
Joe Grahe, Miami (Fla.)	167	154
Linty Ingram, Ariz. St.	181	153
Gerald Alexander, Tulane	127	151
Erik Schullstrom, Fresno St.	146	146
Joe Slusarski, New Orleans	160	146
Ben McDonald, LSU	119	144
Eric Stone, Texas	133	140
Brian Barnes, Clemson	138	140
Scott Lewis, UNLV	152	135
Wally Trice, USIU	121	134
Kirk Dressendorfer, Texas	136	134
Rich Crane, Fresno St.	161	134
Todd Kemp, Tenn. Tech	87	132
Dave Richardson, MTSU	127	128
Dan Archibald, San Jose St.	147	128
Jeff Gidcumb, Florida	152	126
Brian Rountree, So. Car.	124	125
Longo Garcia, CS Fullerton	148	123
Wes Bliven, Santa Clara	148	123
Tim Mauser, Texas Christian	104	120
Howard Landry, SW La.	123	115
Victor Cole, Santa Clara	137	115
Lee Plemel, Stanford	145	115
Darrell Lindsey, So. Miss	100	114
Keith Richardson, Ga. South.	122	114
Jim Poole, Ga. Tech	71	113
Gregg Olson, Auburn	72	113
Charles Nagy, Connecticut	86	113
John Olerud, Wash. St.	123	113
Renay Bryand, UCSB	118	112

STRIKEOUTS/9 INNINGS
(Minimum 50 Innings)

Name	IP	SO	AVG
Jim Poole, Ga. Tech	71	113	14.3
Gregg Olson, Auburn	72	113	14.1
Todd Kemp, Tenn. Tech.	87	132	13.7
Matt Dunbar, Fla. St.	52	77	13.3
Greg Ferguson, Va. Tech	65	94	13.0
Russ Springer, LSU	119	156	11.8
Charles Nagy	86	113	11.8
Ed Rayburg, Duquesne	68	89	11.8
Bart Barnett, Columbia	57	75	11.8
Scott Centala, Texas A&M	54	71	11.8
Andy Benes, Evansville	146	188	11.6
Jeff Mutis, Lafayette	53	68	11.6
Mike Owens, Mass.	53	67	11.4
Bob Kairis, N'western St.	82	103	11.3
John Ericks, Illinois	87	108	11.2
Kurt Knudsen, Miami (Fla.)	51	63	11.1
Tom Liss, Detroit	63	78	11.1
Ben McDonald, LSU	119	144	10.9

The United States team made off with all the gold medals at the Olympic baseball competition.

'88 team wins first U.S. baseball gold

By DANNY KNOBLER

The 1988 version of Team USA stayed together longer and traveled more than any previous U.S. contingent. The prize at the end of the trip, they agreed, was worth all the trouble.

Mark Marquess
... winning coach

When the U.S. team of college all-stars finally returned home from Seoul, South Korea, on Sept. 29, they came back with Olympic gold medals. A 5-3 win in the final game against Japan, the defending gold medalist, left Team USA with an honor that no previous American team could claim. Not even the 1984 Olympic team, the memories of which hung over the '88 club all summer, won Olympic gold.

From June 13, the day coach Mark Marquess welcomed 43 hopefuls to the team's training center in Millington, Tenn., the goal was to win the final game in Seoul—where baseball had demonstration status for the last time. In 1992, in Barcelona, Spain, baseball becomes a full gold medal sport.

Quest for gold

Marquess, coach of Stanford's national collegiate champions, maintained all along that he didn't consider the U.S. the Olympic favorite, but even the players—many of whom were No. 1 draft picks—would have regarded anything less than a gold medal as a failure.

By the time they got to the Olympics, though, Team USA was a tired group that looked forward to a chance to go home. Having played at the world championships in Italy and the Kobe Invitational in Japan before the Olympics, the players hadn't been on U.S. soil in a month.

The U.S. quickly guaranteed itself a spot in the medal round however, beating Korea 5-3 and Australia 12-2. They sleepwalked through a meaningless 8-7 loss to Canada.

U.S. Olympic Team

Members of the 1988 United States Olympic Team included front row, l to r, Tom Goodwin, Doug Robbins, Billy Masse, Jim Campanis, Bret Barberie, Jeff Branson, Mike Fiore. Second row, Scott Servais, Tino Martinez, Ty Griffin, Robin Ventura, Dave Silvestri, Ted Wood, Mike Milchin, Mickey Morandini. Third row, trainer Herb Amato, assistant coach Ron Polk, pitching coach Skip Bertman, head coach Mark Marquess, assistant coach Dave Bingham, assistant coach Rich Alday, business manager Bob Milano, publicist Bob Bensch. Top row, Pat Combs, Joe Slusarski, Mark Beck, Andy Benes, Ben McDonald, Jim Abbott, Charles Nagy, Ed Sprague.

— 250 —

Ventura top player

Robin Ventura, Oklahoma State's three-time All-American third baseman, capped a brilliant amateur career by being named winner of the 1988 Golden Spikes award, symbolic of the top amateur player in the United States.

Ventura, a product of Santa Maria, Calif., hit .423 overall with 67 home runs in three seasons for the Cowboys, and also was a member of the gold medal-winning U.S. team at the Seoul Olympics. He was picked in the first round of the June draft by the Chicago White Sox.

Among nine finalists for the award, eight played with Team USA at the '88 Olympics. Pitcher Gregg Olson, who elected not to play with the team, was the ninth nominee.

Then the team, which Marquess often said was the hardest-working all-star club he'd ever been associated with, focused on the goal at hand.

Team USA scored four first-inning runs in the semifinal against Puerto Rico, and righthander Ben McDonald (Louisiana State) responded with his second complete-game win of the tournament.

In Abbott's court

That set up the gold medal game against Japan, the same nation that had ended the '84 team's gold-medal hopes. Japan went undefeated on its side of the bracket, and beat Korea in the other semifinal to reach the final.

Marquess, the last U.S. coach to win a major international competition (Intercontinental Cup, 1981), gave the ball to lefthander Jim Abbott (Michigan), probably the best-known amateur baseball player ever. Abbott, who was born without a right hand, won the 1987 Golden Spikes Award as the nation's top amateur player, then added the Sullivan Award as the top amateur athlete in any sport.

Marquess also had chosen Abbott to pitch the final game of the world championships, and he took a three-hitter into the ninth inning before Cuba rallied for a 4-3 win.

This time, Abbott finished it off. He struggled in the sixth inning, giving up two runs on two hits and two walks, but worked through it and ended up with a seven-hitter.

First baseman Tino Martinez (Tampa) provided the U.S. offense. His two-run home run in the fourth was the first of the tournament to clear Chamshil Baseball Stadium's 410-foot center field fence. An inning later, he singled home the fourth U.S. run, and he added a second home run in the eighth—his team-high 20th of the summer.

Where were the Cubans?

When Team USA took a victory lap waving the U.S. flag, then took the stand to receive its gold medals, no one was concerned that Cuba had again missed the party. The Cubans, who followed the Soviet-led boycott of the 1984 Olympic Games in Los Angeles, this time honored North Korea's less effective boycott.

Cuba still had a major impact on international baseball in 1988, however. It won a hard-fought seven-game exhibition series, 4-3, from the U.S., then mounted major ninth-inning rallies to take both meetings in Italy to win the world championship.

The first USA-Cuba meeting was played the last day of round-robin play. Both teams went into the game undefeated against the rest of the 12-team field.

Team USA took a 9-6 lead into the ninth, but Cuba rallied for four runs. Lourdes Gurriel hit a game-tying home run, then Alejo O'Reilly's solo shot gave the Cubans the win.

Cuba (11-0) won its semifinal game against fourth-place Japan (7-4), and the U.S. (10-1) beat Taiwan (8-3), setting up another meeting for the title.

Summer baseball

INTERNATIONAL CHAMPIONS

1988 Olympics at Seoul, South Korea. **Champion:** United States. **Runner-up:** Japan.

1988 World Amateur Championships at Parma, Italy. **Champion:** Cuba. **Runner-up:** United States.

International Friendship Series (18 and under) at Rapid City, S.D. **Champion:** Taiwan. **Runner-up:** United States.

NATIONAL CHAMPIONS

National Baseball Congress World Series (unlimited) at Wichita, Kan. **Champion:** Everett, Wash. **Runner-up:** Midlothian, Ill.

American Legion World Series (19 and under) at Middletown, Conn. **Champion:** Cincinnati, Ohio. **Runner-up:** Boyertown, Pa.

All-American Amateur Baseball Association (20 and under) at Johnstown, Pa. **Champion:** New Orleans, La. **Runner-up:** Reston, Va.

National Junior Championships (18 and under) at Sioux Falls, S.D. **Champion:** USA West. **Runner-up:** USA North.

Junior Olympic Super Series (16 and under) at Youngstown, Ohio. **Champion:** Santa Clarita, Calif. (Colt League World Series champions). **Runner-up:** Cincinnati, Ohio (Mickey Mantle League World Series champions).

LITTLE LEAGUE

Big League World Series (16-18) at Ft. Lauderdale, Fla. **Champion:** Taiwan. **Runner-up:** Broward County, Fla.

Senior League World Series (13-15) at Kissimmee, Fla. **Champion:** Taiwan. **Runner-up:** Maracaibo, Venezuela.

Little League World Series (13) at Taylor, Mich. **Champion:** Mexicali, Mexico. **Runner-up:** Hilo Coast, Hawaii.

Little League World Series (11-12) at Williamsport, Pa. **Champion:** Taiwan. **Runner-up:** Pearl City, Hawaii.

AMERICAN AMATEUR BASEBALL CONGRESS

Stan Musial World Series (unlimited) at Battle Creek, Mich. **Champion:** Dallas, Texas. **Runner-up:** Eau Claire, Wis.

Connie Mack World Series (17-18) at Farmington, N.M. **Champion:** Madison Heights, Mich. **Runner-up:** Chicago Heights, Ill.

Mickey Mantle World Series (15-16) at Danbury, Conn. **Champion:** Cincinnati, Ohio. **Runner-up:** Norwalk, Calif.

Sandy Koufax World Series (13-14) at Guaynabo, Puerto Rico. **Champion:** Guaynabo, P.R. **Runner-up:** Bayamon, P.R.

Pee Wee Reese World Series (11-12) at Forest Park, Ga. **Champion:** Paramount, Calif. **Runner-up:** Rio Piedras, P.R.

Willie Mays World Series (9-10) at Hapeville, Ga. **Champion:** Memphis, Tenn. **Runner-up:** Denver, Colo.

NATIONAL AMATEUR BASEBALL FEDERATION

Major World Series (unlimited) at Louisville, Ky. **Champion:** Dayton, Ohio. **Runner-up** Chicago, Ill.

College World Series (21 and under) at Youngstown, Ohio. **Champion:** Northville, Mich. **Runner-up:** Falls Church, Va.

Senior World Series (17-18) at Youngstown, Ohio. **Champion:** Randallstown, Md. **Runner-up:** Chicago, Ill.

Junior World Series (15-16) at Northville, Mich. **Champion:** Baltimore, Md. **Runner-up:** Bayside, N.Y.

Sophomore World Series (13-14) at Northville, Mich. **Champion:** Brooklyn, N.Y. **Runner-up:** Warren, Mich.

BABE RUTH LEAGUE

Babe Ruth World Series (16-18) at Newark, Ohio. **Champion:** Marietta, Ga. **Runner-up:** Alameda, Calif.

Babe Ruth World Series (13-15) at Lebanon, Mo. **Champion:** Honolulu, Hawaii. **Runner-up:** Brazoswood, Texas.

Babe Ruth World Series (13 Prep) at Vallejo, Calif. **Champion:** Sarasota, Fla. **Runner-up:** Honolulu, Hawaii.

Bambino World Series (12 and under) at Oakland, Calif. **Champion:** Oakland. **Runner-up:** Longview, Wash.

PONY LEAGUE

Palomino World Series (17-18) at Greensboro, N.C. **Champion:** Carmichael, Calif. **Runner-up:** Oahu, Hawaii.

Colt League World Series (15-16) at Lafayette, Ind. **Champion:** Santa Clarita, Calif. **Runner-up:** Caguas, P.R.

Pony League World Series (13-14) at Washington, Pa. **Champion:** Seoul, South Korea. **Runner-up:** La Mesa, Calif.

Bronco League World Series (11-12) at Pacific Grove, Calif. **Champion:** Levittown, Pa. **Runner-up:** Miami, Fla.

DIXIE BASEBALL ASSOCIATION

Majors World Series (17-18) at Alexandria, La. **Champion:** Alexandria, La. **Runner-up:** Hattiesburg, Miss.

Pre-Major World Series (15-16) at Texarkana, Texas. **Champion:** Montgomery, Ala. **Runner-up:** Midlands, S.C.

Boys World Series (13-14) at Scottsboro, Ala. **Champion:** Alexandria, La. **Runner-up:** Texarkana, Ark.

Youth World Series (11-12) at Montgomery, Ala. **Champion:** Brent, Fla. **Runner-up:** Ville Platte, La.

Louisiana State righthander Ben McDonald won two games, with a 1.00 ERA, at the Olympics.

The U.S. led 3-1 going to the bottom of the ninth, but a controversial call at first gave the Cubans a runner, and Gurriel followed by hitting another game-tying home run. Five batters later, Lazaro Vargas singled over a drawn-in outfield to win the game for Cuba, 4-3.

Martinez homered twice in the final game for the U.S., and finished the tournament with a .407 average, six home runs and 21 RBIs. He was named the most valuable player. U.S. third baseman Robin Ventura led the tournament with 32 RBIs. But the Cubans took home the big trophy.

"We thought we should have won," Martinez said. "We played better than Cuba."

Searching for gold—down under

The U.S. junior national team had an even longer wait for its shot at a championship.

Because it was played in Sydney, Australia, the 1988 world junior tournament—which the U.S. has never won—was played in December.

The junior team, selected from players participating in the National Junior Baseball Championships, played one international tournament during the summer—the International Friendship Series, in Rapid City, S.D.. The U.S. finished second to Taiwan, which led the final game 12-5 in the seventh inning when it was stopped by lightning.

The U.S. team was composed primarily of incoming college freshmen—like catcher Troy Tallman (Stanford), and pitchers Tyler Green (Wichita State) and Doug Bennett (Arkansas)—and a selection of top high school players.

In addition, Reid Cornelius, one of the nation's top prep players from the spring of '88, elected to stay with the team for its excursion to Australia—even after signing a bonus contract with the Montreal Expos late in summer that was to pay him more than $200,000.

NBC: Everett, surprise champions

With most of the big-name college players heading to Seoul for the Olympics, amateur baseball at home took on a slightly different look in 1988.

The National Baseball Congress World Series final matched a team of ex-professional players against an old-time "town

Olympians Robin Ventura (left) and Ty Griffin were Baseball America's co-summer players of the year.

Olympians share honor

Ty Griffin and Robin Ventura, the twin Chicago first-round draft picks who led Team USA in its successful bid for Olympic gold, were selected co-Summer Baseball Players of the Year for 1988 by Baseball America.

Both Griffin and Ventura played dominant roles for the Olympic squad—Griffin as the team's second baseman and leadoff hitter; Ventura as the club's third baseman and No. 3 hitter.

Eight other members of the U.S. Olympic team also were named to Baseball America's summer All-America squad. The team is limited to players with college eligibility remaining—even though most members of the Olympic team decided to forego their final college season by signing pro contracts.

Griffin, Ventura, first baseman Tino Martinez, outfielder Ted Wood and pitcher Jim Abbott—all No. 1 picks in June—were selected to the team for the second year in a row.

Others top amateur leagues represented on the team included the Cape Cod, Alaska, Great Lakes, Shenandoah Valley, Jayhawk, Western International and Atlantic Collegiate Leagues.

Following is Baseball America's summer All-America squad, with colleges, and statistics in brackets:

C—Troy Rusk (South Florida), Everett, Western International League (.467, 12 homers, 38 RBIs).

1B—(tie) *Tino Martinez (Tampa), Team USA (.402-20-70); John Olerud (Washington State), Pullman/Kenai, Alaska League (.477-22-56). **2B**—*Ty Griffin (Georgia Tech), Team USA (.416-16-52, 21 steals). **3B**—Robin Ventura (Oklahoma State), Team USA (.380-12-77). **SS**—Chuck Knoblauch (Texas A&M), Wareham, Cape Cod League (.361-1-29, 23 steals).

OF—*Ted Wood (New Orleans), Team USA (.405-5-43); Tom Goodwin (Fresno State), Team USA (.318-2-16, 20 steals); *Shawn Hare (Central Michigan), Toledo, Great Lakes League (.427-5-19, 20 steals).

DH—David Staton (Orange Coast, Calif., JC), Brewster, Cape Cod League (.359-16-46).

P—Ben McDonald (Louisiana State), Team USA (8-2, 2.61 ERA); *Jim Abbott (Michigan), Team USA (8-1, 2.55); *Andy Benes (Evansville), Team USA (7-2, 3.29); John Thoden (North Carolina), Wareham, Cape Cod League (9-1, 2.43); *Charles Nagy (Connecticut), Team USA (3-1, 1.05, 6 saves).

*signed professional contract

Tino Martinez
... top gun for U.S.

Jim Abbott
... final-game winner

team"—the first such pairing in 25 years. College-stocked teams had dominated the 32-team NBC tournament in recent years.

Everett, Wash., a team composed entirely of "local" players, defeated the Midlothian (Ill.) White Sox 14-11 in a 12-inning marathon to clinch the title. Catcher Troy Rusk (South Florida, by way of Burien, Wash.) hit a three-run homer to finish the double-elimination tournament.

Rusk ended up 15-for-30 in the tournament, while Everett outfielder O Sobotka (Washington) hit five homers, but MVP honors went to 27-year-old teammate, pitcher Dave Wong. Wong won his fourth game of the tournament in the semifinals, then pitched 8⅓ innings of relief in the final.

Meanwhile, another Washington state product, pitcher-first baseman John Olerud (Washington State), was selected winner of the NBC's annual Baseball America award for being the tournament's top major league prospect, in a poll of scouts.

Olerud played most of the summer with Pullman, Wash., of the Alaska League, but went to Wichita as a pick-up player with the Alaska League's Peninsula Oilers. Olerud, named Baseball America's 1988 college player of the year, won his only start as a pitcher and went 14-for-29 at the plate, with six home runs (including three in one game) and 13 RBIs.

Branching out

The NBC tournament received a challenge, of sorts, in 1988, as the Boardwalk and Baseball amusement park in Florida staged its own tournament of top summer college teams in August. The Summer Collegiate League Shootout matched all-star teams from four leagues—Cape Cod, Central Illinois, Great Lakes and Shenandoah Valley—that don't participate in the NBC event.

The Cape Cod League defended its reputation as the top summer league by winning the tournament, but the Cape needed two wins over the Great Lakes League on the final day to do it. Texas A&M shortstop Chuck Knoblauch, already voted the Cape League's best professional prospect, won the Shootout MVP award by driving in six runs in five games.

Knoblauch also led the Cape Cod League in hitting (.361), while Brewster's David Staton narrowly missed winning the league's Triple Crown, leading in home runs (16) and RBIs (46), but falling two points short in the batting race (.359).

The traditionally strong Alaska League, suffering financial problems brought on by a stagnant economy, saw four of its member clubs suspend operations for the 1988 season, including the 1987 NBC World Series champion, Mat-su Miners. Also biting the bullet were the Anchorage Glacier Pilots, Anchorage Buccaneers and North Pole Nicks.

Marietta wins again

The East Cobb Astros of Marietta, Ga., added to their remarkable string of youth baseball championships in 1988, when they defeated Alameda, Calif., 2-0 to win the Babe Ruth 16-18 World Series.

The win was the fifth World Series crown in six years for the Astros, who won the Colt League (15-16) World Series in 1987, the Babe Ruth 13-15 World Series in 1986, the 1985 Pony League World Series, and the 1983 Little League (11-12) World Series.

TEAM USA
(Cumulative summer statistics)

BATTING	AVG	G	AB	R	H	2B	3B	HR	RBI	BB	SO	SB
Bob Hamelin, 1b	.429	4	7	2	3	0	0	0	1	3	1	1
Ty Griffin, 2b	.416	51	185	69	77	18	3	16	52	34	31	21
Ted Wood, of	.405	50	158	46	64	15	4	5	43	25	28	7
Tino Martinez, 1b	.402	52	199	48	80	12	1	20	70	20	32	2
Jim Campanis, c	.385	17	26	7	10	3	0	1	4	4	6	0
Robin Ventura, 3b	.380	51	184	48	70	17	2	12	77	26	22	1
Doug Robbins, c	.353	34	85	25	30	7	0	2	19	8	25	4
Thayer Swain, of	.333	1	3	1	1	1	0	0	0	0	1	0
Tom Goodwin, of	.318	50	148	38	47	11	1	2	16	17	19	20
Billy Masse, of	.314	47	137	34	43	7	0	6	32	14	20	11
Scott Servais, c	.295	31	78	16	23	5	0	2	17	4	15	2
Ed Sprague, 3b	.290	39	93	21	27	9	0	4	24	14	26	0
Bret Barberie, inf	.288	41	59	15	17	2	0	4	13	12	7	1
Dave Silvestri, ss	.285	49	158	30	45	9	2	2	23	13	36	5
Mike Fiore, of	.268	48	149	39	40	8	0	5	26	23	32	5
Mickey Morandini, of	.256	37	82	26	21	7	3	3	9	14	22	5
Jeff Branson, inf	.207	30	58	7	12	2	0	2	9	8	17	0
Eddie Zosky, inf	.171	18	41	7	7	1	0	0	3	0	6	1
Mike Milchin, 1b-p	.154	15	26	1	4	0	0	0	2	5	9	1
Brent Mayne, c	.000	2	4	0	0	0	0	0	0	0	0	1
Benny Colvard, of	.000	1	2	0	0	0	0	0	0	0	1	0
Totals	**.330**	53	1882	480	621	134	16	86	441	244	359	88

PITCHING	W	L	ERA	G	GS	CG	SV	IP	H	R	ER	BB	SO
Charles Nagy	3	1	1.05	19	4	0	6	51	23	11	6	24	51
Mark Beck	1	0	1.13	3	2	0	0	16	9	5	2	5	18
Mike Milchin	4	1	1.93	12	1	0	2	33	18	11	7	15	29
Jim Abbott	8	1	2.55	15	13	3	0	88	63	28	25	39	74
Ben McDonald	8	2	2.61	13	13	4	0	79	70	28	23	31	61
Pat Combs	6	1	2.52	8	6	0	0	39	34	19	11	21	35
Jim Poole	0	0	2.79	7	0	0	1	10	8	3	3	4	17
Andy Benes	7	2	3.29	14	11	1	2	77	57	31	28	30	77
Joe Slusarski	5	3	4.05	20	2	0	2	53	59	28	24	7	52
Mark Smith	0	0	6.74	1	1	0	0	3	7	5	2	1	1
Tim Mauser	0	0	6.75	1	0	0	0	4	5	3	3	2	5
Mike Gullickson	0	0	8.11	1	0	0	0	3	6	3	3	1	4
Totals	**42**	**11**	**2.69**	53	53	8	13	458	359	175	137	180	424

Players in **bold** represented the U.S. in the Olympic Games

1988 OLYMPICS
Seoul, South Korea

Blue	W	L	For	Ag.
Japan	3	0	17	5
Puerto Rico	2	1	10	11
Netherlands	1	2	11	14
Taiwan	0	3	4	12
White				
United States	2	1	24	13
South Korea	2	1	10	9
Australia	1	2	10	20
Canada	1	2	17	19

Final Round Robin Standings

Semifinals: United States 7, Puerto Rico 2; Japan 3, South Korea 1.
Gold Medal Game: United States 5, Japan 3. **Bronze Medal Game:** Puerto Rico 7, South Korea 0.

INDIVIDUAL BATTING LEADERS
(Minimum 10 At-Bats)

	AVG	G	AB	R	H	2B	3B	HR	RBI	BB	SO	SB
Greg Duce, Canada	.538	3	13	3	7	1	0	0	3	1	1	0
Terushi Nakajima, Japan	.476	5	21	5	10	3	2	1	5	1	2	1
Ted Wood, USA	.474	5	19	3	9	2	0	0	8	2	2	0
Tino Martinez, USA	.471	5	17	6	8	0	0	2	8	4	0	0
Anthony Garcia, PR	.467	5	15	2	7	1	1	0	1	1	0	0
Robert Knol, Neth	.417	3	12	3	5	2	0	0	1	0	1	0
Robin Ventura, USA	.409	5	22	6	9	3	1	0	4	1	0	0

INDIVIDUAL PITCHING LEADERS
(Minimum 8 Innings)

	W	L	ERA	G	GS	CG	SV	IP	H	R	ER	BB	SO
James Figueroa, PR	1	0	0.00	1	1	1	0	9	5	0	0	1	1
Ben McDonald, USA	2	0	1.00	2	2	2	0	18	16	5	2	4	17
Tetsuya Shiozaki, Japan ..	1	0	1.04	4	1	0	0	9	5	1	1	1	10
Jesus Feliciano, PR	2	0	1.26	2	2	1	0	14	12	3	2	5	12
Parris Mitchell, Aust	0	1	1.46	2	1	1	1	12	9	2	2	3	2
Takehiro Ishii, JPN	2	1	1.90	4	3	1	0	24	17	5	5	2	11
Jim Abbott, USA	1	0	2.25	2	2	1	0	12	11	4	3	5	11

World Amateur Championships
Italy

	W	L	For	Ag.
Cuba................	11	0	112	35
USA	10	1	120	22
Taiwan	8	3	77	32
Japan	7	4	65	29
Canada	7	4	73	72
Puerto Rico	6	5	77	46
Nicaragua	5	6	46	61
South Korea........	5	6	59	47
Italy	4	7	51	78
Netherlands........	2	9	49	93
Neth. Antilles........	1	10	44	115
Spain	0	11	9	160

Final Round Robin Standings

Semifinals: Cuba 7, Japan 3; USA 6, Taiwan 3.
Final: Cuba 4, USA 3.

INDIVIDUAL BATTING LEADERS
(Minimum 25 At-Bats)

	AVG	G	AB	R	H	2B	3B	HR	RBI	BB	SO	SB
Antonio Pacheco, Cuba ...	.500	11	42	12	21	3	0	1	8	3	6	3
Mike Fiore, USA	.480	9	25	9	12	1	0	1	6	7	4	0
Robin Ventura, USA	.435	11	46	15	20	8	1	2	28	7	5	0
Daisuke Tsutsui, Japan ..	.424	11	33	8	14	6	0	3	11	5	4	2
Ty Griffin, USA	.421	11	38	17	16	2	0	4	13	12	6	3
Luis Casanova, Cuba	.419	11	43	13	18	3	0	7	20	5	5	1
Tino Martinez, USA	.413	11	46	10	19	2	0	4	18	5	5	0
Efrain Garcia, PR	.409	11	44	8	18	2	0	0	10	3	6	0
Takeshi Omori, Japan	.405	11	37	7	15	3	1	0	5	5	8	0
Warren Sawkiw, Canada ..	.405	11	37	4	15	3	0	2	11	3	5	0
Angel Morales, PR	.395	11	38	14	15	2	1	3	14	9	3	3
Giuseppe Carelli, Italy	.389	10	36	9	14	3	1	1	9	9	3	0
Jorge Robles, PR	.379	9	29	7	11	3	0	0	2	2	4	2
Luis Ulacia, Cuba	.378	9	37	12	14	1	1	1	5	2	2	2
Lin Tzung-Chiu, Taiwan ..	.371	11	35	6	13	3	0	3	12	5	3	1
Wu Fu-Lien, Taiwan	.371	11	35	7	13	3	1	0	9	10	4	1
Terushi Nakajima, Japan ..	.364	11	44	9	16	4	3	1	11	2	7	3
Omar Linares, Cuba	.362	11	47	17	17	2	0	6	15	1	9	2
Matt Stairs, Canada......	.362	11	47	8	17	4	0	1	9	1	7	3
Greg Duce, Canada	.359	11	39	12	14	3	0	1	7	6	4	0
Greg Roth, Canada	.359	11	39	11	14	4	1	4	10	9	6	0
Jim Kotkas, Canada	.357	11	42	9	15	4	3	1	11	5	10	0
Victor Mesa, Cuba	.350	11	40	7	14	4	0	1	15	1	4	0
Ariel Delgado, Nic	.341	11	44	5	15	2	1	2	8	4	10	0
Dave Silvestri, USA	.341	11	41	8	14	3	0	2	6	5	9	2

INDIVIDUAL PITCHING LEADERS
(Minimum 11 Innings)

	W	L	ERA	G	SV	IP	H	R	ER	BB	SO
Ben McDonald, USA	2	0	0.00	2	0	16	6	0	0	5	12
Lee Kang-Chul, Korea ...	2	0	0.00	2	0	14	7	1	0	3	16
Charles Nagy, USA	1	0	0.00	5	0	13	6	0	0	4	18
Takehiro Ishii, Japan	3	0	0.33	4	1	27	13	1	1	2	32
Kuo Cheng-Cherng, Taiwan	2	0	0.40	3	0	23	16	3	1	4	12
Fulvio Valle, Italy	0	0	0.52	5	1	17	11	1	1	3	6
Kuo-Lee Chien-Fu, Taiwan .	1	0	0.75	6	0	12	4	1	1	4	11
Barry Parisotto, Canada ..	2	0	1.10	3	0	16	15	2	2	3	5
Jim Abbott, USA.........	2	0	1.20	2	0	15	8	3	2	5	13
Lazaro Valle, Cuba.......	2	0	1.50	3	0	18	11	5	3	9	19
Eloy Morales, Nic	0	0	1.50	2	0	12	7	2	2	0	5
Paolo Ceccaroli, Italy	1	0	1.98	3	1	14	12	4	3	3	12
Rolando Cretis, Italy	0	0	2.03	2	0	13	13	4	3	10	12
Omar Ajete, Cuba	1	0	2.08	5	0	13	8	3	3	4	15
Yang Chien-Jen, Taiwan ..	0	0	2.18	5	0	12	10	4	3	1	6
Lee Kwang-Woo, Korea ..	2	1	2.33	5	0	19	22	10	5	3	9
Massimo Fochi, Italy	2	0	2.45	2	0	11	12	4	3	2	6
Pat Combs, USA	3	0	2.57	3	0	14	13	6	4	7	14

Cape Cod League

East	W	L	T	Pts.
Yarmouth-Dennis ...	22	18	3	47
Orleans............	22	20	1	45
Harwich...........	21	22	0	42
Chatham..........	19	24	1	39
Brewster..........	17	25	2	36

West	W	L	T	Pts.
Wareham	29	13	2	60
Hyannis	26	17	1	53
Cotuit	21	18	5	47
Falmouth	18	21	4	40
Bourne	12	29	4	27

Playoffs: Wareham defeated Orleans 2-1 in best-of-3 final for league championship.

INDIVIDUAL BATTING LEADERS
(Minimum 119 Plate Appearances)

	AVG	G	AB	R	H	2B	3B	HR	RBI	BB	SO	SB
Chuck Knoblauch, War ...	.361	44	169	38	61	17	2	1	29	24	22	23
David Staton, Bre	.359	42	145	35	52	12	0	16	46	32	36	1
Terry Taylor, Hya	.348	43	158	20	55	10	1	3	26	33	40	1
David Arendas, War	.346	37	133	23	46	7	2	1	26	13	18	11
J.T. Bruett, Cot	.333	29	111	24	37	3	1	0	10	24	9	30
Joe Delli Carri, Bou	.327	32	110	14	36	4	0	0	9	16	18	4
Nolan Lane, Y-D	.318	43	157	28	50	10	2	4	33	18	35	7
Casey Waller, Orl	.318	41	148	27	47	13	1	4	30	13	30	4
Jeff Bagwell, Cha	.318	44	146	26	46	9	1	6	22	33	28	5
Mark Johnson, Bou	.313	43	163	24	51	5	1	3	23	18	15	7
Kevin Long, War	.306	44	157	34	48	9	2	5	31	20	22	13
Mitch Hannahs, Y-D	.302	44	159	30	48	9	0	1	21	35	19	13
Timothy Salmon, Cot	.297	44	165	24	49	14	2	2	23	20	38	2
Brian Shabosky, Cot	.297	44	165	23	49	7	1	0	14	23	24	10
John Farrell, Fal	.296	39	152	21	45	7	1	3	14	12	23	9
Jesse Levis, Orl	.293	38	123	17	36	7	0	3	17	26	14	3
John Byington, Har	.292	43	171	21	50	15	0	4	22	16	27	2
Henry Manning, Bre	.292	39	144	18	42	6	0	2	22	7	12	0
Darryl Vice, Bre	.290	44	162	34	47	10	0	1	23	26	18	12
Warren Sawkiw, Bou	.288	30	111	11	32	4	1	3	20	9	25	2
Michael Weimerskirch, War	.285	42	158	30	45	9	1	0	19	19	17	25
Alan Zinter, Har	.285	39	144	18	41	8	0	6	23	15	32	1

INDIVIDUAL PITCHING LEADERS
(Minimum 35 Innings)

	W	L	ERA	G	GS	CG	SV	IP	H	R	ER	BB	SO
Mark Smith, Hya	4	1	1.03	13	2	1	2	44	37	14	5	13	41
Buddy Jenkins, Y-D	5	0	1.39	7	7	3	0	45	36	10	7	18	37
David Krol, Cot	6	2	1.51	11	11	4	0	84	60	17	14	30	79
Tom Hickox, Fal	0	2	1.80	21	0	0	6	35	28	9	7	15	21
Jason Klonoski, Orl	3	3	2.19	10	10	2	0	74	61	27	18	21	60
Brian Dour, Cha	2	5	2.27	10	10	4	0	79	69	26	20	25	37
Michael Myers, Bre	5	3	2.30	14	6	4	0	70	53	28	18	47	52
Kirk Dressendorfer, Hya ..	5	0	2.32	9	8	4	1	54	40	20	14	31	55
John Thoden, War	9	1	2.43	10	10	7	0	89	71	36	24	15	69
Kevin Morton, Hya	4	3	2.44	13	10	1	0	74	69	31	20	40	62
Brian Ahern, Har	6	2	2.46	10	10	5	0	80	77	28	22	27	62
Tim Smith, Bre	3	2	2.54	10	4	1	0	50	43	19	14	13	46
Pat Leinen, War	6	1	2.64	10	10	4	0	72	72	33	21	18	34

Great Lakes League

	W	L	Pct.	GB
Toledo.............	33	8	.805	—
Columbus	31	10	.756	2
Muncie	18	22	.450	14½
Lima	17	25	.405	16½
Cincinnati..........	13	25	.342	18½
Bowling Green	9	31	.225	23½

Playoffs: Columbus defeated Bowling Green in championship game of six-team double-elimination tournament.

INDIVIDUAL BATTING LEADERS
(Minimum 70 At-Bats)

	AVG	AB	R	H	2B	3B	HR	RBI	BB	SB
Shawn Hare, BG	.427	110	29	47	10	1	5	19	25	20
Matt Mieske, Tol	.352	125	34	44	12	5	4	31	18	6
Jason Welch, Tol	.347	75	16	26	2	3	0	11	10	1
Henry Threadgill, Col	.343	134	39	46	12	2	3	22	18	21

	AVG	AB	R	H	2B	3B	HR	RBI	BB	SB
Dennis McNamara, Tol	.331	124	32	41	9	1	0	16	10	20
Tom Eiterman, Col	.331	118	27	39	7	3	2	24	17	6
Jay Semke, Col	.328	134	30	44	11	3	1	24	17	14
David Larson, Col	.317	126	16	40	3	2	1	31	10	4
Terry Rupp, Lima	.311	106	14	33	9	1	5	25	7	0
Dan Masteller, Tol	.308	130	28	40	5	5	3	22	22	8
Jay Kvasnicka, BG	.306	72	14	22	2	2	0	11	12	12

INDIVIDUAL PITCHING LEADERS
(Minimum 30 Innings)

	W	L	ERA	CG	SV	IP	H	ER	BB	SO
Eric Jaques, Tol	9	1	1.50	6	2	60	37	10	20	59
Rich Capparelli, BG	4	4	2.01	4	0	58	47	13	23	60
Chris Fugitt, Col	4	1	2.03	3	0	31	23	7	4	30
Glen Leaveau, Tol	7	0	2.09	5	1	56	39	13	26	50
Kevin Parrish, Col	4	1	2.21	2	0	41	28	10	14	29
Richard Brandon, Col	4	1	2.25	1	0	32	26	8	12	18
Randy White, Col	6	1	2.31	4	0	47	34	12	25	30
Brad Stuart, Tol	4	4	2.61	4	0	52	47	15	12	35
Dan Rambo, Tol	7	2	2.66	3	1	61	55	18	22	40

Shenandoah Valley League

	W	L	Pct.	GB	
Waynesboro	27	15	.643	—	1988 Final Standings
Madison	25	17	.595	2	
Front Royal	23	19	.548	4	
***Staunton**	19	23	.452	8	
Winchester	19	23	.452	8	
New Market	18	24	.429	9	
Harrisonburg	16	26	.381	11	

*Won one-game playoff for fourth place

Playoffs: Waynesboro defeated Madison 3-2 in best-of-5 final for league championship.

INDIVIDUAL BATTING LEADERS
(Minimum 100 At-Bats)

	AVG	G	AB	R	H	2B	3B	HR	RBI	BB	SO	SB
Bill Jerich, Wayne	.404	35	136	39	55	8	0	11	25	18	20	5
Mike Rolfes, FR	.389	42	175	42	68	13	4	12	48	11	11	7
Brad Hollencamp, Staun	.375	42	168	43	63	11	1	18	43	25	54	1
Chris Turner, Mad	.361	45	180	51	65	12	2	10	33	30	41	13
Mike McGee, FR	.360	43	172	62	81	13	0	2	22	19	24	13
Randy Hood, FR	.357	42	154	39	55	13	0	7	38	31	15	12
Ronnie Plemmons, FR	.352	42	176	43	62	10	2	12	49	20	26	8
John Thomas, Wayne	.347	45	199	37	69	9	3	7	29	19	21	15
Geoff Flinn, Harr	.341	42	164	34	56	11	1	0	26	21	20	15
Pat Kelly, Staun	.332	41	190	37	63	10	2	1	16	8	23	12
Jon Anderson, Win	.329	42	167	32	55	9	0	8	27	20	37	1
Juan Serrano, Mad	.328	45	183	38	60	13	1	20	64	8	44	1

INDIVIDUAL PITCHING LEADERS
(Minimum 35 Innings)

	W	L	ERA	G	GS	CG	SV	IP	H	R	ER	BB	SO
Chris Nabholz, FR	5	2	2.86	10	9	5	0	66	75	28	21	15	55
Dan Smith, Staun	6	4	3.00	11	10	7	0	84	65	34	28	30	65
Joe Ganote, Wayne	5	2	3.61	10	8	4	0	62	66	33	25	21	49
Greg Naquin, Wayne	4	2	3.67	10	5	2	1	49	52	22	20	19	31
Jay Eck, NM	4	1	3.79	6	5	1	0	36	40	21	15	14	36
Scott Renner, Win	5	4	4.06	10	10	3	0	75	80	47	34	19	61
Tom Conners, Mad	4	1	4.26	7	7	2	0	44	43	24	21	21	33
Jake Jacobs, Mad	7	3	4.27	13	11	6	0	91	89	53	43	43	60
Tim Peele, Staun	2	0	4.32	14	0	0	1	42	56	23	20	16	28
Steve Renko, Win	3	5	4.44	13	11	4	0	75	85	52	37	31	69

Atlantic Collegiate League

Kaiser	W	L	Pct.	GB	
Nassau	21	18	.538	—	1988 Final Standings
Long Island	21	19	.525	½	
New York	17	23	.425	4½	
Brooklyn	15	24	.385	6	
Wolff					
Scranton	25	15	.625	—	
Quakertown	22	18	.550	3	
North Plainfield	21	19	.525	4	
New Jersey	17	23	.425	8	

Playoffs: Nassau defeated Scranton 3-1 in best-of-5 final for league championship.

INDIVIDUAL BATTING LEADERS
(Minimum 80 At-Bats)

	AVG	G	AB	R	H	2B	3B	HR	RBI
Mike Palys, Scrn	.473	40	146	66	69	9	8	16	58
Tom Nuniviller, Qkrtn	.441	29	102	24	45	8	1	3	25
Helmut Bohringer, Nass	.431	39	123	32	53	10	5	3	29
Mike Mecca, Scrn	.426	35	115	32	49	2	5	9	44
Eric Young, NP	.420	28	88	41	37	6	1	8	29
Bob Yager, NY	.411	36	112	15	46	8	2	3	33
Mike Valinotti, Brkln	.411	29	90	22	37	8	3	2	19
Dennis Tarantino, NY	.407	34	118	30	48	17	2	6	35
Steve Gatti, NJ	.407	36	108	21	44	4	0	6	27
Sam Champi, NJ	.400	36	124	30	49	5	0	3	23

INDIVIDUAL PITCHING LEADERS
(Minimum 40 Innings or 8 Games)

	W	L	ERA	G	IP	H	R	ER	BB	SO
Bob Migliosi, LI	4	2	1.06	8	42	14	11	5	14	22
Bob Aylmer, LI	4	1	1.75	13	36	14	9	3	6	10
Lynn Priest, Scrn	1	1	2.30	17	24	30	9	6	15	20
Wayne Masters, NP	5	2	2.51	12	43	40	16	12	15	22
Craig Connolly, NY	3	2	3.14	6	43	21	19	15	15	17
Jim Gallen, Nass	0	1	3.24	12	25	28	17	9	20	14
Joe Sottalano, Qkrtn	4	2	3.40	11	45	45	35	17	25	41

Central Illinois League
FIRST HALF

	W	L	Pct.	GB
Springfield	16	8	.667	—
Twin City	15	9	.625	1
Decatur	14	10	.583	2
Fairview Hts.	13	11	.542	3
Lincoln	11	13	.458	5
Quincy	9	15	.375	7
Danville	6	18	.250	10

SECOND HALF

	W	L	Pct.	GB
Twin City	17	6	.739	—
Springfield	14	9	.609	3
Fairview Hts.	13	10	.565	4
Lincoln	11	12	.478	6
Quincy	11	13	.458	6
Danville	10	13	.435	7
Decatur	5	18	.217	12

1988 Final Standings

INDIVIDUAL BATTING LEADERS
(Minimum 130 Plate Appearances)

	AVG	G	AB	R	H	2B	3B	HR	RBI	BB	SO	SB
Melvin Biankowski, Dan . . .	.393	41	135	32	53	7	1	7	38	13	12	3
Mark Dalesandro, Dec	.389	46	175	51	68	14	4	6	37	17	13	3
Ken Simonich, FH	.366	44	145	31	53	6	1	9	42	30	14	13
Tom Vantiger, TC	.362	44	174	49	63	17	4	5	35	21	24	12
Brian Filosa, Dec	.359	45	156	27	56	10	0	1	24	19	17	0
Mike Stevenson, Spr	.355	43	152	27	54	12	0	8	25	15	18	4
Phil Mundy, Dan	.348	43	138	32	48	4	3	3	31	24	13	9
Mark Neff, Dec	.344	41	151	33	52	11	3	6	40	16	36	7
Andy Weis, Spr	.343	46	178	45	61	7	2	7	30	21	21	10

INDIVIDUAL PITCHING LEADERS
(Minimum 40 Innings)

	W	L	ERA	G	GS	CG	SV	IP	H	R	ER	BB	SO
Jerry Oetting, Spr	5	2	1.77	10	9	5	0	71	58	23	14	33	49
Jeff Borski, Spr	3	1	2.45	18	0	0	3	40	35	19	11	26	29
Jeff Richards, Dan	4	2	2.68	33	0	0	4	74	51	27	22	47	68
Bill Wertz, Lcn	5	3	3.38	11	10	5	0	69	60	33	26	28	71
Roger Popplewell, TC	5	1	3.55	9	7	4	1	58	69	29	23	14	29
Don Green, TC	3	3	3.99	16	3	1	5	47	42	26	21	31	52
Scott Brown, Spr	6	3	4.15	10	9	8	0	65	59	38	30	28	46

Alaska League

	W	L	Pct.	GB
Kenai Peninsula	21	14	.600	—
Fairbanks	25	19	.568	½
Pullman, Wash.	18	16	.529	2½
Hawaii	12	14	.462	4½
San Francisco	11	24	.440	10

1988 Final Standings

Andy Benes rose from obscurity to become the top choice in baseball's 1988 draft.

Benes is first chosen; 1,431 others follow

By KEN LEIKER

The 24th June amateur free agent draft began when the San Diego Padres selected Andy Benes, a 6-foot-6, 230-pound righthanded pitcher from the University of Evansville.

Two days and 74 rounds later, 1,432 players had been selected—169 more than the previous record total, set in 1987.

The process yielded 855 new professional players, 60 percent of those drafted. The most notable exception was righthanded pitcher Alex Fernandez of Miami (Fla.) Pace High School, who was selected by the Milwaukee Brewers in the first round.

Despite a bonus offer of $150,000, Fernandez decided to honor a commitment to the University of Miami. He was the first high school player with first-round status to choose a college baseball scholarship over a pro contract since 1979. The Boston Red Sox lost Greg McMurtry, their first-round choice in 1986, but not to college baseball. He accepted a football scholarship from Michigan.

Fernandez was the only first-round selection who did not sign.

The only second-round selection who passed up a pro contract was righthanded pitcher Jeff Seale of Fairview High School in

Boulder, Colo. He chose the University of Texas over the New York Mets.

On the mark again

The Padres' selection of Benes marked the sixth straight year that Baseball America correctly forecast the No. 1 pick. He was the first pitcher since Tim Belcher in 1983 to be the first player chosen.

The Padres previously had spent the first pick in the draft on Mike Ivie (1970), Dave Roberts (1972) and Bill Almon (1974). This time, they were intent on a pitcher who could advance to the big leagues quickly.

San Diego pared its list to Benes and righthander Gregg Olson of Auburn University. The Padres decided on Benes after watching him shut out top-ranked Arizona State, 1-0, in Tempe, Ariz., in the NCAA West II Regional, six days before the draft.

Benes was among nine first-round selections who made the U.S. Olympic team that won a gold medal at the Seoul Games, delaying the start of their pro careers until at least the fall instructional league programs.

The others were pitchers Jim Abbott, Charles Nagy and Pat Combs, first baseman Tino Martinez, second baseman Ty Griffin, third basemen Robin Ventura and Ed Sprague, and outfielder Ted Wood.

Righthanded pitcher Dave Wainhouse of Washington State, the Montreal Expos' first-round selection, was a member of Canada's Olympic team.

Olson, meanwhile, became the first player from the Class of '88 to play in the big leagues, making his debut Sept. 2 after 16 minor league appearances. He was drafted by the Baltimores Orioles, who held the fourth selection and reportedly pressured Olson to forsake the Olympics, although they vehemently denied the charge.

Olson was the only player from the draft class to play in the major leagues in 1988.

Between Benes and Olson, players widely regarded as the top high school prospects were selected. The Cleveland Indians took shortstop Mark Lewis of Hamilton, Ohio, and the Atlanta Braves picked lefthanded pitcher Steve Avery of Taylor, Mich.

The top lefthanded pitching prospects went quickly. Avery, Abbott, Combs and Tom Fischer were among the first 12 selections.

Abbott, who had a spectacular career at the University of Michigan and pitched the gold medal-winning game in Seoul, was considered a risk by many clubs because he was born without a right hand. But the California Angels, convinced that he had no handicap, spent the eighth selection on Abbott.

Jim Abbott
... Angels draftee

The other southern California team also gambled. The Dodgers, choosing fifth, selected righthander Bill Bene, who was regarded as the hardest thrower available but had limited success at Cal State Los Angeles because of control problems.

The high selections of Abbott and Bene were not the only surprises in the first round.

Fischer (12th, Red Sox), third baseman Stan Royer (16th, Athletics) and Wainhouse (19th) were not considered first-round material by many clubs.

College pitchers in demand

The first round was comprised of 16 college players, eight from high schools and two from junior colleges. Ten righthanded pitchers were selected, four lefthanders, four shortstops, three

Reliever Gregg Olson, Baltimore's top pick, became the first 1988 draftee to make the majors.

third basemen, two first basemen, two outfielders and one second baseman.

For the first time, no catchers were selected in the first round, although Royer and Sprague (Toronto) were drafted with the idea that they had the skills to be converted into receivers. Six catchers were selected in the second round.

Toronto drafted the most players (73), followed by the New York Yankees (72), Atlanta (69), Pittsburgh (66) and Houston (65).

Three schools each contributed nine players: Oklahoma State, Texas and San Jacinto, Texas, a two-year school. Eight players came from the University of Miami, Fla., and junior colleges Indian River (Fla.), Seminole (Fla.) and Rancho Santiago (Calif.).

A preference for college talent that began earlier in the decade continued. College selections totaled 625, high school 515 and junior college 274. Eighteen draft choices were not affiliated with any school.

Only 168 high school players, or 32 percent of the total number selected, had signed by Oct. 1, but those unsigned players who elected to attend junior college remained under control of the club drafting them. They will be free to sign after completion of their junior college season in the spring, or go back into the draft pool again.

Big year for bonuses

Four players reportedly received signing bonuses of at least $200,000, a sum that is believed to have been granted to a drafted player only once previously.

Bo Jackson, a fourth-round selection in 1986, received more than $300,000 from the Kansas City Royals, who were competing against the National Football League for the former Heisman Trophy winner.

Benes, who finished his junior year at Evansville with a 16-

3 record and a 1.42 ERA, received $230,000—$70,000 more than Ken Griffey Jr. received a year earlier from the Seattle Mariners as the first selection.

Avery, bartering with the strength of a scholarship from Stanford, received $211,000.

Olson's bonus reportedly was $200,000.

The most expensive player in the draft may have been Reid Cornelius, a righthanded pitcher from Thomasville (Ala.) High School, selected by the Montreal Expos in the 11th round.

Cornelius signed in August, receiving "in the neighborhood of $240,000," according to his father. "He got the highest bonus ever paid a high school player."

Cornelius was expected to be among the first five players chosen until announcing that it would take at least $200,000 to buy him away from a scholarship to Mississippi State. A straight-A student, he intended to pursue a degree in aeronautical engineering.

No first-rounder again

Several other high school players were drafted considerably lower than their talent level because of college commitments. Most were selected by the Yankees, who did not have a turn until 104 players were gone. They lost their choices in the first three rounds because they had signed major league free agents Jack Clark, John Candaleria and Jose Cruz during the offseason.

The Yankees' draft list included Troy Tallman (36th round), who would have been the first catcher selected if clubs thought they could sway him from a commitment to Stanford; John Cummings (32nd round), the top lefthanded pitching prospect on the West Coast, but holding a scholarship from Southern Cal; and outfielder Pat Maloney (37th round), who had a football scholarship from Michigan. All opted for college.

The Yankees did, however, sign their first 27 selections—the most consecutive such picks in draft history.

Other top talents who honored college commitments were outfielder Tommy Adams (Arizona State), selected by Atlanta in the 10th round; and lefthanded pitcher Steve Worrell (Stanford), chosen by Boston in the 37th round.

Pete Rose Jr.
. . . late signee

Outfielder Deion Sanders, a 30th-round selection with first-round talent, did accept a summer job in the Yankees' minor-league system, then returned to Florida State, where he had been an All-America defensive back as a junior. Barring injury, Sanders is expected to be among the first five players chosen in the 1989 NFL draft.

Another two-way talent, outfielder Brian Jordan, was selected by St. Louis as a supplemental pick after the first round. After signing with the Cardinals and playing briefly in their farm system in 1988, he returned to the University of Richmond to play football. A top wide receiver prospect, he had NFL scouts watching him closely.

The Oakland Athletics drafted Rodney Peete in the 14th-round and reportedly offered him $100,000 and would have paid for his final year at Southern Cal, where he was pursuing the Heisman Trophy as a quarterback. Peete, a third baseman on the Trojans' baseball team, did not sign.

The Angels spent their 43rd-round choice on celebrated high school quarterback Todd Marinovich, even though scouts said they had never seen him play baseball. Marinovich is Peete's heir apparent on the Southern Cal football team.

The most famous baseball name in the draft was infielder Pete Rose Jr., who was chosen by the Orioles in the 12th round.

Rose rejected early offers and eventually announced that he would attend Cerritos College, a two-year school in California. But after playing for the Cincinnati team that won the American Legion World Series, he signed for $20,000.

Other players in the draft with familiar names were Pedro Oliva (Minnesota), son of former American League batting champion Tony Oliva; and John Kuehl (San Diego), son of former big league manager Karl Kuehl.

Team-by-Team Selections

(Boldface type indicates player signed with selecting club; order of selection in parentheses after team name)

ATLANTA BRAVES (3)

1. **Steve Avery, lhp, Kennedy HS, Taylor, Mich.**
2. **Jim Kremers, c, University of Arkansas.**
2. **Matt Murray, rhp, Loomis Chaffee HS, Windsor, Conn.** (Choice from Philadelphia as compensation for signing Dave Palmer as a 'Class B' free agent).
2. **John Kupsey, 3b, Gloucester Catholic HS, Gibbstown, N.J.** (Compensation for loss of Glenn Hubbard as a 'Class C' free agent).
3. **Preston Watson, rhp, University of Texas.**
4. **Kevin Tyson, c, Jefferson HS, Lafayette, Ind.**
5. **Steve Wendell, rhp, Quinnipiac College.**
6. **Jimmie Pullins, of, Tyler (Texas) HS.**
7. **Lee Heath, of, LaSalle HS, Cincinnati, Ohio.**
8. **Mark Wohlers, rhp, Holyoke (Mass.) HS.**
9. **Edwin Alicea, 2b, Florida State University.**
10. Tommy Adams, of, Capistrano Valley HS, Mission Viejo, Calif.
11. **Sean Hutchinson, c, Northview HS, Covina, Calif.**
12. Fred Cooley, rhp, University of Southern Mississippi.
13. **David Waldenberger, 3b, Rowland HS, Rowland Heights, Calif.**
14. Mike Hostetler, rhp, Sprayberry HS, Marietta, Ga.
15. **Anthony Tarasco, of, Santa Monica (Calif.) HS.**
16. Russell Brock, rhp, Lockland (Ohio) HS.
17. **John Greenwood, 1b, San Francisco State University.**
18. **Tom Rizzo, ss, North Adams State College.**
19. **Randy Simmons, of, University of Delaware.**
20. Mike Lopez, rhp, Sheridan HS, Denver, Colo.
21. **Steve Lopez, 3b-of, Vacaville (Calif.) HS.**
22. **Donovan Campbell, of, Texas Southern University.**
23. Greg Perschke, rhp, University of New Orleans.
24. **Ramces Guerrero, 2b, Dominican (N.Y.) College.**
25. Thomas Neff, of, Magnolia HS, Anaheim, Calif.
26. Craig Bradshaw, lhp, Alexandria (La.) HS.
27. Ron Hazl, of, Alhambra HS, Glendale, Ariz.
28. **Rickey Rigsby, of, Angelina (Texas) JC.**
29. Scott Stice, rhp, Wake Forest University.
30. **Gary Schoonover, ss, Brigham Young University.**
31. Mark Dressen, rhp, La Serna HS, Whittier, Calif.
32. **James Kortright, rhp, Snow College.**
33. Chris Gaskill, rhp, Westfield HS, Houston, Texas.
34. Adam Schulhofer, 3b, Canoga Park HS, Woodland Hills, Calif.
35. **Alan Thomas, of, Ventura (Calif.) JC.**
36. William Morris, ss, St. Francis HS, Glendale, Calif.
37. **William Lange, lhp, Rio Hondo (Calif.) JC.**
38. **Scott Goselin, 2b, Olivet Nazarene (Ill.) College.**
39. Scott Ruffcorn, rhp, Austin (Texas) HS.
40. Mike Smith, of, Woodward HS, Cincinnati, Ohio.
41. Mike Solar, 1b, Covina HS, West Covina, Calif.
42. John Keller, c, Westwood HS, Austin, Texas.
43. **Calvain Culberson, of, Armstrong State University.**
44. **Wallace Gonzales, c, Rosemead (Calif.) HS.**
45. **Rodolfo Gardey, rhp, Canada (Calif.) JC.**
46. Steven Dailey, of, Ventura (Calif.) HS.
47. Jason Gonzales, ss, Cuero (Texas) HS.
48. **Mark Eskins, rhp, Jacksonville State University.**
49. **Chris Jones, 1b, Southern Tech Institute.**
50. **Pat Stivers, ss-2b, Mesa (Colo.) College.**
51. **Brent McCoy, ss, Howard University.**
52. Doug Kimball, ss-p, Shadow Mountain HS, Phoenix, Ariz.
53. David Cronin, of, LaSalle HS, Cincinnati, Ohio.
54. **David Plela, c, Western Carolina University.**
55. Craig Triplett, c-1b, Paradise Valley HS, Phoenix, Ariz.
56. **Marco Paddy, c, Southern University.**
57. Jeff Blanks, ss, Del Rio (Tex.) HS.
58. Greg Viks, rhp, DeSoto (Texas) HS.
59. **Glen Gardner, of, Rutgers University.**
60. Roy Gamez, c, Casa Grande (Ariz.) HS.
61. **Joe Saccamanno, ss-2b, Bloomfield College.**
62. **Paul Bacosa, rhp, San Jose State University.**
63. **Eric Kuhlman, of, Bradley University.**

1988 Draft: First Round

Team, Player, Pos.	School	Yr.	B-T	Ht.	Wt.	Avg.	AB	R	H	2B	3B	HR	RBI	SB
2. Indians, Mark Lewis, ss	Hamilton (Ohio) HS	Sr.	R-R	6-1	170	.600	105	65	63	10	5	15	66	23
6. Rangers, Monty Fariss, ss	Oklahoma State	Jr.	R-R	6-4	180	.397	242	95	96	14	4	30	114	6
7. Astros, Willie Ansley, of	Plainview (Texas) HS	Sr.	R-R	6-2	195	.458	83	42	38	7	2	7	31	23
9. Cubs, Ty Griffin, 2b	Georgia Tech		B-R	6-0	180	.345	261	81	90	16	8	14	68	38
10. White Sox, Robin Ventura, 3b	Oklahoma State	Jr.	L-R	6-1	170	.391	256	96	100	16	1	26	96	2
13. Pirates, Austin Manahan, ss	Horizon HS, Phoenix	Sr.	R-R	6-1	175	.526	78	51	41	8	3	9	23	23
14. Mariners, Tino Martinez, 1b	Univ. of Tampa	Jr.	L-R	6-2	190	.452	188	68	85	16	2	25	74	8
15. Giants, Royce Clayton, ss	St. Brnd HS, Inglewood, Ca.	Sr.	R-R	6-0	175	.513	78	43	40	8	0	10	32	22
16. A's, Stan Royer, 3b	Eastern Illinois Univ.	Jr.	R-R	6-3	195	.335	170	44	57	12	0	17	54	1
18. Royals, Hugh Walker, of	Jacksonville (Ark.) HS	Jr.	L-R	6-1	190	.512						11	37	
25. Blue Jays, Ed Sprague, 3b	Stanford Univ.	Jr.	R-R	6-2	190	.339	257	62	87	16	0	22	81	5
26. Tigers, Rico Brogna, 1b	Watertown (Conn.) HS	Sr.	R-R	6-2	190	.655				5	5	4	35	9

Team, Player, Pos.	School	Yr.	B-T	Ht.	Wt.	W	L	ERA	G	Sv	IP	H	BB	SO
1. Padres, Andy Benes, p	Evansville Univ.	Jr.	R-R	6-5	230	16	3	1.42	24	2	146	87	36	188
3. Braves, Steve Avery, p	Kennedy HS, Taylor, Mi.	Sr.	L-L	6-4	185	11	0	0.29	12	1	71	15	19	160
4. Orioles, Gregg Olson, p	Auburn Univ.	Jr.	R-R	6-4	210	7	3	2.00	36	10	72	43	27	113
5. Dodgers, Bill Bene, p	Cal St. Los Angeles	Jr.	R-R	6-4	190	6	3	5.80	17	0	50	40	51	45
8. Angels, Jim Abbott, p	Univ. of Michigan	Jr.	L-L	6-3	200	9	3	3.32	17	0	98	88	56	82
11. Phillies, Pat Combs, p	Baylor Univ.	Jr.	L-L	6-3	200	7	6	2.16	19	2	100	77	46	97
12. Red Sox, Tom Fischer, p	Univ. of Wisconsin	Jr.	L-L	5-11	190	6	6	5.00	13	0	77	87	36	80
17. Indians, Charles Nagy, p	Univ. of Connecticut	So.	L-R	6-4	205	6	4	2.40	15	1	86	51	37	113
19. Expos, Dave Wainhouse, p	Washington St. U.	Jr.	R-R	6-2	182	7	6	3.90	27	6	81	78	33	57
20. Twins, Johnny Ard, p	Manatee (Fla.) JC	So.	R-R	6-5	215	10	3	2.51	18	3	125	88	41	114
21. Mets, Dave Proctor, p	Allen Co. (Kan.) CC	So.	R-R	6-3	200	8	2	2.80	11	1	72	49	33	86
22. Cardinals, John Ericks, p	Univ. of Illinois	Jr.	R-R	6-7	215	7	5	4.33	13	0	81	55		108
23. Cardinals, Brad DuVall, p	Virginia Tech	Sr.	R-R	6-1	185	11	3	3.82	17	1	99	89	47	94
24. Brewers, Alex Fernandez, p	Pace HS, Miami	Sr.	R-R	6-1	205	14	0	0.45	17	2	94	94	22	189

Oklahoma State shortstop Monty Fariss was the No. 1 choice of the Texas Rangers.

64. Drayton Reedy, 1b, Towers HS, Decatur, Ga.
65. Michael Eiffert, of, Lewisville (Tex.) HS.
66. **Kevin Thomas, rhp, Rockdale HS, Conyers, Ga.**
67. **Kevin Henry, 3b, Auburn University.**

BALTIMORE ORIOLES (4)

1. **Gregg Olson, rhp, Auburn University.**
1. **Ricky Gutierrez, ss, American HS, Hialeah, Fla. (Special supplemental choice—28th—for failing to sign 1987 No. 1 choice Brad Duvall).**
2. **Arthur Rhodes, of, La Vega HS, Waco, Texas.**
3. **Stacy Jones, rhp, Auburn University.**
4. **Aman Hicks, of, Gardena (Calif.) HS.**
5. **Steve Nicosia, of, Bishop Gallagher HS, St. Clair Shores, Mich.**
6. **Tom Martin, lhp, Bay HS, Panama City, Fla.**
7. **Keith Lee, of, Glassboro State College.**
8. **Mike Deutsch, rhp, Rider College.**
9. **Mike Linskey, lhp, James Madison University.**
10. **Doug Robbins, c, Stanford University.**
11. Cris Allen, 3b, Florida Southern College.
12. **Pete Rose, 3b, Oak Hills HS, Cincinnati.**
13. **Rodney Lofton, ss, Grambling State University.**
14. Jim Robinson, rhp, Northwestern University.
15. Gustavo Miranda, 3b-ss, Miami HS.
16. **Bob Bretwisch, lhp, Bradley University.**
17. **Mike Richardson, 1b, Portland State University.**
18. **Joe Redman, 2b, Paulsboro (N.J.) HS.**
19. **Scott McNaney, ss, Elizabethtown College.**
20. Robert Doman, lhp, James Madison University.
21. Rene Francisco, of, Indian River (Fla.) CC.
22. **Roy Gilbert, of, Centenary College.**
23. **Chris Burgin, rhp, University of Oklahoma.**
24. **Zach Kerr, rhp, New Mexico State University.**
25. Brian Barnes, lhp, Clemson University.
26. **Carey Metts, c, Mars Hill College.**
27. **Chris Shebby, rhp, Georgetown University.**
28. John Hamilton, rhp, Statesboro (Ga.) HS.
29. Michael Place, rhp, Seminole (Fla.) HS.
30. **Brian Janutolo, ss, Bluefield State College.**
31. **Mark Withers, of, North Carolina State University.**
32. Baylor Alexander, c, Wolfson HS, Jacksonville, Fla.
33. **Jeff Champ, c, San Diego State University.**
34. **Dell Ahalt, 3b, North Carolina State University.**
35. Bobby Lamm, of, Hunt HS, Wilson, N.C.
36. **John Fowler, 3b, Frederick (Md.) CC.**
37. Mark Brockell, 3b, James Madison University.
38. Aaron Van Scoyoc, ss, Norway (Iowa) HS.
39. **Robert Block, of, Southern Arkansas University JC.**
40. **Chris LaFollette, of, Southview HS, Fayetteville, N.C.**
41. Brian Cornelius, of, Southern University.
42. David Marshall, ss, Cooper HS, Abilene, Texas.
43. Chris Finley, of, Lamar HS, Houston.
44. **Earl Williams, c, Catonsville (Md.) CC.**
45. **Don Marett, rhp, Owen HS, Black Mountain, N.C.**

BOSTON RED SOX (12)

1. **Tom Fischer, lhp, University of Wisconsin.**
2. **Andy Rush, rhp, Somerset (Pa.) HS.**
3. **Mickey Rivers, of, Bacone (Okla.) JC.**
4. **Dan Kite, rhp, Louisiana State University.**
5. **John Valentin, ss, Seton Hall University.**
6. **Ed Riley, lhp, St. Peter-Marien HS, Worcester, Mass.**
7. **Dave Owen, lhp, Carson-Newman College.**
8. **Tim Naehring, ss, Miami (Ohio) University.**
9. **Willie Tatum, 3b, University of the Pacific.**
10. **Meredith Moore, of, Nogales HS, La Puente, Calif.**
11. David Stuart, rhp, Indian River (Fla.) CC.
12. **James Sanders, rhp, Lower Columbia (Wash.) JC.**
13. **Richard Witherspoon, of, Nogales HS, La Puente, Calif.**
14. **Garrett Jenkins, of, Steubenville (Ohio) HS.**
15. **Howard Landry, lhp, University of Southwestern Louisiana.**
16. **Bernard Dzafic, rhp, Lincoln Land (Ill.) CC.**
17. Eric Slinkard, c, Chula Vista (Calif.) HS.
18. **Billy Hathaway, lhp, Sandalwood HS, Jacksonville, Fla.**
19. **Kevin Crowder, 2b-3b, Keene (N.H.) HS.**
20. Corey Powell, of, Patrick Henry HS, San Diego.
21. Gary Kinser, rhp, Columbia State (Tenn.) CC.
22. **Chris Whitehead, 3b, Middle Tennessee State University.**
23. Scott Bakkum, rhp, Aquinas HS, LaCrosse, Wis.
24. **Bernard Doyle, of, North Newton HS, Morocco, Ill.**
25. **John Flaherty, c, George Washington University.**
26. Jason Blasucci, ss, South Broward HS, Hollywood, Fla.
27. Mark Mitchelson, lhp, Hillsborough (Fla.) CC.
28. **Rodney Taylor, lhp, Bowling Green State University.**
29. **John Sowell, of, University of Lowell.**
30. Andrew Flagler, 1b, Valencia (Fla.) CC.
31. Dan Robinson, 3b, San Jacinto (Texas) JC.

32. Michael Rebhan, rhp, Lake City (Fla.) CC.
33. Peter Hoy, rhp, LeMoyne College.
34. Barton Moore, 2b, Jefferson State (Ala.) JC.
35. Gary Posey, of, Gulf Coast (Fla.) CC.
36. Thomas Wiley, of-p, Westmar College.
37. Steve Worrell, lhp, Lower Cape May (N.J.) Regional HS.
38. Roger Luce, c, San Jacinto (Texas) JC.

CALIFORNIA ANGELS (10)

1. Jim Abbott, lhp, University of Michigan.
2. (Choice to Giants as compensation for Type A free agent Chili Davis).
3. Glenn Carter, rhp, Triton (Ill.) JC.
4. J.R. Phillips, lhp-of, Bishop Amat HS, Rowland Heights, Calif.
5. David Neal, lhp, Montgomery HS, Semmes, Ala.
6. Gary Disarcina, ss, University of Massachusetts.
7. James Edmonds, of, Diamond Bar (Calif.) HS.
8. David Partrick, of, Tate HS, Cantonment, Fla.
9. Jeff Kelso, rhp, Missouri Western State.
10. Dave Sturdivant, c, University of Nevada-Las Vegas.
11. Scott Lewis, rhp, University of Nevada-Las Vegas.
12. Jeff Kipila, of, Elon College.
13. Mike Robertson, of, Servite HS, Placentia, Calif.
14. Damon Mashore, of, Clayton Valley HS, Concord, Calif.
15. Mike Sheehy, of, Penn State University.
16. Dirk Skillicorn, of, St. Francis HS, Los Altos, Calif.
17. Marcus Moore, rhp, Kennedy HS, Richmond, Calif.
18. L.V. Powell, rhp, Poly HS, Long Beach, Calif.
19. Thomas Bates, ss, Paris (Texas) JC.
20. Kirk Dulom, 3b, Miami.
21. Paul Borse, of, Sacramento (Calif.) CC.
22. Larry Gonzales, c, University of Hawaii.
23. Bill Minnis, ss, Mesa (Ariz.) CC.
24. Jeff Oberdank, 2b, UC Irvine.
25. Gary Cooper, 3b, Scottsdale (Ariz.) CC.
26. Wes Bliven, rhp, Santa Clara University.
27. Bruce Vegely, lhp, Cal State Dominguez Hills.
28. Frank Dominguez, c, University of Miami.
29. John Marchese, rhp, Grand Canyon College.
30. Jacinto Easley, ss-2b, Long Beach (Calif.) HS.
31. Darrin Gleiser, ss, Sandpoint (Idaho) Legion HS.
32. Robert Dodd, lhp, Sacramento (Calif.) CC.
33. Charles Lloyd, ss, Miami-Dade New World Center CC.
34. Jim Henry, lhp, Placer HS, Forest Hill, Calif.
35. Donald Vidmar, rhp, Grand Canyon College.
36. Steve Kirwin, of, Lewis University.
37. Michael Hartnett, c, Borah HS, Boise, Idaho.
38. Raul Rodarte, ss, Ganesha HS, Diamond Bar, Calif.
39. Rodney Eldridge, 1b-of, Scottsdale (Ariz.) CC.
40. Randolph Kapano, ss, Azusa (Calif.) HS.
41. Mark Roberts, rhp, Brewton Parker (Ga.) JC.
42. James Pedicaris, of, Lake Gibson HS, Lakeland, Fla.
43. Todd Marinovich, lhp, Capistrano Valley HS, Mission Viejo, Calif.
44. Jon Anderson, c, Indian River (Fla.) CC.
45. William Jones, c, Triton (Ill.) JC.
46. Brian Goodwin, rhp, Indian River (Fla.) CC.
47. Rene Delgado, ss, Miami-Dade North CC.

CHICAGO CUBS (9)

1. Ty Griffin, 2b, Georgia Tech.
2. (Choice to Expos as compensation for Type B free agent Vance Law).
3. Roberto Ventura (Smalls), rhp, St. Thomas, Virgin Islands.
4. Brad Huff, c, Monroe (Ga.) Area HS.
5. John Salles, rhp, Fresno State University.
6. Troy Bailey, of, T.C. Williams HS, Alexandria, Va.
7. Billy St. Peter, 3b-ss, University of Michigan.
8. Robert Bonneau, ss, Gonzaga Prep HS, Spokane, Wash.
9. Dennis Gray, lhp, Banning (Calif.) HS.
10. David Goodwin, rhp, Xavier University.
11. Billy Paynter, c, Coronado HS, Tempe, Ariz.
12. Roger Burnett, ss, Broken Arrow (Okla.) HS.
13. James Murphy, of, Portland State University.
14. Rick Hirtensteiner, of, Pepperdine University.
15. Todd Borders, c, Lake Wales (Fla.) HS.
16. Kevin Roberson, of, Parkland (Ill.) JC.
17. Luis Sierra, of, Dupont HS, Wilmington, Del.
18. Daren Burns, rhp, Birmingham-Southern.
19. Andrew Croghan, rhp, Servite HS, Yorba Linda, Calif.
20. Woody Smith, 3b, Spartanburg Methodist (S.C.) JC.
21. Kraig Washington, of, Rancho Santiago (Calif.) JC.
22. Mathew Leonard, 3b, Benedictine College.
23. Jason Doss, rhp, Westwood HS, Fort Pierce, Fla.
24. George Browder, c, Zephyr Hills (Fla.) HS.
25. Juan Figueroa, of, Laredo (Texas) JC.
26. Dan Johnston, rhp, Creighton University.
27. Greg Kessler, rhp, North Idaho JC.
28. Tim Ellis, lhp, Rosemont (Calif.) JC.

Top Draft Picks

Tom Fischer
...No. 1, Bosox

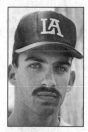

Bill Bene
...fifth pick

Pat Combs
...first pick, Phils

29. **Mike Sodders, lhp, University of Alabama.**
30. **John Jensen, of, University of Texas.**
31. **Albert Stacey, 1b, Cleveland State University.**
32. **Ronnie Rasp, rhp, University of Montevallo.**
33. **Shannon Jones, rhp, Southeastern Louisiana University.**
34. **Ben Shreve, ss, West Virginia University.**
35. Rodney Pedraza, rhp, Cuero (Texas) HS.
36. **Richard Mundy, c, Pattonville HS, Bridgeton, Mo.**
37. Chris Pritchett, ss, Central Catholic HS, Modesto, Calif.
38. Bill Judge, 3b, Brother Rice HS, Oak Forest, Ill.
39. **Tracy Smith, rhp, Miami (Ohio) University.**
40. Jessie Hollins, rhp, Willis (Texas) HS.
41. **Eric Williams, of, University of North Carolina, Charlotte.**
42. **Marvin Cole, ss, Alexandria (La.) HS.**
43. **Chris Lutz, rhp, University of Michigan.**
44. Mathew Johnson, ss, Arvada (Colo.) West HS.
45. Peter Gardere, 1b, Robert E. Lee HS, Houston.
46. **Rusty Crockett, ss, University of Texas.**

CHICAGO WHITE SOX (10)

1. **Robin Ventura, 3b, Oklahoma State University.**
2. **Lenny Brutcher, rhp, Cicero-North Syracuse (N.Y.) HS.**
3. **Mike Mitchener, rhp, Armstrong State College.**
4. **Johnny Ruffin, rhp, Choctaw County HS, Butler, Ala.**
5. Joey Eischen, lhp, West Covina (Calif.) HS.
6. **Mark Chasey, 1b, Florida Southern College.**
7. Richard Batchelor, rhp, University of South Carolina.
8. **Wayne Moye, of, Princeton HS, Cincinnati.**
9. **Jerome Wolak, of, South Hills HS, West Covina, Calif.**
10. **John Hudek, rhp, Florida Southern College.**
11. **Dennis Walker, 3b-c, Grambling State University.**
12. **Scott Egan, c, Glen Ridge (N.J.) HS.**
13. **Scott Middaugh, rhp, San Diego State University.**
14. **John Zaksek, of, University of Cincinnati.**
15. **Fred Dabney, lhp, Seminole (Okla.) JC.**
16. **Frank Merigliano, rhp, University of Pittsburgh.**
17. Todd Hobson, of, Lawrence North HS, Indianapolis.
18. **John Chafin, rhp, Marshall University.**
19. **Michael Busby, ss, Mississippi College.**
20. **James Pague, rhp, Central Florida CC.**
21. **Scott Tedder, of, Ohio Wesleyan University.**
22. **Michael Galvan, lhp, Louisiana Tech University.**
23. **John Furch, 1b, Duke University.**
24. Brian Noack, ss, Pensacola (Fla.) JC.
25. **Dwayne Harvey, rhp, Sherrills Ford, N.C.**
26. **Arthur Thigpen, rhp, Flagler College.**
27. **Patrick Hulme, rhp, Hanna HS, Anderson, S.C.**
28. Chris Fruge, rhp, Mississippi Delta JC.
29. Anthony Pritchett, c, Mobile County HS, Grand Bay, Ala.
30. John DeSilva, rhp, Brigham Young University.
31. **James Garrett, rhp, Southern University.**
32. **Paul Abbatinozzi, c, Flagler College.**
33. Craig Teter, of, Seminole (Okla.) JC.
34. Carl Dorsey, lhp, Hanna HS, Anderson, S.C.
35. Keith Morrison, rhp, North Gwinett HS, Suwanee, Ga.
36. Brian Whittal, rhp-3b, Marysville, Wash.
37. Brian Stephens, of, Hillsborough (Fla.) CC.
38. **Scott Fuller, rhp, University of Wisconsin.**
39. Marvin Benard, of, Bell HS, Cudahy, Calif.
40. Jack Johnson, c, St. Rita HS, Chicago.
41. Jeff Graff, of, Texarkana (Texas) CC.
42. **Derek Lee, inf-of, University of South Florida.**
43. Jeff Ingram, c, University of New Orleans.
44. Osborne Timmons, of, Brandon HS, Tampa, Fla.

45. Todd Bargman, 1b, Oklahoma State University.
46. Ronald Plemmons, of, Spartanburg Methodist (S.C.) JC.
47. Lane Mallett, of, University of Houston.
48. Brian Cordero, lhp, St. John's University.
49. Timothy Sheriff, ss, West Oak HS, Westminster, S.C.
50. Robert Fletcher, 3b, University of Alabama.
51. Robert Thompson, c-of, Indian River (Fla.) CC.
52. Steve James, 1b, Mississippi Valley State University.
53. Brett Berry, of, Emporia State University.
54. Hart Lee Dykes, lhp, Oklahoma State University.
55. Jeff Buell, 1b, Indiana State University.
56. Alex Alvarez, rhp, Gulf Coast (Fla.) CC.
57. Dwayne Wade, of, Washington HS, Greenville, Miss.
58. Ron Stephens, rhp, University of Cincinnati.
59. Wayne Johnson, ss, Leuzinger HS, Gardena, Calif.
60. Brian Gennings, of, Texarkana (Texas) CC.
61. Michael Carlsen, ss, St Anthony's HS, Jersey City, N.J.

CINCINNATI REDS (15)

1. (Choice to Giants as compensation for Type B free agent Eddie Milner).
2. Jeff Branson, ss, Livingston University.
3. Tyler Green, rhp, Thomas Jefferson HS, Denver.
4. Gaetano Giani, c, Gordon Tech HS, Chicago.
5. Ken Gillum, 3b, Westerville (Ohio) North HS.
6. Kurt Dempster, rhp, Arizona State University.
7. Shane Coker, of, Asher (Okla.) HS.
8. Carl Stewart, rhp, Plano (Texas) East HS.
9. Kevin Digiacomo, c, Choate College HS, Ithaca, N.Y.
10. Roosevelt Williams, 3b, Taylor (Texas) HS.
11. Mark Arland, of, Central Valley HS, Spokane, Wash.
12. Steve Foster, rhp, University of Texas, Arlington.
13. Paul Byrd, rhp, St. Xavier HS, Louisville, Ky.
14. Johnny Almaraz, rhp, Southwest Texas State University.
15. Craig Rapp, lhp, Red Land HS, Lewisberry, Pa.
16. Scott McCarty, lhp, San Jacinto (Texas) JC.
17. Benny Colvard, of, Southeastern Oklahoma State University.
18. Kyle Reagan, of, East Lyme (Conn.) HS.
19. Jerry Spradlin, rhp, Fullerton (Calif.) JC.
20. Earl Coachman, 3b, George C. Wallace (Ala.) CC.
21. Brian Nichols, c, University of Southern California.
22. Doug Bond, 1b, Quinnipiac College.
23. Chris Keim, lhp, Taft (Calif.) JC.
24. Chris Hart, of, Harrisonburg (Va.) HS.
25. Duane Mulville, c, Bakersfield (Calif.) JC.
26. Charles Sullivan, 3b, Greenwich (Conn.) HS.
27. Jason Satre, rhp, Abilene (Texas) HS.
28. Agustin Gonzalez, c, Orosi (Calif.) HS.
29. Edward Klamm, lhp, Bishop Ludden HS, Syracuse, N.Y.
30. John Weeks, c, University of Miami.
31. Clarence Thomas, rhp, Western Kentucky University.
32. Meredith Sanford, rhp, University of Alabama.
33. Brett Roberts, rhp, South Webster (Ohio) HS.
34. Dwayne Van Horne, rhp-3b, University of South Carolina.
35. Derrick Copes, of, Angelina (Texas) JC.
36. Michael Malley, lhp, University of Connecticut.
37. Issac Jackson, of, Victor Valley HS, Victorville, Calif.
38. Jon Fuller, c, Bellevue (Wash.) CC.
39. Dan Cholowsky, ss, Bellarmine Prep HS, San Jose, Calif.
40. John Edward, lhp, New Mexico State University.
41. Cary Moore, inf-of, Sulphur Springs (Texas) HS.
42. Brian Landy, lhp, Quinnipiac College.
43. Glen Osinski, 3b, Triton (Ill.) JC.
44. Mike Mulvaney, 1b, University of Wyoming.
45. Jason Cornell, of, Iowa Western CC.
46. Greg Siberz, rhp, Westmar College.
47. Barry Leavell, of, Washington HS, Chicago.
48. David Williams, rhp, Westark (Ark.) CC.
49. Brian Carie, rhp, Vincennes University (Ind.) JC.
50. Lawrence Moore, of, Rend Lake (Ill.) JC.
51. Adrian Jones, of-rhp, University of Missouri.
52. Mark Healy, rhp-1b, Iowa Western CC.
53. Dan Schwader, lhp, Kishwaukee (Ill.) JC.
54. Ben Blake, c, Indianola (Ind.) HS.
55. Phil Zimmerman, 2b, Regis HS, Denver.
56. Tim Boge, c, Dyersville-Beckman HS, Dyersville, Ia.
57. Rick Freehling, of, Regis HS, Denver.
58. Sam Austin, of, Triton (Ill.) JC.
59. Robert Robinson, rhp, Circleville (Ohio) HS.
60. Don Wengert, rhp, Heelan HS, Sioux City, Iowa.

CLEVELAND INDIANS (2)

1. Mark Lewis, ss, Hamilton (Ohio) HS.
1. Charles Nagy, rhp, University of Connecticut (Choice from Giants as compensation for Type A free agent Brett Butler).
1. Jeff Mutis, lhp, Lafayette College (Special supplemental choice—27th—as compensation for losing Type A free agent Brett Butler to Giants).

The Cleveland Indians made shortstop Mark Lewis the second player chosen, and the first high school player.

2. Brian Johnson, c, University of Texas.
3. Clyde Pough, rhp-ss, Avon Park (Fla.) HS.
4. Daren Epley, 1b, Bradley University.
5. Ty Kovach, rhp, Central Arizona JC.
6. Don Young, of, Grossmont (Calif.) JC.
7. Greg McMichael, rhp, University of Tennessee.
8. Olonzo Woodfin, lhp, Sylmar (Calif.) HS.
9. Brett Merriman, rhp, Grand Canyon College.
10. Thomas Duffin, 3b-of, Miami-Dade North CC.
11. Jorge Fabregas, c-1b, Christopher Columbus HS, Miami.
12. Keith Millay, rhp, Apollo HS, Owensboro, Ky.
13. Tommy Boudreau, rhp, Chaparral HS, Las Vegas, Nev.
14. Josh Lowery, ss, Laney (Calif.) JC.
15. Charles Alexander, lhp, Western Michigan University.
16. Joey James, of, UCLA.
17. Barry Blackwell, c, Florida State University.
18. Darrin Paxton, lhp, East HS, Wichita, Kan.
19. Sean Baron, 1b, University of San Diego.
20. Ed Leger, rhp, Ventura (Calif.) JC.
21. Jason Geis, of, Hudson Bay HS, Vancouver, Wash.
22. Darin Campbell, 3b, University of North Carolina.
23. Bob Kairis, rhp, Northwestern State University.
24. Rick Falkner, of, University of Portland.
25. Javier Murillo, 2b, Azusa Pacific University.
26. Martin Eddy, of-1b, Dallas Baptist University.
27. Lawrence Smith, 2b, Bethune-Cookman College.
28. Randy Mazey, of, Clemson University.
29. Kraig Constantino, 1b-c, Branham HS, San Jose, Calif.
30. William Scarborough, rhp, Ferrum College.
31. David Keating, of, UCLA.
32. Rouglas Odor, ss, University of New Orleans.
33. Alex Ferran, of, Coral Park HS, Miami.
34. Andy Baker, rhp, Cook HS, Lenox, Ga.
35. Troy Eklund, of, University of Arkansas.
36. Cecil Pettiford, rhp, Jackson State University.
37. Dan Williams, c, Western Oregon State College.
38. Lenny Gilmore, of, Cal State Northridge.
39. Marc Tepper, 1b, Lubbock Christian College.
40. Keith Bevenour, lhp, Penn State University.
41. Brad Hebets, rhp, University of Southwestern Louisiana.
42. John Abercrombie, c, Eisenhower HS, Houston.
43. Teryl Morrison, rhp, Contra Costa (Calif.) JC.

44. Jeff Bonchek, 3b, Michigan State University.
45. Steve Harrell, of, Hamilton (Ohio) HS.
46. Todd Mraz, c, University of Texas, Arlington.
47. Brian Cofer, ss, University of Montevallo.
48. Douglas Egloff, rhp, Denver.
49. Greg Fowble, 2b, University of Arizona.
50. Dean Meddaugh, of-2b, Victor Valley (Calif.) CC.
51. John Eierman, of, Leo HS, Chicago.
52. Michael Ashworth, rhp, Westmont College.
53. Bill Kull, of, Florida Southern College.
54. David Ferrell, 2b, DeAnza (Calif.) JC.
55. Jason Pfaff, 1b, St. Xavier HS, Cincinnati.
56. Michael Bonetto, lhp, Big Bear HS, Bear Lake, Calif.
57. Erik Young, of, Baldwin-Wallace College.
58. Mark Smith, rhp, San Jacinto (Texas) JC.

DETROIT TIGERS (26)

1. Rico Brogna, 1b-lhp, Watertown (Conn.) HS.
2. Scott Livingstone, 3b, Texas A&M University.
3. Tookie Spann, of, Tulane University.
4. Lance Shebelut, 1b, Fresno State University.
5. Mike Lumley, rhp, Eastern Michigan University.
6. Eric Stone, rhp, University of Texas.
7. Tim Brader, lhp, Shelton State (Ala.) JC.
8. Thomas Aldrich, ss, Bowdoin College.
9. Kurt Knudsen, rhp, University of Miami.
10. Chris Gollehon, rhp, Medical Lake HS, Fairchild, Wash.
11. Michael Brown, of, Pensacola (Fla.) Catholic HS.
12. Mickey Delas, c, Eastern Michigan University.
13. Michael Rendina, 1b, Grossmont HS, El Cajon, Calif.
14. Linty Ingram, rhp, Arizona State University.
15. David Haas, rhp, Wichita State University.
16. Brett Roach, c, Eastern Michigan University.
17. Richard Rowland, c, Mendocino (Calif.) CC.
18. Ronald Howard, 2b, Palomar (Calif.) JC.
19. Todd Taylor, c, Lakeland (Fla.) HS.
20. Kurt Shea, rhp, Southwestern Michigan JC.
21. Robert Thomas, rhp, Sonoma State University.
22. William Warrecker, lhp, University of California.
23. John Barton, rhp, University of Nevada-Reno.
24. Benny Castillo, of, Oklahoma State University.
25. Robert Frassa, of, CC of Morris (N.J.).
26. Brian Dour, rhp, Bradley University.
27. Michael Pfeifer, rhp, Stevens HS, Edison, N.J.
28. Lee Shoup, rhp, Point Park College.
29. Jimmy Hitt, rhp, Florida Southern College.
30. Mike Davidson, of, Michigan State University.
31. James Hill, ss, University of the Pacific.
32. Joseph Niedinger, rhp, Monroe (Mich.) Catholic Central HS.
33. Brian Eubanks, rhp, Marysville (Calif.) HS.
34. Ed Bustamonte, of, Fresno State University.
35. Mike Jones, rhp, Loyola Marymount University.
36. Travis Kinyoun, c, Royal HS, Simi Valley, Calif.
37. Duane Walker, of, University of South Florida.
38. Bert Patton, lhp, Eastern Michigan University.
39. Todd Winston, c, Marysville (Mich.) HS.
40. Bobby Holley, ss, UCLA.
41. Don Pedersen, 1b-of, JC of the Canyons (Calif.).
42. David Brink, rhp, Lake Michigan JC.
43. Joe Arredondo, 1b, Bellflower (Calif.) HS.
44. Derric Taylor, of, Muir HS, Altadena, Calif.
45. Kirk Piskor, c, Plano (Texas) East HS.
46. James Wolfe, c, Spanish River HS, Boca Raton, Fla.
47. Anthony Muser, 2b, Los Alamitos (Calif.) HS.
48. Robert Welch, c, Horizon HS, Scottsdale, Ariz.
49. Andrew Watson, rhp, Vashon HS, St. Louis.
50. Russell Gaston, rhp, Belleville Area (Ill.) CC.

HOUSTON ASTROS (7)

1. Willie Ansley, of, Plainview (Texas) HS.
2. Mica Lewis, ss, Cal State Los Angeles.
2. Dave Silvestri, ss, University of Missouri (Choice from Yankees as compensation for Type B free agent Jose Cruz).
3. Scott Servais, c, Creighton University.
4. Luis Gonzalez, 1b, University of South Alabama.
5. Terry Christopher, rhp, University of Kentucky.
6. Chris Gardner, rhp, Cuesta (Calif.) JC.
7. Bernard Jenkins, of, St. Francis College (N.Y.).
8. Gordy Farmer, rhp, Arizona State University.
9. Brian Griffiths, rhp, Mt. Hood (Ore.) CC.
10. David Klinefelter, lhp, Allegheny (Pa.) CC.
11. Maurice Jones, of, Edgewater HS, Orlando, Fla.
12. Dave Shermet, of, University of Arizona.
13. Bill Gearhart, rhp, Armstrong State College.
14. Larry Lamphere, of, Central Michigan University.
15. Walter Trice, lhp, U.S. International University.

16. Edward Quijada, 3b, Rio Vista (Calif.) HS.
17. Kenny Loftin, of, University of Arizona.
18. Rod Windes, lhp, Cal State Los Angeles.
19. Mike Durant, c, Watterson High School, Columbus, Ohio.
20. Eric Given, c, University of South Carolina, Spartanburg.
21. Rick Dunnum, rhp, William Penn College.
22. Kenneth Morris, rhp, Northwestern State University.
23. James Desapio, lhp, St. Francis College (N.Y.).
24. David Metheney, rhp, Dixie Hollins HS, Seminole, Fla.
25. Kevin Schula, c, El Dorado HS, Placentia, Calif.
26. Rod Scheckla, rhp, Oregon State University.
27. Ben Gonzales, rhp, Cypress (Calif.) JC.
28. Mark King, of, Mt. Carmel HS, San Diego.
29. Anthony Gutierrez, lhp, Englewood HS, Littleton, Colo.
30. Mike Kirk, of, Shasta (Calif.) JC.
31. Robert Hurlbutt, c, Monroe (N.Y.) CC.
32. Matthew Lackie, rhp, Rancho Santiago (Calif.) JC.
33. Mark Rudis, Clear Creek HS, League City, Texas.
34. Eric Gray, rhp, Bloomington HS, Rialto, Calif.
35. Dan Tiumalu, 3b-of, Helix HS, Lemon Grove, Calif.
36. Scott Spurgeon, 3b, Northwest Missouri State University.
37. Clinton Brown, rhp, South Umpqua HS, Myrtle Creek, Ore.
38. Elgin Bobo, c, Cabrillo (Calif.) HS.
39. Mark Hudgins, ss, Plantation (Fla.) HS.
40. Richard Czajkowski, ss, Haverling HS, Bath, N.Y.
41. Chris Tremie, c, South Houston HS.
42. William Wissler, rhp, Central Dauphin HS, Harrisburg, Pa.
43. Troy Dovey, rhp, Miami-Dade South CC.
44. Luis Navarro, lhp, Southwest HS, Miami.
45. Heath Daniel, of, Central HS, Phenix City, Ala.
46. Craig Fairbanks, rhp, Morello Prep HS, Boulder Creek, Calif.
47. Scott Mowl, 1b, Bellflower (Calif.) HS.
48. David Lacroix, rhp-ss, Los Angeles Harbor JC.
49. Placido Vicente, c, Southwest HS, Miami.
50. Anthony Dunnahoe, 1b-of, Haines City (Fla.) HS.
51. Ross Macaluso, ss, Hillsborough (Fla.) CC.
52. James Simpson, of, Lake Worth (Fla.) HS.
53. Steven Schuerman, rhp, Spokane Falls (Wash.) CC.
54. Joe Burnett, of, Delgado (La.) JC.
55. John Hercholcz, rhp, Miami-Dade North CC.
56. Patrick King, of-inf, Don Lugo HS, Chino, Calif.
57. Jose Rubiera, of, Howard (Texas) JC.
58. Nelson Izquierdo, 2b, Pace HS, Hialeah, Fla.
59. Grady Garrow, rhp, Butte (Calif.) JC.
60. Matthew Morgan, of, Creskill (N.J.) HS.
61. Jon Newville, rhp, Bishop Montgomery HS, Palos Verdes Estates, Calif.
62. Jim Greenlee, lhp, Pinole Valley HS, San Pablo, Calif.
63. Joe Church, rhp, Santana HS, Santee, Calif.
64. Michael Ballerelli, of, Castle Park HS, San Diego.

KANSAS CITY ROYALS (18)

1. Hugh Walker, of, Jacksonville (Ark.) HS.
2. Bob Hamelin, 1b, Rancho Santiago (Calif.) JC.
3. Joel Johnston, rhp, West Chester, Pa.
4. Greg Harvey, rhp, Seminole (Okla.) JC.
5. Tim Spehr, c, Arizona State University.
6. Jim Smith, rhp, Jacksonville State University.
7. Franklin Watson, of, Longwood College.
8. Jerry Vaughn, rhp, Shelton State (Ala.) JC.
9. Jeff Hulse, c, Kansas State University.
10. Jeff Garber, 2b, James Madison University.
11. Mike Magnante, lhp, UCLA.
12. Steve Otto, rhp, St. Xavier College.
13. David Rolls, c, University of San Diego.
14. Victor Cole, rhp, Santa Clara University.
15. Kyle Balch, rhp, Vanderbilt University.
16. Kerwin Moore, of, King HS, Detroit.
17. John Conner, rhp, Rose State (Okla.) JC.
18. Stan Bowling, rhp, Desales HS, Louisville, Ky.
19. Marvin Mayberry, c, Cody HS, Detroit.
20. John Cuda, rhp, Penn Hills HS, Verona, Pa.
21. Milt Richardson, of, Skyline (Calif.) JC.
22. Frank Halcovich, of-1b, University of Arizona.
23. Kyle Irvin, rhp, Oral Roberts University.
24. Kelvin Davis, ss, Longwood College.
25. Zach Kimbell, rhp, Kansas State University.
26. Chad Stombaugh, c, Rend Lake (Ill.) JC.
27. Rich Gonzales, lf-1b, Rancho Santiago (Calif.) JC.
28. Gerald Ingram, of, Western Kentucky University.
29. Ronald Collins, 1b, Mt. San Jacinto (Calif.) JC.
30. John Gilcrist, of, Indian River (Fla.) CC.
31. John McCormick, lhp, Ohio State University.
32. Stephen Osik, rhp, Long Island University.
33. Mike Beall, 1b, St. Thomas University.
34. Mike Gillette, c, University of Michigan.
35. Steve Preston, 2b, Michigan State University.

36. Greg Prusla, of, Alfred University.
37. Brad Seitzer, ss-3b, Lincoln Land (Ill.) CC.
38. Dean McMillin, lhp, Ventura (Calif.) HS.
39. Brad Hopper, rhp, Fullerton (Calif.) JC.
40. James Austin, of, Mater Dei HS, Mission Viejo, Calif.
41. Mickey Kerns, ss, Hancock (Md.) HS.
42. Greg Blevins, c, Northeastern Oklahoma JC.
43. John Gross, rhp, Clovis HS, Fresno, Calif.
44. William Melvin, of, Pace HS, Milton, Fla.
45. David Fletcher, rhp, Yucca Valley (Calif.) HS.
46. Jerome Beyers, of, Washington HS, Kansas City, Kan.
47. Kim Cornist, of, Solano (Calif.) CC.
48. Jose Fernandez, c, University of Florida.
49. Jason Bryans, rhp, Macomb (Mich.) CC.

LOS ANGELES DODGERS (5)

1. Bill Bene, rhp, Cal State Los Angeles.
2. (Choice to A's as compensation for Type A free agent Mike Davis).
3. William Ashley, of, Belleville (Mich.) HS.
4. Anthony Collier, of, Muir HS, Pasadena, Calif.
5. Paul Branconier, rhp, Covina (Calif.) HS.
6. Eric Karros, 1b, UCLA.
7. Jeff Hartsock, rhp, North Carolina State University.
8. Scott Erwin, rhp, Georgia Tech.
9. Jim Poole, lhp, Georgia Tech.
10. Ed Pye, ss, Middle Tennessee State University.
11. Robert McMurray, of, Southeastern Louisiana University.
12. Jerry Brooks, of-3b, Clemson University.
13. Chris Morrow, of, Skyline (Calif.) JC.
14. Dana Allison, lhp, James Madison University.
15. Lance Rice, c, Oregon State University.
16. Brian Traxler, 1b, University of New Orleans.
17. Mike Chiusano, c, Nazareth HS, Brooklyn, N.Y.
18. Russell Smith, of, Conestoga Valley HS, Talmage, Pa.
19. James Wray, lhp, Troy State University.
20. Sean McKamie, ss, Central HS, St. Paul, Minn.
21. Steve Finken, ss, University of Michigan.
22. Michael St. Estaben, lhp, Chino (Calif.) HS.
23. Bill Wengert, rhp, Iowa State University.
24. Rod Harvell, of, Fairfield (Calif.) HS.
25. Michael Sampson, rhp, Holyoke (Mass.) CC.
26. Ernie Carr, 3b-of, Jacksonville University.
27. Mike Munson, rhp, University of Illinois.
28. Eric Ganino, c, Fontana (Calif.) HS.
29. John Braase, rhp, College of Southern Idaho.
30. Sean Snedeker, rhp, Texas A&M University.
31. Clayton Enno, lhp, Des Moines Area (Iowa) CC.
32. Bryan Beals, 2b-of, Chapman College.
33. Cam Biberdorf, rhp, Mayville State College.
34. Napoleon Robinson, rhp, Columbus College.
35. Hector Ortiz, c, Ranger (Texas) JC.
36. Jeff Castillo, rhp, Mesa College.
37. Bradley Boggetto, rhp, Parkland (Ill.) JC.
38. Wendall Zink, 3b-ss, Dixie (Utah) JC.
39. K.G. White, of, Georgia Tech.
40. Felix Rios, 3b, George Fox College.
41. Todd Reische, c, Minooka (Ill.) HS.
42. James Blackwell, of, Spartanburg Methodist (S.C.) JC.
43. Garey Ingram, c, Columbus (Ga.) HS.
44. Brent Miller, 3b-1b, Jordan HS, Columbus, Ga.
45. Brad Cohen, of, Starkville (Miss.) Academy.
46. Wilfred Brown, ss, Lurleen B. Wallace State (Ala.) JC.
47. Garrett Beard, of-3b, Spartanburg Methodist (S.C.) JC.
48. Terry Miller, of, Compton (Calif.) CC.
49. Deon Montgomery, ss, Compton (Calif.) CC.
50. Jose Fernandez, of, CC of San Francisco.
51. Daniel Hancock, rhp, Bremen HS, Midlothian, Ill.
52. Gaither Bagsby, rhp, Dickson Co. (Tenn.) HS.
53. Michael Emmons, rhp, Pensacola (Fla.) JC.
54. Shannon Zerlang, of-3b, JC of the Redwoods (Calif.).
55. Craig Thomas, of, Northside HS, Warner Robins, Ga.
56. Daniel Frye, ss-2b, Logansport (Ind.) HS.
57. Dennis Frye, 1b-of, Logansport (Ind.) HS.
58. Michael Vdovkin, rhp, Merced (Calif.) HS.
59. Chris Harding, of, Louisburg (N.C.) JC.
60. Robert Hoffman, c, Kennedy HS, Richmond, Calif.
61. Erik Boddie, of, Creighton University.
62. Michael Piazza, 1b-c, Miami-Dade North CC.

MILWAUKEE BREWERS (24)

1. Alex Fernandez, rhp, Pace HS, Miami.
2. Randy Snyder, c, Washington State University.
3. Joe Andrzejewski, rhp, Chesapeake HS, Pasadena, Md.
4. Ken Kremer, 1b, Rider College.
5. Pat Listach, ss, Arizona State University.
6. Greg Landry, rhp, University of Texas.

7. Chris George, rhp, Kent State University.
8. Mike Ignasiak, rhp, University of Michigan.
9. Bert Heffernan, c, Clemson University.
10. Charlie Fiacco, of, UCLA.
11. Danny Kapea, lhp, University of Hawaii.
12. Donald Meyett, of, Catonsville (Md.) CC.
13. Leon Glenn, 1b, East Central (Miss.) JC.
14. Kenneth Hokuf, rhp, Golden West (Calif.) JC.
15. Sylvester Love, of, University of Southern Mississippi.
16. Heath Lane, rhp, University of Arizona.
17. Robert Scott, of, Mankato (Minn.) West HS.
18. Stewart Lee, 3b, Jacksonville State University.
19. Dave Volt, rhp, University of Kentucky.
20. Ruben Rodriguez, of, University of Southwestern Louisiana.
21. Brian Dodd, lhp, Arizona State University.
22. Robert Lipscomb (Muhammad), of, University of Hawaii.
23. Tim Snow, 2b, East Carolina University.
24. Troy Bradford, rhp, Cochise County (Ariz.) CC.
25. Kevin Carmody, lhp, North Adams State College.
26. Javier Brown, ss-of, Morse HS, San Diego.
27. David Fitzgerald, lhp, Davidson College.
28. Doug Vander Weele, rhp, Bonanza HS, Las Vegas, Nev.
29. Rich Pfaff, of, Essex (Md.) CC.
30. Larry Odewaldt, c, U.S. International University.
31. Michael Grayson, rhp, Florida International University.
32. Robert Jakubik, 1b, St. John Bosco HS, Cerritos, Calif.
33. Chris Norton, c, Lake Howell HS, Maitland, Fla.
34. Donald Culberson, of, Neshoba Central HS, Philadelphia.
35. Dwayne Wilson, of, Oceanside (Calif.) HS.
36. Brad Tilly, 2b, Bradley University.
37. John Littlewood, 3b, Brigham Young University.
38. Bryan Parks, c, Catonsville (Md.) CC.
39. Chris Tacik, rhp, Thomas Johnson HS, Frederick, Md.
40. Bryan Hastings, rhp, East Forsyth HS, Kernersville, N.C.
41. Edgar Anderson, of, Logan HS, Dolton, Ill.
42. Scott Craven, 3b, Punahou HS, Kailua, Hawaii.

MINNESOTA TWINS (20)

1. Johnny Ard, rhp, Manatee (Fla.) JC.
2. Alan Newman, lhp, Fullerton (Calif.) JC.
3. Mike Harrison, c, Campolinda (Calif.) HS.
4. Steve Dunn, 1b, Robinson HS, Fairfax, Va.
5. Steve Dean, of-rhp, Ada (Okla.) HS.
6. Pat Mahomes, rhp, Lindale (Texas) HS.
7. Doug Sutton, rhp, University of Kentucky.
8. Jay Kvasnicka, of, University of Minnesota.
9. Doug Simons, lhp, Pepperdine University.
10. Jody Harrington, lhp, Armijo HS, Fairfield, Calif.
11. J.T. Bruett, of, University of Minnesota.
12. Greg Gross, of, University of the Pacific.
13. Mike Pomeranz, lhp, Clemson University.
14. Steve Muh, lhp, University of Georgia.
15. Tony Tucker, of, Tate HS, Cantonment, Fla.
16. Gary Tatterson, rhp, Glendale (Ariz.) CC.
17. Gary Resetar, c, Rutgers University.
18. Vince Palyan, of, University of Minnesota.
19. Carl Fraticelli, 2b, Loyola Marymount University.
20. Loy McBride, of, Cal State Los Angeles.
21. Jeff Milene, c, Mayo HS, Rochester, Minn.
22. Angel Lugo, ss, Grady HS, Brooklyn, N.Y.
23. Jeff Edmunds, 1b, Plantation HS, Sunrise, Fla.
24. Jody Hurst, of, Mississippi State University.
25. J.P. Wright, of, Washburn University.
26. Steven Gill, lhp, Cypress (Calif.) JC.
27. Scott Stahoviak, rhp, Carmel Mundelin HS, Grays Lake, Ill.
28. Peter Raether, rhp, Edina (Minn.) HS.
29. Jon Bellamy, 3b, Lafayette (La.) HS.
30. Will Vespe, 1b, University of Miami.
31. Chris Hmielewski, lhp, Leyden HS, Franklin Park, Ill.
32. Dom Rovasio, rhp, Quinnipiac College.
33. Pat Hope, rhp, Oklahoma State University.
34. George Behr, of, Hill Murray HS, Maplewood, Minn.
35. Steven Morris, of, University of Hawaii.
36. Michael Teron, rhp, Santa Clara HS, Oxnard, Calif.
37. Aaron Sele, rhp, North Kitsap HS, Poulsbo, Wash.
38. Marc Pak, of, Valley HS, Las Vegas, Nev.
39. Sheldon Forehand, of, American HS, Fremont, Calif.
40. Pedro Oliva, of, Kennedy HS, Bloomington, Minn.
41. David Baine, lhp, San Marin HS, Novato, Calif.
42. Willie McKinnon, of, Nicholls (Ga.) HS.
43. Jeremy Kendall, lhp, Towns Country HS, Hiwassee, Ga.
44. Carl Johnson, rhp, North Thurston Johnson HS, Frederick, Md.
45. Troy Hoerner, of, Milaca (Minn.) HS.
46. John Jackson, of, Washington State University.
47. Jerome McGerry, of-rhp, Liberty Elyau HS, Texarkana, Texas.
48. Frederick Smith, rhp, Venice HS, Culver City, Calif.

MONTREAL EXPOS (19)

1. **Dave Wainhouse, rhp, Washington State University.**
2. **Ben Howze, rhp, Washington HS, Pensacola, Fla. (Choice from Cubs as compensation for Type B free agent Vance Law).**
2. **Chris Nabholz, lhp, Towson State University.**
3. **Marquis Grissom, of-rhp, Florida A&M University.**
4. **Scott Davison, rhp-ss, Redondo Union HS, Redondo Beach, Calif.**
5. **Tyrone Woods, 3b, Hernando HS, Brooksville, Fla.**
6. **Tim Laker, c, Oxnard (Calif.) JC.**
7. **Bret Barberie, ss, University of Southern California.**
8. **Bryn Kosco, 3b, North Carolina State University.**
9. Martin Martinez, rhp, Cochise County (Ariz.) CC.
10. **Joe Klancnik, rhp, University of Florida.**
11. **Reid Cornelius, rhp, Thomasville (Ala.) HS.**
12. **Isaac Elder, of, Cal State Los Angeles.**
13. **Rod Boddie, of, James Madison University.**
14. **Dan Archibald, rhp, San Jose State University.**
15. Rafael Adame, rhp, Bell HS, Maywood, Calif.
16. **Steve Whitehead, rhp, Brawley (Calif.) HS.**
17. **Dan Freed, rhp, Illinois State University.**
18. **Darrin Winston, lhp, Rutgers University.**
19. Richard Busch, c, St. Petersburg (Fla.) HS.
20. **Brian Sajonia, lhp, Washington State University.**
21. **Eric Nelson, 3b-rhp, San Jose State University.**
22. Brian Pease, lhp, Bonny Eagle HS, Cornish, Maine.
23. **Pat Heiderscheit, rhp-c, Iowa State University.**
24. **Michael Farrell, rhp, LeMoyne College.**
25. **Dale Buzzard, rhp, University of LaVerne.**
26. **David Oropeza, rhp, University of Alabama.**
27. Mitchell Banton, of, Virginia Commonwealth University.
28. **Keith Kaub, 1b, Cal State Fullerton.**
29. Robert Langer, ss, Carmel HS, Mundelein, Ill.
30. Danny Parente, 1b-lhp, Los Angeles Harbor JC.
31. Vernon Slater, of, Brandon HS, Tampa, Fla.
32. Justin Heinold, lhp, Stroman HS, Victoria, Texas.
33. Dan Stanley, ss, Lindberg HS, Renton, Wash.
34. Marvin Cobb, rhp, University of Oklahoma.
35. Preston Virden, of, Lee (Texas) JC.
36. Antonio Grissom, of, Lakeshore HS, Red Oak, Ga.
37. Todd Manly, rhp, San Jose (Calif.) CC.
38. Mike Lane, 1b, Indian River (Fla.) CC.
39. **Ken Lake, of, University of Wyoming.**
40. **Ricardo Cartwright, of, Florida A&M University.**
41. Paul Hutto, rhp, Auburndale (Fla.) HS.
42. Brad Erdman, 3b, Douglas (Ariz.) HS.
43. Gary Young, rhp, San Jacinto (Texas) JC.
44. Jesus Molina, lhp, Pima (Ariz.) CC.
45. **Jeff Tuss, rhp, Capital HS, Helena, Mont.**
46. Stephen Day, rhp, Indian River (Fla.) CC.
47. Cord Corbitt, lhp, Palm Beach (Fla.) JC.
48. Frank Giunta, 1b-lhp, Martin County HS, Palm City, Fla.
49. Jared Snyder, c, Saugus (Calif.) HS.
50. Norman Montoya, lhp, Newark (Calif.) Memorial HS.
51. Jeff Ramsey, ss-of, Northampton East HS, Rich Square, N.C.
52. Robert Yonker, rhp, CC of Morris (N.J.).
53. **Doug DeKock, c, University of Miami.**
54. Keith Hopkins, of, Brandon HS, Tampa, Fla.
55. **Marion Correa, 2b, Carol City (Fla.) HS.**
56. James Wallkvist, rhp, Lincoln HS, San Francisco.
57. John Fleischer, rhp, Benedictine HS, Richmond, Va.
58. John Halverson, rhp, Brookwood HS, Snellville, Ga.

NEW YORK METS (21)

1. **Dave Proctor, rhp, Allen County (Kan.) CC.**
2. Jeff Seale, rhp, Fairview HS, Boulder, Colo.
3. **Doug Saunders, 2b, Esperanza HS, Yorba Linda, Calif.**
3. Derrick Warren, of, Washington HS, Pensacola, Fla. (Choice from Yankees as compensation for Type B free agent John Candelaria).
4. **Dan Furmanik, rhp, Palm Beach (Fla.) JC.**
5. **Tim Howard, 2b, Imperial Valley (Calif.) JC.**
6. **Kyle Washington, of, Kishwaukee (Ill.) JC.**
7. **Kevin Baez, ss, Dominican College (N.Y.).**
8. **Mike Lehnerz, rhp, Regis HS, Denver.**
9. Pat Leinen, lhp, University of Nebraska.
10. **Andrew Fidler, lhp, Methacton HS, Audubon, Pa.**
11. **Greg Langbehn, lhp, Everest HS, Schofield, Wis.**
12. Doug Bennett, rhp, Hillcrest HS, Springfield, Mo.
13. **Jeff Thompson, ss, Newnan (Ga.) HS.**
14. Mike Anaya, rhp, Valley HS, Albuquerque, N.M.
15. **Nicky Davis, 1b, Merritt Island (Fla.) HS.**
16. Andrew Reich, rhp, Louisburg (N.C.) JC.
17. **Mason Rudolph, c, Dobson HS, Mesa, Ariz.**
18. **Michael Noelke, 2b, University of Wisconsin.**
19. Beau Campbell, c, Lindberg HS, Renton, Wash.
20. **Jon Hudson, lhp, University of Kentucky.**
21. **Paul Johnson, rhp, Rutgers University.**

Dave Proctor   Johnny Ard

... juco players chosen in first round

22. **Chris Butler, rhp, McEachern HS, Marietta, Ga.**
23. **Dale Plummer, rhp, University of Maine.**
24. Mike Kelly, of, Los Alamitos (Calif.) HS.
25. **Fred Brown, rhp, Navarro (Texas) JC.**
26. Sean Lawrence, lhp, Oak Park (Ill.) River Forest HS.
27. Paul Perkins, rhp, Fairfield (Calif.) HS.
28. **Deron Sample, rhp-of, Paris (Texas) JC.**
29. **Chris Dorn, rhp, San Jacinto (Texas) JC.**
30. Robert Guzik, of, Allegheny (Pa.) CC.
31. Phillip Essex, rhp, McLennan (Texas) CC.
32. **Richard Bristow, rhp, Geneva (Ill.) HS.**
33. **Brian Zimmerman, lhp, North Central (Ill.) College.**
34. **David Parouse, c, Dominican College (N.Y.).**
35. Gary Wilson, ss-2b, Arcata (Calif.) HS.
36. Scott Ellrich, lhp, Crystal Lake (Ill.) South HS.
37. **Devin Moore, of, Madison HS, San Antonio, Texas.**
38. Joe Vitko, rhp, Central Cambria HS, Ebensburg, Pa.
39. **Bryan Rogers, rhp, Sonoma State University.**
40. Jeff Herrington, rhp, Northeastern Oklahoma A&M JC.
41. **Reid Hartmann, 2b, St. Louis CC, Meramec.**
42. Steve Hinton, lhp, Elgin (Ill.) HS.
43. Danny Auchard, lhp, Tracy (Calif.) HS.
44. Brian Buzard, lhp, Neodesha (Kan.) HS.
45. **James Harris, c, St. John the Baptist HS, North Babylon, N.Y.**
46. **Tom Becker, ss, Pratt (Kan.) CC.**
47. Joseph McCann, rhp, DeKalb (Ga.) JC.
48. Alejandro Garces, rhp, Westminster HS, Miami.
49. Mark Moore, c, Shawnee Mission East HS, Overland Park, Kan.
50. Nathaniel Benson, rhp, Leo HS, Country Club Hills, Ill.
51. John Bentley, rhp, Trinity HS, Weaverville, Calif.
52. Michael Sell, 2b, Capital HS, Helena, Mont.
53. James Mathis, of, Cuero (Texas) HS.
54. Mark Bonini, of, Pinole (Calif.) Valley HS.
55. Patrick Kokora, ss, Boulder (Colo.) HS.
56. Michael Kundrat, rhp, Thornwood HS, Calumet City, Ill.
57. Greg Akerman, 3b, Bradley-Bourbonias HS, Bradley, Ill.
58. Perry Amos, of-lhp, Orland HS, Willows, Calif.
59. Chuck Foster, of, San Jacinto (Texas) JC.
60. Jerome Tolliver, of, Lincoln Academy HS, Kansas City, Mo.

NEW YORK YANKEES (22)

1. (Choice to Cardinals as compensation for Type A free agent Jack Clark).
2. (Choice to Astros as compensation for Type B free agent Jose Cruz).
3. (Choice to Mets as compensation for Type B free agent John Candelaria).
4. **Todd Malone, lhp, Casa Robles HS, Citrus Heights, Calif.**
5. **Don Sparks, 3b, Loyola Marymount University.**
6. **Jeff Johnson, lhp, University of North Carolina, Charlotte.**
7. **Billy Masse, of, Wake Forest University.**
8. **Bobby DeJardin, ss, Loyola Marymount University.**
9. **Pat Kelly, ss, West Chester University.**
10. **Kenneth Greer, rhp, University of Massachusetts.**
11. **Andy Cook, rhp, Memphis State University.**
12. **Frank Seminara, rhp, Columbia University.**
13. **Jeff Livesey, c, Auburn University.**
14. **Jeff Hoffman, rhp, Vanderbilt University.**
15. **Robert Munoz, rhp, Palm Beach (Fla.) JC.**
16. **Herb Erhardt, inf-c, Pan American University.**
17. **Jay Knoblauh, of, Rice University.**
18. **Gerald Nielsen, lhp, Florida State University.**
19. **Steve Perry, lhp, King HS, Detroit.**
20. **Craig Brink, rhp, UC Irvine.**
21. **Bruce Prybylinski, rhp, Illinois State University.**
22. **Skip Nelloms, of, Western Carolina University.**

23. Bob Zelhen, of, Indiana State University.
24. John Seeburger, 1b, UC Irvine.
25. Jason Bridges, of, University of Alabama.
26. Michael Draper, rhp, George Mason University.
27. Curtis Ralph, rhp, Sacramento (Calif.) CC.
28. Michael Rhodes, of, University of Houston.
29. Russell Davis, ss, Shelton State (Ala.) JC.
30. Delon Sanders, of, Florida State University.
31. Joe Vitiello, 1b-rhp, Stoneham (Mass.) HS.
32. John Cummings, lhp, Canyon HS, Anaheim, Calif.
33. Todd Youngblood, ss, Farmington (N.M.) HS.
34. David Tuttle, rhp, Los Gatos (Calif.) HS.
35. Mark Kingston, of, Potomac HS, Dumphries, Va.
36. Troy Tallman, c, Napa (Calif.) HS.
37. Pat Maloney, of, Lyons Township HS, LaGrange, Ill.
38. Deshon Brown, of, Modesto (Calif.) HS.
39. Thomas Quinn, rhp, South Florida JC.
40. Matthew Barker, of, Brevard (Fla.) CC.
41. Chad Ogea, rhp, St. Louis HS, Lake Charles, La.
42. Brian Faw, rhp, DeKalb (Ga.) CC.
43. Orlando Palmeiro, of, Miami-Dade South CC.
44. Donald Robinson, of, Killian HS, Miami.
45. Brad Stoltenberg, rhp, Cal State Sacramento.
46. Arthur Canestro, lhp, New York Tech.
47. Brian Reimsnyder, of, University of Florida.
48. Michael Gonzalez, rhp, Sul Ross State University.
49. Kurt Pfeffer, rhp, JC of Marin (Calif.).
50. Allen Popowitz, rhp, Saddle River County HS, Upper Saddle River, N.J.
51. Fernando Vina, ss-2b, Cosumnes River (Calif.) JC.
52. Franklin Lacy, c-of, Laney (Calif.) JC.
53. Alexander Kuhn, c, Eldorado HS, Albuquerque, N.M.
54. George Day, 2b, LaGrange HS, Lake Charles, La.
55. Keiver Campbell, of, Greenville (Miss.) HS.
56. Joe Smith, rhp, Paris (Texas) JC.
57. Michael Eckert, lhp, Pan American University.
58. John Broxton, rhp, Mercer University.
59. Jeff Pickett, c, Blue Springs (Mo.) HS.
60. Matthew Michael, lhp, Morehead State University.
61. Rodney Huffman, rhp, Lake Highlands HS, Dallas.
62. Philip Mendelson, rhp, Grand Junction (Colo.) HS.
63. James Mauldin, rhp, Seminole (Okla.) JC.
64. Mark Ohlms, rhp, Grand View College.
65. Jay Gravens, rhp, Dallas Baptist University.
66. Mark Futrell, rhp, Miami-Dade South CC.
67. Mark Zeratsky, c, Grand View College.
68. (selection voided) Wayne Weinheimer, of, Sacramento (Calif.) CC.
69. Leonard Thigpen, of, Monticello, Fla.
70. Rob Bargas, 3b, Sacramento (Calif.) CC.
71. Scott Thoma, rhp, Texas Wesleyan College.
72. Dan Rambo, rhp, Central Michigan University.
73. Michael Boyan, rhp, Bradley University.
74. Oscar Rivas, lhp, San Jacinto (Texas) JC.
75. Robert LeFebre, of, Florida Southern College.

OAKLAND ATHLETICS (16)

1. Stan Royer, c-3b, Eastern Illinois University.
2. Wynn Beck, c, South Brunswick HS, Southport, N.C. (Choice from Dodgers as compensation for Type A free agent Mike Davis).
2. Joe Slusarski, rhp, University of New Orleans.
3. John Briscoe, rhp, Texas Christian University.
4. Enoch Simmons, of, Loyola Marymount University.
5. Joe Grahe, rhp, University of Miami.
6. Dan Eskew, rhp, University of Tennessee.
7. Ron Witmeyer, 1b, Stanford University.
8. Rich Rozman, rhp, Michigan State University.
9. Nicholas Venuto, rhp, Kent State University.
10. Tom Carcione, c, Texas A&M University.
11. Joel Chimelis, ss, University of Texas.
12. James Lawson, rhp, Huntington College.
13. Mike Messerly, 1b, Middle Tennessee State University.
14. Rodney Peete, 3b, University of Southern California.
15. Ron Correia, ss, Southeastern Massachusetts University.
16. Mike Butler, lhp, North Caroline HS, Denton, Md.
17. Gerard Rizza, rhp, Long Island University.
18. Darren Lewis, of, University of California.
19. William Love, of-lhp, Lassen (Calif.) JC.
20. Dean Borrelli, c, University of Massachusetts.
21. Anthony Floyd, rhp, Southwest Missouri State University.
22. Ray Harris, lhp, University of Arkansas.
23. Bronswell Patrick, rhp, Conley HS, Winterville, N.C.
24. Jim Buccheri, of, Golden West (Calif.) JC.
25. Joe Hillman, of, Indiana University.
26. Tony Ariola, lhp, Northwestern University.
27. Michael Mungin, rhp, Norfolk State University.
28. Greg Ferguson, lhp, Virginia Tech.
29. Dewayne Jones, 2b, University of South Alabama.

30. Steve Whitaker, lhp, Atwater (Calif.) HS.
31. Jeff Webber, of, Merced (Calif.) JC.
32. Lyndon Wright, c, Caesar Rodney HS, Camden, Del.
33. Mike Raskind, rhp, Granite Hills HS, El Cajon, Calif.
34. Tim McDonald, rhp, Central Michigan University.
35. Bobby Jones, of, Cal State Fullerton.
36. Chris Butterfield, of, Cal Poly Pomona.
37. Eric Gruben, rhp, Citrus (Calif.) JC.
38. Brian Foster, 1b-of, Farragut HS, Knoxville, Tenn.
39. Tim Vannaman, of, Rice University.
40. Jim Foley, rhp, Cal State Fullerton.
41. Graham Miller, rhp, Laney (Calif.) JC.
42. Clifford Jones, lhp-of, Oakland HS, Richmond, Calif.
43. Steven Peck, rhp, Mesa (Ariz.) CC.
44. Randy Brown, ss, Alief Elsik HS, Houston.
45. John Pricher, rhp, Winter Park HS, Orlando, Fla.
46. Pat Tozier, Clayton Valley HS, Concord, Calif.
47. Pat Sullivan, lhp, Notre Dame HS, Signal Mountain, Tenn.
48. Blase Sparma, rhp, Watterson HS, Columbus, Ohio.

PHILADELPHIA PHILLIES (11)

1. Pat Combs, lhp, Baylor University.
2. (Choice to Braves as compensation for Type B free agent David Palmer).
3. Tim Mauser, rhp, Texas Christian University.
4. Joe Ciccarella, 1b, Mater Dei HS, Huntington Beach, Calif.
5. Mickey Morandini, ss, Indiana University.
6. Albert Bennett, c, Lee (Texas) JC.
7. Michael Owens, lhp, University of Massachusetts.
8. Gary Wilson, rhp, St. Mary's (Texas) University.
9. Anthony Lozinski, c, University of the Pacific.
10. Jeff Etheredge, cf, Panola (Texas) JC.
11. Mike Sullivan, rhp, North Lake (Texas) JC.
12. Scott Hatteberg, c, Eisenhower HS, Yakima, Wash.
13. Chris Lowe, of, University HS, Johnson City, Tenn.
14. Nick Santa Cruz, 2b-ss, Rancho Santiago (Calif.) JC.
15. Tim Churchill, 1b-of, Cypress (Calif.) JC.
16. Thomas Marsh, of-p, University of Toledo.
17. Brian Walker, lhp, Capistrano Valley HS, Mission Viejo, Calif.
18. Eric Bratlien, rhp, Cal Poly San Luis Obispo.
19. Sam Calarusso, rhp, Orange Coast (Calif.) JC.
20. Todd Goergen, rhp, Trinidad State (Colo.) JC.
21. David Boss, rhp, UC Santa Barbara.
22. Mathew Current, c, Middletown (Ohio) HS.
23. Mark Steffens, of, Germantown Academy HS, Fort Washington, Pa.
24. Calvin Talford, of, Castlewood HS, Dante, Va.
25. Chris Toney, 3b, Hiram Johnson HS, Sacramento, Calif.
26. Jamie Allen, lhp, Hillsborough (Fla.) CC.
27. James Short, 1b, Esperanza HS, Yorba Linda, Calif.
28. Tim Dell, rhp, Huntington College.
29. Gregory Rehkow, lhp, Blue Springs (Mo.) HS.
30. Brian Harper, lhp, Southeast Missouri State University.
31. Craig Johnston, lhp, Napa (Calif.) HS.
32. Ray Walker, ss, Madison HS, Houston.
33. John Marshall, 1b-3b, University of Kentucky.
34. Darryl Vice, 2b, University of California.
35. Michael Dafforn, rhp, Fort Wayne, Ind.
36. Brian Archer, rhp, Kearny HS, San Diego.
37. Rod Klopfer, 3b, Fullerton (Calif.) JC.
38. Darrell Lindsey, rhp, University of Southern Mississippi.
39. Tom Crowley, 2b, Deptford (N.J.) HS.
40. Edward Fletcher, rhp, West Virginia State College.
41. Andrew Barrick, 2b-3b, Elizabethtown College.
42. Joseph Tenhunfeld, of, University of Cincinnati.
43. Paul Anderson, rhp, San Diego Mesa JC.
44. Reggie Garcia, rhp, JC of the Sequoias (Calif.).
45. Todd Pick, rhp, Lassen (Calif.) JC.
46. Troy Kent, rhp, UC Riverside.
47. Greg Breaux, 2b, Waltrip HS, Houston.
48. David Willman, c, Hill HS, Boyertown, Pa.
49. Nick Macaluso, 2b, University of New Orleans.
50. Brian Cummings, 1b-of, Panola (Texas) JC.
51. Thomas Doyle, 1b, Redondo Beach (Calif.) HS.
52. Gary Balderas, 3b, Madison HS, Houston.
53. Stephen Cooke, lhp, Tigard (Ore.) HS.
54. Chris Walker, 1b, University of Montevallo.
55. Rodd Hairston, rhp, Angelina (Texas) JC.
56. Willie Navarette, lhp, Rancho Santiago (Calif.) JC.
57. Dallas Monday, lhp, Jefferson County HS, Strawberry Plains, Tenn.
58. Jeff Patterson, rhp, Cypress (Calif.) JC.
59. Charles Smith, rhp, Rubidoux HS, Riverside, Calif.
60. Carey Newton, rhp, Christian Brothers HS, West Sacramento, Calif.
61. James Davis, c, University HS, Johnson City, Tenn.
62. Juan Price, c, Sweetwater HS, San Diego.
63. David Richison, ss, Spiro (Okla.) HS.
64. Randall Graves, ss, Riverside (Calif.) Poly HS.
65. Gil Valencia, of, Camarillo (Calif.) HS.

PITTSBURGH PIRATES (13)

1. Austin Manahan, ss, Horizon HS, Scottsdale, Ariz.
2. Keith Richardson, rhp, Georgia Southern College.
3. Glen McNabb, 2b-ss, Millikan HS, Long Beach, Calif.
4. Steve Buckholz, rhp, Fresno State University.
5. Daryl Ratliff, of, Santa Cruz (Calif.) HS.
6. Blas Minor, rhp, Arizona State University.
7. John Wehner, 3b, Indiana University.
8. Tim Wakefield, 1b, Florida Institute of Technology.
9. Jeff Payne, lhp, University HS, Morgantown, W.Va.
10. Jon Martin, of, Golden West (Calif.) JC.
11. Joe Ausanio, rhp, Jacksonville University.
12. Chris Estep, of, University of Kentucky.
13. Michael Huyler, 2b, Golden West (Calif.) JC.
14. Deryk Hudson, 3b, Fullerton (Calif.) JC.
15. Mitchell Burke, c, Florida A&M University.
16. James Heins, rhp, Vanderbilt University.
17. Bobby Underwood, lhp, University of South Carolina.
18. Randy Tomlin, lhp, Liberty University.
19. Armando Romero, c, Brevard (Fla.) CC.
20. Lawrence Gilligan, ss, Lakeland HS, Ringwood, N.J.
21. Valentine Henderson, of, Bellevue (Wash.) CC.
22. David Staton, 1b, Orange Coast (Calif.) JC.
23. Renald Datcher, 1b, Lackey HS, La Plata, Md.
24. Scott Cowley, of, St. Leo College.
25. Greg Sims, of, St. Leo College.
26. Chris Sheffield, 2b, Pine Forest HS, Pensacola, Fla.
27. Paul McGhay, of, Montana State University.
28. Jeff Osborne, c, Kent State University.
29. Matthew Udell, rhp, Southwestern Michigan JC.
30. Jeff Kuder, lhp, Mt. Vernon Nazarene College.
31. Troy Clemens, c, Foothill (Calif.) JC.
32. Brian Purvis, of, Noblesville (Ind.) HS.
33. Paul Spalt, ss, North Carolina State University.
34. Steven Roeder, rhp, Mishiwaka (Ind.) Penn HS.
35. Derek Tinnin, of-ss, Anderson College.
36. Albert Molina, ss, Pan American University.
37. Darwin Pennye, of, Southwest Texas State University.
38. Mike Thompson, 1b, North Texas State University.
39. Ken Buksa, c-of, St. Xavier College.
40. Michael Fortuna, of, Coastal Carolina College.
41. Richard Haupt, lhp, Bald Eagle Area HS, Milesburg, Pa.
42. Ronald Way, lhp, Henry Ford (Mich.) CC.
43. Mark Hummell, 3b, Arizona Western JC.
44. Richard Wilson, lhp, Columbus College.
45. Benjamin Burlingame, rhp, Newton (Mass.) South HS.
46. Fernando Arguellas, c, Florida Southern College.
47. Craig Juran, lhp, Colorado State University.
48. Steve O'Donnell, 3b, LaSalle University.
49. Wade Lytle, 3b, Bellmont HS, Decatur, Ind.
50. Keith Mays, rhp, Louisburg (N.C.) JC.
51. Michael LeBlanc, rhp, University of Maine.
52. Joseph Pagan, rhp, Chicago State University.
53. Bryan Arnold, c-1b, Florida Southern College.
54. Dan Nielson, rhp, Western Michigan University.
55. Cary Elston, rhp, Green River (Wash.) CC.
56. Scott Sharts, 1b, Simi Valley (Calif.) HS.
57. Robert West, of, Brewton Parker (Ga.) JC.
58. Kenneth Baurle, rhp, North Allegheny HS, Pittsburgh.
59. Troy Trollope, of, Bellevue (Wash.) CC.
60. Thomas Owen, c, Brewton Parker (Ga.) JC.
61. Jon Fisher, c, Brenham (Texas) HS.
62. Jerry Summers, of, Beaver County (Pa.) CC.
63. David Silvernail, rhp, Columbia Basin (Wash.) CC.
64. Jessie Torres, c, JC of Southern Idaho.
65. Burk Cromer, 3b, Lexington (S.C.) HS.
66. Randy Martin, ss-of, Godby HS, Tallahassee, Fla.

ST. LOUIS CARDINALS (23)

1. John Ericks, rhp, University of Illinois (Choice from Yankees as compensation for Type A free agent Jack Clark).
1. Brad Duvall, rhp, Virginia Tech.
1. Brian Jordan, of, University of Richmond (Special supplemental choice—30th—as compensation for losing Type A free agent Jack Clark to the Yankees).
2. Mike Hensley, rhp, University of Oklahoma.
3. Charlie White, of, University of New Orleans.
4. Mike Ross, 2b, Cal State Fullerton.
5. Lee Plemel, rhp, Stanford University.
6. Rheal Cormier, lhp, CC of Rhode Island.
7. Steve Fanning, ss, Troy State University.
8. Jerry Davis, ss, Lincoln HS, San Diego.
9. Mark Clark, rhp, Lincoln Land (Ill.) JC.
10. Joe Hall, 3b, University of Southern Illinois.
11. Rodney Brooks, rhp, Troy State University.
12. Tom Malchesky, 3b, Western Carolina University.

Top Draft Picks

Dave Wainhouse
...Expos' No. 1

Brad DuVall
...Cards' twin No. 1 picks

John Ericks

13. William Decker, of, Iowa Central CC.
14. John Cebunar, lhp, University of Arkansas.
15. Mike Flore, of, University of Miami.
16. Steve Corry, rhp, Cedar City (Utah) HS.
17. David Richardson, lhp, Middle Tennessee State University.
18. Julio Mendez, ss, University of Florida.
19. Mark Battell, c, Mercy College.
20. Steve Callahan, lhp, Lewis-Clark State College.
21. Fred Langlotti, c, University of Tampa.
22. Tim Pettengill, c, University of Nebraska.
23. Jeff Shireman, ss, Georgia Southern College.
24. John Lepley, lhp, University of Nebraska.
25. Randy Berlin, 1b-3b, Virginia Tech.
26. Corey Satterfield, rhp, Campbell University.
27. Sean Grubb, rhp, Oral Roberts University.
28. John Stephens, 3b, The Citadel.
29. David D. Adams, rhp, Auburn University.
30. Joe Federico, 1b-of, University of Nebraska.
31. Richard Hoffman, rhp, Long Island University.
32. Verlon Grimes, rhp, Arkansas Tech University.
33. Steve Graham, of, Ithaca College.
34. Brian Golden, rhp, Gettysburg College.
35. John Kroeger, c, Fairleigh Dickinson University.
36. David C. Adams, rhp, Ohio University.
37. William Henderson, rhp, Volunteer State (Tenn.) CC.
38. David Bell, of, Volunteer State (Tenn.) CC.
39. Scott Buchheit, lhp, St. Dominic HS, St. Peters, Mo.
40. Kenneth Phillips, of, Pasadena (Calif.) CC.
41. Steve DiBartolomeo, rhp, University of New Haven.
42. Jerry Lutterman, rhp, St. Louis CC, Meramec.
43. George Calhoun, rhp, Spartanburg Methodist (S.C.) JC.
44. Derron Spiller, lhp, Rio Mesa HS, Camarillo, Calif.
45. Joe Philpot, rhp, Volunteer State (Tenn.) CC.
46. David King, 1b-3b, Northeastern Oklahoma A&M JC.

SAN DIEGO PADRES (1)

1. Andy Benes, rhp, University of Evansville.
2. Kelly Lifgren, rhp, Glendale (Ariz.) CC.
3. Ray Holbert, ss, Jordan HS, Long Beach, Calif.
4. Squeezer Thompson, rhp, Mt. Dora (Fla.) HS.
5. Bryce Florie, rhp, Hanahan (S.C.) HS.
6. Bob Brucato, rhp, Northwestern University.
7. Mike Grace, rhp, Joliet (Ill.) Catholic HS.
8. Nikco Riesgo, 3b-of, San Diego State University.
9. Matt Witkowski, ss, Deer Valley HS, Glendale, Ariz.
10. Anthony Sager, rhp, University of Toledo.
11. Scott Welsh, 1b-of, San Diego Mesa JC.
12. Chris Ebright, of-1b, University of Oklahoma.
13. James Noland, of, Central Florida CC.
14. Eric Harris, ss, Roosevelt HS, Dallas.
15. Mike Humphreys, of, Texas Tech University.
16. Brian Cisarik, 1b-of, University of Texas.
17. Vance Tucker, rhp, Seminole (Okla.) JC.
18. Joseph Murdock, lhp, Southern Arkansas University.
19. Greg Ebbert, lhp, Lake Brantley HS, Longwood, Fla.
20. Brian Span, of, Seminole (Fla.) CC.
21. Pedro Lopez, c, Arizona Western JC.
22. Scott Bigham, ss, Willamette University.
23. David Briggs, 3b, Brookdale (N.J.) CC.
24. Brad Hoyer, lhp, Cal Poly San Luis Obispo.
25. Renay Bryand, lhp, UC Santa Barbara.
26. Greg Conley, c, Rollins College.
27. Chris Haslock, rhp, Cal State Dominguez Hills.
28. Stanley Tukes, rhp, Broward (Fla.) CC.
29. Darrin Hart, ss, Harding HS, Charlotte, N.C.

30. Rob Cantwell, lhp, North Idaho JC.
31. **Chad Kuhn, 1b-of, University of New Mexico.**
32. Craig Pueschner, of, Sahuaro HS, Tucson, Ariz.
33. **John Kuehl, 1b-3b, University of California.**
34. Randy Tanner, of, University of Southern California.
35. **Robert Curnow, c, Cal Poly Pomona.**
36. **Craig Proctor, 2b, Cal Poly Pomona.**
37. Jason Farrell, rhp, Kennedy HS, Granada Hills, Calif.
38. Heath Jones, c, El Segundo HS, Hawthorne, Calif.
39. **Walter Wilkerson, rhp, Clermont (Fla.) HS.**
40. Ramey Brooks, c, Blanchard (Okla.) HS.
41. **Richard Peacock, of, Ernest Ward HS, Walnut Hill, Fla.**
42. **Jeff Hart, rhp, University of Central Arkansas.**
43. Brian Looney, lhp, Cunnery HS, Cheshire, Conn.
44. Michael Basse, of, Mater Dei HS, San Juan Capistrano, Calif.

SAN FRANCISCO GIANTS (17)

1. **Royce Clayton, ss, St. Bernard HS, Playa del Rey, Calif. (Choice from Reds as compensation for Type B free agent Eddie Milner).**
1. (Choice to Indians as compensation for Type A free agent Brett Butler).
1. **Ted Wood, of, University of New Orleans (Special supplemental choice—29th—as compensation for losing Type A free agent Chili Davis to Angels).**
2. **Scott Ebert, rhp, Edmond (Okla.) Memorial HS (Choice from Angels as compensation for Type A free agent Chili Davis).**
2. **Chris Hancock, lhp, Fontana (Calif.) HS.**
3. **Reuben Smiley, of, Los Angeles CC.**
4. **Carl Hanselman, rhp, Merritt Island (Fla.) HS.**
5. **Scooter Tucker, c, Delta State University.**
6. **Jeffrey Kaiser, ss, Southwest Missouri State University.**
7. **David Horan, rhp, Eastern Oklahoma State JC.**
8. **Gary Sharko, rhp, Grand Canyon College.**
9. **Charles Rogers, lhp, Mississippi Delta JC.**
10. Turtle Zaun, 1b, North Carolina State University.
11. **Longo Garcia, rhp, Cal State Fullerton.**
12. Michael Adams, rhp, Juanita HS, Kirkland, Wash.
13. **Andre George, 2b, Mt. Hood (Ore.) CC.**
14. **Adam Smith, c, Oklahoma State University.**
15. **Shannon Coppell, of, Eastern Illinois University.**
16. **Mark Standiford, 2b, Wichita State University.**
17. **Mitchell Ferrick, rhp, UC Riverside.**
18. **Adell Davenport, 3b, Southern University.**
19. **David Slavin, c, University of Missouri.**
20. **Shane Durham, lhp, Wichita State University.**
21. **Steve Decker, c, Lewis-Clark State College.**
22. **Steven Gray, ss, Cuesta (Calif.) JC.**
23. **John Patterson, 2b, Grand Canyon College.**
24. **George Penrod, of, Florida Atlantic University.**
25. **Reggie Williams, of, University of South Carolina, Aiken.**
26. **William Gibbons, rhp, University of Delaware.**
27. **David Wuthrich, lhp, Troy State University.**
28. **Adam Hilpert, ss, Cal State Stanislaus.**
29. **Ken Brauckmiller, rhp, Portland State University.**
30. **Glenn Warren, of, Mount Olive College.**
31. **William Berry, lhp, Glendale (Calif.) JC.**
32. **Michael Sanderson, of, University of Alabama.**
33. **David Cantrell, rhp, Chapman College.**
34. **Pat Brady, of, St. Mary's College (Calif.).**
35. **Don Brock, rhp, University of South Carolina, Spartanburg.**
36. **Brett Hewatt, 1b-of, Seward County (Kan.) CC.**
37. **David Booth, of, West Virginia State College.**
38. Rodney Billingsley, c, George Mason University.
39. **Lance Burnett, of, Crowder HS, McAlester, Okla.**
40. **Richard Thompson, of-3b, Los Angeles Valley JC.**
41. **Gregory Lee, inf, Hancock (Calif.) JC.**
42. Basilio Ortiz, of, Buckley HS, Hartford, Conn.
43. Michael Scialo, ss, Saguero HS, Scottsdale, Ariz.
44. Jason Hendricks, rhp, Kincaid HS, Houston.
45. Danny Lane, inf, Laguna Beach (Calif.) HS.

SEATTLE MARINERS (14)

1. **Tino Martinez, 1b, University of Tampa.**
2. **Greg Pirkl, c, Los Alamitos (Calif.) HS.**
3. **Jim Campanis, c, University of Southern California.**
4. **Lee Hancock, lhp, Cal Poly San Luis Obispo.**
5. **Willie Romay, of, Miami HS.**
6. **Kelvin Thomas, of, Smiley HS, Houston.**
7. **Julio Reyan, of, Southridge HS, Miami.**
8. Mike Smedes, rhp, Laguna Hills (Calif.) HS.
9. Steve Chitren, rhp, Stanford University.
10. Ted Devore, rhp, University of Portland.
11. James Allen, rhp, Lake Washington HS, Kirkland, Wash.
12. **Nick Felix, lhp, Texas A&M University.**
13. **Jeff Darwin, rhp, Alvin (Texas) CC.**
14. **Michael Beiras, rhp, Texas Tech University.**
15. Scott Taylor, rhp, University of Kansas.
16. **Mark Razook, ss, Cal State Fullerton.**

17. James Kosnik, lhp, Oakland (Mich.) University
18. Delvin Thomas, ss, Smiley HS, Houston.
19. James Clifford, 1b, Ingraham HS, Seattle.
20. Thomas Liss, lhp, University of Detroit.
21. Michael McLaughlin, ss, Glassboro State College.
22. Johan Miller, c, Normandale (Minn.) CC.
23. Joseph White, rhp, Mesa College.
24. Todd Krumm, of-rhp, Michigan State University.
25. Jim Price, rhp, Stanford University.
26. Jorge Robles, 2b, University of Miami.
27. Doug Davis, 1b-3b, Grossmont (Calif.) JC.
28. Scott Cline, 3b, UCLA.
29. Kerry Woodson, rhp, San Jose (Calif.) CC.
30. Scott Bibee, rhp, Carson City (Nev.) HS.
31. Joel Wolfe, 3b, Chatsworth HS, Northridge, Calif.
32. Dusty Madsen, rhp, Sacramento (Calif.) CC.
33. Tim Stargell, 2b, Southern University.
34. Ben Burnau, lhp, Miami (Ohio) University.
35. Michael Cloutier, of, University of Detroit.
36. Michael Kerber, c, Canoga Park HS, West Hills, Calif.
37. Shawn Brown, of, Granada Hills HS, Los Angeles.
38. John Kohli, lhp, University of Nebraska.
39. Glen Raasch, c, Mt. San Antonio (Calif.) JC.
40. Felix Gurruchaga, lhp, Miami-Dade New World Center CC.
41. Chris Howard, c, University of Southwestern Louisiana.
42. Dean Haskins, c-3b, Montgomery HS, Santa Rosa, Calif.
43. Rob Callistro, rhp, Concord (Calif.) HS.
44. Damian Torino, c, North Marion HS, Sparr, Fla.
45. John Burton, rhp, Mt. San Antonio (Calif.) JC.
46. Tom Brock, of, University of Michigan.
47. Mark Ringkamp, rhp, Palomar (Calif.) JC.
48. Eddie Christian, of, Salesian HS, San Pablo, Calif.
49. Arthur Bass, cf, Westfield HS, Houston.
50. Daniel Donovan, rhp, Brookdale (N.J.) CC.
51. Keith Barrett, of-inf, Cal Poly Pomona.
52. Brent Lutz, 3b, Issaquah (Wash.) HS.

TEXAS RANGERS (6)

1. Monty Fariss, ss, Oklahoma State University.
2. Tim Morrow, of, South Alamance HS, Graham, N.C.
3. Darren Oliver, lhp, Rio Linda (Calif.) HS.
4. Everett Cunningham, rhp, Northwestern University.
5. Cliff Williams, c, East St. Louis HS, Fairview Heights, Ill.
6. Rob Maurer, 1b, University of Evansville.
7. Dominic Pierce, 3b, Skyline (Calif.) JC.
8. Travis Law, of, Oklahoma State University.
9. Trey McCoy, of, Virginia Tech.
10. Eric McCray, lhp, Farmerville (La.) HS.
11. David Wallace, ss-of, Brandeis HS, New York.
12. Cedric Shaw, lhp, Grambling State University.
13. Tim MacNeil, rhp, Rancho Santiago (Calif.) JC.
14. Mike Patrick, c-3b, University of Texas.
15. Peter Lawrence, of, Logan HS, Union City, Calif.
16. John Sipple, lhp, Oregon State University.
17. Carl Randle, rhp, Huston-Tillotson College.
18. Thomas Mileski, rhp, San Jacinto (Texas) JC.
19. Jim Hvizda, rhp, Old Dominion University.
20. Joey Wardlow, 2b, University of Tampa.
21. Mark Bowland, rhp, Memphis State University.
22. Doug Cronk, 1b, University of Southern Mississippi.
23. Mike Reitzel, lhp, Northeastern Oklahoma State University.
24. Mark Tolbert, rhp, Dixie (Utah) JC.
25. Rod Morris, of, Southeastern Louisiana University.
26. Kyle Spencer, rhp, Missouri Valley College.
27. Jeff Shore, c, University of North Carolina, Charlotte.
28. Todd DeVaughan, rhp, Seminole (Okla.) JC.
29. Robert Gamez, lhp-1b, Chabot (Calif.) JC.
30. Jeff Frye, 2b, Southeastern Oklahoma State University.
31. Jonathan Huth, rhp, Waldorf (Iowa) JC.
32. Lindsey Robinson, 3b, University of South Carolina, Spartanburg.
33. Sean Wills, of, Hanford (Calif.) HS.
34. Thomas Urbani, 1b, Cabrillo (Calif.) JC.
35. David Schmidt, 2b, Montgomery HS, San Diego.
36. Anthony Berry, of, Rust College.
37. Steve Allen, rhp, University of Massachusetts.
38. Jeff Simmons, rhp, Rend Lake (Ill.) JC.
39. Brian Evans, rhp, Jacksonville University.
40. Kenneth Penland, lhp, University of South Carolina, Spartanburg.
41. Anthony Peeler, lhp, Paseo HS, Kansas City, Mo.
42. Greg Kuzma, lhp, Princeton University.
43. William Shorr, rhp, Nicholls State University.
44. Fred Collins, lhp, Manatee (Fla.) JC.
45. (selection voided) Americo Loera, rhp, Dallas Baptist University.
46. Edward Ohman, rhp, Auburn University.
47. Donald Parker, of, Rangeview HS, Aurora, Colo.
48. Brian Mouton, of, Hayward HS, Oakland, Calif.

49. Pat Underhill, rhp, Valencia (Fla.) CC.
50. Shannon Albright, rhp, Fruita HS, Grand Junction, Colo.
51. (selection voided) Mike Easley, 3b, Texas A&M University.
52. Jeff Hainline, 1b, Gonzaga University.
53. Daniel Robinson, of, Crossett (Ark.) HS.
54. Henderson Mosley, ss, H.D. Woodson HS, Washington, D.C.
55. Paul Spyhalski, of, Howard (Texas) JC.
56. Brett Snyder, rhp, Rancho Santiago (Calif.) JC.
57. Anthony Tijerina, c, Long Beach (Calif.) CC.
58. Shannon Penn, ss, Lakeland (Ohio) CC.
59. Joe Caruso, rhp, Casa Grande HS, Petaluma, Calif.

TORONTO BLUE JAYS (25)

1. Ed Sprague, 3b-c, Stanford University.
2. Tim Hodge, c, Callaway HS, Jackson, Miss.
3. David Weathers, rhp, Motlow State (Tenn.) CC.
4. Eric Brooks, c, LaMirada (Calif.) HS.
5. Billy Parese, ss, Owasso (Okla.) HS.
6. Michael Ogliaruso, rhp, Countryside HS, Palm Harbor, Fla.
7. Robert Montalvo, ss, Memorial HS, West New York.
8. Tim Pugh, rhp, Oklahoma State University.
9. Brent Gilbert, rhp, Blinn (Texas) JC.
10. Anthony Ward, lhp, Oral Roberts University.
11. Pat Pesavento, ss, Notre Dame University.
12. William Fuller, rhp, Eau Gallie HS, Melbourne, Fla.
13. Curtis Johnson, rhp, University of Washington.
14. Eric Persinger, rhp, Marion (Ind.) HS.
15. Greg Kobza, 1b, Blinn (Texas) JC.
16. Matthew Wilke, ss, Beaver Dam (Wis.) HS.
17. Michael Brady, rhp, Nassau (N.Y.) CC.
18. Rick Vaughn, c, Oral Roberts University.
19. Timothy Bruzdewicz, lhp, Allegheny (Pa.) CC.
20. Daniel Berthel, of, El Camino (Calif.) JC.
21. Marshall Holifield, of, Ganesha HS, Montclair, Calif.
22. Mario Baker, of, Gulf Coast (Fla.) CC.
23. Terrance Jones, ss, Monroe (N.Y.) CC.
24. Michael Daniel, c, Connors State (Okla.) JC.
25. Timothy Brown, rhp, St. Petersburg (Fla.) JC.
26. Richard Nowak, rhp, UC San Diego.
27. Greg McCutcheon, rhp, Kent State University.
28. Woody Williams, rhp, University of Houston.
29. Greg Harding, 1b, University of Richmond.
30. Scott Hutson, rhp, Arizona State University.
31. Michael Matheny, c, Reynoldsburg (Ohio) HS.
32. Greg O'Halloran, c, Orange Coast (Calif.) JC.
33. George Tsamis, lhp, Stetson University.
34. Jeff Lawrence, lhp, Fallbrook (Calif.) HS.
35. Michael Harris, 1b, Tates Creek HS, Lexington, Ky.
36. Chris Kerr, rhp, California Baptist College.
37. Jeff Mooney, rhp, Chapman College.
38. Ray Giannelli, 3b, New York Tech.
39. Eric Reichenbach, rhp, Sachem HS, Farmingville, N.Y.
40. Eric Bradley, rhp, Laney (Calif.) JC.
41. Andrew Carlton, 1b-rhp, Providence HS, Frankfort, Ill.
42. Brian Brazier, inf, Hanford (Calif.) HS.
43. Matt Sines, rhp, Hillsborough (Fla.) CC.
44. Scott Erickson, rhp, San Jose (Calif.) CC.
45. Wayne Williams, c, Chesapeake HS, Pasadena, Md.
46. Thomas Irwin, rhp, Victor Valley HS, Victorville, Calif.
47. Eric Carter, rhp, Louisburg (N.C.) JC.
48. Greg Goushan, c, Orange Glen HS, Escondido, Calif.
49. Dax Jones, of, Waukegan (Ill.) West HS.
50. Greg Davis, rhp, North Torrance HS, Gardena, Calif.
51. Michael Boyd, ss, Clearwater Catholic HS, Largo, Fla.
52. Gordon Purvis, rhp-ss, Berrien County HS, Ray City, Ga.
53. Jeff Kidwiler, ss, Chapman College.
54. Terre Woods, of-3b, Utica (Miss.) JC.
55. Anthony Mills, inf-of, Taft (Calif.) HS.
56. Jason Wood, inf, McLane HS, Fresno, Calif.
57. David Edwards, of, East St. Louis HS, Brooklyn, Ill.
58. Darrell Whitmore, ss, West Virginia University.
59. Michael Lustyk, 1b, Interlake HS, Bellevue, Wash.
60. William Abare, 1b, Polk (Fla.) JC.
61. Brad Raulston, of, La Jolla (Calif.) HS.
62. Jesse Cross, rhp, Middle Georgia JC.
63. Thomas Hamilton, of, Forest Hills HS, Marshville, N.C.
64. Warren Holt, rhp, Cabrillo (Calif.) JC.
65. Walter Heckel, 2b, St. John's University.
66. Jeff Borgese, ss, San Jose (Calif.) CC.
67. Ross Urshan, rhp, Lyman HS, Altamonte Springs, Fla.
68. Louis Williams, rhp, Benton Harbor (Mich.) HS.
69. Jerry Worley, of, Miami Springs HS.
70. James Lewis, rhp, Terry Parker HS, Jacksonville, Fla.
71. Kenneth Koon, of, Orange Park (Fla.) HS.
72. Dennis Stachura, c, Downers Grove (Ill.) North HS.
73. Anton Mobley, of, Yule, Fla.

INDEX

American League Clubs

National League Clubs

Independent Clubs

"If you are in this game or are a true fan, you can't afford to miss Baseball America . . ."

— Lou Gorman
VP/General Manager
Boston Red Sox

OFFER:

Send in this coupon and get the next issue of **BASEBALL AMERICA** absolutely **FREE!!!**

— Yes, please send me the next issue of Baseball America **FREE!**

NAME

ADDRESS

CITY _____ STATE_____ ZIP_____